Behavior Therapy

Application and Outcome

Behavior Therapy

Application and Outcome

Second Edition

K. DANIEL O'LEARY

State University of New York at Stony Brook

G. TERENCE WILSON

Rutgers University

PRENTICE-HALL, INC.   ENGLEWOOD CLIFFS, N.J. 07632

Library of Congress Cataloging-in-Publication Data

O'Leary, K. Daniel, 1940–
  Behavior therapy.
  Includes bibliography and index.
  1. Behavior therapy.   I. Wilson,
G. Terence, 1944–   .   II. Title.
RC489.B4038 1987   616.89'142   86-22615
ISBN 0-13-073875-1

Editorial/production supervision and interior design: Sylvia Moore
Cover design: Wanda Lubelska
Manufacturing buyer: Barbara Kelly Kittle

© 1975, 1987 by Prentice-Hall, Inc.
A Division of Simon & Schuster
Englewood Cliffs, New Jersey 07632

Prentice-Hall Series in Social Learning Theory
  Albert Bandura, Editor

Printed in the United States of America
10 9 8 7 6 5

ISBN   0-13-073875-1   01

Prentice-Hall International (UK) Limited, *London*
Prentice-Hall of Australia Pty. Limited, *Sydney*
Prentice-Hall Canada, Inc., *Toronto*
Prentice-Hall Hispanoamericana, S.A., *Mexico*
Prentice-Hall of India Private Limited, *New Delhi*
Prentice-Hall of Japan, Inc., *Tokyo*
Prentice-Hall of Southeast Asia Pte. Ltd., *Singapore*
Editora Prentice-Hall do Brasil, Ltda., *Rio de Janeiro*

To

Michael and Kathryn

Austen and Douglas

Contents

PART II   BEHAVIOR THERAPY WITH CHILDREN

PART III   BEHAVIOR THERAPY WITH ADULTS

PART IV   EVALUATION: CLINICAL AND ETHICAL ISSUES

Behavior Therapy
as a Humanistic Science **416**
Summary **417**

Contents

K. Daniel O'Leary, University of Illinois, is Professor and past chairman of Psychology at the State University of New York at Stony Brook. His books include: *Principles of Behavior Therapy* (with G. T. Wilson), *Classroom Management* (with S. G. O'Leary), *Mommy I Can't Sit Still: Coping with the Aggressive and Hyperactive Child, Assessment of Marital Discord*, and *Marital Therapy in the Treatment of Depression* (with S. R. Beach & E. E. Sandeen). He received the Distinguished Scientist Award from the clinical division (Div. 12, Section 3) of the American Psychological Association, and he received the Distinguished Practitioner Award from the National Academies of Practice. He was President of the Association for Advancement of Behavior Therapy. He was Editor of *Journal of Applied Behavior Analysis* and is Associate Editor of the *Journal of Abnormal Child Psychology*. He has served on a number of editorial boards including *Journal of Consulting and Clinical Psychology, Behavior Therapy, Behavior Assessment, The Journal of Interpersonal Violence*, and *The Journal of Family Violence*.

G. Terence Wilson, Ph.D., State University of New York at Stony Brook, is the Oscar K. Buros Professor of Psychology at Rutgers University. Among his other books are *Principles of Behavior Therapy* (with K. D. O'Leary), *Evaluation of Behavior Therapy: Issues, Evidence, and Research Strategies* (with Alan Kazdin), and *The Effects of Psychological Therapy* (with S. Rachman). He has co-edited the *Annual Review of Behavior Therapy: Theory and Practice*, since 1973. A Fellow at the Center for Advanced Study in the Behavioral Sciences, Stanford, California (1976–77), he was also president of the Association for Advancement of Behavior Therapy and of the Experimental-Clinical Section of Division 12 of the American Psychological Association. He has served on the editorial boards of several journals, including *Journal of Consulting and Clinical Psychology* and *Behaviour Research and Therapy*. He was associate editor of *Journal of Applied Behavior Analysis*, and is co-editor (with S. Rachman) of *Advances in Behaviour Research and Therapy*. Aside from teaching and research, he is also a practicing clinical psychologist.

Preface

Behavior therapy has had a dramatic impact on the assessment and treatment of psychological disorders. Within the roughly 25 years since it emerged as a formal therapeutic approach, behavior therapy has come to rival the psychoanalytic tradition as the single most important theoretical orientation of mental health professionals. There are over 3,500 members of the Association for Advancement of Behavior Therapy, and there are now behavior therapists in almost all countries throughout the world. Australia, Europe, North America, and South America have their own behavior therapy organizations. There are behavior therapy organizations within Africa, and The People's Republic of China hosted its first official delegation of behavior therapists in 1983.

The influence of behavior therapy has been seen clearly in professional journals. In the early 1960's the main psychological and psychiatric journals were reluctant to accept articles on behavior therapy because the behavior therapy model was not yet accepted. By 1983, behavior therapy research was the preponderant clinical method published in the American Psychological Association's clinical journal, *Journal of Consulting and Clinical Psychology*. In addition, behavioral treatment research was very well represented in the nonpharmacological treatment studies of the American Medical Association's official psychiatric journal, *Archives of General Psychiatry*.[1]

The literature on behavior therapy continues to burgeon. The volume of clinical material on behavior therapy is tremendous, and the clinical and non-clinical problems that have been addressed by behavior therapists span a wide area. This rapid growth and expansion of behavior therapy is underscored by

1. O'Leary, K. D. (1984). The image of behavior therapy: It is time to take a stand. *Behavior Therapy*, 15, 219–233.

comparing the current volume with our first edition, published in 1975. Essentially, this is a new book. We have added new chapters to accommodate the clinical advances in areas such as depression, behavioral medicine, and marital discord. Clinical research in these important areas was only beginning in the early 1970's. We have also included separate chapters on research methodology and clinical issues to reflect the increased sophistication and maturity of behavior therapy. In some instances we have drawn upon material published in our book, *Principles of Behavior Therapy*, published by Prentice-Hall[2], but all of the original chapters have been completely rewritten and updated. It is an encouraging sign of advances in the field when, within a mere decade, new and continuing research developments require such radical revision of the contents of a previous edition. We have chosen to cover the clinical problems that are most common in frequency and in the practice of behavior therapy.

We have used a social learning theory orientation throughout the book to conceptualize both the etiology and treatment of various problems. More specifically, we have included affective, behavioral, cognitive, and environmental variables in our conceptualization of many of the etiological and treatment presentations. We have also tried to cover the biochemical and genetic research regarding the etiology of various disorders such as hyperactivity, delinquency, mental retardation, anxiety, depression, schizophrenia, and alcoholism. In brief, we presented evidence regarding etiologies of various disorders from various perspectives when there was research evidence to support such views. Since the book is about behavior therapy, naturally a learning orientation was given particular emphasis in the discussion of all disorders. However, when the evidence did not support a learning position regarding the etiology of a disorder (e.g., autism and many forms of mental retardation) or when genetic factors had stronger supporting evidence than did a learning position for the etiology of a disorder (e.g., schizophrenia), we have gone beyond traditional learning conceptualizations in our analysis of the disorder.

An introduction and an overview of behavior therapy and a chapter on assessment begin the book in order to acquaint the reader with the general principles and concepts in behavior therapy and in the clinical assessment of a problem. Following a presentation of the types of treatment used to treat various problems, we provide chapters on evaluation, clinical, and ethical issues. The reader should keep in mind that a researcher often examines one treatment procedure in isolation from others to evaluate critically the efficacy of that particular procedure. Clinicians, on the other hand, will treat an individual using a number of different procedures at one time to maximize their effectiveness in helping the client. Both of us are therapists as well as clinical researchers. We subscribe to the scientist-practitioner model of clinical training and hope in this volume to indicate how a knowledge of the relevant clinical findings and methods of experimental psychology and expertise in clinical prac-

2. Wilson, G. T. & O'Leary, K.D. (1980). *Principles of Behavior Therapy.* Prentice-Hall, Englewood Cliffs, N.J.

tice can combine to create maximally effective treatments. All too often the much publicized gap between experimental research and clinical practice results in the two sets of activities being described in relative isolation from each other. We have tried to blend these two domains throughout this book. Aside from the usual emphasis in behavior therapy on controlled research and evaluation of methods, we have highlighted clinical topics such as the therapist-client relationship and the problem of resistance or client noncompliance. We have tried to show that these issues can be usefully conceptualized and integrated within a broad social learning approach to behavior therapy.

This book is intended for upper level undergraduates, graduate students, and clinicians. We believe that it is the most comprehensive behavior therapy book that provides both etiological and treatment outcome data on the major psychological and mental health problems of children and adults. We hope that practicing clinicians will find the book a ready source of information on the etiology and treatment of the most important problems they face. Behavior therapy is the dominant theoretical orientation of child therapists in the United States, and behavior therapy is second only to an eclectic or psychodynamic orientation of adult therapists in the United States.[3] Given the increasingly positive attitude toward behavior therapy by our clients and the public media, we can expect that a behavioral model will become even more prominent in the next decade. Approximately 30% of American citizens purchase some form of psychological or psychiatric services in their lifetime, whereas only 13% of our citizens did so in the 1950's.[4] Given this trend, we can expect that behavior therapy services will be even more readily utilized in the future than they are now. We hope that this book will be a very valuable source for the potential consumer of behavior therapy services and a comprehensive text for the students and service providers of behavior therapy.

3. O'Leary, 1984.

4. Meredith, N. (June, 1986). Testing the Talking Cure. *Science '86*, 30–37.

Acknowledgments

Many individuals have contributed to this book and we gratefully acknowledge their help. Barbara Honig, Kerry Knauf, and Cecelia Koenig greatly facilitated the preparation by continual word processing, reference checking, and editorial aid. Mark Durand and George Nelson provided special editorial and substantive aid on the developmental disabilities and depression chapters respectively, and Raymond Rosen made several valuable suggestions about the chapter on sexual disorders. Susan Geiss and Steven Beach aided in reference selections for much of the material in the aggression and depression chapters, respectively. Sylvia Moore supervised production. We are especially grateful to Albert Bandura, the general editor of this Prentice-Hall series on social learning, for his detailed, substantive feedback and suggestions for revisions of all chapters.

We are thankful for the support of NIMH grant MH35340 (Etiology of Spouse Abuse), NIMH grant MH38390 (Treatment of Marital Discord and Depression), and NIAAA grant AA00259 (Alcoholism/Behavioral Treatment: Research and Developmental Factors in Alcohol Abuse) for allowing us to continue as active researchers and for facilitating the writing of this book. We thank our respective research teams and, most importantly, our postdoctoral colleagues, Doctors Arias, Barling, Beach, and Sandeen, and administrative assistants Mary Samios and Barbara Honig for allowing us to fulfill our writing and administrative commitments. We believe that our clients have significantly expanded our knowledge across the past decade, and we hope that they have gained commensurately from our services. We thank them for their input and insights into the problems that they and many others face.

Finally, we thank our families for their patience while this book was in preparation. The writing of this book took significantly longer than we anticipated because of the information explosion in the behavior therapy field and because of unexpected administrative responsibilities that each of us faced at our respective universities. We thank our wives, Susan and Elaine, for their emotional support and for absorbing many household and child/adolescent care reponsibilities, and we thank our children, Michael and Kathryn, Austen and Douglas, for being there and for being young but terriffic companions.

K. Daniel O'Leary

G. Terence Wilson

1

Behavior Therapy: Introduction and Overview

A BRIEF HISTORY OF BEHAVIOR THERAPY

Behavior therapy[1] has a long past but a short history. Many of the concepts and procedures that are part of current-day behavior therapy were described in the first half of this century. It was only in the late 1950s, however, that behavior therapy emerged as an explicitly formulated, systematized body of knowledge. More important, it was not until the 1960s that behavior therapy was widely recognized as an alternative model of etiology and therapy to the prevailing psychodynamic approach.

Two historical events overshadow all others in the development of behavior therapy.

---

1. The term "behavior therapy" is used synonymously with "behavior modification" throughout this volume. Some writers have distinguished between these two terms (Eysenck, 1982; Krasner, 1971). It is often suggested, for example, that behavior modification refers primarily to the application of operant conditioning procedures, whereas behavior therapy refers to primarily classical conditioning methods. However, there has been no consistent use and little has been gained in the process.

The first is the rise of behaviorism in the early 1900s. The key figure in the United States was J.B. Watson, who criticized the subjectivity and mentalism of the psychology of the time and put forward behaviorism as the basis for the objective study of behavior. His emphasis on the overriding importance of environmental events; his rejection of private, mental phenomena that could not be observed directly; and his claim that all behavior could be understood as a result of learning became the formal bases of behaviorism.

Watson's extremist position has been widely rejected, and more refined versions of behaviorism have been developed. Preeminent in this regard has been the contribution of Skinner, whose radical behaviorism has had a significant impact not only on behavior therapy (particularly applied behavior analysis) but also on psychology in general. Like Watson, Skinner insisted that overt behavior is the only acceptable subject of scientific investigation and rejected mentalistic concepts. He also embraced an ultra-environmentalist position that gives short shrift to genetic or biological influences on behavior. In contrast to the behaviorist tradition of Skinner, Eysenck (1959, 1982) has always argued that behaviorism need not be logically linked with an extreme environmentalist approach. His influential neobehaviorist theory combines an emphasis on genetic influences on behavior with an insistence on learned habits.

The second major historical event was the growth of experimental research on the laws of learning. In Russia, around the turn of the century, Pavlov, a Nobel Laureate in physiology, established the foundations of classical conditioning. At roughly the same time in the United States, pioneering research on animal learning by Thorndike showed the influence of consequences (rewarding and punishing events) on behavior. Beginning in the late 1930s, this process of instrumental learning was elaborated upon by Skinner in his research on operant conditioning. Research on conditioning and learning principles, conducted largely in the animal laboratory, became a dominant part of experimental psychology in the United States after World War II. In the traditions of Pavlov and Skinner, workers in this area were committed to the scientific analysis of behavior using the laboratory rat and the pigeon as their subjects.

During the first half of this century, many articles appeared in both the United States and Russia describing the application of conditioning principles to a wide variety of problem behaviors (Kazdin, 1978a). Among other examples, Watson and Rayner (1920) experimentally induced a phobic reaction in the famous case of Albert by using a simple classical conditioning procedure, and Mary Cover Jones (1924) antedated later investigations by describing the use of several different procedures for overcoming children's fears. Dunlap (1932) devised methods for breaking maladaptive habits, including stuttering, and Mowrer and Mowrer (1938) reported the successful treatment of enuresis by direct con-

ditioning procedures. In Russia, Bekhterev (1923) and Kantorovich (1930) devised conditioning techniques for treating sexual perversions and alcoholism respectively.

Nevertheless, these early applications had no impact on the field of psychotherapy for reasons we will discuss.

Modern Origins of Behavior Therapy

The modern origins of behavior therapy as an explicitly formulated alternative approach to the treatment of abnormal behavior can be traced to independent but clearly related developments which occurred in South Africa, England, and the United States during the 1950s and 1960s. An important landmark in the development of behavior therapy was the publication in 1958 of Wolpe's book *Psychotherapy by Reciprocal Inhibition*. In this classic text, Wolpe introduced several treatment techniques based upon the principles of conditioning developed by Pavlov and Hull, and his own research on the elimination of experimentally produced neurotic reactions in cats (Wolpe, 1948, 1954). Included among these clinical techniques was systematic desensitization, an anxiety reduction procedure which has since become one of the best known and most widely used techniques of behavior therapy with adults. In many ways Wolpe's introduction of systematic desensitization and the technique of assertion training followed earlier proposals of the application of conditioning principles to clinical disorders by Salter (1949). Lazarus (1958), a South African associate of Wolpe's, used the term "behaviour therapy" to describe the application of objective, laboratory-derived therapeutic techniques to the treatment of neurotic patients. It was the pioneering clinical studies and writing of Wolpe and Lazarus in South Africa which, more than any other factor, established the foundations of the clinical practice of modern-day behavior therapy with adults.

Another milestone in the development of behavior modification was the heavily publicized work of Eysenck and his students at the Institute of Psychiatry, London University. In a seminal paper in 1959, Eysenck defined behavior therapy as the application of "modern learning theory" to the treatment of psychiatric disorders. The phrase "modern learning theory" referred directly to the learning principles and procedures of behaviorists such as Pavlov, Hull, Mowrer, Miller, and, to a lesser extent, Skinner. Behavior therapy was said to be a scientific approach based on experimentally demonstrated methods that were more effective than traditional psychotherapy, which was characterized as unscientific, based on purely speculative theories and procedures, and lacking any acceptable evidence of efficacy. In sum, according to Eysenck, behavior therapy was an applied science, the defining feature of which was that it was testable and falsifiable. A testable theory can be specified with precision and subjected to experimental investigation. A falsifiable theory specifies experimental conditions that could be disproved or falsified. Eysenck argued that, in contrast to learning theory, psychoanalysis was too vaguely formulated to be really testable and that it was impossible to identify conditions under which it could be falsified.

In 1963, Eysenck and Rachman established the first scientific journal devoted to developments in behavior therapy: *Behaviour Research and Therapy*. As a result of the continuing research and writings of Eysenck, Rachman, and their colleagues at the Institute of Psychiatry in London, this has remained one of the foremost centers of behavior therapy in the world.

A third major development in the emergence of behavior therapy in the 1950s was the growth of operant conditioning in America and the extension of operant principles to human problems. This development was spurred by Skinner's 1953 *Science and Human Behavior*, in which he criticized psychoanalytic methods and reconceptualized psychotherapy in behavioral terms.

> The field of psychotherapy is rich in explanatory fictions. Behavior itself has not been accepted as subject matter in its own right, but only as an indication of something wrong somewhere else. The task of therapy is said to be to remedy an inner illness of which the behavioral manifestations are merely "symptoms". . . . It has encouraged the therapist to avoid specifying the behavior to be corrected or showing why it is disadvantageous or dangerous. By suggesting a single cause for multiple disorders it has implied a uniformity which is not to be found in the data. Above all, it has encouraged the belief that psychotherapy consists of removing inner causes of mental illness, as the surgeon removes an inflamed appendix or cancerous growth or as indigestible food is purged from the body. . . . It is not an inner cause of behavior but the behavior itself which—in the medical analogy of catharsis—must be "got out of the system."

The reconceptualization of clinical and educational problems with the primary emphasis on accepting behavior as the critical subject matter in its own right provided a decisive impetus for the establishment of behavior modification as a treatment-oriented approach. The first use of the term "behavior therapy" was recorded by Lindsley, Skinner, and Solomon in 1953 in describing their research on how behavior is affected by reinforcement in psychotic patients. The use of operant principles in behavior modification has continued to be especially prominent in the treatment of children and psychotic individuals. The most important initial clinical application of operant conditioning was with children, carried out under the tutelage and direction of Bijou at the University of Washington (e.g., Bijou & Baer, 1961). As described in subsequent chapters, a wide range of behavior of normal and retarded children and preschoolers, including the completion of academic work and facilitation of peer interactions, was changed by altering the manner in which adults reinforced these children. The broad application of operant conditioning to the whole range of psychiatric disorders reached full expression in the influential book by Ullmann and Krasner, *Case Studies in Behavior Modification*, published in 1965. This book presented contrasting descriptions of the medical and psychological models of treatment and illustrated how learning principles, particularly operant conditioning, could be used to modify a wide range of clinical problems. In 1968, the *Journal of Applied Behavior Analysis* was published, providing the premier outlet for research on the modification of socially significant problems through the use of operant conditioning procedures.

Behavior Therapy: A Scientific Revolution

The emergence of behavior modification as an independent therapeutic approach in the late 1950s was explicitly identified with learning theory. Yet, as we have pointed out, there had been previous applications of learning principles to behavioral problems. These were relatively isolated and sporadic efforts which had little impact on psychotherapy, partly because conditioning principles, which had been demonstrated with animals, were rejected as too simplistic and irrelevant to the treatment of complex human problems. Under the influence of psychoanalysis and its derivative psychodynamic approaches, conditioning treatments were rejected as superficial, mechanistic, and naïve. A schism existed between academic-experimental and clinical psychologists. The former were trained in

scientific methods, with an emphasis on controlled experimentation and quantitative measurement; the latter concerned themselves with projective tests, intrapsychic inferences, and speculative hypotheses about the unconscious motives behind human behavior.

Students enrolled in doctoral clinical programs gained their clinical training in a medically oriented setting, such as a state hospital, Veterans Administration Center, or psychiatric clinic. Essentially abandoning their academic training in psychology as a behavioral science, students in these psychiatric settings learned to apply quasi-disease analogies in treating mental illness. Some efforts were made to integrate conditioning principles with psychodynamic theories of abnormal behavior, but these eclectic formulations had little effect and only obscured crucial differences between the respective behavioral and psychodynamic approaches. Dollard and Miller (1950), for example, translated psychodynamic therapies into the language of Hullian learning theory but with little consequence for any clinical innovation, since they were merely reinterpreting psychotherapy rather than advocating different concepts and procedures. The advent of behavior therapy was marked by its challenge of the prevailing status quo and the presentation of a systematic and explicitly formulated clinical alternative that attempts to bridge the gap between laboratory and clinic.

Behavior therapy grew out of dissatisfaction with traditional psychodynamic procedures, which had completely dominated psychiatry and clinical psychology. This opposition largely started after World War II. As early as 1952 Eysenck had stirred up heated controversy by pointing out that no evidence existed to support the widely accepted view that psychotherapy helped the adult patient, arguing that the onus was on psychotherapists to justify their continued practice. Eysenck's criticism of adult psychotherapy was echoed by similarly negative evaluations of the psychodynamic treatment of children (Levitt, 1957, 1963). In like fashion, the associated use of psychoanalytically oriented projective tests for personality assessment was severely criticized as lacking reliability and validity (Zubin, Eron, & Schumer, 1965). These developments within clinical psychology resonated with the trend of psychology as a whole toward a scientific approach to human behavior.

Behavior therapy is rooted in the development of behaviorism, which has as its aim the prediction, modification, and understanding of behavior (Skinner, 1953; Watson, 1930). Krasner (1971) likened this move away from the traditional psychodynamic approach to a scientific revolution or paradigm clash (Kuhn, 1962), i.e., the confrontation of one model of abnormal behavior and its treatment with another radically different and competing model. According to Kuhn the decision to change paradigms is determined not only by professional insecurity deriving from the failure of existing rules and procedures, but also by the availability of an alternative paradigm. The emergence of behavior therapy during the late 1950s and early 1960s was the product of the convergence of these two factors.

These early developments in behavior therapy represented an accommodation of interests rather than an identity of views. The dominant psychoanalytic establishment was the common foe, and its shortcomings were emphasized. Aside from the natural bond deriving from concerted opposition to a common enemy, the different approaches of Wolpe, Eysenck, and Skinner had some common fundamental assumptions, such as the commitment to an applied science. Although it received little attention at the time, there were also important differences in the type of problems they treated, the methods they used, and most important, in the assumptions about human behavior under which they operated.

As behavior therapy developed and matured throughout the 1960s and 1970s, these theoretical differences became more evident. Behavior therapy today is considerably more sophisticated and complex than in its earlier stages. A simple definition of behavior therapy in terms of conditioning principles is now outdated. As the following chapters will make clear, the current practice of behavior therapy goes well beyond the application of classical and operant conditioning principles that were derived from laboratory research with rats and pigeons.

CURRENT CONCEPTUAL APPROACHES

Contemporary behavior therapy cannot be simply defined because it is marked by a diversity of views, a broad range of heterogeneous procedures with different rationales, and debate about its theoretical underpinnings (Wilson & Franks, 1982). A useful way to characterize the field is to point out the different conceptual approaches within contemporary behavior therapy. It is important to remember that while these approaches can be separated, they are not necessarily in opposition to each other and may usually be seen as different emphases, rather than different approaches.

Applied Behavior Analysis

This approach is philosophically consistent with Skinner's (1953) radical behaviorism and relies upon the principles and procedures of operant conditioning. Overt behavior is regarded as the only acceptable subject of scientific investigation. The extent to which Skinner takes account of subjective experience in his formulation of behavior has generated considerable controversy. The question is not whether subjective experience exists but what role it plays in the regulation of human behavior. Skinner (1963) himself has stated that private events should be included in an experimental analysis of behavior. Nevertheless, this recognition of the role of private events in behavior has always been carefully limited in Skinner's behaviorism. In his view, subjective processes such as thoughts or images can never exert a causal effect on behavior. In its strict form, the operant conditioning viewpoint assumes that apart from genetic influences, human behavior is controlled exclusively by environmental events that are ultimately beyond personal control.

Another defining characteristic of the operant approach has been its methodology, with its emphasis on the study of the individual organism. Repeated objective measurement of a single subject under highly controlled conditions has been the hallmark of operant conditioning methodology. Skinner rejected statistical comparisons between groups of subjects, arguing that group averages do not adequately reflect the actual behavior of individual subjects. His approach became known as the experimental analysis of behavior or applied behavior analysis, terms used to distinguish it from the traditional scientific strategy of the statistical analysis of group data.

In addition to a set of philosophical assumptions about behavior and a methodology for studying it, the operant approach provided a number of learning principles that have had a decisive impact on the field. It assumes that behavior is a function of its environmental consequences and that behavior is strengthened by positive and negative reinforcement but weakened by punishment.

Positive reinforcement refers to an increase in the frequency of a response that is followed by a favorable event. If the behavior is emitted, *then* the reward is given. No behavior, no reward. Negative reinforcement refers to an increase in behavior that avoids or reduces an aversive event. Punishment is the presentation of an aversive event or the removal of a positive event contingent on a response that results in a decrease in the frequency of that response.

Operant conditioning techniques have been applied to a wide range of problems in all age groups in clinical and community psychology, education, rehabilitation, and even medicine (Kazdin, 1978b). In the main, however, operant conditioning procedures have been found most useful in changing the behavior of young children, retarded persons, and institutionalized populations, such as chronic mental patients. In general, behavior therapists in clinical practice, particularly with adult disorders, would not describe themselves as applied behavior analysts, but would draw upon much broader theoretical and empirical bases in their work (Barlow, 1985; Lazarus & Fay, 1984; Wilson, 1982b).

The Neobehavioristic Stimulus-Response Approach

This approach derives from the pioneering contributions of Wolpe and Eysenck and is an attempt to apply the S-R learning theories of Pavlov, Guthrie, Hull, Mowrer, and Miller to the treatment of clinical problems. Unlike the nonmediational nature of applied behavior analysis or operant conditioning, in which the focus is exclusively on observable behavior, it includes an emphasis on mediational variables in the explanation and modification of human behavior. For example, while anxiety disorders are assumed to be caused by an underlying fear or anxiety drive, anxiety is a hypothetical construct that cannot be observed directly. However, the attempt is made to anchor this type of hypothetical construct to antecedent and consequent environmental events that can be measured directly. The principles and procedures of classical and instrumental conditioning have been the backbone of this approach. Cognitive formulations of the mediational processes assumed to intervene between stimulus and response have been consistently rejected. This emphasis on conditioning as opposed to cognitions can be traced to the early emphasis on principles from the animal conditioning laboratory and the initial reaction of behaviorism and behavior therapy against the mentalistic concepts of traditional psychodynamic approaches. However, advances in experimental research and psychological theory during the past 20 years have revealed the limitations of conditioning models of complex human behavior (Bandura, 1977b; Mahoney, 1974; Rosenthal, 1982). Conditioning principles, while still seminal, are of more limited utility today. Many behavior therapists, especially those with a social learning approach as discussed next, have sought broader bases of knowledge (Wilson, 1982b). It must be remembered, however, that the contribution of conditioning concepts went well beyond the introduction of particular treatment techniques. A more fundamental benefit was the conceptual and methodological emphasis that the study and application of conditioning principles brought to clinical research and practice. The detailed specification of therapeutic techniques, the focus on behavior *per se* in assessment, treatment, and evaluation of therapy outcome, and the advances in measurement and methodology were all directly associated with the methodological behaviorism that characterized the conditioning approach.

Cognitive Behavior Modification

This approach rests on the fundamental assumption of the importance of cognitive or symbolic processes in the development, maintenance, and modification of abnormal behavior (Mahoney, 1974; Meichenbaum & Cameron, 1982). Cognitive behavior therapy cannot be simply defined, and it incorporates different views and therapeutic techniques. Some of these techniques were developed independently of behavior therapy while others are relatively familiar methods in behavior therapy that are now emphasized more or conceptualized differently. Important concepts include a person's subjective perceptions of events, interpretations and attributions of one's own behavior, thought patterns, self-statements, and cognitive strategies. The treatment techniques that best characterize it are known collectively as *cognitive restructuring*. Mahoney and Arnkoff (1978), although acknowledging the many differences among the proponents of cognitive-behavior therapy, have distilled the defining features of the approach. First is the assumption that cognitive processes mediate adaptive and maladaptive behavior and experience. These processes, in turn, can be activated by procedures that parallel those used in the laboratory study of human cognition. The therapist must be both a diagnostician who assesses the features of the cognitive system that underlie the target problem and an educator who arranges experiences that will alter these processes and contents, and therefore the patterns of behavior and experience with which they are causally associated.

Cognitive-behavioral treatment strategies have been applied to a number of childhood and adult disorders. A good example of this approach can be seen in the conceptualization and treatment of depression. Beck's (1976) cognitive therapy, the most sophisticated and best developed cognitive-behavioral approach, has shown great promise as an effective means of treating depressed patients.

Social Learning Theory

In his influential text *Principles of Behavior Modification* (1969) Bandura presented a comprehensive and innovative account of behavior therapy within the conceptual framework of social learning theory. Each of the approaches already summarized places primary emphasis on one dimension of psychological functioning to the relative neglect of the others. Thus, applied behavior analysis is concerned with observable, overt behavior. The neobehavioristic approach emphasizes classical conditioning of responses of the autonomic nervous system. Cognitive behavior modification has focused preeminently on the role of faulty thought patterns in clinical disorders. One of the advantages of the social learning approach is that it integrates these three separate regulatory systems in a theoretically consistent framework (Bandura, 1977b). In terms of a social learning analysis, some response patterns are regulated primarily by external stimulus events and are affected largely by paired experiences. The influence of environmental consequences, which is the main focus of operant conditioning, is a second form of behavioral regulation. The third and most important system of regulatory influence is assumed to operate through cognitive mediational processes.

According to social learning theory, the influence of enviromental events on the acquisition and regulation of behavior is largely determined by cognitive processes. These are based on prior experience and determine what environmental influences are attended to, how they are perceived, whether they will be re-

membered, and how they might affect future action. To quote Bandura (1969)

> At this (cognitive) level stimulus inputs are coded and organized; tentative hypotheses about the principles governing the occurrence of rewards and punishments are developed and tested on the basis of differential consequences accompanying the corresponding actions; and, once established, implicit rules and strategies serve to guide appropriate performances in specified situations. Symbolically generated affective arousal and covert self-reinforcing operations may also figure prominently in the regulation of overt responsiveness. (p. 63)

Symbolic modeling is one of the best known and most widely used methods derived from the social learning approach. In modeling, learning is assumed to occur through coding of representational processes based upon exposure to instructional, observational, or imagined material. Learning occurs through observation alone without the need for direct reinforcement of the specific behavior acquired. Other traditional learning principles are also interpreted within a cognitive framework. For example, in contrast to operant conditioning analyses, reinforcement is seen not as an automatic strengthening of behavior. Rather, learning from response consequences is attributed to the informative and incentive functions of rewards (Bandura, 1977b, 1986). By observing the consequences of behavior, the person learns what action is appropriate in what situation. By symbolic representation of anticipated future outcomes of behavior, the person helps to generate the motivation to initiate and sustain current actions.

Expectations play an important role in social learning theory. Often, people's expectations and hypotheses about what is happening to them may affect their behavior more than the objective reality of the rules and contingencies associated with the behavior. Clinical problems often arise when a significant discrepancy between a person's perception of events and objective reality develops. Social learning theory distinguishes between efficacy and outcome expectations. The former concern people's confidence that they can cope with a particular situation; the latter address people's belief that their actions will result in a particular outcome. Self-efficacy theory is an important component of the social learning approach, and is discussed in detail in Chapters 8 and 14. In addition, a social learning approach to behavior therapy draws heavily on other cognitive concepts, such as attribution theory and information processing (Bandura, 1977b; Marlatt & Gordon, 1985; Wilson, 1982b, in press). Finally, the social learning theory of personality places major emphasis on cognitive processes as discussed in the following chapter (Mischel, 1973, 1981).

Psychodynamic theories assume that behavior is a product of largely autonomous unconscious forces within the individual. From an operant conditioning perspective, behavior is a function of the environment. As Skinner (1971) put it, "a person does not act upon the world, the world acts upon him" (p. 211). Both of these views are one-sided or unidirectional causal models of behavior. They can be shown schematically as follows: B = f(P,E), where B = behavior; f = function; P = cognitive and other internal events, and E = the external environment. The problems with this position have been summed up by Bandura (1978).

> Personal and environmental factors do not function as independent determinants; rather they determine each other. Nor can "persons" be considered causes independent of their behavior. It is largely through their actions that people produce the environmental conditions that affect their behavior in a reciprocal fashion. The

experiences generated by behavior also partly determine what individuals think, expect, and can do, which in turn, affect their subsequent behavior. (p. 345)

A second distinguishing feature of social learning theory is that psychological functioning involves a reciprocal interaction among three interlocking sets of factors: behavior, cognitive factors, and environmental influences. This view can be shown schematically.

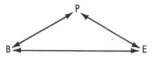

In this conceptual scheme a person is neither driven by internal forces nor a passive reactor to external pressure. Rather, a person is both the agent and the object of environmental influence.

A third characteristic of social learning theory emphasizes the human capacity for self-directed behavior change. Operant conditioning accounts of behavioral self-control ultimately reduce to analyses of external situational control and fundamentally deny the notion of self-control. In addition to the acquisition and maintenance of behavior, activation and persistence of behavior are based mainly on cognitive mechanisms. The importance assigned to cognitive processes enables social learning theory to explain the fact that people initiate behavior that at least in part shapes their own destinies.

In addition to these conceptual advantages of social learning theory, it also offers practical benefits to the therapist. As a broad-based framework that emphasizes the multidimensional nature of psychological functioning, the social learning approach is especially useful in the treatment of diverse and complex clinical problems. Accordingly, the social learning approach to behavior therapy is emphasized throughout the remainder of this book.

CORE CHARACTERISTICS OF BEHAVIOR THERAPY

Instead of searching for a simple definition of behavior therapy it is more useful to view it in terms of a number of common core characteristics (Erwin, 1978). Although the preceding approaches to behavior therapy often involve conceptual differences, there remains a common core of fundamental assumptions that all behavior therapists hold. In the ultimate analysis, behavior therapy: (1) differs fundamentally from the traditional intrapsychic, psychodynamic, or quasi-disease model of mental illness; and (2) is committed to scientific method, measurement, and evaluation. Each of these characteristics has several specific implications for assessment, modification, and evaluation.

A Model of Abnormal Behavior

To understand fully the significance of the behavioral model, it is important to indicate briefly how it differs from the traditional quasi-disease or psychodynamic model. According to the latter model, abnormal behavior is symptomatic of an underlying illness. This illness is not a physical one, such as a brain tumor or a viral infection; it is a mental illness, a psychic disturbance or personality conflict that functions like a medical disease. A person who has an emotional disorder is said to be "sick" and can be restored to "health" only by treating the underlying, unconscious motivational conflicts of which abnormal behavior is a function. These conflicts are traced back to early childhood development and in-

trapsychic processes that interfered with normal or "healthy" personality development. The focus of treatment is on these historical causes of personality malfunction, not the present behavior. However, abnormal behavior is not merely symptomatic of "something wrong somewhere else." It is important in its own right and can be treated directly.

Abnormal behavior cannot usually be traced directly to any physical or psychic disease processes; the underlying intrapsychic conflicts which are assumed to cause maladaptive behavior can only be inferred from behavior itself. The frequent logical error in the quasi-disease formulation is that once these inferences are made, they attain the status of autonomous causal events which are assumed to be valid and are invoked to explain the very behavior from which they were derived. An example of this circular reasoning is concluding that a person is abnormal because he acted in a bizarre or unusual fashion: Why does the person act in a bizarre and unusual manner? Because he is abnormal! Adoption of this model has major consequences for one's interpretation of the development of clinical disorders, their classification or assessment, and their treatment.

In the behavioral model, abnormal behavior that is not a function of specific brain dysfunction or biochemical disturbance is assumed to be governed by the same principles that regulate normal behavior. Many types of abnormal behavior often regarded as illnesses or symptoms of illness are viewed as nonpathological problems of living.

Not all forms of abnormal behavior are considered to be the result of social learning experiences. Among others, autism, schizophrenic disorders, certain types of depression (for example, manic-depression), and mental retardation have important organic determinants. While these disturbances are not "cured" by behavior therapy, they are none-theless subject to the effects of social learning influences within limits. Behavior therapy has been useful in helping individuals afflicted with some of these disorders to lead more fulfilling lives.

Whereas psychodynamic therapies focus on the historical determinants of clinical disorders, behavior therapy emphasizes their current determinants. Treatment directed towards these current determinants is the most powerful and efficient means of eliminating the client's problems. Since behavior therapy emphasizes the continuing interaction between clients' cognitions and behaviors and the particular life situations in which they occur, explicit strategies are employed to ensure that treatment-produced change generalizes to the client's natural environment, and that it is maintained over time. The cessation of a problem behavior in one situation (for example, in a hospital ward or classroom) does not necessarily mean that the client will show similar improvement in other situations (for example, at home). The quasi-disease model makes no provision for this. The problem is assumed to be a psychic disturbance or personality disorder in the patient. "Curing" this disorder should lead automatically to improved behavior across different situations.

An Applied Science

Behavior therapy is defined by a commitment to an applied science of clinical treatment. As a result there is a heavy emphasis on the precise specification of therapeutic methods that are replicable across different therapists and can be objectively evaluated. The experimental evaluation of treatment methods and concepts is essential. This is not to say that all behavior therapy treatment is based on solid scientific evidence. Some methods are fully developed and have this support; others are still in early stages of development and neither the procedure nor its effects have been adequately evaluated.

Two other points should be stressed. First, the path between laboratory and clinic is two-way (see Chapter 18). Developments in clinical practice can exert and have exerted an important reciprocal influence on basic and applied research. Second, no one would assert that there is a simple relationship between experimental research and clinical practice. Behavior therapists have borrowed concepts and treatment methods from other therapeutic approaches that are not directly connected with experimental psychology (e.g., communication training, widely used in contemporary behavioral marital therapy, as discussed in Chapter 12). Nevertheless, the attempt is constantly made to relate treatment methods to the available experimental evidence. Behavior therapy has radically changed the nature of research on psychological treatment methods. Both the quantity and quality of studies on therapy outcomes have increased dramatically. Innovative research strategies allow rigorous evaluation of specific techniques applied to particular problems, in contrast to inadequate global assessments of poorly defined procedures applied to heterogeneous problems.

Behavioral treatment methods are either derived from or at least consistent with the content and method of experimental-clinical psychology. Behavior therapy should not be confused with the somatic or medical methods of behavior change, such as psychosurgery or electroconvulsive therapy (ECT). These latter methods may modify behavior, not on the basis of psychological principles and procedures, but through direct physical intervention.

Box 1–1 *Core Characteristics of Behavior Therapy*

1. Most abnormal behavior is acquired and maintained according to the same principles as normal behavior.
2. Most abnormal behavior can be modified through the application of social learning principles.
3. Assessment is continuous and focuses on the current determinants of behavior.
4. People are best described by what they think, feel, and do in specific life situations.
5. Treatment is derived from the theory and experimental findings of scientific psychology, particularly social learning principles.
6. Treatment methods are precisely specified, replicable, and objectively evaluated.
7. Innovative research strategies evaluate the effects of specific therapeutic techniques on particular problems.
8. Treatment outcome is evaluated in terms of the initial induction of behavior change, its generalization to the real life setting, and its maintenance over time.
9. Treatment strategies are individually tailored to different problems in different individuals.
10. Extensive use is made of psychological assistants, such as parents and teachers, to modify problem behavior in the settings in which it occurs.
11. Behavior therapy is broadly applicable to a full range of clinical disorders and educational problems.
12. Behavior therapy is a humanistic approach in which treatment goals and methods are mutually contracted, rather than arbitrarily imposed.

COMMONLY ASKED QUESTIONS ABOUT BEHAVIOR THERAPY

1. Does Behavior Therapy Ignore Subjective Experience?

Clients' expectations, imagery, emotional reactions, symbolic self-regulatory processes, and self-perception are all fundamental features of the analysis and treatment of clinical problems. The social learning approach to behavior therapy emphasized in this book stresses the importance of the cognitive mediation of human behavior.

Behavior therapy should not be equated with behaviorism. Philosophical behaviorism is the doctrine of J.B. Watson who, in the second decade of this century, attempted to reduce all experience to glandular secretions and muscular movements. He denied the existence of mental events or the mind. Although Skinner has labeled himself a radical behaviorist, he has stated that the study of subjective events (that is, images and thoughts) should not be rejected simply because they are private events. Nonetheless, operant conditioners have consistently deemphasized or ignored cognitive processes because they are neither directly observable nor have any causal status. They have tried to explain all behavior in terms of observable effects of the external environment on overt behavior. We have noted that this operant conditioning approach has proved extremely valuable in the study and treatment of clinical disorders. Yet most behavior therapists today adopt a broader approach that emphasizes the importance of cognitive factors in the treatment of complex clinical disorders.

2. Is Behavior Therapy a Superficial Form of Treatment?

Behavior therapy is not a superficial treatment, since both behavioral and psychodynamic treatments attempt to deal with the causes of behavior. The difference is in what these respective approaches regard the causes of behavior to be. Psychodynamic theories focus on historical, unconscious determinants of behavior; behavior therapy emphasizes the current causes of behavior—the antecedent, mediational, and consequent variables that presently maintain the client's problems. Psychodynamic approaches ask about their patient, "Why did he or she become this kind of person?" Behavioral approaches ask, "What is causing him or her to function this way now, and what can be done to change that level of functioning?" An adequate behavioral assessment of the problem results in multifaceted treatment that deals with the full range of maintaining determinants (causes).

3. Does Behavior Therapy Result in "Symptom Substitution"?

Behavior therapy was once widely criticized as a superficial form of treatment that only treats the "symptoms" while leaving the real causes of the problem untouched. As a result it was alleged that behavioral treatment would lead to symptom substitution, that is, the replacement of the symptom that was treated with another because the underlying problem had not been resolved. This was a misguided criticism, and many psychodynamicists now agree that problematic behavior can be modified without substitute problems emerging.

The charge of symptom substitution has been a confused and confusing notion. Many conceptual problems make it well-nigh impossible to investigate this notion experimentally (Kazdin, 1982). For example, even if a new problematic behavior emerged following treatment, it would be difficult to determine whether or not it was a new problem or a substitute symptom. It is more constructive

to concentrate on objective assessment of therapeutic change. In this connection it is clear that changes in treated problems or behavior may be associated with changes in nontreated behavior, changes that are usually positive. Consider the following examples. In the first, it has been shown that behavioral treatment of phobic disorders not only eliminates avoidance behavior, but also phobic thinking, physiological distress, and associated nightmares (Bandura, 1977b). In the second example, discussed in Chapter 13, behavioral treatment of obesity not only produces weight loss, but also results in reductions in depression and in blood pressure and cholesterol levels (Wilson & Brownell, 1980).

Several well-controlled therapy outcome studies have directly examined the nature of correlated changes in nontreated behavior. Typical of the evidence in this regard are the results from Sloane, Staples, Cristol, Yorkston, and Whipple's (1975) widely quoted study of the comparative efficacy of behavioral and psychoanalytically oriented treatments for neurotic and personality disorders. These investigators summarize their findings as follows: "Not a single patient whose original problems had substantially improved reported new symptoms cropping up. On the contrary, assessors had the informal impression that when a patient's primary symptoms improved, he often spontaneously reported improvement of other minor difficulties" (p. 100). The results of a study of the behavioral treatment of patients with complex phobic disorders, over 60 percent of whom had previously undergone psychoanalytic therapy without success, showed that the vast majority were moderately to markedly improved at the end of treatment (Zitrin, 1981). Of importance in the present context is Zitrin's observation that no symptom substitution occurred. "On the contrary," she comments, "we found a significant improvement in the quality of their lives; better functioning at home and at work, increased social life, expanded interests and activities, improved interpersonal relationships; in general there was a greater richness in the fabric of their lives. With stresses and traumas, there often was a recurrence of the old phobic behavior, rather than the emergence of new symptoms" (p. 13).

In some rare instances correlated changes in nontreated behavior have been negative rather than positive. Kazdin (1982) refers to these as response covariation. Psychodynamic theory fails to provide an adequate explanation. As Kazdin observes, "response covariation refers to clusters of behavior that exist concurrently in the individual's response repertoire. Several behaviors co-exist and change together. . . . The changes are not necessarily the emergence of new problems; some of the changes are improvements in positive or desirable behaviors. Also, the behaviors that form a cluster are not obviously related or interconnected by a single psychodynamic theme" (p. 356).

Precisely how these clusters of behaviors are organized is still poorly understood. Traditional conditioning explanations of stimulus and response generalization have proved inadequate. A more promising approach is social learning theory, with its emphasis on the reciprocal interaction between cognitive variables and environmental influences. In terms of this theory, the person actively selects and organizes experiences in ways that influence subsequent performance. Since it is the individual's "perceptions of the environment that determine the functional equivalence of the different stimuli and responses and influences performance" (Kazdin, 1982, p. 358), it becomes necessary to assess cognitive processes in order to understand or predict response covariation.

4. What Is the Relationship between Psychological Theory and Clinical Practice?

Behavior therapy incorporates a wide range of innovative and distinctive therapeutic techniques. More fundamental to a definition of behavior therapy, however, is that it derives from a particular conceptual model of human behavior that has direct implications for the understanding, assessment, and modification of clinical disorders. Behavior therapy is a way of thinking about clinical disorders, a problem-solving orientation in which different principles and procedures are flexibly tailored to each individual client's specific problem. Procedures are based on empirical data wherever possible. Theoretical considerations help determine what techniques the therapist selects, guide general treatment strategies, and direct clinical research.

Behavior therapists are professionals well-versed in the scientific foundations of behavior therapy who possess the clinical and/or interpersonal skills required to design and implement effective behavior change methods. The variables that determine the therapist-client relationship are important for behavior change and can be fruitfully integrated with more formal behavioral techniques within the conceptual framework of social learning theory (Wilson & Evans, 1977).

5. What Problems Are Suitable for Behavior Therapy?

Behavior therapy is broadly applicable to the full range of clinical disorders. Areas of successful application of behavior therapy include psychological disorders, education, rehabilitation, and medicine (Franks & Wilson, 1973, 1978). The evidence shows that behavior therapy is not only generally useful across a wide range of different disorders, but also that it might be the treatment of choice for more complex and more resistant problems (Kazdin & Wilson, 1978; Sloane et al., 1975).

6. Does Behavior Therapy Overlap with Other Treatment Approaches?

Behavior therapy differs fundamentally from traditional psychoanalytic therapy, but it does share many commonalities with other psychological therapies, particularly those that are briefer and more directive. The broader and more complex behavior therapy has become, the greater has been the overlap (Goldfried, 1980a; Wilson, 1981).

In terms of clinical practice, behavior therapy and multimodal therapy are similar. The majority of the techniques that Lazarus (1981) lists as the most frequently used in multimodal therapy are standard behavior therapy strategies. This is not surprising since Lazarus (1971) was one of the pioneers of clinical behavior therapy, helping to broaden its conceptual bases and introducing innovative clinical methods. Whether or not the multimodal techniques that receive no attention in behavior therapy add to therapeutic efficacy is unclear, since there are no controlled studies or even acceptable uncontrolled clinical trials to help decide the issue.

One of the appeals of multimodal therapy is the flexibility it appears to give the therapist. According to Lazarus, the therapist is free to use "any technique, derived from any system, without subscribing to any theoretical underpinnings which do not have the benefit of empirical support" (1968). Lazarus defends this approach, which he calls technical eclecticism, by stating that therapeutic advances are more probable if therapists remain free of the restrictions of any one theoretical position. Although Lazarus points out

that the therapist's choice of techniques must be determined by "well-conceived guiding principles and general theories of human behavior," neither technical eclecticism nor multimodal therapy makes clear what these guiding principles are. The point at issue here is the importance of operating within an explicit conceptual framework that furnishes an understanding of the disorder in question, which then provides the guide for choice of treatment. If therapists do not work from a basis of clearly stated principles of the processes governing behavior change, they act as a result of personal hunches. Behavior therapy represents an attempt to move beyond idiosyncratic practices to base clinical practice on more secure scientific foundations. Of course, this does not mean that the clinical practice by behavior therapists is always based on solid empirical evidence. Behavior therapists, like therapists from other approaches, have developed their own clinical lore. Lacking sufficient information and guidelines from research, behavior therapists frequently have to conduct informal clinical tests, trying different procedures and altering them on the basis of the effects they produce.

The clinical necessity of using multifaceted or multimodal treatment programs is emphasized repeatedly throughout the remainder of this book, yet behavior therapy cannot be defined so broadly as to include anything that is reportedly effective. In behavior therapy, the therapist draws upon a broad range of principles and procedures within the general framework of social learning theory in designing specific treatment interventions. Inevitably, although this particular theoretical framework is broad enough to incorporate recent advances in personality, social, and cognitive psychology and allows the creative therapist considerable flexibility, it is necessarily limited. Behavior therapy does not try to do everything, and it is a truism that effective, nonbehavioral methods might be developed within alternative theoretical perspectives. Despite the continuing lack of evidence of the therapeutic efficacy or efficiency of traditional psychotherapeutic treatment methods (Rachman & Wilson, 1980), it would be surprising if some strategies from some approaches are not shown to be useful in the course of future outcome research.

All therapists have their particular conceptual assumptions (biases). These biases come into play from the moment the therapist begins the often arduous task of making sense of a client's problem, and include the questions that are asked or not asked, the choice of assessment methods, the framing of goals, and the selection of treatment strategies. The real issue becomes an analysis of the nature of these different conceptual sets and the implications they carry for treatment and the development of the field. Success, as in therapy itself, hinges upon recognizing, accepting, and correcting distorted assumptions. The therapist and the technique are easily confounded, and faith and expectation can exert a powerful influence on therapeutic outcome. Treatment techniques must be distinguishable from the therapists who use them, and must be communicable to other therapists for whom they are also successful. Treatment conditions must be explicitly defined if they are to be testable and replicable across different individuals and different settings. Otherwise, it becomes difficult to decide which features of therapy contribute to its success and which are irrelevant and better discarded.

The self-corrective process is the very essence of the scientific method, and is greatly facilitated by systematically relating treatment methods to a consistent theoretical orientation such as the social learning framework. The advantages of remaining within the social learning approach are that it integrates the currently known facts of behavior change, it is formulated in such a way that its assumptions are testable and its procedures replicable, and it is of heuristic value in generating novel predictions about what might be therapeutically effective. Behavior therapy is a scientific approach, the guiding philosophy of which is succinctly expressed in Francis Bacon's enduring observation that "truth is more likely to emerge from error than from confusion." In brief, with systematic research and treatment, it will become evident what works and what does not.

CURRENT STATUS OF BEHAVIOR THERAPY

Within the space of only two decades, behavior therapy has established itself as a major form of psychological therapy. It has helped to transform graduate training in clinical psychology in the United States in that among highly regarded doctoral training programs several are predominantly behavioral in orientation and few have no behavioral training component at all. Counseling programs in schools of education and doctoral programs in schools of psychology also reflect the influence of behavior therapy. In a recent survey of a random sample of clinical and counseling psychologists, Smith (1982) concluded that "No single theme dominates the present development of professional psychotherapy. Our findings suggest, however, that cognitive-behavioral options represent one of the strongest, if not *the* strongest, theoretical emphases today" (p. 808). Related surveys of other groups of professionals indicate that Smith's was not an isolated finding. Tuma and Pratt's (1982) survey of clinical child psychologists showed that their two major orientations were behavioral and psychodynamic. A similar survey of pediatric psychologists indicated a stronger influence of behavior therapy. Fifty-nine percent of these pediatric psychologists indicated that behavioral psychology was their primary orientation, with 39 percent expressing a preference for psychodynamic therapy (Tuma & Cohen, 1981). In assessing the prevalence of a behavioral or cognitive-behavioral orientation among clinicians, O'Leary (1984) concluded that "with children, a behavioral orientation seems to be a clearly dominant trend with approximately half of all child clinicians identifying with this orientation. With adults, no single theoretical orientation is ascribed to by most professionals; eclecticism is the most popular identification and a wide variety of orientations are mentioned. However, a behavioral orientation is clearly emerging as one of the top three ranked orientations" (p. 5).

O'Leary (1984) also analyzed the treatment outcome research of the 1983 journals of the three major mental health organizations in the United States: *Archives of General Psychiatry*, published by the American Medical Association; *The Journal of Consulting and Clinical Psychology* (*JCCP*), published by the American Psychological Association; and *Social Work*, published by the National Association of Social Workers. The results showed that of the nonpharmacological treatment studies in *Archives* and *JCCP*, most involved behavioral methods. (There were no outcome studies in *Social Work*.) These findings demonstrate that contemporary outcome research on psychological treatment is dominated by behavioral investigators. O'Leary's further analysis of the treatment research funded by the National Institute of Mental Health underscores this conclusion. This dominance in the research arena might be impressive, but it does not necessarily translate into influence on the professions in the broader sense. The limited impact of research findings on the practice of psychotherapy is a well-advertised

fact (Barlow, 1980). The impact of behavior therapy on psychiatry has been far less (Brady & Wienckowski, 1978), although the American Psychiatric Association issued a report concluding that "behavioral principles . . . have reached a stage of development where they now unquestionably have much to offer informed clinicians in the service of modern clinical and social psychiatry" (Birk, Stolz, Brady, Brady, et al. 1973, p. 64).

SUMMARY

Behavior therapy has developed out of the systematic application of experimentally derived principles of learning to the modification of problem behaviors. The contemporary history of behavior therapy dates from the 1950s. During this decade, the pioneering work of Wolpe in South Africa, of Eysenck and his group in England, and the extension of operant conditioning principles to human disorders by Skinner and his students in the United States resulted in the emergence of behavior therapy as a distinctive alternative model of etiology and therapy to the prevailing psychodynamic approach.

Behavior therapy matured and became more complex during the 1960s and 1970s. The initial definition of behavior therapy as the application of conditioning principles is now outdated. Current conceptual approaches within behavior therapy include applied behavior analysis in which the emphasis is on operant conditioning, the neobehavioristic approach, cognitive behavior modification, and social learning theory.

Bandura's social learning formulation is the most comprehensive and sophisticated conceptualization of behavior therapy. In addition to external events, it stresses the influential role of cognitive mediating variables in regulating behavior. By emphasizing the constant reciprocity between personal actions and environmental consequences, it provides an analysis of and generates procedures for self-directed behavior change.

The distinguishing characteristics of contemporary behavior therapy include the rejection of the quasi-disease model and personality trait theory, and the recognition that much abnormal behavior is developed and maintained in the same manner as normal behavior and can be treated directly, and that treatment is derived from the theory and experimental findings of scientific psychology. Contemporary behavior therapy focuses on specificity in assessment, treatment, and measurement; the precise specification of treatment conditions; and the objective evaluation of therapeutic outcome.

Behavior therapy is not synonymous with behaviorism. Symbolic events are included in causal analyses since they are closely tied to observable antecedent and consequent events. Behavior therapy is not superficial or symptomatic treatment. A thorough behavioral assessment indicates all the current determinants of the person's problem; several different techniques are then selectively included within a multifaceted treatment program aimed at modifying all aspects of the problem. Behavior therapy has broad applicability to diverse behavior problems in clinical psychology, psychiatry, education, rehabilitation, and medicine.

Assessment

2

INTRODUCTION

Assessment in behavior therapy began to receive highly significant attention in the late 1970s. The Association for Advancement of Behavior Therapy considered the topic important enough in 1979 to create a special and distinct assessment journal, *Behavioral Assessment*. Previously, the journal *Behavior Therapy* was the repository for both assessment and treatment research. *Behavioral Assessment* though, would provide a special outlet for assessment research and bring methodological and measurement rigor into behavioral assessment by focusing on matters separate from intervention or therapy. In addition to *Behavioral Assessment*, which was officially sponsored by the behavior therapy organization of the United States, a private journal of behavior assessment was also established in 1979: *Journal of Behavior Assessment*.

Special attention has also been given to assessment with the revision of the American Psychiatric Association's *Diagnostic and Sta-*

tistical Manual (DSM III, 1980). This official diagnostic manual for all mental health professionals is used throughout the United States in both public and private clinics. Furthermore, all insurance companies with mental health coverage require that a diagnosis be used in submission of any forms for fee reimbursement to the client. While the *Diagnostic and Statistical Manual* is an official publication of the American Psychiatric Association, decisions about diagnostic classifications are made by a group of psychologists and psychiatrists, with the latter group having the larger number of members on various committees. The continuing revision of the *Diagnostic and Statistical Manual* is made to reflect changes in information about psychological problems and mental disorders, but ultimately committees decide whether a disorder will be part of the manual or not. On occasion there are vehement battles about the labels given various problems. In 1973, there was a great debate about whether homosexuality would continue to be classified as a mental disorder. Under pressure from gay rights groups and the Association for Advancement of Behavior Therapy, homosexuality was no longer a diagnosable entity under a mental disorder classification. Furthermore, in 1985 another heated battle occurred in which the diagnosis "Masochistic Personality Disorder" was the topic of debate, because women who were physically abused by their husbands were likely targets of the diagnosis. Freud thought women were naturally masochistic, and a natural extension of the Freudian view is that victims of wife-beating stay with their mates because of a desire for punishment. Because of pressure from Dr. Lenore Walker, a behavior therapist who represented the women's caucus of the American Psychological Association, the diagnosis was dropped. These debates about revisions of the manual have focused attention on assessment issues, although many decisions about the existence of certain "disorders" appear to be more the result of political climate and pressure groups than of scientifically generated data. Fortunately, as exemplified by the debates on diagnostic issues regarding homosexuality and masochism, some emphasis inevitably does center on data or the lack thereof that may support or fail to support a diagnosis (Holden, 1986).

The premier issue of *Behavioral Assessment* set the stage for more interchange between behavior therapists and psychologists trained in traditional measurement methodology. In a series of six articles by Marvin Goldfried, Eric Mash, Daniel O'Leary, Frederick Kanfer, Stephen Hayes, and Richard Jones, the nature and directions of behavior assessment were discussed. Most apparent was a clear need to look carefully at traditional approaches to assessment for their psychometric sophistication, but the writers also sounded the need for multimethod assessment. More specifically, they called for an emphasis on standard validation approaches,

item and test construction, multiple reliability measures and their various meanings, and the use of many methods of assessment to measure the same construct. Finally, the need for theory was noted by Kanfer (1979): "The future task of behavioral assessment . . . lies in an expansion of measurement instruments and of theory to encompass both dependent and independent variables of greater complexity than those with which behavioral assessment has dealt in the past" (pg. 39).

Anyone in clinical practice regularly assesses clients and their problems. When a client comes to a clinic, a therapist has to make a judgment about whether or not emergency measures are necessary (e.g., hospitalization); whether the case should be assigned a high, low, or moderate priority for treatment; and whether the problem presented by the client is serious enough to warrant any treatment. The latter issue is often of import with child cases in which the parents want to know whether the child's problems (e.g., bedwetting in young children) will change as a simple function of maturation. In making these judgments, a therapist relies on prior experience with clients who have had similar problems, psychological test data, comparisons with normative populations, and the client's distress. If the therapist and the client conclude that therapy is warranted, the therapist then must decide whether the treatment should be directed at the problem presented by the client (e.g., behavior problems of a child) or at other issues (e.g., marital discord). He or she must also determine what treatment procedures should be used, whether the treatment would have any undesirable side effects, and what regular assessments are necessary to ascertain whether the treatment procedures are having the intended effect. All of these decisions require a thorough initial assessment.

In this chapter we discuss the behavioral

model for assessment, survey the types of clinical assessment currently used by behavior therapists, and evaluate these practices.

MODEL FOR ASSESSMENT

Interpreting Presenting Problems

During the intake interview a client almost always identifies certain problems that he or she wants help with or wants to change. These problems are called *presenting problems*. A therapist must first decide whether the presenting problems are the problems to be addressed directly, i.e., the targets for intervention. Generally, presenting problems are important, and behavior therapists, in particular, have viewed them as legitimate targets for direct intervention. However, on occasion certain presenting problems should not receive primary attention. For example, sometimes alcohol abuse may be best treated by focusing on a client's interpersonal relationships, rather than on reducing or eliminating drinking per se. In a case in which drinking occurs each time the client is depressed and the depression reliably follows fights with the spouse, the marital relationship would be a focus of the therapy. Drinking, of course, can be addressed as an issue in therapy, but depending on its severity and frequency, it may not be the primary treatment focus. With a hyperactive child, focusing on increasing academic and social skill may be preferable to emphasizing decreased fidgeting and gross motor movements. The choice of treatment targets is based on a thorough knowledge of the history of the problem, how various treatments affect presenting and related problems, and what appears to be the central or critical cause of the presenting problems.

A related issue is the decision about whether or not there is a central or *higher order* problem. For example, a man may report that his problem is that he gets very angry when his eight-year-old son does not obey him. Upon further questioning, it is learned that the man frequently fights with his wife and receives negative evaluations from his boss because he is overly critical of fellow employees. In such a case, a therapist may conceptualize all of the presenting problems within the context of the common themes: the inability to accept others' faults and to cope with anger. Sharing this interpretation with the client and structuring the therapy to address the higher order problems enables the client to deal simultaneously with many problems. In contrast, focusing solely on his interactions with his son would leave several related issues untouched and would reduce the likelihood both of maintaining treatment gains and of having changes in treatment generalize to other areas.

Another example of a higher order problem is the case of a woman who presents depression as her major problem. However, upon inquiry it is discovered that the woman also has serious marital problems. Since marital problems predispose women to depression, it may be best to request that the woman have her husband come to the clinic with her to receive marital therapy. As will be documented in Chapter 12, treatment for women with both marital problems and depression seems most effective when it focuses on the marital problems, not the individual depression (Beach & O'Leary, 1986).

The decision process about the specific targets for intervention has become quite complex, and Evans (1985) has argued that the term "target behavior" perpetuates a simplistic monosymptomatic view of therapy that fits well with the view of therapy as an experiment but is grossly unlike clinical practice. Evans's point reflects a desire to move beyond a finite target response or set of responses to a systems model that represents interacting behaviors. This approach is similar to that of Patterson and Bank (1986), who documented the interactive nature of parental and child behaviors. In brief, behavior therapists should consider their treatment in light of the social system in which they operate and the interactive nature of various "target behaviors" of an individual and his or her significant others.

Antecedent, Concurrent, and Consequent Events

A general strategy for analyzing presenting problems in a learning theory framework is to assess the antecedent, concurrent, and consequent events of the presenting problem. To assess these events, three general questions should be kept in mind.

1. What events usually precede the client's problem behavior? The events may be overt or covert, so that it is often necessary to assess both the client's thoughts and actions prior to the occurrence of problem behavior. Precipitants of behavior are usually sought in occurrences of the recent past, but on occasion it is necessary to assess early developmental history. In elementary school, complications at birth may be the original determinant of childhood problems such as hyperactivity associated with motor and neurological dysfunction. With couples in marital distress, it is important to discover what each of the spouses expected when the marriage began (Sager, 1976), because discord often emanates from changing or unfulfilled expectations that are not clearly communicated. In every case, assessment of what occurs just prior to the presenting problem is essential. If excessive drinking is the problem, it is important to find out whether the drinking is preceded by feelings of anger or depression or whether the drinking occurs in a jovial social atmosphere. If insomnia is the problem, it is important to assess the daytime stresses, mood, and negative self-statements during the day (Coates & Thoresen, 1984).

The extent to which an individual perceives that he or she can successfully execute a course of behavior is also predictive of how well he or she will perform. This belief about one's success is called a "self-efficacy judgment" (Bandura, 1986). Self-efficacy beliefs have been predictive of such diverse behavior as overcoming fears, stopping smoking, and tolerating pain. Of course, such predictions may be merely a function of one's skill level, but it has been shown that self-efficacy beliefs can predict better than skill level alone can.

2. What thoughts and feelings usually occur simultaneously with the problem behavior? When a person is anxious in social situations, it is important to know what he or she is thinking about when the anxiety occurs, since those thoughts can either exacerbate or ameliorate the anxiety. If a subject is instructed to attend to external cues rather than to his or her physiological state, fear will be reduced (Borkovec & O'Brien, 1977). Insomniacs report more presleep thoughts that are rated as "worried" and negative than good sleepers do (Borkovec, 1982). In short, the cognitions themselves appear to exacerbate the problem.

The import of assessing a client's thought patterns is illustrated in the case of Mr. B, an exhibitionist (Wilson & O'Leary, 1980). Before treatment, Mr. B's feelings could change from an initially weak sexual urge into an overwhelming compulsion to exhibit himself if, once he had an urge, he attended to a particular woman and her anticipated reactions. Treatment consisted, in part, of teaching Mr. B to attend to nonsexual thoughts and feelings as soon as he felt a temptation to expose himself.

In a series of interesting studies, Mischel and his colleagues (e.g., Mischel, Ebbesen, & Zeiss, 1972) showed that what preschool children think about while tempted can strongly affect their self-control. Children were placed in an experimental situation in which they were asked to wait alone in a room while the experimenter left on "an errand." During the waiting period two food treats were accessible, a very desirable one and one less so. The children were told that to obtain the more desirable treat, they had to wait until the experimenter returned. Children who were taught to think about something other than the desired food were much more effective in delaying gratification than children who were not given this suggestion.

3. What events follow the client's problem behavior? The therapist must look for a pattern of particular events that might follow from the problem behavior, because the client may not be aware that some of these events play a significant role in the maintenance of the problem. Consider a woman debilitated by a hysterical paralysis in her leg. Such a paralysis may allow her to avoid addressing a sexual problem with her husband, while her husband dutifully attends to her by preparing meals and doing housework. Psychodynamically oriented therapists call this set of circumstances "secondary gain" (Cameron, 1963). In this case, the secondary function of the paralysis is to keep the husband serving as a caretaker. A behavioral analysis of the wife's paralysis might lead to the interpretation that the hysterical paralysis is reinforced by two events, the attending and caretaking behaviors of the husband and the absence of sexual intercourse.

Another reason skillful interpretation of the client's report of consequences of certain behaviors is critical is that a client may report a series of events as negative, yet those very events may actually reinforce the problem behavior. A mother may repeatedly yell "Stop it!" or "Cut it out!" when her child cries or clings to her skirt. Such attention, even though negative, may unwittingly reinforce the undesired dependent behavior. Similarly, elementary school teachers can inadvertently encourage or reinforce overly active behavior by simply telling the child repeatedly to sit down (Madsen, Becker, Thomas, Koser, & Plager, 1968).

For children with severe developmental disabilities, disruptive behavior often serves an avoidant function. A child in a speech therapy session can remove himself or herself from a difficult session by throwing a temper tantrum. In exasperation, the therapist may simply terminate the speech training session. To alter this pattern, the teacher can teach the child to say, "This material is too hard" through verbal or nonverbal means (Carr & Durand, 1983).

Hallmarks of Behavioral Assessment

Behavioral assessment emphasizes current behavior of interpersonal import and situational determinants of that behavior. A behavior therapist focuses primarily on what a person *does* in particular situations rather than on inferences about general personality attributes (e.g., introversion, defensiveness). It is assumed that people exhibit different behaviors in different situations, and if a therapist wishes to know whether a person is unassertive, dependent, or depressed, the therapist must carefully ascertain in what situations the problematic behavior occurs. (Does the client cower in a supervisor's presence? Is the client afraid to criticize a spouse?) This emphasis on establishing covariation between behavior and its situational determinants may be contrasted with the psychodynamic approach, in which a behavior is almost always interpreted as a sign of some underlying personality characteristic or unconscious conflicts.

While behavior therapists focus on the assessment of the current problems reported by the client as well as on current determinants of those problems, they also seek to determine some history of the problems. In contrast to much traditional assessment, however, with most adult problems there is limited discussion of very early childhood experiences. Assessment is conducted to describe precisely current problem behaviors, to analyze their determinants, and to decide which treatment procedure should be used. Finally, assessment is a continuing process in behavior therapy. It does not occur simply when the client initially comes to the therapist's office; instead progress throughout therapy is monitored and treatment strategies are adjusted accordingly.

TYPES OF ASSESSMENT DATA

Swan and MacDonald (1978) conducted a survey of the assessment practices used by a large sample of behavior therapists. The ten most common practices and the percent of clients with whom the procedures were used are as follows:

Assessment Procedures	Percent of Usage
1. Client interview	89%
2. Client self-monitoring	51%
3. Interview with client's significant others	49%
4. Direct observation of target behaviors in situ	40%
5. Information from consulting professionals	40%
6. Role playing	34%
7. Behavior self-report measures	27%
8. Demographic questionnaires	20%
9. Personality inventories (tests)	20%
10. Projective tests	10%

Clearly, an interview with the client is almost universally employed. The reason the interview was not used 100 percent of the time is that with young children, a therapist may sometimes choose to interview the parents instead of the child.

After obtaining demographic information and conducting the initial interviews with the client or significant others (e.g., parents, teachers, physicians), a therapist will often collect more specific quantitative data. Other than interviews and demographic questionnaires, the assessment practices most frequently used by behavior therapists can be subsumed under four rubrics: self-recording, observing the problem in situ, taking personality inventories and self-report measures, and role playing. We will consider the advantages and disadvantages of the assessment interview as well as these assessment practices and, because of the theoretical import of physiological data, we will briefly note the role of physiological assessment.

The Assessment Interview

During assessment interviews, clinicians move from general descriptions of a client's problem to specific areas that should become the focus of treatment. To allow a client to feel free to divulge information that may be stressful and embarrassing, the clinician builds a relationship of trust and mutual understanding. Because of the crucial nature of mutual rapport, some guidelines for establishing such rapport will be briefly discussed, then the natural progression through intake interviews will be examined to illustrate how a therapist obtains critical assessment data and establishes the groundwork for treatment. Finally, methodological issues regarding reliability and validity of interviews will be explored.

Rapport Building.   Bernstein, Bernstein, and Dana (1974) provided some useful guidelines:

1. *Be Especially Attentive.* Try to follow the client's description of the problem, encourage his or her talking, and don't talk too much yourself.
2. *Be Emotionally Objective.* While remaining attentive and interested, try to keep the therapist's values from influencing the client—especially in the initial interview. The therapist should also be nonjudgmental, for if the client believes that the therapist dislikes what he or she has to say, the client may not speak openly.
3. *Be an Empathic Listener.* Try to understand the problem from the client's point of view and let him or her know you understand by accurately reflecting or restating the feelings or thoughts expressed.

4. *Make Clear that the Therapeutic Relationship is Confidential.* A client should know that information conveyed to a therapist will not be shared with anyone else.

Progression through Intake Interviews. Upon meeting the client for the first time, a therapist eases the client's anxiety by asking simple questions regarding demographic matters, for example, name of spouse, place of work, and educational background. Asking the client to talk about factual matters early in the interview not only relieves his or her anxiety, but also allows the therapist to compare the client's behavior in problematic and nonproblematic discussions. The therapist then focuses more directly on the presenting problem by learning:

1. When did the problem begin?
2. How frequently does it occur?
3. When and in what situations does it occur?
4. Generally, what occurs before and after it?
5. What does the client think about while the problem is occurring?
6. What has been done to change it thus far?

After obtaining detailed information about the nature of the presenting problem, the therapist should ascertain the client's strengths or assets. This is an excellent way to conclude the first interview so that the client leaves feeling more optimistic. Clients often do not pay sufficient attention to their assets, and having them discuss their strengths is a first step toward the frequent therapeutic goal of enhancing confidence in themselves.

Methodological Issues.   Interview data are often unreliable and subject to distortion, particularly if information is being obtained about past events. However, when the behavior of interest is about current events and is easily quantified (e.g., a child wet the bed,

a spouse cried), and when global and inferential judgments are minimal, interview data can be quite reliable (Linehan, 1977). Clinic and nonclinic children can be distinguished on the basis of structured interviews, and Herjanic, Herjanic, Brown, and Wheatt (1975) found 80 percent agreement between mothers and their children when they answered comparably structured interview questions.

Further, a client's self-report in an interview is often highly predictive of critical future behavior. Asking a young engaged couple how well they will succeed in marriage was more predictive of marital stability two years later than a number of personality or marriage tests (Markman, 1977). Similarly, asking college students to predict their grade point average was as predictive of that average as were complex personality and interest inventories (Mischel & Bentler, 1960). Finally, in predicting vocational choice, expressed interests in the job or vocation are superior to psychological tests (Shrauger & Osberg, 1982). In brief, clients may be much more aware of their own ability to do things than psychologists have assumed. If the right questions are asked in an interview, a client can provide information that may allow the therapist to integrate assessment and treatment skillfully.

Self-Recording

Self-recording is one of the oldest methods of obtaining information used by psychologists, and its use by well-known individuals to monitor the change or maintenance of behavior is interesting. For example, here is Skinner's (1967) autobiographical account.

In general I write very slowly and in long hand. It took me two minutes to write every word of my thesis and that is still about my rate. From three or four hours of writing each day I eventually salvage about one hundred publishable words . . . . I induce myself to write by making production as conspicuous as possible (by keeping a chart on the wall showing number of words written). (pp. 403, 408)

Skinner spends a specific amount of time per day in his office and daily records the number of pages he has written.

Irving Wallace, noted author of *The Prize* and *The Man*, depicted his own self-recording as well as that of other novelists in an especially intriguing article written with a behavioral psychologist (Wallace, 1977):

> With my fifth book, I started keeping a more detailed chart which also showed me how many pages I had written by the end of every working day. I am not sure why I started keeping such records. I suspect that it was because, as a free lance writer, entirely on my own, without employer or deadline, I wanted to create disciplines for myself, ones that were guilt-making when ignored. A chart on the wall served as such a discipline, its figures scolding me or encouraging me.

The use of self-recording in behavior therapy has become increasingly prevalent in the past few years for a number of reasons:

1. Self-control procedures have been developed which incorporate self-monitoring as an integral part of the therapeutic strategy (e.g., weight reduction programs which involve daily recording of caloric values of food consumed, times and places eating occurs, and feelings associated with eating).

2. Using observers in the natural environments of many clients, particularly adults, can be an invasion of privacy, is often extremely expensive and impractical, and sometimes produces changes in the behaviors observed.

3. Self-monitoring permits the assessment of extremely infrequent but important behaviors (e.g., seizures) that an independent observer could not record unless he or she followed the individual throughout the day.

4. The only way to assess the frequency of feelings, thoughts, and fantasies is to have the client monitor and record such events. (See Table 2-1.)

Current methods of self-recording vary from simple checks on a note pad to electronic devices that the client simply turns on to record his or her behavior. Many studies have used a simple golf-stroke counter to record the frequency of discrete events, such as number of cigarettes smoked, number of urges to hit someone, and number of supportive comments made to one's child. To avoid the conspicuousness of the golf-stroke counters, decorative wrist bands designed as miniature abacuses have been used to record several events at one time. The bands are designed with leather and a series of small decorative beads which can be moved from one side to another as the events in question occur.

Azrin and Powell (1968) developed a cigarette case that automatically records the number of times it is opened. Gravity-sensitive watches have been worn by hyperactive children to measure their activity levels (Schulmann & Reisman, 1959). Finally, as a result of space-age technology, very sophisticated telemetry devices allow a client to wear a sensor that sends a signal to a recording device at home, so that physiological measurements such as heart rate can be obtained in the natural environment. While these devices record events for the subject, the subject decides whether or not to use them; they are therefore often considered to be self-recording.

Reliability.   Reliability here refers to the percent of time that two individuals, usually a client and another observer, agree that a particular event has occurred. The reliability rates of self-recording have varied from approximately 50 to 100 percent. Lipinski and Nelson (1974) found that the reliability of the

Table 2–1 Daily Log of Depressed Feelings

PRECEDING EVENTS	FEELINGS	CONSEQUENT EVENTS
Monday Got a 65 on chemistry exam.	Had no energy. Didn't want to talk to anyone.	My boyfriend said I was a bore.
Tuesday Had a good night's sleep.	Good Day!	Caught up on Bio homework.
Wednesday Saw my boyfriend eating lunch with another girl.	Felt angry and jealous.	Cut class and took a nap.
Thursday Couldn't do Chem lab assignment.	Just can't learn Chemistry.	Called teaching assistant to ask about tutoring.
Friday Roommate got a permanent— looked great.	I'm ugly! (cried a lot)	She said she would cut my hair tomorrow.
Saturday My parents called.	Lonely—nothing to do here.	Listened to records and went to bed early.

self-recording of face touching was 52 percent. McFall (1970) found that self-recordings of smokers agreed with the observations of nonsmoking peers 61 percent of the time over a seventy-day period. Azrin and Powell (1969) obtained an agreement rate of 98 percent between hospital employees' records and self-recorded pill taking.

When the reliability of self-recording is low, procedures can be implemented to increase the agreement between self- and others' records. First, telling the client that his or her recording will be intermittently checked almost always leads to increased accuracy (Ciminero, Nelson, & Lipinski, 1977). Second, the reliability of self-recording rates can be improved if clients are reinforced for accurate self-recording (Ciminero, et al., 1977). Even with elementary school children, the relia-

bility of self-recordings of social and academic behavior in a classroom has been as high as 75 to 85 percent across a two-month period if the children are reinforced for accurate recordings (O'Leary, 1978).

Reactivity. If a client is simply asked to record minutes spent studying and then finds that there is an increase in study time, the self-recording is said to be *reactive*, in that the use of this procedure prompts a behavior change. Reactivity is a double-edged sword. If the therapist wishes to obtain a stable baseline of certain behaviors before instituting treatment so that the therapy can be evaluated, then reactivity is a clear disadvantage. On the other hand, since the therapist's goal is to help the client change, the reactivity of self-recording can be beneficial. Whether self-monitoring is reactive or not depends upon the specific behavior or factor being monitored. For example, monitoring calories is reliably associated with weight reduction, whereas monitoring of eating habits is not (Green, 1978).

Observation in Vivo

Observing problem behaviors in natural environments has been a hallmark of behavioral psychologists. Bijou (1965) emphasized the need for precise recordings of children's behavior in their home and school environments, and urged psychologists to use the frequencies of observable behaviors as their major dependent measures. This orientation is widespread. In fact, one of the major psychological journals, the *Journal of Applied Behavior Analysis (JABA)*, often requires authors to provide some in vivo observational measure of the behavior in question. Such observations have generally proven reliable, valid, and sensitive to treatment changes in a wide variety of settings, including homes,

schools, and hospital wards (Kent & Foster, 1977; Paul & Lentz, 1977). See Table 2-2 for an example of an observational system with children by Patterson, Cobb, and Ray (1972).

While assessment devices such as self-reports and psychological tests have long been known to suffer from a lack of reliability and the inability to predict the occurrence of behavior in the natural environment, the methodological problems of in vivo observation of behavior have become apparent only in the past decade. Problems of interest have been observer bias (the likelihood that an observer will be influenced by his or her expectations about what should occur), the effects of feedback on observational data, and the reactivity of the subjects to the observational process itself.

Observer Biases. Rosenthal (1969) was one of the first investigators to document the problem of observer biases. He and his associates showed that when observers were told to expect certain events in an experiment (e.g., one group of animals should learn faster),

---

Table 2–2 Observation Procedures in the Classroom Examples of Codes Used by Patterson, Cobb, and Ray, 1972.

Children are continuously observed in the classroom, and every six seconds the presence or absence of behaviors is noted by a specially trained observer.

AT Attending. This category is used whenever a person indicates by his behavior that he is doing what is appropriate in a school situation, e.g., he is looking at the teacher when she is presenting material to the class; he is looking at visual aids as the teacher tells about them; he has his eyes focused on his book as he does the reading assignment; he writes answers to arithmetic problems.

PN Physical negative. Use of this category is restricted to times when a person attacks or attempts to attack another person with the possibility of inflicting pain. Examples include slapping, spanking, kicking, biting, throwing objects at someone, etc.

NC Noncompliance. To be coded whenever the person does not do what is requested. This includes when teacher gives instructions to entire class and the subject does not comply.

LO Look around. Coded when person is looking around the room, looking out the window, or staring into space when an academic activity is occurring.

From Patterson, G. R., Cobb, J. A., and Ray, R. S. (1972). Direct intervention in the classroom: A set of procedures for the aggressive child. In *Implementing behavioral programs in educational and clinical settings*, eds. F. N. Clark, D. R. Evans, and L. A. Hamerlynch. Champaign, Ill.: Research Press, 151–201.

they reported the events even though unbiased measures indicated that the events did not occur. These findings, as well as studies by Azrin, Holz, Ulrich, and Goldiamond (1961) and Scott, Burton, and Yarrow (1967) led investigators to question the objectivity of observational recordings. We now know that the expectation effect or knowledge of experimenters' hypotheses is critical only when the behavior being observed is evaluated in a global fashion. In contrast, if an observer is asked to record the presence or absence of a behavior in small time units (e.g., every 30 seconds or every two minutes), no observer biases are found (Kent, O'Leary, Diament, & Dietz, 1974).

Feedback Effects on Observational Data. In many clinical situations, investigators may be very enthusiastic and indicate sincere relief and delight when an observer reports that the problem behavior (e.g., severe self-destructive behavior or intense tantrums) has decreased. O'Leary, Kent, and Kanowitz (1975) assessed whether this kind of experimenter feedback could artificially alter or bias an observer's recordings. They trained observers to record reliably the disruptive behavior of children in a classroom and then showed them videotapes that were purportedly of baseline and treatment phases of a recently completed study. The experimenter told the observers that certain of the behaviors were expected to decrease with the onset of treatment and other behaviors were not expected to change. In fact, as you might guess, the videotapes showed almost identical rates of behavior during the purported "baseline" and "treatment" phases. When an observer gave the experimenter data that indicated the "expected" decrease, the experimenter made comments such as "The treatment really seems to be working," or "Dr. Kent will really be glad to see the changes you are finding!" The expecta-

tions and feedback led the observers to report decreases in the "problem" behaviors which were expected to decrease, and no decreases in the behaviors which were expected to remain stable. The implication of this study is that investigators must be careful not to give feedback to observers that might artificially bias the data collection.

Reactivity of Observation. The potential effect of an observer's presence on the behavior being observed has been a concern for over twenty-five years (Kent & Foster, 1977). One of the first systematic investigations of reactivity was conducted by Roberts and Renzaglia (1965), who found that counselors made more interpretive statements when they knew that their sessions were obviously recorded than when the sessions were surreptitiously recorded. (The counselors knew that there was always some chance that sessions would be recorded.)

White (1977) evaluated the effects of observer presence on the interactions and activity levels of family members in a simulated living room setting by placing observers both in the room and behind a one-way mirror. He found lower rates of disruptive behavior for older children and less movement for all family members during the times an observer was in the room. His study is limited by the brevity of observation periods (four consecutive half-hour intervals), but it points to the need for an adaptation period in which the effects of observers would diminish. For example, when the effects of observers were evaluated in studies lasting at least ten days in institutions for the retarded (Mercatoris & Craighead, 1974), psychiatric hospitals (Hagen, Craighead, & Paul, 1975), elementary schools (Dubey, Kent, S. O'Leary, Broderick, & K.D. O'Leary, 1977), and junior high schools (Nelson, Kapust, & Dorsey, 1978), very few effects of observers were found. While there is no systematic research evaluating the factors that increase reactivity, the authors feel that the reactivity effect will be strongest when brief observations are made of normal adolescents and adults and of children with conduct disorders.

Self-Report and Personality Inventories

Role of Personality Tests.   Psychologists have used personality tests or inventories for decades, but behavioral psychologists have often been reluctant to use them. In fact, as noted in the Swan and MacDonald (1978) survey, behavior therapists use personality tests with only 20 percent of their clients. One of the personality tests most widely used by psychologists, the Minnesota Multiphasic Personality Inventory (MMPI), is used largely to classify patients into diagnostic categories, such as schizophrenic, depressive reaction, or psychopathic personality (Box 2.1). In fact, a survey of behavior therapists about assessment by Piotrowski and Keller (1984) indicated that 70 percent of the respondents felt that professional practitioners should be familiar with the MMPI. The test was held to be the most important for a practitioner to know. It has been more empirically investigated than any other objective personality assessment and has

been subject to computer profile analyses so that a clinician can obtain objective summaries of his or her client based on its data. These summaries are available commercially for individual use through data centers or computer programs using the two to three scales on which the individual scores the highest (high point codes). If an individual scores higher than the upper 2 percent of the population on various scales, such as depression or psychopathy, a clinician will be more confident that the individual is, in fact, providing statistically deviant responses. A second example of a frequently used personality test is the Taylor Manifest Anxiety Scale (MAS) which is used to determine the level of anxiety of adults. Tests such as the MAS were developed to describe individuals in terms of personality traits, that is, enduring psychic structures or stylistic consistencies in social behavior. Thus, individuals are asked to make statements about themselves that would apply in diverse situations (e.g., I generally perspire, I feel uneasy in the presence of others).

While there have been many legitimate criticisms of the utility of personality tests in the measurement of traits and the assignment of individuals to diagnostic categories (Kendall & Norton-Ford, 1982), the tests have been useful in predicting how people will behave in certain situations and in estimating the se-

---

Box 2–1   *Minnesota Multiphasic Personality Inventory: Selected Items from a 60-item Depression Scale*

If an individual answers as indicated, True or False, the item is scored positively for depression.

F   I have a good appetite.
T   I am easily awakened by noise.
F   I am about as able to work as I ever was.
F   My daily life is full of things that keep me interested.
T   I find it hard to keep my mind on a task or job.

(Psychological Corporation, New York, N.Y., 1970.)

verity of their problems. It is compatible with a behavioral approach to use personality tests for this purpose and to do so does not necessitate adopting a trait theory of personality (Hogan, Desoto, & Solanto, 1977). For example, on the basis of a hyperactivity index (Conners, 1969) completed by a parent or teacher, the therapist can compare the referred child with a large normative population of a particular country and say, "Your child scores in the upper 5 percent of the school population with regard to his activity level" (Arias & O'Leary, 1983). Similarly, normative profiles are available for college men and women on a 122-item Fear Survey Schedule used to assess diverse fears of a client (Tasto, Hickson, & Rubin, 1971). The score a client receives can be compared to those of a nonclinical population, and as noted above, this comparison can aid the therapist in determining the severity of the problem.

Behavioral psychologists such as Eysenck recommended personality inventories as a means of placing an individual on a particular dimension (Eysenck & Eysenck, 1976) and Peterson and Quay (Quay, 1979) developed a children's assessment device which involves having a parent complete a fifty-five-item checklist on which he or she indicates whether or not the child exhibits certain behaviors. On the basis of the parent's responses, a child can be described on four basic dimensions: conduct disorder, personality disorder, subcultural delinquency, and inadequacy-immaturity. This assessment device is sensitive to change from both psychological and pharmacological treatments and has been validated in scores of studies using both laboratory measures and observations in vivo (Quay & Werry, 1986).

Specific Self-Report Questionnaires. While traditional personality tests were designed to measure the modes of responding

characteristic of an individual in diverse situations (e.g., anxiety and fear), behavior therapists have placed a strong emphasis on assessing responses to specific situations (e.g., fear of public speaking). Some examples of self-report questionnaires are fear surveys to assess fear of small animals, pain, death, and aggression (Geer, 1965; Wolpe & Lang, 1964) and social anxiety tests (Rathus, 1973). These self-report devices are designed to measure relatively focal areas of clients' problems and, as such, may be used more frequently by behavior therapists. The specificity of the assertiveness assessment is seen in the Spouse-Specific Assertion Scale (O'Leary & Curley, 1986; Table 2-3), a self-report device used to assess the ease with which one spouse can communicate with the other.

Methodological Issues

Validity. In general, validity refers to the relationship or correlation between a test score and a criterion. Personality tests and specific self-report inventories have long been plagued by low validity. The correlations between individuals' scores on personality tests and outcome criteria are seldom greater than 0.40 (Wiggins, 1973). Further, even individuals' scores on self-report inventories such as a fear survey (Geer, 1965) often correlate only slightly higher with outcome criteria than more general personality tests' measures. For example, Geer (1965) reported correlations of 0.39 and 0.55 between Fear Survey Schedule and the Taylor Manifest Anxiety Scale (MAS) scores for men and women, respectively.

Client Distortion. A client can easily consciously overdramatize or deny his or her problems and complete a personality test or self-report inventory accordingly. Certain personality tests such as the MMPI contain scales to measure client distortions such as

Table 2–3   Spouse-Specific Assertiveness Inventory

Directions: Please use the scale described below to indicate how characteristic or descriptive each of the following statements is of you. After reading each statement, choose a number from the scale and place it in the space provided.

CODE: +3   extremely descriptive, very much like me
+2   quite descriptive, rather like me
+1   slightly descriptive, somewhat like me
−1   slightly nondescriptive, somewhat unlike me
−2   quite nondescriptive, rather unlike me
−3   extremely nondescriptive, not at all like me

STATEMENTS:

_____ Confronting my mate with problems as they come up is seldom a problem for me.

_____ I frequently find that I am able to ask my mate to do me favors without any difficulty.

_____ Challenging my mate's beliefs is something I can do with little difficulty.

_____ I can express a differing point-of-view to my mate without much difficulty.

From O'Leary, K.D., and Curley, A.D. (1986). Assertion and family violence: Correlates of spouse abuse. Journal of Marital and Family Therapy, *12 (3), 281–90.*

"faking good," and such distortion is used to make corrections on separate subtests of the MMPI. However, these correction indices are often difficult to devise and do not always lead to increases in the validity of the test (McCrae & Costa, 1983).

Lack of Specification of Problems for Treatment.   Even a specific self-report inventory, such as one which requires that a parent or teacher complete a questionnaire regarding the hyperactivity of a child, does not necessarily give a therapist clear notions of the problems to be treated. A child may receive a score on a rating scale of hyperactivity which places him or her in the upper 5 percent of the population of elementary school children. However, such knowledge does not provide the therapist with enough information to delineate problem behaviors or make various decisions regarding a treatment program [e.g., (1) Completion of math assignments should receive first priority; (2) cooperation with other children on in-class

projects is of secondary importance; and (3) an increase in frustration tolerance regarding siblings' late bedtime should not be addressed until some progress is made in school]. Such treatment goals generally come only from detailed clinical interviews and/or in vivo observation.

Role Playing

Role playing, as the name implies, consists of having a client enact various interpersonal encounters (e.g., asking a friend for a date, questioning a supervisor's judgment, complimenting a family member, responding to a job interviewer in a confident manner, or communicating without hostility with spouse). Role playing has long been used by therapists of varying persuasions. In fact, role playing was made popular by Moreno, a psychodynamically oriented psychiatrist, who introduced psychodrama in the United States in 1925. Psychodrama involves the enactment of interpersonal experiences in a group therapy context. The therapist serves as a director, fellow group members assume various roles, and clients are prompted to express feelings associated with critical interpersonal experiences—often related to early childhood interactions (Moreno, 1946). Similarly, Gestalt therapists use role playing games or exercises (Levitsky & Perls, 1970) to help clients in groups experience feelings in the "here and now." In assessing a client's problem, a behavior therapist uses role playing in an individual therapy context as a series of mini-experiments in which he or she tries to systematically expose the client to relevant, largely current, interpersonal encounters likely to be associated with the client's problems. Behavior therapists use role playing both to assess interpersonal problems and as a treatment procedure, but we will restrict our discussion primarily to role playing as an assessment procedure.

Functions in Assessment. As noted by Swan and MacDonald (1978), role playing is used with 34 percent of the clients seen by behavior therapists. The assessment of a client's behavior is facilitated by the therapist taking the role of the person with whom the client has difficulty (e.g., the supervisor, child, or employer). Using role playing, a therapist can quickly assess a client's skills in a wide variety of interpersonal situations. While direct in vivo observation of a client's interpersonal skills is often desirable, such observations may be impractical with an employer, a grandparent, or a girlfriend or boyfriend. The role playing encounter allows a therapist to discover how a client reacts and feels when presented with situations that resemble his or her most anxiety-provoking real-life encounters.

Factors Influencing Role Playing. The enactment of roles by client and therapist pro-

vides for a direct and very specific assessment of the client's behavior. The validity of this approach is partly a function of the client's ability to assume roles and to do so in a manner that captures some of the emotional tenor of encounters with critical persons in his or her life. Fortunately, after some practice and guidance, most clients are able to overcome uneasiness they have about the "acting" role and can simulate their significant encounters quite well. When such is not the case, the therapist can ask the client to give detailed verbal descriptions of what he or she would say in situations which cause difficulty.

The therapist's ability to utilize role playing effectively is dependent upon his or her knowledge of typical problems presented by the significant other individuals in the client's life. For example, if a therapist has a mother role play her interactions with her teenager, the therapist should know both characteristic problems presented by the teenager as well as the verbal style and idiomatic expressions which are likely to elicit emotional responses in the mother. Similarly, if a therapist has a client assume the role of a job applicant, the therapist should have some clear knowledge of the types of questions asked by an employment interviewer and the interpersonal styles of such interviewers.

Role playing as an assessment procedure has not received as much research attention as other assessment methods. As Goldfried and Linehan (1977) noted, there is a trend toward assuming that role playing itself serves as an adequate assessment of the actual encounters of the client. The assessment of assertive behavior is one of the few areas in which the validity of role playing has been examined empirically, and there is evidence that it is useful in the assessment of assertion of adolescents and college students (Friedman, 1974; MacDonald, 1978; McFall & Lillesand, 1971). Since role playing is a widely used procedure, research on its reliability and validity is clearly needed.

Physiological Measurement

Physiological measures have been increasingly used in behavioral assessment research in recent years, but they are infrequently used by clinicians. Temperature, respiration rate, penile erection measures, and vaginal blood flow have been used to measure sexual arousal. Measurements of heart rate, blood pressure, and skin resistance responses have been used extensively in studies assessing fear. While certain physiological measures, such as blood pressure and heart rate, could easily be obtained in any behavior therapist's office, most physiological measures require expensive instrumentation not usually found in psychological or psychiatric clinics. In addition to cost factors, many physiological measures do not correlate highly with self-report and observational measures. This does not mean that physiological measures are less valid than self-report or observational measures, but a client's self-report is the report clinicians generally attend to most seriously, since self-report of problems is almost always the criterion for entry into and termination of therapy (Barlow, 1977). Despite the infrequent use of physiological measures by clinicians, several examples of their role in clinical research and/or treatment follow.

The type and duration of women's sexual responses have long been the subject of debate largely because there were no devices that allowed a clinician to assess women's genital responses. Fortunately, Geer, Morokoff, and Greenwood (1974) developed a device that measures blood flow in the vaginal wall. A clear, light-sensitive probe (one-half-inch diameter by one-and-three-fourths-inch length) allows a clinician to measure the amount of light reflected by vaginal wall tis-

sue (See picture below). As arousal and blood flow increase, less light is transmitted through the probe. For some women, change in vaginal blood volume is a reliable indicator of orgasm (Geer, 1977). This technological development has enabled researchers to assess sexual arousal in females. Variations of this device for vaginal photoplethysmography have been developed to minimize error due to positioning, probe size, and vaginal contractions (Hoon, Murphy, Laughter, & Abel, 1984).

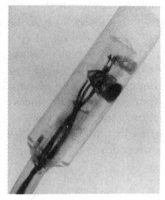

Vaginal probe containing light source (light circular area) and photocell (dark circular area) that is used to measure vaginal blood volume changes. Reflected light passes through the vaginal wall tissue and is reflected to the photocell surface. When viewing erotic films, the blood volume increases markedly over a resting period. (Geer, Morokoff, & Greenwood, 1974.)

Men with serious problems of low sexual desire who do not experience erections while awake are candidates for sleep laboratory assessment. This involves the use of a penile plethysmograph, a device attached to the penis during sleep which measures the engorgement with blood of the penis during erection. The physiological assessment is conducted because if erections do occur in sleep it is highly likely that the man's erectile problem is psychological. However, if there are no erections during sleep, physical and/or biochemical factors need to be addressed (LoPiccolo & Daiss, in press).

The role of physiological measurement is highlighted in the treatment of certain enuretic children (bedwetters) with night terror. Such children have frightening dreams; they awaken abruptly, sometimes screaming (e.g., "I won't do it!"); and then they wet their beds (Sperling, 1971). Dreams usually occur during a period of sleep in which there is a great deal of electrical discharge in the brain and the eyes move rapidly (REM sleep). It is possible to detect REM sleep by placing a small sensing device near the corner of the eye (electro-oculogram). When the clinician has a suspicion that night terror and REM sleep are precursors to bedwetting, a physiological assessment can be made to confirm or reject the clinician's hunches. If night terror and REM sleep are precipitants of the enuresis, the therapist can address the child's fears and dreams rather than focusing on toileting habits and exercises designed to increase bladder size.

Physiological assessment has also been used in the assessment of marital conflict by Levenson and Gottman (1983). They had couples talk about issues that had been a major source of disagreement. On another occasion, the spouses returned to the laboratory to view a videotape of their discussion, during which each provided a continuous self-rating of affect on a rating dial that utilized a "positive-neutral-negative" scale. During both the initial discussion and the sessions in which the spouses viewed their videotaped discussions, four physiological measures were obtained: heart rate, finger pulse, skin conductance, and general somatic activity. Not only were these physiological indices correlated with marital dissatisfaction, they were also predictive of decline in marital satisfaction across a three-year period. To many investigators' amazement, the husband's heart rate during the conflict resolution correlated .92 with declines in marital satisfaction. This research has been very valuable in conceptualizing marital distress and in providing some tentative explanations for some of the frequently noted clinical descriptions about the differences between men and women. More specifically, men have been described as likely to attempt to terminate negative affect in problematic encounters with their mates. In contrast, women have been described as less conciliatory, more conflict-engaging, and less likely to withdraw from negative affect. On the basis of their data, Levenson and Gottman propose that males show a greater autonomic nervous system response to stress, respond more rapidly to this stress, and recover from it more slowly than females do.

MULTIMETHOD ASSESSMENT

It should now be clear that no assessment method is superior. Each has its particular advantages and disadvantages, and sometimes there is only moderate agreement between the various assessment methods. With regard to the measurement of sexual behavior of women by the vaginal probe, it has been shown that alcohol decreases actual sexual arousal, but increases women's self-report of sexual arousal (Wilson & Lawson, 1976). In the assessment of anxiety, Lang (1977) has shown that behavioral, physiological, and subjective reports are not always significantly correlated and sometimes change differentially in response to different treatment methods. Given this lack of correspondence between various assessment measures and the advantages and disadvantages of each assessment domain, numerous behavioral clinicians, such as Lazarus (1976), Lobitz and Johnson (1975), and O'Leary and Johnson (1979; 1986), have argued for a multimodal or multimethod assessment approach using a combination of demographic questionnaires, interviews, personality inventories, and when possible, naturalistic observations of the problem behavior.

FUTURE DIRECTIONS

Computer-Assisted Assessment

Computer-assisted assessment has been used since the mid-1960s by mental health personnel. The majority of these assessments were focused on personality testing, and, in particular, the MMPI received the greatest interest by clinicians. Personality assessment was out of favor by psychologists for some time, and by behavior therapists, in particular. Nonetheless, most behavior therapists feel that their colleagues should know how to use the MMPI. The sympathy with the MMPI was natural for behavioral psychologists because of its empirical approach to assessment. Moreover, since clinics and court systems often require some empirical assessment approach, the MMPI and similar personality scales have grown in favor. For example, Johnson and Williams (1980) developed a computer-based assessment which included the MMPI, a test of intelligence and memory, a social history and problem checklist, the Beck Depression Inventory, and a structured mental status examination. This assessment approach was designed so that a client/patient could punch his or her own answers directly into a computer terminal. Results with this approach have shown it to be superior to and more reliable than traditional methods and to cost half as much as standard evaluations.

Computer-assisted assessment has not been used to any great extent by behavior therapists outside their clinical practices. However, in almost any comprehensive assessments that remain standardized for several years,

the use of computer-assisted assessment is economical and clinically sound. It is a direct and reliable method of data gathering. A review of such assessment by Fowler (1985) indicated that clients, in fact, often prefer taking personality tests by computer, and even phobic patients (Carr & Ghosh, 1983) showed no apprehension about completing a full behavioral assessment by computer. In brief, professionals have been more reluctant to use computer-assisted assessment than have their clients and patients.

Despite the increase in the use of computerized assessment, there is a growing concern about its commercialization. The concern stems from the "pages and pages of today's neatly typed, valid-sounding narrative interpretations that are the products, for the most part, of secretly developed disks of software that have not even been offered for scientific evaluation" (Matarazzo, 1986; p. 15). The clinician cannot be left out of the process of assessment; computerized psychological interpretations are but one element of a psychological assessment. Like other scientific developments in screening and assessment in health care, the cost of computerized assessment has been increasingly borne by third party payments in the public sector. Matarazzo is concerned that if psychologists do not act to monitor their own professional behavior, government agencies and consumer groups will. Finally, he argues that simply because the results of a test are objectively scored does not mean that the interpretation of the results is objective. Interpretation of test results, regardless of their source, requires a well-trained and experienced practitioner.

Research on Temporal Stability

The emphasis by behavior therapists on assessing specific behaviors in different situations has been evident for years. This emphasis was prompted in part by a rejection of psychodynamic trait notions and by research which indicated little consistency in behavior across situations. As Mischel and Peake (1982) noted, "Few assumptions are simultaneously more self-evident, yet more hotly disputed, than that an individual's behavior is characterized by pervasive cross-situational consistencies" (p. 730). On one hand, they said that there appears to be compelling intuitive evidence that supports the notion that people are characterized by broad dispositions that seem to be stable across situations. On the other hand, "the history of research in the area has yielded persistently perplexing results, suggesting much less consistency than our intuitions predict" (p. 730). Because of the problems of not finding consistency of behavior in personality research, two approaches have become prominent. First, there are those that challenge and/or reject trait theories and then look for methods of studying person/situation interactions. Second, others, such as Bem and Funder (1978), have felt that the trait assumptions may be valid but the methods of assessing behavior across situations may be inadequate. Third, Mischel has argued that a reconceptualization utilizing a cognitive prototype enables one to find consistency in behavior across time though not necessarily across settings. As Mischel and Peake (1982) argued, "Instead of seeking high levels of cross-situational consistency—instead of looking for broad averages—we may need, instead, to identify unique bundles or sets of temporally stable prototypic behaviors—key features—that characterize the person even over long periods of time but not necessarily across many or all possibly relevant situations" (p. 574). Mischel and Peake obtained data on conscientiousness/studiousness from sixty-three student volunteers at Carleton College in Minnesota. To qualify as a measure of temporal stability, the correla-

tion had to consist of two observations of the same type of measure. For example, "lecture attendance on day one correlated with lecture attendance on day six" is a measure of temporal stability, and approximately half of the tests of association reflected stability. An example of cross-situational consistency was the correlation of appointment punctuality with lecture punctuality. Only 20 percent of the tests of the association of cross-situational consistency were significant. When subjects' self-perceptions of their own consistency were taken into account, differential prediction was possible. Temporal stability was highest for those high in perception of self-consistency. Further, when the most prototypic behaviors of conscientiousness were selected by the subjects themselves, correlations for the subjects with high perception of consistency were even higher. In short, the findings of Mischel and Peake suggest that individuals judge their degree of consistency from the temporal stability of the relevant prototypic behavior. Such research is intriguing because it poses the possibility of looking at consistency of behavior from a new vantage point.

Need for Construct Clarity

The concern for construct clarity was made especially apparent in a manuscript by Bradbury and Fincham (1986), who critically evaluated standardized tests of marital satisfaction. Essentially, they argued that standardized tests of marital adjustment and marital satisfaction are confounded with varied measures of communication, affect, family relations, and sexual interaction. While it can be argued that marital satisfaction encompasses attitudes, affect, and behavior, Fincham and Bradbury argue that it is necessary to separate satisfaction itself as a criterion from the component constructs that might correlate with marital satisfaction. Until it is known how to decide rationally or empirically the weight of various components of marital satisfaction, it was felt that "pure" measures of satisfaction should first be developed which rate satisfaction alone—not aspects of communication, sexual behavior, affectionate interactions, and daily companionship.

The cogency of this argument is apparent when one reviews the marital literature and finds that groups of couples have been selected because of their scores on marital adjustment tests (high satisfaction versus low satisfaction) and that their investigators evaluate whether the groups differ on various measures such as communication. However, as Fincham and Bradbury (1986) note, the satisfaction measure used to select the groups initially contains many items that assess communication. In brief, there is a circularity in the validation process, in that selection is confounded by the communication items because the investigator is attempting to assess whether satisfied versus dissatisfied couples differ on communication measures. The need, therefore, to have a pure measure of satisfaction becomes apparent. This example was taken from the marital therapy literature, but construct clarity is critical in any area in which one wishes to develop reasonable theoretical models of behavior.

Patterson and Bank (1986) proposed a theoretical model for "Basic Training In Home For Antisocial Behavior." The model building of Patterson is exemplary in child behavior therapy in that theoretical constructs are well defined and assessed with several measures. The relationships among the constructs are specified in the model prior to empirical testing. The model is then evaluated by examining whether or not the proposed relationships relate well to the obtained data. In brief, there is a testing of the model by a procedure called "goodness of fit." If the data are consistent with the model, it does not mean that other models would not also explain the data. Therefore, investigators like Patterson attempt to see how well alternative models "fit" the obtained relationships.

The model of training in antisocial behavior is presented below:

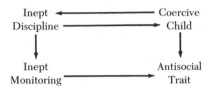

Inept discipline is said to be related to inept monitoring and to having a coercive child. Inept monitoring of children is held to be related to inept discipline and antisocial traits. Discipline is the key variable in the model but children also serve to increase a parent's inept discipline as indicated by the bidirectional arrows. To evaluate the model, several measures of a construct are used, as exemplified by the evaluation of coercion by three measures of observation obtained in the home:

1. The probability of a child starting a conflict given that the parent had acted in a positive or neutral way,

2. The probability of a child starting a fight with a sibling given that the sibling was positive or neutral with the child,

3. The length of the child's negative interactions with family members.

Support for the model of training in antisocial behavior was provided by Patterson and Bank (1986), who used a number of different statistical procedures, including comparing obtained data with the model and path coefficients. As hypothesized, inept monitoring leads to antisocial traits; inept discipline and the coercive child patterns interact upon each other; inept discipline leads to inept monitoring and the coercive child. The paths (path coefficients) and magnitude of the relationships are noted below:

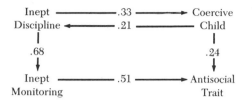

To evaluate relationships among constructs one has to have several measures which should have conceptual clarity. Without such clarity, the ability to arrive at reasonable conclusions would be significantly impaired. The Patterson and Bank (1986) research is an excellent example of the need for conceptual clarity of varied constructs in the model-building stage of research.

SUMMARY

All therapists assess clients and their problems. If a decision is made that a client's problems warrant treatment, the therapist must carefully decide whether the problems presented should be addressed directly in therapy or whether some unmentioned or "higher order" problem should be the primary treatment target. A general framework for analyzing presenting problems in behavior therapy is to assess antecedent, concurrent, and consequent events. In addition, however, recent emphasis in behavioral assessment has been to analyze common everyday problems and

their determinants in order to aid individuals in preventing the development of problems which require intensive individual therapeutic aid.

The assessment interview is the most important step in analyzing any clinical problem, but it should be supplemented by other assessment data. Whenever possible, direct observations of behavior are desirable. Alternatively, daily self-recordings often can provide a useful account of behavior. Self-report and personality inventories have been used by behavior therapists to place an individual in some normative group and sometimes as dependent measures to evaluate the effectiveness of a treatment. Physiological measures have proven very informative in that—particularly through the assessment of anxiety and sexual responsiveness—they have highlighted the lack of convergence of assessment data from different domains (e.g., self-report, observational, and physiological data). Such imperfect correspondence is undoubtedly the case in the measurement of most other behavior, and it is apparent that each assessment method has unique advantages and disadvantages. Consequently, whenever practically feasible, several assessment methods should be used in assessing any clinical problem. There undoubtedly will be an increasing reliance on computerized assessment, but such assessment should be executed by an experienced clinician who can place any computer results within a broad context of the client's social and emotional assets and deficiencies.

3

Fears and Phobias

To go through life without fear is impossible. More importantly, life without fear would be exceedingly dull. We all have experienced situations with some fear, such as a first dive from a high diving board, a first flight in an airplane, or a first public speech. We all have experienced situations such as examinations in which a certain amount of fear is obviously useful. Caution, prompted by fear, regarding dangerous water, streets, and knives, in fact, may be particularly useful for children. When fear becomes great, however, it can be debilitating. Children may be terrified of water, of being alone, of being in the dark, or of going near a dog. They may be frightened of dentists, doctors, and hospitals and terrified of needles or "shots." A fear is a normal response to a real or imagined threat. As Miller (1951) noted, the behavioral effects of fear are often strikingly different. On one hand, certain animals and humans may remain motionless. On the other hand, one may verbalize a great deal, pace the floor, or flee. Apparently, both patterns are prompted by fear, and the patterns may alternate from one to the other as exemplified by animals who at one moment freeze and at another run for shelter (Marks, 1969).

A phobia is a special kind of fear. The word phobia is derived from a Greek word *phobos* meaning flight, panic-fear, or terror. It also has roots in the deity of the same name, who could provoke fear and panic in one's enemies. In fact, according to Marks (1969), the Greeks made masks on their weaponry depicting the god Phobos, who purportedly frightened off the enemy. When reviewing the terminology concerning fears from the nineteenth century to the present, Marks found considerable agreement among the definitions and he thus defined a phobia as "a special form of a fear which: (1) is out of proportion to the demands of the situation, (2) cannot be explained or reasoned away, (3) is beyond voluntary control, and (4) leads to avoidance of the feared situation" (Marks, 1969, p. 3). Further, with children one would have to add a fifth criterion, namely, the fear is age inappropriate.

On the basis of data from England and the

United States, it appears that 1 to 4 percent of childhood cases are referred to clinics for fears, and 7 percent of a behavior therapist's referrals are for fears (Graziano, DeGiovanni, and Garcia, 1979). All children develop certain specific fears, and an evaluation of their etiology and means by which a parent and/or clinician may most effectively deal with such fears will be discussed below. School phobias, on the other hand, represent a unique and often highly serious problem for parents, teachers, and clinicians, and their etiology and treatment will be considered in a separate section.

ACQUISITION OF FEARS AND PHOBIAS

Innate Fears

When a child is born he displays fearful responses to only two stimuli: loud noises and falling. His response to such stimuli is called a Moro reflex, which is characterized by a fanning of the arms in a clutching fashion and simultaneous arching of the back. It is believed that the Moro reflex had adaptive survival features in that its display would alert a mother who was carrying an infant about to fall from her hip. The Moro reflex is a significant reflex of a newborn, and it is one of the reflexes used to assess a child's neurological development; its absence in a newborn or its failure to later develop into a startle reflex would indicate a serious lag in development.

Jersild and Holmes (1935) detailed the extent and development of children's fears and documented how a young child shows an innate startle response to sudden intense or unexpected stimuli. As soon as a child can crawl he or she can discriminate and avoid depth. At one year a child becomes particularly fearful of strangers, as many house visitors or relatives will attest. They peer into a child's crib awaiting a smile only to find a wailing infant. Jersild and Holmes depicted the relative frequency of various fears in their classic 1935 monograph (see Figure 3–1). Most interesting is the change from fears of specific physical events and situations (left portion of figure) to fears of imaginary objects and creatures (right portion of figure) at forty-eight to seventy-one months. As the fears of physical objects decrease, fears of imaginary objects increase. It is generally felt that the fears of loud noises, falling, pain, and depth are largely innate mechanisms. Though they do not occur invariably each time a stimulus is presented, they are so uniform across cultures with highly different infant environments and so generally consistent to most stimuli that they are probably the result of inborn mechanisms which mature in the first year of life. We will discuss why some fears long felt to be universal are not now viewed in that manner when we consider the environmental context in which fears are assessed.

Classical Conditioning

In 1920, the famous radical behaviorist, John B. Watson, and his graduate student, Rosalie Rayner, published the first conditioning experiment of emotional behavior. A healthy nine-month-old male, Albert, was confronted for the first time with a white rat, a white rabbit, masks with and without hair, a dog, a monkey, and burning newspaper. He displayed no fear when presented with any of these objects. However, when a loud hammer struck a large steel bar, the child startled. He showed a change in breathing and a raising of the arms characteristic of the startle reflex of young children. On later strikings of the hammer, Albert's lips trembled and he

PERCENT OF FEARS

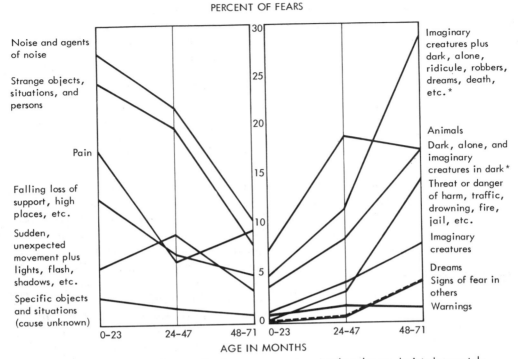

Figure 3–1 Relative frequency of various fear responses. (From Jersild and Holmes, *Children's Fears* (1935), 54.)

began to cry (Watson & Rayner, 1920). Watson had a stimulus which elicited a reliable fearful response and which could be used to test whether Albert would learn by association with the noise of the hammer to be afraid of other objects. At eleven months of age, Albert's conditioning trials began. As Albert reached out to touch the white rat, the hammer was struck behind Albert's head. Albert was obviously frightened; he fell forward and began to cry.

One week later he was again exposed to the white rat without the noise of the striking hammer. Albert reached for the rat but did not touch it. After seven simultaneous presentations of the rat and striking hammer, however, Albert was presented with the rat alone and began to cry. In brief, it was felt that an emotional response of fear had been conditioned to the white rat. To assess whether this fear generalized or transferred, Albert was presented with cotton, wool, a white rabbit and a Santa Claus mask. Albert displayed varying degrees of fear to all of these stimuli to which he was impervious at nine months, and thus it was felt that a learned generalized fear had been established. Finally, one month later, all the stimuli were again presented to Albert, and though his reactions were less extreme than they had been previously, he clearly showed some fearful responses to them.

Watson and Rayner concluded that they had established conditioned fear which had generalized across time and objects.

Those experiments would seem to show conclusively that directly conditioned emotional responses as well as those conditioned by transfer persist, although with a certain loss in the intensity of the reaction for a longer period than one month. Our view is that they persist and modify personality throughout life. (Watson & Rayner, 1920, p. 12)

Watson was dealing with an exceedingly healthy boy. Had he been a fearful child or otherwise emotionally unstable, the investigators felt the conditioned response would have persisted throughout the one-month interval without diminution. Albert left the hospital earlier than expected, and Watson and Rayner were not able to decondition Albert's fear of white objects. Because anxiety was held by most psychiatrists and psychologists to be the precursor of all neuroses, the induction of experimental fear was held to be an ignoble, dastardly act. It was held that Albert might later fear white lab coats, doctors, and dentists because he could have developed a generalized fear of all white things. God forbid, he might even be afraid of platinum blondes or his gray-haired grandmother! While we do not know of Albert's later history, Mary Cover Jones (1924a), showed that children's fears could be reduced via a number of procedures. She studied seventy children aged three months to seven years and assessed various means of reducing fears in laboratory surroundings. Interestingly, she found that presenting the feared object, ridiculing or teasing the child about his fears, and verbal exhortation and appeal did not reduce fears. On the other hand, direct conditioning and social imitation were notably successful in reducing fears. By associating the feared object with the pleasure of eating, the child's fears were reduced; similarly, by placing the child with youngsters without fear, the fear was abated.

In a now famous sequel to Albert's case, Peter, a thirty-four-month-old healthy child with exaggerated fears, was evaluated by Dr. M.C. Jones in 1924. Peter's fears ranged from a rabbit or fur coat to cotton wool. The child was an ideal subject for the study of whether a fear could be "unlearned" in a manner similar to the way in which Watson and Rayner demonstrated that fears could be "conditioned." Because Peter had a greater fear of the rabbit than the rat, the rabbit was selected as the object for deconditioning. Peter was brought into a playroom daily with three other children who had been selected because of their absence of fears. The rabbit was always present during these play periods. To facilitate the "unconditioning," Peter was seated in a highchair and given food which he liked while the rabbit was gradually brought closer to him. As Peter was deconditioned, he was observed in a detailed sequence of toleration steps as follows:

1. Rabbit anywhere in room caused fear reaction.
2. Rabbit three feet away in cage tolerated.
3. Rabbit close in cage tolerated.
4. Rabbit free in room tolerated.
5. Rabbit touched when experimenter held it.
6. Rabbit allowed on tray of chair.
7. Held rabbit on lap.
8. Let rabbit nibble his fingers.

This successful experiment, as we shall see later, was a critical precursor to Wolpe's use of systematic desensitization, a procedure used to reduce fears in adults in which gradual steps in a feared hierarchy are imagined by a patient while in a relaxed state.

It appeared that fears in young children could be conditioned and deconditioned with relative ease. In addition, Harold Jones (1931) demonstrated the acquisition of a conditioned fear in a fifteen-month-old child within a very brief time. However, Bregman (1934) of the

Institute of Educational Research at Teachers College of Columbia University failed to replicate the conditioning effect with fifteen infants, ranging in age from eleven to sixteen months. Bregman used quite different stimuli from those of the earlier experiments and attempted to ascertain whether a child's reaction to neutral stimuli could be conditioned via association with other positive and negative stimuli. As neutral objects she chose geometric forms; the positive stimuli were a baby's rattle and a music box, while the negative stimulus was a loud cowbell mounted on the back of a child's chair. The positive stimuli were paired with one half of the geometric shapes and the negative stimulus was paired with the other half. Though this study has been strongly and legitimately criticized by Yates (1970) because of the very difficult discriminations an infant would have to make, the study did raise serious doubts about the generality of conditioning of fears.

English (1929) also failed to obtain a conditioning effect with a fourteen-month-old girl. He placed this child in a highchair and gave her a large wooden toy duck. As in the Watson and Rayner experiment a large metal bar was struck with a hammer behind the child's head as soon as the girl reached for the duck, after which the duck was withdrawn. After fifty trials of pairing the child's reaching for the duck with the clanging of the hammer, English terminated this part of the experiment. He stated, "the writer must express his surprise—and admiration—at the child's iron nerves." Later the metal bar was sounded with a two-pound hammer which made such a resounding blow that professors in other parts of the building complained to English. Nonetheless, the child remained unafraid. Since this girl had three older brothers, it was felt that she was probably deconditioned to noise because of the racket and commotion to which she was regularly accustomed in her

house. A month later this child showed fear of patent leather boots and the fear generalized to objects near the boots. English felt that the child's fear response was intact, but if one were to condition a fear he had to pick carefully an unconditioned stimulus which was truly effective in eliciting a fearful reaction.

In summary, while Watson and Rayner (1920) and Harold Jones (1931) did demonstrate the learned acquisition of a fear, it was apparent that care had to be taken in the selection of the unconditioned stimuli. Several investigators have noted that it seems easier to condition fears to furry objects than to other stimuli (Valentine, 1930; English, 1929).

From various standpoints, it would be predicted that certain objects are more likely to arouse fear than other objects. According to Seligman (1971) humans are predisposed to fear things that have threatened the survival of the race. The fears are not necessarily believed to be innate. It is thought that we are highly prepared to learn certain fears and that this learning is probably "non-cognitive." According to Bandura (1986), "There are certain properties of events—agential hurtfulness, intensity, unpredictability, and uncontrollability—that make them especially phobogenic. Among the things that are correlated with aversive experience, animals are more apt to produce phobias than are inanimate ones. This is because animate threats, by virtue of their ability to act and roam around, can appear at unpredictable times and places and inflict injury despite self-protective efforts" (p. 201).

It is difficult to separate biological preparedness and psychological preparedness. One can associate shock with objects of evolutionary significance such as snakes or objects of neutral valence from an evolutionary standpoint such as geometric shapes. If biological preparedness were accounting for rapid fear learning, certain objects would be feared quickly whereas others would not. However, even if humans learned to fear snakes more readily than geometric shapes in conditioning studies with shock, it would be necessary to account for the social reasons that snakes would be more readily feared. Research attempting to disentangle biological and psychological preparedness does not lead one to conclude that biological preparedness affects learning.

From experiments with both animals and humans, however, it is clear that direct classical conditioning or pairing of a neutral object with an unconditioned stimulus is one means of acquiring a fear (Kennedy, 1971). A child is born with innate fears to a few stimuli, and other innate responses appear to manifest themselves during the first year of life. During the early years of life, as a child acquires language, new fears develop by a complex learning process. For example, children acquire fearful reactions to myriad verbal stimuli. They are facile in their symbolic thought processes, and these symbolic processes can serve as fertile ground for the development of new fears. The development of such fears

has been referred to as "higher order conditioning" by Pavlov. For example, young children referred to Dr. O'Leary have initially been very fearful of him because he was referred to as "Doctor." The children were fearful of this particular person not because of any direct associations with him but because of their fearful reaction to the word "doctor" and its attendant connotations. In brief, they responded to the symbol or word, not to a white coat, a needle, or an examining room.

Classical conditioning may account for the development of some fears, but lasting fears have not been reliably conditioned and experimentally conditioned fears are easily extinguished. In contrast, phobic reactions seen in clinics are very difficult to extinguish. Even more important, many individuals experience intense fear-provoking conditions that do not produce phobias. For example, many children in severe automobile accidents do not develop car phobias. Certain attempts to reformulate or modify classical conditioning principles with concepts such as preparedness have not received much documentation.

Box 3–1 *Dr. Mary Cover Jones REFLECTS ON WATSON AND BEHAVIOR THERAPY*

In 1978 Mary C. Jones presented an intriguing address about her recollections of the early experiments on conditioning and deconditioning fears and on the negative reception they had (Jones, 1978). Interestingly, Jones was a Vassar roommate of Rosalie Rayner. Watson later married Rayner, who was his graduate student at Johns Hopkins. Through Rayner, Mary C. Jones met Watson, who encouraged her to extend his conditioning work with a large sample of infants.

According to Jones, Watson was handsome, self-assured, able, and ambitious. However, many of his contemporaries found him dogmatic and inclined to exaggerate. He made the now famous quotation: "Give me a dozen healthy infants, well-formed, and my own specific world to bring them up in and I'll guarantee to take any one at random and train him to become any type of specialist I might select— doctor, lawyer, artist, merchant-chief, and yes, even beggarman and thief, regardless of his talents, penchants, tendencies, abilities, vocations, and race of his ancestors" (1924, p. 82). Such statements, even when placed in context, led people to reject his positions. Freudian psychology's goal was to rid the person of anxiety, and Watson's conditioning of fear was anathema to many. As Jones indicated, the loss of leadership, an immature theoretical position, and the appeal of alternative forms of therapy all contributed to the failure of Watson's position to receive wide acceptance.

In short, classical conditioning has not received much empirical support that adequately explains the fears of children seen in clinics. Regardless of the absence of clear support for the classical conditioning model of the acquisition of children's fears observed in clinics, the classical conditioning model did pave the way for a number of treatments of fear as we will show.

Modeling

It has long been known that children have similar kinds and number(s) of fears as their mothers have (Hagman, 1932). In an extensive study of forty-seven phobic adults (Solyom, Beck, Solyom, & Hugel, 1974), it was found that 30 percent of the mothers of these patients were also phobic. With dog-phobic children, 35 percent of the parents of the children also had serious fears and/or phobias (Bandura & Menlove, 1968). It has been found that anxiety about children's reactions in medical and dental settings is related to mothers' anxieties (Johnson & Melamed, 1979). In an experimental study, Venn and Short (1973) showed nursery school children a film of a five-year-old boy who screamed and withdrew when the mother presented a Mickey Mouse figure. In contrast, when the mother presented a Donald Duck figure, the boy in the film showed only a neutral reaction. When children who viewed the film were later tested, they avoided the Mickey Mouse figure more than the Donald Duck figure. In brief, the children had acquired an avoidance response through modeling or observation of a parent-child interaction.

The data regarding the relationship between children's fears and the fears of their parents suggest that some of these fears are modeled. For example, when a young girl is very afraid of spiders or insects, you often find that her mother is also afraid of insects. Of course, there may be genetic or constitutional factors within families that lead members of some families to react to potentially fearful objects in a stronger fashion than members of other families. Further, Thomas, Chess, Birch, Hertzig, and Korn (1963) showed that children vary greatly in their responses to stimuli at birth and that these personality or stylistic differences have some stability in childhood. Even if we accept these personality differences in responsiveness to external stimulation at birth and during the first four years of life, it seems evident from case studies that children can acquire the *specific* fears of their parents by observing their parents displaying such fears.

Evidence for the acquisition of fearful behavior via observational learning also comes from rhesus monkeys. Because of obvious ethical concerns, children cannot be exposed to highly fearful situations to assess the induction and maintenance of intense fears. In addition, it is often unclear whether certain fears in animals and children are innate and evolutionarily determined or learned. Mineka, Davidson, Cook, and Keir (1984) showed that young monkeys raised by parents who have a fear of snakes do not acquire this fear without specific experience with snakes. In contrast, adolescent monkeys do acquire intense and persistent fears of snakes if they observe their wild-reared parents interacting with either a real or a model snake for a brief period. The learning was so rapid that the investigators speculated that fears of snakes among primates may be a good example of "prepared learning" or learning which certain species are biologically equipped to learn rapidly. In this vein, it was thought that the monkeys would not acquire intense fears of neutral objects as rapidly as they would of snakes when they saw their parents react with fear to the neutral objects and to the snakes.

Reinforcement

When a child is afraid of venturing out on his or her own to the store or school and a parent tells the child that he or she need not go to these places, the child is rewarded for avoiding the new situation. For example, a number of years ago, one of the authors saw a child referred for school phobia who was allowed to remain in his home that had an electric pinball machine. Furthermore, the mother said she could not stop her son from playing the pinball machine even when he did not attend school. In essence, this boy was heavily rewarded for avoiding school by playing with the pinball machine, which few if any children of his age had in his town. Interestingly, it is commonly reported that parents of school-phobic children often allow the children to remain at home, to watch TV, and to engage in entertaining activities (Johnson & Melamed, 1979).

A more common example of reinforcing fearful behavior is the attention and praise a young child often receives for reporting to parents that he or she didn't touch a dog that came into the yard. If a child receives frequent instruction not to touch any strange animals and is praised for avoidance of such animals, the child *may* learn to fear animals if the intensity of the parental instruction and reinforcement is great.

Environmental Context

Fear of strangers was once thought to be universal, but it has become apparent that fearful reactions to strangers are not universal and do not occur at all times even in societies in which such fearful behavior is usual. A fearful response to strangers depends upon a number of environmental variables. Infants are more likely to show fearful behavior to a stranger when they are a few feet from their mothers than when they are in their mothers' laps. Similarly, the distance the stranger is from the child is a predictor of the fearful response. However, when a four-year-old child approaches an infant, the infant often has a mildly positive rather than a negative reaction. Finally, the actions of the stranger to the infant are important. If a stranger smiles and talks, he or she will be more likely to receive a positive response from the child than if the stranger is quiet and passive (Hetherington & Parke, 1979).

TREATMENT OF CHILDREN'S FEARS AND ANXIETY

Fear of Dogs

Bandura and his associates (Bandura, Grusec, & Menlove, 1967; Bandura & Menlove, 1968) emphasized that learning variables are not only critical in modifying the behavior of a single child, but are also influential in changing the behavior of other children who watch a learning process. It was thought that if a fearful child simply watched another child play fearlessly with an object, the fearful child would become less afraid. With a debt owed to Mary Cover Jones, who treated Peter's rabbit phobia, Bandura and his colleagues utilized two principles noted by Jones in the treatment of fear of dogs. They emphasized modeling of fearless behavior by a peer and also assessed whether the modeling of fearless behavior would be performed in a positive context, such as a party, or in a neutral context.

We have seen that Mary Cover Jones treated fears by placing children in the presence of a feared object while eating, gradually bringing the object closer to the child. This procedure used by Jones antedated Wolpe's treatment of adult fears through systematic desensitization, and her influence in the Bandura studies will be apparent. Masserman (1943) had also observed the influence of modeling in diminution of fearful behavior of cats who earlier had been shocked as they approached a food dish. When the fearful cats were placed in a cage with another cat who had never been conditioned to fear the food dish, they gradually overcame their fears. In short, from several experiments with cats (Masserman, 1943) and from studies with children (Jones, 1924a, 1924b) it would be predicted that children's fear of dogs could be reduced by watching a fearless model play with a dog and possibly by watching the model in a positive context, such as a party.

In the first study (Bandura, Grusec, & Menlove, 1967), children were selected for treatment on the basis of a parental interview and an objective test in which the child was requested to engage in a series of fourteen tasks which brought him into increasingly more intimate contact with the dog. For example, initially the child was asked to walk up to the playpen in which the dog, a brown cocker spaniel, was leashed; later he was asked to walk the dog on a leash. The last task required the child to climb into the playpen with the dog to pet her and to scratch her stomach while no one else was in the room. After ascertaining both from the parents and the objective test that the child was fearful of dogs, forty-eight children were then divided into four different groups.

Group 1, called a modeling-positive context group, involved having the child watch a fearless model display progressively more approaches to the dog in the context of a birthday party. Group 2, the modeling-neutral context group, watched a fearless model approach the dog without the party atmosphere. Group 3, the dog-positive context group, simply watched the dog in a party context, but there was no modeling of approaches to the dog by a peer. Group 4, the positive context

group, experienced the party atmosphere without a dog or a model. Following exposure to these various experiences, the children were reassessed with the same fourteen-item approach test they had been given earlier to determine the effectiveness of the procedures in decreasing the dog phobia.

As can be seen in Figure 3–2, the children who had been exposed to a model exhibiting fearless behavior with the dog reduced their fear regardless of whether the modeling was done in a positive or neutral context (i.e., model + positive context or model + neutral context). At the follow-up assessment, obtained one month following the post-test, the two model groups were still exhibiting more approach behavior (less fearful behavior) than the no-model groups. The model and positive context group, though slightly superior at follow-up, was not significantly different from the model plus neutral context group.

In a second study Bandura and Menlove (1968) assessed the value of multiple filmed models in reducing children's fears. Forty-eight three- to five-year-old children were divided into three groups. The first group observed a single film model display progressively more intimate interactions with a cocker spaniel. The child observed essentially the same process as depicted by the live model in the previous study. A second group of children observed a similar set of films depicting a variety of models interacting nonanxiously with numerous dogs varying in size and fearsomeness. A control group was shown movies containing no animals. The same fourteen-item approach test given in the earlier study was given in this study. Both the multiple model and the single model groups showed many more approach responses than did the control group, but the multiple model group had a more lasting effect than the single model group (see Figure 3–3). Of clinical interest was the finding that those children who not

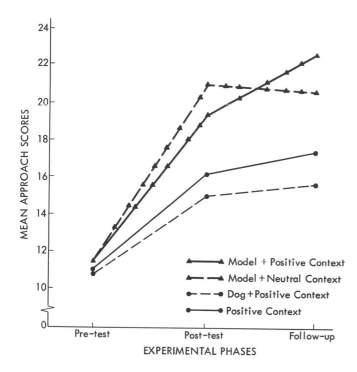

Figure 3–2   Mean approach scores achieved by children in each of the treatment conditions on the three different periods of assessment. (From Bandura, A., Grusec, J. E., & Menlove, F. L. (1967). Vicarious extinction of avoidance behavior through symbolic modeling. *Journal of Personality and Social Psychology, 5,* 16–23. Copyright 1967 by the American Psychological Association. Reprinted by permission of the publisher and author.)

only had fear of dogs but fears of other personal situations showed less improvement than children with singular fears. This finding is similar to that of Lang, Lazovick, and Reynolds (1965) who found that adult phobic patients did less well if they had multiple fears.

Lazarus and Abramovitz (1962) used a procedure they called emotive imagery to treat a fourteen-year-old boy with a strong fear of dogs. The boy was encouraged to imagine his favorite heroes and desired goals while the therapist gradually brought the anxiety-provoking scenes into the fantasy story. The boy, who had a strong interest in racing cars, was told to close his eyes and imagine he was racing an Alfa Romeo at the Indianapolis 500. Initially he was asked to visualize standing outside his house with his car nearby. Later he was to visualize driving through a small town in which people came out to admire his car. Then while visualizing this pleasant event

a dog was to come out to sniff his car. If he felt any anxiety the image was to be erased. With nine public school children Lazarus and Abramovitz were able successfully to reduce fears of seven children with emotive imagery in an average of 3.3 sessions. Follow-up inquiries indicated no relapses or symptom-substitutions.

Fear of Medical and Dental Settings

Some of the best research on fear reduction has been conducted by Melamed and her colleagues. The work is exemplary because it uses multiple assessments of fearful behavior in children, namely, direct observation, self-reports by the children, and physiological measures. For children undergoing elective surgery, Melamed and Siegel (1975) used a film entitled "Ethan Has an Operation," which

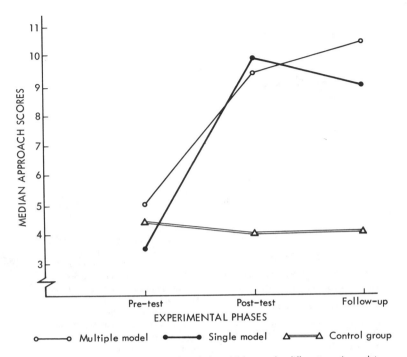

Figure 3–3 Mean approach scores of dog-phobic children under different movie-model treatment conditions. (From Bandura, A., & Menlove, F. L. (1968). Factors determining vicarious extinction of avoidance behavior through symbolic modeling. *Journal of Personality and Social Psychology, 8,* 99–108. Copyright 1968 by the American Psychological Association. Reprinted by permission of the publisher and author.)

depicts the experiences of a seven-year-old boy undergoing a hernia operation. In the film, Ethan describes his fears, concerns, and coping methods. He is seen in the admission room, the ward orientation room, surgery, the recovery room, and the hospital discharge area. Thirty children about to undergo elective surgery for hernias, tonsillectomies, or urinary problems were shown this film about Ethan or a control film about a boy's trip to the country. All children received the usual preoperative hospital preparation which included demonstrations and explanations of surgery and the recovery room process, as well as a visit from the surgeon who explained the surgery to the child and his or her parents. Children who saw the experimental film showed greater reductions of anxiety in all

three measures of fearful behavior: direct observation of the children's anxieties by hospital staff, self-reports of anxiety by the children, and a physiological measure of anxiety, the Palmer Sweat Index. It should again be emphasized that all the children undergoing the surgery received the usual hospital preoperative procedures. Therefore, the effect of viewing the modeling film was over and above the usual hospital means of aiding children to overcome their fears about surgery.

Fortunately, other investigators such as Vernon (1973) and Vernon and Bailey (1974) found that modeling films are effective in reducing a child's fear of general anesthesia or injections. Melamed and her colleagues (Melamed, 1979) have also shown that film models can be useful in reducing fears of dentists and dental situations. Further, they have begun to assess the factors that will enhance or lessen the effects of the film modeling procedure. Children who have been hospitalized previously show less responsiveness to the film, and the pattern of a child's responses while watching a film viewing is important. Heart rate deceleration while watching the film is associated with retaining information about the film.

Fear of the Dark

A very interesting study was conducted by Graziano and Mooney (1980) with six- to twelve-year-old children who had severe nighttime fears. The study is of special interest because, as you may recall from the Jersild and Holmes study, fear of the dark is one of the most common fears of children between the ages of four and six years. In addition, the fears of the children in this study were long-standing (two years or more). Further, "in each family 'going to bed' had become a highly emotional and disruptive nightly event, with delays and battles often lasting well beyond midnight" (p. 209). Thirty-three families were assigned either to a treatment or to a waiting list control group that would receive treatment in three to four weeks. The rationale given to the children in the first group

meeting with their therapist is important because of the message to the children that they can overcome their fears:

> All of you have told us that you are afraid of the dark or of being alone. As you know, some kids are afraid of the dark and others are not. The main difference between you and those other kids who are not afraid is that those other kids know how to *make* themselves not be afraid. In this class, we are going to teach you how to make yourselves less afraid. We are going to teach you how to relax, think pleasant thoughts, and say special words, all of which will help you become braver.

Nightly exercises for the children included (1) muscle relaxation, (2) imagining a pleasant scene, and (3) reciting "brave" self-statements (I am brave, I can take care of myself when I am alone). The parents monitored the exercises and gave the children tokens for conducting their exercises and for being brave during the night. The tokens were exchangeable for a treat at a famous fast-food service.

The treated children improved more than the waiting list children, as judged by parental reports of number of minutes it took the child to get to bed and go to sleep, and the proportion of days the child argued, got out of bed, and asked for a drink of water (see Figure 3–4). Despite the clear success of this

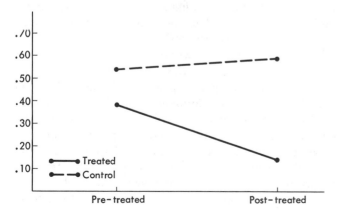

Figure 3–4 Proportion of days child afraid at bedtime. (Data taken from Graziano, A. M., & Mooney, K. C. (1980). Children's nighttime fear reduction, *Journal of Consulting and Clinical Psychology, 48*, 211. Copyright 1980 by the American Psychological Association. Reprinted by permission of the publisher and author.)

program, the investigators reported that the effects of the treatment were specific to the nighttime fear. That is, the treatment did not lead to reductions in fears in school or social situations. Such results indicate that to reduce diverse fears of young children, the treatment has to be directed toward changing fears in varied situations. Fortunately, this research provides an excellent model for building such a treatment program.

Test Anxiety

Scores of studies with adults have shown that desensitization is effective in reducing test worry and anxiety, and several studies with children and adolescents confirm the value of relaxation, meditation, and desensitization with test-anxious children. Mann and Rosenthal (1969) found that desensitization was effective in reducing test anxiety of anxious adolescents. Barabasz (1973, 1974) found significant reduction in a physiological measure of anxiety, the galvanic skin response, and an increase in intelligence test scores after treating highly anxious fifth- and sixth-graders with desensitization. Young children, as you might expect, cannot easily imagine a fearful scene and hold the image in their minds while in a relaxed state. Therefore, meditation or relaxation alone can be used with youngsters six to nine years old to reduce their concerns about tests (Linden, 1973).

Social Withdrawal

While most of the initial research involving modification of withdrawn children utilized adults as the change agents, peers as potential helping agents became recognized as ingredients of intervention programs for withdrawn children. Furman, Rahe, and Hartup (1979) drew upon intriguing research with monkeys which demonstrated that infant monkeys reared by several peer monkeys (i.e., similar or slightly older monkeys) in the absence of a mother monkey showed no later behavioral disturbances. However, infant monkeys raised by a mother monkey in the absence of peer monkeys showed long- and short-term affective and behavioral problems (Harlow & Harlow, 1965). Interestingly, when they tried to erase the social withdrawal of the socially withdrawn monkeys, they found that adult monkeys were not effective "therapists," whereas monkeys who were three months younger were. Drawing upon this body of research, Furman et al. (1979) used child "therapists" with preschool children identified as withdrawn because they interacted with peers less than 33 percent of the time they were observed. Twenty-four withdrawn children or social isolates were assigned to three conditions: (1) unstructured play sessions with a same-age "therapist," (2) unstructured play sessions with a therapist who was 12 to 14 months younger, and (3) a control group, i.e., no intervention. Children who were assigned to either of the unstructured play sessions with child "therapists" improved while children assigned to the control group did not. However, the children who played with the younger therapists improved more than those children who played with same-age therapists. The authors felt that the opportunity to practice initiating and directing social activity was critical in the children's improvement. This research fits well with our clinical observations of withdrawn and immature children. They naturally seek out children who are younger to play with because they can exert some influence over the younger children. In brief, with younger children, the shy, immature child can practice initiating activities, directing the actions of others, and can engage in those actions without fear of reprisal from a same-age or older child.

Social withdrawal is generally thought to

be the result of anxiety in social situations, and the DSM III (APA, 1980) classifies social withdrawal under the rubric Avoidant Disorder. Children with avoidant problems often also lack the social skills necessary to deal with their peers and receive relatively low scores on measures of peer acceptance, i.e., they are unpopular. Because of the diverse problems of socially withdrawn and often unpopular children, investigators have attempted to ascertain critical characteristics of these children. Unpopular children lack skill in perspective-taking or ability to take another's point of view (Gottman, Gonso, & Rasmussen, 1975). There are interventions that can improve this skill but, importantly, there is also suggestive evidence that improvement in perspective-taking is also related to overall adjustment. In addition, socially withdrawn children are not as likely to respond to initiations of other children and, when they do respond, their responses are likely to be nonverbal (Hops & Greenwood, 1981).

` Interventions for withdrawn children have been developed using a variety of approaches but the central themes in most of the programs have been instruction, modeling, and reinforcement. As early as the mid-1960s it was apparent that shaping and reinforcement of behaviors involving other children could result in increases in participation with peers in nursery school children (e.g., Allen, Hart, Buell, Harris, & Wolf, 1964). Filmed models were also used successfully to increase interactive behaviors of preschool children (O'Connor, 1969, 1972), but it was unclear from this research whether the effects were due to observation of a model, coaching, or direct instruction (Conger & Keane, 1981).

In part because of the ambiguity about the critical ingredient in these interventions for withdrawn children, other investigators decided to use purposively more directive and more varied approaches to treating withdrawn children. For example, LaGreca and Santogrossi (1981) developed a social skills training program with eight skill areas: smiling, greeting, joining, inviting, conversing, sharing and cooperating, complimenting, and grooming. Treatment emphasized modeling, coaching, and behavioral rehearsal. Thirty children with low peer acceptance ratings were assigned to (1) the social skills program, (2) an attention placebo group which listened to television programs and played games such as charades, and (3) a waiting list group. Because of the previous research demonstrating the usefulness of observing models who were the same age as the observers, children in the social skills group observed peer models demonstrate each of the eight skills. A discussion followed each tape observation about how the children could use the skills with their classmates. Next the children were asked to role play while the trainers coached them regarding their interactions.

Treatment outcome was measured by skills knowledge assessment in which the children were asked to respond to a peer model with a social problem by describing what they *should* do and what they *would* do in a similar situation. The children were also assessed in a role play situation in which they were required to role play making friends with a new child in school. Finally, the children were also observed during activities in their school which involved possible peer interactions, namely, gym, recess, and club meetings.

The skills training group performed much better than the attention placebo group and the waiting list group on all three dependent measures: the social skills knowledge test, the role playing situation, and the school observations. Of special interest, however, was the subsidiary finding that there were no differences in peer acceptance as a function of the skills training. This finding of no change in peer ratings is not unusual in studies of social skill training and points to the need for longer and more varied treatments. The central aims of the treatment, nonetheless, were achieved and the research exemplifies how peer models, role playing, and direct coaching can be used very effectively in teaching social skills to elementary school children.

Obsessions and Compulsions

Obsessions are unwanted repetitive thoughts; compulsions are behaviors a person feels compelled to perform. Often the obsessions and compulsions follow anxiety about various issues, but after the obsessions and compulsions have been established for a year or so the thoughts and actions appear to assume a status often unrelated to anxiety. Young children often have bedtime rituals; older children develop rituals about dressing and school work. Approximately 2 percent of children who attend psychiatric clinics have obsessive-compulsive problems (Adams, 1973); boys and girls seem to be equally represented. Engaging in childhood games such as "Step on a Crack: Break Your Mother's Back" is not seen as a compulsive problem unless engaging in a number of such behaviors begins to interfere with the child's overall functioning.

There is little systematic research on the treatment of obsessive-compulsive problems of children. As you will see in the chapter on the treatment of obsessions and compulsions in adults, preventing the actual behavior has been shown to be the most effective intervention.

An anxious, obsessional, twelve-year-old boy, Rob, the only child of an agoraphobic mother and an alcoholic father, was referred to the Behavior Therapy Unit of Temple University Medical School (Phillips & Wolfe, 1981) by a psychiatrist who had little or no treatment progress with the boy in two years of psychoanalysis. Rob would not let his parents out of his sight unless he was playing ball in

his backyard with friends. Otherwise, his parents always had to be visible. When Rob was first seen he had been out of school five months and he engaged in approximately fifty ritualistic behaviors per day. The rituals included kicking things as he passed them (eleven times per day), doing things in threes (twelve times per day), waving his arms (thirteen times per day), and phoning his father in a repetitive way many times per day. There had been several highly stressful events in Rob's life starting at the age of three when his father had a heart attack. Rob himself had an operation when he was four, and his mother had an operation when he was five. When Rob was nine his father had heart surgery and subsequent and repeated hospitalizations. Rob worried that his father might die and that his parents might abandon him because he was such a great burden to them.

The treatment consisted of eighty-eight sessions over a two-year period involving relaxation, systematic desensitization, and "in vivo desensitization"—especially in the school. The phasing out of rituals was addressed by having Rob use muscle relaxation whenever he had the urge to engage in the ritualistic behaviors. He said he did so because he believed that by performing them he prevented a catastrophe from striking his parents. Instead of attacking the irrationality of this belief, Rob was shown how he used the behaviors to reduce his anxiety and how he could substitute relaxation as an alternative. In addition, Rob was asked to monitor or record his daily rituals and was rewarded for reducing the rituals.

The treatment of this boy was long and tedious. It involved extensive consultation with school personnel, having his mother go to the school and gradually remain there only a small portion of the day, and highly varied scenes which Rob was to imagine while relaxed (systematic desensitization). Fortunately, the treatment was successful. Rob eventually attended school regularly; two years following treatment he went to Europe with his classmates, and all compulsive rituals ceased.

Initial Conclusions

In summary, fear of dogs, hospitals, dentists, dark, and tests have all been treated using a variety of behavior therapy procedures. With younger children, a particularly effective procedure involves the use of several peer models who are rewarded for playing with dogs without fear or gradually approaching dentists, doctors, or hospitals without fear. Where possible, it is helpful to have multiple models interact with varied feared objects. Having the child eat his favorite foods (e.g., an ice cream cone) while gradually approaching the feared stimulus may be useful in certain cases. Having the child repeat to himself that he or she can overcome the fear may be useful. Rewarding a child directly (in vivo) for approaching a feared object can also be used to diminish fears. Where it is difficult to use in vivo treatment, emotive imagery with heroic fantasies intermeshed with brief themes of anxiety would be an alternative treatment mode for older children. Older children and adolescents who have the ability to imagine feared items and to relax can be treated with desensitization, though where possible, it is best to have the treatment take place in vivo so the person is exposed to the real, rather than the imagined, feared object.

SCHOOL PHOBIA

Definition

The term *school phobia* is fraught with oversimplification. It is generally used in connection with a refusal to attend school and refers to an assumption that the child is irrationally afraid about something surrounding the school. However, as any reader knows, many of us have refused to go to school for reasons other than fear. School truants, for example, repeatedly refuse to attend school. Thus, whether a child is labeled a school phobic or not is based on an assumption that a child is afraid of returning to school. Fortunately, according to Yates (1970), there is little difficulty in distinguishing a school-phobic child from a truant. A study by Hersov (1960) compared children labeled school phobics with children labeled truants. He matched children with respect to age, sex, and intelligence and found that the school-phobic child, not the truant child, was characterized by maternal overprotection, eating disturbances, abdominal pain and nausea, sleeping problems, and clinical indications of anxiety. The truant child was characterized by inconsistent home discipline, juvenile court appearances, persistent lying, wandering from home, and stealing. A description of the school phobic somewhat similar to that of Hersov was given by Kennedy (1965) who said such children have (1) morbid fears associated with school attendance, (2) frequent somatic complaints, (3) a symbiotic relationship with the mother, and (4) conflict between parents and the school administration. In summary, a school-phobic child appeared to be best described by factors relating to fear and anxiety whereas the truant is best described by delinquent behavior.

Incidence

Figures on the incidence of school phobia vary with the length of time a child is absent from school before he is labeled a school phobic. In children's psychiatric clinics the figure varies from 1 percent (Chazan, 1962) to 1.7 percent (Eisenberg, 1958). Higher estimates are found in the general population with estimates generally ranging from 5 to 8 percent (Kahn & Narsten, 1962).

Etiology

Psychodynamic theorists have long maintained that school phobia is essentially a problem of separation anxiety (Eisenberg, 1958). It is stated that there is never any real fear of school; the fear of leaving the mother is the critical etiological variable. Others have said that even if a fear of school were present it was a displacement of unconscious transference of anxiety from the fear of separation from the mother (Berryman, 1959). Thus many feel that the term *school phobia* is a misnomer; they argue it should be called *separation anxiety*.

Arguing against a separation-anxiety view, Levental and Sills (1964) maintain that if a child were really school phobic, the phobia would manifest itself very early in the child's school history. However, many children do not become labeled school phobic until the third or fourth grade. Furthermore, many children diagnosed as school phobic can readily be away from their mother with friends and relatives. Their position essentially is that certain children view themselves very highly as they enter school and feel that they can do anything academically. When their self-image is contradicted, the children develop somatic complaints which enable them to justify not attending school.

Yates (1970) provided an integration of the various explanations for school phobia which seems both sound and lacking in the myopia often seen in etiological explanations based upon a single factor. While his explanation lies largely in a learning framework, he does not deny that a child's self-image can have important consequences for the development of a school phobia and, in fact, argues that the work of personality theorists and child

psychologists on need for achievement and fear of failure should receive serious attention by those concerned with school phobia. According to Yates's integrative interpretation, almost all mothers become very strong reinforcing stimuli to a young child in the preschool years and the mother also becomes a haven for refuge in all times of stress. When the child is separated from his mother and becomes anxious, he will do whatever possible to find solace while away from the mother. As Yates put it " 'Growing up,' in one sense, consists essentially in gradually obtaining rewards while separated from the parents to the point at which 'separation situations' are at least as rewarding as 'being-with-mother-at-home' " (p. 152). Occasionally, a mother may feel undue concern when her child is away from her and may comment, "Be careful not to hurt yourself on the jungle gym," "Take care not to get lost in the woods," "Be a very good boy when Mommy is not around to help you." Such statements coupled with the child's own natural tendency to fear separation may exacerbate the child's fear of any separation from mother. Whether or not an intense fear of school develops depends on the mother's reactions to the child's fears, the rewards available to the child at school from academic subjects and friendships, or occasional traumas at school such as being forced to engage in homosexual activity.

At this point no theoretical account of school phobia has been documented with sufficient supporting evidence to enable one to place particular credence on any one position. While many problems can be treated successfully without much knowledge of their etiology, it is obvious that specific information about the cause of the problem may prove fruitful in developing treatment plans. Since the etiological stresses of various people differ widely (e.g., separation anxiety, unrealistic self-image), further research concerning the development of the problems seems sorely needed.

Treatment

One of the most striking successes in treating school phobias was obtained by Kennedy (1965) with what was called a "rapid treatment procedure for returning a child to school." The essence of this procedure is based on a close liaison between a school and a clinic facility for the early identification of the problem. Another critical factor in Kennedy's approach is the identification of two types of school phobia. These will be considered in some detail since the two types of phobias appear to warrant different treatment programs (see Table 3–1).

Kennedy treated what he labeled Type I school phobia or a "true phobic reaction." The Type II school phobia was described by Kennedy as a "way-of-life phobia" with an extremely complex pattern of fearful reactions to almost any situation, the school phobia being only one aspect of a complex fabric of maladaptive behaviors. While there is overlap between Type I and Type II phobias, a Type I phobic child is generally from the lower grades, kindergarten through third grade, whereas Type II phobics are generally found in the upper grades. Type I phobias represent an acute onset often following an illness. Aware that he has missed work the child becomes apprehensive and refuses to go to school on Monday morning. In Type I families communication is good, whereas in Type II families the father is often irresponsible, uncommunicative, or even out of the home. There is a clear resemblance between a Type II phobic and the school truant formerly discussed.

Table 3–1 Differential School Phobia Symptoms*

TYPE I	TYPE II
1. The present illness is the first episode.	1. Second, third, or fourth episode.
2. Monday onset following an illness the previous Thursday or Friday.	2. Monday onset following minor illness not a prevalent antecedent.
3. An acute onset.	3. Incipient onset.
4. Lower grades most prevalent.	4. Upper grades most prevalent.
5. Expressed concern about death.	5. Death theme not present.
6. Mother's physical health in question: actually ill or child thinks so.	6. Mother's health not an issue.
7. Good communication between parents.	7. Poor communication between parents.
8. Parents well adjusted in most areas.	8. Mother shows a neurotic behavior; father, a character disorder.
9. Father competitive with mother in household management.	9. Father shows little interest in household or children.
10. Parents achieve understanding of dynamics easily.	10. Parents very difficult to work with.

Reprinted from Kennedy, W.A. (1965). School phobia; rapid treatment of fifty cases, *Journal of Abnormal Psychology, 70*, 286. Copyright 1965 by the American Psychological Association. Reprinted by permission.

*While there are no published data on the reliability of Type I and Type II diagnostic categories, it seems useful to distinguish types of problems where there are differential treatment implications. Age, for example, is one factor which is generally felt to be a prognostic indicator of treatment responsivity, and both Kennedy (1965) and Gittleman-Klein and Klein (1973) have some evidence supportive of this notion.

The rapid treatment program for Type I school phobics is comprised of the following six components.

1. Establishment of good professional relations between the school, physicians, and a clinic to provide early detection and rapid referral.

2. Avoidance of emphasis on somatic complaints by a cooperating pediatrician who will matter-of-factly handle the child after school and reassure the parents and the child that medical complaints are not a problem.

3. Forced school attendance by assuring the parents that the child will become desensitized to his fear, and that further time away from school will simply reinforce the child's fears.

4. A structured interview with the parents designed to give the parents confidence to execute the program even in the face of strong resistance from the child.

The formula for the parents is as follows:

Do not discuss attendance in any way over the weekend. There is nothing a phobic child does better than talk about going to school. Don't discuss going to school. Don't discuss phobic symptoms. Simply tell the child on Sunday evening, "Well, tomorrow you go back to school."

On Monday morning get the child up, dressed, and ready for school. Give the child a light breakfast to reduce the nausea problem. Have the father take the child matter-of-factly to school. Don't ask how he or she feels, or why he or she is afraid to go to school or doesn't like school. Simply take the child to school, turn him or her over to the school authorities, and go home.

On Monday evening, compliment the child on going to school and staying there, no matter how resistant the child has been, no matter how many times he or she has vomited, cried, or started to leave. If the child has been at school for thirty minutes on Monday, progress is being made. Tell the child Monday evening that Tuesday will be much better and make no further mention of the problem.

Tuesday can be expected to be a repetition of Monday but with everything toned down considerably. On Tuesday evening, encourage and compliment the child strongly for doing so much better.

Wednesday should be virtually symptom-free. Wednesday evening, with considerable fanfare, give a party for the child in honor of having overcome the problem.

5. A very brief interview with the child is conducted after school, stressing the advantage of facing fear directly, e.g., getting right back on a horse after a fall.

6. A follow-up with the parents is conducted by phone to check on other phobias, academic progress, and possible other emotional problems.

In a twelve-year period, sixty cases were successfully treated using this method, and follow-ups indicated that the children remained symptom-free. While it can be argued that the Type I phobic would eventually go to school with any treatment, obviously this procedure alleviates the family stress quickly, the child does not miss much schoolwork, and fears or manipulative ploys are not reinforced by allowing him to stay home until he is ready to go to school.

Although no large-scale studies using behavioral interventions specifically dealing with Type II phobias have been conducted, several cases which could be classified as such or which have greater similarity to Type II than Type I phobias have been treated successfully. Lazarus, Davison, and Polefka (1965) treated a nine-year-old child with a history of repeated school refusal. After a summer vacation before entering the fourth grade, the child, Paul, refused to go to school. In kindergarten he climbed over an extremely high wall and fled home. His first grade teacher considered him disturbed. Paul's third grade teacher, according to many parental reports, intimidated the children and was very free with physical punishment. During the course of the third grade year, Paul refused to go to school and despite occasions when Paul was dragged to school by the truant officer, he persisted in his refusal. Paul's father was moody, anxious, and under great stress because of his job. Paul's father was severe in his use of punishment, and he overly emphasized extreme consequences which might befall Paul (e.g., "Don't touch that fluorescent bulb, Son; there's poison in it and it will kill you!") Paul's mother was in good health, but she frequently quarreled with Paul and was inconsistent in her discipline.

Paul was a small, frail child whose emotional reactions to stress were an easily discernible postural stoop, a general constriction of movement, tear-filled eyes, mild trembling, and when stress was severe—sobbing. A death theme was present because of a near-drowning at the age of five, a serious appendectomy with postoperative complications, the witnessing of a drowning, and the death of a twelve-year-old girl who was a close friend of an elder sister. In summary, Paul more closely represented a Type II phobic than a Type I phobic because (1) his was a repeated school refusal which was not initially exhibited on Monday following a minor illness, (2) Paul was entering fourth grade, and despite a number of death-related events, was not reported to complain of such, (3) his mother's health was not an issue and communication between the parents was not reported as "good," (4) the parents were not described as well adjusted in most areas. Two criteria of a Type II phobia were difficult to judge from the published report, but according to the second author, Davison, the father did show interest in the household and children and the parents achieved an understanding of the dynamics of the problem rather quickly. Nonetheless, Paul more closely resembled a Type II than a Type I phobic.

The treatment consisted of emotive imagery (picturing subjectively pleasant images such as Christmas or a visit to Disneyland while relating them to the school situation), in vivo desensitization, and rewards for school attendance. The in vivo desensitization ranged from walking past the school on a Sunday through increasing amounts of time spent with the therapist in school, and finally a gradual withdrawal of the therapist from the school. The reward or token reinforcement program established to maintain school attendance following the removal of the therapist from the class consisted of variously colored tokens which Paul could eventually exchange for comic books and a baseball glove. Within four-and-one-half months Paul was attending school regularly and follow-ups at ten months and nine years indicated there was no further school refusal and that Paul was progressing exceptionally well.

Another case which would likely have been unamenable to Kennedy's rapid treatment approach was Valerie, treated by Ayllon, Smith, and Rogers (1970). When Valerie's mother took her to school Valerie became very stiff and began shaking and hollering. Valerie stated she was afraid to go to school because she thought about the time she was molested at four years of age. Valerie was an eight-year-old girl with forty-one absences in the second grade. After four days of school in the third grade, Valerie refused to go to school any more. Ayllon et al. (1970) treated the school phobia as if the essential issue were to deal with a low-rate operant behavior, viz., school attendance. The treatment tack was to decrease the positive consequences for staying home and to increase the positive consequences for school attendance.

After a detailed observation in the house, observations at a neighbor's house where she stayed when she did not attend school, and two visits to her school, a treatment plan was implemented which emphasized (1) a prompting-shaping procedure of school attendance, when Valerie visited the school only at the close of the day to be dismissed with the rest of the class, and (2) a home-based motivational system in which Valerie earned a star for voluntary school attendance, with five stars exchangeable for a special treat or a weekend visit. In addition, each day Valerie went to school voluntarily she received three pieces of candy; if she had to be taken she received only one piece of candy. (3) Her mother also left for work ten minutes before the children went to school and met the children at school to give them a reward for attending (the siblings were six, nine, and ten years of age). If Valerie failed to arrive at school, her mother had to return home to get her. Since the latter procedure would obviously cause aversive consequences for her mother, it was felt that she would become more actively interested in conveying the importance of going to school. Interestingly, on one rainy day that Valerie's mother had to go back home to get Valerie, her mother literally pushed her out of the house and scolded her all the way to school. That was the last day Valerie stayed away from school.

The first treatment procedure worked—but only temporarily. The second procedure resulted in some school attendance but failed to encourage voluntary school attendance. The combination of the second and third procedures, a home-based incentive program and aversive consequences for the mother for Valerie's failure to voluntarily attend school, appeared to be the crucial variables in obtaining normal school attendance. Within one-and-one-half months of the initial referral, the school phobia was cured.

Of particular interest were the other positive features associated with her school attendance. While she was formerly a C student, at a nine month follow-up she had A's and B's. While she was earlier described as showing no interest in friends, Valerie was thrilled at being asked to join the Brownies. At home, Valerie no longer complained of nausea, and despite the initiation of divorce proceedings against the father by the mother, continued

to attend school without any disruption in her academic or social progress. In brief, according to the teachers and her mother, there was clearly no "symptom substitution." Nonetheless, following a routine post-treatment psychodiagnostic evaluation the examiner noted the following: "Her emotional development is characterized by deviations in the area of maturity and aggression. Her reality testing is marred by an extreme overconcern with sexuality and men, whom she sees as attacking, ever-fighting, animal-like creatures. On the basis of the recent results, without consideration to results previous to behavioral management, it would seem that the school phobia may have been treated successfully, but it has not meant anything to this girl" (p. 136). There is little wonder that such evaluations are received as little more than pedantic poppycock! The teacher hardly needed to be told that Valerie was immature. The overconcern about men and sexuality was mere conjecture. Gittleman-Klein and Klein (1973) found that therapist and parent persuasion and desensitization techniques coupled with a placebo or imipramine resulted in school attendance after six weeks of treatment in 47 percent and 81 percent of the children, respectively. This study is one of the few controlled studies combining a behavioral approach with a pharmacological agent in the treatment of any childhood problem. Given the brevity of the treatment and the relative success of the imipramine and behavioral-persuasion intervention, it is likely and desirable that further studies of this nature be conducted.

SUMMARY

Short-term school phobics can be readily treated utilizing the "rapid treatment method" outlined earlier. However, controlled research evaluating behavioral interventions with school phobics is notably lacking. The natural or spontaneous remission rate is unknown and results comparing various treatment approaches are almost completely absent. In this regard it is important to note Yates's (1970) summary of psychotherapy with relatively severe school phobics. Taking data provided by his summary of individual studies and using a criterion of success of "return to school," the treatment was apparently quite successful. On the basis of four psychodynamically oriented psychotherapy studies, 72 percent of the children returned to school. On the basis of four studies in which psychotherapy was combined with pressure to return to school (length of phobia was not stated), 84 percent of the children returned to school. Further, a survey of ninety-nine school-phobic cases seen in a child guidance clinic in England revealed that complex therapeutic inventions for chronic or long-standing school phobics can be relatively successful. Pressure to return to school immediately, and long-term psychotherapy support for parents and the child resulted in a return to school in 89 percent of the cases (Baker & Wills, 1978). There have been no studies—even of a clinical demonstration nature—in which direct behav-

ioral intervention with many subjects has been used. A study by Miller, Barrett, Hampe, and Noble (1972) compared desensitization, psychotherapy, and waiting list controls and found no evidence that either treatment was superior to non-treated controls. Forty-six percent of the children had school phobias while other children had assorted phobias. Given the heterogeneity of the phobias, the questionable use of desensitization with young children, and a self-admitted rigidity of the treatment, one can only reiterate the need for further research in the area. Thus, we can only conclude that for Type I phobias there is clinical evidence that behavioral intervention seems to be a particularly efficacious approach; unfortunately, the spontaneous remission rate of such children is unknown. For relatively severe phobias, the most detailed information relating specific behavioral procedures to school attendance has been provided by Ayllon et al. (1970), but controlled behavioral research on such procedures with school phobias simply does not exist. Finally, psychodynamic psychotherapy and medication with persuasion have shown very respectable school attendance rates. Any responsible clinician should be familiar with such treatments.

4

Enuresis and Encopresis

DEVELOPMENT OF CONTINENCE

Before considering enuresis and encopresis we will discuss the development of continence. The custom of toilet training varies markedly from one culture to another. Primitive African tribes allow their children to be trained solely by imitation and such children are not trained until they are six years of age (Baldwin, 1955). In contrast, inhabitants of Western cultures, where toilet training has been a topic of heated controversy since 1900, begin training much earlier. Fifty percent of the mothers in Western European cities begin toilet training before one year, with the median age in London, for example, being 4.6 months (Hindley, Fillozat, Klackenberg, Nicolet-Meister, & Sand, 1965). Amazingly, Douglas and Bloomfield earlier (1958) found that 60 percent of the mothers in London began toilet training by the first two weeks of life.

Although two weeks is clearly too early an age at which to begin toilet training, children in urban societies must learn at one time or another to use toilets. Whereas our great-grandparents may have been willing to allow children to go behind the nearest bush, the plush decor of many contemporary bathrooms serves to point out why parents yearn to have their children toilet trained.

Because of the emotion generated by Freud's postulation that an adult's personality is in part determined by the manner in which he is toilet trained, and because many parents have heard of the difficulty other parents have had, parents are often frightened at the prospect of toilet training their own children. This fear is to some extent justified. Initially, a child simply defecates and urinates at will, and when taught that it is necessary to conform to certain toilet routines may balk at such a notion. Despite the fact that our personalities are not formed on the potty chairs of the world, it is true that the manner in which a child is trained to go to the toilet can influence later adjustment. If parents nag and ridicule a child in the course of toilet training, long-term negative consequences may ensue. This first major teaching encounter for a parent may set the stage for many other interactions; the battle over toilet training may be the forerunner of instances in which the parent sees the child as negativistic and uncooperative. Similarly, the child may learn to see his parents as punitive ogres. Research that consists principally of surveys about toilet training and focuses on the age or manner in which that training was done strongly suggests that severe or punitive toilet training results in hostility on the part of the child. The child learns to bite, kick, and more important, to refuse to go to the toilet. Chronic bedwetting is said to be associated with "training that was started too early maturationally, to be followed by success" (MacFarlane, Allen, & Honzik, 1954).

Although it is apparent that the manner in which a child is toilet trained can affect his later adjustment, the difference between Freud's contention concerning this influence and the viewpoint of the present authors should be made clear. Freud felt that there was some qualitative difference between the possible results of toilet training and the results of teaching a child any other behavior. The adult behaviors associated with Freud's hypothesized "anal personality" (e.g., stinginess, obstinacy, excessive orderliness, etc.) were considered to be a function of harsh and punitive toilet training; Freud did not feel that these behaviors would result from harsh parental training of any behavior other than continence. In contrast, it is our belief that there is no qualitative difference between the potential results of toilet training a child and the potential results of teaching a child any other skill. The manner in which a child is taught a skill, be it reading, hitting a ball, or sewing, can influence the child's later adjustment. The toilet training of a child is thus held by us to be no more important than the early teaching of other social or academic skills except that this early training sets the stage for teaching other skills.

Fortunately, the value of positive reinforcement procedures for toilet training has been clearly demonstrated with normal children, as well as with retarded and psychotic children. The earliest extensive study with normal children evaluated the relative effects of various behavior modification techniques in toilet training a child (Madsen, Hoffman, Thomas, Koropsak, & Madsen, 1969). Children were randomly assigned to the following five different training conditions:

1. Maturational Control Group: Parents were asked to make no attempts at toilet training.
2. Parents' Methods Control Group: Parents were told to do as they had planned to do before they heard of the project.
3. Reward Group: Parents were given instructions first to shape the child to spend time on the potty by using candies to increase slowly the amount of time spent on the potty. They were to give candy only when the child eliminated successfully in the appropriate place. The parents were told never to reprimand the child for accidents or refusals. Finally, the parent was asked to have a dish of candy in the bathroom out of the child's reach so that the child could be rewarded within two seconds after successful elimination.
4. Buzzer Pants: Parents were asked to use a transistorized signal package sewn into training pants that made a low-intensity buzzing sound whenever liquid touched the circuit sewn in the pants. The buzzer sound was to alert the mother to take her child to the bathroom as quickly as possible to remove his training pants, to put him on the potty, and to disconnect the buzzer. The buzzer pants apparatus consisted of a miniature transistorized speaker of cigarette-case size (4.5 ounces). Each parent also had twelve pairs of training pants into which were sewn two wires covered by terry cloth sewn into the crotch.
5. Reward and Buzzer Pants: Instructions here included the instructions used for both the reward and the buzzer pants group.

Seventy children, volunteered by their mothers, were divided into four separate age groups: 1) twelve– to fourteen-month-old children, 2) sixteen– to eighteen-month-old children, 3) twenty– to twenty-two-month-old children, and 4) children over twenty-four months. Frequency of elimination, number of successes (elimination initiated by the child in the proper place), and number of accidents (any liquid or solid waste in the diaper) were recorded. The evaluation of the program was made by comparing increases in successes and decreases in accidents one week after the four-week training program.

The reward and the reward plus buzzer-pants groups were significantly different from the other three groups in successes but were not significantly different from one another. Considering decreases in accidents, all three experimental groups—reinforcement, buzzer pants, and reinforcement plus buzzer pants —differed from the two nonexperimental groups but did not differ from one another. Age of the children proved to be especially important in the success of the training. All three older groups exceeded the twelve- to fourteen-month group in increases in successes. Children older than twenty-four months produced the greatest number of decreases in accidents, while the sixteen- to eighteen and twenty- to twenty-two-month-old groups were not different from one another but were different from the youngest group.

Of particular interest was the report by the researchers that the effective parents in the parental methods group (four of the thirteen parents) did approximately what the reward group did. That is, they used praise and/or candy to reward appropriate toilet behavior. As the experimenters expected, the maturational control group was not at all effective in increasing successes. In summary, the results of this study clearly demonstrate the effectiveness of using principles of contingent reinforcement in toilet training. The buzzer pants added to the efficiency of the training though the increase was not statistically significant.

Nonetheless, the mothers reported general satisfaction with the buzzer pants as they eliminated the need for scheduling toilet time.

While this study does not specifically answer the question of when a child can best be trained, the results do indicate that training can be accomplished at a much younger age than most child-rearing manuals suggest. Many manuals suggest that parents wait until the child is two years old, yet children in the sixteen- to eighteen-month-old range in this study seemed very amenable to training. On the other hand, given the large number of continued accidents after training, it may well be a mistake to train twelve- to fourteen-month-old infants. A large Swiss study of parents' own training practices indicated that whether one decides to place a child on the pot in the first six months of life or the second six months merely leads children to have bowel control a few months earlier but it has no effect on bladder control (Largo & Stutzle, 1977).

Whatever the specific methods used, there are several steps a parent can take in order to maximize the probability of success in training. It is helpful to have a potty chair rather than a seat which fits on the toilet, since a toddler can go to it himself without help. Additionally, many toddlers are frightened by the height of the average toilet seat and by the whirling, gushing noises of the flushing toilet. Occasionally, a child may also be reticent to sit on the cold potty chair seat; it is then helpful to warm the seat with a hot cloth before asking the child to sit down. Once the child has learned to use the potty chair successfully, it is a good idea to ask him occasionally to use the "big potty" so that the parent is not forced to carry the potty chair everywhere the child goes.

Regularity in bowel movements and urination provide advance warnings for some parents. Occasionally, one can tell from grimaces or from "ants in pants" and "crotch clutching" that the child has to go to the toilet. If the child can be caught in time, he can be assured some success. Miniature marshmallows, raisins, or other edibles should be kept handy so that the "correct" behavior can be quickly reinforced. Most important, appropriate praise and a helpful, cheerful manner indicate concern for the child's welfare and are critical in facilitating the toilet training.

Bowel and bladder training differ in both the rapidity of their onset and the manner in which they are taught. Bladder control begins somewhat earlier in girls than in boys. While there seem to be occasional children who train themselves almost instantly, in general, the process is a gradual one. Waking bladder control appears somewhere around two years of age but sleeping control lags somewhat behind. With girls as well as boys, it is easiest to train bladder control sitting down. (With boys the penis must be held downward because a boy may often have an erection just before he urinates.) Observation of Daddy may produce some mixed feelings on the part of the child, since Daddy urinates standing up. Several misses and a wet leg or two are usually enough to convince the boy that it is easier to urinate sitting down.

Night bladder control usually follows daytime control automatically. Those who fail to develop nighttime bladder control are considered specifically in the section on enuresis (bedwetting). Contrary to popular belief, varied quantities of fluid imbibed at bedtime do not appear to facilitate the establishment of bladder control. It is helpful to waken the child for urination before the parents go to bed. After bladder control is established, occasional lapses should be expected, particularly under novel situations and in times of stress. Even older children, if subjected to severe traumas, often revert to bedwetting. In Great Britain during World War II, chil-

dren who were separated from their mothers were said to wet their beds so much that "half of England was awash" (Stone & Church, 1973).

One novel and intriguingly rapid approach to toilet training of normal children was demonstrated by Foxx and Azrin (1973). From forty-three referred children they selected a sample of thirty-four children for treatment. They eliminated nine children who could not follow simple verbal instructions or imitate simple motor tasks, because, as will become apparent, these skills were prerequisites for participation in the treatment. The mean age of the children was twenty-five months with a range of twenty- to thirty-six months.

The treatment involved providing a very intensive learning experience that maximized factors known to facilitate learning and later fading out those factors as learning progressed. Those facilitative factors included a distraction-free environment, a large number of learning trials, frequent and immediate reinforcement for appropriate responses, a wide variety of reinforcers, manual guidance, verbal instruction, imitation, and verbal and symbolic rehearsal of benefits of toileting correctly.

An important component of the treatment was imitation, which was used in the following manner. A professional toilet trainer gave each child a doll that could be filled with water through the mouth and would release the water through a hole between its legs. The therapist taught the child to praise and feed the doll, to raise and lower its pants, and to allow it to urinate in the potty chair. The child was encouraged to imitate what the doll had done. This directed imitation was done continuously between the child's own practice trials.

Other components of the treatment package, verbal and symbolic rehearsal, were implemented by creating a desire in the child to remain dry in order to please parents, family, and friends. The children were told intermittently during the training that each of these persons would be delighted with the child's success.

The treatment proceeded along the following lines: The therapist-trainer asked the parents to leave their child for the day. The therapist began by making friends with the child. They conversed about such topics as the child's favorite foods, television programs, and people. After establishment of rapport, the therapist gave the child a large quantity of soda pop and subsequently urged the child to give a drink to the large doll we have described. The doll then urinated (simulated) on a potty, and the child was taught to reward the doll with a piece of candy or a potato chip and say, "The doll behaved like a big girl!" Following sequences with the doll the child was asked to sit on a small potty chair. When he or she finally urinated in the small potty, the therapist rewarded the child lavishly with hugs and potato chips. Then the child was asked, "Does Santa pee in his pants? Does the policeman wet his pants?" Obviously the child responded in the negative, and the training progressed. The child's pants were checked every few minutes. If they were dry, he was rewarded; if they were wet, he was not rewarded. The entire process took about four hours. The range of training time was one-half hour to 14 hours, with a mean time of 3.9 hours.

Following the training, the therapist contacted the parents by telephone or visit every month for four months. The parent was asked to inspect the child's pants several times a day: before each meal or snack, at naptime, and at bedtime. If the child was dry, he or she was to be lavishly praised. If an accident had occurred, the parent reprimanded the child, made him change his pants, and required him to practice going to the toilet.

The number of accidents (averaged for the whole group) before and after training are presented in Figure 4–1. Accidents were noted by counting the number of times the child had to be changed each day. Prior to training, the child averaged six accidents per day. Accidents decreased to 0.2 accidents per day or about one per week within the first post-training week. For both bowel movements and urinations, the near-zero level of accidents was maintained for the four-month follow-up period. The only parent who did not express marked pleasure at the results of the procedure was one who had bet a friend $100.00 that his child could not be toilet trained in one day.

An interesting ancillary benefit of the training procedure was the fact that 30 percent of the children stopped wetting their beds at night during the first week following daytime training. A four-month follow-up indicated that all ten of these children remained dry at night as well as during the day. This positive side effect occurred despite the fact that there was no specific training to decrease bedwetting.

A book *Toilet Training in Less Than a Day* by Azrin and Foxx (1974) describes the procedures in detail. The book is designed for parents' use, but evaluations of parents' attempts to implement the procedures indicate that professional supervision appears necessary to achieve success rates between 80 and 100 percent, and adverse emotional reactions may occur without such supervision (Matson & Ollendick, 1977).

ENURESIS

There are occasional reports of children who seem to learn bowel or bladder control spontaneously, but most data on toilet training indicate that this learning is a gradual process. Even so, most children are bowel trained at

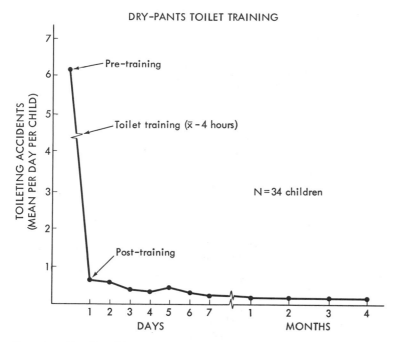

DRY-PANTS TOILET TRAINING

Figure 4–1 The effect of the "Dry Pants" toilet training procedure on the frequency of toileting accidents, both bladder and bowel, of 34 normal children. The toilet training period is shown as an interruption in the curve and required an average of 4 hours per child. The "Pre-training" data point represents the children's accident rate per day during the week prior to training. Data points are given for the first 7 days after training and monthly thereafter. Each datum point is the average number of accidents per day per child. (From Foxx, R. M., & Azrin, N. H. (1973). Dry Pants: A rapid method of toilet training. *Behavior Research and Therapy, 11,* 446. By permission of Pergamon Press.)

two to three years of age and bladder trained at three to four years. Bowel training usually comes first, followed by waking bladder control, and finally by control of bladder function during sleep. The next section will focus on a persistent problem of toilet training, namely, enuresis or night wetting.

Enuresis refers to the involuntary discharge of urine in the absence of organic pathology after a child has reached the age of six years (DSM, III, APA, 1980). There are two types of enuresis: diurnal enuresis (during waking hours) and nocturnal enuresis (during sleeping hours). We shall focus on the problem of nocturnal enuresis (i.e., bedwet-

ting), because it is the subcategory of enuresis with which most investigations of treatment procedures have been concerned. Furthermore, nocturnal enuresis is a more persistent problem and a more vexing one for parents than is diurnal enuresis.

The age at which children stop bedwetting varies from culture to culture and also from social class to social class. Generally, in Western countries, approximately 20 percent of children still wet their bed at a high frequency at the age of four to five years. This percentage decreases to 13 percent at six to seven years of age and to 2 or 3 percent at fourteen years. Enuresis is more prevalent in

---

Box 4–1 *Some Interesting Historical Treatments*

In Western Nigeria toads were tied to a child's penis so that the toad would croak when the child wet the bed. Presumably, the child would awaken at the sound or movement of the toad.

Navaho Indians made enuretic children stand naked over the burning nest of the Phoebe, a swallow that was known not to wet their nest (Salmon, 1975).

A bed was built with special springs and a child was unceremoniously rolled out on a mattress on the floor if he or she wet the bed. This method was devised and perfected but never used with bedwetters because Mowrer feared adverse publicity from its use (Mowrer, 1980).

Thomas Phaer, father of modern pediatrics, advised enuretic children to eat various entrails in a section of his book called "Of Pyssing in the Bedde" (Lovibond, 1964).

---

children from lower than from higher socioeconomic classes and also more frequent in children who have a history of enuresis in their families. It occurs roughly twice as often in boys as it does in girls. There is also some evidence to suggest that enuretics have smaller functional bladder capacities than nonenuretics (Starfield, 1972).

The problem of bedwetting constitutes a very difficult situation for both the parent and the child. The parent is frustrated by the presence of daily soiled linen and the feeling that the child is able but too lazy to control the bladder; the child, in turn, suffers from the embarrassment and discomfort that accompany urine-soaked clothing as well as from the ill feeling generated between himself and his parents. The problem of enuresis is often critical; child abuse research indicates that physical assaults on children are due first to crying and second to bedwetting (Anthony, 1978). Because the problem causes so much concern, there have been a host of remedies reported to deal with it, including raising the foot or the head of the bed, waking at hourly intervals, scolding, beating, and even procedures as extreme as eating entrails. In addition to these, however, a number of medical and psychological treatments have been advanced. Such treatments have involved drug therapy, hormone injections, hypnosis, and psychotherapy. None of the above approaches has proven as effective as direct learning approaches in teaching the child to become continent (Johnson, 1981).

A TREATMENT METHOD AND ATTITUDES REGARDING ETIOLOGY

The first practical learning device for enuresis was developed by Mowrer and Mowrer at Yale University in 1938.[1] The Mowrer apparatus consists of a pad which is sensitive to the ions in the urine and connected to a bell. When the child begins to urinate, the bell rings in an alarm box beside the child's bed. (See Figures 4–2 and 4–3.) The alarm must be turned off manually by the child, after which he goes to the bathroom to complete the voiding process. Often the parent is asked to assure that the child is awake when he is in the bathroom by having the child wash his face. The child then returns to his bedroom to change the sheet, reset the alarm, and go to bed. A daily chart is kept of the child's progress, and each day the child is dry, a gold

---

1. A similar device was developed by Pfaundler, a German pediatrician, in 1904 to alert nurses that a child had urinated. However, that device was inefficiently designed.

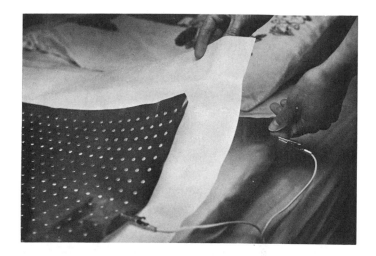

Figure 4–2 Two metal foil sheets separated by an insulating pad; the metal foil sheets are connected to an alarm which awakens the child when he or she urinates.

star is placed on his chart. It usually takes three to eight weeks before the child is dry repeatedly for two weeks. If there is a relapse, the child is given the bell and pad device until he is again dry for two consecutive weeks. In the original Mowrer and Mowrer study it was reported that all thirty children treated by this learning method reached the criterion of fourteen consecutive dry nights within two months after the beginning of treatment. This constitutes a very high success rate for any form of intervention.

It is interesting to speculate about why a method developed in 1938 and seemingly so successful failed to be further developed and utilized by pediatricians and child psychologists for three decades. A major reason for the reluctance of physicians and psychologists

Figure 4–3 Child being aided by mother to shut off the Bell and Pad Alarm and go to the bathroom.

to use the Mowrer device was the attitude that the bedwetting problems represent a symptom of some underlying emotional disturbance. In fact, a long-accepted view of enuresis was that it is a symptom of some emotional conflict. For example, in a case treated in 1956, Robertiello described enuresis as a cooling of the penis, the fire of which was condemned by the superego. Inhof, in 1957, suggested that enuresis usually expresses a demand for love and that it may be a form of weeping through the bladder. Freud, in 1916, explained enuresis as a form of direct sexual gratification and, as seen by Freud and his associates, enuresis was a regressive problem set in motion as a consequence of extreme anxiety resulting from the repression of some basic desires. Although we shall not discuss in detail the psychoanalytic conception of enuresis, the notion of the treatment of enuresis as a symptom of an underlying problem is presented to give one the flavor of the psychodynamic view of the enuretic problem and some indication why the highly successful Mowrer device was not widely adopted by practicing psychologists and physicians. In fact, the Mowrers were involved in Freudian psychoanalysis and were worried about symptom substitution (Mowrer, 1980).

Despite the success of the Mowrers, behaviorally oriented treatment approaches of almost any sort had little prominence until the 1960s, in part because the most popular conception of abnormal behavior, the psychoanalytic conception, was almost antithetical to the use of such treatment. Learning devices like those of the Mowrers were viewed as mechanistic and the treatment model was seen as oversimplified. In addition, according to Mowrer,[2] although six commercial firms began to produce the device almost immediately, they did not advertise widely or

2. O.H. Mowrer, personal communication, 1974.

provide the consultation service frequently rendered by firms today. Thus, parents were only minimally aware of the device and its successful treatment results.

Most therapists, rather than regarding enuresis as a habit deficiency which could be corrected by a direct learning approach, felt that the individual's attitudes, feelings, and thoughts needed modification. Because many of the basic principles of learning had originally been demonstrated with rats or other animals, many practitioners saw learning therapy as synonymous with rat therapy and thus inadequate to solving problems of human concern. In fact, the Mowrers' device is often referred to as a conditioning device though the precise mechanisms of learning may not be due to any simple classical conditioning as the Mowrers imagined. Mowrer was one of the first well-known proponents of the point of view that in a majority of cases, enuresis may be regarded as a simple habit deficiency. According to the Mowrers, "there is a relatively large group of enuretic children in whom faulty habit training is the predominant, perhaps exclusive causal factor" (Mowrer and Mowrer, 1938, p. 456). In a study of 134 enuretics attending a special treatment facility, Young and Turner (1973) found no evidence that enuretic children were more neurotic than normal children, as measured by the Junior Eysenck Personality Inventory. On the other hand, mothers of enuretics had significantly higher introverted and neurotic scores than standard normative populations.

According to the psychodynamic or symptom model, the child who is enuretic should be given psychotherapy aimed at improving his general adjustment. That is, it is necessary to treat the disturbance as a disturbance of the total personality. Thus, the treatment should be directed primarily toward the individual and only secondarily toward the enuresis. In fact, according to some, direct treatment of enuresis is considered undesirable because it would result in an exacerbation of the underlying personality conflict of the individual and a subsequent expression of the underlying conflict in some other way (i.e., symptom substitution).

Alternatively, when one views enuresis as a habit deficiency, the treatment is directed specifically toward developing the habit of continence. This may be accomplished by using one of several possible treatments, including the drug imipramine, learning devices, direct bladder training, and complex learning treatments involving learning to awake to minimal cues, punishment for wetting, and rewards for continence. All of these treatments will be discussed below.

CONDITIONING TREATMENT

The first conditioning device developed by Mowrer and Mowrer in 1938 was described earlier. Conditioning devices in use today are basically similar to the type developed by Mowrer and Mowrer with a few minor variations. Lovibond's (1963) device, for example, uses a twin signal rather than a single alarm; a brief but loud signal is followed by a buzzer similar to that used in the Mowrer apparatus. The theory behind Lovibond's modification of the Mowrer device is that the child has the impression that he is terminating the initial aversive signal when he terminates his micturitional response (urination) and will learn to avoid the alarm and waking up by controlling his micturitional responses. Since most studies have found the Mowrer device to be generally as effective as Lovibond's (Turner, Young, & Rachman, 1970), we will concern ourselves almost solely with research utilizing the Mowrer apparatus. Furthermore, the Mowrer device is readily available in the United States from commer-

cial firms and costs one third as much as the Lovibond device (Turner, Young, & Rachman, 1970).

Beginning with the Mowrer and Mowrer report (1938), a large number of studies investigating the effectiveness of conditioning devices have been conducted. Mowrer and Mowrer reported an unusually high success rate (100 percent) in the initial study using their device. The usual success rate reported over the past three decades is an 80 percent initial arrest of bedwetting when a conditioning device is used in the treatment of nocturnal enuresis (Doleys, 1977; Jones, 1960; Lovibond, 1964; Young, 1965).

Deleon and Sacks (1972) provided follow-up data on twenty-one of forty-four enuretic children who had been successfully treated using the conditioning procedures. The group included subjects of both sexes whose age range at follow-up was twelve to twenty years. All subjects had reached the cure criterion four years earlier with a conditioning procedure earlier employed by Deleon and Mandell (1966). All mothers of the children were contacted by phone and asked if there had been a recurrence of bedwetting since the last contact. The mothers reported that 81 percent of the subjects were virtually symptom free; that is, there were no nights of wetting in the past year. For the subjects who were wetting, the severity of wetting had significantly diminished as compared with the pretreatment level. Unfortunately, though there was an initial control group, no data were presented from this group in the follow-up.

Extensive research has made it clear that the rapid successes produced by the conditioning procedures are maintained in a large percentage of the subjects. Despite the general success of the conditioning treatment, approximately 20 to 30 percent of the children relapse following the initial treatment (Young and Morgan, 1972a; Johnson, 1981). Several investigators have made attempts to reduce these relapse rates. Intermittent reinforcement, that is, having the device always present but activated only part of the time, has been utilized by Finley, Besserman, Bennett, Clap, and Finley (1973), who found fewer relapses in an intermittently reinforced group than in a continuously reinforced group. Central nervous system stimulant drugs such as amphetamines have been used to increase the speed of conditioning and retard the extinction of the learned response (Young & Turner, 1965). These drugs were effective in reducing the duration of the treatment, but after twelve months the relapse rate was higher than the relapse rate of patients treated only by the conditioning process.

Young and Morgan (1972a) utilized a procedure of "overlearning" in which the child was instructed to drink two pints of liquid in the last hour before going to bed as a means of strengthening the resistance of the newly acquired habit of continence following the use of a conditioning device. Overlearning therapy was given to sixty-one cases randomly selected from a total sample of 144 patients at a special treatment clinic. The overlearning procedure was found to significantly reduce the relapse rate without increasing the likelihood of parents terminating the treatment prematurely. In a second study Young and Morgan (1972b) found that of 126 children who used the overlearning procedure only 10 percent relapsed; without overlearning after utilization of the conditioning device, the relapse rate was 20 percent. It is possible that the overlearning helps increase bladder capacity and thus decreases the frequency of bedwetting. However, as Johnson (1981) noted, the overlearning procedure has not always proven to be significantly better than the standard procedure, and some children experience high rates of wetting when it is introduced. Therefore, it may be best to gradually increase fluid intake before retiring rather than to drink two pints of liquid before bedtime (Johnson, 1981).

SYMPTOM SUBSTITUTION

Since the issue of symptom substitution is central to the question of the efficacy of the conditioning treatment versus the psychodynamic treatment, let us examine what some individuals feel might result from the use of a conditioning device. In a book on child care, Salk (1972) stated that he is unalterably opposed to conditioning devices. He feels that it is important for children to learn to use their own resources to achieve control rather than to rely on an external device. He is wary of automatic conditioning devices "because I have seen too many instances where they have affected the child's personality. I have seen cases where male youngsters trained in this way become sexually impotent later in life. I think they have become unconsciously accustomed to an external cue, passively offered to start some internal mechanism of bodily control. These men always expect some external signal to set off a physiologic response. They do not expect to exert any effort" (p. 59). Homan (1969), following the emotional symptom model, says that enuretic children "are urinating on the world about them, in retaliation for the discomforts and tribulations that the world has imposed upon them" (p. 117). He warns against the use of a conditioning device for children under the age of 12 or 14 on the grounds that they may substitute for bedwetting some other socially unacceptable habit such as "masturbating in school or undressing little boys and girls in cellars" (p. 121).

Let us consider whether there is any real evidence suggesting that there are, as Salk and Homan imply, negative side effects resulting from the use of a conditioning treatment. In 1969, Baker obtained a sample of thirty enuretic children by placing a newspaper advertisement describing a study involving the treatment of bed-wetters. His sample consisted of elementary-age schoolchildren, all but four of whom had been bedwetting since birth, and more than half of whom were wet seven nights a week. The children were matched in triads according to information gathered over the phone such as sex, number of nights of wetting, and age. The children from the triads were randomly assigned to each of three experimental groups: (1) behavior therapy, i.e., the Mowrer device; (2) a wake-up treatment, i.e., parents awaken the child at a fixed but unspecified time; and (3) a waiting list which served as a control group. Parents of children in groups 1 and 2 aided the children in getting up at night and kept records of their progress; all children kept star charts and were visited once a week by the experimenter. The child was designated as cured after four weeks of dry nights. In order to evaluate whether symptom substitution occurred, Baker obtained measures of adjustment in the form of a parent checklist designed to assess attributes such as confidence, anxiety, and responsibility. He also obtained a behavior record from the parents which consisted of a list of twenty-six childhood problems, many of which have traditionally been associated with enuresis in the psychiatric literature. Each child's teacher filled out a rating form for the enuretic child and for two randomly selected control children in her class. In addition to measures of overt behavior reported by the parent and the teacher, the child was assessed through a projective test battery and a self-report questionnaire which measured neurotic problems.

The results of the study were as follows: the waiting list control group made no progress, the wake-up group was significantly better than the waiting list group, and the conditioning group was significantly better than the wake-up group. Eventually both the children in the wake-up and the waiting list control group were assigned to the conditioning treatment, at the end of which 74 percent were designated as cured and another 15 percent showed marked improvement. At a six-month follow-up, four cured subjects relapsed, but two of these who were treated became dry again. Of critical concern here is what happened to the children as viewed on projective measures and on reports by the teacher and parent. Contrary to expectations derived from psychoanalytic theory, the children showed significant improvement as seen both in the home and school and on projective ratings. The most frequently reported observation was the children's increased happiness at becoming dry. Many of the children were able to sleep overnight with friends or go to summer camp. Three boys immediately joined the Scouts.

Baker's study presents objective data which convincingly demonstrate that, contrary to the subjective opinions of Salk and Homan, no negative side effects and no instances of symptom substitution result from the proper use of a conditioning device. Instead, the elimination of the bedwetting problem is associated with an increase in the child's happiness and well-being. This finding is consistent with the results reported by other researchers investigating the issue of symptom substitution and reinforces our earlier conclusion that, although it may be associated with other problems, in many instances a target problem can be attacked directly without adverse side effects.

CONDITIONING TREATMENT FOR DEAF CHILDREN

A very interesting variation of the basic Mowrer device was used by Baller and Giangreco (1970) for enuretic deaf children at a large residential school. A light was focused as nearly as possible on the face of the child so that when the child urinated the light shone in his or her face. In brief, instead of having the bell and pad connected to a buzzer, it was connected to a light. A thorough explanation of the purpose of the treatment was given to the children by an experienced counselor with the aid of an interpreter before the apparatus was placed in the bedroom. Twenty-one children, fifteen boys and six girls, all became completely dry within thirty days of treatment. One child relapsed, but with two subsequent uses of the apparatus he became completely dry. As reported by other investigators treating hearing children, the deaf children treated with the variation of the Mowrer procedure also improved in their relations with other children.

COMPARING CONDITIONING AND PSYCHOTHERAPY

In 1966, Deleon and Mandell obtained a sample of eighty-five children, ages 5 to 14, who were referred with a diagnosis of enuresis. During an initial period of two weeks, the mothers were asked to record whether or not the child's bed was wet three times per night: before the mother went to sleep, at 3:00 a.m., and after the family awakened in the morning. The children were assigned to one of three groups: a conditioning group, a psychotherapy or counseling group, and a control group. The instrument used in the conditioning treatment was of the Mowrer type. Success was defined as (1) seven consecutive dry nights on the operative pad, (2) three successive dry nights with the instrument and pad on the bed but disconnected, and (3) three successive nights with the instrument and pad out of the room, for a total of thirteen consecutive dry nights. Subjects in the psychotherapy group were seen for twelve sessions on a weekly basis. A session consisted of forty min-

utes with the child and twenty minutes with the mother. The precise form of therapy was unspecified in the report, although it was stated that it was carried out by a psychologist or a psychiatrist. Subjects in the control group received no treatment but simply had nightly data obtained for ninety days. As in the conditioning group, success in the psychotherapy and control group was defined as thirteen consecutive dry nights. The average follow-up period was thirty weeks and the range was four to eighty-eight weeks. For those who completed treatment, the percentage of subjects reaching the success criterion in the three groups was as follows: conditioning, 86 percent; psychotherapy, 18 percent; and control, 11 percent. The difference between the success of the conditioning group and the other two groups was, of course, highly significant.

Werry and Cohrssen, in 1965, made a similar comparison of conditioning and psychotherapy. The mean age of the sample of children, all of whom were referrals to an enuresis clinic, was ten years. These investigators compared psychotherapy of a psychodynamically oriented nature with a no-treatment control and with a Mowrer-type treatment device. The apparatus was set up only once a night, and after the initial interview, no contact was made with the parents apart from an occasional telephone call. At the end of four months, parents were telephoned to see how many times the child had wet in the preceding months. Whereas brief psychotherapy (six to eight sessions) was ineffective, conditioning treatment resulted in a significantly higher rate of improvement than no treatment. It is interesting to note that Werry and Cohrssen had an initial arrest of enuresis considerably lower than usually reported: only 30 percent of their conditioning treatment subjects were reported cured. As the authors noted, however, a relative lack of supervision may have been responsible for the lowered success rate (after the initial interview no contact except an occasional phone call took place). These results suggest that simply having parents buy a conditioning device is relatively ineffective in treating the enuretic problem. Bollard and Nettelbeck (1981) confirmed this hypothesis when they found that bell and pad use without therapist supervision had resulted in only 60 percent of the cases becoming dry as compared to 80 percent with therapist supervision. Much earlier, Lovibond (1964) reported that commercial use of the Mowrer device without supervision was associated with success rates as low as 56 percent.

Cautions Regarding Success Rates and Relapses

A clinician who treats enuretics with multiple problems such as enuresis and conduct disorders or enuresis and mild mental retardation should be alert to the possibility that the commonly reported success rates of approximately 80 percent may not apply. The success rates usually reported refer to percentages of children with a focal problem of enuresis who become continent. Most authors have found that no particular patterns of behavioral problems or emotional disturbance are associated with enuresis. Furthermore, even in those studies in which higher rates of behavior problems were found, the extent of those problems was of limited clinical significance (Couchells, Johnson, Carter, & Walker, 1981). When multiple problems exist, however, the success rates of behavioral interventions such as the conditioning device and dry bed training are likely to be lower than 80 percent.

It has long been known that approximately 30 percent of children who are successfully treated (become continent) later have at least occasional relapses. Further, children with multiple problems may require special understanding and support from their parents.

In an intriguing case study of a successfully treated enuretic child with noncompliance problems and aggression, a mother was asked to record instances of behavior problems and nocturnal wetting (Vivian, Fischel, & Liebert, in press). Following the successful treatment, there were occasional relapses, and it was learned that the probability of behavior problems was significantly greater on days following a wet night than on days following a dry night. This case study is informative because it indicates that child management problems are more likely following wetting accidents than on days when there are no accidents. The reasons for the association are unclear. The child could be unhappy as soon as he or she awakened and learned that the bed was wet, the parents could have been angry and punitive because of the accident, the child might have been anxious because of some upcoming event in school and that anxiety in turn might lead to problem behavior. Regardless of the factors that might account for such an association between wetting and behavior problems, a parent should be alert to the possibility that problems may be more likely on days following a wet night, should accept occasional relapses, and should be very supportive of the child. Finally, in those cases in which there is a demonstrated relationship between conduct problems and bedwetting, behavioral treatments for enuresis may have to continue for longer periods than standard treatments for simple enuresis, and both parents and children should be aware of such treatment length to eliminate possible frustrations.

DRUG THERAPY

In spite of their high success rate, Lovibond (1964, 1972) has noted that there are problems inherent in the utilization of the conditioning treatment devices. One rather obvious problem concerns the use of a conditioning device in a home in which several children have to share a bedroom. Imagine yourself as a twelve-year-old child who has to sleep in a room with his brother, an eight-year-old, who for two months is awakened nightly by an alarm. While it may be possible to have such a child sleep in the living room or some other isolated place in the house, it is apparent that on occasion the utilization of the device may cause particular inconvenience. This inconvenience may be reflected in high drop-out rates reported by a number of investigators. For example, a sizable portion of Turner, Young, and Rachman's sample in 1970 were removed from therapy presumably because of inadequate cooperation from the parents. Although outright rejection of treatment by a parent is exceedingly rare according to Lovibond, it is important to evaluate whether there are alternatives to the bell and pad procedure which might prove successful when the parent is reluctant to give the child such a treatment because family factors, such as a large number of children in a small house, make the treatment untenable.

Forrester, Stein, and Susser (1964) compared the effectiveness of a conditioning treatment with an amphetamine treatment designed to lighten the child's sleep. Enuresis was completely relieved in 80 percent of the children receiving the conditioning treatment and in 23 percent of the children receiving the amphetamine treatment. The difference between the two cure rates is obviously significant. In another study, Young (1965) found that bedwetting was arrested in 65 percent of the conditioning group and in 36 percent of a varied drug treatment group (e.g., antidiuretics and amphetamines). Not only did they find that the arrest rate was higher in the conditioning group but also that the arrest rate was more rapidly achieved in the conditioning group and relapses were less frequent.

The major drug that has been used for treating enuresis is imipramine (Tofranil). Imipramine is an antidepressant drug whose effects in the treatment of enuresis are not well understood, but Esson, a psychologist, noticed that depressed patients treated with imipramine had difficulty urinating (MacLean, 1960). Hagglund and Parkkulainen (1965) demonstrated an increase in bladder capacity and disappearance of involuntary contractions of the bladder in children who were treated with imipramine. This finding suggests that the nervous input which causes bladder contraction or tension is blocked by imipramine. While the specific nature of the imipramine effect is not exactly clear, Poussaint and Dittman, in 1965, found that eight weeks of imipramine were superior to a placebo in reducing the frequency of enuretic nights. Unfortunately, only 24 percent of children were "cured" of their enuresis with the aid of imipramine (using a period of two months of dryness without medication as criterion for cure). The dosage level was 50 to 75 mg. for children between twelve and sixteen years of age, a dosage level considered high by some (Werry, 1972). Kardish, Hillman, and Werry, in 1968, used 25 mg. of imipramine for children five to nine years of age, and 50 mg. for children ten years and over, with increases to a maximum of 75 mg. if no improvement was obtained at the lower dosage levels. They found that eight weeks of imipramine treatment was statistically superior to placebo therapy. Again, using a two-month dry period following drug termination as a "cure" criterion, 30 percent were designated cured.

As an alternative to psychological intervention, imipramine therapy is not a very valuable alternative because of its relatively low cure rates, frequent resumption of wetting when medication is stopped, and possible side effects. Some clinicians feel the side effects (nervousness, dermatitis, and insomnia), although infrequent and reversible, are important enough to cause one to be cautious when using this form of treatment. In addition, the effectiveness of treatment with imipramine decreases with continued drug use, and the safety of long-term use has not been established. It is important also to note that imipramine has not been judged safe or effective in children under six years of age, and "the safety of the drug for *long-term, chronic* use as adjunctive therapy for nocturnal enuresis in children 6 years of age or *older* has not been established" (Physicians Desk Reference, 1984, p. 969; emphasis added). In addition, the increasing prevalence of drug abuse and addiction among children makes it incumbent upon a physician to consider carefully every instance of the use of medication. The physician should be particularly concerned about the use of any medication which could alter a child's mood, as is the case with imipramine. Finally, prior treatment with imipramine has been associated with relapse after initial arrest of bedwetting following behavioral treatment (Houts, Peterson, & Liebert, 1984).

BLADDER TRAINING

The notion that it was possible to cure bedwetting by having a child engage in a series of exercises for bladder training was mentioned as early as 1885 by Stein. Muellner, in 1960, successfully treated enuretics by requiring bedwetters to practice holding their urine after they had taken a certain amount of water. The purpose of this treatment is to increase the capacity of the bladder, which Muellner saw as the essential cause of enuresis. Following Kimmel and Kimmel's 1970 observation that nocturnal enuresis is often accompanied by a higher rate of urination during waking hours, Paschalis, Kimmel, and Kimmel (1972) examined the frequency of urination in an enuretic group and a non-

enuretic control group during a baseline period. The nonenuretic control group had an average urination rate of 3.5 times daily with a range of 3 to 5 times, whereas the enuretic groups had a mean urination rate of 5.8 with a range of 4 to 12. These observations tend to confirm the notion that enuretics may have a smaller bladder capacity which triggers their urination. Consequently, it has seemed plausible to various investigators to examine direct bladder training designed to increase the bladder capacity.

Starfield, in 1972, reported the results of an outcome study on direct bladder training which consisted of seven basic steps. Those steps are as follows:

1. Once every day the child practices holding his urine as long as he can before going to the bathroom; on school days the best time for him to hold his urine is when he comes home after school.
2. The child drinks large amounts of water, milk, or juice while holding his urine, as this helps to stretch the bladder.
3. After the child has held his urine as long as he is able, he urinates into a cup with ounces marked on it so a record can be kept of his progress in treatment.
4. The child keeps a calendar record of the number of ounces of urine he passes in each daily session; he also checks on the calendar whether he was wet or dry on the day.
5. Because it is sometimes difficult for a child to hold his urine, the family helps him by keeping him busy by playing a game of some kind.
6. After the child has increased his bladder capacity, the parent supervises him in the practice of starting and stopping his urine stream; this will help the child gain control over his bladder.
7. Finally, the child himself practices the stopping and holding of his urine several times each day.

Starfield used this treatment procedure in a six-month program with a large number of families. A total of 198 children were treated and approximately one-third of them were reportedly free of enuresis at a follow-up examination.

Bladder training or retention control training as first reported by Starfield (1972) and Paschalis and others (1972) seemed to be a reasonable alternative to the bell and pad treatment. However, its use has been seriously questioned because of controlled research. For example, Doleys, Ciminero, Tollison, and Wells (1977) found that nine weeks of bladder training, or retention control training as they called it, was essentially ineffective. As can be seen in Figure 4–4, the children given bladder training did not reduce their frequency of wetting, whereas the children who received the multifaceted treatment of Azrin, Sneed, and Foxx (1974) (herein referred to as Dry Bed Training) reduced the frequency of their wetting very markedly. Half

of the children treated by Doleys and colleagues (1977) had previously received other treatments such as the bell and pad, rewards, and nightly awakenings, and one-third of the children had medical treatment for enuresis, such as medication or surgery. Therefore, the children in this study had already received unsuccessful treatment and this previous unsuccessful treatment could account for the relatively poor success rate of the bladder training compared to the previous studies. Another factor that may have accounted for the differences was noted by Doleys and colleagues, who used a maximum retention interval of thirty minutes, whereas Paschalis and colleagues (1972) used a retention interval of forty-five minutes, and Starfield (1972) had the child hold his or her urine for as long as possible. Nonetheless, Harris and Purohit (1977) used children who had received no other

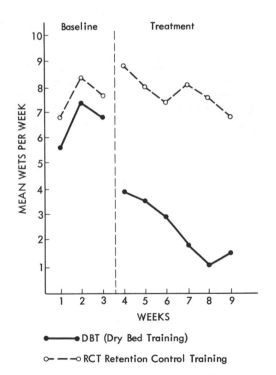

Figure 4–4 Mean wets per week during baseline. (From Doleys, D. M. et al. (1977). Dry bed training & retention control training: A comparison. *Behavior Therapy, 8,* p. 545.)

previous treatment except medication (50 percent of the children) and had used retention intervals "as long as possible." Like Doleys and colleagues they found that thirty-five days of bladder training was relatively ineffective in reducing enuresis despite the fact that bladder capacities increased significantly.

In sum, bladder or retention control training has had mixed results. The success or cure rates have ranged from 43 percent (Paschalis et al., 1972) to essentially zero (Doleys et al., 1977). Even though enuretic children have bladder capacities that are approximately 100 ml (cc) less than nonenuretic children (Starfield, 1972), some enuretic children do not need such training. Allen and Hasazi (1978), found practically significant increases in bladder capacities only with children with capacities less than 200 ml (cc) and that bladder capacity was predictive of awakening at night in enuretics successfully treated with the bell and pad intervention.

MULTIFACETED LEARNING TREATMENTS

A successful method of treating retarded adults with a number of procedures designed to teach continence was developed by Azrin, Sneed, and Foxx (1973). Azrin et al. (1973) supplemented the bell and pad device with specific operant interventions, such as positive reinforcement for having a dry bed, positive reinforcement for nighttime urination in the toilet, practice and reinforcement for arising to urinate, and punishment for accidents (i.e., reprimands and having to clean and remake the bed). Ninety-five percent of the retarded adults learned to toilet themselves at night in an average time period of three days. The methods just described were then modified for use with normal children by Azrin et al.

(1974). Unlike other interventions used to teach continence, the Azrin et al. procedure involved a full night of intensive training followed by the continued use of the bell and pad for one week. The modifications included giving rationales to the child and parents for each of the aspects of the program, having the child drink large amounts of fluid to increase the desire to urinate, using minimal cues from a trainer to arouse the child hourly to go to the toilet, using the bell and pad ringing in both the child's and parents' rooms, reprimanding for wetting the bed, having the child change the sheets after each wetting incident, and using twenty practice trials in which the child lay in bed and got up to make trips to the bathroom to attempt to urinate. After one all-night training session, the twenty-four treated children had an average of only two bedwetting accidents after two weeks of consecutive dry nights. There was a relapse rate of 29 percent, but following booster sessions with the bell and pad, no further relapses occurred. In summary, the all-night training program produced rapid treatment effects that maintained more than six months, and the treatment was more efficient than the standard bell and pad treatment.

The Azrin et al. (1974) method called Dry Bed Training (DBT) was modified by Bollard and Woodroffe (1977), who had parents rather than professional trainers administer the intensive all-night training program. All fourteen children treated ceased bedwetting, but the median time to the last night of wetting was twelve days. Doleys, Ciminero, Tollison, and Wells (1977) also found that Dry Bed Training was effective in reducing the frequency of wetting, but only five of thirteen subjects had fourteen consecutive dry nights by the end of six weeks. Finally, Bollard and Nettlebeck (1981) found that Dry Bed Training was effective in reaching the criterion of dryness in sixty children but that the mean number of wet nights for the DBT was thirteen and the average time taken to the last wet night was thirty-five days.

There are several general conclusions one can draw from the research regarding the utility and efficiency of Dry Bed Training. It is clearly a very effective procedure, but investigators not associated with Azrin have found that it takes them much longer than Azrin and his colleagues to reach a dryness criterion. Nonetheless, the DBT method has been consistently superior to the bell and pad treatment alone in terms of speed of treatment and number of children who achieve continence.

A comprehensive, low-cost, multifaceted learning treatment was developed by Houts, Liebert, and Padawer (1983). The treatment consisted of bell and pad training, cleanliness training, retention control, and overlearning. In contrast to most other interventions, this treatment for primary enuretics was implemented on a one-hour group basis. Each case required fifteen minutes of professional time. As Houts and colleagues (1983) noted, despite the longstanding success of psychological treatments for enuresis (Mowrer, 1938), problems of treatment cost and parent cooperation have contributed to the underutilization of bell and pad interventions. Sixty children participated in the study (forty-eight males and twelve females). The mean age of the children was eight years and the majority of the children had been wetting every night of the week.

The one-hour group sessions were conducted in a university classroom on the weekends so that parents could attend with their child. Ten families attended any one session. Central to the treatment was a behavioral contract in which parents agreed to administer rewards on a specific schedule when the child postponed urination (retention training). In addition, the child agreed to place any soiled bedclothes and sheets in a specific place and to remake the bed (cleanliness training). Finally, the child agreed to drink up to 16 ounces of water during the hour before bedtime after he or she had been continent for fourteen consecutive nights (overlearning). Following the one-hour group session, parents were told to contact the clinic at the end of two months to report whether the child had achieved fourteen consecutive days of dryness and whether the fourteen days of overlearning had occurred.

Eighty-one percent of the children were dry at the end of treatment. This percentage of successfully treated cases is essentially identical to the rates reported in many reviews of enuresis treatment. Further, the relapse rate was only 18 percent. In brief, the study exemplifies how enuresis treatment can be delivered on a cost-effective basis.

CONCEPTUALIZATIONS REGARDING TREATMENT SUCCESSES

There is no single model of enuresis treatment which adequately accounts for the successes in behavioral treatment. The most frequently used model for years was the classical conditioning model espoused by Mowrer and Mowrer (1938). (See Box 4–2.) A serious problem with the Mowrer model is that it depicts how a child can learn to awaken when in fact many children learn to sleep through the night. Approximately 75 percent of children successfully treated with the bell and pad device learn to sleep through the night, whereas 25 percent of children learn to awaken.[3] In addition, a conditioned stimulus loses its effectiveness if the unconditioned

---

3. Personal communication, Dr. Arthur Houts, Memphis State University, January 26, 1982.

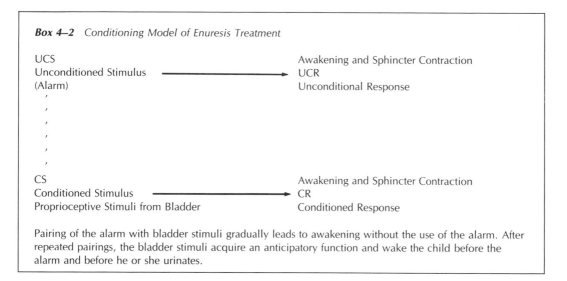

Box 4–2   *Conditioning Model of Enuresis Treatment*

UCS
Unconditioned Stimulus ⟶ Awakening and Sphincter Contraction
(Alarm)
UCR
Unconditional Response

CS
Conditioned Stimulus ⟶ Awakening and Sphincter Contraction
Proprioceptive Stimuli from Bladder
CR
Conditioned Response

Pairing of the alarm with bladder stimuli gradually leads to awakening without the use of the alarm. After repeated pairings, the bladder stimuli acquire an anticipatory function and wake the child before the alarm and before he or she urinates.

stimulus is not paired with it. Therefore, it is unclear with this model why the child should continue to awaken from a bladder signal (CS) when the alarm (UCS) is no longer present.

An alternative conceptualization of enuresis treatment is an operant avoidance response (Lovibond, 1964; Kalish, 1981). Basically, it is held that the child learns to avoid the aversive aspects of sleep interruption—the alarm in the bell and pad treatment—and the aversive aspects of the Dry Bed Training—the awakening trials, sheet changes, and verbal reprimands. Several investigators have not been able to produce significant treatment successes with the dry bed procedure without the bell and pad device (Nettlebeck & Langeluddecke, 1979; Bollard & Nettlebeck, 1981). Some argue (Kalish, 1981) that the alarm device is useful for the effective detection of wetting, and that the bell and pad device "enhances the association of signals from the bladder with the annoyance of being awakened" (p. 204). Kalish's conceptualization of avoidance learning is that the child learns to avoid waking up through control of the sphincter muscle, which in turn

prevents urination. He depicted the process as follows: "Distended bladder produces sphincter contraction (an active avoidance response), and the children learn to be dry through the night simply because they do not want their sleep disturbed" (p. 202). This avoidance conceptualization applies directly to those children who learn to awaken to urinate but could be extended to those children who learn to sleep through the night. It could be said that they learn to avoid sleep interruption.

A third conceptualization of successes in enuresis treatment is that the child learns to retain fluid and sleep through the night with direct bladder training. More specifically, a child is taught to hold his or her urine for a longer period, and in turn, it is expected that bladder capacity will increase (Starfield, 1972). In fact, there is clear evidence that enuretic children have smaller functional bladder capacities and that enuretic children's bladder capacity can increase with direct bladder training (Harris & Purohit, 1977. See Figure 4-5.), but it is not clear that bladder training and in turn, an increase in bladder capacity,

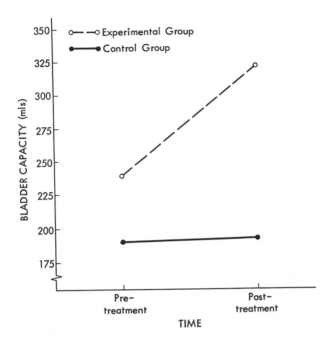

Figure 4–5 Mean bladder capacity for each group at each time period. (From Harris, L. S., Purhoit, A. P. (1977). Bladder training and enuresis: A controlled trial. *Behaviour Research & Therapy, 15,* 488. Copyright 1977 by Pergamon Journals Ltd. Reprinted with permission.)

is necessary or sufficient for all enuretics. Harris and Purohit (1977) in fact had no significant reduction in bedwetting associated with the increases in bladder capacity. However, Allen and Hasazi (1978) found significant increases in bladder capacities only with children whose capacities were less than 200 cc (ml). Further, as noted earlier, they found that in children who were successfully treated with the bell and pad device small bladder capacities were predictive of awakening at night.

As stated at the outset of this section, there is no single model of enuresis treatment which adequately accounts for all successes in behavioral treatment. Although the Azrin et al. multifaceted intervention clearly involves many treatment principles, the other major behavioral alternatives (bell and pad treatment and bladder training) also involve many treatment procedures and principles. More specifically, positive reinforcement, avoid-

ance learning, and increases in bladder capacity are only a few of the factors involved in these treatments. Perhaps much more detailed assessment of the particular needs of individual children prior to treatment will lead to programs which are even more successful and which provide better theoretical conceptualizations of the treatments. Some children may require bladder training while others may not, some may need primary emphasis in their training on awakening, and some children may require positive consequences for being continent and aversive consequences for wetting. Finally, while the evidence does not always support the notion that enuretics have significantly more behavioral and/or emotional problems than nonenuretics (Johnson, 1981), the children brought to psychological and psychiatric clinics with enuresis as a problem often report other significant problems. With such children, sensitive clinical judgment must be used to decide which problem(s) likely occurred first (enuresis or emotional problems) and which problem(s) should become the initial treatment focus.

INITIAL SUMMARY

The two major conceptualizations of enuresis have been discussed. In the first view, enuresis is seen as a symptom of an underlying emotional disorder; in the second, enuresis is seen as a habit deficiency. We have presented data which suggest that the latter is more appropriate for most cases. The implications that the two opposing views hold for the treatment of enuresis were reviewed and the utility of a treatment that consists primarily of the direct training of the habit of continence was demonstrated. In fact, most of the data indicate that direct behavioral treatment of the habit of continence, rather than producing negative side effects, produces many benefits as seen in both the child's self-image and the evaluations of the child by others.

ENCOPRESIS

Encopresis is officially defined as repeated voluntary or involuntary passage of feces in inappropriate places more than once per month after the age of four. Such fecal passage is not due to a physical disorder (DSM III, APA, 1980).

Soiling can result from a multitude of causes, which paradoxically include chronic constipation. On occasion, a child may soil simply to obtain a reaction—even a negative one— from parents. The soiling problem may also be a function of various organic problems, including spina bifida (a defect of the spinal canal) and myelitis (inflammation of the spinal cord following injury). Infrequently, an imperforate anus (malformation of the anus and rectum) may cause soiling; operations to correct this problem may result in scarring of the sphincter which is later associated with soiling (Santulli, 1972). Soiling children should undergo a thorough physical examination to determine whether or not the soiling is a function of organic problems before it is assumed that parental training methods— whether laxness, severity, or absence of such methods—are causing the soiling. If physical problems are the cause of soiling, it would not be diagnosed as encopresis.

Several case studies using behavior modification procedures to treat encopresis have appeared in the last decade (Conger, 1970; Edelman, 1971; Madsen, 1965; Neale, 1963; Peterson & London, 1964; Tomlinson, 1970; Young & Goldsmith, 1972). The study by Conger provided strong evidence that the procedures used were in fact responsible for the observed changes in soiling behavior.

Conger (1970) hypothesized that soiling behavior of a nine-year-old physically healthy encopretic boy was maintained by his mother's attention. When the child was brought to the clinic the mother washed him and changed him each time he soiled and consoled him with comments such as "Oh, that's too bad, don't worry about it." In addition, the boy successfully demanded that his mother change him immediately upon soiling. She did so partly because she thought the boy was a "nervous child" who could not control himself. The child soiled between one and four times per day prior to treatment. With the treatment, ignoring the soiling and refusing to change soiled clothing, rapid extinction of soiling occurred. It can be seen in Figure 4–6 that the child soiled once on the first day of treatment and on one other occasion in the ninety-day program.

Another example of a behavioral approach in which stool holding was successfully treated

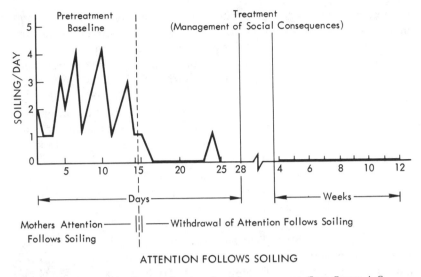

Figure 4–6 Frequency of soiling as a function of social consequences. (From Conger, J. C. (1970). The treatment of encopresis by the management of social consequences. *Behavior Therapy, 1,* 388.)

is provided by Tomlinson (1970). Toilet training was accomplished at about two years of age without administration of a laxative. The child's operant level of elimination without the aid of a laxative was once per week. When the boy was three he complained that elimination was painful, and because he would retain stools for ten days, his parents sought professional advice. A series of physiological examinations, including barium x-rays, indicated no physiological dysfunction. Changes in diet were only temporarily effective in inducing regular bowel movements. Psychological treatment consisted of making the elimination response the only response that would be followed by a particular reinforcer, bubble gum (the only item requested by the child at least once per day). Once the elimination response had been made in any given day, he could have as many pieces of gum as he wanted for the remainder of the day—with the stipulation that he could not save any from one day to the next. Because of the

chronic constipation, a mild laxative was administered daily to increase the probability of the desired behavior and to reduce the likelihood that defecation would be painful. As can be seen from Figure 4–7, the treatment was highly successful, producing elimination on an average of six times per week. The drop in elimination in the fourteenth week occurred when the child visited the grandmother, who was not told of the given contingency. Upon the child's return home, the contingency was re-established and the rate immediately increased. The gum was gradually removed from the bathroom to the kitchen and later was replaced by dessert following the evening meal if defecation had occurred during the day. A two-year follow-up revealed that the child defecated six times per week.

Controlled research on encopresis treatment is sparse, but two studies with reasonably large groups of children indicate that a combination of positive reinforcement and

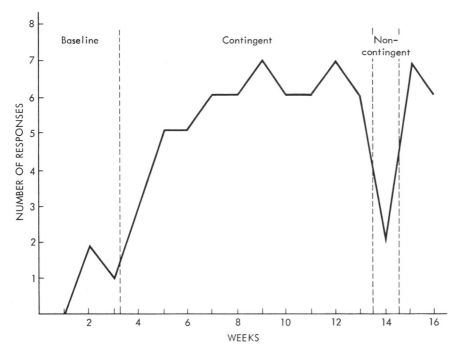

Figure 4–7 Number of voluntary defecations per week during baseline and gum contingency conditions. About the 14th week voluntary defecations decreased when the dispensing of gum did not depend on defecation. (From Tomlinson, J. R. (1970). Bowel retention. *Behavior Therapy and Experimental Psychiatry*, *1*, 84. By permission of Pergamon Press.)

glycerine suppositories is effective in overcoming the problem. Glycerine suppositories are used for two reasons: (1) the suppositories generally prompt defecation in fifteen to twenty minutes so the mother can use them to anticipate when the child should go to the toilet, and (2) the child could become more aware of the cues of rectal distension that precede elimination. Ashkenazi in Israel (1975) successfully trained sixteen of eighteen children who were at least thirty months old. The training took an average of four weeks in which parents implemented the procedure on their own after an initial clinic visit. A six-month follow-up indicated that the successes were maintained. Wright and Walker (1976) treated fourteen children successfully in fifteen to twenty weeks using positive reinforcement

methods and suppositories in a manner similar to that described by Ashkenazi.

SUMMARY

Behavior therapy procedures are successful in teaching children initial toileting habits and in treating cases in which toileting habits are delayed. In fact, toilet training procedures can result in continence in four to eight hours in two-year-old children.

Enuresis has been very successfully treated with a multifaceted learning treatment and the bell and pad treatment. While the bell and pad treatment has been most thoroughly investigated, the multifaceted learning treatment is clearly a viable and more rapid treatment alternative. A third procedure, the use of imipramine, leads to some reduction in wetting, but the low cure rates obtained and the negative side effects it may cause dictate caution in its use.

Encopresis has not received as much research attention as enuresis, but controlled case studies and some reasonably large treatment outcome evaluations indicate that encopresis can be successfully treated in approximately four weeks with a combination of positive reinforcement procedures and suppositories.

5

Developmental Disabilities

AUTISM AND MENTAL RETARDATION

During the past decade, the term *developmental disabilities* has been used to subsume disorders such as autism, mental retardation, and what was formerly called childhood schizophrenia. *Developmental disabilities* has been used as a general rubric for this chapter since the types of treatments for children with various severe problems of childhood are often not very different. As we will discuss, the etiology of autism and certain types of mental retardation are clearly different, but the behavioral treatments are very similar in teaching self-help skills, reducing self-stimulatory behavior, and teaching language. Childhood schizophrenia is no longer an accepted diagnosis in the official Diagnostic and Statistical Manual of the American Psychiatric Association (1980), and the use of this diagnosis in the research literature is now very infrequent. The elimination of the childhood schizophrenia diagnosis was due to the belief

that very few adult schizophrenics were what was described as childhood schizophrenics.

DEFINITIONS

Autism. Autism refers to a disorder which begins before thirty months of age. It is characterized by pervasive lack of responsiveness to people, gross language deficits, peculiar speech patterns such as parroting of others' speech (echolalia), and bizarre responses to the environment (twirling objects). Severe developmental disabilities like autism present a perplexing and frustrating dilemma for parents; they face a plethora of professionals who disagree on the diagnosis of the problems and who often offer little, if any, effective treatment advice. The following material details parental reactions to an autistic child and the professional advice they received.

July, 1970 The balding father pushes the shopping cart down the supermarket aisle, his four-year-old son sitting on the shelf within, sneakered feet dangling through the wire rungs. A fat and friendly woman stops and smiles at the boy. "You're beautiful," she says, bending over him. "He's beautiful."

"Thank you," says the father.

"What's your name?" she asks the boy. He turns his head away making some unintelligible sounds. "What's your name?" she asks again. The boy begins to rock back and forth in the shopping cart. "Don't be shy," the woman continues, "Can't you tell me your name?" "No," says the father, "he can't." The woman looks up with sudden concern. "Doesn't he talk?"

"Not any more," says the father.

"I'm sorry," says the woman, gently reaching out to pat the boy, who ducks his head away. "What's the matter with him? He's so beautiful."

"We don't know," replied the father.

"Oh," the woman recovers her natural joviality, "don't worry, whatever is bothering him, he'll grow out of it, I'm sure."

I wish I could be sure, [Mr. Greenfeld said]. This boy is my son Noah.

At the age of four Noah is neither toilet-trained nor does he feed himself. He seldom speaks expressively, rarely employs his less-than-a-dozen-word vocabulary. His attention span in a new toy is a matter of split seconds, television engages him only for an odd moment occasionally, he is never interested in other children for very long. His main activities are lint-catching, thread pulling, blanket-sucking, spontaneous giggling, inexplicable crying, eye-squinting, wall-hugging, circle-walking, bed-bouncing, jumping, rocking, door-closing, and incoherent babbling addressed to his finger-flexing right hand. But two years ago, Noah spoke in complete sentences, had a vocabulary of well over 150 words, sang the verses of his favorite songs, identified the objects and animals in his picture books, was all but toilet-trained, and practically ate by himself.

What's the matter with Noah? For the longest time it seemed to depend upon what diagnosis we were willing to shop around for. We'd been told he was mentally retarded, emotionally disturbed, autistic, schizophrenic, possibly brain-damaged, or that he was suffering from a Chinese-box combination of these conditions. But we finally discovered that the diagnosis didn't seem to matter; it was all so sadly academic. The medical profession was merely playing Aristotelian nomenclature and classification games at our expense. For though we live in one of the richest states in the nation, there was no single viable treatment immediately available for Noah, no matter what category he could eventually be assigned to. (Greenfeld, 1972, *A Child Called Noah*, pp. 3–5.)

Mental Retardation.   Mental retardation refers to subaverage intellectual functioning as defined by an IQ less than 70 and impairment in social functioning. Other "Pervasive Developmental Disorders" refer to the presence of at least three unusual behavior patterns in children with serious impairment in their social functioning. The unusual behaviors might include extreme anxiety, lack of affect, unusual motor movements, and speech abnormalities. If a child has delusions, is incoherent, or has very loose associations, he or she would simply be called schizophrenic, not childhood schizophrenic. Fortunately, agreement on the diagnosis of mental retardation and infantile autism is quite high (Matison, Cantwell, Russell, & Will, 1979).

PROGNOSES

The prognosis for developmental disabilities varies with the particular type of disorder. Autism has traditionally been one of the most difficult childhood disorders to treat and rarely if ever is thought to improve spontaneously. More specifically, when eighty-five children were followed into adulthood, a very large percentage was found to be educationally impaired and 42 percent were institutionalized (DeMyer, Barton, DeMyer, Norton, Allen, & Steele, 1973). Interestingly, 1 to 2 percent of the children had a recovery judged to be normal, 5 to 15 percent were deemed borderline, 16 to 25 percent fair, and 60 to 75 percent poor. The best predictors of final outcome for autism are language facility and IQ.

The prognosis for mental retardation in childhood varies with the extent of initial retardation. Mentally retarded children are classified into four broad categories according to their IQs: Mild Retardation (IQ 50–70), Moderate Retardation (IQ 35–49), Severe Retardation (IQ 20–34), and Profound Retardation (IQ below 20). Without intensive treatment, individuals with mild retardation when followed into adulthood are able to live independently in the community, have some regular unskilled occupation, and learn some of the three Rs (reading, writing, and arithmetic). Individuals with moderate retardation go to special schools and are generally semidependent in adulthood, often functioning in sheltered workshops. Individuals with severe and profound retardation usually live in institutions (Bakwin & Bakwin, 1967).

ETIOLOGY

Genetic and Biochemical Factors

Autism. Attempting to determine the influence of genetic factors in autism is problematic. First, because the incidence of autism is so low (approximately two to four children out of every 10,000), it is difficult to study enough children to make firm conclusions regarding the role of genetic factors. Second, autism appears to have multiple causes, thereby further complicating its study. Folstein and Rutter (1977), however, conducted an extensive search of schools, associations, and hospitals all over England for records of autistic twins. Using strict diagnostic criteria, eleven monozygotic (one egg) and ten dizygotic (two egg) twins were found. As Table 5–1 illustrates, four of the eleven monozy-

Table 5–1 Pair-wise Concordance by Zygosity

	MZ PAIRS (n = 11)	DZ PAIRS (n = 10)
Concordance for autism	36%	0%
Concordance for cognitive disorder (including autism)	82%	10%

gotic (MZ) twins were concordant, i.e., possessed the trait for autism. None of the dizygotic (DZ) twins, however, showed concordance for autism. This relationship increases if you include those twins in which one of the pair is autistic and the other is either autistic or has some other cognitive disorder (e.g., mental retardation or language disorder). Since monozygotic twins have identical genetic material, those findings support the importance of genetic factors in autism. Because autistic children rarely have children of their own, studying the exact genetic mechanism or mechanisms which lead to autism is extremely difficult. On the basis of twin research, genetic factors appear to play a part in the etiology of autism, but its precise role awaits future investigation.

Data indicating that autistic children are unlikely to have siblings who are autistic also are used to support the view that the causative role in autism is not psychological but biological. Family histories of autism are rare. Interestingly, Rutter and Garmezy (1983) noted that although only 2 percent of the siblings of autistic children are autistic, that rate is fifty times the average for the general population. While autism per se does not appear frequently in siblings of autistic children, siblings of autistic children are more likely to have lower IQs than expected on the basis of demographic variables. Using data both from the twin studies and the research noted above, Rutter and Garmezy (1983) argue "that (probably) it is not autism as such that is inherited but rather some broader predisposition to language and cognitive abnormalities of which autism constitutes but one part," (pg. 792).

Biochemical investigations with children who have been labeled autistic or developmentally disabled have not produced clear-cut results. Investigators in this area have assumed that the bizarre behaviors of these children may be due to underlying biochemical and/or physiological disturbances (Cohen & Shaywitz, 1982). In this light, biochemical research has included studies of specific enzymes (e.g., Cohen, Young, & Roth, 1977), serotonin levels (e.g., Ritvo et al., 1970), indoleamine (e.g., Cohen, Caparulo, Shaywitz, & Bowers, 1977), catecholamines (Young, Kavanagh, Anderson, Shaywitz, & Cohen, 1982), and chromosomal aberrations, such as the fragile-X syndrome (Pueschel, Herman, & Groden, 1985). Disturbances in all of these biochemical or genetic areas have been observed in some autistic and developmentally disabled children and these children differ from normal children in those biochemical factors. However, it is clear that some of these children do have chemical abnormalities and these biochemical factors have not been linked to specific syndromes (Piggott, 1979). Nonetheless, the prevailing theoretical conceptualization of the etiology of autism is a biological one (Cohen & Shaywitz, 1982). It is held that there are multiple biological causes of autism though there is no single common pathway by which the disorder is made manifest.

Mental Retardation. In the 1950s developments in tissue staining and other cytological techniques led to the discovery of the relationship between chromosomes and retardation. A normal person has twenty-three pairs of chromosomes. It has been found that deviations from this number may cause mental retardation. One of the most common

chromosomal deviations, the presence of a small, extra chromosome in the twenty-first or twenty-second pair, results in a condition labeled Down's Syndrome or Mongolism.

The term *Mongolism*, although in common use, is a misnomer. The only similarity between a child with Down's Syndrome and a member of the Mongolian race is the epicanthic fold of the eyelid (Kirk, 1972). The pathonomic feature of Down's Syndrome is a distinct round face with slanted eyes. The condition can generally be diagnosed at birth. Generally, though not exclusively, children with Down's Syndrome have an IQ in the range from 30 to 50. Although Down's Syndrome children are born to women of any age, the rate is significantly higher in older mothers than in young mothers—the peak age for mothers of Down's Syndrome children is about twenty years older than for other mothers. Carter and McCarthy (1951) noted that the incidence of Down's Syndrome births is 1 in 3000 for mothers under thirty years of age, but 1 in 40 for mothers from forty-five to forty-nine years of age. In fact, the increase in the incidence of Down's Syndrome as a function of the mother's age is described as a logarithmic function (see Table 5–2).

In addition, the age of the father has some impact on the likelihood of having a child with

Table 5–2   The Frequency of Mongolism According to Maternal Age*

AGE OF MOTHER (YEARS)	RISK OF MONGOLISM PER PREGNANCY
Under 30	1 in 3000
30–34	1 in 600
35–39	1 in 280
40–44	1 in 70
45–49	1 in 40
All ages	1 in 665

*(Adapted from Carter, C., & McCarthy, D. (1951). Incidence of mongolism and its diagnosis in the newborn. *British Journal of Preventative Social Medicine, 5,* 83.)

Down's Syndrome. Although the effect of paternal age on Down's Syndrome is not as great as that of maternal age, the increasing age of the father after 35 years is associated with some increased risk. (Stene, Stene, Stengel-Rutkowsky, & Muiken, 1981).

It should be emphasized that there is a type of Down's Syndrome called mosaic Down's Syndrome in which the abnormality is much less apparent both phenotypically and intellectually. In fact, some mosaic Down's Syndrome children have average IQs and function normally in their environment.

Rubella (German Measles). It was found in the early 1940s that if German measles (rubella) were contracted by the mother during the first three months of pregnancy, her child might be born with congenital defects including mental retardation. The most important congenital defects were cataracts, deafness, and heart disease. The frequency of children who are defective varies according to the month in which the rubella is contracted. If rubella is contracted during the first month of pregnancy, the likelihood of having an abnormal child is approximately 50 percent. If rubella is contracted in the second month, this frequency decreases to 25 percent, and to 12 percent if the mother contracts rubella during the third month of pregnancy (DeKaban, O'Rourke, & Cornman, 1958). Figure 5–1 presents the statistics found by DeKaban et al.

Fortunately the rubella virus has been isolated and a vaccine has been developed to prevent its occurrence. As a consequence, it is expected that in the future the number of children who become mentally retarded as a result of rubella will greatly decrease.

Phenylketonuria. Phenylketonuria (PKU) is a well-known inherited disease which causes mental retardation. It is caused by a recessive gene inherited from both parents, is characterized by the excretion of phenyl acids in the urine, and is usually associated with fair skin and light-colored eyes. The essential problem in phenylketonuria is a metabolic error in the liver; there is an absence of a liver enzyme which mediates the conversion of phenylalanine to tyrosine. The mental defect caused by this condition becomes evident during the first few months of life. Most patients ultimately learn to walk but only occasionally to talk. The principal damage of PKU, which is to the central nervous system, occurs during the first two years of life. The mental defect is usually severe, with IQs generally below 20 (Bakwin & Bakwin, 1967).

Fortunately there are simple, rapid blood or urine tests which can detect pheylketonuria that are now compulsory in most hospitals in the United States. Given at birth or shortly thereafter, they enable the physician to know whether a diet low in phenylalanine is necessary. Such a diet can prevent retardation. Several other genetic disorders, such as cretinism, Tay-Sachs disease, and Niemann-Pick disease can result in retardation, but these disorders are less frequent than Down's Syndrome.

Of the three types of developmental disorders discussed in this chapter, perhaps the most specific and detailed information on biochemical influences is available in the area of mental retardation. Other biochemical disorders which can lead to intellectual retardation include hypothyroidism and galactosemia. With more detailed information on the specific nature of these disorders, early detection and prevention of their damaging effects is now possible. For example, galactosemia, which involves the inability to digest the lactose in milk, can be detected through a simple urine test after birth and is treated by eliminating lactose in the child's diet.

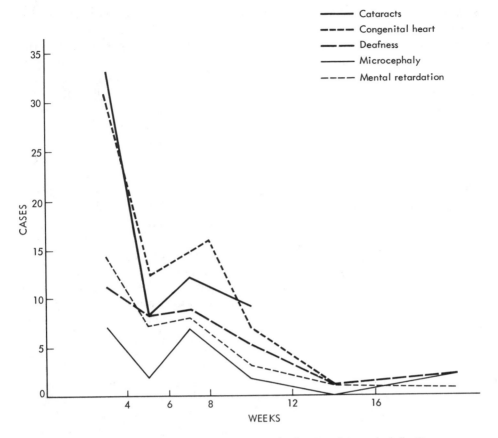

Figure 5–1   The frequency of abnormalities in 100 offspring related to time of maternal rubella. (From DeKaban, A., O'Rourke, J., & Corman, T. (1958). Abnormalities of offspring related to maternal rubella during pregnancy. *Neurology, 8,* 390. Copyright, The New York Times Media Co., Inc.)

Social Influences

It was hypothesized by Kanner and Bettelheim that cold personality styles of mothers of autistic children led them to withdraw from their parents (Rimland, 1964). Specifically, Kanner referred to a "refrigerator-parent" who interacts in a cold detached manner. Variations of the theme of disturbances in the mother-child relationship have been proposed by many psychodynamic therapists but there is no evidence to support this view (Cantwell, Baker, & Rutter, 1978). There had

been concern that early studies of personality styles of parents were methodologically flawed because the parents might react to severe handicaps of the children. However, even when studies were conducted with ratings of home movies of children in infancy, some who later became autistic and some who did not, there were no conclusive differences between the groups (Rutter & Garmezy, 1983). In brief, there is no unequivocal evidence to support the view that the personality styles of the parents, particularly the mother, play a causative role in autism. Further, an analysis of the communication and language environments of autistic children did not indicate any major differences in their environments as compared to matched controls (Wolchick & Harris, 1982).

Overselective attention has also been held to be a cause of autistic behavior. This conceptualization resulted from analyses of error patterns during discrimination training; overselecting occurs when one irrelevant cue of a compound stimulus controls responding on a large number of trials (Lovaas, Schreibman, Koegel, & Rehm, 1971). Overselectivity has been found to occur in autistic and mentally retarded children. It has been linked to the failure of autistic children to form lasting personal relationships, and many researchers have developed training programs to remediate or ameliorate this handicap (Hedbring & Newsom, 1985). While overselectivity has been found to occur in autistic children, it does not explain autism per se since overselectivity occurs in almost all very young children and in mentally retarded and learning disabled children.

While the origin of developmental disabilities (i.e., autism, childhood schizophrenia, and retardation) may be genetic or biochemical, the social environments of these children can also influence the way they behave. Some evidence suggests that many of the deviant behaviors may be maintained by reinforcement from other individuals. Behaviors such as aggression, self-injury, and psychotic speech may unwittingly be encouraged by the very people most concerned with the welfare of the children (e.g., parents and teachers).

An interesting study by Lovaas, Freitag, Gold, and Kassorla (1965) illustrates the role other people can play in the deviant behavior of developmentally disabled children. Severe self-injurious behaviors (head and arm banging, self-pinching and slapping) of a nine-year-old schizophrenic girl were the focus of the investigation. In one phase of their study, they responded to the child's self-injury with an empathetic statement typically emitted by teachers, parents, and institutional staff (e.g., "I don't think you are bad"). These dangerous, self-injurious behaviors *increased* with this form of attention. When adult attention was withdrawn (extinction), self-injury decreased. Thus, a very humanistic response actually served to reinforce self-injurious behavior.

Of the critical behavioral characteristics of autism and childhood schizophrenia, several appear to be highly influenced by reinforcement contingencies. The pervasive lack of responsiveness to other people, for example, a defining characteristic of autistic children, is amenable to change through the reinforcement of social behavior (e.g., Hingtgen, Saunders, & DeMyer, 1965). Further, as we have already seen, self-injury in childhood schizophrenics may be maintained by interactions with other individuals. These and other findings suggest that although developmentally disabled children may have genetic or biochemical disturbances, the social environment in which they live may also determine how they will behave as they grow older.

TREATMENT OVERVIEW

A classic case study by Wolf, Risley, and Mees (1964) was a precursor to later behavioral treatment research. The targets for treatment (i.e., reducing disruptive behavior, increasing self-help, developing social and verbal skills, and training parents) have been the focus of study for behavior therapists working with developmentally disabled children for the past twenty years. As such, this case study has become a prototype both for research and clinical work.

Wolf, Risley, and Mees (1964) worked with a three-and-a-half-year-old boy who did not eat well and lacked normal social and verbal skills. In addition, and possibly more important, he exhibited extreme tantrums and self-destructive behavior which often left him bruised and bleeding. Sedatives, tranquilizers, and restraints were tried without success. The child was diagnosed autistic.

Dicky was the son of middle-socio-economic-class parents, with one younger and two older normal female siblings. According to hospital records, Dicky progressed normally until he was nine months old, at which point cataracts developed in the lenses of both eyes and severe temper tantrums and sleeping problems began to develop. During the second year he had a series of eye operations which culminated with the removal of his occluded lens. At this point it became necessary for Dicky to wear glasses, but for more than a year his parents could not make him wear them. He was admitted to a children's mental hospital at three years of age because his ophthalmologist predicted that unless Dicky began wearing his glasses within the following six months he would permanently lose macular (central) vision.

Wolf et al. (1964) were invited by the hospital staff to be consultants in training Dicky to wear his glasses. Thus, glasses-wearing was a target behavior of the first part of this intervention; further, the consultants concurrently developed procedures for dealing with Dicky's tantrums, eating problems, and inappropriate social and verbal behavior. Since early research strongly suggested that temper tantrums will decrease with extinction procedures (Williams, 1959), it was thus decided that Dicky should be placed in a room with the door closed until the tantrum ceased. This procedure was first initiated in the institution in which Dicky spent most of his time. Later it was taught to his parents to be carried out in the home. Dicky's tantrums involved head-banging, hair-pulling, or face-scratching. Fortunately, after two-and-a-half months such severe self-destructive behavior was nearly eliminated.

The consultants instituted a shaping procedure to get Dicky to wear his glasses. During the first few sessions the therapists attempted to establish a conditioned reinforcer (an acquired or learned reinforcer, such as food) by having the clicks of a toy noise-maker followed by Dicky's receiving small bits of candy or fruit. The click then would become a cue for Dicky to go the bowl where the reinforcers (candies) were placed. Since Dicky had worn the prescription glasses for only a few seconds on only one occasion, it was assumed that wearing the glasses was not immediately reinforcing. In fact, it was felt that glasses-wearing might be mildly aversive since they would drastically change all visual stimuli as well as force his eyes into greater accommodation. In addition, there had been previous physical attempts to force Dicky to wear glasses. As a consequence, it was decided not to begin the procedure by having Dicky wear his actual prescription glasses; instead, several glass frames without lenses were placed around the room and Dicky was reinforced for picking them up, holding them, and carrying them about. Slowly, by successive approximations, he was reinforced for bringing the frames closer to his eyes. This shaping procedure was not particularly effective and the beginning of the treatment was marred by several failures. The clicks failed to become conditioned reinforcers through pairing with bits of fruit, and an attendant failed to follow appropriate instructions to shape Dicky's behavior.

In order to facilitate Dicky's glasses-wearing, it was decided to add several bars to the glasses to serve as a cap and, thus, prevent the glasses from sliding easily off Dicky's face.

One day Dicky seemed most interested in the ice cream the experimenters brought to the session. As a consequence, the experimenters decided to try to teach Dicky to wear the full-prescription lens, since it was obvious that the ice cream would serve as a powerful reinforcer. He was shaped very systematically, and at the end of approximately thirty minutes Dicky was holding the ear pieces properly over his ears and the nose piece at the tip of his nose. He was looking through the lens at objects like the clicker and soon was wearing his glasses continuously during the meal sessions. At the end of Dicky's release from the hospital he had worn the glasses for a total of more than 600 hours (approximately twelve hours per day).

After glasses-wearing was established, the investigators attempted to generate a verbal repertoire in Dicky. Like the glasses training, the verbal training consisted of a series of sessions in which an attendant administered food reinforcers. Fruit and candy had been tried unsuccessfully, but when the attendant used breakfast and lunch as training sessions they began to have dramatic and rapid effects. Dicky's verbal behavior was originally limited to occasional echoic responses in the form of jargon and song. In order to teach him meaningful verbal behavior, the therapist required Dicky to display on demand the desired behavior in order to receive bites of his meals. He was taught to match and label letters and then to mimic the names of a series of five pictures. Gradually the teacher stopped saying the word first. Then Dicky began to say the word in the presence of the picture alone. He progressed to naming picture books, common household objects, and finally to past events.

In addition to his verbal deficit, Dicky lacked appropriate eating skills. His eating problems involved snatching food from other children's plates and throwing food around

the room as well as eating with his fingers. Treatment observation indicated that at least 55 percent of his mealtime was involved in such inappropriate eating. Intervention consisted of "having the attendant remove Dicky's plate for a few minutes whenever he ate with his fingers, and after a warning, remove Dicky from the dining room (and the remainder of his meal) whenever he would throw food or take food from others' plates." As a result of these procedures, Dicky learned appropriate mealtime behavior.

In summary, through the use of a variety of behavioral techniques, Wolf and colleagues (1964) were able not only to stop Dicky's self-destructive tantrums and to prevent Dicky's loss of eyesight, but also to teach him speech and appropriate social and self-help behaviors. This success was achieved both in the institution in which Dicky lived and later at home with his family. Their study is significant because it was one of the first systematic and successful applications of behavioral techniques to the treatment of an autistic child. Dicky's treatment did not end after these initial successes, however.

In 1972, Nedelman and Sulzbacher made a presentation entitled "Dicky at Thirteen Years of Age: A Long Term Success Following Early Application of Operant Conditioning Procedures." Dicky's treatment history from 1959 to 1972 is outlined in a diagram (see Figure 5–2). The treatment begun by Wolf and colleagues (1964) was continued as Dicky attended the pre-school at the University of Washington Developmental Psychology Laboratory, then directed by Sidney Bijou. Nedelman and Sulzbacher reported that when he finished two years at the University Laboratory preschool Dicky entered public school in a special education class for the mentally retarded. He adjusted well to the setting and in 1967 entered a special class for the physically handicapped. At this time, Dicky was

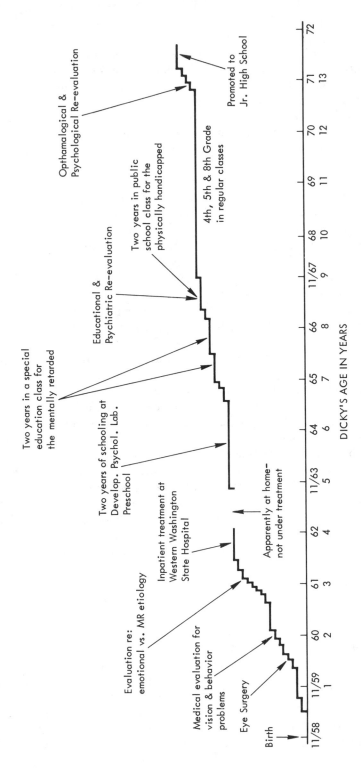

Figure 5–2 Dicky's treatment history. (From Nedelman, D., & Sulzbacher, S. I. (1972). Dicky at thirteen years of age. In G. Semb (ed.), *Behavior Analysis and Education, 4,* XX.)

Birth

Eye Surgery

Medical evaluation for vision & behavior problems

Evaluation re: emotional vs. MR etiology

Inpatient treatment at Western Washington State Hospital

Apparently at home— not under treatment

Two years of schooling at Develop. Psychol. Lab. Preschool

Two years in a special education class for the mentally retarded

Educational & Psychiatric Re-evaluation

Two years in public school class for the physically handicapped

4th, 5th & 8th Grade in regular classes

Opthamalogical & Psychological Re-evaluation

Promoted to Jr. High School

DICKY'S AGE IN YEARS

11/58 11/59 60 61 62 11/63 64 65 66 11/67 68 69 70 71 72
        1   2   3   4   5   6   7   8   9   10 11 12 13

reevaluated at the Child Development and Mental Retardation Center at the University of Washington, and significant progress was found in all areas of behavior, though extreme overprotectiveness by the mother was noted. At three years of age it was not possible to give Dicky an intelligence test; at five years of age his overall IQ was approximately 60; at 13 his IQ score was 81. Looking only at his verbal intelligence, his IQ score was 106. Dicky's ability to handle elementary school had evolved so significantly that in 1969 he began attending regular classes.

While Dicky displayed some behavior which might be labeled autistic (e.g., rocking in his seat and inappropriate hand clapping), it is clear that Dicky made marked progress. He participated in prolonged conversation and had a relatively sophisticated vocabulary for a boy of his age. The continued effort of these psychologists suggests that the lives of severely handicapped children can be significantly enriched by early intervention using a behavior modification approach, and by systematic follow-up work over a period of years to ensure maintenance of behavior and continued acquisition of significant new behaviors.

Language

During the 1960s and 1970s, language skills were taught largely by form through discrete trial training. More specifically, in discrete trial training a child was taught to label objects presented to him or her. The setting was determined by the teacher and the training was usually in massed trials. Changes in the approach to language training have taken place over the past decade because treatment gains often failed to persist or generalize beyond the immediate setting and there were dramatic differences in the responses of children to treatment (Carr, 1985). While maintenance and generalization problems are not unique to behavior therapy, these problems are salient in behavioral therapy because of the emphasis that behavior therapists have placed on developing treatments that are enduring. A contemporary solution to solving the problems of maintenance and generalization is incidental teaching (Hart & Risley, 1982). Such teaching takes place in the natural context of a child's interactions. The child initiates the episode and the content is determined by both the child and the adult. For example, a child may point to or look at a ball and the parent or teacher may say "What do you want?," or "What is that?" If the child responds correctly the adult will give the child the ball. If not, the adult will prompt the correct response. As Carr (1985) noted, incidental teaching does not invalidate the discrete trial method. Rather, it should be viewed as an extension of behavioral language intervention to the domain of teaching children to use previously acquired forms communicatively (p. 53). There are no comparative outcome studies using an incidental approach to teaching language, but studies using this approach indicate promise in producing maintenance of behavior, in using natural reinforcers to teach communication, and in using parents and teachers as the primary mediators of change.

Disruptive Behavior

It has been estimated that over 70 percent of developmentally disabled children exhibit some form of disruptive behavior, including aggression, tantrums, and self-injurious behavior (Jacobson, 1982). These behaviors create a major obstacle to efforts at teaching the children appropriate skills and are, therefore, frequent first targets in treatment.

Researchers have been concerned with the elimination of a number of negative behaviors. Self-injurious behavior is frequently exhibited by childhood schizophrenics, autistic children, and retarded children, often taking the form of severe scratching, biting, head-banging, and face-slapping. In a case reported by Tate and Baroff (1966), Sam, a self-injurious nine-year-old boy, banged his head forcefully against walls, floors, and other hard objects. Further, he often slapped his face with his hands, punched his face with his fists, hit his shoulder with his chin, and kicked himself. During five twenty-minute strolls on the hospital grounds with a ward attendant, Sam injured himself approximately seven times per minute. From initial observations, the therapist noted that physical contact (e.g., holding hands) with an attendant was reinforcing for Sam. The therapist hypothesized that this physical contact was maintaining the self-destructive behavior. Consequently, during the experimental intervention, the attendant was told to immediately withdraw from any verbal or physical contact with Sam for three seconds at the occurrence of any self-injurious behavior, a punishment procedure called "time-out from reinforcement." After five days of this intervention the attendant was told to resume his former manner of walking with Sam. Finally, as can be seen in Figure 5–3, the attendant was asked to return to his former time-out procedure, i.e., jerking his hands away from Sam and withdrawing attention from him when he injured himself. When the time-out procedure began, the self-injurious behavior decreased to one per minute. When the time-out procedure was stopped and the ward attendant reverted to his former natural way of interacting with Sam, the self-injurious behavior again increased. Finally, with the reinstatement of the time-out procedure, the self-injurious behavior decreased to one per minute. It was particularly interesting to note that Sam appeared more alert and responsive on experimental than on control days. In contrast to his usual whining and crying during the control periods, Sam smiled more and displayed more acceptable behavior during the time-out procedure.

Despite Sam's marked improvement with the time-out procedure, he continued to engage in such severe self-injurious behavior on the ward that he was restrained in his bed. Consequently, Sam was given a half-second electric shock when he injured himself. He was told that each time he hit himself he would receive a shock. During several months of this procedure, the self-injurious behavior declined steadily and was gradually eliminated even though shock was discontinued. Throughout the use of the shock procedure, the authors praised all desirable behavior. As noted earlier, with the treatment intervention—albeit a punishment—Sam became more socially responsive.

Generally punishment is used as an adjunct to time-out from reinforcement and reinforcement of appropriate behavior. When certain behaviors are ignored, however, they often show an initial increase in rate and intensity. consequently, it is sometimes especially dangerous to use ignoring (extinction) alone or even ignoring with reinforcement for appropriate behavior. It should be emphasized here that self-injurious behavior is not simply a mild behavioral problem; it is displayed in extremely severe forms of scratching, setting one's hair on fire, and biting one's flesh to the bone. Thus, electric shock is sometimes used at the outset of treatment with children who display very high rates or severe types of self-injurious behavior. A seven-year-old schizophrenic boy who had been self-injurious since the age of two displayed 3000 self-injurious behaviors during a ninety-minute period when his physical restraints were removed. With four sessions and twelve shocks, the self-pummeling behavior was almost completely eliminated (Bucher & Lovaas, 1968). Again, there was less whining

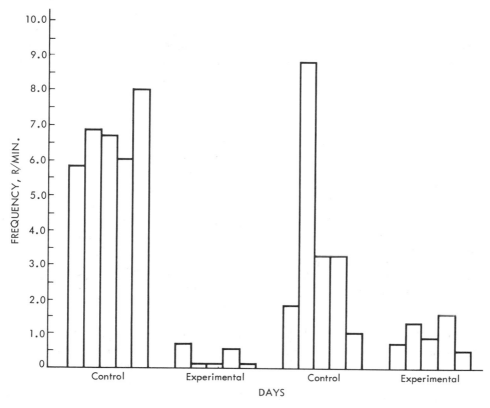

Figure 5–3 Effect of the punishment procedure of Study I on the daily average frequency of SIB's. On experimental days SIB's were followed by withdrawal of human physical contact after a minimum interval of 3 sec. On control days the SIB's were ignored. (From Tate, B. G., & Baroff, G. S. (1966). Aversive control of self-injurious behavior in a psychotic boy. *Behavior Research and Therapy, 4,* 283. By permission of Pergamon Press.)

and more attending with the onset of the treatment.

In some very interesting new research, investigators are attempting to treat severe behavior problems (e.g., aggression, self-injurious behavior, and tantrums) without punishment (Durand & Carr, 1982). The researchers have found that behaviors such as head-banging and hitting others can be conceptualized as nonverbal forms of communication (e.g., "I don't want to do that"). This work involves teaching these children to "communicate" more appropriately; that is, training them to request assistance or attention from adults

through short phrases such as "Help me." One autistic boy was found to be engaging in severe tantrums and self-injurious behavior in order to avoid his classwork. Specifically, Hal would become very upset and agitated whenever any new or difficult tasks were introduced by his teacher. His language ability was very limited and he could only speak in one- or two-word phrases. It was decided to teach Hal to say, "I don't understand" whenever he got an answer wrong in class. The teacher would respond by giving him extra assistance to help him come up with the right answer. This procedure, called Differential

Reinforcement of Communication Behavior (DRC), resulted in virtually eliminating his disruptive behavior in the classroom. The power of this technique is also illustrated by a letter received by his teacher from Hal's mother one week following the start of the program at school.

> When Hal came home from school yesterday he asked for a snack. After he finished he asked for more, and I told him, "No, not now." Instead of getting upset, he looked at me and said, "I don't understand." I immediately remembered that this was part of the program you were telling me about. Even though I couldn't give him the answer he wanted, I could see that he was trying to cope with it in this new way. I was very excited. After a while I gave him another snack. I can't believe he generalized it to such a different type of situation at home.

Work using DRC to treat the behavior problems of autistic, retarded, and schizophrenic children is continuing, including a long-term follow-up of its effects on children in their classrooms. Procedures such as this may ultimately provide alternatives to punishment for many of these children.

Socialization Skills

A major deficit in retarded children and a defining characteristic of autistic and other developmentally disabled children is their inability to appropriately interact with others. Autistic children, for example, will often actively avoid social interactions, while even less impaired children lack any of the basic skills required for successful social contact (e.g., making appropriate requests and eye contact). In order for those children to function adequately in society, it is important that they learn socialization skills.

In children with severe handicaps, social skills training often involves teaching very basic skills. A study by Cone and his associates (Cone et al. 1978), for instance, focused on teaching profoundly retarded boys to toss a ball to one another. By prompting and rewarding ball tossing, they found that they could increase the likelihood of this behavior in the training setting. Unfortunately, these children did not engage in ball tossing in a play area, a setting in which they were not specifically trained. In other words, no generalization of ball tossing occurred in a nontrained study. These investigators found that they had to prompt and reward ball tossing specifically in the play area in order to get these children to engage in social interaction in this setting.

According to operant learning principles, if a behavior is not reinforced, it will decrease in frequency. Stability of behavior is due to some continuing level of reinforcement in one's natural environment. In brief, when one teaches a behavior to a child, one has to place the child in a situation in which there is continuing reinforcement if the newly acquired skill is to remain stable. In the social cognitive view, stability of behavior depends upon more than situational rewards and punishments. "Social cognitive theory expands what constitutes rewards for action and posits varied factors, both personal and situational, that contribute to the generality and stability of human behavior . . . the satisfactions and benefits derived from mastering events figure prominently in the generality and steadfastness of human pursuits." (Bandura, 1986, p. 255)

How applicable the above notion is to the maintenance of behavior of children with severe developmental disabilities is unclear. It is known that even reasonably well developed speech skills will decline if the skills are not reinforced, as was evidenced by the dramatic decline in speech of autistic children who had to be returned to institutions because of absence of highly supervised day care or foster care (Lovaas, Koegel, Simmons, & Long, 1973). According to Bandura (1986), "Under such adverse conditions, the decline in functioning reflects disuse, rather than the loss, of acquired competencies . . . The resultant decreases in behavior are reversible, so that unused skills are quickly reinstated in responsive social environments" (p. 256). In fact, autistic children who lost their speech following institutionalization had their speech reinstated rather quickly. Lovaas et al. (1973) felt that their problem was essentially motivational. It is now moot whether the problems of these children can be reasonably conceptualized in the social cognitive sense described by Bandura. Clearly, mastery, or a sense of efficacy, has been shown to be a valuable concept in predicting behavior of both children and adults (Barling & Abel, 1983; Godding & Glasgow, 1985). Whether perceived self-efficacy will prove to be a valuable concept in developing treatment programs for developmentally disabled children is not clear.

Self-Help Skills

The teaching of very rudimentary skills, such as dressing and feeding, becomes crucial for developmentally disabled children. In shaping dressing skills it is necessary to break the task into small discrete units. Watson (1973) described in detail how a child can be taught to take off a short-sleeved pullover shirt. The child is taught through a procedure called chaining. More specifically, the child is first taught to complete the last sequence of the chain of behaviors, i.e., to take his shirt off his left wrist. In subsequent sessions the child is taught to add, one at a time, each step preceding the steps he already knows. The parent or aide requires the child to add an immediately preceding step in the sequence before the child is reinforced. This procedure continues until the child is able to complete the entire sequence of behavior. The child always has to complete the undressing act before he is reinforced and reinforcement always occurs as he removes his shirt from his left hand. Another example of shaping dressing skills using the same techniques was de-

Figure 5–4 Child in Lovaas' speech therapy program. (Photograph by Allan Grant)

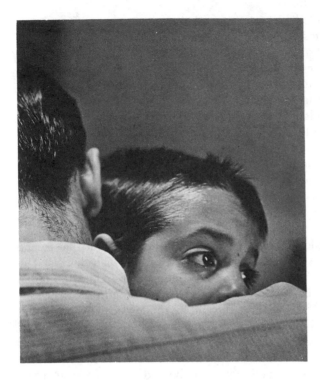

Figure 5–5 Child being comforted by therapist in the Lovaas program. (Photograph by Allan Grant).

scribed by Watson. The child is completely dressed except for his shoes. The child is then asked to put on his shoes and is reinforced for doing so. Later the child is required to put on his socks and shoes before he is reinforced. Next, he already has his pants and underpants on and he is required to put on his shirt followed by his socks and shoes before he is reinforced.

Roos and Oliver (1965) compared operant conditioning with two alternative procedures, viz., special education class teaching and traditional hospital care in the teaching of self-help skills in severely retarded children. The group receiving operant training procedures showed greater gains than the other two groups. The authors noted that the greatest gains with the operant training procedures were produced during the first six months of the program. As Ullmann and Krasner (1969)

noted, when such gains are found in programs using operant conditioning procedures, be they on a hospital ward or in a classroom, the task of the program administrator is to constantly change the behaviors to be reinforced as well as the type of reinforcers for the children.

One of the most interesting programs to teach self-help skills was described by Girardeau and Spradlin (1964) and Spradlin and Girardeau (1966). Mentally retarded girls with IQs ranging from 20 to 50 were trained in skills necessary to live successfully in their home environment. Tokens were used to reward behaviors such as making beds, setting their hair, taking a shower, and being on time. Undesired behavior was disapproved by having the child be deemed unable to earn tokens for a fixed period of time. The girls made important changes and the staff morale significantly improved as a result.

Toilet Training

Parents often find toilet training a frustrating, messy, and difficult task. Generally parents wait until they think a child is "ready," then place the child on a potty. If the child learns to eliminate on the toilet then other aspects of training are undertaken, e.g., walking to the toilet and removing clothing. Mahoney, Van Wagenen, & Meyerson (1971) selected five male retardates with IQs ranging from 10 to 45 for toilet training. Each child wore a pair of pants equipped with a transistor which signaled the child to go to the toilet on the occurrence of urine flow. The retarded children reached criterion in an average of twenty-nine training hours, i.e., they walked to the toilet, lowered their pants, urinated in the toilet, and pulled up their pants without any prompts or auditory signals.

In 1971, Azrin and Foxx noted that despite some degree of success in teaching retarded children "habit training" or successful elimination in the toilet when the child was placed there regularly and frequently (Dayan, 1964; Baumeister & Klosowski, 1965), quantitative data regarding the enduring success of these procedures have not been proffered. Azrin and Foxx thus designed a program to toilet train nine profoundly retarded males. Although these retardates were adults, the basic components of this program have been outlined for retarded children by Foxx and Azrin (1973a) and for normal children by Foxx and Azrin (1973b). Like the Mahoney et al. (1971) procedure, the investigators used wet alarm pants which sounded a signal when the resident urinated or defecated (Azrin & Foxx, 1971, p. 91).

The distinctive features of the procedures, according to the authors, were artificially increasing the frequency of urinations, positive reinforcement of correct toileting but a delay for "accidents," shaping of independent toi-

leting, cleanliness training, staff reinforcement procedures, and the use of pants which set off an alarm when wet.

In order to detect appropriate elimination in the toilet, a second detection apparatus was used. The immediate detection of elimination allows a trainer to teach several residents at once and eliminates the need to look between the resident's legs to see if he is voiding. Reinforcers for correct toileting were a piece of candy bar, a big hug, and praise. Reinforcers for remaining dry were sugar-frosted cereal, small candies, and praise for dry pants every five minutes for as long as they remained dry.

Following the general notion advanced throughout this text that maintenance of behavior must be programmed, posttraining maintenance procedures were devised. As Azrin and Foxx noted, the benefits of toilet training would not be expected to endure unless the ward staff was sufficiently motivated to encourage proper toileting and to discourage accidents. Thus posttraining ward maintenance procedures were devised which specified six regular inspection periods for the resident each day. If dry, the attendant praised him; if wet, the resident was reprimanded, required to clean himself and wash his pants, and had his snack omitted or was slightly delayed in his entrance to the forthcoming meal. Eight weeks after training, a minimal maintenance procedure was introduced which involved a variation of the above program but only mealtime and bedtime inspections were held. When four weeks had elapsed without a single accident, the program was discontinued. Each resident was no longer inspected regularly but was required to clean himself, his pants, and the floor if necessary. In addition, a meal was delayed by one hour if an accident occurred prior to a meal or a snack was omitted if an accident occurred after a meal.

The average number of accidents was reduced from two per day to almost zero after an average of four days of training. One hundred and forty days following training, incontinence was virtually eliminated in a group of retarded residents with a median IQ of 14 (range 7 to 45).

While toilet training may seem an insignificant problem for people far removed from institutional life, there can be little doubt that a change in toileting behavior has a significant effect on the pleasantness of an institutional environment. The frequent stench of institutional wards is so strong that visitors to wards for profoundly retarded children often recoil and withdraw. Teaching children to be continent not only eliminates foul odors but the retarded child's self-esteem is markedly increased when he learns to control his eliminative functions.

Mealtime Behavior

Undesirable mealtime behavior is a frequent problem in any hospital unit. Using a natural punishment contingency (interruption of the behavior as soon as it began to occur), Henricksen and Doughty (1967) focused on the reduction of five types of undesirable behaviors: (1) eating too fast, (2) eating with the hands, (3) stealing food from other patients' trays, (4) hitting other patients at mealtime, and (5) throwing food trays or deliberately spilling food. Four profoundly retarded boys who frequently displayed these behaviors were placed at a single table with two aides stationed at opposite corners of the table. The aides were to comment positively if the patients ate well; they were to verbally disapprove of the aforementioned undesired behaviors and interrupt them as soon as they began. Research on timing of punishment has repeatedly shown that punishing early in a sequence of behaviors is more effective in reducing the behavior than punishing late in that sequence (Walters & Demkov, 1963; Walters, Parke, & Cane, 1965). The training period lasted for thirteen weeks, during which training occurred at all three meals each day. However, the aides were gradually phased out by increasing their distance from the table and the children were returned to the normal dining room situation. The results were particularly impressive. The frequencies of undesirable eating behaviors per week for each of the four subjects respectively were 350, 265, 150, and 125 before treatment, and 50, 25, 10, and 20 after treatment.

Undesirable mealtime behaviors of sixteen retardates in a hospital cottage were reduced by time-out procedures applied successively to one undesirable behavior after another in a multiple baseline design (Barton, Guess, Garcia, & Baer, 1970). The time-out procedures included removal of a child from the room until the meal was finished and a fifteen-second removal of the child's meal tray. The undesirable behaviors were similar to those mentioned by Henricksen and Doughty (1967), viz., messy use of utensils, stealing food from others, and "pigging" (eating directly with mouth). In all instances there was a marked reduction in the undesired behaviors. As the inappropriate behavior declined, neat mealtime behaviors increased. There was no change in the weights of the children throughout the study.

Unsightly, messy table manners will almost guarantee that a retardate will be viewed as an undesirable person. Fortunately, there have been a number of successful attempts to teach appropriate eating styles to children. Mild punishment in the form of time-out, physical restraint, removing the child's food for short periods of time, and reinforcing nonstealing all have been shown to help in the teaching of eating skills.

INSTITUTIONALIZATION

Willowbrook, on Staten Island, is a New York State institution for the mentally retarded. In 1972 it had 5268 residents and severely overcrowded conditions. Of 2750 employees only 1850 were involved with patient care; the rest were support staff and custodial workers, office personnel, etc. According to Rivera (1972), the patient to attendant ratio was thirty to one. The story of Willowbrook became an award-winning television documentary that engendered a great deal of emotional response from the public. Dr. Michael Wilkins, a physician, and Ms. Elizabeth Lee, a social worker, were fired from Willowbrook purportedly because they had been organizing the parents of patients to improve the children's conditions. At the request of Dr. Wilkins, Geraldo Rivera, a New York television reporter, was asked to take an ABC film crew to document the conditions. An unannounced visit to the institution found naked children leading lives of filth and abandon.

An excerpt from Rivera's book *Willowbrook* describes the conditions he discovered.

> There were perhaps sixty or seventy severely and profoundly retarded children living (another word which flatters the state of being in Building 6) in a room that looked like the unfinished basement of a cheap home in the suburbs. Wooden benches and hard chairs were scattered randomly around the room. Plaster was peeling off the dirty, greenish cement walls. There was one sign hanging up. It said, "Merry Christmas." That was the only concession to humanity. Aside from that there wasn't a single toy or distraction in the place. The other walls were barren except for the misery that they contained. (p. 17)

The Willowbrook story was no isolated incident. Shortly after its publication, twenty-four attendants were arrested at the Rome State School, another New York State school for the retarded, for abusing forty mentally retarded patients ranging in age from 7 to 75.

The treatment of retarded children, both inside and outside of institutions, however, is not uniformly bad. Fortunately, during the last decade there has been an increase in concern about the plight of retarded and developmentally disabled children. As a result of parental and legislative efforts, there have been obvious improvements in certain aspects of health care and education for these children. This public interest has been prompted in part by prominent people such as the Kennedys and the Humphreys, who have retarded children in their families. In October, 1961, President John F. Kennedy appointed a panel of experts to assess the treatment and research relating to mental retardation and to recommend national policy changes. In 1962, the twenty-seven-member panel published a report, "A Proposed Program for National Action to Combat Mental Retardation." One month before President Kennedy's death, he signed legislation to implement the panel's report.

Also of great import is the rapid rise in enrollment in parents' organizations for retarded and autistic children. Many of these organizations have pressed to have their children deinstitutionalized, and only 2 percent of children with IQs between 50 and 70 are institutionalized; 25 percent of all retarded children with IQs between 25 and 50 are institutionalized; and only 35 to 40 percent of children with IQs less than 25 are institutionalized (Conley, 1973). The remainder live at home with their parents. Parent training and involvement thus becomes an important aspect of care for retarded children. The Association for Retarded Children was formed in 1953; by 1983 it had over 300,000 members and approximately 2500 chapters. The National Society for Autistic Children was formed in 1965. It has 7000 members and 200 chapters in the United States. Concerned groups like the American Association on Mental Deficiency have done much to dispel incorrect impressions and change public attitudes regarding mental retardation, as well as to promote legislation and community programs for retarded children. Probably one of the positive changes in attitudes toward mental retardation has been the Special Olympic program for retarded children. (Figure 5–6).

While there are certain types of retardation that result from some organic dysfunction, there are a number of psychologists who contend that societal factors produce the intellectual-developmental deficit (Robinson & Robinson, 1965; Braginsky & Braginsky, 1971). The latter investigators found that a large number of institutionalized "retardates" said that they were placed in the facility because of rejection, family disorder, and disintegration. Braginsky and Braginsky (1971) presented a model which suggests that, given certain social events, any child can be transformed into a mental retardate. The most important social reason for such a transformation was held to be family rejection. If the costs to a family both psychologically and economically are great, there is a high probability of being rejected and discarded. Unfortunately, the ease of being placed in an institution for retarded persons is in many places phenomenal. It is even more astounding when one considers the institutional role children learn to play.

In many instances, instead of teaching children social skills that will enable them to function in their own communities, institutions for psychotic and retarded children become, as Patterson (1963) noted, vast teaching machines that help maintain patients as patients. That is, staff members may have such low expectations that they may convey to the child that it is not worthwhile even to attempt to make progress. Since progress for the children is often reflected in an increase in activity, question asking, and interaction between the patients, the ward attendants essentially teach the children to become passive and dependent in order to make them less of a burden on the ward. As Ullmann and Krasner (1965) emphasized, once in the hospital, there are very strong pressures on an individual to assume a "good patient role." That is, the pressures are on the patient to become properly passive and dependent. The nursing attendants have the responsibility of keeping large numbers of people clean, safe, and quiet. They exert a rather explicit set of contingencies in order to obtain this quiet, dependent behavior. Among the explicit reinforcers available to the attendants are privileges (such as the freedom to move), passes, better accommodations, and the threat of punishments (such as electro-convulsive therapy and transfers to a ward peopled by more disturbed patients). Ullmann and Krasner further noted that the apathy and withdrawal which are the most prognostically unfavorable symptoms of a patient may well arise from the training not to be assertive or to insist upon his or her legitimate rights. It has been well documented that aides in certain institutions not only fail to train children in self-help skills and independent behavior, but actually promote dependent behavior (Klaber, 1969). More disquieting still was the explicit reinforcement contingency for keeping a person in such an institution. In the British medical journal *Lancet* (1966), it was noted that secretaries, engineers, and senior nursing officers in English mental deficiency institutions were paid according to the number of beds in the hospital. Thus "the harder the matron or chief

Figure 5—6 Three pictures of Special Olympics for Retarded Children, Stony Brook, N.Y. (Photographs courtesy of Louis Manna)

male works to rehabilitate patients, the more they undermine their own salaries" (pp. 532–533).

Thus children in institutions learn to behave in ways that often assure that they will be deemed retarded, i.e., they act dependent, servile, and "dull." They stay out of the attendants' way and lose whatever skills they had when they entered the institution. With the astounding rise in child abuse in the last five years it is even more likely that, at least temporarily, some children will be removed from their homes. Let us reiterate our view that institutionalization should be a last resort in treating developmentally disabled children.

This cautious approach is reflected in the changes in some states regarding institutionalization procedures and conditions. For example, in California a parent can only put a child into an institution with the consent of the Department of Education, and then only after it has been determined that the child is absolutely untrainable. According to Dr. Richard Koch, director of the Los Angeles Regional Center for Mentally Retarded, only 1.5 to 3 percent of the most profoundly retarded children fall into this category (Rivera, 1972). The philosophy of the treatment of mentally retarded children in California is to avoid the problems found in large caretaker institutions by shifting the care and training of retarded children to their own communities. Instead of being directed at custodial care, time and effort are spent providing the parents of retarded children and their communities with the knowledge and resources to care for the children in a humane setting. Perhaps most important, emphasis is focused on prevention of developmental disabilities. For example, because prenatal problems are among the greatest causes of profound retardation, much effort is directed toward teaching parents proper prenatal care.

The California system, with its emphasis on family and community care, has produced benefits which exemplify humane, well-planned treatment. A description of the Developmental Center for Handicapped Minors, a state-run facility for severely and profoundly retarded children in Van Nuys, California, serves to illustrate the striking contrast between humane treatment and the stark institutionalization of Willowbrook.

> It was a refreshing change from Letchworth (state institution in New York) and Willowbrook. The kids were sparkling and smiling. The walls were brightly colored; toys were everywhere. In Willowbrook, one of the greatest dangers to children is their hurting themselves. In the developmental center, they are protected against falls and self-inflicted injuries. The rooms are filled with water beds and cushions, and many of the children wear padded helmets. One room had so many helmeted boys that it looked like a Little League football squad. But as far as I was concerned, there was something even nicer. The place smelled good. It was lunchtime. Some of the children were being fed; others were feeding themselves. One little boy had one bean left on the plate and was trying to get it on his spoon. He pushed the bean across the plate, but it fell onto the table. Knowing that he wasn't supposed to eat it with his hands, he picked the bean up, placed it on the spoon, and then ate it. He looked up at me for the first time and smiled a triumphant smile. (Rivera, 1972, p. 101)

Changes can be made in existing institutional practices which would enable a child to learn a great deal and make institutions pleasant for children. And just as important, beyond improving institutions, the retarded child has been integrated into the community through sheltered workshops and vocational rehabilitation programs. In these programs, a state department of vocational rehabilitation pays an employer to have a retarded person work for a period of time. This inducement ensures that the employer will hire more retarded people to work in an industry or a factory.

Another alternative to institutionalization which places some clear responsibility on the family is a "Five-Two Plan" described by Drabman, Spitalnik, Hageman, and Van Witsen (1973) for a low functioning child. Although the program was implemented with autistic and childhood schizophrenic children, its relevance to populations of retarded children is clear. The "Five-Two Plan" consists of a joint effort of the residential institution, a special school, and the family. Within the program, a child lives at home for a minimum of five days per week, and, generally on weekends, resides in the hospital. As the authors note, hospitals must change from being places where one is "put away" to facilities that serve as a functional part of an integrated treatment approach. Both from the standpoint of economics and efficiency, the hospital must be extended into the community. The hospital staff can serve, as they did here, as consultants to the school and family for an integrated behavioral treatment. Realistically, the hospital can also serve as a temporary (weekend) respite for the parents from their daily problems of rearing a low-functioning child. In such cases, where the child cannot reside at home full time, the "Five-Two Plan" would appear to be a viable alternative both to full time institutionalization and to foster home placement.

MAINSTREAMING

A current trend in work with the developmentally disabled is an effort to integrate these children into regular classroom environments. Placing them in separate special education programs may prevent their obtaining the benefits of observing normal peers and regular education curricula. Russo and Koe-

gel (1977) describe one systematic attempt to integrate a five-year-old autistic girl into a normal kindergarten classroom. A therapist initially sat next to her in this classroom and employed a token economy to increase social behaviors and verbal responses and decrease self-stimulatory behavior. Following the success of the token economy, the therapist's involvement was reduced over several weeks, with control of the program transferred to the teacher. The child's improvement in classroom performance was evidenced across the three targeted behaviors. This child later went on to regular first, second, and third grades, with minimal additional training. Behavioral techniques have been employed to allow some developmentally disabled children to benefit from regular education settings.

EARLY INTERVENTION

Currently, efforts are being directed towards treating very young developmentally disabled children. This recent trend reflects a concern that some of the characteristic deficits displayed by these children may be more easily remediated if treated at a young age. A pioneering project in the field of early intervention began in 1970 at the University of California at Los Angeles under the direction of Dr. Ivar Lovaas. The goal of this project has been to assess the effects of intensive behavioral treatment on children under 4 years who are diagnosed as autistic. The Young Autism Project places autistic children in one of two treatment groups. An intensive treatment group received more than forty hours of individual one-to-one behavioral treatment per week for two to four years. Treatment was conducted by graduate students in psychology from UCLA, with the child's parents participating as co-therapists. Treatment included reinforcement and shaping of compliance, self-help, and social and language skills, as well as the use of contingent aversive procedures (e.g., reprimands and slaps) to reduce disruptive behavior. A second group of children received less intensive treatment, that is, ten hours or less of individual behavioral therapy per week. While both groups received behavioral training, the amount of therapist contact was significantly less in the less intensive treatment group. Pretreatment measures revealed no significant differences between the groups.

Reports on the results of the Young Autism Project (Lovaas, in press) showed that 47 percent of the children in the intensive behavioral treatment (N = 19) "made substantial recovery with IQ scores within the normal range of intellectual functioning and successful first grade performance in public schools. By contrast, only 2 percent of the control children (N = 40) had evidenced such recovery. Both in the intensive treatment group and in the control group approximately 43 percent of the children were mildly retarded and assigned to special classes for the language delayed. Finally, in the intensive treatment group, 10 percent of the children were profoundly retarded and in classes for autistic/retarded whereas 53 percent of the children in the control group were so classified and assigned at post intervention."

SUMMARY

The term developmental disabilities has been used to subsume disorders such as autism, mental retardation, and what was formerly called childhood schizophrenia. While the etiology of autism and mental retardation may differ, treatments for children with such problems are often very similar. Autism is a disorder which begins before 30 months and is characterized by a pervasive lack of responsiveness to people, gross language deficits, peculiar speech patterns (e.g., echolalia), and unusual responses to the environment (e.g., twirling objects). Mental retardation refers to subaverage intellectual functioning as defined by an IQ less than 70. Prognoses for autistic individuals have been rather bleak; roughly 40 to 50 percent of such individuals are institutionalized as adults. The best predictor of long term outcome for such persons is language facility and IQ. The prognoses for retarded individuals also depend upon their IQ. Individuals with moderate to mild mental retardation are able to live independently in the community, whereas those with severe and profound retardation usually live in institutions.

The causes of autism appear to be biological but the precise nature of the specific biochemical problem is unclear. It is clear from twin studies that monozygotes have much higher concordance rather than dizygotes. Further, it is rare to have a sibling of an autistic child also be autistic. Mental retardation, particularly of a severe nature, is caused frequently by diseases such as rubella, PKU, and Tay-Sachs. While the causes of developmental disabilities may be largely biochemical, there is also evidence that social reinforcement may serve to maintain some highly unusual behaviors of these children, like self-injury.

Behavioral treatment for children with developmental disabilities has been shown to be effective in improving language, socialization skills, self-help skills, and toileting. Institutionalization should be a last resort treatment for it is often associated with a *deterioration* in social functioning. Mainstreaming of children with developmental disabilities and early intervention appear to be two key methods for ameliorating the conditions of these children.

As Lovaas (in press) noted in summarizing his views on this intervention, "These data imply a major relief in the emotional hardships of families of autistic children." The intensive treatment involving forty hours of one-to-one intervention per week for as much as four years may seem costly—the cost of a full-time teacher/therapist for two years could cost as much as $60,000. However, as Lovaas argued, the cost of long-term institutionalization for an autistic child could be as much as two million dollars.

6

Conduct Problems: Aggression and Hyperactivity

DEFINITION

Conduct problems refer to a wide variety of behaviors that disturb others and often impede academic learning. Sometimes conduct problems are called antisocial behaviors because they include fighting, temper trantrums, verbal aggression, defiance, destruction of others' property, and restlessness. However, aggression is the most salient characteristic of conduct problems; in all studies of children with conduct problems, verbal and physical aggression are the central problems associated with conduct problems. Further, in long-term follow-up studies of individuals diagnosed as having had conduct problems as children, the greater the level of aggression the greater was the likelihood of significant adolescent and adult problems. Young children with extreme forms of aggression do not simply "outgrow" their problems, and studies of delinquents repeatedly indicate that they had serious antisocial behavior as young children.

Aggression is one of the most stable of all human characteristics. Kagan and Moss (1962)

found a correlation of 0.61 between general aggressive behavior at age six and aggressive behavior toward the mother at age 14. Eron, Walder, Huesmann, & Lefkowitz (1974) found a correlation of .32 between aggression scores at grade 3 and grade 13. However, when Patterson (1982) reanalyzed Eron's data for extreme scorers (at the 95th percentile) at grade 3, he found that *all* of the sample was at or above the mean on aggression at grade 13. As Patterson argued, "These studies assert that extremely coercive children do not outgrow their problems. . . . Given extreme deviance plus social skills deficits, then the extremely antisocial child would be likely to grow up as an adult who, at *best*, makes a marginal adjustment." In a fourteen-year follow-up study by West and Farrington (1973), a boy rated as extremely aggressive at 9 had a .14 chance of being a violent adolescent delinquent. Furthermore, 70 percent of the violent adolescent delinquents were rated as aggressive at age 13; 48 percent of these children received such a rating at age 9 (Patterson, 1982). In short, the message regarding aggression and conduct problems is clear. The problems should be diagnosed and treated at a young age.

Hyperactivity, or hyperkinesis, is a childhood problem that has received widespread discussion in the professional and public literature since the mid-1970s. Hyperactivity refers to a combination of behavioral and cognitive factors, but most notably it refers to motor restlessness and overactivity, inattention, and poor frustration tolerance. As hyperactive children get older they also begin to have serious learning problems which are, in part, a function of their difficulty in sustaining attention. Hyperactivity received widespread attention in the United States when it was learned that a large number of children in some schools were receiving medication for this problem. The alarm came because the medication generally given was a psychostimulant with some properties similar to those drugs taken by adolescents and young adults to "get high," although it is not the case that children "get high" from receiving psychostimulants. It was estimated that approximately 2 percent of all elementary children in the United States were receiving psychostimulant medication in 1979 (Krager, Safer, & Earhardt, 1979). In some cases, school systems allegedly required that children receive such medication to attend a regular class. Such a requirement was challenged in court by parents in Taft, California, and struck down (Whalen & Henker, 1980).

Among others, educators and journalists were concerned that psychostimulant medication would become widespread in schools and that children receiving it would be prone to using various forms of medication as adults. Neither of these concerns has been borne out. In the early 1980s there was a slight leveling off of the percentage of children receiving psychostimulant medication (O'Leary, 1984), and several follow-up studies of young adults

who had received it as children did not find that they used any medications at a higher rate than a group of individuals matched for age, sex, and socioeconomic class who had not received the medication as children (Gadow & Loney, 1981).

The hyperactivity issue, however, had a ripple effect among behavior therapists. It prompted them to attempt to develop treatments which might enable hyperactive children to function without medication and to seek some of the central causative factors of hyperactivity so that those causes might be addressed in various treatments. We will turn to those treatments later in this chapter.

DIFFERENTIATION OF AGGRESSION AND HYPERACTIVITY

The need to differentiate between aggression and hyperactivity became apparent when pharmacological treatment for hyperactive children became widely used in the United States. Parents, teachers, and mental health professionals all asked experts in the field of assessment and diagnosis how one could distinguish between these two problems. From the definitions given earlier you may not suspect a problem, but in daily clinical practice the two problems, hyperactivity and aggression, often occur together. That is, children with motor restlessness, overactivity, and attention problems often are also verbally and physically aggressive. However, it is clear from both research and clinical practice that the two problems are sometimes separate. Such differentiation is important because there are different factors which lead to aggression and hyperactivity and the treatments for these problems are different. More specifically, medication is used much more readily with a hyperactive child than with an aggressive child and psychological therapy is used more frequently with aggressive children and their families.

It is not clear exactly why hyperactive children are more responsive to medication than aggressive children, but it appears that medication for hyperactivity improves attention and fine motor skills. Children with aggression problems and little or no hyperactivity need aid in learning to tolerate frustration and to control their tempers. Therefore, children with primarily aggression problems are generally not given the type of medication given to hyperactive children (i.e., psychostimulant medication).

The percentage of children with conduct problems varies somewhat across countries, but teachers in the United States repeatedly indicate that 10 percent of children in an elementary class have marked problems with aggression, impulsivity, and overactivity—conduct problems. Such problems interfere with classroom learning so that about half of the children with conduct problems have significant academic learning deficits. According to the U.S. Department of Health, Education, and Welfare, in 1971, approximately 5 percent of children in the United States were hyperactive. In Britain a much smaller percentage of children are diagnosed hyperactive, although when rating a child's behavior the clinicians observing the child would likely rate the child similarly. The differences from one country to another result from different decision rules for assigning a diagnosis to a case. Further, in 1971 there was no empirical method for differentially diagnosing hyperactive and aggressive children. At present, it appears that if one breaks down the overall conduct problem category into aggression and hyperactivity, about 30 percent of children would be hyperactive, 20 percent would be primarily aggressive, and 50 percent would have both hyperactive and aggressive char-

acteristics (Steen, 1982). In recognition of the need to deal with complex but realistic clinic cases, the World Health Organization and the American Psychiatric Association encourage clinicians to provide both primary and secondary diagnoses. In the interest of simplifying the presentation of etiology and treatment, the general term *conduct problem* will be used frequently, but you should keep in mind that when possible, differential diagnoses or primary and secondary diagnoses may be necessary in clinical practice.

Differentiating between hyperactivity and aggression has not been easy. On the basis of many research studies, it has been found that children's scores on measures of aggression and hyperactivity correlate quite highly (0.60–0.70). These correlations have led some researchers to conclude that the conditions overlap so markedly that a general category of conduct disorder should be the overall category. However, some empirical research involving the weighting of certain items that typify hyperactivity and aggression allow for reliable classification of these two problems (Loney, Langhorne, & Paternite, 1978; S. O'Leary & Steen, 1982; Barling, S. O'Leary, & Cowen, 1985). The types of behaviors that receive greatest weighting for hyperactivity are fidgetiness, judgment deficits, and inattention. The types of behaviors that receive greatest weighting for aggression are control deficits, negative affects, and aggressive interpersonal styles.

LONG-TERM PROGNOSIS

In a classic study by Robbins (1979), it was found that children with conduct problems who had attended a general mental health clinic were most likely to have problems as adults. Robbins studied approximately 500 children referred to a child guidance clinic between 1924 and 1929. Most of these children were referred for antisocial behavior and about half had some contact with the juvenile court. Robbins's cases were therefore more severe than the average conduct-problem case in a mental health clinic, but with these cases she stated the following: "Serious antisocial behavior . . . presages lifelong problems with the law, inability to earn a living, defective interpersonal relationships and severe personal stress" (p. 509). On the other hand, if children with serious antisocial behavior like contact with courts are eliminated from the larger group of conduct-problem children, the prognosis for a child is quite good (Shepard, Oppenheim, & Mitchell, 1966). As indicated, a primary predictor of later social difficulty is level of aggression as a child.

Excellent long-term evaluations of hyperactive children who were diagnosed but not treated were conducted in Canada by Weiss and her colleagues (Weiss, Hechtman, Perlman, Hopkins, & Wener, 1979). This team compared adolescents who had been formerly diagnosed as hyperactive with adolescents who were matched on age, sex, IQ, and social class. The matched adolescents had never failed a grade and neither parent felt the matched adolescent had been a behavior problem. The adolescents who were diagnosed hyperactive as children had lower self-esteem, poorer socialization skills, and greater impulsivity than the comparison children. Interestingly, the formerly diagnosed hyperactive children also had more car and motorcycle accidents, and, as you might expect, poorer marks in school.

One-hundred-and-one individuals diagnosed as hyperactive in childhood were followed when they were young adults (aged 16 to 23 years) and compared to normal controls by Gittelman, Mannuzza, Shenker, & Bonagura (1985). The controls in this research were composed of individuals who attended the Adolescent Medicine Department of the hospital where the hyperactive children had been treated. The controls were included if they sought medical attention for routine problems, such as flu and sore throats, and if their histories did not indicate school problems. All subjects were assessed by examiners who were unaware of the previous condition of the subject. The parents of experimental and control subjects were similar on demographic characteristics, such as age, education, and socioeconomic status. The problem of attention deficits, a key factor of hyperactive children, was found in 31 percent of the individuals at follow-up and in 3 percent of the controls.

There were also greater percentages of experimental subjects with conduct problems and substance abuse disorders. Of special interest was the finding that 20 percent of the control subjects received some official psychiatric diagnosis as compared to 48 percent of the previously diagnosed hyperactive children. Clearly, children diagnosed in youth as hyperactive have almost twice the chance of having some psychiatric problems. It may be surprising that 20 percent of individuals in late adolescence and young adulthood would have received a psychiatric diagnosis. However, in the United States the rate of psychiatric diagnoses in late adolescent males, generally found in epidemiological or survey studies, is between 15 and 20 percent, and research in England also leads us to see adolescence as a turbulent time for many (Gittelman et al., 1985).

In summary, children with conduct and/or hyperactivity problems do have more problems in adolescence and adult life than the average child. Whether the child is hyperactive or not, aggression is a foremost predictor of problems in adolescence (Langhorne & Loney, 1979). Further, if a child has had contact with the juvenile courts, the likelihood of having adult problems is considerable.

ETIOLOGY

Physiological and Biochemical Factors

Genetic Predisposition. Active, impulsive, aggressive parents often have children who display the same traits, and parents will report that they feel their child obtained their "bad" characteristics from them. In fact, studies involving twins and adopted children indicate that genetic predispositions do influence activity levels. Reports of mothers of same-sex twins indicate that activity level is much more alike for monozygotic (same egg) twins than for dizygotic (different egg) twins. The correlation of activity level for monozygotic twins was 0.92 whereas for dizygotic twins it was 0.60 (Willerman, 1973).

Self-reports of natural parents of hyperactive children who were adopted were compared with self-reports of the foster parents of hyperactive children. Self-reports of natural and foster parents indicated that natural parents of hyperactive children reported higher activity levels as children than did foster parents (Morrison & Stewart, 1973). Such data provide suggestive evidence for genetic factors in the development of hyperactivity.

There are methodological problems with adoption and twin studies of humans because adoptions usually do not take place at birth and parental reports of monozygotic and dizygotic twins may be biased by parents' experiences and expectations. Nonetheless, these studies provide interesting leads, and animal studies confirm the position that predispositions to high or low activity levels are inherited. Studies with rats and dogs show that such animals can be selectively mated to produce certain temperaments or activity levels (Fuller & Thompson, 1978). Similarly, animals can be selectively bred for aggression. On the other hand, there is no clear evidence

that aggression per se is inherited. Whether aggression is displayed or not depends upon a host of environmental conditions, such as victory or defeat, and the reinforcement value assigned to winning. There is a clear relationship between testosterone levels (male hormone) and aggression in young men between 17 and 28, but there is no relationship between testosterone and aggression in adolescents (Moyer, 1976) from general populations. Therefore, it seems most reasonable to conclude that children inherit a predisposition to be active or inactive. Although animal research indicates that animals can be selectively bred for aggression, the environmental influences on aggressive behavior are so great that it is not clear that aggression in children is influenced to any practically significant degree by genetic factors.

Brain Dysfunction. Since the turn of the century, hyperactivity was thought to be a result of brain dysfunction (Still, 1902), and in fact some serious childhood illnesses such as encephalitis and meningitis were causes of hyperactivity. Unfortunately, however, brain dysfunction became viewed as "the" cause of hyperactivity, and this view has been a dominant one in the United States until recently. After the development of the electroencephalograph (EEG) it became apparent that most hyperactive children had no unusual brain wave patterns. A significant percentage of hyperactive children had motor coordination problems revealed in writing, maze tracing, and use of small mechanical objects, but the majority of hyperactive children did not even have such motor coordination problems. It was the search for causes and the desire to explain the reasons for the motor coordination problems of hyperactive children that led medical professionals in the 1960s and 1970s to view hyperactivity as synonymous with Minimal Brain Dysfunction. In short, while there was no obvious brain dysfunction revealed on a neurological exam or EEG, it was hypothesized that some minimal brain dysfunction was the cause of the hyperactivity and motor coordination problems. Fortunately, use of the term MBD is waning since there is little or no evidence for it in most hyperactive children.

Dietary Factors

In an era of physical fitness, concern about diet is natural. In fact, slogans and by-lines of newspapers often reflect the notion "You Are What You Eat." The notion that a relationship exists between diet and hyperactivity was proposed by Dr. Benjamin Feingold in his book *Why Your Child Is Hyperactive* (1975). Basically, he felt that children have a physiological sensitivity to food additives, such as red and yellow dyes and food preservatives. Therefore, he placed hyperactive children on diets free of such substances and reported that 30 percent of such children showed a "dramatically positive response" and another 18 percent had a "very favorable response." When a number of controlled studies were conducted comparing the Feingold diet to alternative diets, however, there was no clear evidence that the diet led to any improvement (Conners, 1980). Only when children consume very large amounts of dye (100–150 milligrams) or were selected because of a presumed dye sensitivity has there been any adverse effect (Swanson & Kinsbourne, 1980). According to the U.S. Food and Drug Administration, about 10 percent of children between five and 12 years consume approximately 150 milligrams of food dye daily. We are not arguing that because a small percentage of children shows an adverse effect that food dyes should remain in our diets. In fact, even if a very small percentage of children have adverse reactions to

food coloring, it seems reasonable to question their use. They have no nutritional value and in high amounts the dyes may have adverse effects.

A related dietary concern that grew out of the Feingold diet studies were the concern about sugar ingestion. Prinz and his co-workers (Prinz, Roberts, & Hantman, 1980) suspected that some children might have shown a positive response to the Feingold diet because of a reduction in sugar in the diet. Prinz and colleagues found a significant relationship between amount of sugar eaten daily and the rates of aggression and restlessness exhibited in a playroom containing several hyperactive children. Even when the researchers controlled for general parental competence, educational level, and socioeconomic status, it was still clear that sugar consumption was correlated with rates of aggression and restlessness in the young hyperactive children. It is not possible to conclude from this research that all children, especially nonhyperactive children, are adversely affected by ingestion of sugar. In fact, there was not a significant correlation between sugar ingestion and aggression and activity level in nonhyperactive children. However, it did appear from this research that if a child has a problem with restlessness and aggression, it would be advisable to place reasonable limits on amount of sugar consumed. A survey of pediatricians and family practitioners by Bennett and Sherman (1983) indicated that 43 percent of them periodically recommended low sugar diets when treating these children.

Since the Prinz et al. (1980) research, there have been a number of studies which involved changes in the amount of sugar in children's diets. These studies have yielded inconsistent results. Some show an increase in hyperactivity associated with sugar ingestion (e.g., Conners & Blouin, 1983; Rosen, Booth, Bender, et al., 1985). Other investigators have found no changes in attention and behavior associated with sugar ingestion (e.g., Milich & Pelham, 1985; Wolraich, Milich, Stumbo, & Schultz, 1986). It appears that the inconsistencies across the studies may be due to differences in amount of sugar ingested in challenge (experimental) diets, differences in number of days the children were examined or observed, the type of situation in which the children were observed (e.g., playroom or experimental testing room), and the age of the subjects. The best conclusion one can currently draw from this research is that ingestion of dietary sugar may have some effect on the behavior of young children but that the magnitude of the effect is small (Rosen et al., 1985). Of course it is possible that certain *individual* children may have an adverse reaction to sugar, and we are probably best advised to keep an open mind about the issue. However, the effects of sugar ingestion, in the form of several candy bars, are in general very small and would not lead a practitioner automatically to restrict sugar ingestion in all hyperactive and/or aggressive children.

Social Factors

Reinforcement. All children, especially males, learn that aggression pays off. Aggression is rewarded in courtrooms, businesses, playgrounds, and athletic fields. Even in nursery schools, aggression pays off more often than not. Patterson, Littman, and Bricker (1967) observed thirty-six nursery school children over a nine-month period and coded consequences of aggression in positive and negative categories, i.e., categories of behavior that would presumably reward (positive) or punish (negative) the aggression. Positive categories of aggression including crying, being passive, and acting defenseless; negative categories included telling the teacher, retaliation, and teacher intervention. Aggressive

behaviors were generally likely to be followed by positive consequences for aggression. Even children who were initially passive and unassertive often experienced positive consequences for their aggression and became more assertive. In examining the behavior of aggressive children and their families, Patterson (1982) drew upon the differentiation made by Knutson and Hyman (1973). They distinguished instrumental and irritable aggression. Instrumental aggression is controlled by its positive consequences, whereas irritable aggression is elicited by an aversive event. Patterson (1982) believes that two-thirds of children referred for conduct problems have aggression that can be classified as instrumental aggression. They display behaviors that are coercive; they whine, yell, hit, and refuse to comply. These behaviors are used in such a fashion that they have a reliable effect upon their victim and a clear effect upon the aggressor. Children with high rates of these behaviors use them to control others fairly consistently across their childhood and adolescent years. Their whining and crying will change, however, to yelling, sarcasm, and argumentativeness. Children with conduct problems often lack many social skills and therefore are even more inclined to use coercive means of controlling their environment. As Patterson observed, "An increasing number of people report experiencing him as unpleasant. At this point he is labeled 'deviant' " (p. 25).

One may reasonably ask why coercive behaviors of aggressive children "pay off." Why are they not punished? First of all, many aggressive children will pick on targets they are likely to dominate. Second, while parents certainly do punish aggressive children for coercive behaviors, they often do so in a fashion that is ineffective. They threaten, scold, and yell, but they infrequently use punishment that works. Given that children can often get away with aggressive behavior without negative consequences, the result of parental yelling and scolding is often to increase the undesired behavior.

Direct rewards for aggression are also apparent in parent-child interactions. One might hear a father say, "I don't want to hear that you have hit your brother, but if John Jones hits you at school, I want you to beat the hell out of him." Not all children follow such parental imperatives, but it is known that children praised for hitting do increase their attacks more than children who were not praised for hitting (Patterson, Ludwig, & Sonoda, 1961). In the same vein, Bandura and Walters (1963) found that parents of aggressive boys explicitly rewarded their sons' aggression when it was directed at children outside the home.

Modeling.   Children imitate their friends, parents, and heroes. We even confuse the voices of teenagers for those of their parents because their speaking styles—pace, enunciation, and timbre—are so similar. We also see the adverse effects of modeling when we hear our children utter four-letter words we have inadvertently uttered in their presence. Bandura and his colleagues in the early 1960s conducted a series of experiments which unequivocally demonstrated how young children readily imitate aggressive models. Children who viewed movies depicting children behaving aggressively displayed more aggressive behavior in their classes than children who viewed movies without aggressive scenes. This research also revealed how young children learn to display novel sequences of aggressive behavior after simply watching a child model behave aggressively toward a life-sized plastic Bobo doll. The child model sat on the doll, punched the doll repeatedly, kicked the doll around the room, and made statements like, "Sock him in the nose." To assess the effect of observing the child model,

Bandura, Ross, and Ross (1963) compared the children who viewed the model with children who did not view the model but had the same objects with which to play (e.g., Tinkertoy set, mallet, five-foot Bobo doll). Both boys and girls were dramatically influenced by the aggressive model.

The effects of watching TV violence were illustrated in a classic study by Lefkowitz, Eron, Walden, and Heusmann (1977). These researchers collected data from 400 nine-year-old boys, including peer ratings, television viewing habits, and parental disciplinary practices. Ten years later, data were obtained on the 400 individuals, who were then nineteen years old. Boys who watched a high level of TV violence at age 9 were likely to be more aggressive at age 19 than boys who were not exposed to high levels of TV violence at age 9.

Marital Discord.   It has long been recognized by therapists of varying theoretical orientations that marital discord has a negative impact on children. Comparisons of marital status of the parents of children who attend psychological clinics with the marital status of parents of randomly selected children of the same age and sex indicate that marital discord is higher among clinic families than nonclinic families (Oltmanns, Broderick, & O'Leary, 1977). Family systems theorists have strongly implicated marital discord in the development of childhood problems as exemplified by Framo's (1975) statement: "Whenever you have a disturbed child, you have a disturbed marriage" (p. 22). Our own data in several studies does not support such a statement and, in fact, such broad generalizations seem myopic when one considers the host of variables that can lead to childhood problems. We have found, however, that marital discord is most highly associated with conduct problems of boys (Emery & O'Leary,

1982) and this finding was also obtained in a large-scale investigation in England (Rutter, 1975). Marital discord has some negative effect on girls but the research with clinic samples indicates that the effect is much smaller than the effect on boys. Finally, there is suggestive evidence that girls' anxiety and withdrawal problems are more closely associated with marital discord than are their conduct problems. It is unclear whether hyperactivity per se (hyperactivity without aggression) is associated with marital discord, but clinical studies suggest that hyperactivity without aggression would be less likely to correlate with marital discord than would aggression alone or aggression and hyperactivity (Prinz, Myers, Holden, Tarnowski, & Roberts, 1983).

The traditional way of viewing the association between marital discord and childhood problems has been largely one of marital discord leading to childhood problems. It must be recognized also that disagreements about childrearing and the impact of a child with serious psychological problems can also lead to marital stress. In brief, the relationship between marital and childhood problems can be a reciprocal one.

Strong Punishment and Inconsistent Discipline.   There is a large amount of evidence indicating that parents who use strong, frequent punishment are likely to have aggressive children. Sears, Maccoby, and Levin (1957) interviewed approximately 400 mothers of 5-year-old children and found that both severity of punishment by parents and the extent of disagreement between parents were associated with aggression of the young children. Bandura and Walters (1959) interviewed mothers, fathers, and their aggressive teenagers and compared the results of these interviews to interviews of nonaggressive youths and their parents. The nonaggressive youths were matched on the basis of age, eduction, social status, and residential area. Like Sears and colleagues (1957), Bandura and Walters found that parents of aggressive youths were more punitive, more often disagreed with each other, and were more likely to be cold and rejecting. There are numerous studies which confirm the results just mentioned; in fact, the finding is so clear that most clinicians who treat children with conduct problems assess types and frequency of punishment in some detail.

TREATMENT

Psychological

Home Interventions.   Patterson and his colleagues at the University of Oregon began conducting research on treating aggressive boys in the mid-1960s, and his work has been replicated in England by Martin Herbert (1978). This work has focused on home and family interactions. We will first cover home-based treatment for children. Patterson's teaching manual for parents, *Living with Children*, has been translated into Dutch, French, German, Spanish, and Swedish. The initial efforts of Patterson and his research colleagues were designed to develop a practical treatment program based on behavioral principles that could be used by others. The program generally included the following components (1) *Rewarding desired behavior* such as cooperating, sharing, and requesting aid rather than demanding help. Rewarding could take many forms but most importantly it emphasized praise and other supportive comments. (2) *Ignoring undesired behavior.* Most aggressive children have many behaviors that are annoying, and it is ridiculous to attempt to punish all undesired behavior—even though many parents tell you they would like to do so. A relatively aggressive 10-year-old boy might yell too much at his brothers and sisters, fail to dress "properly," fail to have his hair cut or wash it regularly, swear at his mother, and refuse to do homework. If a parent attempts to reprimand all these behaviors consistently the parent will be hoarse and exhausted. Instead, the parent must decide which behaviors are most important to change and which can be ignored—at least temporarily. (3) *Punish undesired behavior.* Certain behaviors such as swearing and insolent back-talk require firm consequences. They generally cannot be ignored because if they occur often they can generalize to school and other social interactions. Firm, nonphysical consequences include loss of privileges, isolation in a room for a fixed period, or removal from a preferred activity (e.g., a family game or a game in the yard with friends). Whenever the first author hears that there is too much arguing between parent and child, he indicates that parents are probably taking too little action. Extensive arguing and screaming in parent-child interactions with aggressive children usually means that parents are teaching their children to become "Philadelphia Lawyers," i.e., rewarding aggressive verbal counter acts.

Patterson and Fleischman (1979) found that when there is an aggressive child in the family, the family members are more coercive than family members who do not have an aggressive child. *Coercive* here refers to engaging in physical and verbal attacks as a means of changing behavior. The implication of this work is that one should be alert to the possibility that "the aggressive child" may be the subject of attacks by family members and that at least some of the aggressive child's problem arises from attempts to defend himself or herself.

Patterson and Fleishman (1979) reviewed the effects of behavioral treatment as well as

the maintenance of treatment gains and found that behavioral programs were better than no treatment, client-centered treatment, or traditional treatment. In a behavioral treatment program at the Oregon Social Learning Project, 114 families with aggressive children were studied over a ten-year period. There was a 17 percent dropout rate during baseline, which is comparable to many other studies, and another 41 percent refused to participate in the twelve-month follow-up after treatment. Deviance was clearly reduced from baseline to termination of treatment, and at a twelve-month follow-up, 84 percent of the children were observed to function in the normal range. Further data from a number of investigators with programs similar to Patterson's have also found significant treatment effects, and Patterson and Fleishman found that mothers reduced their punitiveness and had more positive perceptions of their children following treatment. After treatment, mothers saw their children as more relaxed, less withdrawn, less aggressive, more effective in the classroom, and having fewer conduct problems.

Baum and Forehand (1981) also have provided evidence that oppositional behavior and noncompliance can be changed with a parent training program that puts its emphasis on rewarding compliance and appropriate behavior. Time out from reinforcement was also used as a means for highly inappropriate behaviors, such as destruction of property and cursing. While there was suggestive evidence that treatment gains were maintained when the authors looked at pre-, post-, and follow-up data, there was no control group treated with an alternative intervention. The absence of such data provides only suggestive evidence regarding the long-term effects of the treatment. As Kent (1976) has emphasized, the frequency of overt aggression and similar disruptive behaviors generally decreases during the school years. Without control groups to deal with this change one cannot un-equivocally say that the intervention was effective.

Verbal 10- to 12-year-old children and ad-olescents who are aggressive require more than rewards, supportive comments, and punishment with minimal reasoning; they need to participate in the problem-solving process. Foster, Prinz, and O'Leary (1983) success-fully utilized the following problem-solving model with adolescents and their parents:

1. Define the problem.
2. Generate alternative solutions without eval-uation.
3. Evaluate the alternatives by projecting pos-itive and negative consequences, including compromise and choice of solution(s) to try.
4. Plan to implement the agreed-upon solu-tion.

This model sounds simple, but when a ther-apist attempts to put it into effect, the emo-tional outbursts and blockages become readily apparent. Since emotionally charged issues are often impossible to discuss initially with-out a great deal of therapist intervention, it is best to discuss a relatively small problem before proceeding to major issues. As this progression occurs, the therapist gives feed-back to the parents and adolescents about constructive communication. Good listening and correct restatements of what the other person said are especially encouraged. Fam-ily members also give feedback regarding destructive communication styles such as name-calling, repeated criticism, and avoid-ing issues.

Robin, O'Leary, Kent, Foster, and Prinz (1977) compared treated mother-adolescent dyads using the above model and obtained impressive increases in problem-solving be-haviors in the therapy session, but they ob-tained only minimal evidence from self-report

measures that the effects generalized to the home. Foster, Prinz, and O'Leary (1983) placed greater emphasis on producing gen-eralization via repeated practice of skills and graduated homework assignments. They found that self-report measures of behavior at home did change as a function of treatment and that the treatment effects were maintained at fol-low-up. On the other hand, observation of problem-solving behavior did not change during treatment. In brief, the results allow cautious optimism regarding the potential of communication training with parents and ad-olescents. The effects obtained depend upon the measures used, and it is necessary to ob-tain more than self-report of change to have unequivocal confidence in the intervention. However, research on communication with parent-adolescent dyads is relatively new and is likely to occur in various places in the next decade.

With hyperactive children there is also evidence that a focus on enhancing commu-nication is valuable (Dubey, S. O'Leary, & Kaufman, 1983). We believe that the type of communication enhancement described here would be useful to incorporate in any ther-apy program. The communication emphasis included the following types of guides for parents:

1. Use "I" statements rather than "you" state-ments. State how you feel yourself rather than making inferences about how your child feels. Let your child speak for himself or herself. For example, it is better to say, "I get discouraged when I see your breakfast dishes on the table every day," rather than, "You are deliberately trying to get me upset by leaving your breakfast dishes on the table every day."
2. Listen carefully and try to be able to restate what the other person has said. Parents can learn a great deal about a child's feelings if they simply listen more to their children. They can learn about a child's concerns, fears, and wor-ries as well as his or her likes and dislikes.

3. Invite the child to talk.
4. Do not interrupt the person speaking.
5. Acknowledge that you heard a comment.

One of the key aspects of this communication enhancement program is active listening, i.e., being able to understand what the speaker means or feels. Aggressive and hyperactive children often have poor self-esteem, receive more criticism than the average child, and very frequently feel that their parents do not understand them. Therefore, any communication program which can foster understanding between parents and children is laudatory.

School Interventions. There is very convincing evidence that aggressive and hyperactive behavior can be changed in classrooms. Generally, the treatment programs designed to change such behaviors focus on rewarding academic production and appropriate classroom behavior. Teachers are bothered most by aggression, running around the room, and defiance and are initially most interested in reducing the rates of such behavior. Reducing them, though, does not necessarily lead to increases in appropriate behavior, and increases in academic production do not always lead to decreases in disruptive behavior. Of course, if you are sitting in your seat and working diligently, it is less likely that you will create disturbances in the classroom. However, even diligent workers can find time to create considerable classroom havoc. Such findings have led clinicians to place primary focus on increasing academic output while at the same time having clear methods for decreasing highly disruptive behavior.

Kent and O'Leary (1976) designed a four-month intervention in which a therapist consulted weekly with the parent and child and approximately biweekly with the teacher. The program focused on (1) daily goal-setting with the child, (2) praise and other forms of positive teacher attention for completion of work, (3) soft rather than loud reprimands, (4) daily report cards (3 × 5 index cards) on which the teacher indicated how well the child had completed the daily goals, (5) parental rewards such as praise and extra privileges for receiving a good report, and (6) parental support and guidance for the child on a programmed workbook series to teach academic skills related to his or her problems in the classroom. The children in this study were almost exclusively boys chosen because of high rates of aggressive behavior, as judged by teacher ratings and classroom observations. This selection resulted in children whose aggression scores before treatment were in the upper 1 percent of the population on a standardized teacher rating of aggression. Because of the high rates of aggressive behavior, the treatment program provided for somewhat variable contact with families, but all therapist contact with families ended after a three- to four-month period. In order to ensure the maintenance of academic gains, the children and their parents met with a certified teacher on four occasions during the summer regarding reading or math—whichever subject with which they had most difficulty. These meetings were held to encourage parents to continue to support their daily tutorial sessions with their child.

At the end of treatment, both observational data in the classroom and teacher ratings of social and academic behavior demonstrated that there was greater behavioral improvement in the treated than in the control children. At a nine-month follow-up, the control group had improved to the point that there were no differences in social behavior between the treated and control subjects, but in contrast, the treated children had significantly greater achievement scores and grades than the untreated children. From a clinical standpoint, it is important to note that while Kent and O'Leary had demonstrated significant effects, they noted the need for longer treatment (i.e., more than three to four months) and additional consultation about family problems. As they emphasized, "It appears that certain clients were very well served by twenty hours of consultation, whereas others may need at least double that number to produce lasting improvement in school" (p. 595).

A classroom intervention for hyperactive children was devised by O'Leary, Pelham, Rosenbaum, and Price (1976), who evaluated the effects of a behavioral consultation program for teachers. The program involved a weekly group meeting with the teachers, which was occasionally attended by a very supportive principal. In the context of this supportive atmosphere, teachers were asked to do the following with the hyperactive child in their class:

1. Establish daily academic and social goals for the child each morning which can be met fairly readily.

2. Praise appropriate behavior.

3. Ignore as much disruptive behavior as possible.

4. If reprimands are necessary, use a reprimand audible only to the child being reprimanded.

5. Have the child keep a 3 × 5 index card (Daily Report Card) on which the teacher can indicate whether or not the child met the daily goals. In addition, place a check on the allotted space if the child should receive praise and other reinforcers from the parent, such as extra TV or a special dessert.

Nine hyperactive children were assigned to the treated group and eight hyperactive children were assigned to the control group, a no-contact group. As was evident from the teacher ratings of problem behavior and hyperkinesis (hyperactivity), the treated children improved significantly more than the nontreated children. Furthermore, the gains obtained were clinically significant.

Behavior therapy programs have been designed to change cognitive strategies of aggressive children to encourage self-control by such children. Camp (1977) taught children to ask themselves the following questions: What is my problem? What is my plan? Am I using my plan? How did I do? In order to teach the children to verbalize and use the cognitive strategies, a teacher had the children play "copycat" and repeat each question. Later, the child was taught to verbalize the strategies whenever a social or academic problem arose. Interestingly, the children were also taught a problem-solving strategy to help them recognize the emotions of oth-

	Name of Child _____	
	Yes	No
1. Finished math assignment	_____	_____
2. 80 percent correct in spelling	_____	_____
3. Cooperated with others;	_____	_____
Should get reward:	_____	_____
Date: _____	Teacher's Signature: _____	

Figure 6–1   Daily Report Card (submitted daily by teacher to parents) (From O'Leary, K. D., Pelham, W., Rosenbaum, A., & Price, G. (1976). Behavioral treatment of hyperkinesis. *Clinical Pediatrics, 15,* 512.)

TREATMENT OF HYPERKINESIA

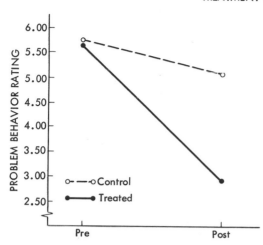

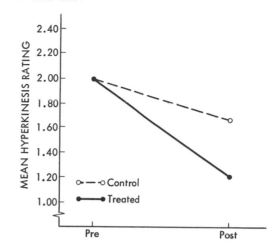

Figure 6–2 Comparison of the mean problem behavior ratings of nine hyperkinetic children treated with behavior therapy, and of eight similar controls.

Figure 6–3 Mean hyperkinesia ratings of the same children, obtained from the Teacher Rating Scale (TRS). The data reflect the mean item ratings (range 0.0–3.0) on the ten-item TRS.

(From O'Leary, K. D., Pelham, W., Rosenbaum, A., & Price, G. (1976). Behavioral treatment of hyperkinesis. *Clinical Pediatrics, 15,* 513.)

ers, predict the outcomes of interpersonal situations, and evaluate the fairness of those outcomes.

This self-control or cognitive strategy program was taught daily for six weeks by specially trained teachers. To facilitate the children's use of the strategies in the classroom, teachers strongly encouraged strategy-use in completing schoolwork or dealing with problems in the classroom. The aggressive children who received the program were compared with aggressive children who did not receive such a program, and the treated children improved more on laboratory measures of impulsive behavior, such as completing mazes. On the other hand, teacher ratings of aggression in the classroom did not indicate that treated children fared better than untreated children.

Relaxation Interventions. Several single-subject studies have used relaxation with hyperactive children, but there have not been consistent effects with progressive muscle relaxation or with biofeedback to the frontales muscle on the forehead. One problem with evaluating relaxation interventions, especially with children, lies in not knowing whether or not the subjects become relaxed. To deal with this problem, Behavioral Relaxation Training, consisting of ten overt postures and behaviors, was developed for hyperactive children (Raymer & Poppen, 1985; Schilling & Poppen, 1983). The postures and behaviors were taught by modeling, prompting, and feedback. Modeling trials consisted of having the experimenter demonstrate an unrelaxed and a relaxed behavior. Tokens and praise were given for successful imitation of the experimenter. The children were taught to maintain the relaxed behavior for periods of ten, twenty, thirty, and sixty seconds. After relaxation was learned, the training was discussed with the parents, who were then trained in relaxation. While there was objective evidence of decreases in muscle tension as measured by the EMG and relaxation ratings by the experimenter, there was no conclusive evidence that parental ratings of hyperactivity changed in response to decrease in muscle tension in the therapy office. However, there was suggestive evidence that when mothers began to implement the relaxation exercises in the home, the children became less hyperactive. This research, like much research with aggressive children, suggests that interventions should be made in the place where the desired behaviors occur.

Direct training of relaxation and self-control for aggressive/hyperactive children has been effected through the use of a self-control procedure called the Turtle Technique, involving relaxation and, later, social problem-solving to help choose appropriate responses to situations like name-calling (Robin, Schneider, & Dolnick, 1976). Young children are taught to withdraw from a scene in which they feel anger building and to imagine that they are turtles pulling into their shells. Then they are taught to use progressive relaxation and, following their showing a relaxed body to their teacher, they begin to engage in social problem-solving. While relaxation alone and relaxation and problem-solving have shown some promise with hyperactive/aggressive children, the procedures must be regarded as having suggestive support from clinical case studies and several individual subject designs.

There has been considerable controversy about the role of self-control and cognitive strategies in behavioral programs. In fact, extensive reviews of self-control or cognitive behavioral strategies with children conclude that such programs per se do not have enough promise to be employed as a singular strategy for changing the aggressive behavior of children in the home or classroom (Hobbs, Mo-

guin, Tyroler, & Lahey, 1980; S. O'Leary & Dubey, 1979; Rosenbaum & Drabman, 1979; Whalen, Henker, & Hinshaw, 1985). In their answer to the question, does cognitive behavioral therapy facilitate short-term behavioral improvements?, Whalen, Henker, and Hinshaw (1985) stated the following:

"The effectiveness of cognitive behavioral therapy has been demonstrated for specific behavioral domains, in circumscribed contexts, for brief periods of time, and primarily with non-clinical samples of children considered deficient in self-control skills. Regarding clinically diagnosed attention deficit disorder children, however, an admittedly overgeneralized and perhaps controversial 'bottom line' is that the results of CBT are not very strong, somewhat inconsistent, difficult to replicate, and decidedly disappointing. On the plus side, delimited short-term gains have been documented in numerous studies. But on the minus side, the findings are neither as predictable nor as widespread as once expected." (p. 393)

At this point, pitting self-control against external programs of some nature seems ridiculous if one is treating children. Feedback, rewards, praise, and other forms of social support are necessary in any program with children who have conduct problems. Similarly, teaching self-control strategies, such as goal-setting, self-evaluation, and self-reward, are reasonable in most clinical settings of behavior therapists working with children. Programs to change children's self-control and cognitive strategies can be especially useful if combined with consultation to parents and teachers about behavior management (Douglas, 1979).

An example of the efficacy of self-evaluation procedures in the context of a token reinforcement program was provided by Hinshaw, Henker, and Whalen (1984). Boys with a diagnosis of attention deficit disorder with hyperactivity participated and were evaluated with regard to observations of appropriate and negative social interactions. A matching procedure was used in small groups in which the children were taught to match a teacher rating of their behavior on a 1 to 5 scale. The object was for the boys to monitor their own behavior, evaluate their performance in comparison with the criteria, and then match the trainer's ratings. Matching the trainer's rating eventually led to reinforcement only if the behavior also received a positive rating. (A boy would not get bonus points for agreeing that he did an absolutely terrible job.)

Psychostimulant medication or placebos were used throughout the study. It was found that reinforced self-evaluation and medication were both associated with increases in positive social behavior. The study involved only short-term assessments, but it suggests that self-control procedures *in combination with* token reinforcement and psychostimulant medication can be effective in altering the behavior of hyperactive children.

An area that has been neglected in research is the use of negative feedback or punishment in classrooms. The emphasis in child behavior therapy has been on various forms of positive reinforcement since the ascent of child behavior therapy. One of the ardent proponents of positive reinforcement was Skinner; he argued against the use of punishment of almost any kind. In fact, his utopian world *Walden Two* was based solely on positive reinforcement. Child behavior therapists often were influenced by Skinner or individuals who translated his work into forms that could be applied in clinical and educational settings (e.g., Bijou, 1965; Ullmann & Krasner, 1965). Such translations involved positive reinforcement (e.g., shaping, praise, and token reinforcement programs).

A series of studies across a five-year period by S. O'Leary and associates (S. O'Leary, 1985) has shown that prudent negative conse-quences in classroom settings are critical in maintaining appropriate behavior of hyperactive children. In five separate studies S. O'Leary demonstrated that when negative consequences are totally withdrawn, a reliable and marked increase in off-task behavior occurs. In contrast, however, when positive consequences are withdrawn, no change in the rate of off-task behavior occurs for a period of five days. These findings occur reliably with different teachers, different children, phases of varying lengths, and different types of negative consequences (Rosen, O'Leary, Joyce, Conway, & Pfiffner, 1984).

Since some form of negative consequences seems necessary, albeit at a low frequency, to maintain appropriate classroom behavior, it seemed useful to evaluate the types of negative feedback most likely to produce the desired reduction in inappropriate behavior. It was found that negative consequences which were calm, concrete, and consistent were more effective than negative consequences which were loud, emotional, and inconsistent (Rosen et al., 1984). The studies conducted on negative feedback noted previously took place following a period after which teachers had established good working relationships with classes of hyperactive children and after high rates of appropriate classroom behavior had been established. It should be emphasized that these high rates of appropriate behavior were obtained by teachers who used a combination of positive and negative consequences during the baseline periods. It certainly is not argued that negative consequences alone are advised. As the authors noted, "An all-negative approach to classroom management could have cumulative and adverse effects on the teacher's attitude, perhaps resulting in generally reduced interaction rates with the students and less active teaching" (p. 602). Finally, they also caution that children's attitudes toward school and the teacher could be adversely affected if all negative consequences were used in a classroom.

Thus far discussions of changing the behavior of young aggressive children have focused on reinforcing appropriate behavior, ignoring disruptive behavior, and occasionally punishing especially disruptive behavior. An important alternative or complementary approach is to arrange activities and transitions to activities for young children so that they will become so engaged that they will not indulge in disruptive behavior. This approach, called *activities planning*, was described by Saunders and Dadds (1982). It initially consists of identifying child-care settings in which parents frequently report difficulties (Quilitich & Risley, 1973). The parents are taught "a broad range of stimulus control and organizational skills such as advance planning of an activity or outing, how to organize oneself to prevent last minute rushing, how to establish and discuss ground rules specific to the setting, how to role-play and rehearse the correct behavior with the child, and how to select and arrange activities to engage the child in the setting. Parents were then taught to apply these general skills across multiple parental situations both in the home and the community (e.g., visiting grandparents, shopping)" (p. 102).

Saunders and Dadds (1982) compared child management training alone (reinforcement, ignoring disruptive behavior, and time out from positive reinforcement) with child management training plus planned activities training. Five families with a preschool aged child participated. All children displayed high rates of disruptive, noncompliant, and demanding behavior. Children were observed in training settings (family homes) and generalization settings (community environments and home areas not used in training). Using a multiple baseline design it was found that child management training procedures resulted in changed parent behavior in both the training and generalization settings. However, only one of the five parents was effective in reducing levels of deviant behavior. Planned activities resulted in further improvements in child behavior in both the training and generalization settings for three families. For one family, neither of the interventions was effective in changing the child's behavior.

This work by Saunders and Dadds (1982) drew upon the conceptualizations of Risley and colleagues (Quilitich & Risley, 1973), who had shown the importance of planning activities and transitions from one activity to another. This conceptualization is important for changing behavior problems of all kinds and points to the possibility that many behavior problems can be eliminated with some forethought by parents.

The role of extrafamily environment factors on parents and, in turn, on children, was illustrated by Dumas and Wahler (1985). These researchers were interested in the extent that types of interaction mothers had with people outside the family might influence their interactions with their children. Mothers who had few and/or negative social contacts on a daily basis, defined as insular mothers, were more aversive with their children than noninsular mothers. As Dumas and Wahler argued, when an insular mother responds to any one of her coercive partners (e.g., child or spouse), her response does not seem to be influenced by that person but by *all* the other persons who regularly engage her in coercive interchanges. Such research points to the need to analyze the social stressors of parents and to look more closely at the factors outside the parent-child interactions that influence such interactions. When mothers were asked to change their interactions with their children (Wahler, 1980), those mothers who had few and/or negative interactions with relatives or friends were less able to be positive in their interactions with their children (see Fig 6-4) and had to deal with a greater percent of oppositional occurrences on the days where they had "Low Friendship Days." This finding extends the research, which shows that parents with marital problems and overt hostility are more likely to have children with conduct problems than parents without marital difficulty (Emery & O'Leary, 1984).

Pharmacological

Psychostimulant medication has been used for hyperactive and some aggressive children since the early 1940s. The mechanism of the stimulant medication is not clear, but the drugs have an excitation effect on the central nervous system. The reticular arousal system (RAS) is activated by psychostimulants, which are thought to lead to enhanced attention. They are given to 2 percent of all elementary school children in the United States, in part because the effects of the medication are rapid and clear. Enhanced attention and compliance in the classroom have been documented in scores of studies. Interestingly, the psychostimulants used with children, such as dextro-amphetamine and methylphenidate, do not lead to general increases in motor activity. Whether motor activity is increased or decreased depends on the situation in which the motor activity is assessed. According to highly respected psychiatric specialists in child pharmacology, it appears that "in the usual clinical situation, the effect [of receiving psychostimulant medication] is a beneficial one" (Cantwell & Carlson, 1978, p. 180).

While the positive effects of psychostim-

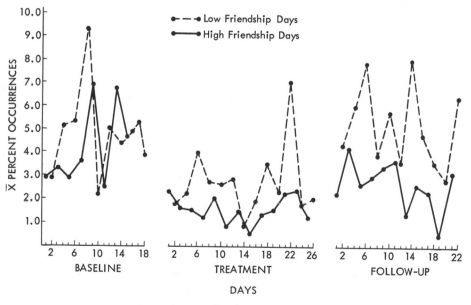

Figure 6–4 Mean percentage occurrence of target child oppositional actions. These means are presented for two sets of observation sessions over three phases of this study. Low friendship sessions are those occurring on days in which the mothers reported friend contacts to be less than 20% of their extra-family contacts. High friendship sessions refer to days comprised of 80% friend contacts. (From Wahler, R. G. (1980) The insular mother: Her problems in parent-child treatment. *Journal of Applied Behavior Analysis, 13,* 216. Copyright 1980 by the Society for the Experimental Analysis of Behavior, Inc.)

ulant medication on social behavior in classrooms are clear, it is ironic that despite better social behavior and enhanced attention, children treated with psychostimulants do not improve more academically than children not receiving psychostimulants (Barkley & Cunningham, 1978). Further, the positive effects of the medication (e.g., enhanced attention) are immediately lost when the medication is withdrawn—even after the child has received such medication for months. Finally, since stimulant medications increase the arousal systems, children cannot take such medication late in the day or they will not sleep at night. Therefore, parents must learn ways to cope with behavior problems at home after school and in the evening. These problems associated with psychostimulant use have led to the need for alternatives and adjunctive treatments.

Behavior therapy approaches have been used successfully with children clearly diagnosed as hyperactive who had never taken medication (O'Leary, Pelham, Rosenbaum, & Price, 1976) and with hyperactive children who were receiving medication but whose pediatricians felt they should not take it any longer (S. O'Leary & Pelham, 1978). There is only one major study comparing behavior therapy with medication (Gittleman-Klein, Klein, Abikoff et al., 1976). In an eight-week evaluation, it was found that psychostimulant medication was superior to behavior therapy in classroom observations and teacher ratings. Both behavior therapy and medication individually were associated with significant improvements in the children's behavior, but the gains were greater for the medicated group. The only place in which the combined treatment of psychostimulant medication and behavior therapy was superior to behavior therapy alone was on global teacher ratings. The treatments were in effect for eight weeks, which in the mid-1970s seemed reasonable since other research had shown that hyper-

active problems could be reduced within eight to ten weeks (O'Leary, Pelham, Rosenbaum & Price, 1976; Rosenbaum, O'Leary, & Jacob, 1975). A major difference in the studies by O'Leary and his colleagues and Gittleman-Klein and her colleagues is that the studies by O'Leary's group were conducted in a school with principal cooperation and teacher participation. The teachers met with the investigators, and sometimes with the principal. The esprit de corps in those studies was probably a key factor in some of the successes obtained. In contrast, the Gittleman et al. research was conducted in a hospital clinic attended by individuals from many diverse school districts. The two clinicians, who had been well-trained in behavior therapy principles, then had to visit the schools and attempt to obtain teacher cooperation on their own. It appears that the delivery systems of the two programs may account partly for their successes. The outpatient clinic model, while a very common one, may be problematic. Further, it now seems clear that eight weeks of behavioral therapy treatment is but a small portion of the needed intervention for such problems. It appears that hyperactive and/or aggressive children may need psychological therapy for one to two years. If they are given medication alone, even for two years, they will have better school adjustment as judged by teachers, but they will not do any better academically than if they had not received the medication.

The study that best represents what happens clinically when children receive both medication and behavior therapy and some tutoring indicated there was an "unexpectedly good outcome." More specifically, there were academic gains of approximately 1.6 years in mathematics and reading during the year-long treatment program (Satterfield, Cantwell, & Satterfield, 1979).

The Satterfield and colleagues (1979) study provides suggestive evidence for a combined intervention of medication, behavior therapy, and tutoring. This study was a clinical treatment demonstration, not a true experiment. There was no attempt to discern the effects of the components of the year-long treatment or to show that the compound treatment was better than the individual components. The study is noted here because there are few treatment studies with hyperactive children which simulate what happens in actual clinical practice. That is, few studies last for more than three to four months, despite the fact that hyperactive children have to be treated for several years. In addition, treatment in the best of actual practice may often involve several types of intervention, such as tutoring and medication or behavior therapy and tutoring. However, a problem with studies like that of Satterfield is that the treatments are highly varied. For example, the psychological therapy involved mixtures of behavior therapy, family therapy, parent training, and individual supportive therapy for parents. Without a treatment manual and observations of the therapy per se it is impossible to determine the critical treatment ingredients. Nonetheless, the posttreatment gains of 1.6 years in mathematics and reading in one year are truly impressive for hyperactive children, and the gains were evident at a one-year follow-up, during which time most of the children continued to receive relatively low doses of psychostimulant medication (0.32 mg/Kg) and some psychotherapy (Satterfield, Cantwell, & Satterfield, (1979).

Selection of Treatments

The results of the studies of psychostimulant medication with hyperactive children lead different investigators to different conclusions. Researchers who are likely to prescribe medication in their practice or work with individuals who evaluate drugs as a major aspect of their research efforts are most likely to conclude that medication is the treatment of choice for hyperactive children. As Gittelman-Klein et al. (1976) concluded, should the pattern obtained so far persist in the completed study, the data will support the conclusion that stimulant treatment is the intervention of choice for hyperactive children. If the medication is not enough, behavior modification should be added" (p. 377).

On the other hand, researchers who are likely to practice behavior therapy or conduct research evaluating behavior therapy are more likely to advocate it as the treatment of choice. For example, O'Leary (1980), in an article titled, "Pills or Skills in Hyperactive Children," argued that behavior therapy approaches emphasizing reinforcement of desired classroom behavior, teacher consultation, and parent consultation have shown consistent positive effects. He further states that he "would not initially use pharmacological intervention with most hyperactive children because the behaviors that characterize the hyperactive syndrome are so dramatically, although fleetingly, changed by psychostimulants that the parents, teachers, and children may view the medication as a panacea and we know that such is very far from the truth" (p. 201). In short, data issues are not the only factors which influence professionals to advocate one treatment or another. We know from the data that there are varied and somewhat contradictory effects of different dosage levels: the medication effects that seem best to improve social behavior may be the worst to improve academic behavior, the effects of medication are usually lost when it is discontinued, and behavior therapy is generally associated with improved conduct and grades.

The consumer should be as educated as possible regarding the medical and psychological treatments for various problems. As is apparent in the treatment of several problems common in psychological and psychiatric clinics, the same studies can lead different investigators to different conclusions. Often these conclusions are influenced by professional biases about presumed causes of problems and beliefs about both short- and long-term advantages of the treatments. The consumer should remember that professionals have often given treatments which later seem utterly ridiculous (e.g., treatment of schizophrenia by prefrontal lobotomies or surgical ablation of various areas of the brain in the 1930s, and play therapy for almost any child problem in the 1940s). Ultimately, consumers seeking treatment should garner information from magazines, from professional journals, and from talking to professionals whom they respect. Keeping in mind the professional biases that might influence the individuals with whom they speak, the consumer can then make an informed judgment.

SUMMARY

Conduct problems refer to a wide variety of behaviors that disturb others and interfere with academic learning. Aggression is the primary characteristic of conduct problems, but impulsivity, temper tantrums, defiance, and destruction of property are also common characteristics of children with conduct problems. Hyperactivity is characterized by motor restlessness, overactivity, and inattention. Some research has shown that hyperactivity can be diagnosed separately from aggression, but historically aggression and hyperactivity have been seen as subgroupings of conduct problems. While hyperactivity and aggression often occur together in a child, it is important to diagnose these problems separately where possible, as they have somewhat different etiologies and often warrant different treatments.

Conduct problems, aggression, and hyperactivity all have multiple determinants. With the exception of an inherited predisposition to be active or inactive, brain dysfunction in a very small percentage of hyperactive children, and occasional sensitivities to dietary factors that influence aggression and hyperactivity, social factors appear to be the primary causative factors of aggression and hyperactivity. Reinforcement, modeling, marital discord, and inconsistent discipline have all been shown to be clearly related to aggression and/or hyperactivity. The greater the rate and intensity of aggression in a child, the more difficult it is to treat the child.

Behavioral treatment of aggression and hyperactivity has been successful in both the home and school. Originally, the emphasis in behavioral treatment was on reinforcement of appropriate behavior, ignoring inappropriate behavior, and occasional soft reprimands, but the treatment programs for such children have become more multifaceted and now include family consultation about reciprocal effects of parent-child interactions, academic tutoring, and sometimes marital therapy. In addition, self-control programs have shown promise in changing academic behavior when combined with consultation to teachers regarding classroom management. A reasonable approach by a clinician would be to combine self-control strategies with an approach that includes overt reinforcement in the form of teacher and parent praise and positive feedback, decreases in threats and punishment, academic tutoring if necessary, and therapy for parents if marital problems seem to be obviously related to the child's problems. Psychostimulant medication can be used successfully as an adjunct to behavior therapy if the child has serious problems with fine motor control, coordination, overactivity, and impulse control. However, generally psychostimulant medication, in our opinion, is an alternative to be used after psychological therapy and academic tutoring have been tried and found to be unsuccessful or minimally effective. This result occurs in a small number of cases.

Delinquency

INCIDENCE AND DEFINITION

Hardly a night passes in any city in which some delinquent act is not portrayed on television. Our increasing awareness of such acts is not simply the result of better mass communication; delinquency is increasing at an alarming rate. Acceleration in juvenile crime from 1965 to 1975 was four times greater than the increase of juveniles in the population (Gibbons, 1976). In 1978, juvenile offenders between 10 and 17 years of age accounted for 50 percent of all arrests for serious offenses (U.S. Uniform Crime Reports, 1979). Arrests, of course, are only part of the story. Anonymous questionnaires of "normal" adolescents suggest that 75 percent had engaged in behavior which would have been labeled delinquent had they been caught (Offer, Sabshin, & Marcus, 1965). Further, while numerous studies show that delinquency rates are higher in urban than in rural areas, criminal activity is increasing at a much faster rate in rural areas. Between 1963 and 1977, U.S. Uniform Crime Reports indicated a 287 per-

cent increase in crime in urban areas and a 351 percent increase in rural areas (Lyerly & Skipper, 1981).

In 1967, the Commission on Law Enforcement and Criminal Administration of the U.S. Government concluded that institutionalization, the main treatment from 1955 to 1965, had not proven effective. Further, research in England on residential treatment has also yielded primarily negative findings (Clarke & Cornish, 1978). As you might expect, such institutionalization programs are extremely costly and sometimes inhumane. In 1986, it cost approximately $35,000 per year to keep a youth in an institution with other juvenile offenders.[1] Efforts to keep delinquents free of crime are hampered by a strong peer culture that maintains the delinquent behavior. Even those treatments which are successful on a short-term basis have usually failed to document any long-term difference over similar nontreated youths in such variables as number of offenses. As such, the treatment

1. Personal communication, June 13, 1986. Dr. Kathryn Kirigin, University of Kansas, Lawrence, KS.

133

of delinquent youth represents one of the greatest challenges to the fields of psychology, psychiatry, and social work. It is not now possible to predict accurately whether or not any single youth will commit a crime at a later date, but as will be documented in this chapter, we do know that the presence of certain risk factors makes it more likely that an individual will engage in criminal behavior. The use of such risk factors, however, is not precise enough to allow one to say that a particular youth will almost definitely commit delinquent acts later in his or her life. In addition, definitional problems concerning the term *delinquent* are often myriad. At one end of the spectrum, the term covers any "problem youth," whereas a more stringent definition involves a legal infraction. However, what is a legal infraction in one state may not be in another. Generally, however, in this chapter, the term *delinquent* refers to a youth who has committed a legal offense. Since the offenses for which a youth is labeled delinquent vary a great deal from state to state, and since treatment efficacy may be related to type and frequency of offense, the type of offenses committed by the youth will be specified wherever possible.

An interesting trend is taking place in the U.S. legal system in which juveniles are beginning to be prosecuted as adult criminals. According to some, such a trend might lead to a demise of the term *delinquency* and in its place the term *young criminals* might appear. There is an increasing attitude by the public favoring more severe punishment (e.g., mandatory sentences and capital punishment). Western governments are cutting social programs, turning to more conservative leadership, and eliminating programs such as summer work, any of which may increase criminal activity among youth. Our guess is that whether the term *juvenile delinquency* is changed or not, issues of criminal activity among youth will still be viewed differently than such activity among adults. The social fabric of youth is clearly different from that of adults and presumably the etiology of criminal activity among youths and adults differs. As you will see, however, delinquency presents one of the most difficult challenges that social, behavioral, and biological scientists face.

ETIOLOGY

Theories of delinquency can generally be subsumed under the following headings: biological, sociological, and social learning. As in previous chapters, theories other than the psychological, particularly the social learning approach, will be presented to give the reader an idea of other conceptualizations, and where possible, to point to possible rapprochement between theories of delinquency.

Biological Theories

In 1965, Jacobs, Brunton, Melville, Brittain, and McClemont published a study which had a profound impact on the legal and mental health professions. They reported that instead of the usual forty-six chromosomes, some tall, mentally retarded, aggressive criminals had an extra Y chromosome, number forty-seven. This abnormality is known as the XYY genotype. As Jarvik, Klodin, and Matsuyama (1973) noted, with the exception of mental deficiency, this was the first time a specific behavioral abnormality had been linked to a chromosomal aberration. Further, it was known that persons with XYY genotypes were six inches taller than XY men and that there is evidence that tall youngsters are arrested at earlier ages than short youngsters.

In 1965, Daniel Hugon was charged with the brutal strangulation murder of a prostitute in France; he was found to have an XYY chromosomal constitution. In 1969, a six-foot-eight-inch, 240-pound man named John Farley beat, strangled, raped, and mutilated a Queens, New York, woman. His attorney defended him on the grounds of "reason of insanity resulting from a chromosome imbalance." Similar gory crimes have been committed by men with XYY genotype and, in certain instances, they have been acquitted on that basis.

Despite the identification of the XYY syndrome in some criminal populations, it was readily learned that many XYY men were normal law-abiding citizens. As important, for our purposes here, the frequency of the XYY genotype in a criminal population is only about 2 percent. Furthermore, as Bandura (1973) noted in one study, XYY prisoners had a lower incidence of physical and sexual assaults than did suitably matched XY's (Price & Whatmore, 1967). He added, "Perhaps the most striking aspect of the chromosome story is the ready proclivity to blame crime on 'bad genes.'"

The largest study regarding XYY was conducted in Copenhagen, Denmark, where all men born between 1944 and 1946 were studied. From this large group, the tallest 15 percent was selected for the study of sex chromosome aberrations. They found that the XYY men as a group were mildly retarded. When the researchers controlled for intelligence and social class by statistical methods, they found that the number of criminals expected was only two. Since five XYY men actually had criminal records, the XYY chromosome abnormality was seen as a factor that may account for some increased risk of crime (Walzer et al., 1978). The way in which the risk is mediated is not clear, but follow-ups with newborn children with XYY suggest that expressive speech and language development is severely impaired and reading deficits appear evident.

While it is possible that the XYY pattern has a role in risk for criminal behavior, it is clear that this chromosomal abnormality should not be seen as a major factor in the etiology of crime. The incidence of XYY in a general population is only 1 percent, and, as noted earlier, the frequency of XYY in a criminal population is only 2 percent.

A much earlier biological approach to delinquency was of physiological typing according to height and weight. In 1883, the Anthropometric Committee of the British Association for the Advancement of Science reported on the physical characteristics of 1874 delinquent children (placed in training schools) and 51,000 nondelinquent children. Their results showed the delinquent children to be shorter and lighter in weight than the nondelinquent children. Similar reports appeared throughout the early twentieth century, and many criminologists thus accepted the view that the delinquent was inferior in stature. On the other hand, the studies of somatotypes begun by Sheldon (1949), which placed individuals in three general categories, endomorphs (heavy), mesomorphs (athletic), and ectomorphs (thin), found that delinquents are more mesomorphic than nondelinquents (Cortes & Gatti, 1972). The earlier physiological typing studies showing delinquents to be shorter and lighter than nondelinquents may have obtained different results from the more recent somatotype research because the delinquent in the 1800s was largely a lower class, impoverished delinquent. The current delinquent is often from the middle and upper classes and even today's lower class delinquent is usually not on the same survival diet as the nineteenth-century delinquent.

Finally, a number of twin studies have been conducted in which criminal behavior is reported to be more likely in the twin of an incarcerated criminal who is a monozygotic (same egg) twin than in the twin of an incarcerated brother who is a dizygotic (different egg) twin. For example, in a classic study conducted by Lange in 1931, thirty pairs of twins were examined (thirteen identical, seventeen fraternal) in which one twin in each set was known to have been imprisoned. Of the thirteen identical twins, ten sets had had both twins imprisoned, whereas only two of the seventeen sets of fraternal twins had both been imprisoned. Studies with similar results were reported by Eysenck (1964) and Christensen (1968). The latter study was the better methodological study in that it was based on a thirty-year follow-up of all twin births in Denmark. He found that if one twin was a known criminal the likelihood of the other twin being criminal was three times greater in monozygotic than dizygotic twins.

While the child-rearing practices of parents of identical twins may differ from those of fraternal twins, there is an increasing belief by many professionals that criminal behavior is determined in part by constitutional factors (Wilson & Herrnstein, 1985). In one study of offenses in Philadelphia, 60 percent of all offenses were committed by less than 10 percent of the offenders. That is, a small number of delinquents and adult criminals commit a large percentage of the crimes, particularly violent crimes (*Science Times*, New York Times, September 17, 1985). Neurological deficits and brain dysfunction are seen as critical variables in the behavior of repeat offenders, who account for a large portion of the crimes.

In arriving at the conclusion that criminal behavior is influenced by constitutional factors, Wilson and Herrnstein (1985) noted that most repeat offenders begin their misdeeds at an early age, have somewhat lower intelligence than average, and are impulsive and deficient in socialization. They emphasize that criminals are generally antisocial children

grown up and that criminality gives its signals in early childhood. Despite the evidence one can marshal to support the notion that criminal behavior is constitutionally determined, it is difficult to reach unequivocal conclusions about the role of constitutional factors. Twin studies and autopsies of criminals with brain tumors or dysfunction can lend credence to the belief that criminal behavior is biologically influenced. However, few criminals have diagnosed brain dysfunction, and follow-ups of many twin studies have often revealed that identical twins have much more similar postnatal environments than fraternal twins have. Psychologists and criminologists have long been willing to accept the view that many of our behaviors are environmentally determined and that criminal behavior is heavily influenced by environmental factors; however, they should also keep an open mind about the possibility that constitutional factors may be important in violent criminal behavior. In the long run, it seems most likely that both constitutional and environmental factors are important (Hutchings & Mednick, 1974).

A twin study using self-reports of delinquency surveyed all twins in the eighth to twelfth grades in almost all school districts in Ohio in 1978 to 1980 (Rowe, 1983). Among other things, the youths were asked if they engaged in various behaviors that were later labeled delinquent by the investigators. Concordance rates for self-reported delinquent behavior were greater for monozygotic than dyzgotic twins in both males and females. Further, those twins who spent more time with one another did not have higher concordance rates than those twins who did not. Thus, in this study it appears that shared genes were more important than closely shared environments; however, there was a substantial association between the extent of delinquent acts and the number of delinquent friends (Rowe & Osgood, 1984). The authors argued that the genes of the individuals who engaged in delinquent acts prompted them to seek friends who engaged in delinquent behavior. The argument over whether constitutional or environmental factors contribute to or cause delinquent behavior will rage just as did the similar battle over genetic and environmental influences on intellectual behavior. The publication of the highly publicized book, *Crime and Human Nature*, by Wilson and Herrnstein (1985) has fueled this controversy. After reviewing evidence for the role of genetics, they argue strongly for the role of constitutional factors, noting that most repeat offenders begin their misdeeds at an early age, have somewhat lower intelligence than average, and are impulsive and deficient in socialization.

The present authors do not view the problem as an either/or issue. Delinquent behavior appears to be influenced by both environmental and genetic factors (Hutchings & Mednick, 1974). Undoubtedly, there will be a book rebutting the thesis of Wilson and Herrnstein, and it will likely argue for the environmental causes of delinquency. The reader should bear in mind that authors often have prejudices and that the consumer should judge the presentation accordingly.

In summary, various biological factors appear important in the etiology of some criminal behavior. Nonetheless, despite genetic breakthroughs, such as the development of better twin detection methods and the discovery of the XYY genotype syndrome, many XYY holders are not criminal, and even when one-half of the pair of a monozygotic twin set is known to be criminal, a sizeable proportion of the other half is not criminal. As with any other bio-social problem, the issue is not an either/or question. However, at present the question of reducing the incidence of criminal behavior largely resides in psychological and social factors.

Sociological Theories

One of the most famous and influential sociological theories of delinquency is Sutherland's (1939) "theory of differential association." Sutherland died in 1950, but eight editions of his book have now appeared through the aid of Donald Cressy. Numerous variations of this theory have appeared as differential identification, differential role commitment, differential social control, differential selection, and differential association-reinforcement theories (Cortes & Gatti, 1972). Sutherland's theory is essentially a learning theory, in which he noted that criminal behavior is learned as is any other behavior. He stated, "The principal part of the learning of criminal behavior occurs within intimate personal groups. A person becomes delinquent because of an excess of definitions (conditions) favorable to violation of law over definitions (conditions) unfavorable to violation of law." Reformulated by Burgess and Ackers (1966), the latter statement reads, "Criminal behavior is a function of norms which are discriminative for (cues for) criminal behavior, the learning of which takes place when such behavior is more highly reinforced than noncriminal behavior." Despite the general impact of Sutherland's theory, it has been strongly criticized because of, among other things, its vagueness, incompleteness, and superficiality (Cortes & Gatti, 1972). As Cortes and Gatti noted, Sutherland's theory does not explain why some persons with certain pressures and associations become criminals whereas others with similar pressures and associations do not. Burgess and Ackers (1966) similarly criticize Sutherland's theory on the basis of its little empirical support and absence of practical applications.

Another influential sociological theory is Cohen's "subcultural" theory of delinquency (1955). Essentially he states that behavior can be viewed as problem-solving and that many youths who cannot achieve the accepted societal values devise their own criteria of success which they can more readily obtain. In brief, they reject middle-class standards and adopt an alternative subculture which legitimizes their own values. The theory thus is an explanation of gang delinquency resulting from the failure of the delinquent to obtain societal rewards through legitimate means, an explanation which is particularly applicable to youths from the lower classes. It does not, however, explain the reasons why men such as Eric Hoffer, Horatio Alger, and James Baldwin became successful, not delinquent.

Control theory by Hirschi (1969) assumes that delinquency occurs when bonds between an individual and society are broken. In particular, the bonds are attachment to others, commitment to conventional lines of action, involvement in conventional activities, and belief in the moral validity of normative order. Hirschi does not claim that all adolescents with weakened bonds with prosocial peers will resort to delinquency; he simply says that such adolescents are more likely to be involved in delinquent activity. Unlike Sutherland's theory, Hirschi's analysis does not take into account the importance of delinquent friends, but there is some empirical support for control theory. There is a strong negative relation between composite commitment scores based on the bonds described above and delinquency (Lyerly & Skipper, 1981). Although it would be foolish to ignore sociological factors in the etiology of delinquency, such as the difficulty of acquiring legitimate goals and the bonds of an individual with his or her society, the sociological

theories have yet to have their impact in psychological treatment.

Learning Theories

There have been two primary trends in the behavioral literature concerning the etiology of delinquency: the conditionability approach espoused by Eysenck (1964) and the modeling and operant reinforcement approach espoused by Bandura and Walters (1963). Essentially, Eysenck's position is that the delinquent—especially the psychopathic delinquent—has a poor constitutional capacity for socialization, in that he does not acquire conditioned fear responses as readily as the average individual does. The term *psychopath* has been generally supplanted by the term *sociopath*, reflecting the increased tendency on the part of professionals to recognize social forces which prompt and reinforce unlawful behavior (Ullmann & Krasner, 1969). Although the term *psychopath* is replete with problems, it is used to refer to two primary features: a lack of emotional responsiveness and an irresistible tendency to act on impulse (Yates, 1970). (Though not all delinquents are regarded as psychopaths, many are, and much of the discussion of conditionability relates to the psychopathic delinquent.) The lower conditionability for fear combined with poor socialization is said to be a critical etiological factor in delinquent behavior. Studies by Hare (1965, 1968a) and Hare & Quinn (1971) have shown that psychopaths do show less reactivity than nonpsychopaths in a learning situation involving shock or anticipation of shock. In another study, Hare (1968b) found that psychopathic prisoners detected shock in a signal detection experiment less readily than a group of nonpsychopathic prisoners. However, verbal conditioning experiments using rewards and not involving shock or any type of punishment do not show any differences between psychopaths and nonpsychopaths (Johns & Quay, 1962; Schacter & Latane, 1964). In summary, psychopaths are not defective in the learning of skills influenced by reward, but do appear to be deficient in learning influenced by punishment or threat of punishment.

Quay (1964) evaluated 115 delinquents on the basis of various behaviors noted in their case histories. Using factor analysis, a statistical procedure designed to summarize a large body of data into smaller dimensions, Quay found the following three types of delinquents:

1. Unsocialized psychopathic; characterized by defiance of authority and assaultiveness
2. Neurotic disturbed; characterized by shyness, worrying, and timidity
3. Subcultural socialized; characterized by gang activities, bad companions, and strong allegiance to select peers.

Quay and his associates have found the same three patterns of delinquency in a series of studies, and thus the pattern appears highly replicable (Peterson, Quay, & Cameron, 1959; Quay & Quay, 1965; Quay, 1972). The conditionability notions espoused by Eysenck do not account for the neurotic disturbed delinquent, who *is* influenced by praise and punishment (Quay, 1964), or the subcultural socialized delinquent. An approach to the etiology of delinquency that can account for these different "types" of delinquent behavior is the social learning approach. Although Eysenck (1964) certainly recognized and discussed the interaction of conditionability and socialization factors, Bandura and Walters (1963) were among the first proponents of an explicit socialization approach to delinquency based on modeling and reinforcement. In studies by Andry (1960), Bandura and Walters (1959), and McCord and McCord (1958), a pattern of parental rejection combined with

a criminal role model by the father or a harsh, punitive father has been found in aggressive or delinquent boys. Interestingly, while fathers of delinquent or aggressive boys often demand complete obedience at an early age at home, they simultaneously instruct their sons to "beat the tar out of anyone who aggresses against or crosses them." In addition, parents of delinquents provide models of physical aggression as they discipline their own children—contravening their very objectives. As Bandura and Walters stated, "If a parent punishes a child physically for having struck a neighbor's child, the intended outcome of the training is that the child should refrain from hitting others. Concurrently, with the intentional training, however, the parent is providing a model of the very behavior he is attempting to inhibit in the child. Consequently, when the child is thwarted, in subsequent social interactions, he may be more, rather than less, likely to respond in a physically aggressive manner" (pp. 68–69). In addition, Bandura and Walters (1963) explained that while punishment often works with other populations, it usually fails with delinquents because they have continuing models of delinquent behavior and/or a lack of prosocial modes, which lead to greater reinforcement than does their antisocial behavior.

In addition to the familial determinants of aggressive and delinquent behavior, Bandura (1973) has stressed the role of subcultural and community determinants of aggression. Of interest is his analysis of a social agency, namely the military establishment, which, he argues, can transform people who have been taught to abhor killing into combatants with little compassion for human life. In this regard, it has been found that the longer one was a Marine drill instructor at Paris Island, the more likely he was to physically aggress against his wife (Neidig, 1985). Finally, Bandura discussed the role of the mass media in providing repeated and novel forms of aggression and cited airline hijacking as an example of the role of aggression modeling.

Integrated Theoretical Stances

Rutter's (1984) stance on the etiology of delinquency places dual stress on biological and social determinants. Most important to Rutter is the criminality of the parent, which he believes has a predisposing genetic effect on offspring. Second, there is intrafamily discord as evidenced by frequent and prolonged quarreling, temporary or permanent home break-up, expressed hostility, and rejecting attitudes of the parents toward the children. Third, lack of family activities and a warm family atmosphere are held to be risk factors for delinquency. Fourth, harsh and inconsistent discipline along with lack of parental supervision will place a youth at risk for delinquency. The fifth risk factor is a negative peer group. As is evident from this position, which has been supported by research on risk factors, very similar points have been made regarding the etiology of conduct disorders, and as we have stated, some professionals believe that delinquents generally are antisocial children grown up.

Another theoretical stance regarding the etiology of delinquency was proposed by Patterson (1982), who presented a model to account for the etiological factors likely to lead to "social aggressors" and "stealers." The similarity between the social aggressor and the stealer is noncompliance. In brief, 89 percent of the parents of antisocial children report that the children are disobedient, and the rate of noncompliance of social aggressors and stealers was approximately 10 to 15 percent; the rate of noncompliance for normals is less than 5 percent. Another similarity of social aggressors and stealers is arrested socialization. These groups of children maximize short-term gains and ignore the long-term costs of

their actions. A third similarity that is especially frustrating for parents is reduced responsiveness to social reinforcers of parents and scolding. Finally, both social aggressors and stealers lack skill in peer relations and academic achievement.

Factors that differentiate the two groups are parental variables. Parents of social aggressors are more coercive; parents of stealers, particularly mothers, are more distant and less friendly. Further, parents of stealers ignore minor property violations, such as taking money from siblings or themselves.

There are children who are both socially aggressive and stealers. According to Patterson (1982), these children are from homes characterized by the worst features of the parents of both groups. As Patterson notes, "These parents are poorly motivated to do anything for the child, and they are irritable in their face to face contacts with [their children] . . . The parents are generally unskilled in their use of punishment. They are committed to the here and now. If the child steals from a neighbor, let the neighbor take care of himself, but do not *bother* the parent. If the child is making noise, yell at him until he stops" p. 249.

Social and Academic Risk Factors

As we noted in the introduction to this chapter, treatment programs for delinquents have been largely unsuccessful. Henn, Bardwell, and Jenkins (1980) proposed that this lack of efficacy could be due to a failure to differentiate types of delinquents. They separated 207 delinquents into undersocialized aggressives, undersocialized unaggressives, and socialized delinquents, and followed them ten years after their discharge from a detention facility. As predicted, the socialized delinquents corresponding to Quay's subcultural socialized delinquents had much less chance of being imprisoned. The differentiating characteristics of the groups were whether or not the youths had developed a caring feeling for others and whether or not there was a loyalty to a group. This research fits well both in terms of sociological (especially Cohen's "subcultural" theory of delinquency) and social learning theories of delinquency.

Finally, poor academic performance, school truancy, and dropping out of school are good predictors of later delinquent behavior (Elliot, 1966). In fact, the delinquency rate for school dropouts is ten times greater than for nondropouts (Knopf, 1979).

TREATMENT

Employment and Diversion Programs

A novel approach to the modification of delinquent behavior was developed by Slack (1960) and expanded by Schwitzgebel and Kolb (1964). Twenty boys ranging in age from 15 to 21 with an average of 15.1 months of incarceration and 8.2 arrests were treated and compared with a control group matched for age of first offense, type of offense, nationality, religious preference, and length of incarceration. The treatment was described to the delinquent youths as an experiment whose purpose was to find out how teenagers feel about things, how they arrive at certain opinions, and how they change. One specific "job" of the delinquent was to talk into a tape recorder for which he was paid one dollar per hour. In response to requests for work, the youths were given jobs answering correspondence or building electronic equipment. Termination of employment was gradual and individual; if a youth got an outside job which went well, the interviews were gradually dropped. If an outside job went poorly, interviews were increased. Generally, youths

were associated with the project for ten months.

The youths employed by the project showed an average of 2.4 arrests three years following project termination; control youths, on the other hand, averaged 4.7 arrests. The project youths averaged 3.5 months of incarceration whereas the control youths averaged 6.9 months of incarceration. Unfortunately, the *number* of persons returned to prison or a reformatory did not differ. In brief, the project was associated with a reduction but not an elimination of delinquent behavior. Of note, however, is the fact that the youths who participated in the experimental project seemed to have less serious offenses and were arrested less frequently.

A natural extension of the approach taken by Schwitzgebel and Kolb was the diversion program in which a youth was diverted from the court into programs emphasizing education, job training, peer counseling, and family involvement. One of the goals of the program was to avoid stigmatization and labeling as a juvenile delinquent. A second goal was minimizing the learning of the culture of crime apparent in facilities for delinquents and jails. There is obvious appeal of these programs to parents, offenders, and legal authorities. They are less costly and they offer the promise of learning new skills without being enmeshed in the crime culture of penal institutions. While there are some reports of success with these diversion programs, it appears that the programs have not reliably fulfilled their original goals of reducing criminal behavior (Lemert, 1981).

Case I and Case II

One of the pioneering efforts to deal with delinquents was made by Cohen, Filipczak, and Bis (1967) in a project called CASE I (Contingencies Applicable for Special Education) at the National Training School for

Boys in Washington, DC. The youths at the National Training School were generally dropouts with crime records including rape, auto theft, and homicide. Sixteen delinquents were involved in a special education day program for six months in which they earned points exchangeable for edibles, items from the Sears Roebuck catalog, time in a lounge, or use of a telephone. All points were earned for studying and achieving 90 percent accuracy on programmed academic materials. The four-and-one-half-month, half-day program resulted in academic gains, as reflected on standardized tests, ranging from nine months to one year and seven months.

The success of this program convinced Cohen and his associates that a twenty-four-hour program (CASE II) would be a logical next step. Though the Training School was a penal institution, choice in CASE II was maximized and arbitrary orders from authority figures were kept to a minimum. To emphasize choice the boys could buy or rent a large number of items, e.g., a private room could be rented and special meals, clothing, and room furnishings could be purchased. Alternatively, if they chose, they could also go on relief, eat standard institutional food, and wear standard institutional clothing. It should be emphasized that the rewards were things other than those provided by the institution, e.g., money, special clothes, bed, and meals; no privileges, food, or beds available to other youths in the school were withdrawn. The goals of this second program (CASE II) were to prepare as many students as possible for public school within one year. The forty-one young men in the program ranged in age from 14 to 18 (mean 16.9) and had been convicted of homicide, rape, automobile thefts, and housebreaking (see Table 7–1). A major way a student-inmate could earn points for money was by studying. As Cohen and Filipczak (1971) put it, the model was "that of a student re-

Table 7–1 Offenses Committed by Case II Students

TYPE OF OFFENSE	CASE II POPULATION	
	Number	Per Cent
Dyer Act (auto theft)	18	43.9
Housebreaking	4	9.8
Postal violations	2	4.9
Petty larceny	3	7.3
Robbery	3	7.3
Assault	3	7.3
Homicide	1	2.4
Other	7	17.1
Totals	41	100.0

From Cohen and Filipczak, *A New Learning Environment* (1971), p. 62. Reprinted by permission of Jossey-Bass, Inc.

search employee who checks in and out of various activities for which he is paid or for which he pays. As a Student Educational Researcher, the student was hired to do a job and paid to learn." In addition, in CASE II, a student-inmate could receive points for exemplary social behavior from officers. A learning environment which guaranteed privacy was available so students could work on self-contained, programmed instructional materials.

The rate of gain in grade levels per year as reflected on standardized achievement tests (Stanford Achievement Test, SAT) was 1.5 or 2.0, depending upon the particular SAT series given. CASE students stayed out of trouble longer than a similar group processed by the National Training School. The first year following release the recidivism rate was two-thirds less than the norm for inmates at the National Training School. Unfortunately, by the third year the total rate of recidivism appeared to be near the norm. As the investigators concluded, CASE delayed the delinquents' return to incarceration, but a special program to maintain their lawful behavior is necessary for the CASE program to have effects after one year. They concluded that "the only effective approach to juvenile delinquency is the development of effective academic and interpersonal programs within our nation's public schools. We must stop building prisons for youths and begin investing our funds and energy to establish preventive systems within our present ongoing schools and community centers" (p. 143). As we shall see, Cohen moved in just that direction, but it should also be emphasized that Cohen and Filipczak were dealing with young men with much more serious offenses than are seen in most studies presented in this chapter. To deal with some convicted offenders an alternative or supplement to changing our school programs is probably necessary, specifically devising programs to maintain lawful behavior outside our institutions. If any theme is apparent in this evaluation of the outcome of present treatment research, it is that maintenance programs are necessary to maintain behavior changes made during treatment. This fact is as true for programs working with delinquents as it is for those dealing with autistic children, alcoholics, and hospitalized schizophrenics.

At the Institute for Behavioral Research in Silver Spring, Maryland, Cohen (1972) developed an academic, vocational, and interpersonal curriculum to teach delinquent youths skills that allow them to compete for accepted societal rewards. Cohen's basic conceptualization of the law-abiding and delinquent behavior is reflected in the following quotation, "Simplistically, the reason most people do not steal to gain their reinforcement is that the present aversive control system—religious moral codes, with their delayed payoffs; police, law, and courts with their delayed payoffs—directs them to seek safer means of getting their rewards. However, this controllable group (the law-abiding citizen) does have other repertoires to gain success and a large enough payoff. Since most of the youthful offenders we have worked with do not have a variety of rational options open to them (such as employable skills, which have a high payoff) they resort to the one choice they are equipped to use—unlawful behavior" (p. 67). The program attempted to reverse the values between the rewards associated with unlawful behavior and those associated with lawful behavior in a half-day, out-of-school program with participants described as predelinquent and emotionally disturbed. They were referred because of disruptive in-school behavior, minimal in-school academic performance, and delinquent community activities. The delinquent youths were in a half-day, out-of-school program and spent the other half of the day in their respective schools in Washington and suburban Maryland. In addition, there was a parent program and a program operative in the schools to help maintain their appropriate school behavior. The morning out-of-school program comprised the bulk of the academic and vocational remediation (and will receive emphasis here). Approximately seventy-five self-instructional courses were available for subjects in grades two through twelve in reading, mathematics, and language. A specially designed automated assessment apparatus was built to teach study skills, such as paying attention and working quickly and accurately. Each student had a private study carrel with accommodated automated programmed learning equipment. At the end of each day a youth was paid a certain amount of money if he completed his educational program at the specified criterion level. One year of the morning remedial program was associated with relatively strong gains in reading and math (1.55 and 1.53 years, respectively), and a mean nine-point increase in IQ scores. Using the youths as their own controls, one other pre-post comparison is of particular interest. During the year of their enrollment in the special program, each student averaged two suspensions from his regular school; whereas the previous year, they had each received an average of ten suspensions. Although there were no matched control data reported, and it was not clear how much professional time per child was necessary to exact these changes, this study is another example of how delinquent youths can be motivated to succeed academically.

Behavioral Contracting

Behavioral contracting is a means of scheduling the exchange of positive reinforcements between two or more people (Stuart, 1971). It increases positive interchanges by assigning responsibilities or duties to various people for which they receive certain privileges. Contracts have been used in behavioral treatment programs for delinquents and other children for years. An example of a behavioral contract for a sixteen-year-old girl, Candy, referred by a juvenile court for promiscuity,

exhibitionism, drug abuse, and truancy is depicted in Table 7–2.

Contracts are renegotiated as necessary to ensure positive attitudes and mutually positive reinforcing effects for all concerned. In fact, the contract depicted here is the second of Candy's contracts. She had become so aversive to her parents that they had sought to have the court assume wardship over her, and in the initial contract they wished to establish virtually total control over Candy's behavior. Although the therapist believed that the parents were expecting too much and that this was too large an initial treatment step, efforts to modify their expectations failed. Within three weeks of the initiation of the contract, Candy was sneaking out of her bedroom window at night, visiting a local commune, and returning home before dawn. Over a twenty-four-day period, it was found that there were eight major contract violations, and thus the contract had to be renegotiated. The more permissive contract (Table 7–2) was thus

Table 7–2 Behavioral Contracting Within the Families of Delinquents

PRIVILEGES	RESPONSIBILITIES
General In exchange for the privilege of remaining together and preserving some semblance of family integrity, Mr. and Mrs. Bremer and Candy all agree to	concentrate on positively reinforcing each other's behavior while diminishing the present overemphasis upon the faults of the others.
Specific In exchange for the privilege of riding the bus directly from school into town after school on school days	Candy agrees to phone her father by 4:00 p.m. to tell him that she is all right and to return home by 5:15 p.m.
In exchange for the privilege of going out at 7:00 p.m. on one weekend evening without having to account for her whereabouts	Candy must maintain a weekly average of "B" in the academic ratings of all her classes and must return home by 11:30 p.m.

Table 7–2 Behavioral Contracting Within The Families of Delinquents (*cont.*)

PRIVILEGES	RESPONSIBILITIES
In exchange for the privilege of going out a second weekend night	Candy must tell her parents *by 6:00 p.m.* of her destination and her companion and must return home by 11:30 p.m.
In exchange for the privilege of going out between 11:00 a.m. and 5:15 p.m. Saturdays, Sundays, and holidays	Candy agrees to have completed all household chores *before* leaving and to telephone her parents once during the time she is out to tell them that she is all right.
In exchange for the privilege of having Candy complete household chores and maintain her curfew	Mr. and Mrs. Bremer agree to pay Candy $1.50 on the morning following days on which the money is earned.
Bonuses and Sanctions If Candy is 1–10 minutes late	she must come in the same amount of time earlier the following day, but she does not forfeit her money for the day.
If Candy is 11–30 minutes late	she must come in 22–60 minutes earlier the following day and does not forfeit her money for the day.
If Candy is 31–60 minutes late	she loses the privilege of going out the following day and does not forfeit her money for the day.
For each half hour of tardiness over one hour, Candy	loses her privileges of going out and her money for one additional day.
Candy may go out on Sunday evenings from 7:00 to 9:30 p.m. and either Monday or Thursday evening	if she abides by all the terms of this contract from Sunday through Saturday with a total tardiness not exceeding 30 minutes which must have been made up as above.
Candy may add a total of two hours divided among one to three curfews	if she abides by all the terms of this contract for two weeks with a total tardiness not exceeding 30 minutes which must have been made up as above and if she requests permission to use this additional time by 9:00 p.m.

Monitoring

Mr. and Mrs. Bremer agree to keep written records of the hours of Candy's leaving and coming home and of the completion of her chores.

Candy agrees to furnish her parents with a school monitoring card each Friday at dinner.

From: Stuart, Behavioral contract, *Journal of Behavior Therapy and Experimental Psychiatry*. (1971) 2.9. Reprinted by permission of Pergamon Press.

negotiated, but it prompted some strong consequences for other people. A court order was obtained by her therapist which forbade Candy from entering the commune. Should she do so, the commune members, not Candy, would be liable to prosecution for contributing to the delinquency of a minor. This contract with its associated contingency for the commune members was quite effective in terms of increasing compliance. Though the contract itself cannot, of course, account for the change in Candy's behavior, it was very helpful in tempering fights because of options made available through negotiations and it ensured privileges such as free time and money contingencies. Stuart recommends that behavioral contracting be supplemented by interaction training for parents, and tutoring or vocational guidance for the youth.

The effects of behavioral contracting for youths who were very disruptive in school and who, in some instances, had prior court contacts were described by Stuart and Tripodi (1973). The exact nature of the offenses and the number of court contacts were not specified. Though the youths were described as predelinquents or delinquents, the total number of prior court contacts for seventy-nine cases was only thirteen, and some of these may have resulted from repeated contacts by an individual youth. Seventy-nine youths and their families were offered contingency treatment of three different time lengths: fifteen, forty-five, or ninety days. The actual number of therapist direct-contact and phone hours with the school and family in the treatments was, on the average, ten hours, sixteen hours, and twenty-eight hours, respectively. The three treatments did not differ with respect to effects on ten dependent measures, including school attendance, tardiness, grades, court contacts, attitudes, or parental evaluation. However, when the treated youths were compared to a group who

declined treatment, the treated youths fared much better in school grades and attendance. While the utilization of control subjects who decline treatment (defectors) is fraught with problems of possible different motivations and types of youths, it should be emphasized that the effort of Stuart and Tripodi was an initial step, and the major evaluations were concerned with a comparison of differing treatment lengths. As Stuart and Tripodi (1973) emphasized, there is some evidence suggesting that short-duration experimental treatments are more effective than longer term treatments with youths in correctional settings, adult neuropsychiatric patients, and social work clients in traditional family service settings. More work of this evaluative nature is sorely needed, because we must be attuned to the possibility that treatments may in fact be iatrogenic, i.e., they may produce adverse effects. For example, a therapist may delve into family problems to justify his continued efforts when in fact further consultation may be of no avail and may deplete the client's finances. Furthermore, though not documented in the Stuart and Tripodi study, it may actually be deleterious to unearth family problems with delinquent youths once day-to-day family conflicts have been resolved.

Contracting as a therapeutic approach has undergone significant changes since its development in the late 1960s. With delinquents and adult offenders, various stages of contracting have been used (Pokalow & Doctor, 1974). More specifically, precontractual agreements are first used in which participants make a material contribution to the program (e.g., a sum of money or a highly valued object). Secondly, the contract enters a managerial phase in which an individualized behavior program is designed in areas such as job procurement and drug abstinence. Third, a transitional contract is written as a means of reducing structure and increasing individual responsibility for the participants. In marital therapy, as will be evident in Chapter 12, there also has been some use of behavioral contracts. However, there is ample clinical evidence that perception of external control of a partner's behavior makes change in the partner's behavior less desirable. Our opinion is that even with delinquents, where more structure may be necessary than with marital problems, the less focus on behavioral control by clearly perceived external constraints the better.

Family Intervention

An interesting family intervention approach for delinquents was successfully employed by Alexander and Parsons (1973). In prior family interaction studies it was found that deviant families, compared to normal families, are more silent, talk less equally, have fewer positive interruptions, and are less active (Alexander, 1970; Stuart, 1968). The treatment goal was thus to increase what Patterson and Reid (1970) describe as reciprocity in the family, i.e., to increase the mutual reinforcement among family members. Patterson and Reid had already demonstrated that when the amount of mutual positive reinforcement in a family with aggressive boys is altered, the frequency of problem behavior decreases. Thus, increases in mutual reinforcement were a decided goal of the treatment program in which therapists modeled, prompted, and reinforced the following in all family members: "(a) clear communication of substance as well as feelings, and (b) clear presentation of 'demands' and alternative solutions; all leading to (c) negotiation, with each family member receiving some privilege for each responsibility assumed, to the point of compromise."

To reach these goals, facilitation of communication was achieved by differentiating rules from requests—the former often being too rigid and frequent in homes of delinquents. Second, family members were trained in solution-oriented communication patterns while they negotiated the specific content of the rules and token reinforcement programs involving an exchange of behaviors, e.g., when a youth agreed to help a parent with some chores, the parent might offer to take the youth and his friends to the bowling alley.

The therapists consisted of eighteen first- and second-year graduate students who had been trained for six hours in this specific family interaction model and who received weekly supervision. The delinquent youths, ranging in age from 13 to 16, were randomly assigned (with some exceptions) to a client-centered family therapy, a psychodynamic family therapy, the behavioral intervention program previously described, or a no-treatment control group. The client-centered therapy focused largely on group discussions of feeling and attitudes regarding the family and was implemented by two therapists hired by the court. The psychodynamic therapy was implemented by a local church group and "insight" was its primary goal. The delinquent youths had been arrested or detained at a juvenile court for offenses such as running away, truancy, shoplifting, and possession of alcohol, soft drugs, or tobacco.

Follow-up data taken six to eighteen months following the termination of the treatment, generally lasting twelve to fifteen sessions, revealed the following recidivism or rearrest rates: behavioral treatment, 26 percent; client-centered treatment, 47 percent; psychodynamic therapy, 73 percent; no-treatment controls, 50 percent. Related to the original therapeutic goals, it was also found that lack of offenses (nonrecidivism) in the behavioral treatment group was related to more talking in the family, more interruptions (presumably positive), and more equality of talk time among family members. In brief, the treatment was significantly related to a reduction in crime and increased reciprocity of reinforcement. While this study contained a number of problems—such as different therapists giving different treatment, unequal treatment lengths, and unspecified alternative treatments (e.g., client-centered and psychodynamic treatment)—it has several interesting implications. First, compared to existing treatments made available by courts or churches, this treatment was superior. Though not mentioned by the authors, the psychodynamically oriented approach was associated with an increase in criminal behavior. Compared to the no-treatment control group recidivism rate (50 percent) or the county-wide recidivism rate (51 percent), the psychodynamic therapy recidivism rate was 73 percent. Though the number of cases was small in the psychodynamic group, these figures should alert one to the possibility that certain forms of treatment may actually be harmful. Finally, though this study is clearly an initial exploratory attempt in the development of an intervention program, the investigators have developed a training manual for therapists so that other researchers or mental health personnel can replicate their work. In addition, an extension of this work by Klein, Alexander, and Parsons (1977) indicates that siblings of the initially referred delinquents had less contact with the courts than did siblings from other treated groups or nontreated controls.

Patterson and Reid (1973) provided evidence that behavioral intervention with families of aggressive boys was successful in significantly reducing deviant behavior in the homes of eleven families. Although the boys were not described as delinquent, stealing was of concern to five of the eleven parents. The median age of the boys was seven years and all had a history of high rates of aggressive behavior. The basic treatment consisted of an instructional program for the teachers (*Living with Children* by Patterson & Gullion, 1968), a token reinforcement program for the children, removal of the child from the classroom or main area of the room for hitting, and a contract system developed with the consent of the parents, teachers, and school administration. In 31.4 hours of professional time per case, there was an observed reduction of 61 percent of targeted behavior (aggression, noncompliance, and teasing). Furthermore, after termination of treatment, eight of the ten mothers contacted reported that their child had improved markedly, eight felt that their family on the whole began to function better, and seven reported that their sons were more happy at home.

Of special interest was a subsequent analysis of twenty-five cases of hyper-aggressive boys by Reid and Hendricks (1973). They found that although the intervention was effective on the average, those boys reported to steal (N = 14) were helped less than nonstealers. With a criterion of success of 33 percent reduction in rate of deviant behaviors from baseline, six of the fourteen stealers compared to nine of the eleven nonstealers were categorized as successes. The parents of boys who had records of stealing were "dismally" unmotivated. Of the twenty-seven most recent stealing referrals to Reid and Hendricks, only five of the referrals actually began treatment. The parents phoned to request treatment immediately following the legal apprehension, but they then missed the initial appointment or cancelled it. There was a great deal of family disorganization, and the boys were usually unsupervised for long periods each day. The difficulties encountered by these investigators point to the need for alternative programs for families with boys who steal.

The effects of treatment programs for stealers have been less positive than the effects of treatment programs for aggressive children and adolescents. The parents were highly unmotivated and they had relatively little concern for property violations: e.g., taking money from mothers' purses. There were reductions in stealing in the family and neighborhood associated with a program designed to teach parent management skills (Reid, Hinojosa-Rivero, & Lorber, 1980). However, the parents did not continue to apply family management practices and follow-ups indicate that 64 percent of the children were chronic offenders (Patterson, 1982).

Achievement Place

The most comprehensive behavioral treatment evaluations of delinquency programs have been made of "Achievement Place," a family-style residential treatment program for pre-delinquent youths. Achievement Place homes consist of a home in a residential community, two parents, and seven or eight boys or girls between twelve and sixteen years of age. The youths are referred to Achievement Place by a Juvenile Court of the Department of Social Welfare. The development of the treatment model started with boys and a married couple, Elery and Elaine Phillips, who were then trained at the masters level in behavior modification procedures, juvenile law, community relations, and remedial education techniques. Because of their professional expertise they were called "teaching parents." Since the development of the first Achievement Place in Lawrence, Kansas, in 1967, 150 homes had been established in the United States as of 1980 (Howard, Jones, & Weinrott, 1982).

The delinquent behavior of the youths in Achievement Place homes has been viewed as the product of inadequate social learning experience. As Phillips, Phillips, Fixsen, and Wolf (1971) stated, "The cause of this disturbing behavior is that the past environment of youths has failed to provide the instruc-

tions, examples, and feedback necessary to develop appropriate behavior . . . and this general behavior failure often forces the youth to become increasingly dependent upon a deviant peer group which provides inappropriate instructions, models, and reinforcement that further expand the behavior problems." In order to correct the behavioral deficiencies of the delinquent youth, a very strong comprehensive token reinforcement system was established to develop specific social skills, such as manners and introductions, academic skills, and personal hygiene habits. Unlike many treatment programs with global aims, the specific treatment objectives were enumerated in great detail. In fact, 188 behaviors for which points could be earned appeared in the Achievement Place manual.

The specific goals of the treatment program are realized through a token reinforcement program based on levels in which behavior is initially very heavily reinforced; later the material reinforcers are gradually diminished as the youth develops desired behavior. The myriad privileges that a boy or girl can buy can be classified under the following general headings:

1. Basics: use of tools, games, and recreation area, and outside privileges
2. Snacks: after school and before bedtime
3. Away Time: permission to leave Achievement Place to go home, downtown, or to a sports event
4. "Allowance": points exchangeable for $1 to $2 per week
5. Bonds: savings for gifts and special clothing
6. Special Privileges: point price negotiable.

Essentially, a youth moves from a system of immediate, concrete rewards to rewards which are remote and common in his or her natural environment. Initially, a youth is placed on a Daily Point System which involves a point card on which he is to record the points given him by the teaching parents. All privileges are free the first day; later he has to earn his privileges, and if he does not display enough desired behavior on the Daily Point System, he is placed on a six-hour, three-hour, or even a one-hour system. As the youth earns points consistently for one week on the Daily Point System, he advances to the Weekly Point System, in which he accumulates points for one week and buys his privileges for the following week. Throughout the Achievement Place Program, a youth can both earn and lose points (a reward and cost system). However, because there are a host of ways in which a youth can earn points, the point losses do not necessarily result in a loss of privileges. In addition, he can always be returned to a former level of the system if he does not succeed at the level to which he has advanced.

In order to integrate study behavior and school behavior, a daily report card is given to the youth's teacher, on which she checks whether or not the youth did his assigned work and obeyed the class rules (Bailey, Wolf, & Phillips, 1970). Later a youth advances to a Merit System after four straight weeks of a desired behavior on the Weekly System. The Merit System is a testing condition in which all privileges are free and in which the youth's behavior is assessed carefully to ascertain whether these behaviors are maintained in the absence of the contingent tangible reinforcers. It is hoped that the praise, approval, and affection of the teaching parents as well as the peer environment will maintain appropriate behavior. Finally, after four weeks of success on the Merit System, the youth advances to the Homeward Bound System, in which he moves from Achievement Place to his own home. Under the supervision of the teaching parents, the youth and his parents negotiate a behavioral contract which

specifies desired behaviors at home and associated privileges that the youth can earn by displaying such behaviors. During the first few weeks of the Homeward Bound System, a youth spends one or two nights or days each week at Achievement Place to discuss any problems he may be having at home. Weekly meetings with parents are reduced to monthly meetings, and after six months to one year, the consultation meetings are discontinued unless there is a problem.

The majority of the original research publications evaluating Achievement Place were individual subject designs (ABAB) or variants thereof. Using such designs Phillips (1968) showed that aggressive statements of three boys were reliably reduced when a fine was made contingent upon each aggressive statement. Verbal reprimands and threats, however, did not decrease such statements. Use of the word "ain't" (Phillips, 1968) and promptness at dinner (Phillips, Phillips, Fixsen, & Wolf, 1971) were also controlled by fines. Bathroom cleaning was also shown to be reliably related to reward and point consequences of the reinforcement system (Phillips, 1968). Although bathroom cleaning may be regarded as nonessential (Phillips, Wolf, & Fixsen, 1973), it allowed the investigators to evaluate the effects of various types of administrative systems at Achievement Place. Bathroom cleaning occurred every day, could be easily recorded, and since it was not a critical behavior, the investigators could permit it to be investigated. From an ethical standpoint, experiments on behaviors of the delinquent youths, such as stealing or aggressing in the classroom, could not have been easily conducted using reversal designs. Therefore, other target behaviors were selected in order to evaluate the effectiveness of varied interventions in changing such behaviors.

A number of arrangements for assigning

Figure 7–1 Youth at Achievement Place group meeting where the peer manager is elected. (Courtesy of Elery L. Phillips).

routine bathroom cleaning chores were compared for their effectiveness in accomplishing the tasks and for their preference by the boys. Among the comparisons studied were (1) assigning tasks to individuals versus assigning tasks to groups, (2) reward and cost consequences for individuals versus groups, and (3) a peer managership which could be earned either by the highest bidder or determined by peers (see Figure 7–1). The system that was both effective and preferred by the youths involved a democratically elected peer manager who had the authority both to give and take away points for his peers' performances (see Table 7–3). As the authors noted, the elected manager system was probably preferred because mutual contingencies were operative under this system, i.e., the manager had immediate contingencies which he could effect on his "workers" and they had the contingency—albeit more remote—of not reelecting the manager if he did not treat them fairly.

Thirteen Achievement Place models were compared with nine comparison group homes by Kirigin, Braukman, Atwater, and Wolf

(1982). The evaluation consisted of during- and post-treatment effectiveness of the Achievement Place and comparison group

Table 7–3 Preferences for Various Systems of Assessing Tasks and Delivery of Consequences

SYSTEM	PREFERENCE RANK
Elected Manager (±500)*	1
Individual Assignment-Individual Consequence (+500)	2
Individual Assignment-Individual Consequence (±500)	3
Elected Manager (+500)	4
Purchased Manager (±500)	5
Purchased Manager (+500)	6

Redrawn from, Phillips et al., *Journal of Applied Behavior Analysis*, (1973), 556.

*Pluses and minuses refer to the opportunity to reward (+) and subtract (−) points.

homes with regard to police and court records and consumer evaluations. In order to assess consistency in thirteen Achievement Place programs, a year-long, in-service training sequence was developed which consisted of two one-week workshops, frequent telephone and periodic in-home consultation sessions, and regular formal evaluations. All homes selected for evaluation were in Kansas because the major research evaluation team was located in Lawrence, Kansas. The comparison homes were selected by two Kansas state agencies as homes they considered representative of residential programs. There were 140 youths (102 boys, 38 girls) in the Achievement Place homes and 52 youths (22 boys, 30 girls) in the comparison homes. All homes served court-adjudicated youths between 12 and 16 years of age; the mean age of first offense was between 12 and 14. During treatment, the Achievement Place youths had fewer alleged criminal offenses, and consumer evaluations (e.g., by the youths and their teachers) favored the Achievement Place model. Unfortunately, in the post-treatment year none of the differences between the groups was maintained. In a subsequent study by Kirigin, Braukman, Wolf, and associates, approximately 160 Achievement Place youths were compared with approximately 200 comparison group youths from various group homes.[2] Like the previous study, during the stay of the youths at Achievement Place or the alternative group homes, the Achievement Place youths had fewer official offenses and fewer self-reported offenses than youths in the alternative homes. As in the previous study, however, there were no differential effects one year post-treatment.

Howard, Jones, and Weinrott (1982) also compared Achievement Place homes (N = 25)

2. Personal communication, K. Kirigin, November 1985.

for predelinquent and delinquent youths. The Achievement Place youths fared no better during- or post-treatment on most measures of self-reported or official delinquency, drug use, performance in school, or self-esteem. However, on ratings of various dimensions regarding the intervention, the Achievement Place homes had higher scores than the comparison homes. Howard and colleagues (1982) interpreted the differences as reflecting differences in the likeability of Achievement Place staff. More specifically, Achievement Place house parents are taught to keep open lines of communication with various agencies, to make school visits, and to have frequent parent conferences. Even though there were no differences in legal offense rates, these rating differences are important in that a program that is positively evaluated by consumers, court officials, and community board members is more likely to be maintained than one which does not receive such evaluations. While the global evaluations favor Achievement Place homes, one should not discount the failure to find differences in offense rates. Numerous therapies with no scientific validity have been liked by patients or clients, and an ultimate decision regarding effectiveness has to be based in part on offense rates.

The current strategy of the Achievement Place research team is to provide very systematic aftercare following a stay at the family-style setting. More specifically, the parents or parent-surrogates of the delinquent are taught parenting skills and communication strategies. This effort has not yet been experimentally evaluated, and we do not know that residence in an Achievement Place home itself is necessary before parent training. However, since Achievement Place has been the subject of more studies than any other behaviorally oriented treatment program for delinquents during the past two decades, it will be especially interesting to see if their treatment effects can be maintained with aftercare for the year following treatment.

An interesting alternative to group homes is to provide intensive home-based programs. Barnard, Gant, Kuehn, et al. (1986) had juvenile offenders randomly assigned to a behavioral consultation program for families or to traditional juvenile court services. The court-adjudicated youths had committed one or more juvenile code violations which would not result in out-of-home placement. All youths were first-time offenders. The intervention implemented by the juvenile court services included psychotherapy at a local mental health center and probation officer monitoring. The latter involved informal counseling, curfew

setting, limits regarding school attendance, and consequences for violating municipal and state ordinances. In the behavioral consultation program, the youth did not have contact with the probation department; instead, all contacts were with the behavioral consultation staff. Treatment generally involved the entire family and was carried out in the family's home. Emphasis was placed on the problem being a family problem rather than focusing on the youth as "the problem." The general strategy was to teach the families ways in which they could overcome skill deficiencies (e.g., interacting with peers appropriately and informing parents of their plans, and negotiating compromises with parents re-

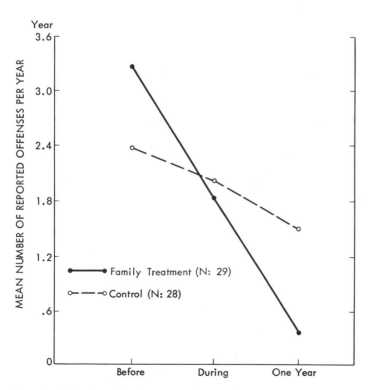

Figure 7–2 From Barnard et al. (1986). Home-based treatment of juvenile probationers. Unpublished manuscript; University of Kansas, Lawrence, Kansas.

garding rules and limits). Parents received consultation about being fair, consistently enforcing household rules, and finding opportunities to be positive to family members. A home token reinforcement system was also used to provide consistent feedback and motivation. Youths earned points for studying, attending school, completing chores, and interacting pleasantly with family members. Points were lost for not coming home on time, not picking up after themselves, and backtalking. Points were exchangeable for use of the family car, extra money, television privileges, and late curfews.

The youths who received the behavioral treatment program had significantly fewer offenses during treatment and one year after than the youths who received traditional court services (see Figure 7–2). In addition, fewer youths in the behavioral consultation program were readjudicated by the court. The actual time spent in active treatment and number of contacts with counselors differed markedly between the two groups. While the average length of time in treatment for both groups was seven months, the mean number of contacts the youths had with the behavioral consultation staff and the traditional services staff was fifty-one and sixteen, respectively. A further complication in interpreting these results is that many parents were uncooperative in completing testing evaluations, and therefore rendered checklist data on parent evaluation of the program and child behavior problems uninterpretable. Despite the methodological problems of this study, it does provide a good example of how interventions can be delivered to families without placement in residential homes. Placement in residential homes often provides a youth with the opportunity to learn bad habits from other offenders, and when parents can provide some stability for children who have had initial

scrapes with the law, the model seems quite useful.

SUMMARY

Unlike many other problems discussed in this book, the incidence of delinquency in both rural and urban settings is dramatically increasing. Delinquency is becoming a problem of younger children, of females as well as males, and of all social classes. The development of delinquent behavior is undoubtedly a multidetermined problem. Biological factors such as the XYY syndrome may be critically influential in certain, though admittedly few, instances. Sociological factors, such as a delinquent subculture, are influential in others. Psychological factors, including parental rejection, parental modeling of criminal or aggressive behavior (if only blatant cheating on income tax), vicarious reinforcement of criminal behavior as depicted on the public media, and lowered fear conditionability are variously influential in other cases. At this point, there is no single unifying theory to adequately explain criminal behavior; rather, the biological, sociological, and psychological principles mentioned above probably account for delinquent behavior in certain situations but not others.

Nonetheless, a number of successful treatments have been derived from psychological learning theory which have led to lowered recidivism, greater school attendance, improved academic performance, and improved family relations.[3] Although the problem for which a youth is referred for treatment is criminal behavior, it has been emphasized that the behavior therapist does not simply

3. See Stumphauzer, 1979, for a collection of behavior therapy approaches to delinquency.

deal with the referring problem. Rather, the treatment is based on the premise that the youth does not have the requisite social, academic, or vocational skills to enable him to obtain, in a socially appropriate fashion, rewards as great as those he can obtain through criminal behavior. As such, the treatment may involve a long-term program including the following components: (1) teaching basic academic skills such as reading and mathematics, (2) teaching certain manners or roles to adopt when dealing with parents and other authority figures, (3) teaching parents and the youths to interact in a way that will allow mutual rewards, (4) occasionally securing financial assistance for a family via social agencies, and finally (5) providing a trusting and supporting relationship with someone so that the youth feels he can rely on that person to discuss difficulties. As with many other problems, no single solution exists, and the greater the multitude of interventions, the more likely the problem will be ameliorated.

Although other types of behavior problems have been successfully changed by behavioral interventions without explicit programs designed to maintain the behavior, explicit programs should be provided for maintaining the appropriate behavior changes obtained in delinquency treatment. The rewards associated with criminal behavior are often potent, immediate, and difficult to resist in the presence of others who ascribe to such a life. Consequently, when intervention programs are devised, they should probably be built in such a fashion that they can be very gradually withdrawn and maintenance procedures implemented.

Criminal behavior in youths is very difficult to change, and it appears that behavior therapists should concern themselves with varying theoretical conceptualizations of crime and multidisciplinary efforts. Our attempts to produce long-term change of adolescents who have been placed in institutions or foster facilities have proven effective but time-limited. As Nietzel (1979) argued, behavioral psychologists have generally not applied their efforts at reducing crime in the communities and settings where the crime occurs. Much more work is needed at the preventative level (e.g., prevention of shoplifting, library theft, and physical assaults) and at analyses of the problems of our legal system (e.g., length of time from arraignment to trial, effects of reparations rather than incarcerations for youths, and programs for first offenders).

Attempts to fit restitutive punishment to a particular transgression have been reasonably successful with both clinical and normal populations. Basically, the offender is requested to engage in restitution of some form while also being taught social skills, perhaps community service in one form or another, such as having a driving while intoxicated (DWI) offender spend significant time in hospital accident wards with patients who have been hospitalized because of auto accidents. The punishment for stealing from an elderly person may involve aiding the elderly by serving meals to house-ridden individuals. According to Martin (1981), offenders generally regard restitution to be an acceptable sanction and performance of restitutive contracts is reasonably high. Such punishments are certainly deserving of very systematic evaluation, especially in recidivism rates.

A sobering but important caution mentioned by Nietzel (1979) is in order as we conclude. "All crimes will not be prevented. Nor will all criminals be cured. . . ." We need to develop programs for offenders who are entitled to rehabilitation that are "neither coercive, punitive, nor unduly restrictive but which encourage their well-informed, active participation" (pp. 254–255).

Anxiety Disorders—I

8

THE PSYCHODYNAMIC APPROACH

The traditional psychodynamic approach regards anxiety as the common mainspring of all neurotic[1] (anxiety) disorders. It is said to be unconsciously and indirectly controlled by a variety of different defense mechanisms, such as repression and displacement. These defenses are said to prevent intrapsychic conflicts and unconscious impulses from threatening the conscious portion of the personality by allowing them indirect and symbolic expression in overt behavior.

It follows from this psychodynamic framework that therapy has to be directed toward resolving the fundamental unconscious conflicts, of which the overt behavior problems are merely symptomatic. This explains why, with rare exceptions (e.g., Klein, Zitrin, Woerner, & Ross, 1983), traditional psycho-

therapy has discouraged attempts to modify phobic and other anxiety disorders directly, in contrast to behavior therapy.

BEHAVIORAL ANALYSES

In the original behavioral formulation, phobic anxiety was viewed as a classically conditioned response (Eysenck, 1960; Wolpe, 1958). (A good example of this formulation was the conditioning analysis of the acquisition of fears by little Albert, discussed in Chapter 3 above.) Subsequently, both research and clinical practice revealed major inadequacies of the classical conditioning model. Currently, two major views about anxiety can be identified within behavior therapy: the three-systems model (Hugdahl, 1981) and social learning theory (Bandura, 1977a).

The Three-Systems Model

Anxiety is a hypothetical construct, not an entity or "lump" (Lang, 1971). Rather, anxiety has been more fruitfully conceptualized

---

1. What used to be known as "neurotic" disorders in the psychiatric classification system in the United States are now referred to as anxiety disorders (American Psychiatric Association, 1980).

as a set of loosely coupled systems which can be directly measured. These response systems are the verbal report of feelings of distress and apprehension, the presence of physiological arousal predominantly involving the sympathetic branch of the autonomic nervous system, and overt escape and avoidance behaviors. But since anxiety is not a unitary phenomenon, these systems often fail to correlate with each other, and this lack of correlation is referred to as desynchrony. These response systems are also modifiable by different methods and at different rates.

In an extension of Lang's (1971) analysis, Rachman and Hodgson (1974) described the ways in which changes in the three systems were either synchronous or desynchronous in response to treatment, and they spelled out a number of hypotheses about conditions under which changes would be synchronous or not. For example, they hypothesized that synchrony would be more likely under conditions that evoke strong emotional responses (e.g., clinically severe reactions), while discordance would be more likely under conditions that evoke weak emotional responses. In general, this prediction has received empirical support (Craske & Craig, 1984; Rachman, 1978). Another hypothesis was that synchrony among the three response systems would increase as time went by. This, too, has received partial support (Biran & Wilson, 1981; Rachman, 1978). A third hypothesis, that synchrony would vary as a function of the specific method used to treat anxiety disorders, has not been confirmed. One prediction suggested that desynchrony among response systems at post-treatment would predispose toward relapse; an initial test failed to support this prediction (Himaldi, Boice, & Barlow, 1985).

The three-systems model orders relationships among different dimensions of anxiety and is simply a description of anxiety, not an explanation of interdependent processes. It has, however, provided testable predictions about these interrelationships. Hugdahl (1981), for example, has suggested that if clients "load differentially" on different fear components, then treatment should be tailored to the precise patterning of the fear response. A client with high physiological arousal and few anticipatory negative self-statements would be predicted to show little benefit from cognitive restructuring, whereas another client with the reverse "loading" would be helped. By way of illustration he suggests that the reader consider three agoraphobics. Client 1 is a "behavioral responder," Client 2 is a "physiological responder," and Client 3 is a "cognitive responder." Assuming that one could quantify phobics in this simple manner—a very debatable proposition—Hugdahl proceeds to match treatments to fear-response patterning: in vivo exposure for Client 1, systematic desensitization for Client 2, and cognitive restructuring for Client 3. At this level there is a marked similarity between the three-systems model and multimodal therapy.

There is, however, no evidence for an assumption of an isomorphic relationship between the way in which a problem is expressed and the form of its treatment. Studies designed to test this notion of matching treatments to "types" of phobic responders have yielded ambiguous or negative results (Ost, Jerremalm, & Johansson, 1981; Ost, Jerremalm, & Jansson, 1984). An example of this sort of study is discussed on page 175. The data show that a performance-based treatment is usually the most effective means of changing both cognitive processes and physiological arousal, as well as actual behavior (Marks, 1981; Wilson, 1982d). Hugdahl (1981) himself, noting that all phobias include a behavioral component, concludes that "treatment methods are probably best 'tailored' to the individual needs of every patient if they also include an exposure-based response prevention" (p. 83), a behavioral treatment we will discuss.

Social Learning Theory

According to the three-systems model, the different response systems are viewed as more independent than interdependent (Hugdahl, 1981). By contrast, in the social learning view, "thought, affect, and action operate as reciprocally interacting factors rather than as loosely linked components or as conjoint events. While recognizing the role of labeling processes in emotional expressions, this approach acknowledges that thought creates physiological arousal as well as providing cognitive labels for it. Arousal can, in turn, influence thought. The relative influence exerted by these three sets of interlocking factors will vary in different individuals for different activities performed under different circumstances" (Bandura, 1977a, p. 257).

The key concept that mediates the reciprocal interaction among action, affect, and thought is self-efficacy. This theory holds that the stronger an individual's sense of self-efficacy, the less his or her avoidance, autonomic arousal, and subjective anxiety will be. It postulates the conditions under which both synchrony (high strength of self-efficacy) and desynchrony (low strength of self-efficacy) among different measures of anxiety will occur (Bandura, 1982).

ANXIETY DISORDERS

There is a huge literature in behavior therapy on the nature and treatment of the anxiety disorders (Bandura, 1982; Barlow & Beck, 1984; Emmelkamp, 1982; Marks, 1981; Mathews, Gelder, & Johnston, 1981; Rachman & Hodgson, 1980). In this and the following chapter, we follow the DSM-III classificatory system in discussing the etiology and treatment of the various anxiety disorders.

Simple Phobias

Simple phobias are unrealistic fears of specific objects or situations, e.g., small animals, heights, enclosed spaces, blood, and vomiting. Simple phobias are the most common form of phobic reaction in the general population, although among people seeking therapy agoraphobia is most common. For many reasons, simple phobias have been the testing ground of a number of the most important treatment methods and the theories proposed to explain their effects.

The Classical Conditioning Model

The early behavioral view of the development of simple phobias, as well as the more complex phobias discussed later, assumed that they were acquired via classical conditioning. However, this model is inadequate on several grounds, as summarized by Rachman (1977):

1. Many people who are exposed to intense fear-provoking conditions do not develop phobias (e.g., not all people involved in car or plane crashes develop phobias about cars or planes).
2. Watson and Rayner's (1920) findings with Albert B have not been replicated. There is no conclusive evidence that lasting conditioned fear reactions can be established in humans in the laboratory (Hallam & Rachman, 1976).
3. In clinical cases it is often difficult, if not impossible, to find any traumatic experience that might have produced a conditioned fear reaction (Marks, 1981).
4. The classical conditioning model does not explain the fact that only certain types of stimuli are usually associated with intense fear reactions (Seligman, 1971). Thus people commonly have phobias about heights, flying, driving automobiles, dentistry, small animals, snakes, and so on, but not about inanimate objects like grass, hammers, electric sockets, and typewriters, al-

though they are frequently associated with trauma such as receiving an unpleasant electric shock.

5. Classically conditioned fear reactions typically extinguish very quickly if the conditioned stimulus is repeatedly presented without the unconditioned stimulus. People with phobias frequently come into contact with situations or objects they fear (the CS) without any adverse effects (the absence of an US), yet their phobias remain intact. For example, an agoraphobic client will often be exposed to what for her are anxiety-eliciting situations like crowds of people, supermarkets, and traffic, and others, but still remain fearful. The classical conditioning model cannot explain the well-known resistance to extinction of anxiety reactions.

Contemporary analyses of classical conditioning have moved away from the notion that what was learned consisted of simple stimulus-response (S-R) bonds. In what is known as a molar account of classical conditioning, it is the learning of a correlational or contingent relationship between the CS and US that defines the conditioning process (Rescorla & Wagner, 1972). Classical conditioning is no longer seen as the simple pairing of a single CS with a single US on the basis of temporal contiguity. Instead, correlations between entire classes of stimulus events can be learned. The advantage of this correlational view of conditioning is that it more closely resembles complex behavior than the one-to-one pairings of CS's and US's traditionally studied in classical conditioning experiments.

The molar view provides an explanation for the first of the problems with the conditioning model of fear reactions. People may be exposed to traumatic events (contiguity) but not develop phobic reactions unless a correlational relationship is formed between the situation and the event. Nevertheless, the learning of fear responses is not automatically conditioned by contingent stimuli. People do not learn contingent relationships between stimuli unless they recognize that the events are correlated. Awareness of the relationship seems to be critical for learning to occur (Bandura, 1985; Dawson & Biferno, 1973). The molar conditioning view also fails to explain fears in which no traumatic events (US) can be identified, the selectivity of phobic fears, or why they are so resistant to extinction.

Two-Factor Theory

Originally proposed by Mowrer (1939) in his attempt to translate Freud's psychoanalytic conception of anxiety into more scientifically acceptable terms, two-factor theory involves two key assumptions: (1) anxiety is an acquired drive established on the basis of a classical conditioning process in which a neutral stimulus is paired with an unconditioned stimulus; and (2) this anxiety motivates instrumental or avoidance behavior, which in turn is reinforced by the reduction of the underlying anxiety drive. Take the case of a compulsive handwasher with an obsession about dirt and cleanliness. It is assumed that his fear about dirt or contamination is a classically conditioned response that causes him to wash his hands repeatedly after touching anything he believes to be contaminated. Handwashing removes any dirt and reduces the fear of contamination. This fear reduction then reinforces the handwashing.

Subsequent research has demonstrated several major problems with two-factor theory. These include the following:

1. The difficulty in explaining the resistance to extinction of phobic behavior is still not resolved. Although an avoidance response removes the conditioned stimuli that elicit anxiety, reducing the amount of nonreinforced exposure to the conditioned stimuli (presentation of the CS in the absence of the US), some nonreinforced exposure occurs. By definition, some classically conditioned anxiety must be elicited in order to motivate the avoidance behavior. Nonreinforced exposure to the conditioned stimulus is the necessary and sufficient condi-

tion for extinction. By this process, anxiety must inevitably extinguish with the result that the avoidance response will disappear. Yet, as we have noted, this does not happen in phobic fears.

2. Experimental and clinical evidence clearly show that avoidance behavior is not causally mediated by an underlying drive state of autonomic arousal (Bandura, 1977a; Herrnstein, 1969; Rescorla & Solomon, 1967). There is no consistent relationship between autonomic arousal and avoidance behavior. Surgical deactivation of autonomic functioning in animals has little effect on the acquisition and virtually no effect on the maintenance of avoidance behavior, which often continues long after any classically conditioned anxiety (autonomic arousal) has been extinguished. Moreover, it can be effectively eliminated without reducing conditioned anxiety. Leitenberg, Agras, Butz, and Wincze (1971), for example, have shown that in the treatment of phobias, avoidance behavior can be eliminated by directly altering its reinforcing consequences without first inhibiting physiologically defined anxiety. Anxiety reduction is sometimes the consequence rather than the cause of behavioral change in both laboratory animals and clinical patients. A more accurate conceptualization is that both autonomic arousal and overt avoidance behavior are correlated coeffects of a central mediating state.

Regardless of the validity of the classical conditioning and two-factor theories of anxiety disorders, they have been extremely influential in the development of therapeutic procedures for the treatment of these disorders. It is quite possible, though, that treatment methods may be effective for reasons other than those put forward by their originators.

Contemporary Conditioning Models

Contemporary conditioning models provide different formulations of the development and maintenance of phobic reactions in an attempt to answer the criticisms above.

In the incubation hypothesis, Eysenck (1982) argues that the basic law of extinction of a conditioned response has to be revised. In his view, presentation of an anxiety-eliciting conditioned stimulus without the unconditioned stimulus can result either in extinction of the anxiety (the usual effect) or its maintenance and enhancement. The latter result is referred to as the incubation effect. According to this hypothesis, the conditioned response of anxiety has drive properties in the same way as the unconditioned response does. Eysenck suggests that incubation is likely to occur under the following circumstances: very short exposure to the conditioned stimulus, very potent unconditioned responses, and certain genetically determined personality characteristics that make the individual susceptible to fear arousal.

Although there are scattered data indicating that brief exposure to anxiety-eliciting conditioned stimuli alone can increase measures of autonomic arousal (Stone & Borkovec, 1975), there is no firm evidence to support Eysenck's position, which has been widely criticized (Levis & Malloy, 1982).

In the preparedness hypothesis, Seligman (1971) has suggested animals and humans are biologically prepared to learn certain fears as a result of our evolutionary past. This would explain the nonrandom distribution of fears and phobias. Phobias about heights or snakes are more common than phobias about hammers or electric outlets because the former, and not the latter, were associated with danger and threats to life in our evolutionary history. According to Seligman, "prepared" fears are often acquired on the basis of a single pairing with an aversive stimulus and are highly resistant to extinction.

There are conceptual and empirical objections to this hypothesis. Conceptually, Bandura (1977b) points out that fears and phobias about sexual activities are among the most common complaints therapists encounter for which there are obviously no evolutionary advantages. More people have drowned than died of snake bites, yet fear of snakes is more prevalent than fear of water. Laboratory studies of classical conditioning have shown that the specific nature of the CS can affect resistance to extinction. Hugdahl (1978) paired pictures of either snakes and spiders (a fear-relevant CS) or circles and triangles (the fear-irrelevant CS) with either electric shock or the threat of electric shock as the UCS. The dependent measure or CR was a change in skin conductance, a widely used measure of fear. All four groups of subjects showed equal evidence of conditioning. During extinction, when subjects were informed that no further shock would be given, the two groups who had been conditioned with the fear-irrelevant CS showed an immediate reduction in fear response. The two groups who had experienced the fear-relevant CS indicated resistance to extinction. However, Seligman's "preparedness" hypothesis is only one possible explanation of these results. An alternative view would emphasize differential social learning experiences. In our culture we learn to react quite differently to salient, fear-relevant stimuli like snakes than we do to stimuli like circles and triangles.

Two findings are particularly damaging to the notion of "prepared" fears. The first is that fear-relevant stimuli do not produce quicker acquisition of conditioned fear than fear-irrelevant stimuli. The preparedness hypothesis would predict faster learning to more dangerous stimuli. The second finding is that, contrary to the hypothesis, they do not appear to be unusually resistant to extinction in actual treatment studies. Later in this chapter we will see that phobias are readily extinguished in clients when the appropriate learning conditions are arranged. In a clinical test of the preparedness hypothesis, de Silva,

Rachman, and Seligman (1977) rated sixty-nine phobic and eighty-two obsessional clients for the "preparedness," or evolutionary significance of their fears and related these measures to therapeutic outcome. The results showed that the "preparedness" ratings failed to predict treatment outcome, stimulus generalization, severity of the problem, suddenness of the onset of fear, or age of onset.

The correlational view of the classical conditioning does not provide an adequate model of phobic anxiety. However, an interpretation of avoidance behavior based on a correlational analysis of the relationship between behavior and its consequences overcomes several of the objections to the two-factor theory of avoidance behavior (Herrnstein, 1969). This correlational interpretation is an operant analysis that assumes that avoidance behavior is learned and maintained because it reduces or eliminates negative consequences. In contrast to two-factor theory, the concept of classically conditioned fear is said to be unnecessary. Avoidance behavior is more parsimoniously explained by analyzing the observable relationship (correlation or contingency) between the organism's responses and environmental outcome, without any reference to an internal mediating state, such as fear.

The advantages of this operant analysis of avoidance behavior are as follows. First, it is consistent with the evidence that fear is probably not a necessary condition for the learning of avoidance behavior and is definitely not necessary for its maintenance. Second, this operant analysis leads to the prediction that the most efficient way to extinguish avoidance behavior is to concentrate on the behavior directly, rather than on the presumed underlying state of fear.

Finally, since a classically conditioned fear response is not the cause of avoidance behavior, extinction will take place only if the correlation between avoidance behavior and outcome is broken. For this to happen, the person has to recognize that the contingency has changed and that it is now safe to stop avoiding.

While this view is an improvement over two-factor theory, a problem still remains. Phobic clients are not always successful in avoiding their feared situations or objects, yet even when nothing terrible happens during an encounter, extinction does not occur. The problem seems to be that it is not the objective or observable relationship between behavior and its consequences that maintains phobic disorders. The client's perception of that relationship may be the critical factor, as emphasized in social learning theory.

Social Learning Theory

In the discussion of two-factor theory we pointed out that autonomic arousal does not directly motivate avoidance behavior. In social learning theory, correlated experiences produce expectations that govern behavior, rather than a drive state that motivates behavior. Autonomic arousal and avoidance behavior are correlated coeffects. According to social learning theory, both are products of expectations of personal harm or threat. A social learning analysis also provides a theoretically consistent framework for integrating what Rachman (1977) called the "three pathways to fear." The first pathway is the acquisition of fear through direct experience with a traumatic event. Such experiences create learned expectations about what cues predict what events. Events viewed as threatening then elicit fear-arousing thoughts which, in turn, evoke fear reactions. Awareness of the relationship between predictor cues and distressing events is critical to emotional learning.[2]

2. An alternative view that has been popular in behavior therapy is that there are two routes through

The second pathway to fear is observing some other person behaving fearfully or being harmed. This cognitive process is known as modeling. It helps explain how people can develop phobias even though they have never had any direct contact with the feared situation or object. Strong evidence of the role of modeling in the acquisition of phobic reactions comes from a study of primates (Mineka, Davidson, Cook, & Keir, 1984). Young monkeys acquired severe and lasting fear of snakes after observing their wild-reared parents behave fearfully in the presence of a snake. The degree of behavioral disturbance (fear) shown by the parental models was more important than behavioral avoidance itself in determining the observer monkeys' fear.[3] As with direct experience, not all observation of fearful behavior results in the acquisition of fear by the observer. Among the factors that de-

which phobic reactions are learned. The first is the cognitively mediated, self-arousal process described here. The second is a nonmediated one in which the phobic response is elicited directly by the external stimulus without any intervening thought or self-arousal process (Bridger & Mandel, 1964). The implication of this position was that fears created via the first route—the self-arousal process—are modifiable by changing thoughts as in cognitive restructuring procedures. Fears established via the second route, through direct, nonmediated experience with aversive events, would require repeated disconfirming experiences to be modified.

Bandura (1986), in his social learning theory, argues that even in cases in which the external cue apparently elicits fear directly, the original learning was cognitively mediated. The fear reaction becomes so powerful and so frequently rehearsed that people begin to react very rapidly at the first sign of a threatening event. Instead of dual routes for modification, performance-based treatment is recommended as the most powerful means of modifying all fear reactions.

3. This last finding led Mineka, Davidson, Cook, and Keir (1984) to conclude that parents who have strong fears or phobias should avoid confronting their phobic situation or object with their children present, since the distress they show would instill fear in their children.

termine this are the extent to which the observer imagines that he or she is in the model's place (Rosenthal & Bandura, 1978).

The third way in which fears are acquired is through instruction and information. Take the case of phobias about snakes and other animals. Our folklore is full of frightening stories depicting snakes as slimy, evil, and deadly adversaries of human beings. Hearing (and believing) these stories from childhood will affect future behavior.

To summarize, direct experience with aversive events, vicarious learning, and verbal instruction are three different ways of conveying information about predictive relationships between cues and their consequences. These different pathways of learning fear reactions vary in the quality and amount of information they provide, but their effects are assumed to be mediated by common cognitive processes, such as self-efficacy.

How does social learning analysis account for the marked resistance to extinction of phobic reactions? Although it is not incompatible with the notion that some people may be biologically vulnerable to acquiring persistent fears, social learning theory emphasizes learned expectations about potentially dangerous events. Bandura (1977b) argues that in many instances phobic expectations are maintained because occasional mishaps occur. Take the person with a fear of flying. Planes do crash from time to time. The phobic focuses selectively on the highly improbable consequence of his or her flight being one of the statistically rare crashes. In addition, the exposure phobics have to their feared situations or objects, which inevitably produces extinction of conditioned anxiety responses, does not automatically alter fearful expectations. Whether these fearful expectations are disconfirmed and phobic behavior hence eliminated will depend on the nature of the information the person derives from exposure with the phobic situation. If the exposure is such that individuals conclude that they can cope effectively, they will stop avoiding and overcome their fear. If the exposure is such that individuals cannot cope and will experience unnerving anxiety, no change will take place. By strengthening phobics' expectations that they cannot cope, the exposure might even enhance phobic sensitivity.

Treatment

Several behavioral methods have proved effective in treating phobias.

Systematic Desensitization

Mary Cover Jones's (1924) treatment of a child's phobia has been discussed in Chapter 3. Wolpe (1958) applied essentially the same principle in introducing systematic desensitization. In experimental research on fears in cats, Wolpe found that conditioned emotional responses could be eliminated by gradually feeding animals closer to the locus of the original fear conditioning. Accordingly, Wolpe formulated his reciprocal inhibition principle which stated that anxiety-eliciting stimuli could be permanently neutralized if "a response antagonistic to anxiety can be made to occur in the presence of the anxiety-evoking stimuli so that it is accompanied by the complete or partial suppression of the anxiety response" (p. 71). This procedure has also been referred to as counterconditioning (Davison, 1968).

In applying these laboratory findings to practical clinical treatment, Wolpe adapted from Jacobson (1938) a technique called progressive relaxation training as a means of producing a response incompatible with anxiety. This consists of training clients to concentrate on systematically relaxing the different muscle groups of the body, which results in lowered physiological arousal and a comfortable subjective feeling of calmness. In another extrapolation from laboratory research findings, Wolpe found that imagined representation of stimulus conditions seemed to be as effective in eliciting anxiety as their actual occurrence. This was of major importance in helping the therapist to arrange conditions for the extinction of maladaptive anxiety reactions generally evoked by stimuli involving past or future events or social situations not easily controlled or dealt with directly in the therapist's office.

To ensure that anxiety is inhibited by muscle relaxation, the client is instructed to imagine anxiety-producing scenes in a carefully graded fashion. Hierarchies of anxiety-eliciting situations are constructed, ranging from mildly stressful to very threatening items, which clients are told to imagine while they are deeply relaxed. In the event that any item produces much anxiety, the client is instructed to stop visualizing the item and restore feelings of relaxation, since the technique is predicated on the rationale that anxiety be kept at a minimal level. The item is then repeated, or the hierarchy adjusted, until the client can visualize the scene without experiencing anxiety. Only then does the therapist present the next item of the hierarchy.

Efficacy of Systematic Desensitization

Systematic desensitization is perhaps the most intensively researched psychological treatment technique on record. For example, in a review of controlled group outcome studies, Kazdin and Wilcoxon (1976) found over seventy such studies in only five of the journals they surveyed. A large majority of these studies consists of laboratory-based investigations with subjects who were only mildly fearful. Consequently, the generalizability of the findings to severely phobic clients is questionable. Nonetheless, the net result of all

these studies shows that systematic desensitization is an effective technique.

A landmark study by Paul (1966) illustrates both the efficacy of systematic desensitization and the sort of research strategy that behavior therapists developed to evaluate treatment methods. College students who experienced debilitating anxiety in public-speaking situations were administered a comprehensive pretreatment assessment encompassing personality questionnaires for both general emotional responsiveness and specific public-speaking anxiety and physiological and overt behavioral measures of anxiety. The latter consisted of highly reliable observations of subjects' behavior under stress during a four-minute speech to an unfamiliar audience. Using within-sample matching, subjects were then randomly assigned to four groups: (1) systematic desensitization, (2) insight-oriented psychotherapy, (3) attention-placebo, and (4) no-treatment control. Five experienced psychotherapists whose orientation was "dynamic and insight-oriented," treated subjects in all groups for five hours over a six-week period. Following treatment all subjects were again given the anxiety-assessment measures. This procedure controlled for therapist bias in favor of systematic desensitization; if anything, it favored the psychotherapy condition, which involved an interview approach, stressing insight and self-understanding of the psychological nature of the subjects' anxiety. The therapists routinely used this approach in their daily work and confidently expected it to be successful, but they were unfamiliar with systematic desensitization and had to be coached in its use.

Subjects in the attention-placebo group were given what they believed to be a "fast-acting tranquilizer" which supposedly helped them to learn to respond nonanxiously while working at a bogus "stressful task." They were told that this training would immunize them against stress reactions in outside social situations. This group controlled for any improvement which could be attributed to nonspecific therapy factors such as suggestion, expectation of relief, and the therapist-patient relationship. Subjects in the no-treatment condition were administered the pre- and posttreatment assessment procedures but received no therapy.

The results, summarized in Figure 8–1, showed that systematic desensitization produced consistently greater improvement on all dependent measures than either the no-treatment control or the insight-oriented and attention-placebo treatment groups. On the behavioral measure of anxiety, for example, 100 percent of the systematic desensitization group improved as against 60 percent of the insight group, 73 percent of the attention-placebo group, and 24 percent of the control group. The psychotherapy and placebo treatments were superior to no treatment in self-report and behavioral measures, but only the desensitization group showed a significant decrease in physiological arousal relative to the control group. There were no significant effects due to the different therapists, the improvement being directly attributable to the treatment procedures. Follow-up evaluations based on subjects' self-report of anxiety, six weeks and two years after therapy, demonstrated essentially the same pattern of results: 85 percent of the systematic desensitization subjects showed a decrement in subjective

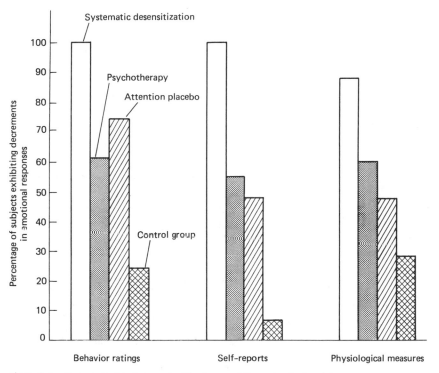

Figure 8–1   Percent of subjects in each of the four conditions who displayed decreases in anxiety as measured by behavior ratings, self-reports of emotional disturbance, and measures of physiological arousal. (Adopted from Bandura, *Principles of Behavior Modification* (1969). Copyright © 1969 by Holt, Rinehart and Winston Publishers. Reprinted by permission of Holt, Rinehart, and Winston.)

anxiety from pretreatment estimates, as compared to 50 percent of both the psychotherapy and placebo groups, and 22 percent of the nontreated controls. Moreover, subjects treated with systematic desensitization not only maintained their therapeutic gains but also showed no sign of any form of symptom substitution.

Why Systematic Desensitization Is Effective. Although it is clear that desensitization is effective, it has been argued that this is not due to specific learning principles but to general placebo factors that characterize all psychological therapies. This argument is often part of the broader view that there are no real differences among the various psychological therapies (Frank, 1979; Smith, Glass, & Miller, 1980).

Systematic desensitization has not always been shown to be superior to a highly persuasive attention-placebo control treatment (Kazdin & Wilcoxon, 1976), but several convincing studies have shown that its effects cannot be explained solely on the basis of placebo influences (Paul, 1985; Rachman & Wilson, 1980). Consider the Paul (1966) experiment described earlier. Critics have argued that the attention-placebo group may not have been as credible or convincing to the subjects as was the desensitization treatment. This would mean that the placebo group did not control satisfactorily for variables like subjects' expectations of therapeutic improvement across groups. However, it must be remembered that systematic desensitization was also significantly more effective than the psychotherapy treatment in the Paul (1966) study. There is no evidence to suggest that subjects in this psychotherapy condition were less enthusiastic about treatment or expected less improvement. Factors such as subjects' confidence in an impressive-sounding therapeutic technique and consequent expecta-

tions of success undoubtedly contribute to the overall efficacy of systematic desensitization. However, the specific procedures used have an effect over and above these general placebo influences.

Another explanation for the success of systematic desensitization is that the interpersonal relationship between therapist and client is the critical agent of change. However, the efficacy of the technique itself is established by studies in which the influence of the therapist is intentionally minimized. Lang, Melamed, and Hart (1970), for example, have shown that desensitization administered by a computer was as effective in reducing snake phobias as therapist-conducted desensitization. Moreover, totally self-directed desensitization has proved as effective as therapist-administered treatment in some studies (Rosen, Glasgow, & Barrera, 1976).

Flooding

Unlike systematic desensitization, which relies on client-controlled graduated exposure to anxiety-eliciting stimulus conditions, flooding[4] involves therapist-controlled, prolonged exposure to high intensity aversive stimulation without the soothing effects of relaxation training. Flooding may be conducted in imagination, but it is more usually done in vivo. The rationale behind this technique was originally based on two-factor theory and the principle of extinction. This principle states

---

4. Flooding should not be confused with implosion therapy, a technique developed by Stampfl (Stampfl & Levis, 1967). A major difference is that implosion therapy involves an emphasis on psychodynamic themes (e.g., aggressive and sexual impulses and Oedipal conflicts) that are assumed to play a role in the etiology and maintenance of anxiety disorders. The evidence shows that these psychodynamic themes are irrelevant to the extinction of phobic reactions (Leitenberg, 1976). Furthermore, whereas implosion therapy relies exclusively on the use of imagery, the current trend is to conduct flooding in vivo.

that a conditioned fear response can be extinguished by repeatedly presenting the stimuli that elicit the conditioned fear response in the absence of actual aversive stimulation. The presentation of feared stimuli is expected to elicit a strong emotional response initially; however, continued exposure should result in a rapid decrease in fearful response. To ensure full exposure, the client is prevented from making an avoidance or escape response. Whether the exposure is presented in imagination or in real life, the client is strongly encouraged to continue to attend to the anxiety-eliciting stimuli despite initial stressful effects. Every effort is made to elicit as intense an anxiety response as possible so that total extinction will ensue. Such a scene would be presented continuously in imagination until the client's anxiety shows a definite decrease and the formerly frightening stimuli no longer elicit much distress.

Flooding has been most frequently used in the treatment of agoraphobia. Its treatment effects are evaluated in the next chapter.

Guided Exposure

Guided in vivo exposure is conducted on a graduated or hierarchical basis. The purpose is to help phobics learn to cope with feared situations or objects without avoiding them. This strategy of guided exposure, or enactive mastery, (Bandura, 1982) is also discussed in the following chapter.

Modeling

Several types of modeling procedures have been shown to eliminate simple phobias reliably (Rosenthal & Bandura, 1978). In symbolic modeling, the client observes a live or filmed model systematically engaging in progressively more threatening interactions with the phobic object (e.g., a small animal). Covert modeling is a method in which the patient does not observe a live or filmed model, but imagines a model engaging in phobic behavior. The following factors enhance treatment outcome: imagination of multiple models, reinforcement of models for overcoming their problem, and imagination of a coping model who gradually overcomes initial fear, as opposed to a "mastery" model who performs fearlessly from the outset. There appears to be little differential effectiveness among symbolic and covert modeling and systematic desensitization (Bandura, 1982).

Modeling may also play a useful role in the treatment of phobics with guided exposure treatment. In this procedure, beyond arranging for systematic exposure to the feared situation, the therapist models specific coping strategies (verbal and behavioral) for the client. Well-controlled studies have shown that an integrated method combining modeling and guided mastery can significantly improve the therapeutic effects of both symbolic and in vivo exposure with simple phobias (Bandura, Blanchard, & Ritter, 1969; Williams, Dooseman, & Kleifield, 1984).

Theoretical Mechanisms.   Well-controlled research has established that the key procedural component of systematic desensitization, flooding, in vivo exposure, and modeling is systematic exposure to the anxiety-eliciting situation. In desensitization, for example, neither the graded hierarchy nor the relaxation training is required for successful treatment. This finding contradicts Wolpe's (1958) theory of reciprocal inhibition, which states that phobic responses cannot be eliminated unless graded anxiety-eliciting stimuli are paired with a physiologically incompatible response, such as relaxation. To the extent that graded exposure or relaxation training is helpful, it is because they facilitate exposure to the anxiety-eliciting situations.

Systematic exposure to anxiety-eliciting

objects or situations is the common denominator among effective fear reduction methods. But this is only a description of a procedure, not an explanation of the mechanisms of fear reduction. It is important to go beyond the mere technology of exposure treatment (Marks, 1981) to an understanding of why it works; such an understanding might well allow us to refine existing treatments into more effective procedures. As we illustrate in the following chapter, different theories of why exposure works have direct implications for the manner in which they are applied in clinical practice. As the social psychologist Lewin (1935) said, there is nothing so practical as a good theory. An explanation of why exposure works will also help us understand the reasons for our failures.

Mowrer's (1947) two-factor theory was successful in helping to generate and guide behavioral treatment procedures such as flooding and in vivo exposure. Nevertheless, it is now clear that the theory is untenable as an explanation of exposure treatments. It runs into several problems:

1. There is not a consistent relationship between level of anxiety during exposure and treatment success (Chambless, Foa, Groves, Goldstein, 1982; Marks, 1981). According to the theory, maximal anxiety should be elicited, and extinguished, during exposure to threatening stimuli for optimal behavioral change.
2. The theory predicts that amount of exposure will be closely correlated with behavior change (Levis & Malloy, 1982), yet amount of exposure is a poor predictor of degree of behavior change.
3. The theory holds that phobics should not leave the feared situation until their fear is reduced or at least decreasing, because it is assumed that if they do, the escape/avoidance behavior will be reinforced by the reduction of anxiety. This has been a basic principle in the literature and practice of behavior therapy (Eysenck & Rachman, 1965; Mathews et al., 1981), yet de Silva and Rachman (1984) have shown that phobics instructed to escape from

an anxiety-evoking situation while still fearful showed improvement—their phobic behavior was *not* reinforced. Phobics who systematically entered and then withdrew from situations while still fearful improved as much as phobics who remained longer in the feared situation.

4. Another problem already referred to is the finding of desynchrony among response systems during treatment. For example, phobic behavior may cease even while autonomic arousal levels remain unchanged or even increase.

The operant analysis which stresses the contingent, or correlational, relationship between avoidance behavior and its consequences fares better in accounting for the results. Flooding, in vivo exposure, and response prevention are all effective methods breaking the existing relationship between phobic behavior and its consequences. By bringing the person into contact with a different contingency (that is, it is safe to stop avoiding or engaging in compulsive rituals), the phobic avoidance or compulsive behavior is extinguished.

However, even this operant analysis falls short of explaining some of the clinical and experimental findings on flooding and in vivo exposure. For example, why does the same amount of exposure result in improvement for one client, no effect for a second client, and perhaps increased fear in still a third client? Evidence also indicates that the objective condition of exposure to the feared situation alone is insufficient for explaining treatment effects. An important consideration seems to be what the person does during exposure (Marshall, Gauthier, & Christie, 1976). In imaginal flooding, for example, treatment outcome may be enhanced by the person imagining realistically coping with the feared situation instead of being passively exposed to it. In other words, how the subject appraises the external situation will be a determinant of behavior.

Is Exposure a Necessary Condition for Anxiety Reduction?   Conditioning theories, such as Mowrer's two-factor theory, hold that exposure to the conditioned anxiety-evoking stimulus is a necessary condition for reducing phobic anxiety. However, de Silva and Rachman (1981) make the case that while exposure is often sufficient for reducing phobic anxiety, it cannot be said to be a' necessary condition.

To begin, what is meant by "exposure" in this context should be defined. De Silva and Rachman (1981) define exposure as "planned, sustained and repetitive evocations of images/image sequences of the stimuli in question." Mere thoughts or fleeting images do not constitute imaginal exposure. Among the strands of evidence that support their position, de Silva and Rachman cite the following: some fears can be reduced by verbal reassurance or verbal forms of cognitive restructuring treatment; fears have been reduced by placebo and nonbehavioral treatment methods that do not involve planned, repeated exposure to feared situations; and fears can be reduced by non-psychological treatment methods, such as pharmacotherapy, that do not involve exposure. These conclusions point out the need for a more integrative theory of fear reduction that accommodates the problems encountered by conditioning models. We turn now to one such possibility—self-efficacy theory.

Self-Efficacy Theory.   The major alternative to the two-factor conditioning theory of behavioral treatments for anxiety disorders is Bandura's (1977b) self-efficacy theory. According to this theory, treatment methods, whatever their nature, are effective because they increase the client's expectations that he or she has the ability to cope successfully with a threatening situation. They are differentiated from outcome expectations, which are defined as the client's belief that a particular behavior will result in a certain outcome.

Efficacy expectations are based on four major sources of information: behavioral performance, vicarious experience, physiological arousal, and verbal persuasion. Figure 8–2 shows the hypothesized mode of operation on efficacy expectations of behavior therapy techniques for fear reduction.

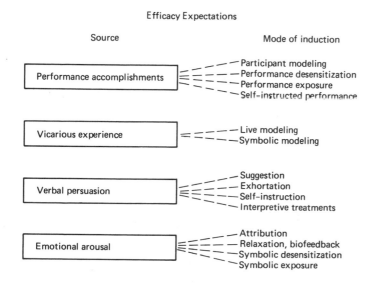

Efficacy Expectations

Figure 8–2 Major sources of efficacy information and the principal sources through which different modes of treatment operate. (Bandura, A. Self-efficacy: Toward a unifying theory of behavioral change (1977). Reprinted by permission from *Psychological Review, 84,* 191 - 215. Copyright 1977 by the American Psychological Association.)

In an experimental test of self-efficacy theory, snake phobic subjects received treatments designed to create differential levels of efficacy expectations and relate them to behavioral change (Bandura, Adams, & Beyer, 1977). The three treatment methods were modeling with guided mastery, symbolic modeling, and a no-treatment control group. Predictably, modeling with guided mastery produced significantly stronger efficacy expectations and more generalized behavioral changes than did symbolic modeling. The latter resulted in greater expectations of personal efficacy and behavioral change than the control condition. As shown in Figure 8–3, the degree of treatment-produced change in efficacy expectations was closely related to a reduction in phobic behavior. The greater the increase in self-efficacy, the greater the reduction in phobic behavior. Consistent with the theory, a detailed analysis shows that increases in efficacy expectations were predictive of behavioral change, irrespective of whether they were created by participant or symbolic modeling.

Bandura and Adams (1977) pitted self-efficacy theory against two-factor conditioning theory in an experiment. They treated snake phobic subjects with systematic desensitization until they completed the stimulus hierarchy so that they showed no anxiety to imagined representation of the most aversive scenes. In addition to measures of behavioral avoidance, subjects' self-efficacy expectations were assessed before treatment, after treatment but prior to the post-test, and following the post-test. Although all subjects had been equally desensitized, their reductions in

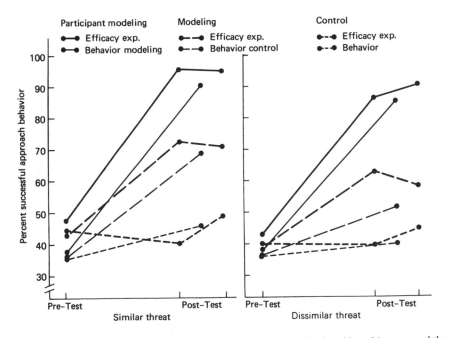

Figure 8–3 Level of efficacy expectations and approach behavior displayed by subjects toward threats after receiving vicarious or enactive treatments, or no treatment. (Bandura, A., Adams, N.E., and Beyer, J. (1977). Cognitive processes mediating behavioral change. *Journal of Personality and Social Psychology,* *35,* 126 - 239. Copyright 1977 by the American Psychological Association. Reprinted by permission.)

avoidance behavior were typically variable. Subjects' self-efficacy expectations, however, were accurate predictors of subsequent performance on 89 percent of the behavioral tasks. These results support the cognitive theory that treatment-induced reduction of physiological arousal changes phobic behavior by increasing efficacy expectations, rather than by extinguishing a conditioned autonomic drive as postulated by the reciprocal inhibition or two-factor theory of avoidance learning.

Self-efficacy is related to measures of fear arousal other than self-report. Phobics who have little self-efficacy and who engage in feared activities show increases in blood pressure and heart rate. With high levels of self-efficacy, phobics engaged in the activities show no increase in blood pressure and heart rate (Bandura, Reese, & Adams, 1982). Self-efficacy is also related to neuroendocrine processes underlying stress reactions (Bandura, Taylor, Williams, Mefford, & Barchas, 1985). Phobics who reported only moderate levels of self-efficacy about specific tasks showed significant increases in plasma epinephrine and norepinephrine. After their self-efficacy was increased through behavioral treatment (guided mastery), these phobic subjects completed the previously feared tasks with little increase in endocrine activity.

Self-efficacy theory can account for the many problems encountered by conditioning theory in explaining clinical and experimental findings on fear reduction.

1. In self-efficacy theory, it is unnecessary to evoke maximally intense anxiety during flooding, since it is not the intensity of the anxiety drive but the informative function of the situation that determines the effects of prolonged exposure. Exposure treatment may or may not increase the strength and generality of efficacy expectations, depending on a number of associated factors like discrimination learning and attributional processes.

2. It is not the amount of exposure to the feared situation, but the impact exposure has on self-efficacy that will determine fear reduction.

3. Self-efficacy theory provides an explanation of de Silva and Rachman's (1984) finding that escape from a situation while fear is high can still result in reductions in phobic behavior. The assumption here is that neither the escape behavior nor the high anxiety is critical, but rather the impact of the exposure on self-efficacy. Physiological arousal is not automatically appraised as a source of inefficacy or lack of controllability. Rather, individuals whose efficacy is high will engage in activities despite arousal, knowing that they can cope and the arousal will likely decline as they keep going.

4. Self-efficacy theory does not require that exposure be a necessary condition of fear reduction, as in conditioning theories. The evidence cited by de Silva and Rachman (1981) showing that fear reduction can occur in the absence of exposure is consistent with emphasis in self-efficacy theory on different sources of information (e.g., verbal persuasion and altered physiological arousal) contributing to efficacy judgments.

Self-efficacy theory has not escaped criticism, particularly from behaviorists who are uncomfortable with cognitive concepts of this general sort (e.g., Borkovec, 1978; Eysenck, 1982; Lang, 1978). In response to an early objection that research on self-efficacy was too narrowly based on work with snake phobics, Bandura and his colleagues subsequently showed that self-efficacy theory can account for the effects of different methods applied to people with other phobic disorders, including agoraphobia (Bandura, Adams, Hardy, & Howells, 1980). In general, the theory has received largely positive support from investigations by researchers treating different types of problems. For example, Biran and Wilson (1981) carried out a self-efficacy analysis of their study comparing guided exposure to cognitive restructuring. Replicating Bandura's results, they found that efficacy expectations were accurate predictors of outcome in the guided exposure treatment. However, the congruence between efficacy ratings and outcome in the cognitive restructuring treatment was less than in the exposure condition. According to the theory, congruence between efficacy expectations and behavior should be comparably high across all methods.

Another criticism has been that outcome expectations alone might predict behavior without the need to invoke the construct of self-efficacy (Carver & Scheier, 1981; Kazdin, 1978c). The evidence from a series of different studies, however, firmly supports the superior predictive value of efficacy over outcome expectations.[5] In two experiments, one on assertiveness and the other on fear of snakes, Lee (1984 a & b) found that efficacy and outcome expectations were correlated, but efficacy expectations alone were better predictors of outcome than either outcome expectations alone or an additive or multiplicative combination of the two. The view that outcome expectations might predict behavior either better than or independently from efficacy expectations received no support. Lee points out that since outcome expectations were highly correlated with performance, therapeutic methods should be designed to alter both efficacy and outcome expectations. Fear

reduction methods such as guided exposure do just this. Williams and Watson (1985) have similarly shown that efficacy expectations independently predict phobic behavior better than patient ratings of the perceived dangerous consequences of being in the phobic situation (i.e., an outcome expectation postulated by Beck [1976] to explain phobic avoidance). To the extent that outcome expectations ever predict behavior change, this effect is due to their being correlated with efficacy expectations. Once this correlation with perceived efficacy is eliminated, using the statistical technique of partial correlation, outcome expectations alone do not predict phobic behavior.

The concept of self-efficacy has also been criticized as being correlated with outcome but not causally related to outcome. To establish the causal relationship, Bandura et al. (1982) treated snake phobic subjects until they reached predetermined levels of low, moderate, or high self-efficacy. This was accomplished by assessing subjects' efficacy levels following the completion of each task on the hierarchically arranged behavioral avoidance test. Finally, increasing levels of self-efficacy were successively induced within the same subjects. Both intergroup and intragroup experimental designs showed that approach behavior varied as a function of self-efficacy, covariation that Bandura interprets as establishing the causal nature of perceived efficacy.

Lang's Bioinformational Theory. Whereas Bandura relies primarily upon subjects' self-report, Lang (1979) tries to index phobics' cognitive processes through physiological assessment. He has proposed a bioinformational theory of emotional imagery that is directly relevant to fear reduction treatment methods. In this propositional analysis, an image is seen as a conceptual network, the

---

5. Efficacy and outcome expectations are necessarily related. The outcomes people expect depend in part on how well they think they will be able to cope with the situation in question. Bandura (1985) illustrates this point with the following example: "The social reactions people anticipate for asserting themselves depend on their judgments of how adroitly they can do it. Tactless assertiveness will produce negative counterreactions, whereas adept assertiveness can elicit accommodating reactions. In social, intellectual, and physical pursuits, those who judge themselves highly efficacious will expect favorable outcomes, self-doubters will expect mediocre performances of themselves and thus negative outcomes" (p. 392).

cognitive structure of which controls specific physiological responding and serves as a prototype for overt behavioral expression. Lang stresses that an image is not an internal stimulus to which the person responds (the former S-R conception of imagery in the behavior therapies). Rather, the person generates a conceptual structure that contains both stimulus and response propositions. Behavior change "depends not on simple exposure to fear stimuli, but on the generation of the relevant affective cognitive structure, the prototype for overt behavior, which is subsequently modified into a more functional form" (Lang, 1979, p. 501).

This theory offers a possible explanation for the variable effects of exposure therapies in the treatment of phobic clients. Only those who generate the relevant affective stimulus and response propositions will respond successfully (Lang, Melamed, & Hart, 1970). Those who are unable to accomplish this primary processing of affective information will show poorer outcomes.[6] However, it is unclear how Lang's theory would explain the findings yielded by studies of self-efficacy. Moreover, one of the implications of this theory is that generating the greatest amount of arousal (anxiety) during therapy should produce the most behavioral change, yet the treatment outcome data show no such relationship.

6. It has long been noted that a client's inability to react with some anxiety during imaginal systematic desensitization limits the use of this method. For example, Bandura (1969) noted that "individuals who are unable, for one reason or another, to visualize threatening stimuli vividly, or for whom imagined scenes fail to evoke emotional reactions, will most likely derive little benefit from an exclusively cognitive form of counterconditioning treatment" (p. 473). And Wolpe (1978) has observed that systematic desensitization does not benefit that "considerable number of people" who "do not have fear when they imagine the things they fear."

Conclusion

The evidence is clear that behavior therapy, particularly in vivo exposure, is the treatment of choice for simple phobias. The major exception to this conclusion is seen in the results of a study by Klein et al. (1983). They found that supportive psychotherapy was as effective as behavior therapy (systematic desensitization) in the treatment of agoraphobia, mixed phobia, and simple phobia. This was not because behavior therapy was ineffective; rather, it was because patients in the supportive psychotherapy condition did "unexpectedly well." Supportive therapy in this study was much more directive than is typically the case in psychotherapy, particularly in psychodynamic therapy. Yet Klein and colleagues concluded that the results of their study are consistent with the therapy outcome literature in showing that there are no significant differences among psychological treatments. For phobic patients, they all achieve their effect by instigating "corrective activity" between therapy sessions in the form of in vivo exposure. There are both practical and theoretical limitations to this analysis.

First, not all psychological therapies, either deliberately or unwittingly, encourage or instigate some form of in vivo exposure. Klein and colleagues themselves note that such a tactic is often proscribed in the more traditional psychotherapies. To the extent that non-behavioral therapies ignore or even discourage in vivo exposure, they will be relatively ineffective at best, counterproductive at worst. On a practical level, this would appear to be an important dimension for differentiating among effective and ineffective therapies.

A second point raises a more fundamental issue. Since it is agreed that some form of corrective activity (in vivo exposure) is central to overcoming phobic disorders, it makes sense to use the most efficient methods for accomplishing this task. Moreover, these methods ideally would be those that follow logically from a theoretically sound conceptualization of the effective ingredients in exposure treatment. Klein et al. reject an explanation of exposure in terms of reciprocal inhibition. But they fail to acknowledge that current conceptualizations of fear reduction processes and exposure treatment are quite different (Bandura, 1977b).

Social Phobias

Clinical Characteristics

Clients with social phobias are characterized by a "persistent, irrational fear of, and compelling desire to avoid, a situation in which (they are) exposed to possible scrutiny by others and fears that (they) may act in a way that will be humiliating or embarrassing" (American Psychiatric Association, 1980, p. 228). In a comparative clinical study of social phobics and agoraphobics, Amies, Gelder, and Shaw (1983) found that the former had an earlier age of onset, typically between 10 and 19 years of age. A greater proportion of social phobics were men. Their most prominent somatic symptoms were blushing and muscle twitching, symptoms which, as Amies and colleagues point out, can be seen by other people. Simple phobias were less often associated with social phobics than with agoraphobics. Phobic disorders were present in the families of 20 percent of both social phobics and agoraphobics. Social phobics showed significantly more excessive alcohol use (20 percent) and suicide attempts (14 percent) than did agoraphobics. Past or present depression is also common among social phobics (Liebowitz, Gorman, Fyer, & Klein, 1985).

Treatment

Relatively little attention has been given to the treatment of social phobias. The evidence from studies which included social phobics, together with simple phobics and agoraphobics (e.g., Gelder, Bancroft, Gath, Johnston, Mathews, & Shaw, 1973) indicate that social phobias can be treated as effectively as simple phobias can by either systematic desensitization or flooding (Emmelkamp, 1982; Marks, 1981). Additional support for this conclusion comes from a four-year follow-up of different phobic patients who had originally been treated with systematic desensitization (Marks, 1971). Over 20 percent of these sixty-five patients suffered from social phobias. No differences were observed between them and their counterparts with simple phobias or agoraphobia, either at post-treatment or long-term follow-up.

Butler, Cullington, Munby, Amies, and Gelder (1984) compared two behavioral methods to a waiting list control group in the treatment of social phobics. One method was exposure plus anxiety management (EX/AM) training. Anxiety management (AM) based on Suinn and Richardson's (1971) technique, consisted of progressive relaxation training, distraction, and rational self-talk. The latter was a form of cognitive restructuring in which clients identified negative or self-defeating thoughts, then rehearsed more constructive alternative thoughts. The other method was in vivo exposure (EX) which focused exclusively on encouraging clients to participate in situations they had been avoiding. No instructions about coping with anxiety were given. Instead of AM training, clients in this method received a comparable amount of a placebo procedure called associative psychotherapy. Treatment comprised seven weekly sessions and two booster sessions at two and six weeks during follow-up.

Both treatment groups improved significantly more than the waiting list control group, which showed no improvement on most measures. Treatment effects were maintained, or increased, at a six month follow-up. At post-treatment, the EX/AM group had lower scores than the EX group on two cognitive measures of social anxiety. Six months later the EX/AM group had lower scores on four additional measures, including patients' self-ratings of phobic severity. Only the EX/AM group showed generalized treatment effects to fear in situations other than social ones. This finding is consistent with the view that AM training provides clients with skills that can be used in different situations. No patient on the EX/AM group requested further treatment within a year, whereas 40 percent of the EX group did so. All patients showed satisfactory compliance with therapeutic instructions, with no difference between the two treatment groups. Patients also expressed comparably high ratings of the credibility and suitability of both treatments.

Biran, Augusto, and Wilson (1981) also found that guided exposure was a most effective treatment for social phobics. Moreover, they showed that exposure was significantly more effective than cognitive restructuring, which produced no benefit, either alone or in conjunction with exposure. These data suggest that the modest but clear effects of AM in the Butler et al. (1984) study may be more attributable to the relaxation or distraction strategies than the rational self-talk. Butler and colleagues themselves suggest that the more varied nature of AM, as opposed to purely verbal cognitive restructuring, might account for its apparent efficacy.

Social skills training, in which patients are helped to become more assertive and effective in coping with interpersonal issues, has also shown promise. Shaw (1979) examined the relative efficacy of systematic desensitization, flooding, and social skills training in the treatment of seriously incapacitated social phobics. Systematic desensitization and flooding were carried out entirely in the imagination, whereas the social skills training was performance-based. Treatment outcome was assessed using multiple measures of subjects' fear and avoidance behavior. The results showed that all three methods produced substantial therapeutic improvement that was maintained at a six-month follow-up. No differences were found between treatments.

It is usually the case in behavioral research on phobic disorders that patients with the same diagnosis are grouped together rather than randomly assigned to different treatment methods. Ost et al. (1981) went beyond this customary design in taking account of individual differences in patterns of fear response. Following participation in a structured social interaction test, social phobics were classified as either "behavioral" or "physiological" responders. The former were rated as high on behavioral indices of social anxiety and showed low physiological arousal. The latter displayed the opposite pattern. Subjects within each of these experimentally structured groups then received either relaxation training or social skills training (a similar procedure to that used by Shaw, 1979). In sum, Ost et al. compared a treatment that corresponded to the subjects' response pattern with a treatment that did not.

Treatments consisted of ten individual sessions. The within-group comparisons showed that both treatments yielded significant improvements on most measures. The between-group comparisons showed that for the behavioral reactors, social skills training was significantly better than applied relaxation on most of the measures; for the physiological reactors, relaxation was significantly better than social skills training on some of the measures. Ost and colleagues concluded that these data indicate that superior treatment effects are obtained when the method meshes with the patient's response pattern. Nevertheless, these results provide little support for the three-systems model of anxiety. First, the classification of phobics as "behavioral" or "physiological" responders can be queried. Second, the advantage of applied relaxation over social skills treatment in the "physiological" responders was small, albeit significant. More important, this advantage washed out during follow-up. Even here, the view that performance-based treatments are more effective is supported.

Conclusion

The meager evidence on behavioral methods for social phobics makes it difficult to reach any firm conclusion, but the treatment of choice for social phobias would appear to be in vivo exposure, together with some anxiety management strategies such as relaxation training. Social skills training might be useful, especially in cases in which the person has deficits in interpersonal skills.

SUMMARY

The three-systems model views anxiety as a set of loosely coupled components, namely, physiological arousal, avoidance behavior, and self-report of fear. This model has provided testable predictions of the interrelationships among these three components, but does not explain the interactions. Social learning theory views these three components as reciprocally interacting factors. The concept of self-efficacy mediates the reciprocal interaction among action, affect and thought. The stronger people's self-efficacy, the less their avoidance, physiological arousal, and subjective anxiety will be.

Conditioning theories of the etiology and development of simple phobias have been shown to be inadequate. Contrary to the theory, classically conditioned fear responses are not unusually resistant to extinction and they do not directly mediate phobic avoidance. Attempts to salvage conditioning theory (e.g., the biological notion of prepared fears) do not fit well with the available evidence.

In terms of social learning theory, phobias may be acquired through conditioning experiences, observational learning, or other means of transmission of frightening information. Autonomic arousal and avoidance behavior are both products of expectations of personal harm. Elimination of phobic behavior will depend on alteration of these expectations, which, in turn, is a function of the nature of the information the person derives from exposure to the phobic situation. Exposure does not automatically reduce phobic fear.

Systematic desensitization is a treatment method in which the client is asked to imagine a hierarchically ordered series of phobic scenes while deeply relaxed. The rationale is that the relaxation will help inhibit the anxiety elicited by the imagery and that this will transfer to real life situations. Systematic desensitization has been shown to be an effective treatment for simple phobias in a number of well-controlled studies. Its success is due to the specific treatment procedures rather than more general factors such as placebo influences or the therapist-client relationship.

Flooding involves prolonged exposure to high levels of phobic anxiety (either in real life or in imagination). Guided exposure is similar to systematic desensitization in that it is carried out on a graduated basis. But it is done in real life situations rather than through imagery, and it is designed to increase the client's coping skills rather than directly reduce underlying anxiety arousal. In modeling methods the client observes a live or filmed model systematically engaging in increasingly more threatening interactions with the phobic object. In covert modeling the client imagines a model engaging in the phobic behavior.

The critical component of techniques such as systematic desensitization, flooding, and modeling is systematic exposure to the anxiety-eliciting material. In contrast to the difficulties encountered by conditioning theories in explaining the effects of this exposure, self-efficacy theory has received much empirical support. According to self-efficacy theory, treatment methods, whatever their nature, are effective because they increase expectations that the client can cope with threatening situations.

There is less evidence on the effectiveness of behavior therapy with social phobias. However, guided exposure, together with anxiety management strategies such as cognitive restructuring or relaxation training, and social skills training, have shown promising results.

9

Anxiety Disorders—II

AGORAPHOBIA

Etiology and Nature

Agoraphobia is the most complex of the phobic disorders and the most difficult to treat. The diagnostic criteria for agoraphobia, according to DSM-III, are as follows:

A. The individual has marked fear of and thus avoids being alone or in public places from which escape might be difficult or help not available in case of sudden incapacitation, e.g., crowds, tunnels, bridges, public transportation. B. There is increasing constriction of normal activities until the fears or avoidance behavior dominate the individual's life. C. Not due to a major depressive episode, Obsessive Compulsive Disorder, Paranoid Personality Disorder, or Schizophrenia. (p. 227)

An additional diagnostic distinction is made between agoraphobics with and those without panic attacks. Panic attacks are acute, terrifying episodes of intense anxiety with somatic symptoms such as palpitations, choking sensations, dizziness, faintness, trembling, and feelings of unreality. Panic is increasingly seen as central in the anxiety disorders, and will be discussed in detail.

The onset of agoraphobia often occurs in late adolescence or early adulthood, but later onset is also common. Unlike social phobia, the majority of agoraphobics are women (roughly 80 percent). Associated features include obsessions, compulsions, and depression. The latter is typically the consequence of the anxiety disorder, due to the despondency and low self-efficacy that follow unpredictable anxiety and panic attacks.

The incidence of phobic and other anxiety disorders among family members of agoraphobics has varied from study to study. On the one hand, Harris, Noyes, Crowe, and Chaundry (1983) found the risk for all anxiety disorders to be 32 percent among first-degree relatives of agoraphobics, compared to 15 percent among non-anxious controls. Female relatives were at greater risk than male relatives. Harris et al. concluded that agoraphobia is familial. On the other hand, Amies et al. (1983) found that only 20 percent of near relatives of their agoraphobic sample were reported to have been phobic. Marks (1981) has reported similar prevalence data. In a well-controlled study of agoraphobics and carefully matched controls, Buglass, Clarke, Henderson, Kreitman, and Presley (1977) found that only 28 percent of the mothers and 17 percent of the fathers of agoraphobics had anxiety disorders of any kind. Buglass et al. concluded that there is no evidence for an increased prevalence of phobic or other psychiatric illness among the parents of agoraphobics, since no significant differences were found between the patient groups and their controls. Based on these and other findings, Mathews, Gelder, and Johnston (1981), in their authoritative review of the literature, stated that there is little support "for any strong genetic influence in agoraphobia, and the findings that reach significance seem, if anything, more amenable to an environmental explanation" (p. 33). Agoraphobia is twice as likely to afflict the poorly educated (Chambless, 1985).

The conditioning model seems inadequate to the task of explaining the etiology of agoraphobia. As Mathews et al. note, "agoraphobics cannot as a rule recall either any event that provoked intense fear or any repeated fearful events that occurred in the circumstances that they subsequently came to avoid. Instead, they report that the first acute anxiety seemed to come 'out of the blue' " (p. 43). Nor do agoraphobics seem to have had the vicarious learning experiences that might account for their disorder on the basis of modeling. However, the evidence consistently shows that agoraphobia usually develops against a background of stress (e.g., physical illness or psychological conflict).

Drawing on the three-systems model, Ost and Hugdahl (1983) investigated the mode of acquisition of agoraphobia in a sample of eighty patients. They found that 81 percent attributed the onset of their disorder to condition-

ing experiences and 9 percent to vicarious learning, while none attributed it to mere transmission of negative information. Only 10 percent failed to recall any specific circumstances surrounding onset. These data would seem, on face value, to contradict Mathews et al.'s conclusion about the inapplicability of conditioning theory in the etiology of agoraphobia, but the contradiction is only apparent. In agreement with Mathews and colleagues' position, Ost and Hugdahl report that the majority of their patients could not identify a traumatic event which caused their first panic attack. They interpret patients' well-known avoidance of situations in which repeated anxiety attacks occur as "conditioning." This still leaves unanswered the reason for the original panic attack, although it highlights the need to modify the patient's phobic avoidance behavior.

Contrary to Rachman's (1977) hypotheses, Ost and Hugdahl (1983) uncovered no relationship between mode of acquisition and patterning of the three dimensions of anxiety. For example, those who attributed their agoraphobia to conditioning experiences did not report or show greater physiological arousal during behavioral testing. Taken in conjunction with the results from these authors' similar study with other simple phobias (Ost & Hugdahl, 1981), these data call into question some of the propositions of the three-systems model.

In sum, the most parsimonious behavioral account of the etiology of agoraphobia has been put forward by Mathews et al. (1981). They hypothesize that the initial panic attack is a function of background stress and the arousal of the immediate situation "provoking an upward spiral of autonomic responses." Once this has occurred, the person increasingly avoids the original and related situations. A learning history of dependence as opposed to self-reliance then predisposes the person to continue avoiding rather than confronting her fears, which are attributed to various external circumstances. Finally, the agoraphobic pattern is maintained by the negative reinforcement of avoiding anxiety-provoking situations and possibly by positive reinforcement of such behavior by significant others in her environment. Alternative theories view agoraphobia as secondary to panic attacks that are directly caused by biological abnormalities. The implications of these theories for treatment are noted below.

Treatment

Clinical experience and experimental research have shown that the most effective procedures are those that rely upon systematic in vivo exposure to the feared situations (Marks, 1981; Mathews et al., 1981). Two major forms of in vivo exposure treatment have been used to treat agoraphobic patients: (1) flooding in vivo, designed to elicit maximum anxiety by confronting patients with their most intense anxiety-eliciting cues as soon as possible; and (2) graduated in vivo exposure, conducted on a graduated or hierarchical basis to confront patients with their feared situations without evoking intense anxiety. An instructive example of the therapeutic benefits of flooding, based on a well-controlled outcome study, is provided by Gelder et al. (1973).

Flooding was compared to both systematic desensitization and an attention-placebo control condition in the treatment of phobic clients. Treatments were carried out by experienced therapists explicitly trained in the administration of the different methods. An attempt was made to induce a high expectancy of success in half of the subjects by describing the treatment and therapist chosen in very favorable terms and showing them a videotape of a patient who had benefited from the treatment they were to receive. Half of the clients were agoraphobics; the other half, a mixed group of specific social or animal phobics. Agoraphobics, who exhibit generalized anxiety reactions, are regarded as more difficult to treat than simple phobics. Clients were assigned to treatments and therapists in an experimental design that permitted an analysis of the possible interactions among treatment effects, therapist differences, types of phobia, and levels of expectancy.

Therapy consisted of fifteen weekly sessions that included both imaginal and real life exposure. Treatment effects were evaluated by multiple measures of behavioral avoidance, blind psychiatric ratings, client self-ratings, physiological responsiveness, and standardized psychological tests at the end of treatment and at a six-month follow-up. The adequacy of the control group in eliciting expectancies of treatment success comparable to those evoked by the two behavioral methods was assessed directly, thereby avoiding the problem with the attention-placebo group in Paul's (1966) study. Expectations of improvement were similar across all three groups.

The results of this study are shown in Figure 9-1. Both behavorial treatments, particularly flooding, produced greater improvement than the control condition on the behavioral avoidance tests, physiological arousal measures, and psychiatric ratings of the main phobia and patients' self-rating of improvement, although only the flooding as opposed to the control condition comparison reached acceptable levels of statistical significance. These treatment gains were maintained successfully at follow-up. Flooding was roughly twice as effective as the powerful attention-placebo treatment. An important finding in this study was that the placebo control treatment was markedly less effective than both flooding and systematic desensitization with agoraphobics than with the other subjects. This result provides additional evidence that the success of

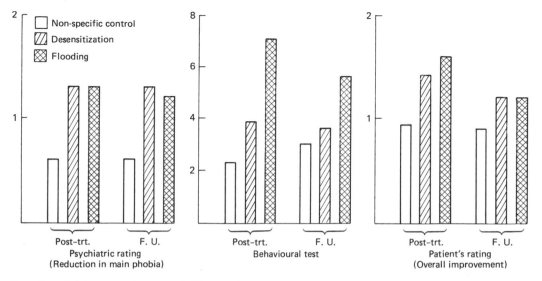

Figure 9–1 Results at post–treatment and follow-up of the three treatments on different measures of outcome. (From Gelder et al. (1973). *British Journal of Psychiatry, 123,* 445–462. Reprinted with permission.)

behavioral methods, such as flooding and systematic desensitization, cannot be attributed solely to the role of placebo factors or expectations of favorable therapeutic outcome.

Controlled clinical research, much of it conducted in the United Kingdom, has significantly furthered our understanding of the clinical practice and effects of in vivo exposure methods. This information may be summarized as follows:

1. Both flooding and graduated exposure in vivo are more efficient and effective than treatments based on imagery. In impressive demonstrations of the efficacy of flooding in the treatment of agoraphobic patients, such as the Gelder et al. (1973) study, imaginal exposure was followed in each session by in vivo exposure to the feared situation.

2. The longer the exposure to the feared situation is, the more effective flooding is likely to be. For instance, Stern and Marks (1973) found that two hours of continuous exposure in vivo was significantly more effective than four separate half-hours in one afternoon in the treatment of agoraphobics.

3. It is unnecessary to elicit intense expression of anxiety during in vivo exposure, since a patient's anxiety level during flooding does not correlate with subsequent outcome. Graduated exposure is as effective as flooding, and is the most widely used method today (Marks, 1981).

4. Flooding and graduated in vivo exposure conducted within a group setting are as effective as individual treatments (Hand, Lamontagne, & Marks, 1974).

5. In vivo exposure treatment in which the exposure is client-controlled may be as effective as therapist-controlled exposure, and is more cost-effective (Barlow et al., 1983). However, it should be stressed that this self-directed exposure was carried out under the intensive weekly supervision of therapists. The same research group has shown that simply providing clients with a treatment manual without regular therapist contact is ineffective (Holden, O'Brien, Barlow, Stetson, & Infantino, 1983).

6. With appropriate patients, home-based treatment, use of a treatment manual, and active spouse involvement produce improvement comparable to that achieved with more intensive therapist-administered treatment in the clinic (Jannoun, Munby, Catalan, & Gelder,

1980). Home-based spouse-assisted treatment is not only cost-effective but might also result in superior maintenance of treatment-produced change (Munby & Johnston, 1980).

7. In vivo exposure treatment conducted by nursing personnel under the supervision of a professional behavior therapist may in some instances be comparable to treatment carried out by clinical psychologists or psychiatrists. This increases the cost-benefit ratio for efficient delivery of treatment services (e.g., Marks, Hallam, Connolly, & Philpott, 1977). Yet it would be well to note that a therapist effect was evident in two major studies, despite the highly standardized treatment format (Jannoun et al., 1980; Mathews, Johnston, Lancashire, Munby, Shaw, & Gelder, 1976).

8. Guided exposure is significantly more effective than a form of cognitive restructuring treatment based on verbal analysis and disputation (Emmelkamp & Mersch, 1982). Adding this cognitive restructuring method to exposure does not increase its efficacy (Williams & Rappoport, 1983).

9. Exposure treatment is not directly comparable from one study to the next. Although exposure treatment is a straightforward method, its effective use frequently depends on success in dealing with clinical issues, such as increasing motivation, facilitating compliance, coping with anticipated anxiety attacks during exposure sessions, and overcoming cognitive distortions (Wilson, in press b). In addition to prescribing the basic behavioral tasks of gradually approaching phobic situations, the clinical practice of exposure treatment occurs in a context of strategies for coping with thoughts and feelings that would otherwise undermine therapeutic progress. These strategies are not addressed by conditioning formulations, which describe exposure as a simple extinction method aimed at habituation of fear, but follow naturally from a social learning view, with its emphasis on active cognitive processing of experience (Williams et al., 1984).

An illustration of the foregoing can be taken from the exposure treatment manual of Mathews et al. (1981). They explicitly address the important question of maintaining improvements clients make in treatment in the following manner:

"Hardly anyone recovers from agoraphobia without having at least one 'setback.' Feelings vary, sometimes from day to day, and what you did successfully yesterday may seem impossible today. Even then, you could make real progress. What counts is how you cope with whatever feelings you experience. So, a little done on a bad day can be worth more than a lot done on a good day." (1981, p. 184)

In these instructions about maintenance of improvement, Mathews et al. (1981) help clients interpret or "reframe" critical events in constructive rather than negative, self-defeating ways. By anticipating the possibility of a "setback," they explicitly attempt to defuse the otherwise detrimental effects of an unexpected anxiety attack just when clients feel they are improved. Little or no mention is made of such specific interventions in the behavioral literature on agoraphobia, but it is plain that Mathews et al. are engaging in what Marlatt and Gordon (1985), in the field of addictive disorders, have described as the cognitive-behavioral strategy of relapse-prevention training (see Chapter 14).

Mathews and colleagues provide clients with a short set of summary rules about what to do if a panic strikes. These include the following: "1. The feelings are normal bodily reactions; 2. They are not harmful; 3. Do not add frightening thoughts; . . . 9. Plan what to do next . . ." (p. 183). These instructions are designed to help clients form adaptive attributions of the cause (and management) of their problems, and then to cope constructively with them.

10. Clinical findings on the use of exposure treatment mesh better with cognitive social learning theory (self-efficacy theory in particular) than conditioning theories (Goldfried & Robins, 1983; Wilson, in press b). The following study shows that guided exposure informed by a social learning approach is more effective than exposure treatment based on conditioning theory. Williams, Dooseman, and Kleifield (1984) compared the conditioning view of exposure treatment, which emphasizes the extinction of conditioned anxiety responses to phobic stimuli, to the social learning model, which emphasizes the development of coping and personal mastery. Degree of overall exposure was equated between the two treatment conditions. The critical procedural difference between the two

studies was the extent to which the therapist provided subjects with driving and height phobias with "mastery induction aids." The latter included active guidance by the therapist during exposure tasks, setting proximal goals to overcome lack of progress, and varied performance. Both treatments were more effective than a non-treatment control condition, and the guided mastery treatment was significantly superior to the exposure model procedure on measures of behavior, self-efficacy, and self-report of fear.

Self-efficacy is a capsule construct that subsumes different subprocesses, such as attention and attribution. Thus, changes in perceptions of efficacy will occur only to the extent that individuals attribute therapeutic improvement to themselves. One of the problems in treating some complex phobic disorders such as agoraphobia is that clients often discount successful instances of nonphobic behavior, explaining them away as "luck" or as one of those rare "good days" that agoraphobics experience—in other words, they attribute their accomplishments not to themselves but to external factors. Clients with complex disorders, including some agoraphobics, typically show distortions in the way they appraise personal and situational information. They attend selectively to cues, mislabel internal sensations, misinterpret events, recall selected information in a cognitively biased manner that emphasizes negative features, and minimize or ignore evidence of progress (Wilson, in press b). For example, although agoraphobics seem no more sensitive to internal cues about their feelings than normals, they mislabel their internal sensations and attribute the causes of these feelings to abnormal aspects of themselves significantly more than nonagoraphobic subjects (Fisher & Wilson, 1985). This pattern of findings fits with Chambless and Goldstein's (1982) concept of an "hysterical" or distinctive attributional style in agoraphobic patients. Agoraphobics also

more easily retrieve phobic experiences from memory than nonagoraphobic subjects (Nunn, Stevenson, & Whalan, 1984). Experimental and clinical findings of this nature require that the therapist address the patient's cognitive and emotional processing of fear-relevant information if treatment is to succeed.

In addressing cognitive processing of information, Bandura (1982) states that individuals' self-efficacy increases when their "experiences disconfirm misbeliefs about what they fear and when they gain new skills to manage threatening activities. They hold weak self-percepts of efficacy in a provisional status, testing their newly acquired knowledge and skills before raising judgments of what they are able to do. If in the course of completing a task, they discover something that appears intimidating about the undertaking or suggests limitations to their mode of coping, they register a decline in self-efficaciousness despite their successful performance" (pp. 125–126). Agoraphobics, may, despite a successful venture into feared territory such as a supermarket, come away from the event as fearful as ever because of some unexpected and unnerving feeling of anxiety.

A clinical view of the cognitive processing of information, based on Beck's (1976; Beck & Emery, 1985) cognitive therapy, dovetails with social learning theory and provides useful leads for the practice of guided exposure treatment. The dysfunctional cognitions that Beck has identified, which are discussed in detail in Chapter 10, illustrate the distortions commonly seen in complex anxiety and depressive disorders.

Affect, or mood, plays a particularly influential role in biasing cognitive processing and efficacy judgments. One well-documented illustration of affect's role in influencing cognitive processing is Bower's (1981) research on the effects of mood on memory, demonstrating a mood-congruity effect (people attend to and learn more about events that match their emotional state). He proposes that emotion "serves as a memory unit that can enter into associations with coincident events." People tend to recall more experiences that are congruent affectively with their feeling state during recall. An agoraphobic's vivid recall of a previous panic attack, when anxious, is an example of the latter process. Subjects who are made to feel sad significantly lower their perceived efficacy about their capabilities across a wide range of different personal and interpersonal activities (Kavanagh & Bower, 1985). This finding shows how different emotional states can affect efficacy judgments, which, in turn, will influence an individual's capacity to cope with threatening or distressing situations. The reciprocal interaction between self-efficacy and negative mood states becomes an important part of social learning theory in understanding and treating anxiety and depressive disorders.

Affect changes cognitive accessibility, making mood-relevant material more available. Kihlstrom and Nasby (1981) note that "while moods are themselves created cognitively. . . . moods affect cognitive processes —thus leaving open the possibility for a vicious cycle that can be highly maladaptive. Consider the case of a clinician who attempts to alter negative cognitions. . . . by leading the client to focus on positive rather than negative features of percepts and memories. This will be difficult to do if the client's mood is having just the opposite effect. The clinician must find some way to break the vicious cycle of affect and cognition before treatment can hope to be successful—either by means of drugs . . . or better, by teaching the client a self-regulatory strategy by which he or she can learn to modulate the effect of mood" (p. 298). Another means of breaking the cycle to which Kihlstrom and Nasby refer would be to prod the person into a series of graded

mastery experiences, as in exposure treatment, which modify both the associated affect and cognition.

Long-Term Efficacy

The effects of exposure treatments have been maintained at lengthy follow-ups. In England, Munby and Johnston (1980) conducted a long-term follow-up of the agoraphobic patients of three major clinical studies, including the Gelder et al. (1973) investigation. Of sixty-six patients treated in these three studies, 95 percent were interviewed by a psychiatric research worker five to nine years later. Follow-up measures, repeating those used in the original studies, were compared with those obtained prior to treatment and six months after treatment ended. On most measures of agoraphobia, the patients were much better at follow-up than they had been before treatment. There had been little change in the patients' agoraphobia since six months after treatment. No evidence of any symptom substitution was found. The patients who showed the greatest reductions in agoraphobia were, at follow-up, among the least anxious and depressed. However, interpretation of these findings must be tempered by the report that a sizeable number had received additional treatment over the follow-up period. Excluding these subjects from the analysis of the data did little to change the outcome, however. Another result that suggests caution in evaluation is that at the end of follow-up, over 50 percent of these patients had received psychotropic medication. Twenty-one patients reported that they had experienced "a period of severe relapse, lasting at least a month."

Four other long-term follow-ups provide further support for the durable effects of in vivo exposure treatments of agoraphobic patients. In Holland, Emmelkamp and Kuipers

(1979) followed up seventy outpatient agoraphobics, derived from a sample of eighty-one patients who had received exposure treatments four years previously. All information was obtained from questionnaires mailed to patients. Improvements in phobic fear and avoidance obtained during treatment were maintained, and on some of the measures further improvement occurred; there was also a reduction in depression in the follow-up period, and no new anxiety disturbances developed. In Scotland, McPherson, Brougham, and McLaren (1980), using a postal follow-up of fifty-six agoraphobics who had shown improvement when treated with in vivo exposure, similarly found that treatment gains were maintained four years later. Finally, in England, Marks (1971) and Thorpe and Burns (1983), respectively, reported satisfactory maintenance of treatment effects in agoraphobics at four and eight year follow-ups.

Clinical Outcome

Although it can be concluded that systematic exposure methods are usually superior to alternative forms of psychological treatment, their limitations must be noted. Barlow, O'Brien, Last, and Holden (1983) estimate that roughly 25 percent of agoraphobics fail to benefit from exposure treatment. Of the remaining 75 percent, some make only limited improvements and continue to experience periodic anxiety problems. This latter point is made clear by long-term follow-ups. Moreover, this estimate must be interpreted in the light of an attrition rate from exposure treatment of roughly 10 to 20 percent, depending on the particular study.

Estimates of this sort are naturally somewhat arbitrary, and a host of moderating factors could affect the treatment outcome across different settings. Nonetheless, given these outcome statistics, what is the extent of improvement achieved? The primary dependent measure in a majority of studies has been independent clinical ratings of treatment outcome using a nine-point scale (Marks, 1981). Although these ratings are reliable, they do not provide an adequate picture of therapeutic improvement. Fortunately, some studies have measured changes in behavioral avoidance more directly, showing substantial improvement in functioning in this domain (Bandura, Adams, Hardy, & Howells, 1980; Mathews et al., 1981; Williams & Rappaport, 1983). As a result of behavioral treatment, agoraphobics are typically helped to drive, use public transport, shop, go to movies and restaurants, and travel—in short, to function independently.

Exposure treatment reduces not only phobic anxiety and avoidance, but also panic. In addition, exposure treatment is usually associated with significant decreases in depression. Marital satisfaction, although not directly treated, has also been shown to improve following exposure therapy (Barlow et al., 1983; Marks, 1981). No evidence of symptom substitution or therapy-induced negative effects has been found. These findings on the treatment of anxiety disorders show that behavior therapy produces broadly based improvement in people's lives. Treatment outcome extends beyond the reduction of specific phobic anxiety to the enhancement of other aspects of personal and interpersonal functioning. (Sloane et al., 1975; Zitrin, 1981). Moreover, these generally positive effects are not limited to the anxiety disorders.

Marital Satisfaction and Agoraphobia. Several theories of agoraphobia, particularly family-systems approaches, emphasize the significance of the marital relationship in the maintenance and modification of the disorder. One popular view is that agoraphobia is intimately linked to marital dissatisfaction; a related view is that agoraphobia is a symptom of a pathological family system. From this it follows that family therapy is necessary to treat the entire family. None of this clinical speculation is supported by acceptable empirical evidence (Mathews et al., 1981; Wilson, 1984b).

Among the many methodological problems in the literature on marriage and agoraphobia are the small number of patients that comprise many studies, the absence of appropriate control groups, questionable measures, and correlational and retrospective studies. An exception is a study by Buglass et al. (1977). They compared thirty married agoraphobic women with normal controls matched for age, sex, social class, and marital status, and found no significant differences between the two groups across a wide range of measures, including decision-making, domestic organization, social relationships, and problems in their children. Both husbands and wives of each group described their marriages in similar terms before the onset of agoraphobia or during the comparable period among the control group. Nor could Buglass et al. unearth evidence indicating that spouses were reinforcing dependency in the agoraphobic partners—no joy here for the systems theorists and their communications conceptions of agoraphobia. Arrindell and Emmelkamp (1985) compared female agoraphobics and their husbands to three comparison groups: nonphobic female psychiatric patients and their husbands, maritally distressed couples, and happily married couples. In terms of marital adjustment, the agoraphobics and their spouses were most similar to the happily married couples. By comparison, the nonphobic psychiatric controls reported significantly more marital distress and resembled the maritally distressed couples. Fisher and Wilson (1985) similarly found no differences in marital ad-

justment between agoraphobics and matched normal control subjects. These results indicate that agoraphobia is a problem that emerges independently from the interpersonal (marital) context.

The allegation that improvement in phobic behavior in one spouse leads to negative changes in the marriage (Hafner, 1976) has been discredited. Marks (1981) pointed out that the evidence is clearly that greatest improvement in phobias was associated with greatest improvement in other areas of function, including marital satisfaction. This result is the opposite of that expected from the symptom substitution model or from general systems theory (1981, p. 238). Other studies have shown that treating marital/interpersonal problems of agoraphobics does not change the phobic disorder, as would be required by theories (Chambless & Goldstein, 1982) which assume that agoraphobia is causally related to marital/interpersonal conflict (Chambless et al., 1982; Cobb, McDonald, Marks, & Stern, 1980).

Marital factors can influence the maintenance of treatment effects, as would be predicted by social learning theory. A caring spouse can provide the emotional support that helps the agoraphobic persist in confronting rather than avoiding treatment situations (Arnow, Taylor, Agras, & Telch, 1985). Agoraphobics with good marriages at the onset of exposure treatment maintain the reductions they make on phobic anxiety and avoidance better than their counterparts with poor marriages (Bland & Hallam, 1981). Including husbands in their agoraphobic wives' exposure treatment program (couples training) produced superior results to treating wives alone in one study (Barlow et al., 1983). A second study, however, failed to show any benefit of including the spouse in treatment (Cobb, Mathews, Childs-Clarke, & Blowers, 1984). Couples training may be particularly useful in treating patients whose marriages are poor to begin with (Barlow et al., 1983).

Behavior Therapy in Practice

The foregoing conclusions are based primarily on research studies which evaluated the effects of a specific therapeutic technique —namely, some form of exposure. The requirements of controlled research militated against individual assessment of each patient's problems, as would be standard clinical practice. Such individual assessment, a cardinal feature of clinical behavior therapy, would in all likelihood have led to multifaceted interventions in many cases. In vivo exposure would have been supplemented with such diverse strategies as assertion training, behavior rehearsal, marital therapy, and self regulatory procedures where appropriate. Thus it can be argued that the therapeutic results obtained in the controlled research described above represent a conservative index of the outcome that might be achieved with clinical practice.

Goldstein (1982) reported the outcome of thirty-four successive agoraphobics using an approach that involved an intensive two-week program, including ten daily group exposure sessions of three hours each, four one-and-one-half-hour group psychotherapy sessions, two one-and-one-half-hour significant other groups, two two-hour couples' group sessions, and four one-hour individual sessions. Each two-week program group was composed of six to eight clients. Aside from the intensive exposure sessions, treatment included cognitive restructuring, teaching of anxiety coping skills, breath control for hyperventilation symptoms, and "Gestalt techniques" (Goldstein, 1982, p. 191). No drugs were used.

At post-treatment, only two clients (6.25 percent) showed no improvement. Twenty-two percent were completely free of agora-phobic symptoms (including no panic attacks). This proportion increased at the succeeding follow-ups as follows: 34.9 percent at three months; 58.9 percent at six months; and 71.4 percent at one year. All other subjects were rated as moderately to much improved at each assessment period following treatment. Goldstein also reports significant improvement in other areas of the clients' functioning, such as depression and obsessive thinking. The elimination of panic attacks in the majority of clients without any medication is noteworthy.

The usual reservations about an uncontrolled clinical series apply to Goldstein's results. The small number of clients at the longer follow-up points is especially limiting. Nonetheless, this report does suggest that the findings of controlled studies of briefer and more limited interventions may provide too conservative an estimate of the actual clinical success that can be obtained with a multifaceted treatment program that is largely but not exclusively behavioral.

Behavioral and Alternative Therapies

Few comparative outcome studies of different psychological approaches to the treatment of agoraphobia have been completed, and those that are available have their methodological limitations (Kazdin & Wilson, 1978; Rachman & Wilson, 1980). The Klein et al. (1983) study, indicating no difference between imaginal desensitization and an unusually directive form of supportive psychotherapy with all phobic disorders, has been discussed above. Gillan and Rachman (1974) found that systematic desensitization was significantly superior to psychotherapy, although the quality of the psychotherapy treatment could be questioned. Gelder, Marks, and Wolff (1967) showed that systematic desensitization was more efficient, and on some measures more effective, than individual or group psycho-therapy. Nevertheless, these sparse data do not permit any definitive conclusions to be drawn.

The comparative effects of behavioral and alternative treatments for agoraphobia have also been evaluated using the statistical technique of meta-analysis (Andrews, Moran, & Hall, 1983). This analysis was based on twenty-six outcome studies published between 1956 and 1982, with 1975 being the median year. These studies involved the treatment of some 850 agoraphobics who had received a median of seventeen hours of therapy over four-and-a-half weeks and were assessed a median of three months later. Most were women and most were treated as outpatients. The designs used in the twenty-six studies varied from retrospective examinations of case material to randomized controlled trials against patients on placebos or waiting lists. The majority of studies were pre-post designs, with subjects being measured before and at various times after treatment. A standard measure of improvement was calculated for each measure in each study. Andrews and colleagues' conclusion? "On balance, therefore, it would appear that the graded exposure techniques are the treatments of choice, with the use of antidepressants being reserved for those unable or unwilling to confront their fears, or for when behavior therapy is unavailable. Certainly, both treatments seem to offer better results than the symptomatic management of panic attacks by anxiolytics, treatment which has no support in the literature, but which is very commonly used."

Behavioral and Pharmacological Therapies

A frequently used treatment for agoraphobia is the administration of antidepressant drugs (both tricyclics [e.g., imipramine] and monoamine oxidase inhibitors). This treatment is based on the theory that agoraphobia is a function of a biological or biochemical disposition to suffer panic attacks. Panic attacks are then followed, secondarily, by avoidance behavior. The antidepressant drugs are believed to remedy directly the biochemical abnormality that causes panic attacks through pharmacological action (Liebowitz, Fyer, Gorman, Dillon, et al., 1985; Zitrin et al., 1983).

Several controlled studies comparing the separate and combined effects of exposure and imipramine treatment have recently been completed. Three of these studies showed that exposure was at least as effective as imipramine; four indicated that imipramine, in the absence of some form of exposure treatment, has little therapeutic effect on agoraphobics (Marks, Gray, Cohen, et al., 1983; Mavissakalian & Michelson, 1983; Mavissakalian, Michelson, & Dealy, 1983; Telch, Agras, Taylor, Roth, & Gallen, 1985). For example, in the Marks et al. (1983) study, not a single significant therapeutic effect of imipramine over placebo was found on ratings of agoraphobic avoidance, self-ratings of anxiety and panic, global improvement, depression, or spontaneous panic attacks. The impact of these strongly negative findings is underscored by Marks et al.'s demonstration that satisfactory plasma levels of imipramine were obtained, together with significantly greater side-effects in the imipramine condition.

It is particularly important to evaluate the effects of antidepressant drugs independent of concomitant exposure to feared situations. Telch et al. (1985) randomly assigned agoraphobics to the following conditions: (1) imipramine alone, (2) imipramine plus in vivo exposure, and (3) placebo plus in vivo exposure. To control for the effects of exposure, subjects in the imipramine-alone condition were given counter-practice instructions, which emphasized the importance of refraining from entering phobic situations for the first eight weeks so that the medication would have time to take effect. The in vivo exposure treatment consisted of a total of nine hours of therapist-assisted group exposure spread over three consecutive days followed by a partner-assisted home-based exposure method described by Mathews et al. (1981).

Multiple behavioral, self-report, and physiological measures of outcome showed that the imipramine-only treatment produced no improvement on any index of phobic anxiety or avoidance. In contrast, the two exposure groups resulted in marked improvements on measures of phobic anxiety, phobic avoidance, self-efficacy, panic, and depression. Comparisons between the combined imipramine-exposure and placebo-exposure conditions revealed an advantage for the combined imipramine-exposure group across different measures. Only patients receiving the imipramine plus exposure treatment showed a significant reduction in panic attacks. These data dispute the notion that imipramine blocks panic attacks directly by its pharmacological action (Klein et al., 1983). Telch et al. suggest that antidepressant drugs such as imipramine add to the efficacy of exposure treatment via their effects on cognitive processing of evidence of improvement. Presumably, the drugs correct the tendency of agoraphobics to distort or discount their successful behaviors and thereby undermine their self-efficacy.

A fifth study (Zitrin, Klein, Woerner, & Ross, 1983), indicated that imipramine was more effective than imaginal desensitization or a drug placebo treatment. This study, however, has been criticized on several methodological grounds, including the lack of a specific measure of panic attacks, the primary target of antidepressant drugs, and the reliance on global clinical ratings of outcome (Emmelkamp, 1982; Mathews et al., 1981).

A sixth study, by Mavissakalian and Perel (1985), showed that at twelve weeks after treatment, imipramine was more effective than a placebo when added to exposure. Improvement was related to the dose of the drug, with high levels required for optimal efficacy.

The failure of imipramine alone to produce greater improvement than exposure on measures of mood and panic attacks has both practical consequences for choice of treatment and theoretical implications for the nature of agoraphobia with panic. The rationale for using antidepressant drugs is that they have specific "anti-phobic" properties. As such, they are said to reduce the primary problem in agoraphobia—spontaneous panic attacks. Phobic anxiety and avoidance are allegedly secondary reactions that may then be treated with behavioral methods. The results from the four studies reviewed here are inconsistent with this conceptualization of the anxiety disorder.

In clinical practice, these comparative outcome data must be evaluated with the following considerations in mind. First, as Telch, Tearnan, and Taylor (1983) point out, many agoraphobics dislike—and avoid—pharmacotherapy. For example, Telch et al. (1985) found that almost 20 percent of all agoraphobics who contacted the clinic expressed an unwillingness to take medication and thus were not accepted into the study. Further evidence for this limitation of drug treatment comes from Norton, Allen, and Hilton's (1982) study of the social validity of treatments for agoraphobia. Both a non-patients group and a group of agoraphobics rated psychological procedures as more acceptable and perceived them to be more effective than drug treatment. Graduated in vivo exposure received the highest ratings on both dimensions. Antidepressant medication was rated as the least acceptable treatment. Although the implications of social validity studies of therapies for actual clinical practice are necessarily limited, Norton et al.'s findings, together with Telch et al.'s clinical experience, must be seriously considered in planning treatment services for the full spectrum of agoraphobic patients.

Second, adverse physical side-effects of drug treatment must be taken into account. These side-effects are undoubtedly a cause of the relatively high rates of attrition associated with drug treatment. According to Telch et al., "drop-out rates from the antidepressant trials published to date consistently average between 35 and 40 percent, well above the mean of 10 percent for drug-free behavioral treatments" (p. 516). (Marks et al. [1983] report an attrition rate of 36 percent; the comparable figure for behavioral treatment studies conducted by this group is 16 percent). This phenomenon, together with the refusal of many agoraphobics to enter into pharmacotherapy in the first place, means that a non-trivial number of agoraphobics must necessarily be treated with psychological methods. This point is particularly important since effective drug treatment requires high dosages that increase the aversive side-effects (Mavissakalian & Perel, 1985). It also means that the success rates of pharmacotherapy with agoraphobics, whatever they are, are based on a somewhat select sample of patients.

The third caveat about the use of antidepressant medication with agoraphobics concerns the problem of relapse. Relapse rates when patients are withdrawn from imipramine are unacceptably high and predictable, ranging from 27 percent to 50 percent. It is important to realize that assertions of the utility of imipramine in the treatment of agoraphobia are based on immediate post-treatment evaluations, since empirical data on the lasting value of pharmacotherapy for agoraphobia do not exist. The long-term stability of behavioral treatment is discussed above.

ANXIETY STATES

Behavior therapy methods for nonphobic anxiety states have not been tested as extensively as in specific phobic disorders. An indication of the value of behavior therapy can be gleaned from the Sloane et al. (1975) study, in which fifty-seven of the ninety-four patients were diagnosed as having anxiety reactions using the DSM-II classification. The findings of this study showed that 48 percent of the control group and 80 percent of the behavior therapy and psychotherapy groups were considered improved or recovered. Behavior therapy produced significant improvement in both work and social adjustment, whereas psychotherapy resulted in only marginal improvement in work. Behavior therapy was significantly superior to the other groups on the global rating of improvement. At the one-year follow-up, there was no overall difference among the three groups on any of the dependent measures. Behavior therapy in this study included a range of methods such as imaginal desensitization, assertion training, direct advice, and relaxation training.

In DSM-III (1980), anxiety states are divided into panic disorder and generalized anxiety disorder.

Panic Disorder

In DSM-III, panic is defined as "the sudden onset of intense apprehension, fear, or terror often associated with feelings of impending doom" (p. 230). Panic appears to be qualitatively different from generalized anxiety, with a different pattern of development. Patients with panic disorder also have a stronger somatic component of their anxiety than patients with generalized anxiety disorder (Barlow, Vermilyea, Blanchard, Vermilyea, et al., 1985). Panics may be predictable or unpredictable, with feelings of loss of control and dizziness characteristic of the latter. Although panic disorder is singled out as a specific diagnostic category, panics occur in all of the diagnostic categories of anxiety disorders (Barlow et al., 1985; Rachman & Levitt, 1985). The immediate effects of panics are an increase in anticipatory anxiety, but not an increase in experienced fear (Rachman & Levitt, 1985). It is this consequence of anticipatory anxiety—a "fear of fear"—that motivates subsequent avoidance behavior, as in the case of agoraphobia.

Behavior therapy for panic disorder is still in its early stages. Exposure treatment may produce significant reductions in panic attacks in agoraphobics, particularly if it is combined with antidepressant drugs. However, exposure treatment may be unsuitable in cases in which there is no avoidance of particular situations. Accordingly, other cognitive-behavioral methods have been developed.

Clark, Salkovskis, and Chalkley (1985) have reported a respiratory control method that appears to be a promising means of substantially reducing panic attacks in those individuals whose panic is linked to hyperventilation.[1] They divided patients with panic attacks into "situationals" and "non-situationals." The latter, whose anxiety and panic were unrelated to any situation, seem similar to panic disorder patients. Treatment consisted of (1) brief, voluntary hyperventilation, which was intended to induce a mild panic attack, (2) explanation of the effects of overbreathing and reattribution of the cause of a patient's attacks to hyperventilation, and (3) training in slow

breathing incompatible with hyperventilation. Substantial reductions in frequency of panic attacks were obtained within two weeks in both groups of patients, despite the documented absence of exposure to feared situations.

Generalized Anxiety Disorder

Relatively few studies have evaluated the behavioral treatment of generalized anxiety disorder. Treatments focusing on its somatic component have consisted mainly of biofeedback and relaxation procedures (Rice & Blanchard, 1982). As in other areas of application, biofeedback (specifically, EMG feedback) is not reliably superior to progressive relaxation training. Moreover, clinical improvement has not been linked to reductions in muscle tension, as required by the logic of EMG biofeedback, indicating that other factors account for therapeutic change. Overall, treatment of generalized anxiety disorder with biofeedback/relaxation procedures has yielded distinctly modest results. For example, Raskin, Bali, and Peeke (1980) suggest that an improvement rate of no more than 40 percent can be expected.

Treatments featuring a combination of relaxation training and some form of cognitive restructuring have shown some positive effects. Woodward and Jones (1980) compared the following four conditions in the treatment of outpatients diagnosed as suffering from anxiety states: (1) cognitive restructuring, consisting of elements of both rational-emotive therapy and Meichenbaum's (1977) self-instructional training; (2) modified systematic desensitization, emphasizing coping rather than mastery imagery; (3) a combination of the two; and (4) a waiting list control. The combined treatment proved to be significantly superior to all others in reducing anxiety. Cognitive restructuring alone had little

---

1. Noting the similarity between the symptoms of panic attacks and the effects of hyperventilation, they suggest that hyperventilation may play a key role in panic. Specifically, they propose that hyperventilation is the basis of the physical symptoms of panic attacks and that cognitive misinterpretation of these symptoms is necessary for the effects to be experienced as panic.

therapeutic effect. Jannoun, Oppenheimer, and Gelder (1982) reported significant success in treating patients with generalized anxiety and panic attacks with a combination of relaxation and self-instructional training. Aside from improvements in anxiety ratings, treatment produced a 60 percent reduction in the medication patients took. Improvement was maintained at a three-month follow-up.

Barlow, Cohen, Waddell, et al. (1984) treated five generalized anxiety disorder and five panic disorder patients with a procedure that combined EMG biofeedback, relaxation training, and cognitive restructuring. Compared to a waiting list control group, treated patients improved significantly on clinicians' ratings, psychophysiological measures, and patients' daily self-monitoring of background anxiety and panic. This improvement was maintained at a three-month follow-up. The waiting list controls did not improve. Although the panic disorder patients showed greater somatic reactions on self-report and physiological measures prior to therapy, both groups of patients responded equally well to the treatment.

The lack of better research precludes any firm conclusion about the efficacy of behavior therapy with these nonphobic anxiety disorders.

OBSESSIVE-COMPULSIVE DISORDERS

An obsession is an "intrusive, repetitive thought, image, or impulse that is unacceptable and/or unwanted and gives rise to subjective resistance. It generally produces distress. Obsessions are difficult to remove and/or control . . . during calm periods the person acknowledges the senselessness of the thought or impulse. The content of an obsession is repugnant, worrying, blasphemous,

obscene, nonsensical—or all of these" (Rachman & Hodgson, 1980, p. 10). Typical clinical examples of obsessional thoughts are "Did I hit someone while driving home today?" "I feel I might hurt my child with a knife," and "I might have contracted venereal disease." Obsessional impulses are often associated with a fear of losing control, although impulses are rarely acted upon.

Compulsions are repetitive, stereotyped acts. They may be wholly unacceptable or, more often, partly acceptable, but are regarded by the person as being excessive or exaggerated. They are preceded or accompanied by a subjective sense of compulsion, and provoke subjective resistance. They generally produce distress. In calmer moments, the person usually acknowledges the senselessness of these activities (Rachman & Hodgson, 1980). The two most frequent classes of compulsions are cleaning and checking rituals. The classic example of the former type is the compulsive handwasher; a common example of the second type is the person who compulsively checks the security of appliances and of entrances to his home.

The disorder begins in late adolescence or early adulthood, with no evidence that it is more likely to afflict women than men. Summarizing the evidence, Rachman and Hodgson (1980) state that the factors that promote obsessive-compulsive disorders include "a nonspecific genetic component, observational learning experiences that promote them indirectly (by fostering dependent, noncoping, fearful behavior), reactive depression, and, in compulsive cleaning disorders, a precipitating event" (p. 51). Precipitating factors commonly involve stressful events (e.g., problems at work, marital difficulties) or a depressive episode. Depression may also cause obsessive-compulsive problems, and seems closely associated with obsessions in particular.

According to two-factor theory, compulsive behavior is maintained, if not originally acquired, on the basis of the anxiety reduction produced by the escape/avoidance response (the ritual). Experimental analyses of the persistence of compulsive behavior have shown that rituals generally do decrease anxiety, especially in the case of cleaning compulsions. But there are numerous instances in which engaging in the compulsion, particularly in checking rituals, does not result in anxiety reduction. The explanation of this pattern of behavior remains unclear. Rachman and Hodgson (1980) conclude that anxiety may be a sufficient condition for the maintenance of compulsive behavior, but it is not a necessary condition.

Treatment of Compulsions

Obsessive-compulsive disorders are among the most severe and disabling psychiatric problems. As in other areas, the behavioral-treatment literature shows a definite progression toward the development of increasingly refined and effective therapeutic techniques. After methods such as imaginal systematic desensitization proved to be largely ineffective, more effective methods were developed—namely, in vivo exposure and response prevention.

These methods may be illustrated with reference to a compulsive handwasher. The different objects or activities which lead the client to wash his hands are first identified through behavioral assessment. Then, following a thorough explanation of the technique and its rationale, and with the client's fully informed consent, he is encouraged, systematically, to touch objects that trigger handwashing. Either graduated exposure or flooding may be used. Once the client has touched what he unrealistically views as a "contaminated" object, he is asked to refrain from washing. In

some in-patient treatments, using strict response prevention, the client might have been asked to agree, beforehand, to be denied an opportunity to wash his hands. The client's anxiety typically rises initially after touching the object, and then decreases over the course of the session. Focusing the client's attention on his fear of contamination facilitates treatment (Grayson, Foa, & Steketee, 1982). As in the case of phobic disorders, the goal of treatment is to break the negative reinforcing value of the compulsion and increase the client's self-efficacy.

Most of the evidence for efficacy of these behavioral methods comes from uncontrolled clinical reports, with few controlled studies of the sort that have characterized research on the phobic disorders. Nonetheless, the consistency of findings by investigators using in vivo exposure and response prevention in different countries, and between controlled and uncontrolled reports, strongly suggests that a behavioral approach is effective with compulsive rituals.

Illustrative of the controlled research on the treatment of obsessive-compulsive disorders are two studies by Rachman, Marks, and their colleagues at the Institute of Psychiatry in London. In the first study (Marks, Hodgson, & Rachman, 1975), three methods were compared: flooding in vivo, guided exposure plus modeling, and a combination of the two. Patients were selected whose disorders were sufficiently severe to merit admission to an inpatient unit. All of them had previously received other forms of treatment. After an initial week's evaluation, all subjects received fifteen one-hour sessions of relaxation training over the next three weeks. This extended period of relaxation therapy was designed to serve as an attention-placebo control. Thereafter, the subjects were randomly assigned to the three treatment conditions for an additional fifteen sessions of therapy during the final three weeks. Subjects were assessed before and after treatment, at the end of flooding or modeling, and at a six-month follow-up. Measurements taken included self-ratings, psychiatric rating scales, attitudinal responses, behavioral avoidance tests tailored to individuals' specific problems, and direct measures of compulsive acts.

Both flooding and modeling were significantly more effective than the relaxation control on all measures, but they did not differ from each other. The combined treatment did not increase the success of either method alone. A subsequent two-year follow-up revealed that of the twenty clients treated, fourteen were judged much improved, one improved, and five unchanged. Subjects who had improved at the six-month follow-up maintained their progress. Improvements in obsessive-compulsive problems were accompanied by improvement in other aspects of the patients' functioning.

The limitations of this important study should be noted. Relaxation is not necessarily a stringent control condition against which to compare the effects of flooding and participant modeling. Furthermore, the latter techniques were administered after the relaxation training, confounding order effects with the effects of different treatments. Finally, the efficacy of the specific behavioral methods at the two-year follow-up is difficult to determine, because many subjects received additional treatment during this period. Eleven subjects had to be treated in their home settings after being discharged from the hospital.

In the second study (Rachman, Cobb, Grey, McDonald, Mawson, Sartory, & Stern, 1979), the effects of behavioral treatment (in vivo exposure with modeling and self-imposed response prevention), alone and in combination with an antidepressant drug (clomipramine), were investigated with forty chronic obsessive-compulsive patients. Consistent with previous findings, the behavioral method

produced significantly greater reductions in compulsive rituals than did a relaxation-training control. The flooding treatment did not, however, result in an improvement in the patients' depressed mood. The use of the clomipramine did produce a general improvement in patients' mood states, as well as some change in compulsive behavior. The specificity of the treatment effects argues against alternative interpretations of placebo factors or the therapeutic relationship. The therapeutic effects of the in vivo exposure treatment were maintained at one- and two-year follow-ups (Marks, Stern, Mawson, Cobb, & McDonald, 1980), and improvement had generalized to social adjustment. Discontinuing clomipramine after forty weeks of treatment resulted in frequent relapses, although the patients improved again after readministration of the drug. As in the previous study (Marks et al., 1975), several patients required additional therapy following the end of the formal treatment period (four weeks of pharmacotherapy as outpatients, followed by six weeks of behavioral treatment as impatients). Furthermore, Marks et al. report that during the two-year follow-up, eight patients had to be readmitted to the hospital (four each from the drug and placebo conditions) and that "extra counseling and support was given to five clomipramine and five placebo patients, to a mean of five sessions" (p. 17).

In both of the foregoing studies, patients were simply instructed to desist from engaging in their rituals during and between treatment sessions, and compliance seemed to affect outcome. Response prevention can be ensured by continuous nursing supervision during inpatient treatment, and those studies that have followed such a procedure have obtained particularly positive outcomes (Foa & Goldstein, 1978; Meyer, Levy, & Schnurer, 1974; Mills, Agras, Barlow, & Mills, 1973). For example, using in vivo exposure and strict response prevention, Foa and Goldstein demonstrated significant improvements in their sample of twenty-one obsessive-compulsive patients after only two weeks of treatment. In the majority of cases, these gains were maintained and even increased during follow-ups ranging from three months to three years. The therapeutic improvements spread beyond the target symptoms to include improvements in occupational adjustment, social life, sexual adjustment, and family relations. The most striking feature of their results is that two-thirds of the patients became asymptomatic after treatment. The therapeutic changes were large, stable, and generalized. Moreover, the major changes took place within the remarkably short time of two weeks of intensive treatment. The possible contribution of nonspecific factors cannot be excluded, given that there was no control group, but the fact that no changes were observed in the pretreatment period, with or without therapist contact, rules out at least some of the commonly encountered nonspecific therapeutic factors.

The Mills et al. study (1973), employing rigorous single-case experimental methodology, demonstrated that response prevention per se, independent of any placebo factors, produces substantial improvements in compulsive rituals. Strictly supervised response prevention conducted with inpatients has yet to be compared to self-imposed response prevention. It may be that the additional resources and practical problems entailed by the former are a relatively small price to be paid if, in the ultimate analysis, it proves to be more efficient and possibly more effective than the latter.

Other findings on the behavioral treatment of compulsions can be summarized as follows:

1. In some cases, self-controlled exposure appears to be as effective as therapist-controlled exposure (Emmelkamp & Kraanen, 1977).
2. Combining self-directed in vivo exposure with cognitive restructuring has not been found to increase therapeutic efficacy (Emmelkamp, van derHelm, van Zanten, & Plochg, 1980).
3. Trainee nurse-therapists working under the direction of psychologists and psychiatrists achieve success with severely incapacitated patients that may be comparable to the outcome obtained by professional therapists in some cases (Marks et al., 1977).
4. Including patients' spouses in self-directed in vivo exposure treatment may produce results superior to those obtained by treating the patients alone (Emmelkamp, 1982).
5. Although in vivo exposure and response prevention seem to be essential elements in eliminating compulsive rituals, effective treatment must often include supplementary behavioral strategies. Recall the additional treatment (visits to patients' home and involvement of family members in the treatment process) given patients in the Marks et al. (1975; 1980) outcome studies. Spouses or family members are not always easily co-opted into the treatment program, and formal marital or family therapy may be necessary to produce treatment effects in the first place, let alone to facilitate the maintenance of therapeutic improvement. Similarly, Emmelkamp (1982), noting that a complete behavioral assessment of individual cases occasionally reveals patients hampered by social anxiety and lack of assertiveness, has reported clinical findings showing that assertion training may be a necessary component of effective treatment.
6. Aside from supplementing in vivo exposure and response prevention with other behavioral methods, therapists may also find antidepressant drugs to be necessary components of many obsessive-compulsive patients. This is especially the case where the obsessive-compulsive disorder is associated with depression (Marks et al., 1980). Nevertheless, tricyclic antidepressants (e.g., clomipramine) have an effect on compulsions that is independent of their impact on depression.

Treatment of Obsessions

Far less progress has been made in the treatment of obsessions than compulsive rituals. In thought stopping, clients are instructed to bring on their obsessional thought or image, at which point the therapist suddenly shouts "Stop!" (Wolpe, 1958). This disrupts the obsession. The procedure is repeated until the client is able to terminate his obsessive ruminations by saying "Stop!" subvocally. The client is instructed that the thoughts will usually return, but that he or she should repeatedly use the technique to interrupt unwanted thoughts as they begin. Although some case studies have yielded successful results with this technique, the little experimental research that is available has failed to show its efficacy (Stern, Lipsedge, & Marks, 1973).

The use of imaginal exposure and response prevention has yielded more promising results. As described by Rachman and Hodgson (1980), clients are systematically instructed to engage in their obsessional thinking for a prolonged period. They are told not to make any attempts to avoid the obsession (e.g., think of, or do, something else), even if they experience anxiety and distress. Clients are required to implement the method at home and keep careful records of their progress. The rationale for this method is that prolonged exposure to distressing material will produce habituation (extinction) of the anxiety response. In our own clinical practice, we find it useful to have clients make a detailed tape-recording of their obsession, and then repeatedly listen to the tape for prolonged periods (e.g., thirty minutes or more). This procedure strengthens the salience of the obsessional content and facilitates response prevention. Controlled evaluations of this technique have yet to be made.

Analyses of Treatment Failures

The evidence from both uncontrolled clinical trials and controlled outcome studies reveals a consistent failure rate ranging from 10 percent to 30 percent (Rachman & Hodgson, 1980). The reasons for this failure are still unclear, although patients who are depressed and who do not believe their obsessions to be irrational have been reported to do poorly (Foa & Tilmanns, 1980).

In an analysis of the predictors of outcome, Foa, Grayson, Steketee, Doppelt, et al. (1983) examined the data from fifty patients treated in their program. These patients had participated in different treatment outcome studies that had evaluated the effects of three main treatment methods alone or in combination: in vivo exposure to situations or objects that trigger obsessive-compulsive behavior, imaginal exposure, and response prevention. Using a composite score of change in both obsessions and compulsions, at post-treatment, 58 percent of the patients were classified as much improved (i.e., an improvement of at least 70 percent); 38 percent as improved (i.e., an improvement of 31 to 69 percent); and 2 percent as failures. Although Foa et al. comment that patients who received both imaginal and in vivo exposure fared better than those who received only in vivo exposure, differences between groups did not reach statistical significance. A correlation of 0.49 was found between outcome at post-treatment and follow-up. Patients rated as much improved maintained their improvement. Patients who were only moderately improved showed unstable patterns of functioning during follow-up.

Reactivity and habituation to feared stimuli within and between sessions were all negatively related to outcome. Reactivity in this context refers to the highest subjective anxiety level reported during the session in which patients were first exposed to their most feared stimulus. Habituation within sessions was defined as the percentage of change between the highest level of anxiety reported in response to the first presentation of the most feared stimulus and the lowest level during the same session. Habituation between sessions was defined as percentage change in self-reported anxiety from the highest level in response to the first presentation of the most feared stimulus in the fifth or sixth session to the highest level in response to the same stimulus in exposure session 10. Consistent with previous studies, pre-treatment level of depression was also negatively related to treatment outcome.

From Research to Clinical Practice

In Chapter 17, on clinical methodology, we raise the question of the generalizability of controlled clinical research to actual clinical practice. We discuss how there may be differences between patients, therapists, and even the ways the same therapy is implemented. Accordingly, it is important to evaluate the correspondence between results of research and those achieved in routine clinical practice.

A good example in the present context is a report by Kirk (1983), who described the treatment of thirty-six consecutive referrals to a National Health Service Clinic in England. In many ways this sample was similar to those treated in research studies, although there were also differences. One such difference was the higher proportion of patients with pure obsessions than has been the case in controlled trials. The patients described by Kirk also had received less previous treatment. As for treatment, there was less time for therapist-assisted in vivo exposure. But there was a heavy emphasis on homework assignments and patients were taught anxiety coping skills more frequently than has been the case in controlled studies that have focused mainly on exposure and response prevention methods. Of the fourteen patients with

obsessions who completed treatment, eleven were treated with thought stopping. Graded exposure was used in seven cases and relaxation training in eleven. All patients received support, encouragement, and reinforcement for homework assignments. In many cases the treatment was brief. Thus, 19 percent had fewer than five sessions and 58 percent received fewer than ten sessions.

Outcome was reported in global improvement ratings based on patients' self-recordings and therapists' judgements. Three-quarters of the sample were rated as moderately improved or better. Only two patients remained unchanged and none became worse. Of the sixteen patients with obsessions, twelve were rated as "goal achieved;" another was moderately improved. Kirk notes that this figure of 81 percent improved is more favorable than outcomes in controlled studies. An examination of hospital files to see if the patients sought subsequent psychiatric help, covering a period ranging from one to five years, indicated that in 81 percent of cases there was no evidence of further contact. Five cases had been referred for more behavioral treatment for obsessional-compulsive problems and one had received antidepressant medication. These results are most encouraging, although the global outcome measure used requires that they be cautiously interpreted.

OTHER ANXIETY PROBLEMS

Cognitive-behavioral methods have been used extensively to modify anxiety problems not easily classified within the DSM-III categories of anxiety disorders. Two examples are social-evaluative and test anxiety. Both have been a common target of mainly analogue research, often using college students as subjects. One of the major methods used to treat these, among other problems, is cognitive restructuring.

Cognitive Restructuring

The therapies in this category are based on the assumption that emotional disorders are the result of maladaptive thought patterns. The task of therapy is to restructure these maladaptive cognitions.

Rational-Emotive Therapy

The oldest of the cognitive restructuring therapies is Ellis's (1970) rational-emotive therapy (RET), which, until the 1970s, existed outside the mainstream of behavior therapy. According to Ellis, the road to hell is paved, not with good intentions, but with irrational assumptions. These assumptions or self-statements are said to be irrational because they are distortions of objective reality. Ellis (1970) lists twelve irrational core assumptions said to be at the root of most emotional disturbance. Examples include "Human misery is externally caused and is forced on one by outside people and events," and "One must have certain and perfect control over things."

Clients do not always consciously or deliberately make these irrational assumptions in everyday situations. These self-statements or beliefs appear to be automatic and pervasive in their influence because they have been repeated so often that they assume the status of an overlearned response.

Treatment consists of assisting the client to identify these irrational ideas and replace them with more constructive, rational thoughts. The therapy consists of the following procedural steps:

1. verbal persuasion aimed at convincing the client of the philosophical tenets of RET

2. identification of irrational thoughts through client self-monitoring and therapist feedback

3. direct challenges to the client's irrational ideas and models and rational reinterpretations of disturbing events

4. repeated cognitive rehearsal aimed at substituting rational self-statements for previously irrational interpretation

5. behavioral tasks designed to develop rational reactions to replace formerly irrational, distress-producing assumptions[2]

Systematic Rational Restructuring

A procedure developed by Goldfried (1979) is a variation of RET. The technique of systematic rational restructuring is more clearly specified and structured than is Ellis's method. In a manner similar to the procedure in systematic desensitization, the client is asked to imagine a hierarchy of anxiety-eliciting situations. At each step the client is instructed to identify irrational thoughts associated with the specific situation, dispute them, and reevaluate the situation more rationally. In addition, clients are instructed to practice rational restructuring in specific in vivo situations that elicit anxiety. Although procedurally differ-

---

2. RET is usually viewed as a therapeutic approach that rests primarily on the use of verbal persuasion, logical analysis, and rational restructuring of faulty thought patterns. Ellis (1977) has argued that this is too narrow a view of RET and that behavioral homework assignments have always been part of RET. In his most recent formulation, Ellis asserts that RET includes the use of all behavior therapy techniques, Gestalt therapy methods, encounter group exercises, and other therapies. If RET is this all-inclusive, it would be impossible to evaluate. For present purposes we concentrate on the specific assumptions about faulty thought patterns that are the basis of RET and the explicitly cognitive techniques that Ellis has repeatedly emphasized as the major methods of therapeutic change (Ellis, 1962, 1970). It is this insistence on the primary role of cognitive processes in clinical disorders and their treatment that distinguishes RET from alternative treatment approaches.

ent, systematic rational restructuring shares the same rationale as RET, and the two methods are not distinguished in the critical evaluation that follows.

RET: A Critical Evaluation. The theoretical framework for RET is not well-developed. RET boils down to the conclusion that thoughts influence behavior. Ellis's theory does not at present provide a formal theoretical model for guiding empirical research. Maladaptive thoughts may contribute to emotional disorders. However, research does not provide support for the loose theoretical assumptions on which RET rests. For example, there is no convincing evidence that Ellis's list of irrational assumptions causes emotional conflicts. Goldfried and Sobocinski (1975) found that the tendency to hold irrational beliefs of this nature was correlated with different forms of anxiety, but this was only a correlation. One cannot argue from correlation to cause. Rogers and Craighead (1977) showed that negative self-statements increased physiological arousal, but their findings suggest that this relationship might be more complex than is noted in RET. Nor is there any evidence that most clients even share the irrational assumptions described by Ellis. Many of them may be irrelevant to a particular client's problems, and many clients protest that they do not hold such beliefs. Goldfried and Davison (1976) report that two of Ellis's notions are especially characteristic of neurotic clients—"everybody must love me" and "I must be perfect in everything I do." Yet these beliefs are too global and imprecise. For example, few clients really believe that "everybody must love me"; rather, this translates to the individual client wishing that a few highly significant people love him or her. Similarly, the desire to be perfect in everything usually means that the client has unduly

high and strict standards of self-reinforcement in specific areas of functioning.

It is difficult to assess the efficacy of RET because the appropriate outcome studies have been sparse, often lacking in the necessary controls, and frequently based on nonbehavioral measures. The following are some examples of the better controlled outcome studies on RET.

DiLoreto (1971) performed a frequently cited outcome study on the treatment of interpersonal anxiety in college students. The different treatment groups in this study were as follows: (1) RET, (2) systematic desensitization, (3) client-centered therapy, (4) attention-placebo, and (5) no treatment. DiLoreto also investigated the interaction between specific treatments and the personality type of the subjects by assigning an equal number of introverted and extroverted subjects to each treatment group. The results indicated that all three treatment groups differed significantly from the control groups on behavioral and self-report outcome measures, with the exception that the client-centered group was not superior on the self-report scale of anxiety. Overall, however, systematic desensitization was significantly more effective in reducing anxiety than either RET or client-centered therapy. For example, systematic desensitization was equally effective with introverted and extroverted subjects. RET, however, proved to be effective only with the introverted subjects. The results of a similar study of the treatment of interpersonal anxiety by Kanter and Goldfried (1979) proved to be more favorable to a variation of RET, namely rational restructuring. Compared to a desensitization treatment and a waiting list control condition, rational restructuring was more consistently effective across a broad range of behavioral and subjective measures of anxiety in interpersonal interactions at post-treatment and at a two-month follow-up. As we have noted, rational restructuring appears to be ineffective with simple phobias and agoraphobia.

Cognitive restructuring has proven effective in the treatment of test anxiety (Rachman & Wilson, 1980). The efficacy of this method with test anxiety is probably due to the fact that cognitive and attentional processes are the critical factors as opposed to motivational and physiological processes.

SUMMARY

Agoraphobia is the most complex and difficult to treat of the phobic disorders. The two main behavior therapy methods used to treat it have been flooding and graduated in vivo exposure. The latter is more commonly used today. Exposure may be cost-effectively conducted by nonprofessional assistants or by the clients themselves under a therapist's supervision. Both flooding and exposure have been shown to be more effective than alternative psychological methods such as cognitive restructuring. Studies have shown that the results of exposure treatment are maintained even at follow-ups ranging from four to nine years.

Clinical findings on the use of exposure fit better with social learning theory than the conditioning model from which it was originally derived. Social learning theory also suggests practical guidelines for the more effective use of exposure treatment with complex phobic disorders. Unlike controlled clinical trials, behavior therapists in clinical practice will supplement exposure with other cognitive-behavioral strategies. These multifaceted programs are arguably more effective than the restricted use of exposure alone.

Agoraphobia is not a manifestation of a pathological family system that necessitates family therapy. Improvements in agoraphobia are usually accompanied by improvements in marital satisfaction; no symptom substitution occurs. Including the spouse in treatment enhances treatment outcome in some cases.

Controlled studies indicate that exposure is as effective as treatment with antidepressant drugs, although a combined approach might be optimal in some cases. However, more clients drop out of drug treatment than from behavior therapy, and even successfully treated clients tend to relapse once the drugs have been discontinued.

Panic attacks are often reduced by exposure treatment, and respiratory control treatment combined with cognitive restructuring has shown promise. Generalized anxiety disorder has been reduced by a combination of relaxation training and cognitive restructuring, although firm conclusions about the efficacy of behavior therapy cannot be drawn.

Exposure and response prevention have proved consistently effective in eliminating compulsive rituals. However, as in the case of complex phobic disorders, complementing exposure with additional behavioral methods, including spouse participation, may be necessary. There is far less evidence on the efficacy of behavioral treatment of obsessions, with imaginal exposure and thought stopping emerging as two of the more widely used methods.

Other forms of social-evaluative anxiety have been treated with cognitive restructuring methods, the oldest of which is Ellis's rational-emotive therapy (RET). The theoretical basis of RET is inadequate, and empirical evidence for its specific claims is weak. There is little evidence that strictly verbal forms of cognitive restructuring are effective. They are significantly less effective than behavioral methods in the treatment of phobias and obsessive-compulsive disorders.

10

Depression

PREVALENCE

Almost all individuals feel sad, apathetic, and listless on occasion. For some, however, these feelings become overwhelming. They experience little enjoyment in people and events, show minimal interest in daily occurrences, lack motivation, feel helpless, and often have suicidal thoughts. Approximately 10 to 20 percent of the population experiences depression to such a magnitude that clinical intervention is warranted (Craighead, 1984). Women experience problems of depression approximately twice as frequently as men do, and about 6 percent of women and 3 percent of men are hospitalized for it (APA, 1980). Depression is most common in the 18 to 29 age range, while 10 to 12 percent of the college population reports moderate depression and 5 percent reports severe depression.

Depression has been recognized for centuries as an important health problem. It was depicted as early as the eighth century B.C. when Saul was shown as despondent and hopeless. Initially, he responded to David's music, but he later became so severely depressed and psychotic that he attempted to kill David and his son. The term "melancholy" was first used in Hippocratic writing in the fourth century B.C., and as early as the time of Christ, melancholy was thought to be a biochemical disturbance.

During the Renaissance, mild depression was considered fashionable (Andreasen, 1984). Aristotle said that those who are eminent in philosophy, politics, poetry, and the arts all have tendencies toward depression. Well-known individuals such as Abraham Lincoln and Winston Churchill were depressed, and their accounts of the influence of depression on their lives exemplify the personal toll that depression can have.

Fifteen percent of seriously depressed individuals commit suicide (Robins & Guze, 1972), and 80 percent of individuals who commit suicide are depressed (Flood & Saeger, 1968). The third leading cause of death among late adolescents is suicide (Craighead, 1985), and depression is prominent in the majority of cases.

Box 10–1   *Abraham Lincoln: "The Fatal First of January, 1841!"*

Where can Abraham Lincoln be? Has he not looked forward to this, his wedding day? No; to Lincoln it is almost his death day. By daybreak, after persistent search Lincoln's friends find him. The mental strain he has manifested all through the engagement now drives him with restless agitation into a state bordering on melancholia. This is not the time to berate him for his delinquency. He is too ill mentally, his suffering is too acute, and his friends take him into their care. (pg. 55)

After a few days, during which he scarcely eats or sleeps, Lincoln appears less agitated, but his thinking is labored and his actions are similarly slow. Periods of silence are broken by lamentations and listlessness. He is indifferent to his surroundings, interrupted by short-lived periods of a pressure of activity, as though he were laboring under an intense inner conflict. His thoughts are filled with gloomy forebodings. On the days when he is less perturbed he is able to attend the sessions of the legislature, yet he is clothed in a constant mood of apathy and gloom. His friends encourage him to attend these sessions, as this activity may take his mind from his recent misfortune. (pg. 56)

A few weeks later, he writes Stuart in Washington, "I have within the last few days, been making a most discreditable exhibition of myself in the way of hypochondriasm." And a few days later, in answer to a letter from his partner, he states, "From the deplorable state of my mind at this time, I fear I shall give you but little satisfaction," but he is able to give his partner briefly the political news. Yet even this little attention to the issues at hand fatigues Lincoln, and he ends, "I am now the most miserable man living. If what I feel were equally distributed to the whole human family, there would be not one cheerful face on the earth. Whether I shall ever be better, I cannot tell; I awfully forebode I shall not. To remain as I am is impossible; I must die or be better . . ." (pg. 57, Clark, 1933)

DESCRIPTION

Depression is generally described as an affective disorder. The American Psychiatric Association's criteria for a "major depressive episode" include the absence of another major psychological disorder and the presence of at least four of the following problems for nearly every day, for at least two weeks:

1. poor appetite or significant weight loss (when not dieting) or increased appetite or significant weight gain (in children under six, consider failure to make expected weight gains)
2. insomnia or hypersomnia
3. psychomotor agitation or retardation (but not merely subjective feelings of restlessness or being slowed down) (in children under six, hypoactivity)
4. loss of interest or pleasure in usual activities, or decrease in sexual drive not limited to a period when delusional or hallucinating (in children under six, signs of apathy)
5. loss of energy; fatigue
6. feelings of worthlessness, self-reproach, or excessive or inappropriate guilt (either may be delusional)
7. complaints or evidence of diminished ability to think or concentrate, such as slowed thinking, or indecisiveness not associated with marked loosening of associations or incoherence
8. recurrent thoughts of death, suicidal ideation, wishes to be dead, or suicide attempt (APA, 1980, p. 214)

There are two major types of depression, bipolar or manic-depression and unipolar depression. Manic depression or manic-depressive disorder, as it is commonly called, refers to the cyclic variation between elation and despondency. Unipoplar depression is diagnosed when there are one or more episodes of major depression without the presence of mania.

At the turn of the century, psychoanalytic explanations of depression were the accepted view of depression, but with the discovery of psychotropic medication in the 1950s and the concomitant use of electroconvulsive shock therapy (ECT), the accepted conceptualizations of depression, whether unipolar or bipolar, became biological. According to Craighead (1984), there was a critical absence of psychological theorizing regarding depression from the 1950s to the mid 1960s.

Bipolar depression is responsive to antidepressant medication or lithium, but there is little evidence that such depression is responsive to any type of psychotherapy (Rush, 1982). In contrast, unipolar depression is clearly responsive to various types of psychotherapy and antidepressant medication.

PSYCHOLOGICAL MODELS

The primary psychological theories of depression that have led to validated treatments are (1) Beck's cognitive distortion and negative self-schema theory, (2) Lewinsohn's behavioral model of depression, (3) Rehm's self-control model of depression, and (4) Weissman's interpersonal theory of depression. One cognitive/psychological account of depression and helplessness (Abramson, Seligman, & Teasdale, 1978) has had significant impact on research regarding the etiology of depression, but this theoretical account has not generated as much treatment research as have the other four theories of depression.

Beck's Cognitive Theory

Central themes held to be critical in the development and maintenance of depression are: concepts of self, world, and future. According to Beck (1967, 1976), these views are negatively distorted in such a way that external events are construed to represent a loss or deprivation to the depressed person.

Negative View of Self

On the basis of a number of case studies, Beck was convinced that depressed persons view many events in the world in terms of failure and rejection, in spite of or independent of disconfirming evidence. In this vein, Beck found a negative association between self-concept and severity of depressive symptoms. He also found that personal inadequacy and failure were common themes in the clinical interviews of depressed patients.

Negative View of the World

Depressed individuals view their world during their waking and sleeping hours as filled with loss. Both during clinical interviews and in reports of dreams, depressed persons report more difficulties and losses than do nondepressed persons (Hauri, 1976). Depressed undergraduates rate common personal problems as more difficult to cope with than nondepressed students do (Funabiki & Calhoun, 1979).

Negative View of the Future

Most cognitive theories of depression emphasize negative expectations about important future events as a major cause of depression. Accordingly, a number of studies have shown an association between depression and measures of pessimism and helplessness. Such studies are correlational. In an attempt to establish a causal relationship between negative cognitions and depression, two research strategies have been utilized: inducing depressive cognitions in initially nondepressed subjects in a laboratory and analyzing the role of cognitive variables and depressive symptoms in longitudinal studies. In the induction studies, subjects read negative statements suggesting either lack of self-worth or the experience of bodily sensations commonly associated with depression, such as fatigue and lack of energy. Subjects who read "elated" or neutral statements reported less frequent lowered mood and other deficits common to depression. While some of the changes obtained may be due to experimental demand characteristics or implied suggestions by the experimenters, it is also plausible that when individuals experience negative statements by various media (reading, TV, or movies), their affect can change. In the longitudinal studies of cognition, researchers have followed the course of depressive episodes and found that the degree of improvement over time is correlated with a concomitant decrease in depressive distortions (Krantz & Hammen, 1979) and more positive expectations about the future. In related research, Seligman and Abramson (cf., Seligman, 1981), found that depressive cognitions predicted depression at a later date in mostly non-depressed subjects. More recently, Peterson and Seligman (1984) provided some support for a general attributional analysis of depression.

Cognitive Distortions

Cognitive distortions, according to Beck, cause many if not all of a person's depressed states. Burns (1980), who presented Beck's theoretical perspective in a popular book, *Feeling Good*, said, "Depression is not an emotional disorder at all! The sudden change in the way you *feel* is of no more causal relevance than a runny nose is when you have a cold. Every bad feeling you have is the result of your distorted cognitive thinking. Illogical pessimistic attitudes play the central role in the development and continuation of all your symptoms. . . . You will learn . . . that the negative thoughts that flood your mind are the actual *cause* of your self-defeating emotions. These thoughts are what keep you lethargic and make you feel inadequate. Your

---

Box 10–2   *Attributional Model of Depression*

When individuals experience uncontrolled negative events, they often display strong emotional responses such as depression. This phenomenon has been described as learned helplessness (Maier & Seligman, 1976). The helplessness model was expanded by Abramson, Seligman, and Teasdale (1978)* to account for the loss of self-esteem in depression and the generality of depressive symptoms. More specifically, when people face uncontrollable, bad events, they ask

1. Is it something about me (internal) or the situation (external)?
2. Is the bad event likely to be persistent (stable) or transient (unstable)?
3. Is the cause likely to affect a variety of outcomes (global explanation) or to be of limited concern (specific explanation)?

In the reformulation of the helplessness model, internal explanations lead to self-esteem loss. Stable explanations were held to cause chronic depressive symptoms following bad events. Global explanations tended to have pervasive depressive effects following bad events. Essentially, the more individuals engage in explanatory styles that are internal, stable, and global the more likely they are to be depressed; suggestive evidence from cross-sectional studies, longitudinal studies, and case studies supports this attributional model of depression (Peterson & Seligman, 1984). Evidence for the consistency of the attributional dimensions across situations is weak (Fincham, Beach, & Nelson, in press) but this attribution research has been very valuable in prompting research.

*Copyright 1978 by the American Psychological Association. Reprinted by permission.

negative thoughts, or cognitions, are the most frequently overlooked symptoms of your depression. The cognitions contain the key to relief and therefore are your most important symptoms" (p. 29).

Beck's ten most important cognitive distortions were summarized by Burns (1980).

1. All-or-nothing thinking: You see things in black-and-white categories. If your performance falls short of perfect, you see yourself as a total failure.

2. Overgeneralization: You see a single negative event as a never-ending pattern of defeat.

3. Mental filter: You pick out a single negative detail and dwell on it exclusively so that your vision of all reality becomes darkened, like the drop of ink that discolors the entire beaker of water.

4. Disqualifying the positive: You reject positive experiences by insisting they "don't count" for some reason or other. In this way you can maintain a negative belief that is contradicted by your everyday experiences.

5. Jumping to conclusions: You make a negative interpretation even though there are no definite facts that convincingly support your conclusion.
   a. Mind reading. You arbitrarily conclude that someone is reacting negatively to you, and you don't bother to check this out.
   b. The Fortune Teller Error. You anticipate that things will turn out badly, and you feel convinced that your prediction is an already-established fact.

6. Magnification (catastrophizing) or minimization: You exaggerate the importance of things (such as your goof-up or someone else's achievement), or you inappropriately shrink things until they appear tiny (your own desirable qualities or the other fellow's imperfections). This is also called the "binocular trick."

7. Emotional reasoning: You assume that your negative emotions necessarily reflect the way things really are: "I feel it, therefore it must be true."

8. Should statements: You try to motivate yourself with shoulds and shouldn'ts, as if you had to be whipped and punished before you could be expected to do anything. Musts and

oughts are also offenders. The emotional consequence is guilt. When you direct should statements toward others, you feel anger, frustration, and resentment.

9. Labeling and mislabeling: This is an extreme form of overgeneralization. Instead of describing your error, you attach a negative label to yourself: "I'm a loser." When someone else's behavior rubs you the wrong way, you attach a negative label to him: "He's a goddamn louse." Mislabeling involves describing an event with language that is highly colored and emotionally loaded.

10. Personalization: You see yourself as the cause of some negative external event which in fact you were not primarily responsible for.

Krantz and Hammen (1979) developed a measure of depressive cognitive distortions that involves having a subject read stories about persons experiencing negative life events, then choosing from among various reactions to such events that he or she might have. One set of reactions represented the realistic-depressed, realistic-nondepressed, nondepressed and distorted. Both psychiatric patients and depressed college students chose a greater number of depressive-distorted responses than nondepressed subjects, thus providing some evidence for Beck's distortion hypothesis.

Related research on the etiology of depression indicates that depressed individuals have much greater anxiety or physiological arousal to bogus or phony negative feedback than nondepressed persons (Golin, Hartmann, Klatt, Munz, & Wolfgang, 1977). Hammen and her colleagues (Hammen & Cochran, 1981) also found that depressed undergraduates report more "uncertainty" in response to recent negative events than nondepressed persons do.

Schemas

"Schemas," rules or assumptions, represent organizing principles for processing information that are based on early learning experiences and are held to account for vulnerability to depression. Research on the role of schemas or rules is not as extensive as the research on cognitive distortions and negative views of self, world, and the future, but there is some evidence that such schemas are different for depressed persons than for nondepressed persons. For example, Derry & Kuiper (1981) found that depressed psychiatric patients remembered a higher proportion of adjectives with depressed content that they judged descriptive of themselves than did nondepressed psychiatric patients or normal controls. In contrast, the nondepressed comparison groups remembered a higher proportion of nondepressed content adjectives judged self-descriptive than did the depressed patients. It has also been found that depression in college students correlated significantly with scores on several factors of the Irrational Beliefs Test (Jones, 1968, e.g., "I have to excel in everything"). The research on schema does not allow one to unequivocally argue that faulty schema cause depression. At best, schema are inferred from data regarding memory for negative adjectives which are held to describe the patients themselves. There have not been independent assessments of schema in research on depression and until such assessments are conducted, we must regard the role of negative schema as presumptive.

Lewinsohn's Behavioral Model

The cause of depression, according to Lewinsohn and Arconad (1981), is assumed to reside in a person-behavior-environment interaction and is explainable by low rates of positive reinforcement and high rates of aversive experiences. These authors view the causes of depression within a general social learning framework in which behavior is an ". . . interacting determinant, not simply an outcome of external events." In accord with

the general position made in the introduction to this book, people are seen as capable of having considerable influence over their behavior; they are not simply passive reactors to external events. "They select, organize, and transform the stimuli that impinge upon them. This conceptualization of human functioning does not cast people in the role of powerless objects controlled by environmental forces, nor does it cast them as free agents who can become whatever they choose. People and environments are reciprocal determinants of one another." (p.35)

A low rate of response-contingent positive reinforcement is assumed to constitute a critical antecedent for the occurrence of depression. The basic assumption is that the low rate of behavior and the associated dysphoric feelings are elicited by a low rate of positive reinforcement and/or high rate of aversive experience. Alternatively stated, the behavior of depressed persons does not lead to enough positive reinforcement to maintain their behavior. Therefore, depressed persons find it difficult to do things; they are listless and appear unmotivated. The rate of their initiating behaviors becomes very low and they are passive. The relatively low rate of positive reinforcement is assumed to cause the feelings of sadness and dysphoria. Thus, in brief, low rates of reinforcement lead to low rates of initiating behaviors, and in turn the person becomes sad and depressed.

A corollary hypothesis is that high rates of punishing experiences also cause depression. As Lewinsohn and Arconad (1981) note, "The punishing events can cause depression directly or indirectly by interfering with the person's engagement in and enjoyment of rewarding activities." There are a number of reasons why an individual may experience aversive events: (1) a person may be in a generally punishing environment, such as a hostile work or family atmosphere; (2) he or she may display behaviors which lead to punishment or aversive feedback by others; (3) the potency of positive events may be reduced and the negative impact of punishing events may be heightened. (See Figure 10-1 for A Social Reinforcement Model of Depression.)

Lewinsohn and his colleagues have found that depressed persons experience lower rates of positive reinforcement and higher rates of punishment than nondepressed persons. Further, they have found that as depression decreases, the rates of positive reinforcement increase and the rates of punishment decrease. They further state that these changes are greatest for depressed persons who im-

prove most during therapy. Let us now look more closely at the evidence regarding the behavioral model of depression.

Low Rate of Positive Reinforcement

Lewinsohn and his associates have concluded the following regarding low rates of positive reinforcement:

1. Depressed individuals display fewer behaviors than nondepressed individuals.
2. The rate of positive reinforcement received for particular behaviors is less than the rate of

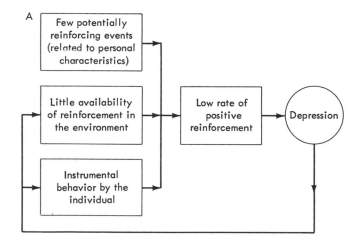

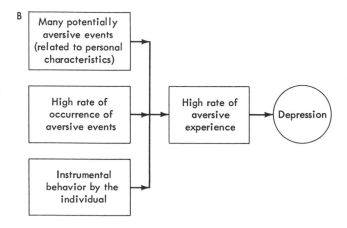

Figure 10–1 Social reinforcement for depression. (From Lewinsohn, P. M., and Arconad (1981). Behavioral treatment of depression: A social learning approach. In J. F. Clarkin, & H. I. Glaser (Eds.) *Depression: Behavioral and Directive Intervention Strategies.* New York: Garland STPM Press.)

positive reinforcement received by nondepressed persons.

3. There is an association between depressed mood and the number of pleasant activities in which individuals engage.

4. Depressed persons have a greater sensitivity to aversive stimuli than nondepressed persons.

5. The rate of positive reinforcement received by depressed individuals increases as a function of clinical improvement.

High Rate of Punishing Experiences

Paykel and his colleagues (1980) have found that depressed patients report approximately three times as many life events (largely negative events) as nondepressed persons in their retrospective reports of events in the past six months. Using female subjects, Brown, Harris, and Peto (1973) found that "markedly threatening events" were elevated over the whole two-year period prior to the onset of depression.

An unpleasant events scale was developed by Lewinsohn (1975) to assess the frequency and aversiveness of unpleasant events. More specifically, the unpleasant events assessed are items related to health and welfare; material and financial events; sexual, marital, and friendship events; achievement-academic-job events; and social events. The typical patterns for depressed persons is a high frequency and high aversiveness of negative events followed by a secondary pattern of high frequency of negative events with average or below average aversiveness.

Rehm's Self-Control Model

The self-control model of depression hypothesizes that there are deficits in three different aspects of self-control: self-monitoring, self-evaluation, and self-reinforcement. More specifically, self-monitoring problems include tendencies to attend to negative events to the exclusion of positive events and to attend to the immediate consequences of behavior. Self-evaluation problems include setting highly stringent criteria for one's behavior and making self-attributional errors consistent with expectations of a negative outcome. Self-reinforcement problems include administering insufficient rewards to one's self and administering excessive self-punishments.

Self-monitoring of negative events by depressed persons is similar to two cognitive distortions described earlier by Burns: mental filtering and disqualifying the positive. In addition to research already noted that depressed persons have depressive/distorted responses to negative events, Nelson and Craighead (1977) found that depressed persons recall less positive feedback and more negative feedback than controls do. However, from this and related research (De-Monbreun & Craighead, 1977) it appears that the most consistent finding is underestimation of positive feedback when it is given at high rates. Overestimation of negative feedback has not been found to be a consistent finding. Another method of assessing self-monitoring is by evaluating the amount of time one attends to positive and negative feedback. Roth and Rehm (1980) found that when depressed subjects were given a choice of feedback in a word association task, they chose to find out which word associations they got wrong more frequently than nondepressed subjects did. Interestingly, an examination of the effects of daily monitoring of negative versus positive events over a four-week period did not result in any differential effect on mood (O'Hara & Rehm, 1979). In sum, there is some evidence for self-monitoring differences among depressed versus nondepressed subjects in memory and choice of feedback studies. However, one of the most relevant studies on potential changes in mood as a function of self-monitoring did not show any negative influence on monitoring negative daily events. Further, according to Rehm (1981), there is little research on the self-monitoring of immediate versus delayed outcomes of behavior.

Rehm (1981) also sees the criterion setting problem of depressed persons as one of being too perfectionistic. The standard may be too high in an absolute sense or too high relative to one's own skills and activities. While there are many clinical anecdotes regarding the problem of standards that are too high, evidence for the comparatively high standard setting is meager. In one study, depressed patients rated their performances as poor even though their actual performances were identical to nondepressed persons (Loeb, Beck, Diggory, & Tuthill, 1967), and in another study there was an association between high standard-setting and low self-esteem in males (Warren, 1976). Attribution errors have already been discussed in the context of the attributional model of depression by Abramson, Seligman, and Teasdale (1978). Essentially, depressed persons are more likely to have attributions about their own behavior that are internal, stable, and global.

Self-reinforcement is less in depressed college students than nondepressed subjects (Nelson and Craighead, 1977), and depressed psychiatric patients reinforce themselves less on a memory task than nondepressed subjects do. Further, the depressed patients also punished themselves more than nondepressed subjects did. Finally, it has also been observed that depressed persons self-reward less when an experimenter is watching, but when the task was performed in private, the depressed persons increased their self-rewards.

In sum, the self-control model of depression is one in which depression is viewed as a function of self-control deficits. As Rehm (1981) noted, "The symptoms [of depression]

are descriptions of either self-control deficits or their consequences. Most of the cognitive symptoms reflect self-control behavior per se. That is, cognitive symptoms represent 'readouts' or descriptions of self-control behaviors and processes. For example, pessimism reflects negative self-monitoring strategies; perfectionism and low self-esteem reflect stringent standard setting; helplessness reflects self-attributional errors; self-deprecation reflects self-punishment" (pg. 79).

Interpersonal Theory

Interpersonal therapy is based on the theoretical assumption that depression occurs in a social context and that an understanding of the interpersonal context associated with the onset of depressive symptoms is critical to know how to treat a depressed person. Interpersonal Therapy (IPT) was developed by Klerman and Weissman in a Boston-New Haven Collaborative Depression Project for the treatment of unipolar depressed persons. The theoretical framework for understanding depression was developed in part from the work of Adolph Meyer (1957) who was one of the first psychiatrists to view adult psychiatric disorders as attempts to adapt to their interpersonal environments. Meyer viewed one's adaptation to the environment as a function of early experiences in the family and in various social groups.

In understanding the roots of depression, it is also important to examine developmental theory, especially attachment theory. Attachment theory emphasizes that the most intense human emotions are associated with the formation and disruption of affectional bonds. As Bowlby (1969) notes, many types of psychiatric disorders result from one's inability to make and keep affectionate bondings, and the way one develops affectionate bonds is determined largely by events within the family. In turn, Bowlby (1977) proposed a system of psychotherapy designed to assist a patient in understanding current interpersonal relationships on the basis of past experiences with attachment figures in childhood, adolescence, and adulthood. In related work on the development of various disorders, especially depression, Henderson, Duncan-Jones, McAuley, and Richie (1978) found that patients with depression had fewer friends and attachment figures, felt that their attachment figures gave them insufficient support, and had more unpleasant interactions with their primary group than nondepressed persons did. Further support for the importance of bonding in depression comes from Brown, Harris, and Copeland (1977). In a large survey of women in London, they found that the presence of an intimate, confiding relationship with a man, usually a spouse, was the most important protection against developing a depression in the face of life stress. Similarly, Miller and Ingham (1976) found that women who do not have intimate confidants report more severe psychological symptoms to general physicians than women who do have confidants. Finally, Paykel, Myers, Dienelt, Klerman, Lindenthal, and Pepper (1969) found that marital friction was the most common event reported by depressed patients prior to the onset of depression.

The role of attachment in the interpersonal theory of depression and its implications for therapy bears striking similarity to the conclusions reached by Lewinsohn. More specifically, in both accounts of depression, relations with significant others, such as spouses, are very important. In the attachment theory of Bowlby, greatest emphasis is placed on attachment figures during childhood and adolescence, whereas in Lewinsohn's theory, greatest emphasis is place on interactions with one's spouse.

Weissman and Paykel (1974) studied the interpersonal relationships of depressed women in some detail and found that depressed women were impaired in *all* aspects of social functioning. They had difficulties as mothers, workers, wives, and friends. Interestingly, however, the impairment was greatest with spouses and children with whom there was poor communication, disaffection, and hostility. Klerman and Weissman (1982) noted that there is some debate as to whether the marital difficulties are the cause or the result of the depression. We will return to that issue later in this chapter.

Interpersonal therapy is also concerned with role impairments. We all have multiple roles (e.g., student, parent, spouse, worker) and impairments in these roles can occur for a number of different reasons. According to Klerman and Weissman (1982) some of the most important pathways to role impairments that may be addressed in therapy are as follows:

1. Psychodynamic conflicts, e.g. a conflict between sexual wishes and restrictive social codes.
2. Regression, the patient may have attained one level of functioning but may have regressed under stress to a previous level.
3. Change in family status, e.g., loss of job, physical illness, and increased consciousness of women may lead to severe tension within the family.

Another interpersonal conception of depression has been described by Coyne (1976, 1985), who placed depression squarely in the context of marriage. As many researchers have found, depression and marital disturbance are associated. As Coyne (1985) noted, "The marriages of depressed women are characterized by friction, poor communication, dependency, and lack of affection." Based on their laboratory observations, Coyne and colleagues (Kahn, Coyne, & Margolin, 1983) describe the marriages of many depressed persons as "characterized by periods of inhibited communication and tension punctuated by arguments involving intense negative affect and then withdrawal, with little constructive problem solving. The aversiveness and futility of efforts to resolve differences encourages avoidance of confrontation until an accumulation of unresolved issues precipitates another negative encounter" (p. 5). Coyne admits that not all depressed persons present with marital problems. However, he proffers that "whether or not depressed persons report dissatisfaction with their marriages, they tend to be facing difficulties renegotiating their relationships so that they meet their wants and needs as they define them, and this recurs as a common theme in therapy with them."

Coyne's (1976) work prompted systematic analyses of the interactions between various individuals and depressed persons. He found that following a phone conversation with a depressed person, naive subjects rated themselves as more depressed, anxious, and hostile than subjects who interacted with a nondepressed person. Interestingly, this finding has been replicated using several methodologies. Negative reactions are obtained to written descriptions presumably of depressed persons, audiotaped interviews of depressed patients, and confederates role playing depressed persons. Spouses of depressed persons also rate themselves as more anxious and hostile after interactions with their spouses, and Biglan, Hops, and Sherman (1985) in their literature review summary state that depressed people engage in a class of behaviors that is clearly aversive to others. Biglan, Hops, Sherman, Friedman, Arthur, and Osteen (1985) have conducted studies which suggest strongly that depressive behavior is functional in reducing the aversive behavior of others.

The interpersonal account of depression by Coyne (in press), is included here because it

has been useful in prompting research on dyadic issues in depression. This account also has an associated treatment program, but there are no outcome studies evaluating the therapy. Further, it should be noted that even in a general marital clinic, only in approximately 50 percent of the couples does at least one spouse score in the depressed range on the Beck Depression Inventory (Beach, Jouriles, & O'Leary, 1985). Finally, in at least three studies, the correlation between marital discord and depression both for men and women is only approximately 0.30 (Beach, Arias, & O'Leary, in press). In brief, it is important to realize that there may be many causes of depression, and marital discord is but one of these important factors.

In summary, interpersonal therapy is based on the premise that it is necessary to explore one's current social adjustment and interpersonal relations. It includes a systematic analysis of relations with significant others in the patient's current situation and implications of those attachments for present functioning. Klerman and Weissman (1982) also note that the first goal of treatment is to ". . . help the patient understand that the vague and uncomfortable symptoms of depression are part of a known syndrome that is well-described, well-understood, and relatively common; that responds to a variety of treatments; and that has a good prognosis. Psychopharmacologic approaches may be used in conjunction with interpersonal therapy to alleviate symptoms more rapidly" (p. 97).

BIOCHEMICAL MODELS

The Amine Hypothesis

One of the major biological hypotheses about the cause of depression is that there is an amine deficiency, and conversely, that mania is caused by an amine excess. The amine hypothesis grew out of serendipitous observations regarding the effects of certain drugs on humans and animals. Amines are derivates of ammonia, in which the hydrogen atoms are replaced by radicals containing hydrogen and carbon atoms.

In evaluating major hypotheses regarding amines the following predictions have been made (Zis & Goodwin, 1980):

1. Drugs that increase the output of monoaminergic systems should possess antidepressant properties and/or precipitate mania.
2. Drugs that decrease the functional output of monoaminergic systems should posses antimanic properties and act as depressants.
3. The concentration of amines and their metabolites in tissues and fluids obtained from depressed patients should be lower than in normal controls.
4. The concentration of amines and their metabolites in tissues and fluids obtained from manic patients should be higher than in normal controls.

Excess Monoamine Oxidase

Levels of the brain enzyme, monoamine oxidase or MAO, are higher in depressed than nondepressed persons. MAO breaks down and metabolizes other substances such as noradrenaline. Noradrenaline is partly responsible for focusing attention, filtering distractions, and experiencing pleasure. Excessive amounts of MAO are held to result in too much noradrenalin being broken down; the consequent low level of noradrenaline is thought to cause the depressed person to have reduced ability to experience pleasure or attend to events. It is commonly agreed that noradrenalin is involved in depression, but it is not clear whether the low levels of noradrenalin are causes or effects of depression.

As you will see in the treatment section of this chapter, neither the amine deficiency or the excess monoamine oxidase model have

led to pharmacological treatments which have become generally accepted. There is evidence for the effectiveness of MAO inhibitors but there are also such negative side effects of these medications that they have not become treatment of choice.

TREATMENT

Antidepressant Medications

Antidepressant medications have been used for more than two decades. The tricyclic antidepressants are the most commonly used medications, and we will restrict our discussion to their use. One of the earliest studies of antidepressants was by Ball and Kiloh in 1959. Forty-eight patients were given daily either 250 mg. of imipramine or a placebo. Comparisons of the effectiveness of the medication were made after four weeks of treatment. Patients were divided into those considered to have endogenous depression (depression with severe "vegetative" symptoms such as listlessness, insomnia, and anorexia) and reactive depression (depression that is in response to external events). Seventy-four percent of the patients with endogenous depression receiving imipramine improved, whereas only 22 percent improved on placebo. Of those individuals with reactive depression, 59 percent of those receiving imipramine improved, whereas only 20 percent improved on placebo. Nonetheless, unwanted side effects of the medication were judged to be severe, such as dryness of the mouth, constipation, difficulty with urination, and blurring of vision. Since 1959, many other studies have been conducted using placebos and imipramine, and the results have generally been the same. Statistical reviews of controlled trials of imipramine in the treatment of acute endogenous depression support the efficacy of this medication for such depression, whereas the utility of the effects of imipramine with chronic or reactive depression is less clear (Rogers & Clay, 1975).

A medication introduced in the late 1950s was amitriptyline. It was evaluated in the early 1960s and was found to be superior to placebos in the treatment of clinically depressed persons (Garry & Leonard, 1963). Comparisons were also made of the effectiveness of amitriptyline and imipramine (Burt, Gordon, Holt, & Horden, 1962). Seventy-three female patients in a psychiatric hospital received 150 mg. of medication daily for one week, 200 mg. daily for the next three to five weeks, and then 100 mg. daily for the next six months. Overall assessment after four weeks of medication did not show either drug to have a superiority over the other. Both imipramine and amitriptyline have antidepressant properties, and in many respects their effects are comparable. Finally, it has also been established that patients who received continued treatment with either of the medications for six months following their initial treatment had a lower rate of relapse than individuals who did not receive continued use of the medication.

The major antidepressant medications are absorbed rapidly and completely when taken orally. Peak levels in blood plasma are reached after one to four hours. Nonetheless, the clinical effects of the medication are often not seen for two to three weeks following the initiation of treatment. It is felt that the onset of the depressive disorder is associated with a change in the synthesis of amine transmitter substances in the nerve cells. Further, it is held that it takes two to three weeks for the amines to cross the "nerve axon to the nerve endings where they become active" (p. 240, Mindham, 1979). With acute depression and depression in which anxiety is also prominent, the evidence regarding the effective-ness of the antidepressant medications indicates a small advantage for the patients receiving the medication.

Monoamine Oxidase Inhibitors (MAO Inhibitors)

According to Klerman (1980), the MAO inhibitors should not be used as a first choice of drugs for most depressed patients. They are useful, he indicates, when the patient has not responded to tricyclic antidepressants or when there is a previous history of positive response to the medication by a family member. The MAO inhibitors appear to be of greatest value with patients who have anxiety and phobias, not early morning awakening and weight loss. Despite the utility of the MAO inhibitors with some patients, they should be used with special caution, as they are generally less effective than the tricyclics and are more toxic. That is, use of the medication is sometimes associated with hypertension, mouth sores, and rashes. Finally, insomnia is estimated to occur in 50 percent of the patients using the MAO inhibitors, and 30 percent report daytime sedation (Nies & Robinson, 1980).

Lithium

The clinical utility of lithium carbonate, a simple inorganic substance, in treating depression caused a great stir in the media in the mid 1970s. The stir was created because it initially was thought that individuals who suffered from depression might take this substance, which in raw form could be taken simply like vitamins. While there is evidence that lithium is effective in the treatment of bipolar depression and, in particular, the treatment of mania, lithium is not a medication of first choice with unipolar depression. As Coppen, Metcalfe, and Wood (1980) noted, "The margin between effective pro-phylactic level and toxic level is narrow" (p. 281). Lithium ingestion has been shown to impair kidney functioning and adversely affect thyroid functioning.

In sum, as Klerman (1980) reported, "Moderately depressed patients are often helped by antidepressant drugs used conjointly with psychotherapy. If the clinician makes the decision to use medication, the tricyclics are the class of drug that has the greatest efficacy and best relative margin of safety. The clearest indication for tricyclic drugs is an endogenous symptom pattern which can be recognized by the following symptoms: sleep disturbance (especially early morning awakening), weight and appetite loss, agitation, psychomotor retardation, and decreased sexual interest" (p. 441).

Electroconvulsive Therapy (ECT)

Electroconvulsive therapy is a means of inducing electrical charges through a person's body with the intent of alleviating a particular disorder. In the 1920s, schizophrenia and epilepsy were thought to be antagonistic. Therefore, it was felt that transfusing the blood of epileptics or inducing seizures like those of epileptics would be useful to ameliorate a schizophrenic condition. In this vein, chemical and electrical means of inducing seizures in schizophrenics were developed. While the original rationale for ECT is now questioned, it is felt by some that depression is caused by some abberation in the chemical and electrical functioning of the brain. Further, ECT is held by some to be the treatment of choice for severely depressed patients with severe psychomotor retardation and/or agitation and delusions. It is also considered the treatment of choice with depressed patients who are intensely suicidal and for whom a physician does not wish to wait two weeks before an antidepressant drug takes effect (Klerman, 1980). Let us now address the issue of the effectiveness and safety of ECT.

The Medical Research Council of England (1965) designed a treatment outcome study comparing ECT, imipramine, phenelzine (a medication), and placebos. As best could be ascertained, the patients were generally suffering from endogenous depression. The improvement rates in the groups after four weeks of treatment were as follows: ECT 84 percent, imipramine 72 percent, phenelzine 38 percent, and placebos 45 percent. A number of other studies have also showed that ECT is superior to placebos (Kiloh, 1980). The improvement rates in these studies are generally measured by self-ratings and ratings by psychiatric personnel regarding the patient's condition.

In an overall summary of the effectiveness of ECT and anti-depressant medication, the following results were reported: in nine studies with ECT, "The response rate varied from 16 percent to 94 percent with a mean of 72 percent. The mean response rate in 131 studies of drug therapy was 65 percent and in 25 placebo groups was 23 percent." (p. 264, Kiloh, 1980). While one can reasonably question mean or average response rates across nine studies with improvement rates from 16 percent to 94 percent, Heshe and Roeder (1976), using a different methodology involving questionnaire results from psychiatrists who gave the ECT, found recovery rates of 80 percent for ECT and 60 percent for anti-depressant medication. These results could certainly be favorably biased toward ECT, but utilizing data from controlled clinical trials in which various treatment methods were used as well as the foregoing studies comparing response rates, it appears that ECT does result in reductions in depression in many patients.

Confusion and memory disturbance have long been known to be dominant problems associated with ECT. The degree and duration of the memory disturbance is reportedly associated with the placement of the electrodes on the scalp and whether the placement is bilateral or only on the non-dominant hemisphere of the brain. Dominant hemispheric placement is reported to be associated with less memory disturbance than bilateral placement. According to Kiloh (1980), "With modern techniques any defective memory function that follows ECT is minor in the majority of patients" (p. 270). Nonetheless, there are other more severe effects of ECT that must be considered. Epilepsy has been reported in a number of patients after ECT, ". . . some patients die in course of, or immediately after ECT from cardiac arhythmias or cardiac arrest." (p. 271, Kiloh, 1980).

According to many researchers in the area of clinical depression, ECT is an effective form of treatment for endogenous depression. Further, with such persons, ECT is held to be more effective than antidepressant medication (Kiloh, 1980; Klerman, 1980). All researchers note the memory loss associated with ECT, but generally report that it is temporary and rarely severe. Nonetheless, the use of ECT is still highly controversial. Many patients will not accept such treatment, and of those who begin treatment, as many as 27 percent will drop out (Abrams, Taylor, Faber, Ts'o, Williams, & Almy, 1983). Even though the initial response to ECT may vary from 60 to 90 percent (Fink, 1977), there is risk of relapse with ECT. Finally, studies comparing ECT to placebo for nonendogenous or reactive depression have failed to demonstrate the efficacy of ECT for these conditions.

Psychotherapy

Psychotherapy is believed to be useful both for depressed persons who receive psycho-pharmacological treatment and for those who do not receive medication. For individuals with bipolar depression, while response to medication may generally be positive, 35 percent to 40 percent of such patients do not respond to initial trials of antidepressants (Beck, 1976). In addition, many of the responders to medication refuse to continue on their medication for a variety of reasons, including adverse side effects and an attitude that medication is not an answer to the psychological problems they face. For these and related reasons, drug treatments often have high dropout rates. For example, in the Rush, Beck, Kovacs, and Hollon study (1977), 36 percent of the subjects in the drug treatment study dropped out. We will now review the evidence for the effectiveness of four types of psychotherapy, viz., Beck's Cognitive Therapy, Lewinsohn's Behavior Therapy, Rehm's Self-Control Therapy, and Weissman's Interpersonal Therapy. All four therapeutic approaches are short-term, i.e., they involve approximately twelve to twenty sessions that occur biweekly or weekly, as determined by the needs of the client and the type of therapy. All four therapeutic approaches involve individual or group psychotherapy for the depressed person, and all four are designed to reduce the depressive symptoms and aid the client/patient in developing more effective strategies for viewing the world and/or dealing with interpersonal problems.

Beck's Cognitive Therapy

The general thrust of cognitive therapy (CT) is to teach the cognitive model to the client in a straightforward didactic sense. Patients are taught to analyze the associations between their thoughts, affects, and behavior and to view their depression as the product of dysfunctional thoughts. The goal of the therapist is to develop a collaborative set with the client to analyze which thoughts are dysfunctional. Finally, the client is taught specific techniques designed to change faulty beliefs and thought processes.

As noted earlier, a person's cognitive assumptions or evaluations of events are basic to the development of depression. The person's negative view of self, world, and the future, likely developed in childhood, are addressed as central elements in therapy. As Coleman and Beck (1981) noted, changing this cognitive triad involves having the person change his or her general negative views ("I'm no good." "The world is unjust." "Things won't work out.") to more specific attitudes and beliefs about the self ("I can't speak coherently." "My memory is not what it used to be.")

Systematic errors in the thinking of the depressed person include the following:

1. Overgeneralization, e.g., "I'm no good" after receiving repeated negative feedback from one person, such as one's spouse.

2. Drawing negative conclusions from a single event, e.g., "People are out to cheat you whenever they can" after receiving the wrong change from a grocery store clerk.

3. Magnification and minimization, e.g., "The poor grade I received on that exam will prevent me from ever getting into a good school."

4. Personalization, or undue inference that external events pertain to oneself, e.g., "The reason that my elementary school science curriculum was shut down was that my principal hated me." (In fact, all funds were cut for science across the district.)

5. Selective abstraction, focusing on a detail of an event taken out of context, e.g., "I am depressed because I saw my child badly hurt in a bicycle accident and I should never have let him learn to ride a bicycle."

6. Arbitrary inference, drawing a conclusion without evidence to support that conclusion, e.g., "Most depression is simply the result of receiving bad genes."

Many dysfunctional thoughts have little basis in reality. However, they are held to exist at a "primitive illogical level," and therefore are thought to be generally unavailable to the client. The thoughts are felt to occur frequently and rapidly, almost as if by reflex. The therapist then aids the client in identifying dysfunctional thoughts. Identifying the thoughts may occur by recording one's depressed moods and noticing the thoughts, images, and memories associated with the depressed mood. Changes in affect throughout the day are excellent markers that can be used to identify automatic thoughts. Identifying common themes, such as thoughts of rejection, are also methods of deciding which thoughts are dysfunctional.

Despite the fact that the therapist's job is to help the client identify dysfunctional thoughts, the therapist must check his or her own tendencies to simply instruct the client about the irrationality of these thoughts. Instead, the therapist must help the client judge the rationality of the thoughts and learn that the thoughts are not based in reality. In brief, the goal of the therapist is to develop a collaborative set with the client.

Cognitive Therapy

The identification of dysfunctional thoughts per se aids the client in that he or she can gain some "distance" from them and begin to evaluate their reality by checking real life data. However, more than simple identification of dysfunctional thoughts is necessary. The therapist must carefully and specifically question the client. For example, the therapist asks questions to help the client discover the maladaptive consequences of holding the assumption that one should *always* work up to one's potential. Let us look at an example of therapist-patient interaction taken from Young & Beck (1982).

"PATIENT: I guess I believe I should always work up to my potential.
THERAPIST: Why is that?

PATIENT: Otherwise, I'd be wasting time.

THERAPIST: But what is the *long-range* goal in working up to your potential?

PATIENT: (long pause) I've never really thought about that. I've just assumed that I should.

THERAPIST: Are there any positive things you give up by always having to work up to your potential?

PATIENT: I suppose it makes it hard to relax or take a vacation.

THERAPIST: What about 'living up to your potential' to enjoy yourself and relax? Is that important at all?

PATIENT: I've never really thought of it that way.

THERAPIST: Maybe we can work on giving yourself permission *not* to work up to your potential at all times."

A second strategy for changing dysfunctional thoughts is to list the advantages and disadvantages of changing an assumption. After making the list, the therapist and client collaboratively evaluate the advantages and disadvantages of the assumption. Additionally, the patient may simply weigh the long-term effects of holding the assumption.

Third, the therapist may help the client overcome a number of "shoulds" that restrict the client's activities. For example, a client may feel she "should" not dress well because her husband has always been jealous and never wanted her to "look too good."

To aid clients in overcoming the "shoulds," the therapist helps him or her devise experiments that assess what will happen if the "should" is disobeyed.

In addition to the cognitive strategies used to change dysfunctional thoughts, behavioral techniques are used as well. More specifically, activity scheduling, mastery and pleasure techniques, and graded task assignments are key behavioral techniques used to alter depression.

Activity scheduling refers simply and straightforwardly to day-to-day, hour-by-hour planning of activities. This scheduling is par-

ticularly helpful because the depressed person as well as his or her family often believes that he or she can do very little. Realizing that daily accomplishments can occur gives the depressed person the belief that he or she can actually do important, though small, things. Recording each activity is part of the intervention, but to avoid having the depressed person feel that he or she has not met goals, the client is encouraged to be flexible in following activity plans.

An initial evaluation of cognitive therapy was conducted by Rush, Beck, Kovacs, and Hollan (1977), who compared antidepressant medication with cognitive therapy for depressed individuals. Nineteen individuals received cognitive therapy and twenty-two received the antidepressant medication imipramine. The cognitive therapy consisted of an average of fifteen psychotherapy sessions given by therapists who had recently received training in the treatment of depression. There were two main measures of therapeutic improvement: self-ratings and clinicians' ratings of depression. At post-therapy, three-month follow-up, and six-month follow-up, cognitive therapy was superior to antidepressant medication in reducing depression both on self-ratings and clinicians' ratings. This was the first outcome study showing the superiority of psychotherapy over antidepressant medication, and the results were greater than expected by the investigators for cognitive therapy (see Table 10-1). Furthermore, at a 12 month follow-up, self-rated symptoms of depression were lower for individuals in cognitive therapy than for those receiving medication. Finally, there was significantly more dropout from the pharmacotherapy than the cognitive therapy group. More specifically, as reflected in Table 10-1 from Rush et al. (1977), eight of the individuals in the pharmacotherapy group discontinued treatment: two withdrew because of medication side effects, one had a suicidal crisis and required a change in treatment, and five terminated against the therapist's advice. Interestingly, the major reason for termination was that they failed to have symptomatic relief.

An evaluation of the efficacy of cognitive therapy for treating depression was also conducted by McLean and Hastigan (1979). In one of the largest studies of its kind, 178 depressed individuals were assigned to psychotherapy, behavior therapy, drug therapy, or relaxation therapy. The depressed individuals had been depressed for two months and were functionally impaired because of depression (e.g., unable to work, socially withdrawn, or suicidally preoccupied). They also met specified diagnostic criteria for clinical depression suggested by Feighner et al. (1972). Twenty-five percent of the individuals had made at least one serious suicide attempt; 54 percent reported frequent suicidal ideation.

The therapists were psychologists and psychiatrists who were selected because of their particular expertise in at least one of the therapeutic approaches being evaluated (with the exception of relaxation therapy, which none of these therapists had used). Ten weekly therapy sessions were established, and mar-

ried individuals were encouraged to have their spouses attend the sessions to "work together on the program." The short-term psychotherapy was modeled on the work of Marmor (1973) and Wolberg (1967). When treatment sessions were attended by both spouses, equal status was given to each person attending. The goal of the therapy was relief of symptoms through the development of insight into the psychodynamic forces that initiated the current depression and the related personality factors. In relatively unstructured treatment, therapists used techniques such as insight, reality testing, emotional support, catharsis, and suggestions regarding self-perception and emotional adjustment.

The relaxation therapy consisted of ten sessions of highly structured relaxation training exercises. As in the short-term psychotherapy, participating spouses were treated in the same fashion as the depressed clients were. That is, both clients were asked to complete the relaxation exercises. The goal of the relaxation therapy was to get the client to "appreciate the relations" between the level of muscle tension and depression and to return to his or her level of pre-episode physical

Table 10–1   Clinical Status of Patients at the End of Treatment

Status[a]	Cognitive therapy	Pharmacotherapy
Markedly or completely improved (0–9)	15	5
Partially improved (10–15)	2	6
Not improved (≥ 16)	1	3
Dropouts[b]	1	8
Total assigned treatment	19	22

[a] Numbers in parentheses indicate Beck Depression Inventory cut-off scores.

[b] According to their Beck Depression Inventory scores, all dropouts had a "not improved" clinical status classification at the time of termination.

From Rush et al. (1977). Comparative efficacy of cognitive therapy and pharmacotherapy in the treatment of depressed outpatients. *Cognitive Therapy and Research, 1*(1), 28.

functioning by developing a significantly increased ability to reduce tension in all muscle groups.

Behavior therapy consisted of 10 hourly sessions over a ten week period. Clients were given the rationale that depression is the result of ineffective coping techniques used to remedy situational life problems. "The task of therapy was to help clients avoid their negative and introspective cognitive habits by gainfully interacting with the environment, despite the temporary experience of depressed mood." A hierarchy of treatment goals was developed and scaled for each client as a function of a behavioral assessment of complaints, personal skills, and goals. Using a graduated practice approach, therapists focused on goal attainment in the following areas: communication, behavioral productivity, social interaction, assertiveness, decision-making, problem-solving, and cognitive self-control.

Drug therapy consisted of eleven weeks of amitriptyline (imipramine) starting at 75 mg. and graduated to 150 mg. per day.

In terms of the Beck Depression Inventory, individuals who received behavior therapy improved most. At the end of treatment, seven percent of the behavior therapy subjects were depressed, whereas approximately 20 percent of the subjects receiving drug therapy or relaxation therapy were depressed (score: >23 on BDI). On measures of mood, complaints, goal attainment, and general satisfaction, the behavior therapy group did significantly better than the other three groups. In brief, this was the second study in which behavior therapy was shown to be superior to psychotherapy. In dropout rates, behavior therapy was clearly superior to the other treatments (5 percent as compared with 26 to 36 percent for the other treatments). Interestingly, not only did the clients improve more on social measures, but also on mood and complaint measures as well.

To assess whether or not individuals assigned to the medication group were taking their medication, blood serum analyses revealed that 100 percent of the clients were doing so. The usual advantage of the drug therapy is its ease of delivery, but the drug group had the highest dropout rate (36 percent) and was not significantly better than the relaxation group on any measure. It should be pointed out, however, that the relaxation therapy was associated with a reduction of Beck Depression Index scores from moderate depression to mild mood disturbance at posttherapy and that relaxation per se should be viewed as an alternative type of treatment—not an inert approach to depression.

Psychotherapy, according to McLean and Hastigan (1979), "proved least effective at both post-treatment and follow-up evaluation periods and, generally speaking, fared worse than the treatment control condition (relaxation therapy)." Thirty percent of the subjects in the psychotherapy condition remained moderately to severely depressed at the end of treatment. According to the authors, general psychodynamic therapy did not prove very successful with these depressed patients. Nonetheless, as was the case with the relaxation therapy, psychotherapy was associated with a decline in Beck Depression Inventory scores from pre- to post-therapy of moderate to borderline clinical depression. This decline, while significantly less than the decline in depression for the behavior therapy group, should be addressed straightforwardly. Unfortunately, without an untreated control group it is not possible to ascertain how much of a reduction in depression scores is due to cyclic variation in depression and how much to spontaneous remission.

Blackburn, Bishop, Glen, Whally, and Christie (1981) also evaluated the effects of cognitive therapy for depressed persons. They found that cognitive therapy was superior to antidepressant medication for depressed out-patients in a general practice. In contrast, cognitive therapy was equivalent to antidepressant medication in psychiatric clinic outpatients. Furthermore, many studies with depressed college students indicate that cognitive therapy is more effective than no treatment (a waiting list control) and nondirective or supportive psychotherapy (cf. Rush & Giles, 1982).

Behavioral Treatment

Currently there is no single behavioral treatment for depression, but the approach that is most clearly behavioral is the strategy developed by Lewinsohn and colleagues at the University of Oregon (cf. Lewinsohn, Sullivan, & Grosscup, 1982). As we have noted, depression is presumed to be a function of low rates of positive reinforcement. The corollary hypothesis is that a high rate of punishing experiences also causes depression. To reiterate three key points, there are three reasons why a person may experience low rates of positive reinforcement and high rates of punishment:

1. The person's immediate environment may have few available positive reinforcers or may have many punishing aspects.
2. The person may lack the skills to obtain available positive reinforcers and/or cope effectively with aversive events (skill deficits).
3. The positive reinforcement potency of events may be reduced and/or the negative impact of punishing events may be heightened.

The absence of reinforcers typically related to depression include: positive sexual experiences, rewarding social interactions, enjoyable outdoor activities, solitude, and competency experiences. (Lewinsohn & Amenson, 1978). Punishing events particularly important to depression include: marital discord,

work-related difficulties, and negative reactions from others. The relevance of the role of reinforcement and punishment to the treatment of depression is reasonably straightforward. Using the model of depression, treatment focuses on increasing the rates of positively reinforcing interactions with the environment and decreasing the person's rate of punishing interactions.

Lewinsohn and colleagues have outlined a Five Step Treatment Plan as follows (Lewinsohn, Sullivan, & Grosscup, 1982):

(1)   Daily Monitoring

Patients are taught to graph and interpret their daily monitoring of data. Apparently, patients often readily see the relationship between negative events and unpleasant moods but seldom see the clear relationship between pleasant events and an elevated mood. However, enabling clients or patients to see that depression is clearly related to many observable events in life is useful for understanding it, and often is enough to comfort the patient to a large extent. As Lewinsohn et al. noted, "Patients, in a very real sense, learn to diagnose their own depression" (p. 69).

(2)   Relaxation Training

Patients are taught to learn how tension can maximize the impact of negative situations and how it interferes with pleasant situations. Individuals are assigned a book on learning how to relax (e.g., Benson, 1975) and are instructed in how to tense and relax major muscle groups. They are asked to practice relaxation twice per day and to keep a record of their relaxation. Finally, they are aided in ascertaining which situations make them feel most tense.

(3)   Managing Aversive Events

Cognitive strategies are described by Lewinsohn et al. (1982) for decreasing unpleasant events. Patients are taught to substitute more positive and constructive thoughts between the events that prompt the dysphoric feeling. They are taught not to take things personally, how to deal with aversive encounters, how to use self-instruction to enhance their coping efforts, and how to reduce the impact of failures.

(4)   Time Management

Depressed persons often have difficulty managing their time. They don't make adequate preparation for daily events and need guidance in planning their days.

(5)   Increasing Pleasant Activities

In brief, patients are aided in increasing their rate of engagement in pleasant activities by setting concrete goals and developing specific plans for what they expect to do.

Essentially, the behavioral treatment described here is an educational intervention whose goal is to teach problem-solving regarding the etiology and amelioration of one's own depression. It is also educational in that specific goals and graduated steps to realize those goals are discussed throughout the therapy.

The effectiveness of behavioral treatments for depression, assessed at the University of Oregon, was discussed by Lewinsohn et al. (1982), who showed that patients on the average decreased approximately 15 points on the Beck Depression Inventory and approximately 20 points on the MMPI Depression scale. These decreases would generally be viewed as clinically significant because they reflect changes from moderate depression to mild mood disturbance.

A comparison of cognitive behavior therapy and a behavioral approach modeled after Ferster (1965) and Lewinsohn (1974) for depressed individuals was conducted by Taylor and Marshall (1977). Subjects were required to satisfy the following criteria for depression:

1. Self-report of depression of not less than two weeks duration.

2. Beck Depression Inventory (BDI) scores of not less than 13 (the cutoff score suggested by Beck as distinguishing depressed and nondepressed persons).

3. MMPI Depression Scale Scores of 70, a score in the highest 2 percent of the population.

4. Not currently taking medication or any other treatment.

Subjects were randomly assigned to one of four groups: cognitive therapy, behavioral therapy, cognitive and behavioral therapy, and a waiting list control group. The subjects were graduate or undergraduate students with a mean age of 22 years. Treatments were six forty-minute sessions given by the senior author of the study (Taylor).

There was significant overall improvement for the treatment groups compared with the untreated controls (waiting list control group). On the main depression measures, BDI and MMPI, the combination of behavioral and cognitive methods was better than either treatment alone.

Lewinsohn, Antonuccio, Steinmetz, and Teri (1984) developed a group treatment for depressed women which was designed as a class for students with problems of behavior and cognitions that can be unlearned. The course employed lectures, class activities, homework assignments and a textbook, "The Coping With Depression Course," by Lewinsohn et al. (1984). The material covered in the course was similar to that of the Lewinsohn and Arconad (1981) program described earlier, but the format was twelve two-hour class sessions scheduled over eight weeks rather than individual therapy. The content included time management, assertiveness, self-control techniques, improving social skills, and reducing anxiety.

On the basis of three outcome studies assessing the efficacy of "The Coping With Depression Course," it was apparent that depression scores of the class members were substantially reduced and gains were maintained at one- and six-month follow-ups. Further, the degree of improvement was similar to the amounts observed in previous studies of individual therapy for depression. While a majority of the depressed individuals improved at the end of treatment, approximately 20 percent stayed depressed. Failure to improve was associated with a high pretreatment level of depression and suicidal behavior. In brief, highly depressed individuals with suicidal ideation and behavior may require more than a class approach to their problems. Interestingly, on the average, participating in treatment other than the class was negatively correlated with improvement. Thus it seems that not all adjunctive therapies are helpful, and in fact some appear to be detrimental. Most important, since depression is such a frequent problem in the general population, "The Coping With Depression Course" offers a cost-effective method of dealing with this mental health problem that seriously affects 10 to 20 percent of the population at some point in their lives.

Rehm's Self-Control Treatment

Like the Lewinsohn treatment program, the self-control therapy model is didactic in nature and is conducted in a group context. Each session ends with a homework assignment that is brought back and discussed at the next session. Each session builds on the previous one, and the participants view the intervention as a class. The groups vary from six to twelve ninety-minute sessions and have been tested with all-women groups. The self-control therapy model of depression has direct implications for treatment; self-monitoring, self-evaluation, and self-reinforcement are discussed with the clients.

Participants are asked to record daily mood

and participation in positive activities. They are given a list of positive activities and are asked to "experiment" by noting how many positive activities occur. By assessing how positive mood correlates with engaging in or simply noting positive activities, clients are expected to feel somewhat better. They are also asked to begin to focus on some long-term effects of their behavior. Instead of focusing on the immediate and sometimes negative aspects of their actions, such as the problems associated with cleaning the house or some other unpleasant job, clients are asked to consider the positive aspects of completing the job.

In self-evaluation, clients are taught to set realistic goals, to define sub-goals, and to establish attainable yet meaninful overall goals. The self-reinforcement phase of the program is meant to increase the participants' use of self-reward. In brief, clients are taught to reward themselves when they feel they have done something well.

In a series of four treatment studies summarized by Rehm (1981), using the Beck Depression Inventory as the major criterion and the depression scale of the MMPI, the efficacy of the self-control treatment method has been demonstrated. Another dependent measure, a self-report of activity level was also obtained, as was a measure of ideal-self and actual-self. The subjects showed statistically and clinically significant reductions in depression reflected both on the BDI and the MMPI depression measures. Subjects also showed increased positive activities. The measure of discrepancy between ideal and actual self did not show significant changes. In brief, however, the results in general showed clear validation of the self-control treatment model, and, in addition, there is some evidence that the effects are maintained up to a full year later.

Interpersonal Therapy (ITP)

The first outcome evaluation of ITP was reported in 1979 by Weissman, Prusoff, DiMascio, Neu, Goklaney, and Klerman (1979). Treatment outcome for ITP is reviewed here because it has been seen as one of the two major psychotherapies for depression, and the U.S. government has a multisite treatment study in progress which involves a comparison of IPT, Beck's cognitive therapy, and antidepressant medication. ITP should not be construed as behavior therapy. It is a variant of psychodynamic therapy and is included here because of its high regard by staff at the National Institute of Mental Health. ITP was used alone, antidepressant medication was used alone, and the two were combined for one treatment group. Eighty-one depressed individuals accepted random assignment to treatment. To be accepted, individuals had to meet research diagnostic criteria for unipolar depression, to be nonpsychotic, and to receive a cutoff score in the severe depression range on the Raskin Depression Scale.

Treatment lasted for sixteen weeks on a weekly basis. Assessment of the treatment was conducted by a clinical evaluator who was not aware of the type of treatment the individual was receiving. The control group had nonscheduled treatment, which essentially meant that individuals could receive a fifty-minute session at a maximum of once per month if his or her needs were of sufficient intensity. Any individual who worsened sufficiently to require other treatment was reassigned to another treatment and withdrawn from the study. In brief, this procedure is an efficient ethical means of studying treatment that takes into account clients'/patients' individual clinical needs.

The decline in depression was greater for the ITP group than for the nonscheduled treatment when evaluated by the clinical evaluator and the patients' self-reports. At one-year follow-up, ITP patients were less impaired in social activities and as family members than those individuals who did not receive ITP. In sum, the investigators found that symptom reduction was obtained at the end of four months of treatment, but that increases in social functioning took six to eight months to obtain with ITP.

Antidepressant medication had been the accepted standard for treatment of depression for many years. Therefore, some of the initial studies of psychotherapy for depressed persons involved the addition of psychotherapy to medication for depressed persons. From the 1960s to the mid 1970s, there was an accepted belief that antidepressant medication would produce relatively immediate symptom relief, whereas psychotherapy would produce overall social adjustment. However, it was also felt that psychotherapy would require much longer to effect change than medication would.

To address this issue, depressed women were randomly assigned to eight months of amitriptyline hydrochloride (imipramine), a placebo, and no intervention. Half of the patients in each group received ITP from psychiatric social workers. All patients in the study had shown a positive response to medication. As reflected in Figure 10-2 from Weissman et al. (1974), the groups were then divided into what was termed high-contact and low-contact groups. The high-contact group received psychotherapy; the low-contact group only saw the psychiatrist monthly for prescribing medication (Weissman, Klerman, Paykel et al., 1974). Treatment protocol allowed for two psychotherapy sessions per week, but patients rarely attended more than one. According to the investigators, "Most

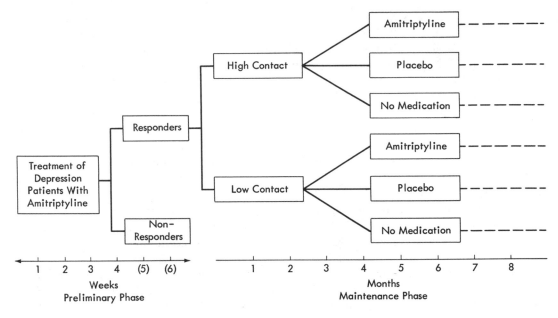

Figure 10–2 Design of study. (From Weissman et al. (1974). Treatment effects on the social adjustment of depressed patients. *Archives of General Psychiatry, 30,* 6, 772. Copyright 1974, American Medical Association.)

psychotherapy was with the patient alone, although a wide range of interventions selectively occurred, such as home visits and family and group therapy." Therapeutic emphasis was on current functioning rather than on reflective discussions or "uncovering of early childhood material." Therapists took a reassuring, helpful, and active stance, not a neutral position. Separately collected data on what patients discussed indicated that descriptive accounts of practical problems, such as employment, housing, finances, and close interpersonal relations, usually spouse and children, comprised most of the discussion.

Patients were all women from working- and lower-middle-class backgrounds. The typical patient was a married housewife with children; one half of the women had experienced one or more serious depressive episodes. Of 150 patients who completed at least two months of treatment, 44 dropped out of the study, leaving a total of 106 patients completing

treatment. After four months, there were essentially no differences between the groups. After eight months, differences between the psychotherapy group and the medication alone group were apparent. Most important, patients in the psychotherapy group showed significantly less work impairment, less interpersonal friction, better communication, and less anxious rumination. In brief, ITP appeared to improve the patients' social adjustment.

In a study comparing cognitive therapy and antidepressant therapy (amitriptyline) by Beck, Hollon, Young, Bedrosian, and Budenz (1985), depressed patients were assigned to either treatment. Treatment consisted of up to twenty sessions across twelve weeks. Both groups showed significant reductions in depression, and the decreases were clinically meaningful. There were no differences in the groups in decreases in depressive symptomatology. Further, combining antidepressant medication with cognitive therapy did not improve the effectiveness of the intervention. However, there was some evidence that combining treatment may provide some advantage in long-term stability.

Mechanisms of Therapeutic Change

The effectiveness of various types of behavioral treatments for depression is clear. Since the behavioral treatments differ in their procedural emphases, it is unclear what the common ingredients of a successful treatment are. For example, some behavioral treatments emphasize social skills, others emphasize cognitive changes, and still others emphasize self-control. Even more divergent from these general methods is marital therapy for depressed persons, another treatment with demonstrated effectiveness for depression. Teasdale (1985) proposed that "depression about depression," or depression about being depressed, is a very important factor in maintaining depression. It was suggested that "anyone who experienced the highly aversive symptoms and effects of depression, who saw these as the result of personal inadequacy, and who felt quite hopeless that their situa-

tion would improve, either through their own efforts or otherwise, would experience depression about depression" (p. 160). Teasdale further proposes that effective treatments for depression reduce "depression about depression by reducing its aversiveness and increasing its perceived controllability" (p. 162). Clinically supportive data for this premise comes from questionnaire data regarding being depressed. In addition, many responders to treatment appear to change in the first four weeks of treatment, and it is argued that if skill training were the critical ingredient, the improvement would not be as rapid. Instead, it is felt that cognitive changes that allow clients to have a sense of efficacy in dealing with depression mediate the relatively rapid improvement.

SUMMARY

Depression is the most common individual problem for which people seek treatment. Women experience depression almost twice as frequently as men do, and 15 percent of seriously depressed persons commit suicide. The major descriptors of depression are poor appetite, insomnia, psychomotor agitation, loss

---

Box 10–3   *Behavioral Marital Therapy: A Viable Treatment for Depression*

Approximately half of depressed women have serious marital problems. It is unclear whether depression causes the marital problems or whether marital problems cause the depression. Interestingly, depressed women who received marital therapy fared better than depressed women who received cognitive behavior therapy. Women in both treatments showed reductions in depression, but women who received marital therapy showed both reductions in depression and increases in marital satisfaction. The focus on marital variables is predicated on three important facts:

(1) Marital difficulties are the most frequent presenting problems of women seeking treatment for depression.

(2) Poor marriages are predictors of depression.

(3) Marital problems are poor prognostic indicators of women receiving antidepressant medication (Coyne, 1985).

of interest in pleasurable activities, and feelings of worthlessness. There are two types of depression, unipolar and bipolar, with the latter referring to depression with mania. Bipolar depression is responsive to antidepressant medication but not to psychotherapy. Unipolar depression is responsive both to medication and psychological therapies. Lithium has been used successfully with bipolar depression, especially mania, but it is not the medication of choice with unipolar depression because it has severe toxicity problems and therefore must be used with extreme caution. Severe unipolar depressives respond and show clinical improvement with ECT, but the method is controversial and many refuse such treatment.

Four theoretical models of depression—Beck's cognitive theory, Lewinsohn's behavioral theory, Rehm's self-control model of depression, and Weissman's interpersonal theory—have some empirical support, and all have led to treatment programs utilized in many places throughout the United States.

The models need not be viewed as competing but rather as complementary. They lead one to conclude that depressed persons view themselves and their world as negative, experience more negative events than nondepressed persons, receive less positive reinforcement, and often have poor attachments with others. There are some biochemical correlates of depression, such as amine and noradrenaline deficiencies.

The largest therapy outcome study yet conducted in the United States was initiated in 1982 under the aegis of the National Institute of Mental Health (Elkin, Parloff, Hadley, & Autry, 1985). The study involves a comparison of Weissman and Klerman's Interpersonal therapy, Beck's Individual Cognitive Therapy, antidepressant medication, and a placebo. The therapies have been conducted at three different universities (George Washington University, University of Pittsburgh, and University of Oklahoma). A total of 240 depressed persons have been treated by 28 therapists. Since the study is ongoing, there is still no official publication regarding the efficacy of the various treatments. However, at the 1986 annual meeting of the American Psychiatric Association, a group of federal researchers presented the initial findings of the 10 million dollar study using the end of therapy evaluations. The results were as follows: At the end of four months of treatment "those who were severely depressed had done just as well with either form of psychotherapy as those who received drug and minimal support therapy (20–30 minutes of supportive talk each week)" (*Newsday*, May 20, 1986, p. 3). So far, only a six-page summary of the findings has been released. Without the actual publication of the study and the presentation of follow-up data it is impossible to draw firm conclusions about the efficacy of the treatments. However, even this initial summary attracted national attention, and it was covered in almost every major magazine. For example, the study was hailed in *Time* (May 26, 1986, p. 60) as a landmark study by which all other psychotherapy research will be assessed, and the *Time* byline was "Talk Is as Good as a Pill." Moreover, the psychotherapies may even fare better than the antidepressant medication at the six-, twelve-, and eighteen-month follow-up periods. Antidepressant medication and behavioral therapies have been found to be approximately equivalent in efficacy in several outcome studies (e.g. Beck et al., 1985; McLean & Hastigan, 1979), and in some studies, cognitive therapy was more effective than antidepressant medication (e.g., Blackburn, Bishop, Glen, Whalley, & Christie, 1981). However, in a number of studies dropout rates from drug treatment are as high as 35 percent, and an equivalent percent does not respond to initial trials of medication. Finally, when medication is terminated, depressive symptoms may return, especially in cases in which there is significant marital discord. In brief, behavior therapy for depressed persons is a highly effective treatment with comparatively few dropouts and essentially no adverse side effects.

11

Psychosexual Disorders

SEXUAL DYSFUNCTION

The analysis and treatment of sexual disorders has been a prominent part of behavior therapy from its earliest days (Wolpe, 1958; Wolpe & Lazarus, 1966). It was, however, the publication in 1970 of Masters and Johnson's influential book *Human Sexual Inadequacy* that led to the professional acceptance of what has come to be called "sex therapy." Masters and Johnson do not identify their methods as "behavior therapy," but their treatment program can be accurately characterized in this way, as discussed below.

DEFINITION AND ETIOLOGY

Sexual Dysfunctions in Men

The two major forms of sexual dysfunction in males are ejaculatory and erectile disorders.

Ejaculatory Disorder. Premature ejaculation is the most common type of ejaculatory disorder and one of the most difficult to define. This is the problem of the male ejaculating "too soon." But what is "too soon"? Masters and Johnson (1970) defined premature ejaculation as the inability to delay ejaculation long enough for the woman to experience orgasm 50 percent of the time, except for those cases in which the female is nonorgasmic for reasons other than rapid ejaculation. Sexually functional women vary greatly in the amount of stimulation required for orgasm; the same woman will vary from time to time depending on a host of changeable physiological and situationally specific psychosocial factors. According to DSM-III, premature ejaculation is defined as occurring before the "individual wishes it, because of recurrent and persistent absence of reasonable voluntary control of ejaculation and orgasm during sexual activity. The judgment of 'reasonable control' is made by the clinician's taking into account factors that affect duration of the excitement phase, such as age, novelty of the sexual partner, and the frequency and duration of coitus" (p. 158). Many sex therapists emphasize the importance of *both* sexual partners feeling satisfaction with the male's ejaculatory control during intercourse.

Masters and Johnson's study of close to 200 premature ejaculators revealed a correlation between a man's educational level and his concern about his wife's sexual satisfaction. The better educated the man, the more likely he was to be troubled by his inability to satisfy his wife sexually. Premature ejaculation seems to be related to early sexual experiences that were unusually hurried.

Erectile Disorders. In DSM-III, problems with erection are classified as "Inhibited Sexual Excitement." The more common label has been "impotence," and because Masters and Johnson and other clinicians have used this term, we use it here. The impotent man cannot have sexual intercourse because his penis does not get hard enough to enter the vagina or because he cannot maintain his erection long enough to ejaculate. Masters and Johnson distinguished between primary and secondary impotence. Primary impotence means that a man has never been able to achieve an erection sufficient to have either vaginal or rectal intercourse with a partner. Cases of this severity seem to be relatively rare. In secondary impotence, the man is currently unable to achieve an erection sufficient to engage in sexual intercourse, either vaginally or rectally, but had been able to do so at least once in the past.

Impotence can have numerous causes, both psychological and biological (e.g., diabetes) in nature. In the majority of cases impotence is a result of psychological problems relating to sexual expression. These psychological determinants can be conveniently divided into factors that are currently maintaining sexual inadequacy and historical influences that have contributed to the person's present problem. Irrespective of the historical causes, it is the person's current fear of sexual performance that seems responsible for most forms of sexual dysfunction. The man is self-conscious. Instead of being open and responsive to erotic stimulation and enhanced sensory input, he is distracted by critical self-evaluation that generates anxiety and undermines his body's natural psychophysiological response (erection) to erotic cues.

Masters and Johnson reported that the single most common factor in the backgrounds of both men and women with different forms of sexual dysfunction was rigid adherence to religious orthodoxy. These dysfunctional individuals were led to believe that "sex is sin." As in all the underlying factors discussed here, it is important to realize that many deeply religious people do *not* develop sexual dysfunction. A dominating, overcontrolling parent who undermines self-esteem; traumatic initial sexual encounters, such as a humiliating failure that destroys self-confidence and heightens fears of inadequacy; and homosexual leanings that compete with heterosexual arousal are some other underlying causes of primary impotence.

The range of causes of secondary impotence is probably broader than that of primary impotence. In addition to the factors noted above, premature ejaculation and alcohol abuse are among the most common antecedents of secondary impotence. A large percentage of men experience occasional erectile problems during the course of their sexual lives. Kaplan (1974) has estimated that this applies to roughly half of the male population. Many of these men cope with these problems with minimal distress and no professional help. Others, however, are deeply affected and probably require specific assistance in overcoming their difficulties.

Organic problems can seriously impair sexual performance and in an important minority of patients these physical factors are directly responsible for sexual dysfunction. Disorders of the vascular, neurological, and endocrinal systems can all affect sexual functioning. Different organic disorders can impair specific aspects of sexual functioning selectively. Thus the sexual problem may involve a lack of sexual desire, erectile difficulties, or interference with orgasm (ejaculation). The erectile response is vulnerable to a variety of noxious physical agents, including drugs and disease, and it is imperative that impotent men be screened carefully for possible organic causes of their sexual dysfunction.

It has been estimated that roughly 90 percent of all cases of erectile dysfunction are due to psychological problems, but the figure may be considerably higher among older men or those with a significant history of chronic illness. For example, one report suggests that some impotent men—perhaps more than the roughly 10 percent previously thought to suffer from organic impotence—may have hormonal abnormalities that can be corrected by appropriate treatment using hormones other than testosterone (Spark, White, & Connolly, 1980). The absence of experimental controls makes this report only suggestive at best. Nonetheless, it emphasizes the importance of an informed diagnosis about the cause of impotence and the preferred treatment.[1]

Sexual Dysfunctions in Women

Inhibited Female Orgasm. The most frequent dysfunctions are what Masters and Johnson called primary and situational or-

1. See Rosen (1983) for an informative summary of the appropriate screening and assessment procedures.

gasmic dysfunction. The former is the failure of a woman to have ever had orgasm by any means, whereas the latter refers to those cases in which a woman is orgasmic in only very limited circumstances, e.g., with masturbation but not during intercourse.

Both biological and psychological factors can produce orgasmic dysfunction. Among the most common causes identified by Masters and Johnson were the same negative influences responsible for male sexual disorders. Restrictive religious prohibitions, homosexual commitments, and negative family influences can all result in sexual difficulties. The most frequent source of sexual orgasmic difficulty was the woman's emotional dissatisfaction with her partner. These negative emotional reactions might include shame, resentment, jealousy, boredom, disappointment, or even disgust, variously reflecting unhappiness over financial failure, physical appearance, social shortcomings, a lack of affection, and reactions to the man's relationships with other women. Sexual problems in women can also be the result of specific trauma, such as rape or attempted rape, being molested as a child, or severe pain or panic during the first sexual encounter.

Although there is clear evidence that various sexual traumas can result in later sexual dysfunction, not all women (or men, for that matter) who undergo traumas of one kind or another subsequently develop sexual problems. In one study, adult rape victims were asked to rate, retrospectively, their satisfaction with different forms of sexual behavior before and after their rape (Feldman-Summers, Gordon, & Meagher, 1979). Two findings are important. First, when compared to a comparable group of women who had not been raped, the victimized group reported significantly less satisfaction with their current sexual experiences. Second, the two groups did not differ in reported frequency of intercourse, masturbation, or orgasm. Both groups indicated that their sex lives were satisfactory.

Women are also vulnerable to the negative influences of sexual inadequacy in their male partners. Men may not even concern themselves with their partner's sexual satisfaction and are physically able to have orgasm through sexual intercourse regardless of their mate's sexual responsiveness. For a woman to achieve orgasm during sexual intercourse, however, her partner must maintain an erection and control his ejaculation for a sufficient period of time. Even then, a clumsy or insensitive lover might interfere with a woman's orgasmic response, the presence of the necessary sexual mechanics of erection and ejaculatory control notwithstanding. Furthermore, women frequently worry about their partner's inability to control ejaculation or maintain an erection, thereby impairing their own sexual response. Of the large number of couples Masters and Johnson treated in which both partners showed sexual dysfunction, the most common combination was premature ejaculation and orgasmic dysfunction.

Fundamental to most forms of sexual dysfunction in women, according to Masters and Johnson, is society's double standard of sexual values in which male sexuality is culturally sanctioned, if not implicitly encouraged, while a woman's sexual nature (other than to satisfy her husband) is ignored or even denied. Sexual responsiveness is not simply an innate drive that automatically unfolds as men and women mature physically. The biological potential for sexual responsiveness with which we are all born is elaborated upon and probably channeled into different directions depending upon subsequent psychosocial experiences (Gagnon, 1977). If the necessary social opportunities for this learning are unavailable, or if the response is systematically punished, a woman will encounter difficulty

in suddenly becoming orgasmic as a result of taking a marriage vow or accepting her first invitation to go to bed with a man.

Related to our society's double standard of sexual mores has been the assumption that the man, as the sexual expert, must take responsibility for initiating and orchestrating sex. A study in the United States of pairs of college students who were seriously dating found that despite the recent breakdown of the double standard of sexual morality, it still tends to be the male who is expected to make the first move in sexual encounters (Peplau, Rubin, & Hill, 1977). Overwhelmingly, women waited for men to make sexual overtures, although 95 percent of both the men and women advocated identical moral standards for sex. The reason? The women's fear that they would threaten their partner's ego were they to be the initiator of sex. In their research on the customary sexual behavior of normal couples, Masters and Johnson found that the typical script, with the man taking the lead, was stereotypically some form (usually desultory) of foreplay, followed by the ultimate objective of vaginal intercourse. This relatively unvarying pattern among heterosexual couples often places the woman at a sexual disadvantage because the timing may be desynchronous with her pattern of sexual responsiveness. At the same time this single-minded emphasis on sexual intercourse as the goal places unnecessary pressure on the man to perform, pressure that can result in impotence.

As in the case of male sexual dysfunction, organic factors can play a role in orgasmic dysfunction, although Kaplan (1974) has stated that the female sexual response is "less vulnerable" to impairment by drugs and illness than the male response. However, the biological basis of sexual dysfunction in women has received less direct research attention than disorders in men.

Vaginismus and Dyspareunia.   Vaginismus refers to the involuntary tightening or spasm in the outer third of the vagina. These spasms can make it difficult if not impossible for the woman to have intercourse. Aside from some of the psychosocial causes of sexual dysfunction discussed above, such as punitive religious prohibitions, vaginismus can be the result of rape.

Painful intercourse, such as aching, burning, or itching sensations during intercourse often indicate an absence of adequate lubrication in the vagina. Lack of lubrication usually means that the woman is insufficiently aroused, suggesting that some emotional or interpersonal factor is responsible and indicating sex therapy. However, vaginal infections and other physical problems are all possible causes of deep pelvic pain during intercourse and require diagnosis by a gynecologist.

Disorders of Sexual Desire.   Many couples consult therapists complaining not of problems with erection and ejaculation in the male, or their counterpart, lubrication and orgasm in the female, but of a loss of interest in sex. Affecting both men and women, this loss of sexual interest has been called inhibition of sexual desire (ISD). Kaplan (1979) provides the following clinical description of ISD:

> "The person with low sexual desire will not feel 'horny' or interested in sex. S/he will not be moved to seek out sexual activity, nor will s/he fantasize about sex. Also, in contrast to normal experience, sexual desire evoked by stimulation of the genitals will be absent or greatly reduced. The reflexes may, in fact, work if stimulation is permitted; i.e., the person may have an erection or lubricate and/or have an orgasm. But this experience is not really satisfying in the presence of a low desire state. Pleasure is fleeting, perhaps just before orgasm, and is limited to and localized in the genitals. Patients

describe such experiences as similar to eating a meal when one is not really hungry" (p. 62).

No consensus exists on an operational definition of low or inhibited sexual desire. Sexual interest between partners will vary over time regardless of how much in love they are with each other, assuming that they are physically healthy and free from pressing psychological problems. Periods of stress and other fluctuating factors will produce transient decreases in one or the other partner's sexual desire. The diagnosis of ISD requires that the therapist take into account the context of the couple's life, their ages, health, and customary sexual pattern. Friedman and Hogan (1985) offer the following diagnostic criteria, "An individual is arbitrarily diagnosed as global low desire if individual or partner sexual experiences (including oral, manual, or penile or vaginal stimulation) occur every two weeks or less and there is evidence of lack of subjective desire for sexual activity (including sex with mate, sex with other partners, masturbation, sexual dreams), lack of fantasies, and an absence of sexual reactions to attractive people of the opposite or same sex. If low frequency and low subjective desire are partner specific, situational low sexual desire is diagnosed" (pp. 423–424).

A Social Learning Analysis

In a social learning analysis, psychosexual dysfunction, except for those cases in which it is due to organic causes, is mainly a function of lack of appropriate knowledge and negative emotional reactions. The absence of an emotional attachment for one's sexual partner may also result in sexual difficulties. The person may be in love with someone else or hostility might exist as the result of interpersonal conflict. Masters and Johnson (1970) primarily emphasized the role of performance anxiety as the proximal determinant of dysfunction. A broader social learning analysis is required, however, in which interpersonal and cognitive-attentional processes are critical elements.

As in the case of the anxiety disorders, the original learning theory explanation of psychosexual dysfunction relied upon the model of conditioned (performance) anxiety. The reduction of this anxiety, via techniques such as desensitization, explained treatment success. However, as Beck and Barlow (1984) have pointed out, a simple anxiety-reduction model cannot fully explain the relevant treatment mechanisms. They note that laboratory studies show that anxiety, operationalized as threat of electric shock or pharmacologically elevated autonomic arousal, does not necessarily decrease sexual arousal. Beck and Barlow suggest that sexual arousal is inhibited by cognitive distraction. Several studies indicate that impotent men are distracted by thoughts which decrease attention to the sexual situation and thereby interfere with sexual arousal (Barlow, 1986; Heiman & Rowland, 1983). This conceptual shift from a simple anxiety-reduction conditioning model to a more cognitive approach parallels developments in the anxiety disorders, as described in Chapters 8 and 9, and is consistent with social learning theory (Bandura, 1977b).

TREATMENT METHODS

Masters and Johnson's (1970) program incorporated several established behavior therapy techniques (Wolpe, 1958) in an innovative approach which fundamentally changed the way sexual dysfunction was treated. Current psychological treatment methods are largely derivative of their program, which was designed to extinguish fear of failure through what is basically an in vivo desensitization procedure.[2]

A key concept is that both marital partners participate in the treatment, since Masters and Johnson consider that the "relationship between the partners is the patient," even if one is clearly dysfunctional and the other is not. Emphasis on treating the sexually dysfunctional couple reflects the importance attributed to shaping up effective interpersonal communication. It also precludes the possibility of the partner not in therapy accidentally or purposefully interfering with therapy because of mutual emotional involvement in the sexual problem. The program is based on abolishing goal-oriented performance. For example, whether he is trying to control his ejaculation or to get an erection, the sexually dysfunctional male is preoccupied with performance pressure. He is worried about achieving a significant goal, namely, adequate sexual intercourse that satisfies both his own ego and his partner's sexual appetite. As a result, the man slips into the "spectator role," in which he self-consciously distracts himself from the physical and psychosocial erotic stimulation that produces erections. The first step in reducing this performance anxiety is to prohibit any sexual activity not specifically sanctioned by the therapists. To begin, sexual intercourse is forbidden, thereby removing the pressure on the man to perform. Thereafter, the couple is instructed in how to embark upon a carefully graduated program of mutually pleasurable sensual and sexual involvement. Since this is conducted at the couple's own pace and involves no explicit goals, performance pressure is effectively undercut.

The mutual, non-goal-oriented sensual interactions between the partners is known as

2. Wolpe and Lazarus (1966) explicitly described desensitization procedures, the "stop-start" technique for premature ejaculation, and other methods, which were later popularized by Masters and Johnson (1970).

sensate focus. The term is self-explanatory—the focus is on physical or sensory stimulation of each other's bodies. The couple is taught to learn to think and feel sensuously by giving and getting bodily pleasure, first by nongenital contact and then by specific genital stimulation. The use of moisturizing lotions has been found to facilitate pleasurable physical interaction between partners. Although clients develop skills in bodily stimulation, the fundamental significance of the sensate focus exercises is in increasing verbal and nonverbal communication between the partners and in teaching them that sexual gratification does not necessarily depend on sexual intercourse. As sexual arousal spontaneously occurs in these "homework" assignments, the treatment is oriented towards the specific form of sexual dysfunction in question.

Sexual Treatments for Men

Premature Ejaculation: The "Squeeze Technique."   In this technique the woman manually stimulates her partner's penis to full erection and then, just prior to ejaculation, using her thumb and first two fingers of the same hand, firmly squeezes the penis on each side of the coronal ridge for three or four seconds. The pressure eradicates the urge to ejaculate, and after about 30 seconds the procedure is repeated. Gradually the man is able to maintain increasingly longer erections. The progression then moves from the woman straddling the man and inserting his penis into her vagina while remaining motionless, to gradually building up to vigorous pelvis thrusting. If at any time the man feels he is going to ejaculate too quickly, the woman, who is in the superior coital position, raises her body, repeats the squeeze technique, and then reinserts the penis.

In a variation of this procedure, the so-called "stop-start" technique, the woman ceases all physical stimulation of the penis as soon as her partner signals her that he is close to the point of ejaculating. His urge to ejaculate will diminish, at which point the couple resumes stimulation. As in the squeeze technique, it is vitally important that the man recognize the point at which he is close to ejaculation and communicate it to his partner. If he waits too long he will reach the point of ejaculatory inevitability, at which stage he will be unable to restrain ejaculation. The man's willingness and ability to make this judgment and communicate it to his partner is critical to the success of treatment.

Impotence.   The treatment of impotence is similar to that of ejaculatory disorders. Couples are instructed to continue with sensate focus exercises until erection spontaneously occurs. Thereafter the wife uses a "teasing technique" in which she manipulates the penis to erection and then relaxes with her partner until the erection disappears. She then repeats the procedure several times, thereby effectively extinguishing the man's fear of losing an erection and not getting it back during sexual interaction. The therapy continues with the woman facilitating nondemanding intromission followed by progressively more vigorous thrusting until orgasm occurs involuntarily.

Relationship Problems.   Impotence, as with any other sexual dysfunction, is often imbedded in a troubled relationship. After months, if not years, of repeated failure to experience satisfactory sexual intercourse, the woman or wife is frustrated and frequently resentful. The husband, his sense of masculinity threatened by his sexual inadequacy, usually feels defensive and insecure. He may harbor hostility towards his wife as a result of these insecurities and belittling comments she might make about him. The longer the problem persists and goes untreated, the greater the likelihood that it will affect their overall relationship. Small disagreements increasingly escalate into drawn out battles as the issue of his impotence is inevitably injected into the discussion.

To illustrate the role of marital difficulties in the maintenance of sexual dysfunction, consider the following clinical case (Brady, 1976). A 27-year-old client was treated for frequent secondary impotence. The now almost standard therapy of graduated in vivo desensitization failed completely. The client went against the therapist's explicit instructions and drank before a session of sensate focus. The man's wife similarly ignored instructions by engaging almost immediately in direct genital stimulation and urging her husband to attempt intercourse. Mutual recriminations inevitably followed. As soon as this self-defeating pattern of behavior became apparent, the therapist delved more deeply into the nature of the couple's marital relationship. This assessment showed that the client was plagued by self-doubt and a lack of assertiveness; his wife, while she expressed warmth and support on occasion, was predominately critical and aggressive. Brady then introduced a number of behavior therapy techniques aimed at improving the couple's relationship. Among the strategies employed were assertiveness training and cognitive-behavioral approaches to marital therapy (see Chapter 12).

As a result of this shift in therapeutic tactics, the couple's marital relationship improved greatly over the following five months of treatment. However, the impotence persisted, and anxiety was still attached to sexual performance. At this point the original in vivo desensitization program was reintroduced with the result that the impotence was eliminated within a few weeks. A six month follow-up indicated successful maintenance of the couple's sexual adequacy.

The foregoing clinical illustration underscores the following point: In several instances the effective treatment of specific sexual disorders will require treatment of other nonsexual aspects of the couple's functioning, such as competitive tendencies and the lack of communication. Sexual dysfunction flourishes in an unhappy relationship, and problems such as impotence invariably place a great strain on any relationship. The pragmatic clinical strategy is to intervene directly in the sexual problem while looking for clues or signs of marital disharmony that might interfere with therapy. This is a more efficient approach than automatically assuming that underlying conflicts must be dealt with first before focusing on the sexual difficulty. As illustrated in Brady's case, the use of behavioral sex therapy methods provide a powerful diagnostic and motivational test. As in this case, it may quickly expose resistances to treatment so that other related features of the total clinical problem can be identified, assessed, and appropriately treated.

Sexual Treatments for Women

The fundamental treatment concepts and procedures are the same for both sexes, including the commitment to treating the woman and her partner as a couple, the use of a dual-sex therapist team, the abolition of performance-oriented sex, and the emphasis on nondemanding mutual pleasuring and improved verbal and nonverbal communication that form the essence of sensate focus.

The sensate focus exercises are designed to create an accepting atmosphere in which the woman has permission to identify, enjoy, and express her own feelings of sexuality, perhaps for the first time in her life. The idea is to encourage the woman to show her partner what she finds sexually arousing, as opposed to passively allowing him to do what he thinks she wants. The therapists instruct the couple in the details of specific sexual positions for stimulation and intercourse and in the importance of timing. For example, Masters and Johnson's observations of heterosexual couples having sex revealed that men typically begin to stimulate their partner's clitoris as soon as sex is initiated. However, this stimulation may be ineffective if not unpleasant unless the woman is psychologically ready for immediate stimulation of this sort. The man is taught to stimulate nongenital areas of his partner's body to build up arousal gradually before moving to more direct genital play. This more varied or imaginative pattern of sexual stimulation, carried out with explicit concern for the woman's sensual and sexual pleasure, contrasts with what has been described as the more typical sexual script between man and woman. This latter pattern has been characterized as "a kiss on the lips, a hand on the breast, and a dive for the pelvis." Following the sensate focus exercises, the couple proceeds gradually to nondemanding penile insertion with the woman in the superior coital position and controlling the pace.

As sex therapy has developed, several additional treatment procedures have been shown to be effective in enhancing female sexual responsiveness. A widely used approach with women who have never experienced an orgasm is a systematic program of directed masturbation (Heiman, LoPiccolo, & LoPiccolo, 1976). Briefly, the woman is first taught to familiarize herself with her body, particularly the genital area, and to identify pleasurable sensations. A female therapist then instructs her in the intricacies of masturbation, including the use of electric vibrators. Once the woman reaches orgasm through masturbation, her husband is introduced to the procedure by observing her masturbate. This not only desensitizes the woman to being sexually aroused in his presence, but also is a learning experience for him, who, in the next step of the program, masturbates the woman to orgasm.

The treatment of vaginismus closely resembles that of orgasmic dysfunction. Therapy involves actually demonstrating the existence of the muscular constriction of the vaginal muscles to the couple by having the man insert his finger into the vagina and feel the constriction. Following this demonstration the man is shown how to slowly insert progressively larger vaginal dilators in a program of gradualness or in vivo desensitization under the guidance of the woman, until she can comfortably accommodate fairly prolonged insertion. All twenty-nine women in the Masters and Johnson program who experienced vaginismus were treated successfully by this gradual insertion procedure.

Resistance to Change. Sex therapy involves considerably more than merely providing information and prescribing specific physical exercises. These mechanics of treatment will be successful only if used in the appropriate therapeutic context. It should never be taken for granted that the sexually dsyfunctional man and his partner are both completely rational people who are committed to change and intent upon actively participating in a cooperative problem-solving venture. Typical problems include patients who do not really wish to change, despite what they might say; hidden agendas; and a partner appearing to express warmth and support, but in fact being critical and aggressive. More often than not, the real task of therapy is to get the couple to the point at which they are both willing and able to implement specific sexual treatment techniques.

An advantage of the Masters and Johnson program is the intensive, daily contact they have with couples who are able to concentrate fully on the program since they are away from their customary routines of daily living. Commenting on their treatment program, Masters and Johnson have pointedly observed that there seemed to be a "cumulative effect when the therapy was conducted on a daily basis. When treatment crises occurred, the clients were never more than 24 hours away from active professional support. Therapy crises can be turned into important teaching opportunities rather than therapeutic setbacks if faced in the relative immediacy of their onset . . . In addition, the importance of continuing therapeutic reinforcement and modeling is maximized in a daily treatment format, drawing upon the underlying principles of social learning theory in a most efficient manner" (1979, pp. 258–259).

Most sex therapy is conducted on an outpatient basis, with treatment sessions once or twice a week. Adherence to therapeutic instructions is often a problem, but this is not due solely to the absence of intensive, daily sessions. Either one—or both—of the partners may resist change. Resistance can take many forms. Missing treatment sessions and failure to complete homework assignments are typical examples. A frequent refrain is "We were too busy this week," and so on. Note that in the Brady case outlined above the husband deliberately drank despite the warnings of the therapist, while the wife pressured him to have intercourse in direct violation of the no-goal-oriented program. A spouse can find many ways of engaging in "sexual sabotage." Most partners know specific actions that either turn on or turn off each other. This knowledge can be used to facilitate or inhibit sexual desire.

Sex may be part of the politics and power arrangements of the marriage and the resolution of a man's impotence might drastically alter this balance, thereby threatening an insecure partner for whom this dysfunction served a controlling purpose. Should a formerly impotent man regain his potency, his wife would be faced with the prospect of greatly increased sexual contact that she may not want

or may even fear. Improvement in a wife's orgasmic responsiveness can produce impotence in her husband, a man whose wife's sexual inhibitions had masked his own problems (Brady, 1971). These are some of the reasons for including both partners in sex therapy.

The sexually dysfunctional man may fail to adhere to treatment instructions himself. This apparent resistance may be motivated by a number of factors, including simple inertia, the belief that treatment will be ineffective, or even what Kaplan (1979) refers to as a "fear of success." Should continued encouragement and repetition of the treatment instructions to engage in specific homework assignments prove unproductive, the therapists will confront the couple directly. The pattern of failure to follow treatment directives is pointed out, and the issue opened up for mutual questioning and discussion. Providing insight into self-defeating patterns of behavior that the sexually dysfunctional man or his partner might not have been aware of usually suffices to overcome resistance.

EFFICACY OF TREATMENT

Uncontrolled Reports

Masters and Johnson (1970) reported that of the 790 patients they treated, only 19 percent were failures at the end of the two-week program. The overall failure rate five years after therapy, including both initial treatment failures and subsequent reversals, was only slightly higher (25.5 percent) than that immediately following treatment. The five-year follow-up figures are based on 313 of the original 790 patients treated. There were no overall differences between failure rates with men and women. Masters and Johnson's innovative and enormously influential research, though, was not without scientific shortcomings (O'Leary & Wilson, 1975). As they themselves pointed out, theirs was a highly select and motivated sample of patients uncharacteristic of the general population. Zilbergeld and Evans (1980) have noted other limitations of this research, including a reliance upon global, imprecise criteria for therapeutic outcome. Systematic evaluation of treatment effects by the patients themselves was not reported. Nor did an independent, neutral assessor who was "blind" to the type of therapy evaluate treatment outcome. Only Masters and Johnson's own judgments of outcome were reported.

Adequate evaluation of treatment outcome must include multiple subjective and objective measures, as pointed out in the discussion of anxiety disorders. The importance of gathering multiple measures of sexual responsiveness is illustrated by Wincze, Hoon, and Hoon's study (1978) of women who participated in a comprehensive sex-therapy program for low levels of sexual arousal. Outcome measures included vaginal photoplethysmographic recordings, clinical interviews, subjective ratings of sexual arousal and anxiety, and self-monitoring records of sexual behavior. At post-treatment, all five women in this study expressed positive attitudes toward the therapists, increased capacity for sexual arousal, increased knowledge and understanding of sex, and general improvement in their sexual relationships, although none of the objective measures showed any clinically significant changes.

Controlled Studies

Several controlled studies have clearly demonstrated the efficacy of behavioral sex therapy for different sexual disorders. Mathews, Bancroft, Whitehead, Hackmann, Julier, Bancroft, Gath, and Shaw (1976) compared three methods—systematic desensitization plus counseling, directed practice (i.e., a modified version of the Masters and Johnson in vivo program) plus counseling, and directed practice with minimal therapist contact—in the treatment of male and female sexual dysfunction. The counseling consisted of discussing sexual attitudes, reviewing treatment progress, and encouraging free communication of sexual feelings between partners. In the minimal-contact condition, therapeutic instructions were mailed to patients, with only two actual treatment sessions (at mid-treatment and at the end of therapy). Counseling was absent from these sessions. All therapy consisted of twelve weekly sessions. Of the thirty-six couples, eighteen presented with primarily male problems, such as erectile failure or premature ejaculation. The most common complaint among the female patients was low interest in and arousal by sexual encounters; thirteen reported failure in achieving orgasm. Both members of each couple were seen together, but half the couples in each therapy condition were treated by a single therapist and half by a two-partner sex-therapy team. Outcome measures included ratings of patients' sexual adjustment by an independent psychiatrist before and after therapy and at a four-month follow-up, patient self-ratings and estimates of sexual activities, and therapist ratings of patients' sexual adjustment.

The Masters and Johnson treatment was approximately twice as effective as the other two treatments. Given the earlier discussion of the importance of specifying therapy outcome criteria, the following observation by Mathews and his colleagues is noteworthy, "The nature of the change occurring in couples whose treatment was rated relatively successful was often surprisingly unclear. This seems particularly true of 'female complainant' couples, where changes in orgasmic function were disappointingly few, even when there was general agreement that the sexual relationship had improved. One possibility is that some parts of treatment, particularly the mutual exchange and communication aspects of directed practice, succeeded in increasing sexual enjoyment, despite failure to attain orgasm" (1976, p. 452).

Impotence and premature ejaculation were the target problems in two outcome studies by Auerbach and Kilmann (1977) and Zeiss (1978). In the Auerbach and Kilmann study, twenty-four men with secondary impotence were matched in age, severity of disorder, cooperativeness of partner, and marital status and assigned either to group desensitization or an attention-placebo control. The latter consisted of relaxation training (unrelated to specifically sexual functioning) and developing rapport. Group desensitization proved to be significantly more successful in improving erectile functioning. This improvement was maintained over a three-month follow-up period, and control subjects who were subsequently treated showed considerable change.

In the Zeiss study, twenty couples who reported difficulties with premature ejaculation received one of three types of treatment. The first treatment consisted of a totally self-administered program based on a written manual. Couples were given copies of a self-help book written by Zeiss and Zeiss (1978) describing a twelve-week program based on the techniques of Masters and Johnson (1970) and requiring approximately three hours of sexual and talking assignments each week. In the second treatment condition, couples received copies of the same manual; in addition, however, they had minimal contact with a therapist, consisting of weekly, prearranged telephone calls. On average, each couple received about six minutes of phone contact per week. The third treatment condition consisted of more conventional therapist-administered treatment. Couples in this group received weekly individual therapy sessions in which the therapist followed the same procedures described in the self-help manual.

The results indicated that the therapist-administered and the minimal-contact treatments were significantly superior to the completely self-administered treatment, but did not differ from each other. All six of the couples in the therapist-administered group and five out of the six couples in the minimal-contact group were treatment successes. The totally self-administered treatment failed to produce any improvement; five of the couples dropped out of treatment in the early stages.

Behavioral sex therapy for women has similarly registered some well-documented successes. In the treatment of primary orgasmic dysfunction, Riley and Riley (1978) compared a directed masturbation program to a control treatment consisting of the sensate focus component of the Masters and Johnson program plus supportive psychotherapy. All patients were seen weekly, together with their husbands, for six weeks and then every two weeks for another six weeks. Of the twenty women in the directed masturbation treatment, 90 percent were orgasmic at post-treatment compared to 53 percent in the control treatment. Eighty-five percent of the directed masturbation group, as opposed to 43 percent of the comparison treatment group, was orgasmic during intercourse at least 75 percent of the time. These results were maintained at a one-year follow-up. Of eight failures in the comparison group who were subsequently offered directed masturbation treatment, seven became orgasmic. Echoing the caution voiced by other responsible sex therapists, Riley and Riley emphasize that "Directed masturbation must be viewed only as an adjunct to therapy and not as the sole element in treatment. The encouragement of communication between sexual partners and sex education is essential" (p. 405).

Symbolic modeling is successful in improving inhibited sexual functioning. Nemetz, Craig, and Reith (1978) compared individual symbolic-modeling procedures, conducted on either an individual or a group basis, with a waiting list control. The subjects were twenty-two inorgasmic women, fifteen of whom suffered from secondary orgasmic dysfunction and seven of whom reported primary orgasmic dysfunction. Treatment consisted of relaxation training followed by the viewing of forty-five videotaped vignettes depicting graduated sexual behavior, with instructions to practice the modeled activities at home. Multiple outcome measures were used, including the frequency of specific sexual behavior as assessed by both the subject and her partner, global and specific measures of sexual attitudes, and subjective measures of anxiety about sexual behavior. Treated subjects improved on all three categories of outcome measures. Women who did not receive treatment showed no improvement and even some evidence of deterioration. Successful treatment effects were maintained at a one-year follow-up.

Primary orgasmic dysfunction can be treated with semi-automated procedures. McMullen and Rosen (1979) developed a series of six videotapes sequentially showing a female therapist instructing an inorgasmic client to become orgasmic through a graduated masturbation program. The videotaped client acted as a coping model, expressing fears, frustrations, and initial apprehension in entering the program. She explicitly modeled specific sexual exercises, reported her weekly progress to the videotaped therapist, and involved her husband in the exercises during the sixth tape. Sixty percent of the treatment groups were orgasmic with vibrator masturbation, whereas no control group subject became orgasmic during the ten-week waiting period. Treated subjects increased the number of times they initiated sexual contact, masturbated more frequently, and showed increased rates of orgasm by manual stimulation from their partners and during intercourse.

Behavioral sex therapy typically takes the form of multifaceted treatment rather than a focus on a single method. For example, Munjack, Cristol, Goldstein, Phillips, et al. (1976) evaluated the effects of a multicomponent program consisting of systematic desensitization, assertion training, cognitive restructuring, and masturbation training in the treatment of married women with primary or secondary orgasmic dysfunction. Compared to a waiting list control condition, the behavioral treatment produced significantly superior results in the percentage of patients experiencing orgasm during at least 50 percent of sexual relations, the percentage of women reporting satisfactory sexual relations at least 50 percent of the time, patients' ratings of positive reactions to various sexual activities, and assessors' global clinical ratings of the women's sexual adjustment.

Few controlled studies comparing behavioral methods to alternative treatments have been conducted, and those that have suffer from a number of methodological limitations. Obler (1973) compared behavioral treatment to traditional group therapy and to no treatment. The behavioral treatment consisted of fifteen weekly sessions of systematic desensitization, supplemented by the use of films of sexual encounters, assertion training, and role playing of situations related to sexual problems. Group psychotherapy, one-and-a-half hours weekly over a ten-week period, was conducted by psychodynamic therapists who focused on reducing misconceptions, promoting greater insight, and interpreting underlying dynamics and repressions associated with sexual dysfunction.

The behavioral treatment produced significantly greater improvement than did either group psychotherapy or no treatment. A total of 42 percent of the female subjects and 61 percent of the male subjects reported successful sexual encounters, as compared to only 3 percent of successful sexual attempts in the other two groups. Unfortunately, no information on treatment outcome for specific sexual problems is reported and outcome criteria are not defined, leaving questions unanswered about the nature of therapeutic improvement.

Crowe (1978) compared three treatments: behavioral marital therapy, an interpretative therapy, and a supportive control procedure. Couples who received the behavioral marital therapy and exhibited sexual dysfunction were treated with a modified Masters and Johnson approach. Therapy lasted from five to ten sessions and outcome was evaluated in terms of marital, sexual, and general adjustment. Crowe established, through independent ratings of taped therapy sessions, that the three treatments were procedurally discriminable. At post-treatment and at three- and eighteen-month follow-ups, the behavioral treatment was significantly more effective than was either the interpretative therapy or the supportive control procedure. The behavioral and interpretative treatments yielded roughly comparable success on ratings of marital and general adjustment, although only the behavioral treatment was significantly superior to the supportive control treatment at the 18-month follow-up.

Conclusion.

1. Behavioral therapy has been shown to provide quick and effective treatment for orgasmic difficulties in women, premature ejaculation, and some erectile problems. It reliably reduces sexual anxiety and can increase sexual responsiveness. Whatever its current limitations, behavioral sex therapy is the preferred form of treatment for psychogenic sexual dysfunction in men and women.

2. Evidence of the long-term efficacy of these methods is limited, since only five controlled studies have included follow-ups of one year or more (Crowe, 1978; Crowe, Gillan, & Golombok, 1981; Nemetz et al., 1978; Obler, 1973; Riley & Riley, 1978).

3. Masters and Johnson's insistence on highly trained two-partner sex-therapy teams is unfounded. Single therapists appear to achieve comparable success (LoPiccolo, Heiman, Hogan, & Roberts, 1985); nor is it necessary to match the gender of therapist with that of client (LoPiccolo et al., 1985).

4. Behavior therapy is efficient as well as effective. Aside from the much-publicized two-week rapid-treatment program of Masters and Johnson, most of the controlled outcome studies reviewed above ranged from approximately five to twenty sessions. Treatment manuals, at least for a relatively straightforward problem such as premature ejaculation, can be helpful, provided that there is some minimal level of therapist contact and direction (Zeiss, 1978). Group treatment of couples has proved feasible and effective in certain cases (e.g., Leiblum, Rosen, & Pierce, 1976). Some data suggest that therapy for primary orgasmic dysfunction is as effective if the women alone are treated as a group as it is if the women are treated together with their male partners (Ersner-Hershfield & Kopel, 1979).

5. Behavioral sex therapy does not result in any symptom substitution or other noticeable negative side effects. Contrary to some concerns, therapy-induced deterioration in the patients' functioning has not been reported (Wilson, 1978b).

6. For optimal efficacy, behavioral sex therapy needs to be used flexibly, following a thorough assessment of each individual patient's (or couple's) problems. Multifaceted treatment programs, including both sexual and nonsexual methods, are usually required (Brady, 1976; Lazarus, 1971; Leiblum & Pervin, 1980).

7. Relationship problems tend to complicate sex therapy and militate against its success (e.g., Brady, 1976; Mathews et al., 1976; Munjack et al., 1976). This finding assumes added significance if, as is widely believed among sex therapists, the population seeking sex therapy today

is somewhat different from and more likely to have fundamental relationship problems than the patients treated in the early 1970s (Friedman & Hogan, 1985; LoPiccolo, 1978).

9. Among contemporary sexual disorders, problems of low or inhibited desire are particularly challenging. Therapeutic success rates with these problems are said to be much lower than with the other forms of sexual dysfunction (Friedman & Hogan, 1985; Kaplan, 1979). For example, Kaplan (1979) has argued that whereas short-term behavioral sex therapy is reliably effective for a number of specific sexual dysfunctions, it is inadequate for a subset of sexual problems characterized by greater psychopathology, as in low sexual desire. For the latter problems, Kaplan advocates an amalgam of behavioral methods and psychodynamic principles she calls "psychosexual therapy," which, she claims, works where behavior therapy fails. Whether or not this is the case is an empirical question. What can be said at this juncture is that the failure of psychoanalytically oriented psychotherapy to have produced therapeutic success with sexual problems in decades past does not augur well for its presumptive efficacy in the subset of patients referred to by Kaplan (Rachman & Wilson, 1980). Similarly, Friedman and Hogan (1985) assert that to treat problems of low desire, therapists must be skilled not only in behavior therapy, but also systems and marital therapy, and be able to use techniques from Gestalt, psychodynamic, and transactional psychotherapy. No data are presented for such ambitious claims.

HOMOSEXUALITY

Few topics of human behavior have generated as much public and professional controversy over the recent past as that of homosexuality. In the United States, the controversy has been ignited by the challenging of traditional views about homosexuality, not only by gay activist groups, but also by behavioral and social scientists. Responding to this pressure, the American Psychiatric Association dropped the term homosexuality from its Diagnostic and Statistical Manual of Mental Illnesses (DSM) in 1973. This action was protested by a large number of psychiatrists within the American Psychiatric Association who insisted that homosexuality was pathological, a view deriving from psychoanalytic therapy (Bieber et al., 1962). In the latest version of the manual (DSM-III), a new category, ego-dystonic homosexuality, refers to those homosexuals who wish to reorient to heterosexuality.

A Social Learning Analysis

The social learning approach holds that human beings are sexual, with the direction of that biologically based potential being influenced by learning and cultural influences. There is still no compelling evidence showing that homosexuality is either genetically determined or hormonally based. Homosexuality is viewed as a variant of sexual expression, an alternative life-style that is not *ipso facto* psychopathological. Labeling homosexuality as "abnormal" or "psychopathological" is not conferring a scientific description but a value judgment. Homosexuals may have sexual and nonsexual psychological problems—just as heterosexuals do—but these are not necessarily either a cause or a symptom of their homosexuality. The social learning view is consistent with available scientific findings on the subject. It explains the historical and cross-cultural data showing that homosexuality has been and still is regarded as "normal" in some societies but not others. It is also consistent with Masters and Johnson's findings that there are no detectable physiological differences in sexual arousal and response between heterosexual and homosexual men and women.

The implications of this view are different from the traditional therapeutic position. Since homosexuality is not regarded as a form of emotional disorder, there is no implicit mandate that homosexuals should be "cured" of their homosexuality. This view accommodates the wide range of sexual and nonsexual differences that characterize homosexuals and heterosexuals alike, and it shifts the emphasis from trying to find the cause of homosexuality to understanding the development of all sexual behavior and studying how homosexuals are affected by their social situations. The following section reviews how the field has developed from trying to alter homosexuals' sexual orientation to helping them with their sexual and nonsexual problems.

Can Homosexuals Become Heterosexuals?

Various forms of psychotherapy and behavior therapy have been used in attempts to assist homosexuals to revert or change to heterosexuality. Psychotherapy has been ineffective (Bancroft, 1974; Bieber et al., 1962). Early behavior therapy treatment approaches relied almost exclusively on the use of aversion conditioning techniques. Typically, these were aimed at decreasing or eliminating homosexual arousal and behavior by repeatedly associating homosexual thoughts, feelings, and activities with an unpleasant or painful event. For example, a male homosexual patient might be shown a photographic slide of a sexually arousing male and then administered a painful but nonharmful electric shock to the forearm. Studies of the effectiveness of this technique by Feldman and MacCulloch (1971) produced a success rate of 57 percent, with success being defined as the cessation of all overt homosexual behavior. Other investigators, however, have failed to achieve comparable results, reporting much lower success rates in reducing homosexual behavior. Bancroft (1974) has estimated that the overall success rate with aversion therapy is roughly 40 percent.

Aversion therapy has drawn intense criticism from the gay community who see it more as a form of punishment than treatment. The majority of behavior therapists, too, have criticized the use of aversion therapy in the treatment of homosexuals and have suggested that its application be discontinued (e.g., Davison & Wilson, 1973). The ethics of helping homosexuals reorient to heterosexuality are discussed in Chapter 19. Rather than resorting to ethically questionable and relatively ineffective forms of aversion therapy, behavior therapists, to the extent that they try to help selected homosexuals reorient to heterosexuality, emphasize methods designed to increase heterosexual arousal, improve heterosexual communication, and facilitate both sexual and nonsexual heterosexual relationships.

Several behavioral treatment techniques have been used to promote an increase in heterosexual behavior directly without any attempt to denigrate or try to suppress the person's pre-existing homosexual orientation. Orgasmic reconditioning, a method we will describe, has been used to enhance heterosexual arousal in cases where the individual was aroused predominantly or exclusively by homosexual fantasies.

The Masters and Johnson Program. An illustration of the use of positive sexual retraining procedures to assist male and female homosexuals in switching to heterosexuality is Masters and Johnson's (1979) treatment program. Sixty-seven dissatisfied homosexuals, fifty-four men and thirteen women, were treated with essentially the same two-week therapy program we have discussed. Clients were accepted only after careful screening to ensure that they were highly motivated and sincere about changing their sexual preferences. In addition, all clients had to have an understanding partner of the opposite sex who was willing to participate in the treatment program and continue to support the client in his or her new-found heterosexual preference in the months immediately following therapy. As in the treatment program for dysfunctional heterosexuals, male and female cotherapist teams were employed.

Masters and Johnson distinguished between those clients (nine men and three women) who were "converting" and the rest who were "reverting" to heterosexuality. The former had little or no prior heterosexual experience; the prior sexual experience of the latter ranged from predominant to considerable heterosexuality. Approximately one out of three dissatisfied homosexuals failed to revert or convert to heterosexuality immediately following therapy. A follow-up ranging from one to five years showed an overall failure rate of 28.4 percent.

Several comments about these findings are in order. First, as Masters and Johnson themselves emphasize, their clients were highly motivated, sincere, and fortunate enough to have a willing and able partner of the opposite sex to provide them with sexual and nonsexual support and guidance. As a result, caution must be exercised in attempting to generalize from these findings to other samples of homosexuals who might seek heterosexual reorientation. Second, the comparable success rates of "conversion" and "reversion" clients is surprising in the light of previous findings by investigators like Bieber and his colleagues and Feldman and MacCulloch (1971) showing that prior heterosexual experience was significantly related to successful treatment outcome.

The limitations of Masters and Johnson's study must be recognized. As in their previous therapy study with dysfunctional heterosexuals, the criteria of treatment outcome are not always clear. Barlow (1980) has pointed out that Masters and Johnson's follow-up data

on these dissatisfied homosexuals are unimpressive. When viewed critically, their follow-up findings are not superior to previous reports in the clinical literature. Sixteen of forty-three men and three of ten women who had responded to the initial therapy could not be contacted. Masters and Johnson did not include their data in their summary statistics, a procedure that probably made their follow-up failure rate of 28 percent appear lower than it actually was. An estimated failure rate of roughly 45 percent is more plausible.

Sexual Dysfunction in Homosexuals

When the concern about their specific sexual preferences is abandoned, and homosexuals are seen as people who share the joys, worries, frustrations and problems of life common to all, the similarities between homosexuals and heterosexuals seem far greater than the differences. As a result of Masters and Johnson's (1979) laboratory studies, we know that physiologically, homosexuals respond the same way to sexual stimulation as heterosexuals do. It should come as no surprise, therefore, that homosexuals also experience the same sexual dysfunctions as heterosexuals do. Taking this correspondence still further, it follows that dysfunctional homosexuals might be helped to overcome their sexual difficulties in the same manner in which heterosexuals have been aided. This is precisely what Masters and Johnson and other therapists have shown.

In the Masters and Johnson (1979) study, eighty-four male and female homosexuals participated in the same two-week rapid treatment program used to treat heterosexuals. All clients were required to have a partner of the same sex who was willing to participate in the therapy. The treatment format was the same as with heterosexuals, including the emphasis on male/female co-therapists for each couple. Sexual adequacy in homosexuals was assessed by how successfully the person responded to sexual stimulation by: (1) masturbation, (2) partner manipulation, and (3) fellatio or cunnilingus.

Using definitions of impotence and orgasmic dysfunction similar to those in their treatment of heterosexuals, Masters and Johnson reported an overall failure rate of only 7 percent at post-treatment and 11 percent at the end of the five-year follow-up.

Clearly, homosexuals can be helped to lead more effective sexual lives. However, we have made the point that it is unwise to view homosexuals' sexual preferences too narrowly. What about the rest of their lives? Their jobs? Their social networks? Traditionally, homosexuals have led secretive and isolated existences. More recently, however, homosexuals have been "coming out of the closet." In taking this important step, homosexuals have to cope with the various pressures, prejudices, and expectations that being a publicly declared homosexual entails. Behavioral treatment strategies have been used to help homosexuals cope better with these nonsexual aspects of their lives. For example, Russell and Winkler (1977) employed assertion training to assist homosexuals in responding to discrimination and other negative or hostile social reactions.

SEXUAL PARAPHILIAS AND GENDER IDENTITY DISORDER

The term sexual deviance has typically been used to describe those patterns of sexual behavior which are disapproved of by a particular society because they are contrary to the cultural mores. There is considerable diversity across cultures as to what forms of sexual expression are labeled deviant, and few patterns have been universally disapproved of as abnormal. Among the several types of sexual behavior judged to be deviant or abnormal in western society are exhibitionism, fetishism, transvestism, sadomasochism, pedophilia, and voyeurism. DSM-III uses the term paraphilias to cover this range of sexual activities. In addition to the paraphilias, another major class of sexual deviance discussed in this chapter is the gender identity disorders, in which a person seeks to assume the physical identity of the opposite sex.

Paraphilias

The paraphilias can be thought of in terms of either the object to which the person is sexually attracted (e.g., an inanimate object in fetishism) or the particular activity the person engages in (e.g., the exhibitionist exposes his genitals to unsuspecting women). Traditional psychodynamic treatment approaches have viewed these forms of sexual disorders as pathological sexuality that derives from unconscious, intrapsychic conflicts created in early childhood. For example, the exhibitionist is seen as defending himself against underlying fears about castration. Reassurance of the fact that he is not castrated is supposedly gained from his reaction to the observer's reaction to the sight of his genitals. In accordance with this model, therapy is aimed at resolving the underlying childhood conflicts with little direct attention focused on trying to modify directly the person's current sexual behavior.

In a social learning analysis, sexual behavior, conventional and unconventional (deviant) alike, is learned. This view was originally espoused by Kinsey:

"Learning and conditioning in connection with human sexual behavior involve the same sorts of processes as learning and conditioning in other types of behavior . . . From its parents, from other adults, from other children, and from the community at large, the child begins to acquire its attitudes toward such things as nudity, the anatomic differences between males and females and the reproductive functions; and these attitudes may have considerable significance in determining its subsequent acceptance or avoidance of particular types of overt sexual activity . . . Even some of the most extremely variant types of human sexual behavior may need no more explanation than is provided by our understanding of the processes of learning and conditioning. Behavior which may appear bizarre, perverse, or unthinkably unacceptable to some persons, and even to most persons, may have significance for other individuals because of the way in which they have been conditioned. . . . The prominence given to classification of behavior as normal or abnormal, and the long list of special terms used for classifying such behavior usually represent moralistic classifications rather than any scientific attempt to discover the origins of such behavior, or to determine their real social significance" (Kinsey et al., 1953).

The treatment of paraphilias is illustrated in the following section with reference to exhibitionism and transvestism. It should be noted, however, that behavior therapy procedures such as aversive imagery and self-control strategies have been used to treat a range of different paraphilias, including child molesting (Kelly, 1982; Quinsey & Marshall, 1983).

Exhibitionism. The general therapeutic philosophy and some of the specific intervention techniques for paraphilias can be illustrated with reference to the treatment of exhibitionism. The exhibitionist exposes his genitals to women but does not attack or molest them. His "victims" may be adults or children. The average age of the exhibitionist at conviction is 30 years; approximately one-third are married; one-third are separated,

divorced or widowed; the remainder were never married. In exposing himself, the exhibitionist acts compulsively. He will report that he feels driven to expose himself, and during the exposure itself he is totally obsessed with his immediate feelings and intentions, with the result that he becomes oblivious to the consequences of his actions and the danger he may be in. His behavior is out of control. The majority of exhibitionists who have committed only one or two exposures usually experience strong guilt feelings, remorse, and embarrassment. They are motivated to regain control of their behavior and respond favorably to treatment. A much smaller number of exhibitionists who may have exposed themselves on numerous occasions over a long period of time are more difficult to treat.

The goal of treatment is to teach the exhibitionist, or any other sexual deviant, to regain control of this behavior. Several self-control techniques are used. On the basis of an assessment of the thoughts, feelings, and events that precede exposure,[3] the patient is shown how he contributes actively to his problem by focusing on inappropriate thoughts and feelings. He is taught to recognize early warning signs about temptation to expose himself and to institute self-control procedures at that point. If he waits too long and the temptation becomes too strong, his chances of self-control are much less. If tension or anxiety precipitate exposure, the patient is taught relaxation procedures that provide an alternative to the act of self-exposure. Exhibitionists typically dwell on thoughts and images related to exposure once this train of behavior is triggered. Self-instructional train-

---

3. See Wilson and O'Leary (1980, Chapter 1), for a detailed clinical illustration of the assessment and treatment of a persistent exhibitionist.

ing is a self-control procedure in which the patient is taught to identify maladaptive thoughts that increase the likelihood he will expose himself (e.g., "I cannot control my impulses." "I really need to expose myself to feel better."), challenge them (e.g., "I can control myself if I try." "My behavior is not involuntary, I can cope if I remember to follow my therapist's advice."), replace them with more constructive self-statements and reward himself for displaying control.

Aversive Imagery.   Aversion therapy has been one of the most frequently used behavioral treatment techniques for the paraphilias. The most serviceable form of aversion therapy employs aversive imagery. In this technique the patient is instructed to imagine engaging in the deviant behavior, then imagine an aversive consequence. The specific content of the images is tailor-made to each patient's particular circumstances. For example, an exhibitionist might be instructed to imagine that just as he approaches the woman he plans to expose himself to, a police car with flashing red lights and blaring siren draws up and he is apprehended, or that he is becoming physically sick and vomiting.

One of the advantages of this technique is that it can be employed as a self-control method by the patient himself any time he senses the urge to expose himself. To be effective the patient must repeatedly and actively rehearse the association between his deviant activities and realistic aversive consequences. Naturally, this will not happen unless the patient cooperates fully with the therapist. Although the data are from an uncontrolled clinical study, and are therefore not definitive, Maletzky (1980) has reported a success rate of roughly 90 percent in treating exhibitionists with aversive imagery, with follow-up evaluations ranging up to two-and-a-half years. Another encouraging finding is that Maletzky obtained equal success with self-referred and court-referred exhibitionists.

Electrical Aversion Conditioning.   Another form of aversion therapy used to treat the paraphilias involves the administration of a noxious but safe electric shock to the patient's arm or fingers. Electrical aversion therapy has been shown to be useful with exhibitionists with histories of chronic exposure (Rooth & Marks, 1974) as well as with other psychosexual disorders.

The use of aversion therapy, particularly electrical aversion conditioning, has generated controversy. If the patient has given genuine informed consent, if other more benign self-control methods, such as covert sensitization, have been tried and proved unsuccessful, and if the technique is carried out by a qualified therapist who is alert to potential side-effects, aversion conditioning might be considered as an appropriate treatment method for exhibitionists. A popular misconception links aversion therapy with the science fiction portrayed in Anthony Burgess's *A Clockwork Orange*. The film shows how an extremely violent rapist is "conditioned" against his will to become a passive, law-abiding citizen. While films like this might make good drama, they distort and vulgarize psychology. Automatic conditioning is largely a myth. The evidence not only suggests that conditioned aversion reactions cannot be developed so easily but also that they cannot be developed without the client's cooperation. If patients fail to rehearse the association between deviant cues and aversive consequences in their minds, then the treatment is unlikely to have any enduring impact. It is clear that considerations of both ethics and efficacy demand that if aversion therapy is to be employed, the client's freely given, informed consent to a therapist he trusts and respects is a minimum necessity.

Aversive Behavior Rehearsal. An unconventional treatment procedure for exhibitionists is known as aversive behavior rehearsal (Wickramasekera, 1976). In this procedure the exhibitionist is asked to expose himself to a group of people under carefully arranged circumstances in the therapist's office. The rationale behind this technique is that the exhibitionist usually obtains gratification by exposing himself as a result of the shocked, disgusted, or horrified reactions of his female victims. In aversive behavior rehearsal the audience of women (and perhaps men too) reacts with indifference or clinical detachment, thereby denying the patient the rewarding consequences he associates with exposure. The idea is to extinguish this deviant behavior under controlled laboratory or hospital conditions.

Most exhibitionists expose themselves to women they do not know; the anonymity of the situation seems to be a crucial precondition of their behavior. Aversive behavior rehearsal requires the exhibitionist to expose himself under conditions that are not anonymous. This makes the situation an extremely aversive one for the patient, one from which he derives no gratification. In some uses of the procedure the audience speaks to the exhibitionist and points out the immaturity of his behavior. Instead of acting in a shocked or offended fashion, they discuss his behavior in rational scientific terms. In a variation of the basic technique, the exhibitionist is shown a videotape of another exhibitionist exposing himself in front of a professional panel in the aversive behavior rehearsal technique.

Wickramasekera (1976) has reported complete success in the treatment of 20 exhibitionists for follow-ups ranging up to seven years. He cautions that the technique is most appropriate for exhibitionists who are introverted and show anxiety and remorse about their behavior. Similarly, Wardlaw and Miller (1978) reported complete elimination of exposure or urges to expose in exhibitionists treated in this manner.

Transvestism

A transvestite is a man who becomes sexually aroused by dressing as a woman. This cross-dressing is usually done under limited circumstances and, for the most part, these men are masculine in appearance and activities. Most are heterosexual and married. The transvestite cross-dresses in secrecy, often with the knowledge and occasionally with the cooperation of his wife. Those transvestites, however, who perform in nightclubs as female impersonators are often homosexuals "in drag."

Therapy for transvestites focuses primarily on helping the individual develop sexual arousal to more conventional heterosexual activities without the aid of cross-dressing. An example of such a treatment strategy is a method that is based on altering the fantasies that invariably accompany masturbation in males. The technique is known as orgasmic reconditioning. Its application to the treatment of transvestism and sadomasochism can be illustrated with reference to a case reported by Brownell, Hayes, and Barlow (1977).

The patient was a policeman, married and 31 years old, who suffered from uncontrollable urges to dress as a woman and appear in public. In addition to this transvestism, he also had a history of sadomasochism. During sexual intercourse with his wife he had tied her to the bed, handcuffed her, and had her wear an animal leash with a collar. He had also tied himself with ropes, chains, handcuffs, and wires while he was cross-dressed. He was concerned that he would injure himself seriously. The man's wife had threatened divorce as a result of the cross-dressing, yet she frequently purchased women's clothing for him and was "compassionate" while he was in female clothing. This collusion by the wife, however grudging, is far from atypical.

The patient was instructed to continue to masturbate to his deviant fantasies of cross-dressing and sadomasochism in his usual fashion. However, just prior to the point of ejaculatory inevitability, that is, that point at which the male ejaculates involuntarily, he was instructed to switch to an erotic fantasy of more conventional heterosexual behavior. This switch was then gradually made earlier in the sequence until the client could initiate masturbation and reach orgasm exclusively using heterosexual fantasies. He was given pictures from magazines of nude women to facilitate the switch to heterosexual arousal.

Prior to treatment the patient had shown virtually no arousal to conventional heterosexual stimuli. Following approximately twenty sessions with orgasmic reconditioning he displayed strong erections to such stimuli (see Figure 17-3 p. 366). During much of this treatment the investigators concurrently assessed the patient's tumescence in response to other deviant sexual stimuli using a multiple baseline single-case experimental design. These responses showed no change, even though his response to conventional heterosexual stimuli was shifting. The specificity of this behavior change indicates that the particular treatment technique was responsible for increasing heterosexual arousal, as opposed to a more general placebo effect.

Developing arousal to more conventional heterosexual activities does not always guarantee that attraction to unusual forms of sexual behavior such as transvestism will diminish.

In the case of this individual, for instance, responses to transvestite and sadomasochistic stimuli were treated successfully using aversive imagery.

Gender Identity Disorders

Transsexualism. A transsexual believes he or she is a member of the opposite sex. This belief (and desire) is summarized in the favorite phrase of the male transsexual: "I'm a woman trapped in a man's body." The ultimate aim of transsexuals is to obtain a "sex change" operation—surgery that will alter their bodies to that of the opposite sex. Initially, more men than women applied for these sex change operations, but recent reports suggest that an equal number of would-be patients are women who wish to become men. They identify completely with the opposite sex. Transsexuals should not be confused with transvestites or homosexuals. Transvestites are almost always heterosexuals who achieve specific sexual satisfaction by cross-dressing. They do not make the fundamental and consistent identification with the opposite sex that the transsexual does. Although a man who is a transsexual is sexually attracted to other men, this is not in the homosexual sense. Rather, the transsexual claims that "she" relates to men as a woman does.

In the 1960s, surgery became an established form of treatment for transsexuals, and some reports have claimed that postoperative evaluations of transsexuals show that they are happier and better adjusted than their counterparts who do not receive surgery (Blanchard, Steiner, & Clemmensen, 1985; Green & Money, 1969). Subsequently, other reports have questioned the value of surgery (Meyer & Reter, 1979). Early behavioral treatment approaches emphasized electrical aversion conditioning. Whereas these techniques proved effective with transvestites, they failed with transsexuals (Marks, Gelder, & Bancroft, 1970). However, in 1973, Barlow, Reynolds, and Agras reported what appears to have been the first successful effort to change gender identity in a transsexual using psychological methods.

The patient was a 17-year-old male transsexual. Several different measures of sexual orientation and gender identity were monitored consistently before, during, and after therapy, including attitudinal responses towards transsexualism, such as "I want to have female genitals"; penile circumference changes to slides of nude males and females; a daily record of the number and nature of sexual fantasies; and detailed behavioral checklists of gender-specific behaviors, like walking and talking. The initial treatment attempt to increase heterosexual arousal by gradually having the client imagine heterosexual stimuli while sexually aroused had no effect. Similarly, forty-eight daily half-hour sessions of punishment of transsexual fantasies with electric shock failed to show any changes. The focus of therapy was then shifted to developing appropriate sex role behaviors. Modeling, behavior rehearsal, and videotaped feedback were used to modify the client's excessively effeminate manner of walking, standing, and sitting, which were the most obvious signs of gender identity confusion, and which elicited social scorn. This gender role reshaping program was then expanded to incorporate typical masculine interpersonal contacts at high school (e.g., discussing football or girlfriends), and finally, to voice retraining. At the end of this phase of therapy, which lasted roughly three months, the client liked his new-found masculine manner of acting, but still reported feeling like a girl, both socially and sexually. Moreover, objective measures of sexual arousal, urges, and

fantasies remained at the pre-treatment level despite the overt behavioral changes.

Accordingly, a direct attempt was made to develop competing gender-appropriate thoughts and fantasies. A female therapist praised the client for fantasizing sexual involvement with a girl for increasingly longer durations. Transsexual attitudes decreased for the first time, while female fantasies predominated over previous male fantasies. In contrast to these subjective reports of sexual fantasies about females, penile tumescence changes indicated no such arousal. A classical conditioning procedure in which female slides (as a conditioned stimulus) were paired with attractive male slides (as an unconditioned stimulus) rapidly increased physiological arousal, which further enhanced masculine aspects of sitting, standing, and walking. Remaining homosexual arousal was eliminated by the use of aversion therapy, which now proved to be effective.

At a one-year follow-up the client's transsexual attitudes had disappeared, subjective and physiological measures showed sexual arousal to female stimuli, and masculine role behavior remained stable. The client had a steady girlfriend. A follow-up six-and-a-half years after therapy by a psychologist who had not been involved in the original treatment revealed stable progress. (Barlow, Abel, & Blanchard, 1979).

Despite the successful use of behavioral treatment in this and a few other cases, relatively few therapists have adopted this approach. There is general pessimism about the effects of psychological (including behavioral) treatment with transsexuals, most of whom have severe psychological problems (Rosen, 1986).

Gender Identity Disorders of Childhood. This disorder is characterized by "a persistent feeling of discomfort and inappropriateness in a child about his or her anatomic sex and the desire to be, or insistence that he or she is, of the other sex . . . This is not merely the rejection of stereotypical sex role behavior, for example, "tomboyishness" in girls or "sissyish" behavior in boys, but rather a profound disturbance of the normal sense of maleness or femaleness" (DSM-III, p. 264). Social learning procedures, especially modeling and differential reinforcement of gender appropriate behavior, have proved highly effective in treating this disorder (Green, Newman, & Stoller, 1972; Rekers, 1975). Box 11-1 presents an illustrative case study and brief discussion of the controversial issues involved in the treatment of this disorder.

SUMMARY

The most common forms of sexual dysfunction in men are ejaculatory problems and erectile difficulties (impotence). Although these disorders are predominantly psychogenic in nature, some are due to organic causes. In women, problems include inability to achieve orgasm under some or all circumstances, painful intercourse, and vaginismus.

Behavioral sex therapy, which was popularized by Masters and Johnson's (1970) landmark research, dates back to Wolpe and Lazarus's (1966) pioneering clinical contributions. Treatment emphasizes education in sexual matters, the reduction of anxiety and cognitive distraction that interfere with nor-

---

Box 11–1 *The Case of Kraig*

Kraig was a physically normal 5-year-old boy who was referred for treatment by the family physician. He had cross-dressed since the age of 2, played with cosmetic items belonging to his mother and grandmother, displayed exaggerated feminine mannerisms, preferred to play with little girls, and emphasized his desire to be a girl. Rekers and Lovaas (1974) helped Kraig's mother alter her behavior to reinforce more masculine activities and decrease gender inappropriate behavior. The result was that Kraig's gender disorder decreased dramatically, and he began to act in a more masculine manner. Using sophisticated methodological control procedures, Rekers and Lovaas were able to show that this behavioral change was due directly to the reinforcement procedures that formed the basis of the treatment program. At a follow-up over two years later, Kraig looked and acted like any other boy his age.

Rekers and Lovaas justified their treatment program on the following grounds: (1) exaggerated feminine behavior of this sort in boys subjects them to social isolation and ridicule by their peers, (2) cross-gender preferences predict severe adjustment problems in adulthood (Most adult transsexuals and transvestites report a history of childhood gender disturbances.), (3) altering cross-gender preferences is most likely to be successful during early development, and (4) the treatment program was consistent with the parents' wishes, the social mores and cultural expectations of the community in which the family lived, the local law, the views of other professionals, and the fact that the child himself was cooperative with the therapist throughout the program. Critics of this sort of program, including other behavior therapists, have argued that adult pathology, such as transsexualism, cannot be reliably predicted from the presence of highly effeminate behavior in early childhood. They also object to the emphasis in these programs on the masculine sex role. As an alternative, these critics advocate the idea of androgyny (Winkler, 1977). Androgyny is behavior that is neither "masculine" nor "feminine" in the stereotyped sense, but includes supposedly desirable attributes from each (e.g., strength and independence from the "masculine" role, affection and compassion from the "feminine" role). They assert that androgynous behavior is more likely to lead to better adjustment than extreme sex-role typing as "masculine" or "feminine."

mal sexual functioning, enhanced communication and sharing between partners, and, where necessary, resolution of nonsexual interpersonal conflict (e.g., marital discord).

The results show that behavioral sex therapy typically provides effective treatment for a range of different dysfunctions in men and women. It is the preferred form of therapy for psychogenic sexual dysfunction. Evidence of the long-term efficacy of these methods is more limited. Relationship difficulties complicate treatment and may reduce success. Problems of low or inhibited sexual desire present particular challenges, and therapeutic effects here are more modest.

Homosexuality is viewed primarily not as a clinical disorder but as an alternative lifestyle. Rather than trying to change gay people's sexual preferences as was once typical of all therapies, contemporary behavior therapy focuses mainly on helping them to cope with both sexual and nonsexual problems of adjustment. Treatment of specific sexual dysfunctions in gay patients produces results comparable to those obtained with heterosexuals.

Sexual paraphilias, or what used to be called sexual deviance, consist of patterns of behavior that are disapproved of by cultural norms. Examples include exhibitionism, child-molesting, transvestism, and rape. In terms of social learning theory, these forms of behavior are learned and maintained accord to the same principles as conventional sexual activities. Treatment methods are varied and include different forms of aversion therapy (e.g., pairing aversive imagery with images of the undesired behavior), self-control strategies, and methods designed to promote more socially acceptable sexual activities. Therapeutic success varies across the different paraphilias, although particularly promising results have been achieved with exhibitionism.

Disorders of gender identity are those in which the person seeks to assume the physical identity of the opposite sex. Attempts to reverse these disorders in childhood have proved effective but controversial.

12

Marital Discord

INCREASING INTEREST IN MARITAL PROBLEMS

Many behavior therapists became interested in marital problems as a result of dealing with children and adolescents (e.g., Kent & O'Leary, 1976; Stuart, 1969; Weiss, Hops, & Patterson, 1973). More specifically, it appeared that many children's problems were maintained or exacerbated by marital discord. While the relationships between marital and childhood problems are quite complex, it is clear that there is an association between marital problems and certain childhood problems, especially conduct problems of boys (O'Leary, 1983). The growing interest in family therapy also has prompted behavior therapists to attend to marital problems. Questions are now being addressed, such as whether marital or childhood problems should be treated first when both exist (Margolin, 1983) and how many family members should be included in the treatment of a "child" or "marital" problem (Turkewitz, 1982). Finally, the emergence of sex therapy as a prominent area

of research has sparked interest in marital therapy. More specifically, the pioneering work of Masters and Johnson (1970) prompted the utilization and evaluation of fairly specific sexual techniques, but it has become apparent that sexual therapy procedures often have to take place in the context of significant and often extensive marital therapy (O'Leary & Arias, 1983). In summary, interest in marital therapy by behaviorally oriented psychologists grew markedly in the late 1970s and early 1980s.

INCIDENCE OF DIVORCE AND MARITAL PROBLEMS

Therapists of all orientations are probably interested in marital problems because of their impact on children, the increasing divorce rate, and the large number of referrals to mental health clinics. Thirty-eight percent of first marriages in the United States are expected to end in divorce (Glick & Norton, 1978). Many problems appear during the first few years of marriage, and 30 percent of all

---

Box 12–1   *Reflections on Marital Treatment*

It was only a decade and a half ago that social learning theory was rising phoenix-like from the ashes of Hullian learning theory. The renewed enthusiasm was in part a reflection of the writings of H.J. Eysenck and J. Wolpe. However, the particular impetus within social learning was provided primarily by B.F. Skinner in a series of volumes beginning with *Behavior of Organisms* (1938). It took some time for his translations of reinforcement theory to make their appearance in the general realm of social engineering. Those were indeed exciting times. Each new visitor coming through the campus at the University of Oregon brought news of some startling new application of operant procedures to some long-standing clinical problem. At first, it seemed that there was not any problem that could not be solved. Many of us went out into the field to apply the existing social technology to problems of severely brain-damaged children, autistic children, psychotic adults, depressed adults, etc.

Some of our creative pioneers in social engineering, such as Richard Stuart, also applied the technology to problems of distressed marital couples. . . .

At that time, our group at Oregon was working with families of severely aggressive children. We were teaching parents simple child management skills—or at least that is what we thought we were doing. Our follow-up data revealed the fact that some families no longer practiced family management skills after termination of therapy. Clinical follow-up with those people revealed that some of them were involved in severe marital conflict, often leading to separation and divorce. Caught up in the enthusiasm of that time, we decided it would be a simple matter to alleviate these problems. One only had to apply the notions inherent in social learning principles; the distressed couples would be relieved and our follow-up data would look as it should.

Reflections of G.R. Patterson, pioneer in the treatment of aggressive boys at the University of Oregon. Taken from Foreword to *Marital Therapy* by Jacobson and Margolin (1979).

---

divorces occur within the first three years of marriage (Vital Statistics, Vol. III, 1978). Marital problems are the most frequent problems for which adults seek treatment in a mental health facility (Gurin, Veroff, & Feld, 1960): 42 percent of the individuals seeking help view their problems as marital. Except for the death of a close family member, divorce and marital separations are the most important stressors in an adult's life (Holmes & Rahe, 1967). Admission rates to psychiatric facilities are lowest among the married, intermediate among the widowed and never married, and highest among the divorced and separated. In addition, motor vehicle accident rates of persons undergoing divorce double during the period from six months before until six months after the divorce. Finally, marital disruption distinguishes persons likely to become physically ill from those who do not (Bloom, Asher, & White, 1978). Even

illnesses such as coronary disease and alcoholism are more prevalent among separated and divorced than among married persons.

ATTRACTION OF MARRIAGE

While the divorce rate has climbed in the United States and Western European countries, marriage still has its attractions. In a poll of approximately 10,000 persons in Western Europe, Jacques-Rehe Rabier found that married persons described themselves as happiest (*Newsday*, March 15, 1976, p. 70). In 1982, Gallup conducted a poll of U.S. citizens in which individuals were asked to rate satisfaction or dissatisfaction in various areas of their lives. Most people indicated they were highly satisfied with their relations with their children (81 percent), and 78 percent rated themselves as highly satisfied with their married lives. Finally, even when marriages do fail, 80 percent of partners remarry, and they usually do so three to five years following divorce (Norton, 1976).

ETIOLOGY OF MARITAL DISCORD

Reinforcement Loss

Consequences of behavior are very important in marriage, as well as in any other human interaction. Positive reinforcers are critical in maintaining a good marriage, and, as you will see, they can be used to increase satisfaction in a discordant marriage. The role of reinforcers in marital therapy is central; a number of studies have shown how daily rates of positive behaviors are related to marital satisfaction. One of the most outstanding examples of this phenomenon is the work of Birchler, Weiss, and Vincent (1975), who found that distressed spouses had a pleasing/displeasing behavior ratio of 4:1, whereas nondistressed spouses had a 30:1 ratio. The distressed and nondistressed couples were obtained via newspaper announcements and later screened by a standardized, well-accepted marital adjustment test. To find out how distressed couples and nondistressed couples differed, they gave couples a checklist consisting of approximately 400 behavioral items which were categorized on a priority basis as pleasing and displeasing. The behaviors spanned a dozen marriage-related topics such as companionship, sex, communication processes, child care, and household manage-

---

Box 12–2　*Daily Behavior Checklist (Sample Items)*

	Did Not Happen	Happened	Rating
1. We spent time walking or playing with the pet together.	_____	_____	_____
2. Spouse interrupted me.	_____	_____	_____
3. Spouse thanked me for something that I did.	_____	_____	_____
4. Spouse called just to say hello.	_____	_____	_____
5. Spouse was critical of something I said or did.	_____	_____	_____
6. Spouse left clothes or dishes around the house.	_____	_____	_____
7. Spouse prepared a meal.	_____	_____	_____
8. We disagreed about how to handle the children.	_____	_____	_____

RATING SCALE

1. Extremely Unpleasant
2. Very Unpleasant
3. Rather Unpleasant
4. Slightly Unpleasant
5. Neutral
6. Slightly Pleasant
7. Rather Pleasant
8. Very Pleasant
9. Extremely Pleasant

ment. Over a five-day period, the husband and wife were asked to check whether these behaviors did or did not occur during the past twenty-four hours.

A number of research reports using daily behavior checklists indicate that daily behaviors correlate significantly with marital satisfaction. In general, the research suggests that the more positive behaviors that occur per day, the more satisfied the couple will be, and the more negative behaviors that occur, the more the couple will evaluate their relationship as unsatisfactory. Of special interest, however, is the repeated finding that daily behavior ratings generally correlate with marital satisfaction, approximately 0.40 for men and 0.25 for women (Broderick & O'Leary, 1986). There appears to be one outstanding reason that daily behavior ratings correlate more significantly with marital satisfaction for men than for women. Men place more emphasis than women on instrumental behaviors of their spouses, such as caring for the house, preparing meals, and child-rearing. Some behavior therapists were so impressed with behavior checklists that their marital therapy clients were required to complete a 400-item checklist prior to entering treatment (Jacobson & Margolin, 1979). This requirement was presumably based on a strong belief that the day-to-day behavioral interactions had a very strong role in marital satisfaction and that changes in these behaviors should be a cornerstone of marital therapy.

One might guess that if all positive and negative behaviors were analyzed across the course of a marriage that marital satisfaction could be predicted almost perfectly. That is, even if one believes that thoughts and feelings are important, some would say that such thoughts and feelings are mere products of the behavioral interactions a couple has. In fact, comparisons of studies in which couples recorded behavior for one day (e.g., Chris-

tensen & Nies, 1980) reveal less significant correlations than studies in which couples recorded behaviors across seven days (Broderick & O'Leary, 1986). However, even in those studies in which approximately 100 daily behaviors are recorded for a one- or two-week period, the correlations between behaviors and the marital satisfaction of their spouses were generally no more than 0.40. The correlation between positive behaviors of women across one week and the marital satisfaction of their husbands was 0.38; the correlation between negative behaviors of women and their husband's marital satisfaction was -0.42. In contrast, the correlation of positive behaviors of men and their wives' marital satisfaction was only .27; the correlation of the husbands' negative behaviors and their wives' marital satisfaction was -0.25 (Broderick & O'Leary, 1986). Even with daily recordings of more than 100 behaviors for seven days, correlations with marital satisfaction are generally less than 0.40. That is, only a moderate amount of variance in marital satisfaction is explained by daily behavioral interactions—at least as those behavioral interactions can now be measured across seven days.

On a clinical level, of course, having couples record all their behaviors across a long period is highly impractical. Therefore, clinicians and researchers attempt to assess behavioral interactions indirectly by gathering ratings of various areas of a marriage (e.g., communication, sex, and finances). A behavior rating differs from a frequency recording in that a rating provides a summary evaluation about a behavior or set of behaviors, whereas a frequency recording involves checking whether a behavior occurred or not during a specific period. Summary ratings provide a reasonable evaluation of past behaviors; rating systems allow a respondent to reflect on experiences shared with a spouse over an extended period and evaluate thousands of behavioral interactions. While summary ratings of behavioral interactions are subject to certain methodological problems such as halo effects, they are very useful in clinical work.

Whether one measures daily behaviors using a checklist or a summary evaluation, it is likely that any practical data-gathering procedure will yield correlations with marital satisfaction that are less than 0.60. Even in research in which subjects were asked to note the impact of their spouse's ten most important behaviors on their marital satisfaction, the correlations between daily recordings of those behaviors and marital satisfaction were at most 0.55 (Johnson & O'Leary, 1986). As expected, the correlation of these ten most important behaviors with marital satisfaction was higher than the correlation between recordings of 100 daily behaviors, from which the ten behaviors and marital satisfaction were selected. Recording from a large behavioral domain is time consuming, and the time demands alone may lead to less careful recording than when a small number of meaningful behaviors are recorded.

Positive Affect Loss and Criticism Sensitivity

When a couple comes to a therapist about a marriage problem, they almost always feel bad about their interactions. When one partner does not feel bad and the other does, the prognosis for change may be especially poor. The way partners feel about each other is especially important in therapy effectiveness. Even if a therapist can help a couple behave in "positive" ways toward each other, if both partners do not feel attracted to or care about each other, the relationship may be doomed to fail or to be stable but unsatisfactory. A number of years ago the first author (KDO) saw a couple, and the wife began to do almost everything the husband had indicated he

wanted. After several months of such progress, the husband said, "My wife could do cartwheels on the lawn every day but it won't make any difference. I don't love her."

Psychologists and psychiatrists have shied away from concepts like love and caring in their research, particularly because they are difficult to define. Some psychologists have even felt that defining concepts such as love should be left to poets and novelists. Our search of all psychological articles published in 1980 revealed that love was a major subject only thirty-one times, whereas aggression—which can be measured in terms of frequency of behavior, such as hitting or verbal insults —was a major subject over 200 times.

It is interesting that wars are fought over love, families separate because of lack of love, and spouses kill each other when love is mixed with hate. Interestingly, as Walster and Walster (1978) note, however, even research on love has aroused bitter debate. More specifically, Dr. Elaine Walster and her colleague, Dr. Ellen Berscheid, received an $84,000 grant to conduct research on passionate and companionship love. Senator William Proxmire discovered this grant and released the following statement to the press: "I object to this not only because no one—not even the National Science Foundation—can argue that falling in love is a science; not only because I'm sure that even if they spend $84 million or $84 billion they wouldn't get an answer they believe. *I'm also against it because I don't want the answer.* I believe that 200 million other Americans want to leave some things in life a mystery, and right on top of things we don't want to know is why a man falls in love with a woman and vice versa . . . National Science Foundation get out of the love racket. Leave that to Elizabeth Barrett Browning and Irving Berlin. Here if anywhere Alexander Pope was right when he observed, 'If ignorance is bliss, tis folly to be wise' " (Walster & Walster, 1978). As most of us may remember, "ignorance is bliss" makes sense when we first fall in love—especially as we remember our first love when we were teenagers. At that point, we didn't want to know why we were in love or exactly what attracted us to our partners. However, when love fades or dies, as it does in most of the 40 percent of marriages that end in divorce, the reasons why love dies become especially important. Therapy for couples is predicated on knowledge that positive feelings toward a spouse (love) can be the subject of research just as other behaviors are legitimate subjects of research.

Despite Proxmire's protests, efforts to carry out research on issues of love and caring have increased dramatically over recent years. Our own research on love and caring was designed to assess whether or not we could predict which couples would progress in therapy and which couples would not. Turkewitz and O'Leary (1981) asked couples questions regarding how they felt toward their spouses that were designed to assess caring or love. Examples of questions appear in Box 12-3. We found that feelings toward the spouse correlated very highly with marital satisfaction and that they were predictive of change in therapy for women ($r = 0.43$). We also know that positive feelings toward spouses are more highly correlated with marital satisfaction than daily behaviors assessed across a one-week period (Broderick & O'Leary, 1986). This result indicates that love or caring is clearly a critical factor to assess in deciding what to change in a marriage.

Research on emotional responsiveness has been conducted by Gottman and Levenson (1983), in which they have shown that spouses' physiological reactions to conflict and criticism are highly correlated with marital satisfaction (0.75). More specifically, the emotional responses of the spouses are re-corded with physiological measures such as heart rate and galvanic skin response. These physiological measures are taken during problem-solving sessions and are then related to the partner's affect and marital satisfaction. This research is particularly important because it is the first of a series of studies in which physiological assessment of affect has been related to general marital satisfaction. Furthermore, in a follow-up of nineteen couples assessed three years earlier, self-report measures of affect during a communication task were correlated with changes in marital satisfaction. That is, decreases in overall marital satisfaction across a three-year period were predicted by the initial affect ratings in the communication task—affect ratings made by individuals as they watched an earlier recording of their conversation during a high conflict task. Interestingly, decreases in marital satisfaction were predicted by less positive affect in the husband and more positive affect in the wife during the ratings of their problem solving three years earlier. The seemingly paradoxical finding was interpreted by the investigators as follows: "the husbands, prior to the wives, become emotionally withdrawn. In turn, the wives may attempt to compensate for this lack of emotional behavior and display a high rate of positive behavior during the problem solving" (Gottman & Levenson, 1985).

Cognitive Factors

Behavioral marital therapists have begun to address the importance of cognitive factors in the etiology of marital problems. As Dember (1974) noted, there is an increasing trend in psychology to "go cognitive," and in behavior therapy this trend is salient (Bandura, 1977; Wilson, 1982). Until the beginning of the 1980s, however, the cognitive trend had

---

Box 12–3 *Positive Feelings Toward Spouse*

1. How do you feel about your spouse as friend to you? 1 2 3 4 5 6 7
2. How do you feel about the future of your marital relationship? 1 2 3 4 5 6 7
3. How do you feel about the degree to which your spouse understands you? 1 2 3 4 5 6 7
4. Touching my spouse makes me feel 1 2 3 4 5 6 7
5. My spouse's encouragement of my individual growth makes me feel 1 2 3 4 5 6 7
6. My spouse's physical appearance makes me feel 1 2 3 4 5 6 7

1	2	3	4	5	6	7
Extremely Negative	Quite Negative	Slightly Negative	Neutral	Slightly Positive	Quite Positive	Extremely Positive

---

not made much of an impact on practicing marital therapists or university researchers in this area. On the other hand, several clinical and research areas involving cognitive factors are likely to have significant impact on marital therapists in the next decade.

Expectations and Irrational Beliefs

In 1976, Sager published a book, *Marriage Contracts and Couples Therapy*, in which he described the expectations that each spouse has when he or she enters a marriage, and noted how these expectations rapidly become solidified. These expectations, in turn, become viewed as contracts which, if violated, cause serious marital discord. Sager discussed the contracts from a psychoanalytic framework and stressed unconscious defenses, but his notion of a marriage contract is consistent with a behavioral approach. In fact, changes in expectations and the problems that result from these expectations are often apparent when one sees a middle-aged couple in which the wife decides to enter college or the work force after staying at home as a housewife for twenty years. Their husbands often have feelings like the following:

1. "Now my wife won't be home when our teenagers come home from school."
2. "My wife will be studying all the time and she won't have enough time for me."
3. "My wife is attractive and she is the kind of woman men will try to date."
4. "I didn't expect her to go to college when I married her and I don't like it now."

Related to the problem associated with dramatic changes in expectations of a spouse is the area of unrealistic expectations. This research received its impetus from Ellis's propositions that most, if not all, psychological disorders arise from irrational thoughts. Basically, Ellis noted that people have faulty assumptions about themselves and the world about them. In turn, these assumptions lead to self-statements or "internal sentences" which are self-deprecating. For example, Ellis stated that a key proposition or belief held by many individuals with psychological problems is: "One should be thoroughly competent, adequate, and achieving in all possible respects if one is to consider oneself worthwhile" (Ellis, 1962, p. 63). In turn, the therapist's goal is to help a client alter such beliefs. Ellis assumes that marital problems result from neurotic disturbances of either or both spouses.

His theory is that most couples enter marriage with two general expectations: the hope for regular sexual satisfaction and the enjoyment of intimate companionship and love. If these two expectations are prejudiced or illogically exaggerated, marriages will be disturbed (Ellis & Harper, 1962).

There is only moderate support for the notion that irrational beliefs like those posited by Ellis are associated with marital discord. Eisenberg and Zingle (1975) compared couples seeking marital therapy with randomly selected couples from the community on a questionnaire designed to assess Ellis's irrational beliefs. They found that clinic couples had significantly higher irrational idea scores than community couples. On the other hand, there was no correlation between the irrational idea scores and a general measure of marital adjustment (i.e., the Locke-Wallace MAT). Epstein and Eidelson (1981) assessed irrational beliefs about relationships rather than irrational beliefs about self. They found that self-report scales designed to measure such expectations about relationships were better predictors of marital distress and desire to terminate the relationship than irrational beliefs about self.

Cognitive Distortions

Couples in distress often interpret messages intended to be positive as neutral or negatively valenced. Distressed and nondistressed couples are asked to sit at a talk table in which the intent and impact of various messages is recorded for the purpose of assessing communication problems. Each time a person stops talking to allow his or her spouse to speak, the speaker rates the intent of the message on a one to five scale (negative to positive) and the listener records the impact of the message on the same scale. Gottman, Notarius, Markman, et al. (1976) found that clinic and nonclinic groups did not differ in their percentages of positive and negative intentions, but clinic spouses recorded greater percentages of negative impacts than did nonclinic spouses.

Schacter and O'Leary (1985) extended the work of Gottman and colleagues (1976), using a talk table format in which the intent and impact of messages were recorded. Of greatest interest was the finding that spouses, whether distressed or not, recorded the impact of their partner's message as more negative than was intended by the spouse. As might be expected, the impact of the messages was more negative when rated by the clinic couples. In contrast to the Gottman et al. (1976) finding, however, the clinic couples had more negative intentions than the nonclinic couples.

An interesting distortion in marital interactions is what is called egocentric bias. For example, if both spouses are asked to rate their participation in some activity, such as planning leisure time, they may give themselves more credit than acknowledged by the partner. Christensen, Sullaway, and King (1982) had young college student couples complete a checklist on which they individually indicated whether certain behaviors occurred in the past twenty-four hours (e.g., spouse was sarcastic with me; I was sarcastic with spouse). One of the most interesting findings was that there was a greater tendency to attribute responsibility for negative events to the partner or to deny them in the self as the length of the relationship increased.

Attribution theory has led researchers to ascertain a subject's reasons for engaging in behaviors or for believing that others engage in certain behaviors. Attribution research began largely in social psychology, and, in particular, such research emphasized attributions for interpersonal behavior, though not with married partners. More recently, however, a series of investigations (Jacobson, McDonald,

Follette, & Berley, 1985) found that distressed married persons tend to attribute their partner's positive behavior to external factors (He was nice to me because my mother was there). Secondly, they found that partners attribute negative behaviors to internal factors (He has a generally mean streak in him). Variations of this attribution research (Fincham & O'Leary, 1983; Fincham, Beach, & Nelson, in press) have shown that partner blame is associated with low levels of marital satisfaction. That is, not only do distressed partners attribute negative behaviors to their partners; they also blame them for engaging in those negative behaviors. From a series of studies by Fincham and colleagues, it became clear that attribution of fault is pivotal in close relationships (Fincham, 1985).

In terms of clinical implications, Fincham (1985) noted that it is probably best to ensure that therapeutic change be seen to occur in the absence of environmental constraints. "Changes in the absence of perceived constraint would make the changes maximally reinforcing. . . . For example, rather than have the spouses request behavior changes from one another . . . each should themselves generate positive changes which might increase his/her spouse's satisfaction. Similarly, implementation of such changes should not be based on reciprocal behavior change contracts . . . but should be unilateral" (p. 23).

EFFECTIVENESS OF BEHAVIORAL MARITAL THERAPY

Case Studies

Evidence of behavioral marital therapy effectiveness began with a series of case studies published by Stuart in 1969. In that series, Stuart had couples complete contracts in which the spouses agreed to behave in certain ways and in which rewards were specified for completion of the behaviors. For example, if a husband agreed to spend twenty minutes per day talking with his wife, the wife might then agree to be affectionate to her husband before dinner. In short, a quid pro quo agreement was completed in which spouses agreed to do things for each other. Behavioral marital ther-

---

Box 12–4 *Prevalence of Physical Aggression in Marriage*

In a longitudinal study of marriages in 393 young couples, assessments were made six weeks prior to marriage. Couples were recruited by advertisements in newspapers and on radio announcements; they received $40 for their participation. Couples were representative of couples in New York State in terms of age of marriage and religious preference. Assessments included information on family of origin, personality styles, relationship satisfaction, caring for partner, and physical aggression toward partner. To ensure confidentiality and to emphasize the importance of the research, individuals were placed in individual offices or in situations where conversations between partners was impossible.

To the investigator's surprise, 41 percent of the women and 33 percent of the men indicated that they had engaged in some form of physical aggression against their partner during the past year. Reports of aggression were assessed regarding the subject's attempts to solve an argument with the partner. Types of aggression included pushing, shoving, hitting with a fist, kicking, and biting. Aggression against one's partner was associated with being from a family in which one saw parents hitting one another. It was also associated with an aggressive personality style, less caring for one's partner, and lower levels of relationship satisfaction than if one did not aggress against his or her partner. (O'Leary, in press; O'Leary, Arias, Rosenbaum, & Barling, 1986)

apists generally do not now use contracts in the fashion that Stuart described in 1969 and Stuart himself no longer uses contracts and reinforcers in the same fashion (Stuart, 1980). The real contribution of Stuart's publication, however, was to show the utility of a behavioral treatment model emphasizing reinforcement of behavior by spouses.

Weiss, Hops, and Patterson (1973) conducted a series of ten case studies in which they combined a problem-solving/communications approach with behavioral contracting. Changes in a spouse were to be reinforced or punished by the other spouse, the therapist, or the individual who made the change (a good faith contract). Interestingly, although problem-solving skills were stressed, they were given emphasis only to allow the couples to complete the behavioral contracts. Couples were seen weekly by a therapist pair (an experienced Ph.D. clinician and a Master's level student) over a period of approximately two months. Significant improvements were found on pre-post measures of self-report, pleasing interactions, and observational measures of problem-solving skills. The Weiss et al. work offered promising leads for others to follow in controlled research, and their emphasis on varied outcome measures was laudatory.

The case studies just reported illustrated the potential efficacy of a behavioral approach to marital treatment. There are numerous problems with case studies, though, such as (1) the absence of a control group to assess natural changes that might occur in a distressed relationship simply as a function of time, (2) the relatively meager evaluation of the success of therapy, and (3) the absence of any experimental verification of the extent to which the treatment program was followed by the therapists. Nonetheless, in any new area, case studies pave the way for controlled research, and these studies provided an excellent prompt.

Controlled Outcome Studies

Jacobson conducted several outcome studies that addressed the role of problem-solving and contingency contracting. In one of these studies (1978), a behavioral treatment group was compared with a nonspecific control group. The behavioral treatment emphasized problem-solving and contingency contracting. An additional comparison was made in that good faith contracts and quid pro quo contracts were compared. As noted earlier, a good faith contract involves specifying what a spouse, therapist, or individual who makes a desired change should do when the behavioral change occurs. As such, the contract may involve a self-reward component. In contrast, a quid pro quo contract involves specifying exactly what a spouse should do when the partner does or does not engage in desired behaviors. The clear-cut reciprocal relationship in the quid pro quo contract has led it to be informally referred to as a "tit for tat" contract. The nonspecific control group emphasized interpretation of the spouse's affect and interactions. There was a clear attempt to ensure that the groups were equivalent on many variables, such as number of homework assignments, activity level of the therapists, and extent of directiveness of the therapists. The couples in each of the treatment groups perceived that they would be helped in overcoming their difficulties equally well. However, the couples in the behaviorally treated groups improved more than the couples in the nonspecific treatment group. Interestingly, there were no differences in the improvements seen in the couples that had good faith contracts and quid pro quo contracts.

In a related study, Jacobson (1977) treated six couples experiencing severe marital distress. Many of the spouses had histories of serious individual problems such as schizophrenia and manic depressive illnesses. A multiple baseline design was used, in which baselines were obtained across a three- to four-week period, during which couples were *generally* instructed to increase desirable behavior and decrease undesirable behavior. However, specific behavior changes were not recommended. Following the three- to four-week baseline, the problem-solving strategy was applied to each of the target behaviors one at a time. Five of the six couples showed evidence of improvement as seen in self-report and observational measures. Problem-solving seemed crucial in the improvement of four of these five clearly improved couples. The other improved couple did not respond favorably to the problem-solving, but did respond to an intensive focus on increasing positive behaviors.

Azrin, Naster, and Jones also reported on the behavioral treatment of couples in 1973. An assessment of marital happiness was obtained by having couples rate their marital happiness on a one to ten scale for each of nine problem areas, as well as a general category of marital happiness. During an initial three-week period, couples simply discussed their problems with a therapist, who did not intervene in any systematic fashion. Following this initial three-week period, a behavioral intervention was followed similar to those described earlier, with special emphasis on doing positive things for the spouse on a daily basis (caring days). Eleven of the twelve couples reported greater happiness at the end of therapy than at the end of the three-week baseline period.

Comparison with Other Treatments

Turkewitz and O'Leary (1981) compared behavioral marital therapy and communication therapy with a waiting list or untreated control group. Communication therapy in-volves teaching listening; accurately reflecting, checking, or validating what a spouse said; emphasizing positive feedback; and decreasing threats and criticism. Communication therapy also often involves teaching problem-solving skills. A couple is taught to define a problem accurately, outline alternative solutions, evaluate the solutions, and decide on a course of action. Our own therapeutic work has led us to believe that problem solving and communication generally should be taught together, although stress can be placed on the one that appears to need greater emphasis for a particular couple.

In the Turkewitz and O'Leary study, both treated groups, a behavioral marital therapy and a communication therapy group, improved more than the waiting list group on a general measure of marital satisfaction and communication. Unfortunately, on a measure of positive feelings toward spouse, while the treated couples showed an overall improvement, the changes were not significantly better than the nontreated group. Interestingly, age was the best predictor of change. Young couples (median age = 29) improved significantly more than older couples (median age = 40).

The above study is of import because it is one of the few marital therapy studies in which independent evaluators assessed whether the therapists had, in fact, acted in accord with prescribed treatment. There were some overlaps in the treatments of the two treated groups, but the analyses of the therapy tapes by independent raters indicated that therapists conducting behavior therapy gave clients more positive feedback on behavior changes other than communication than did therapists in the communication therapy group, whereas such agreements were not made in the communication group.

In Germany, a comparison between reciprocity training and communication skills training was made by Hahlweg, Schindler, and Revenstorf (1980) over fifteen sessions. Like Turkewitz and O'Leary (1981), they made a straightforward comparison between the two therapy approaches, but they also compared conjoint (couple) therapy with conjoint group therapy. All treated couples were compared to a waiting list control group. There was some overlap in treatments as the reciprocity training group received two sessions devoted to communication skills, and of course it could be expected that the clinical psychologists treating the couples would provide at least some feedback regarding communication in the sessions to all couples. While a treatment outline and reading materials for the couples were described, unfortunately, no data were presented to allow one to determine the therapeutic techniques actually utilized.

Couples were assessed pre- and post-treatment, using six outcome measures (1) self-report of quarreling, (2) self-report of tenderness, (3) self-report of communication, (4) self-report evaluation of overall problems, (5) independent judges' evaluation of negative behavior as seen on a video tape, and (6) independent judges' evaluation of positive behavior as seen on a video tape. Couples receiving reciprocity training improved on all six outcome measures, whereas the communication training group improved on only three of the six measures (self-report of communication and independent judges' evaluation of positive and negative behavior as seen on video tape). Couples in the waiting list group did not improve on any of the measures. The authors concluded that the behavioral approach was superior to the communication approach.

The largest behavior therapy outcome study was conducted by Baucom (1982), who assigned seventy-two couples to four treatment conditions: (1) problem-solving communications training plus quid pro quo contracting, (2) problem-solving communications training only, (3) quid pro quo contracting only, and

(4) waiting list. Each couple was seen for one to one-and-a-half hours for ten weeks. Two doctoral students in clinical psychology served as therapists, receiving several hours of weekly supervision during the course of the study.

The problem-solving was similar to the problem-solving communication approaches described earlier. Couples were taught to (1) state their problems in concrete behavioral terms, (2) describe alternative solutions to their problems, (3) execute one of the solutions, and (4) understand communication styles, e.g., using guilt as a way of getting a spouse to accept a solution or getting side-tracked on irrelevant issues. During quid pro quo contracting, the spouses agreed to engage in certain behaviors if their partners behaved in the agreed-upon manner.

There were no overall differences among the three treatment groups regarding therapy effectiveness or in their ability to produce differential results at a three-month follow-up, and no differences between therapists in the changes their clients evidenced. The absence of treatment differences across the groups may be surprising in that simply focusing on quid pro quo contracts appeared as effective as communications training plus quid pro quo contracting. While this study is clearly one of the best conducted outcome studies in the marital therapy area, no data were reported regarding what the therapists actually did. Therefore, we do not know how differently the therapists actually behaved across the three treatment conditions. Based on our own experience (Turkewitz & O'Leary, 1981), it is very difficult to keep therapists from providing what they think will be helpful, irrespective of conditions, and our own therapists feel that providing feedback regarding communication skills is one of the most important therapeutic strategies they can use. In brief, we would assume that some therapist aid in the quid pro quo group occurred and that the therapists' differences across treatment groups were relative, not absolute. Further, there was one important failure of the quid pro quo group: couples did not change on negative interactions in the communication assessment. This failure led Baucom to conclude, "When a couple needs to change their communication patterns, teaching them only contracting skills appears unlikely to be the most effective strategy."

In judging the effectiveness of marital therapy, one wants to know more than whether reliable improvement can be obtained in a relationship. Often two individuals come to a marital therapist with a desire to improve their relationship and a definite goal of attempting to find out how they may feel about the relationship and their spouse following therapy. If they are very dissatisfied with the relationship prior to therapy and only moderately satisfied with the relationship after therapy, they may decide not to stay married. We are not placing any value judgment on that decision; we are simply pointing to the need to critically evaluate the effectiveness of the intervention in a fashion that is clinically significant. Jacobson, Follette, and Elwood (1984) raised this issue in a methodological framework, and have attempted to arrive at a solution for deciding whether or not a treatment is clinically significant. Basically, they argue that a treatment has to produce changes that move a couple from a dissatisfied range to a range that is more likely to be within the range of a control group. Using this criterion, and outcome data from a number of studies, Jacobson et al. (1984) found that approximately 50 percent of couples showed such improvement. Using research from the sex therapy area (Schover & LoPiccolo, 1982) as well as the marital area, O'Leary and Arias (1983) reported that, on the average, clients move from a moderately dissatisfied range at pre-therapy to a moderately satisfied range at post-therapy. In sum, while great strides have been made in behavioral marital therapy, we

have only begun to understand who may be helped in a clinically significant way, who may need to consider alternatives to their marriage, and who may need to consider remaining in a marriage that does not meet at least some of their expectations (Beach & O'-Leary, 1986).

In evaluating the effectiveness of marital therapy, we also have to broaden the scope of our assessments. In a study of which aspects of marriage were considered important to marital happiness, six qualities were judged as extremely important: trust and commitment, love, fidelity, understanding, honesty, and respect (Broderick, 1981). Most marital therapy outcome studies have focused on a general measure of marital satisfaction, along with some observations or recordings of a couples' problem-solving ability. Further, we know that at least one of the six aspects of marriage noted above—commitment—was found to be only moderately correlated with general marital satisfaction. In addition, it is important to assess some aspects of individual functioning, since a purportedly successful marital therapy outcome might be associated with increases in depression or constriction of freedom. Turkewitz and O'Leary (1981) addressed this issue in a subsidiary aspect of their study and found that individual functioning, in fact, increased as marital satisfaction increased. Given the association between marital problems and childhood problems (O'Leary & Emery, 1982), it is also important to ascertain whether increases in marital satisfaction are associated with increases in positive associations of the parents with their children.

Marital Therapy for Depression

It has been known for some time that one of the predisposing factors to depressive incidents is marital discord. Interestingly, however, the standard treatment for depression for several decades has been antidepressant medication. Even following a successful course of treatment with antidepressants, if marital discord exists, the likelihood of a recurrence of depression is much greater than if depression did not exist. Using this information, Beach and O'Leary (1986) compared marital therapy and individual cognitive therapy for depressed persons who, in addition, had serious marital discord. Alternatively stated, individual and marital therapy were compared for women who were both seriously depressed and maritally discordant. Individual cognitive therapy was associated with marked reductions in depression. To some people's surprise, marital therapy was associated with reductions both in depression and marital discord. In contrast, wives receiving individual cognitive therapy did not show as significant reductions in marital discord as did wives receiving marital therapy. As Beach and O'Leary stated, "Behavioral marital therapy may allow a clinician to cast a wider net than individual cognitive therapy when trying to treat co-occurring marital discord and depression. Behavioral marital therapy may prove to help relieve depression while simultaneously providing an improved interpersonal climate which can facilitate personal growth and change. Conversely, cognitive therapy may have less effect on improving the interpersonal environment" (p. 11).

SUMMARY

Interest in marital therapy has increased greatly in recent years, due largely to the apparent relationship between child behavior problems and marital discord and the growing prevalence of marital discord and divorce. In spite of the growing divorce rate, marriage remains an attractive option to most Americans, even those who have previously had an unhappy marriage.

As with any application of behavioral principles, understanding the consequences of behavior plays an important role in behavior marital therapy. Specifically, the finding that happily married couples emit higher ratios of pleasing/displeasing behaviors than unhappily married couples has led therapists to make one goal of therapy to increase this ratio. Such an approach frequently involves the use of behavior checklists, summary ratings, and behavior contracts. Behavior contracts can be either quid pro quo or good faith agreements. Whereas early applications of behavioral principles to marital problems focused almost exclusively on overt behavior, the past few years have brought an increasing interest in variables such as positive affect (love) and cognitive factors. Although some critics believe there is no place in scientific research for the study of such traditionally mysterious matters as romantic love, measures of positive affect can predict marital satisfaction better than strict behavioral measures. The recent popularity of cognitive research has had an impact on marital research as well. Studies have demonstrated an association between marital satisfaction and couples' irrational beliefs and expectations of their relationship. One cognitive distortion found to relate to marital distress is the tendency to interpret messages from one's spouse as negatively valenced. Another is the finding that the longer a couple has been together, the more they tend to blame each other (and deny responsibility in themselves) for negative events.

Evidence of the efficacy of Behavior Marital Therapy was initially provided by case studies which reported improved pre- and post-measures of behavioral interactions and self-reports of satisfaction. Case studies of behavioral marital therapy have had three outstanding methodological weaknesses: (1) absence of a control group, (2) inadequate measures of success, and (3) no verification that the therapist's behavior was in accord with the prescribed treatment program. Outcome studies have also been conducted which have, to varying degrees, remedied these weaknesses. Couples undergoing behavior therapy have shown more improvement than couples on waiting lists or undergoing nonspecific treatment. Studies that have compared behavior contracting to communication and problem-solving interventions have shown them to be about equally effective. The practice of randomly assigning couples to treatment groups irrespective of the nature of their problems in outcome studies has been commented on by researchers. Their observations point up the importance of tailoring therapeutic strategies to meet the needs of each couple in clinical settings.

13

Eating Disorders

OBESITY

Obesity, Disease, and Improved Health

Obesity is a widespread condition in the United States, with estimates of prevalence ranging from 15 percent to 50 percent (Bray, 1976). The prevalence is inversely related to socioeconomic status and increases with age (Stunkard, 1975). These rates are disturbing because obesity entails serious medical and psychological consequences. Studies have clearly shown relationships between obesity and hypertension, hyperlipemia, diabetes, pulmonary and renal problems, osteoarthritis, and complications in recovery from surgery (Bray, 1976; Van Itallie, 1979).

The most commonly used norms for determining ideal body weight are from the Build Study of 1979 (Society of Actuaries, 1983). These norms provide a range of ideal weight rated by sex, height, and body frame. The data from this study show a positive relationship between increasing weight and mortality. Other epidemiological studies have produced conflicting findings, however. Keys (1979) completed a prospective study of coronary heart disease in seven countries and found that both gross obesity and marked leanness were related to increased risk. There was no relationship between body weight and heart disease for all other weight categories. Lew and Garfinkel (1979) investigated the association between weight and mortality in 750,000 men and women as part of the American Cancer Society Study from 1959 to 1972. They found that the lowest mortality was shown by people roughly 10 percent to 20 percent below average weight. Mortality increased 50 percent in people 30 percent to 40 percent above average weight, and 90 percent in those 50 percent above average weight. Coronary heart disease was the main contributor to mortality, but rates of cancer were higher for those 40 percent or more above average weight.

Obesity has been shown to be an independent risk factor for cardiovascular disease in the Framingham Heart study (Hubert, Feinleib, McNaman, & Castelli, 1983). In this epidemiological study of 5209 men and women in Framingham, Massachusetts, relative weight predicted a twenty-six-year incidence of coronary disease (both angina and coronary disease other than angina), coronary death, and congestive heart failure in men, independent of age, cholesterol, systolic blood pressure, cigarettes, left ventricular hypertrophy, and glucose intolerance. Relative weight in women was also positively and independently associated with coronary disease, stroke, congestive failure, and coronary and CVD death. These data further show that weight gain after the young adult years conveyed an increased risk of CVD in both sexes that could not be attributed either to the initial weight or risk factors that may have resulted from weight gain. Based on evidence of this sort, the National Institute of Health (NIH, 1985) recently concluded that obesity is a serious disease, with health hazards becoming significant at 20 percent or more above desirable weight, as shown by the Metropolitan Life Insurance Tables (Society of Actuaries, 1983).

The psychological and social consequences of obesity may be as important as its physical hazards. Society seems biased against overweight people, and obese children, adolescents, and adults all suffer the secondary social sequelae of the condition, such as rejection, isolation, and job discrimination. Obese people are not only stigmatized by society, but are also blamed for their physical condition. They are commonly viewed as lazy, lacking will-power, and gluttonous (Wooley, Wooley, & Dyrenforth, 1979). Not surprisingly, many obese individuals experience depression, lose self-esteem, and become preoccupied with weight in a manner that is damaging to their emotional well-being. Despite the health benefits of weight loss, the women who consistently comprise the majority of participants in weight reduction programs are motivated primarily by cosmetic reasons. They want to look better. In their study of people who join

Weight Watchers in North America, Stuart and Jacobson (1979) found that "85 percent of the men and 91 percent of the women saw improved appearance as an objective . . . while 48 percent of the men and only 20 percent of the women were primarily motivated to lose weight by the goal of achieving better health. Clearly, then, the desire to meet social rather than health challenges is differentially reflected in the structure of decisions reached by men and women" (p. 249).

Psychosocial benefits that may indirectly help to promote improved personal health usually accompany successful weight loss. But the well-being of those obese individuals who fail to lose weight despite repeated struggles will be helped only to the extent that society and the professionals who treat them adopt a more informed and humane view of this refractory condition (Wooley et al. 1979).

Prevalence and Etiology

Using the insurance tables as the norm, roughly thirty-four million adults in the U.S. (one in five people over the age of 19) are obese. Of these, eleven million are severely obese—they exceed the norms by 40 percent or more. There is evidence suggesting that the prevalence of obesity in the United States is increasing. In population-based surveys of the Minneapolis-St. Paul metropolitan area, the prevalence of overweight in 1980–81 was greater than in 1973–74 (Jeffery, Folsom, Luepker, Jacobs, et al., 1984). Dieting to regulate weight was reported by 43.7 percent of men, and 72.5 percent of women, even among those who had never been overweight.

The etiology of obesity is complex. Aside from the role of social learning, genetic and biological factors have been shown to be important determinants of body weight. It has long been known that obesity "runs in families." Genetic influences in animal models of obesity had been established, but only recently has strong evidence of genetic control of obesity in people been produced. Both twin and adoption studies have indicated that obesity can be mainly determined by genetics. In the former, monozygotic twins show significantly greater concordance for overweight than dizygotic twins (Stunkard, Foch, & Hrubec, 1986). In the latter, adopted children were much more likely to weigh the same as their biological than their adoptive parents (Stunkard, Sorensen, Hannis, Teasdale, et al., 1986).

Several strands of evidence suggest that weight is biologically regulated. Studies have shown that most normal-weight individuals are very resistant to significant weight loss or gain over the long term (Keys, Brozek, Henschel, Mickelsen, & Taylor, 1950; Sims, Goldman, Gluck, Horton, et al., 1968). As we shall see, it has proved extremely difficult to produce substantial, lasting weight reduction in obese clients. Neither obese animals nor obese humans appear to consume more calories than their leaner counterparts (Wooley et al., 1979). The behavioral formulation of obesity as a learned habit disorder that is a function of overeating (Ferster, Nurnberger, & Levitt, 1962) has been abandoned. As Garner, Rockert, Olmsted, Johnson, & Coscina (1985) conclude, "Just as some individuals are naturally lean, others have no choice but to be statistically overweight, by virtue of the physiological settings in their bodies that control weight maintenance" (p. 536).[1] The mechanism(s) responsible for this biological

regulation of weight is still a matter of controversy, however (Brownell & Foreyt, 1986).

Evidence of genetic control of obesity does not necessarily mean that obese clients cannot be helped to lose weight. Moreover, despite the evidence of some form of biological regulation of weight, the data show that at least mild to moderate obesity is amenable to treatment.

Behavioral Principles and Procedures

Behavioral treatment departs fundamentally from alternative forms of treatment such as traditional psychotherapy, special diets, drugs, or surgery in that the goal is to alter the person's eating and activity habits. The emphasis is on changing behavior in order to restrict caloric consumption and increase caloric expenditure through physical exercise, thereby producing a negative energy balance and consequent weight loss. The emphasis has been on gradual weight loss (one to two lbs. per week), on the assumption that this reduces the likelihood of increased hunger and enables the person to integrate behavioral changes into his or her life without undue disruption.

Restricting Calories The core of most behavioral treatments, derived from Stuart and Davis's (1972) program, consists of four main elements: self-monitoring and goal setting, stimulus control for restricting external cues, changing eating patterns, and reinforcement of altered behavior. Record keeping, or self-monitoring of specific behavior, thoughts, or feelings in relation to eating and exercise, is a vitally important component of a successful treatment program. Not only is self-monitoring the mainstay of behavioral assessment of obesity (Brownell, 1981), but it is also part of the behavior change process. Self-monitoring of

---

1. This view, plus the general finding that obese people do not eat significantly more than their leaner counterparts, discredits the notion that obesity is an "eating disorder" or form of "substance abuse." We include obesity in this chapter, however, not only to encourage a more accurate understanding of its nature and treatment, but also because there are important overlapping theoretical and clinical concerns among obesity and the eating disorders of anorexia and bulimia nervosa (see Brownell & Foreyt, 1986).

daily caloric intake but not the mere occurrence of eating or its surrounding circumstances is reactive in that it alone can result in significant weight loss (Green, 1978). This reactivity results from people evaluating their performance against the specific goals, or consumption limits, they set for themselves. Failure to remain within the prescribed limits creates dissatisfaction that motivates efforts to reduce subsequent intake. Some performance goals are more effective than others in increasing motivation for change. Goals that are too general, too difficult, or set too far in the future function poorly as incentives. Simple, short-term sub-goals are significantly more effective in producing weight loss than more long-term goals (Bandura & Simon, 1977). Dubbert and Wilson (1983) failed to show that proximal (daily) goals produced greater weight loss than distal (weekly) goals. Nevertheless, as in the Bandura and Simon (1977) study, some subjects failed to adhere to their assigned goal-setting strategy, and subjects' self-reported (as opposed to assigned) goal-setting strategies were significantly related to successful weight reduction. Subjects who reported they followed either a daily or weekly goal-setting strategy lost significantly more than those who set no goals.

There is no direct evidence that restricting food cues or decreasing their salience, as exemplified in stimulus control procedures (e.g., eat only in one place, do nothing else like reading or watching T.V. while eating), actually results in weight change. Although programs based on the general principle of stimulus control have yielded success, Loro, Fisher, and Levenkron (1979) have pointed out that stimulus control has always been evaluated in conjunction with other procedures. Their own data on stimulus control as a single treatment modality indicates that it is "relatively ineffective." Similarly, whereas some studies have shown that changes in eating habits were related to weight loss (Ost & Gotestam, 1976), others have failed to find such a relation (Brownell, Heckerman, Westlake, Hayes, & Monti, 1978; Stalonas, Johnson, & Christ, 1978). Rosenthal and Marx (1978) found that following participation in a standard behavioral treatment program, overweight subjects did alter their eating patterns in the prescribed manner (e.g., they ate more slowly); however, both subjects who were successful and those who were not showed this altered eating pattern to the same degree.

Several forms of reinforcement procedures have been used to modify eating habits. In contingency contracting, the therapist arranges a contract in which a specified outcome, such as habit change or a designated amount of weight loss, is rewarded by the return to the client of portions of a refundable money deposit. Alternatively, failure to meet predetermined goals may result in the client forfeiting a sum of money to his or her most disliked organization or political group. One potential problem with contingency contracting for weight loss is that it may lead to unhealthy dietary practices. Mann (1972) obtained significant weight loss with contingency contracting, but only when subjects resorted to undesirable procedures (e.g., diuretics, vomiting, and starvation). Yet Jeffery, Thompson, and Wing (1978) obtained impressive short-term weight losses without any of the negative dietary practices reported by Mann (1972), while Wing, Epstein, Marcus, and Shapira (1981) found that the prolonged use of strong monetary contracts may also facilitate maintenance of weight loss.

Broadening the Treatment Base. Contemporary behavioral programs rely upon multifaceted interventions that build on the preceding methods. They include cognitive and behavioral skills training for coping with interpersonal situations and emotional states that often trigger eating, cognitive self-control methods, a focus on the interpersonal context of the problem, and increased emphasis on physical activity. Social skills training may assist obese individuals to cope constructively with interpersonal situations that trigger inappropriate eating. Declining a cocktail when dining at a restaurant is no different from refusing dessert. The obese person needs the assertive skills to say "no" without feeling guilt, shame, or rejection. Cognitive factors influence food intake, and there is reason to believe that combining cognitive with behavioral methods might enhance therapeutic efficacy. Rodin's (1980) results from a multifaceted treatment program that emphasized cognitive reappraisal and coping strategies such as self-instructional training are particularly promising, although some negative findings have also been reported (Wilson & Brownell, 1980).

Physical Activity

There are several reasons for emphasizing increased physical activity in attempts to control weight. Perhaps least important is the increase in energy expenditure; possibly more significant is the potential of increased physical activity for increasing basal metabolism. The body reacts to caloric deprivation by reducing metabolic rate, an adaptation that can become permanent with repeated attempts at dieting (Wooley et al., 1979). Several investigators have suggested that this homeostatic reduction in metabolic rate may be offset by increased physical activity (Brownell & Stunkard, 1980; Thompson, Jarvie, Lahey, & Cureton, 1982). Donahoe, Lin, Kirschenbaum, and Keesey (1984) monitored resting metabolic rate (RMR) in overweight women during a phase in which they cut their caloric intake. The dietary restriction lowered RMR by an amount nearly double that expected on

the basis of the resulting weight loss. This finding shows how the body becomes more food-efficient as weight is lost and may explain the typical decline in rate of weight loss in the later stages of many treatment programs. Physical exercise, however, increased the RMR to a level appropriate to the dieters' weights. The available evidence is mixed, and no firm conclusion can yet be drawn (Thompson & Blanton, 1984). Physical exercise also minimizes the amount of lean tissue involved in weight loss and has favorable effects on problems associated with obesity (e.g., high blood pressure and lipid levels) even in the absence of weight loss (Weltman, Matter, & Stamford, 1980).

The beneficial effects of exercise have been demonstrated in several studies. Harris and Hallbauer (1973) compared a behavioral program designed to change eating habits to the same program combined with exercise instructions. Weight losses for the two groups did not differ after twelve weeks of treatment, but the exercise group showed greater weight losses at a forty-month follow-up. Stalonas et al. (1978) found that a structured program contributed to the maintenance of weight loss at a one-year follow-up, although the addition of exercise was no more beneficial than the addition of contingency contracting procedures. Other studies have similarly shown that exercise improved the short-term efficacy of behavioral treatments (e.g., Dahlkoeter, Callahan, & Linton, 1979). Moreover, Miller and Sims (1981) found that exercise was one of the few factors that predicted long-term maintenance of the relatively large weight losses they obtained in their residential treatment program. Compliance with instructions to increase physical activity is a major problem in treatment programs. Rather than prescribing specialized exercise programs, Brownell and Stunkard (1980) have recommended that weight reduction treatments focus on routine activities, such as walking or climbing stairs, that are more easily integrated within existing lifestyles.

Maintenance Strategies

Maintenance of the effects of any program of treatment can be ensured only to the extent that strategies explicitly designed to accomplish this objective are an integral part of the overall intervention.

Booster Sessions.   These sessions, scheduled at various points after the end of treatment, have been the most commonly used maintenance strategy. Yet the results have been disappointing (Ashby & Wilson, 1977). Booster sessions prearranged to occur at fixed intervals may be insufficient to ensure implementation of the self-regulatory strategies the individual acquires during therapy. According to the social learning approach, clients need to monitor problem behaviors and reinstate self-corrective procedures at the first signs of the erosion of treatment-produced improvement. In a maintenance strategy described by Bandura and Simon (1977) clients monitored their weight and used a specific weight level as a cue to reinstate self-regulatory strategies. Stuart and Guire (1978) found that the perception of being "overweight" at no more than three pounds above goal weight was a key correlate of long-term maintenance in Weight Watchers. Although this correlational study precludes definitive conclusions, it is consistent with the view that successful maintenance requires constant vigilance and willingness to prevent problems by the timely reinstatement of self-regulatory procedures.

Successful maintenance of therapeutic change also involves arranging incentives that sustain the reinstatement of self-regulatory measures. Booster sessions may have periodic utility if they happen to occur at the appropriate time and serve as incentives for reinstating waning self-control activities. In other cases, prearranged booster sessions may be too little and too late to shape up deteriorating self-regulatory capacities. In these instances, sources of external support probably need to be tailored to the obese person's particular needs.

Social Support Systems.   Eating and exercise are responsive to social influence, and support from family, friends, and fellow workers may help the obese person to adhere to the rigors of a behavioral treatment program. This possibility has been studied in both home and work settings.

Initial studies found that including the spouses of obese individuals in behavioral programs resulted in superior weight loss. For example, Brownell et al. (1978) demonstrated that the inclusion of spouses in a standard behavioral treatment program produced significantly greater weight loss at three- and six-month follow-up evaluations than treatments in which spouses did not participate. In Brownell et al.'s couples training program, spouses learned to monitor their partners' behavior, model prescribed eating habits, set a good example, and assist their obese partners in coping with high-risk situations by engaging them in an activity incompatible with eating. Subjects in the couples training (spouse present) treatment showed an average weight loss of nearly 30 lbs. eight-and-a-half months after the beginning of treatment. Pearce, LeBow, and Orchard (1981) similarly found that a couples training group produced greater weight loss over a one year follow-up than a group consisting only of the obese clients.

Other studies, however, have failed to replicate these promising findings (Brownell & Stunkard, 1981a; Dubbert & Wilson, 1983). Thus the Brownell and Stunkard investigation, with treatment conditions carefully modeled after those used by Brownell et al. (1978), indicated that couples training did little to facilitate maintenance of weight loss at a one-year follow-up. The inconsistency in outcome among similar studies using the same interventions remains to be explained.

The potential social support and physical convenience of the work-place are being explored as a means of facilitating both treatment of obesity and subsequent maintenance of weight loss (Abrams, Follick, & Thompson, 1983). Behavioral programs have been implemented with union members in urban department stores, hospital employees, and members of the armed services. Brownell (1982) has summarized the available evidence as follows, "Two findings stand out from these studies: Weight losses are somewhat less than those obtained in clinical settings, and 50 percent or more of program participants tend to drop out of treatment within six months or less. Both may result from several factors. First, the lack of a program fee in most instances, and the ease with which patients receive treatment, might attract participants who are less motivated than persons who seek out a clinical program. Second, the potential benefits of social support need to be weighed against the potential drawbacks. For instance, Stunkard and Brownell (1980) assumed that employees in their program would encourage each other to attend sessions, so that any partnership would be as strong as these stronger members. However, employees may influence each other to drop out, so that some partnerships may be only as strong as their weakest member" (p. 195).

Relapse Prevention. Cognitive-behavioral strategies for preventing relapse in the addictive disorders have been incorporated into weight control treatments (Marlatt & Gordon, 1985). Inevitably, even people who have successfully lost weight will begin to deviate from therapeutic prescriptions after the termination of treatment. At this point, whether or not the person relapses will be influenced by the way he or she interprets the violation of post-treatment adherence to a program for control of weight gain. It may not be the violation itself that will determine subsequent behavior but the meaning that the person attaches to it. The typical negative reaction is for the person to attribute failure to adhere to the requirements of the weight control program as an affirmation of his or her personal inability to regulate weight. Previous treatment success is discounted as insignificant. Among the adverse consequences of such an attribution is a sense of helplessness. Other self-defeating cognitions involve rationalization. The obese person who eats too much on occasion might decide that since the treatment program for that day has been "blown," he or she might as well overindulge for the remainder of the day and return to the program the next day. Some never return.

Sternberg (1985) has reported that the addition of a relapse prevention training component to a traditional behavioral treatment program improved maintenance of weight loss. Perri, Shapiro, Ludwig, Twentyman, and McAdoo (1984) showed that behavior therapy plus relapse training and continuing therapeutic contact via mail or telephone significantly facilitated maintenance of weight loss compared to behavioral therapy or nonbehavioral treatments alone. They also found that behavior therapy plus relapse prevention training without continuing professional contact over the one-year follow-up was relatively unsuccessful. These results suggest that both relapse prevention training and continuing contact to encourage subjects to implement the strategies are important in maintaining weight loss.

The degree to which the client will be able to resist these negative cognitive reactions to post-treatment setbacks in adhering to a controlled behavioral routine will depend in part on treatment-induced expectations of self-efficacy. Efficacy expectations are the conviction that one can cope successfully with a given situation (Bandura, 1977a). Self-efficacy theory holds that efficacy expectations will determine whether coping behavior will be initiated, with what effort, and how resolute one will be in continuing to cope in the face of the inevitable pressures and problems that are encountered by the individual struggling to control weight. The client who, as a result of treatment, has strong efficacy expectations about coping with high-risk situations is more likely to overcome the potentially destructive consequences of a post-treatment transgression. Jeffery, Bjornson-Benson, Rosenthal, Lindquist, et al. (1984) found that pre-treatment self-efficacy measures were positively associated with the long-term maintenance of weight loss, while Mitchell and Stuart (1984) showed that members of Weight Watchers who dropped out had significantly lower self-efficacy scores at the beginning of their membership than those who continued.

A number of specific treatment and maintenance strategies derive from these cognitive-behavioral formulations of the maintenance of treatment effects. It is important to anticipate possible or probable setbacks or transgressions during treatment and to equip the client with cognitive and behavioral coping strategies for negotiating such setbacks. Teaching the client the appropriate strategies involves role playing and imaginal rehearsal of high-risk situations. Specific difficulties are confronted and the client's self-statements, self-evaluation, and labeling of the situation carefully monitored.

The importance of patients' attributions of behavior change and weight loss are illustrated by Craighead, Stunkard, and O'Brien's (1981) study. A combined pharmacotherapy (fenfluramine) and behavior modification treatment produced substantial weight loss at post-treatment (32 lbs.). However, where behavior modification treatment alone produced further weight loss at the six-month follow-up, the combined treatment group regained 10 lbs. This maintenance failure is probably due to subjects' attributing their weight loss to the drug rather than their own efforts. A heightened sense of self-efficacy based on self-attribution of behavior change must be the target of obesity control programs.

Evaluation of Treatment Effects

The outcome of weight control treatments is best determined by evaluating the method, the administrator, the problem, the client, the effects, the length of treatment, and the cost (Wilson & Brownell, 1980).

Which Methods Are Most Effective?

In general, controlled outcome studies have shown that behavioral treatments produce greater weight losses than a number of alternative methods in the short-term. The latter have included equally credible attention-placebo treatments emphasizing social pressure and group cohesiveness (Kingsley & Wilson, 1977), nutrition education (Levitz & Stunkard, 1974), relaxation training (Hall, Hall, Hanson, & Borden, 1974), and traditional medical treatment and group psychotherapy (Penick, Filion, Fox, & Stunkard, 1971). The absence of controlled studies of the effects of psychodynamic therapies makes it impossible to evaluate the efficacy of these methods. Stunkard (1980) has reported that psychoanalysis may produce significant, long-lasting weight reduction, but methodological flaws in the studies on which this assessment was based (e.g., the absence of suitable controls) renders them largely uninterpretable.

A noteworthy exception to the superiority of behavioral treatments in producing short-term weight loss has been pharmacotherapy. Craighead et al. (1981) compared four treatment conditions: (1) routine doctor's office treatment with fenfluramine, (2) behavior therapy in groups, (3) fenfluramine with Rogerian nondirective therapy in groups, and (4) fenfluramine combined with group behavior therapy. After twenty-five weekly sessions, the average weight losses for the four conditions were 14.1, 24, 29.9, and 31.9 lbs., respectively (see Figure 13-1). These data suggested that medication can lead to substantial weight loss if used in the context of group therapy. Adding behavior therapy improved weight loss somewhat, and the drug (with or without behavior therapy) was more effective than behavior therapy alone. However, a one-year follow-up revealed a high relapse rate in those individuals who had received fenfluramine. In contrast, the behavioral treatment produced good long-term maintenance of weight loss. Brownell and Stunkard (1981a) have replicated these findings.

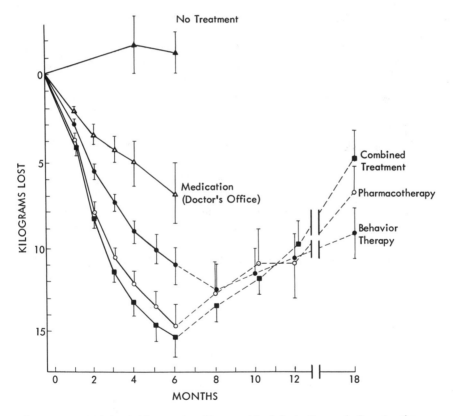

Figure 13–1 Weight loss in kilograms for subjects receiving behavior therapy, fenfluramine, the combination of behavior therapy and fenfluramine, or two control treatments. (From ''Behavior Therapy and Pharmacotherapy for Obesity'' by L. W. Craighead, A. J. Stunkard, and R. O'Brien (1981). *Archives of General Psychiatry, 38*, 763–768. Copyright 1981, American Medical Association. Reprinted by permission.)

Who Should Administer Weight Control Programs?

Behavioral treatments have been carried out by a variety of people with uneven expertise, ranging from experienced therapists to graduate students and dieticians. There is, however, no definitive evidence on the level of experience or professional expertise necessary to obtain the optimal treatment effects. Jeffery, Wing, and Stunkard (1978) found that experienced therapists produced greater weight loss than novice therapists. Similarly, Levitz and Stunkard (1974) demonstrated that professional therapists obtained significantly better results than lay therapists. Yet results obtained with a relatively impersonal self-prescription program manual have been comparable to those obtained with a therapist-administered program in some studies (Hagen, 1974), suggesting that for the most part, the therapist's contribution to successful weight control programs may be quite limited.

Who Are the Best Candidates?

Behavior therapy is the preferred treatment for the mildly to moderately obese. The severely obese appear to be poor risks for behavioral and other treatments (Van Itallie & Kral, 1981). Beyond this, relatively little can be said about predicting outcome. A consistent finding from behavioral studies is that a few people achieve clinically significant weight reduction, some only modest weight loss, and others little if any weight loss during treatment. Reliable psychological prognostic factors in the treatment of obesity remain to be identified. Initial adherence to treatment procedures (e.g., self-monitoring) and weight loss in the first two to four weeks might be the best available predictors of who will lose weight (Wilson, 1985). Yet even these factors account for comparatively small amounts of the variance in treatment outcome. Dubbert and Wilson (1983) reported that a combination of the best six predictor measures available early in treatment (pre-treatment percentage of body fat, initial weight, age, spouse percentage overweight, reported caloric intake during Week 2, and weight lost during the first three weeks) accounted for 59 percent of the variance in total weight loss through their nineteen-week program. The most powerful predictor of weight loss at the end of treatment and the 30-month follow-up was percentage of body fat, a physiological rather than a psychological variable that is less amenable to modification. Jeffery et al. (1978) had found that a combination of six similar subject characteristic variables accounted for about 25 percent of the variance in outcome for clients in their program. The most consistent predictor here was body weight prior to treatment, another physiological variable.

What Effects Does Behavioral Treatment Have?

Attrition. In contrast to other forms of treatment, behavior therapy has dramatically decreased attrition from treatment programs. The average attrition in traditional treatments has been as high as 80 percent (Stunkard, 1975) and in self-help groups the figure is at least 50 percent (Stunkard & Brownell, 1979). By contrast, the attrition rate in studies of behavioral treatment has been approximately 12 percent. Refunds of money deposits contingent on continuing participation in treatment are associated with significantly reduced attrition rates.

Body Weight. The average weight loss in behavioral treatment is ten to eleven lbs. This figure is remarkably consistent across different studies despite different client populations, therapists of varying expertise, and treatment programs of different durations (a range of roughly eight to sixteen weeks). Since the average length of treatment programs is twelve weeks, this mean weight loss is consistent with the usual goal of gradual weight loss of one to two lbs. each week. The extent to which these results can be improved upon is still unclear. In an intensive, multifaceted program lasting nineteen weeks and designed to remedy some of the shortcomings of previous behavioral treatments (e.g., combining standard group treatment with individual treatment sessions), Dubbert and Wilson (1983) obtained an average weight loss of seventeen lbs. Using a sophisticated cognitive-behavioral treatment over a twenty-week period, Rodin (Note 1) has reported some of the best results yet: a loss of 24.4 lbs. or 41 percent of excess weight. However, it is obvious that the vast majority of participants in behavioral treatment programs do not reach their goal weights.

Any weight control treatment faces the challenge of producing lasting, long-term results. Many people can lose weight, but few can keep it off. Unacceptably high rates of relapse characterize virtually all treatments. Pharmacotherapy is a case in point. Both Craighead et al. (1981) and Brownell and Stunkard (1981a) found that fenfluramine produced substantial weight loss at post-treatment, roughly 60 percent of which had been regained at a one-year follow-up. In contrast to most approaches, behavioral treatments show good maintenance of weight loss at a one-year follow-up (Foreyt et al., 1982; Wilson & Brownell, 1980). Although weight loss is maintained for at least a year in most behavioral programs, most participants do not continue to lose weight during this follow-up period. Finally, there is little evidence of maintenance of weight loss beyond the one-year mark. Dubbert and Wilson (1983) found

successful maintenance at thirty months, but five-year follow-ups by Stalonas, Perri, and Kerzner (1984) and Stunkard and Penick (1979) failed to find any evidence of successful maintenance.

Psychological Effects. The results of non-behavioral treatments indicate that depression, anxiety, fatigue, irritability, or similar symptoms occur in at least 50 percent of all dieters (Stunkard & Rush, 1974). No study, however, has shown any adverse emotional effects of behavioral treatment, despite careful assessment of the psychological concomitants and sequelae of weight control. Rather, the psychological consequences of behavioral programs have been positive, including reliable decreases in depression (e.g., Craighead et al., 1981; Taylor, Ferguson, & Reading, 1978) and improvement in body image (Dubbert & Wilson, 1984). Behavior therapy is a safe form of treatment for weight control.

Cardiovascular Functioning. Weight control treatments have had demonstrable health benefits. Among these are clinically significant reductions in blood pressure (Dubbert & Wilson, 1983) and favorable changes in the balance of serum lipids (Brownell & Stunkard, 1981b; Thompson, Jeffery, Wing, & Wood, 1979). Using behavioral treatment plus nutrition education, Brownell and Stunkard (1981b) found that in men, a 10.7 kg. weight loss was associated with a 5 percent increase in the HDL-cholesterol level, a 15.8 percent decrease in the LDL-cholesterol level, and a 30.1 percent increase in the HDL-LDL ratio. In contrast, obese women showed a 8.9 kg. weight loss, a 3.3 percent decrease in the HDL-cholesterol level, a 4.7 percent decrease in the LDL-cholesterol level, and no significant change in the HDL-LDL ratio. These changes in serum lipids in men seemed directly attributable to weight loss and not correlated to changes in alcohol consumption, cigarette smoking, nutrition, or exercise. In contrast to these results with women, Follick, Abrams, Smith, Henderson, and Herbert (1984) found that both total and LDL-cholesterol levels decreased during treatment and remained lower at a six-month follow-up. HDL-cholesterol and the HDL-LDL ratio did not change during treatment but increased significantly above pre-treatment levels at follow-up. Furthermore, long-term changes in lipoprotein levels were significantly correlated with changes in body weight.

Cost-Effectiveness of Treatment

The cost-effectiveness of any treatment depends on the efficacy and cost of each program component and the effectiveness of the delivery system (Yates, 1978). Nothing definitive can be concluded about the efficacy and cost of specific program components, even in behavioral treatments, which have been most intensively studied. More is known about how efficiently behavioral treatments can be delivered. These methods have almost always been implemented on a standardized group basis. Moreover, they seem to have a robust effect that can be achieved by inexperienced therapists under supervision.

Behavioral treatment methods are disseminable because they are well-defined and replicable across settings. An instructive example of the cost-effectiveness of behavioral treatment comes from its incorporation by self-help groups. The most prominent of low-cost self-help groups is Weight Watchers, evaluations of which have generally shown results comparable to those obtained by medical practice (Stuart & Mitchell, 1978). The addition of behavioral methods to the fundamental elements of Weight Watchers—the positive group environment and carefully structured nutrition—may have enhanced its general efficacy. Based on a twelve-week study of over 7000 members, Stuart (1977) showed that the addition of behavioral methods to the traditional Weight Watchers program resulted in greater weight loss. A further idea of the effects of the revamped Weight Watchers program can be gleaned from Stuart and Guire's (1978) correlational analysis of long-term outcome. Fifteen months after members reached their goal weights, 24.6 percent were below goal at the time of follow-up, 28.9 percent were within 5 percent of goal, 17.5 percent were between 6 and 10 percent above goal, and 17.5 percent were 11 percent or more above goal.

Combining Treatments

The likely advantages of emphasizing the cost-effectiveness of standardized behavioral treatment programs, namely, a modest weight loss in a large number of people at relatively low cost, should not detract from efforts to develop more effective but expensive methods. This raises the question of combining behavioral programs with other treatment modalities.

Behavior Therapy and Drugs

The typical pattern of weight loss in behavioral treatment is a decelerating one in which weight loss that is most marked in the early stages of treatment gradually tapers off and often ceases completely when treatment is discontinued. A likely cause of this phenomenon is the body's homeostatic reaction to caloric deprivation in which basal metabolism is slowed (Wooley et al., 1979). Another factor might be that initial weight loss is facilitated by the early enthusiasm and optimism of participants in a new treatment program. Inevitably, this enthusiasm wears off and adherence to treatment demands becomes more taxing. Many individuals become frustrated with weight losses that are too slow, too little, and too variable. Dissatisfaction with the lack of rapid success might contribute to the inconsistent results of behavioral programs. As noted, pharmacotherapy promotes rapid and substantial weight loss but is contraindicated because of its high relapse rate. Combining pharmacotherapy with behavioral treatment has not remedied this problem (Brownell & Stunkard, 1981a; Craighead et al., 1981); however, there are different ways to sequence a combination of behavioral and drug treatment (Lasagna, 1980), and research is only beginning to address these possibilities (Craighead, 1984).

Very-Low-Calorie Diets

Another promising means of producing rapid and large weight loss is the very-low-calorie diet (VLCD) or protein-sparing modified fast (PSMF). Although concerns about its safety have been voiced, the diet is safe if used properly by individuals who are carefully screened and medically monitored on a regular basis (Howard & Bray, 1981; Wadden, Stunkard, & Brownell, 1983). Extended average weight losses of approximately four pounds per week can be expected, with positive effects on blood pressure and lipid levels. Adherence to this diet of 400 to 700 calories per day is better than that obtained with the caloric restriction goals (1000 to 1500 calories per day) of standard behavioral weight control programs.

The problem with a VLCD is how to prevent relapse when the person returns to more normal eating. Combining a VLCD with behavioral procedures designed to facilitate transition to a conventional diet while maintaining weight loss may help overcome the relapse problem. An illustration of how this might be accomplished can be seen in Katell,

Callahan, Fremouw, and Zitter's (1979) use of behavioral treatment in combination with PSMF. They reported a carefully documented case in which the client, finding that weight loss was too slow and too variable under the conventional, behavioral program, resorted to PSMF under medical supervision. Following rapid weight loss during the eight weeks she received this diet, she returned to the behavioral program with successful maintenance of weight loss at six months. Other uncontrolled clinical trials have reported impressive results using a combination of behavioral treatment and PSMF (Bistrian, 1978; Lindner & Blackburn, 1976; Wadden, Stunkard, Brownell, & Day, 1984).

When Treatment Fails

Obesity has remained resistant to most treatment methods and even our most effective procedures have produced relatively modest successes. Far too many obese individuals are trapped in a recurring cycle of losing and regaining weight. This off-again/on-again pattern can have deleterious consequences for the person's physical health and psychological well-being. In a comprehensive behavioral weight control program emphasizing slow weight loss through caloric restriction and increased exercise, the health risks incurred by treatment failure are probably minimal. However, there is evidence showing that the more typical pattern of failure to achieve weight reduction, namely, repeated periods of severe caloric restriction and rapid weight loss followed by excessive overeating and equally rapid weight gain, may have negative effects. Recovery of metabolic rate to pre-diet level may take longer and metabolic rate may fall more rapidly with return to caloric restriction than it did originally (Wooley et al., 1979). Research on two successive cycles of pronounced weight loss and gain in laboratory rats has shown striking effects of these cycles (Brownell, Stellar, Greenwood, & Shrager, 1986). Rats took twice as long to lose the same amount of weight on the second cycle. They also regained the same amount of weight more rapidly during the second refeeding cycle. Compared to the first cycle, food efficiency (weight change per unit of food) was increased significantly in the second cycle, during both the loss and regain phases.

Some of the psychological effects of failure may produce a sense of helplessness and diminished sense of self-efficacy. To the extent that treatment failures suffer these emotional reactions, they are less likely to succeed in subsequent weight control efforts. Yet it is clear that failure to lose weight in one sort of treatment does little to deter a great number of obese people from trying again—and succeeding in some cases (Schachter, 1982). Many of these obese individuals can be helped to lose weight and even to maintain this weight loss. Dubbert and Wilson (1983), for example, found that none of their measures of previous dieting or unsuccessful weight loss history correlated significantly with weight loss at post-treatment.

BULIMIA

In our society today, women, particularly adolescent and young adult women, express significant concern with their weight and physical appearance. A majority report that they are dissatisfied with their body weight, are very self-conscious about eating, and are frequently dieting or restricting their eating in one way or another (Halmi, Falk, & Schwartz, 1981; Pyle, Mitchell, Ekert, Halvorson, et al., 1983). Wooley and Wooley (1986) report that a body image survey in *Glamour* magazine in 1983 showed that 76 percent of respondents considered themselves too fat, including 45 percent of those classified as underweight according to standard measures of weight. Only 13 percent of respondents thought that their mothers had liked their own bodies. There can be little doubt that the societal ideal is to be thin and sexy, and that women experience considerable social pressure to watch their weight. A glance at the svelte, narrow-hipped models on T.V. and in popular magazines will quickly confirm this assertion. The evidence is clear, however, that weight is partly determined by biological processes which, particularly in women, conflict with relatively recent societal ideals about physical beauty. Confronted with this clash between biological and societal forces, many women choose unhealthy means of trying to control their weight. Aside from starvation diets, a large number of women try self-induced vomiting. Some of these women experiment harmlessly with this unnatural form of weight regulation. For others, for reasons not yet fully known (Striegel-Moore, Silberstein, & Rodin, 1986), however, it develops into the clinical disorder of bulimia or bulimia nervosa.

Definitions and Description

The DSM-III criteria for bulimia are listed in Table 13-1. Bulimia nervosa is a more precisely defined form of bulimia (Fairburn, 1984) and is characterized by the following three features: 1. recurrent binge-eating. (a binge is defined not by the amount eaten but by the perception of excessive food intake, and the feeling of loss of control over eating); 2. purging, such as self-induced vomiting or laxative abuse; and 3. excessive concern with body weight and shape, and a fear of gaining weight. Clients with bulimia nervosa are within the range of average weight. Bulimic symptoms also occur in some cases of obesity and in roughly 50 percent of cases of anorexia nervosa. In both obesity and anorexia nervosa, binge eating is associated with a poorer prognosis (Agras & Kraemer, 1984; Keefe, Wyshogrod, Weinberger, & Agras, 1984).

Bulimic episodes usually occur during unstructured time periods, particularly at night and on weekends. Bulimia is a solitary activity and has been dubbed the "secret addiction." Because of feelings of guilt and shame, bulimics conceal their disorder from family, friends, and even their physician.

Bulimia nervosa is frequently associated with a variety of psychopathological features, including depression, anxiety, excessive guilt, intolerance for frustration, and problems with expressing feelings such as anger (Johnson, Lewis, & Hagman, 1984). A minority abuse alcohol or other drugs, show parasuicidal behavior, and shoplift food (Fairburn & Cooper, 1984). Clients with bulimia and bulimia nervosa vary widely in personal characteristics, and it would be premature to "type" a bulimic in a clinical profile. Medical consequences of recurrent bingeing and vomiting have been reported, particularly electrolyte imbalances, kidney and gastric abnormalities, parotid gland enlargement, and erosion of tooth enamel (Pyle, Mitchell, & Eckert, 1981), although other studies have shown no noteworthy blood

abnormalities or other physical symptoms (Jacobs & Schneider, 1985). Menstrual irregularities are common.

Prevalence

Individual studies have indicated different prevalence rates, depending on the sampling procedures and definition of bulimia used, but the evidence is clear that bulimia and bulimia nervosa represent significant clinical problems. Fairburn and Cooper (1984) concluded that the prevalence of bulimia nervosa among adult women in general is 1 to 2 percent. Johnson et al. (1984) estimate the prevalence of bulimia among female high school and college students to be 5 percent. Some studies have estimated prevalence of bulimia, as defined by DSM-III, to be as high as 13 percent among the population of college students (Halmi et al., 1981), and there are data suggesting that the prevalence is increasing (Pyle, Halvorson, Neuman, & Mitchell, 1986). Models, dancers, and athletes—groups for whom weight control is of central importance—are at high risk for bulimia. The overwhelming number of bulimics are women. Men comprise less than 1 percent of those

---

Table 13–1 Diagnostic Criteria for Bulimia

A. Recurrent episodes of binge eating (rapid consumption of a large amount of food in a discrete period of time, usually less than two hours).

B. At least three of the following:
   1. consumption of high-caloric, easily ingested food
   2. inconspicuous eating
   3. termination of such eating episodes by abdominal pain, sleep, social interruption, or self-induced vomiting
   4. repeated attempts to lose weight by severely restrictive diets, self-induced vomiting, or use of cathartics or diuretics
   5. frequent weight fluctuations greater than 10 lbs. due to alternating binges and fasts

C. Awareness that the eating pattern is abnormal and fear of not being able to stop eating voluntarily.

D. Depressed mood and self-deprecating thoughts following eating binges.

E. Bulimic episodes not due to anorexia nervosa or to any known physical disorder.

who suffer from bulimia nervosa (Fairburn & Cooper, 1984).

Onset and Etiology

On average, binge-eating begins around age 18, with vomiting developing roughly a year later. The onset of vomiting intensifies the problem, since bulimics then have a way of coping with the fear of weight gain which had partly restrained bingeing. Once established, bulimia nervosa becomes a chronic disorder. Studies of family histories have shown significant levels of depression and obesity among family members. A personal history of weight disturbance is common in individuals with bulimia nervosa. A large number have been obese, and a minority underweight or anorexic in the past. The majority of bulimics begin binge-eating following a period of severe dieting.

No evidence exists that bulimia or bulimia nervosa is caused by biological disturbance of the food regulatory system. As a result of the significant family and personal history of depression in bulimics, the disorder has been viewed as a form of affective illness (Hudson, Pope, & Jonas, 1984). However, careful analyses of the clinical features of bulimia nervosa and its response to treatment, show that depression is secondary to the eating disorder in most cases (Fairburn & Cooper, 1984; Wilson, 1986).

A primarily cognitive model of bulimia and bulimia nervosa fits the data best. In this view, individuals have abnormal attitudes and beliefs about weight regulation. Evaluating their self-worth mainly in terms of their body shape and weight, these individuals become preoccupied with dieting. They develop rigid, unrealistic, and hence dysfunctional cognitions about eating and weight control, which are part of what Polivy and Herman (1985) call dietary restraint. Clinical experience has

shown that when these cognitive standards are transgressed, typically under stressful circumstances, a binge is triggered. Laboratory studies have confirmed this analysis, showing that individuals high in dietary restraint tend to lose control and overeat when they feel stressed or depressed (Polivy, Herman, Olmsted, & Jazwinski, 1984; Ruderman, 1985).[2] Obsessed with the fear of gaining weight, bulimics try to cope with these binges by vomiting. Figure 13-2 summarizes this model.

Treatment Principles and Procedures

A wide range of different cognitive and behavioral procedures have been used to treat bulimia and bulimia nervosa, including cognitive restructuring techniques, self-control strategies, relaxation training, dietary interventions, assertion training, and exposure and response prevention (Hawkins, Fremouw, & Clement, 1984; Wilson, 1986). The severity and complexity of bulimia nervosa typically requires a multifaceted cognitive-behavioral treatment program. An excellent example of such a treatment program, which is both clinically sophisticated and conceptually sound, is that developed by Fairburn (1984).

Multifaceted Cognitive-Behavioral Principles and Procedures

Fairburn's treatment is a problem-oriented, present-focused approach in which the therapist actively provides information, ad-

---

2. Polivy et al. (1984) have called this loss of control or overeating by restrained eaters, once their rigid dietary code is violated, "counterregulation." Notice that this concept of counterregulation is essentially the same as Marlatt and Gordon's (1985) "abstinence violation affect," which they formulated in the treatment of another substance disorder, alcoholism (see Chapter 14).

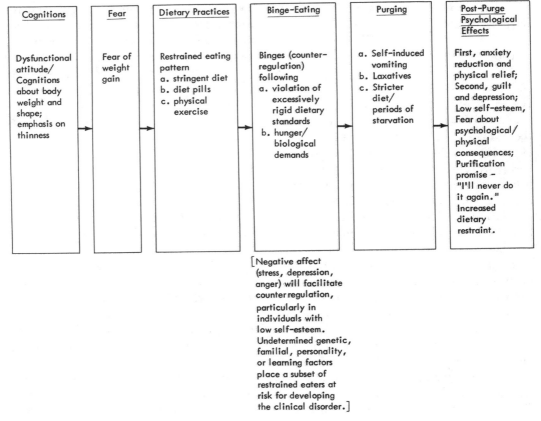

Cognitions	Fear	Dietary Practices	Binge-Eating	Purging	Post-Purge Psychological Effects
Dysfunctional attitude/ Cognitions about body weight and shape; emphasis on thinness	Fear of weight gain	Restrained eating pattern a. stringent diet b. diet pills c. physical exercise	Binges (counter-regulation) following a. violation of excessively rigid dietary standards b. hunger/ biological demands	a. Self-induced vomiting b. Laxatives c. Stricter diet/ periods of starvation	First, anxiety reduction and physical relief; Second, guilt and depression; Low self-esteem, Fear about psychological/ physical consequences; Purification promise – "I'll never do it again." Increased dietary restraint.

[Negative affect (stress, depression, anger) will facilitate counter regulation, particularly in individuals with low self-esteem. Undetermined genetic, familial, personality, or learning factors place a subset of restrained eaters at risk for developing the clinical disorder.]

Figure 13–2 A model of the binge-purge sequence.

vice, and support and requires a good working relationship between therapist and patient. It comprises three stages. In the first, the main emphasis is on establishing some degree of control over eating; the techniques used are largely behavioral. Patients are asked to self-monitor, daily, what, where, and when they eat and to record any binges, vomiting, or laxative use. They are directed to make sure they eat three planned meals each day, with the option of one or two snacks. Virtually all patients with bulimia nervosa try to restrict themselves to fewer meals because they fear gaining weight. The usual result of this deprivation is to increase hunger and temptation, particularly for "forbidden foods," which then increases the probability that they will binge. Developing regular and stable eating patterns is a vital treatment objective. Patients typically object that regular eating will cause them to gain weight and they are reluctant to comply with this request. Fairburn informs them that they are absorbing calories by bingeing, even if they vomit afterwards, and that resumption of regular eating usually does not involve any weight gain. Patients are also urged not to weigh themselves more than once a week, since this only fuels their self-defeating concern with weight.

"Patients are advised of the folly of trying to maintain rigid control over their weight. Instead, they are asked to accept a weight range of approximately 6 lbs. in magnitude, located between 85 percent and 115 percent of the average weight for their age, height, and sex. It is suggested that they should not decide on a specific weight range until control over their eating has been established, since only then will they be able to gauge how much they can eat in order to keep their weight relatively stable. They are advised against choosing a weight which necessitates anything more than moderate dietary restriction since restraint of this type is prone to encourage overeating" (p. 246).

Self-control strategies (e.g., stimulus control and arranging activities incompatible with unplanned eating) are used to counteract urges for unplanned eating.

The second stage of treatment is more cognitively oriented with particular stress being placed on the identification and modification of dysfunctional thoughts and beliefs about eating, weight, and body image. Patients are encouraged to introduce into their meal plans foods they previously tried to avoid. Typically, these are "bad," i.e., fattening, foods. The goal here is to overcome a rigid, dichotomous style of thinking—what Beck (1976) calls all-or-nothing thinking. Bulimics typically take extreme views of themselves and their eating: they are "in control" or "out of control," "fat" or "thin." Food is either "good" or "bad," "allowed" or "forbidden." There are no in-between (more flexible) views, no grey areas. With such rigid, inflexible standards the slightest slip or deviation from their diet is viewed as failure or loss of control. Bulimics refer to this state of mind as being "one bite away from a binge." Learning to be more flexible about what they eat and acquiring a more stable eating pattern are powerful ways of neutralizing their concern with dietary restraint which, because it is so often the precursor of binge-eating, is ultimately self-defeating. The attitudes and values about

women being thin in this society are examined, and bulimics helped to challenge what may be unrealistic societal pressures for slimness.

The final stage of treatment provides patients with specific guidelines for maintaining improvement. The bulk of these instructions emphasize prudent behavioral planning and the use of self-control strategies. Future difficulties are anticipated and coping responses discussed. Patients are informed that setbacks are to be expected, but they need not precipitate full-blown relapse. Fairburn uses essentially the same principles as developed by Marlatt and Gordon (1985) in their relapse prevention social learning model (see Chapter 14).

Exposure and Response Prevention

Bulimia nervosa has been likened to an obsessive-compulsive disorder. The bulimic binges, typically in response to some negative emotional state (e.g., anxiety, depression, or anger). The immediate effect of the binge is to reduce this negative emotional state, but then the act of bingeing itself distresses the person primarily because she fears weight gain. Vomiting reduces this fear and any associated physical discomfort. Thus vomiting can be conceptualized as a negative reinforcer, just as, in a compulsive handwasher for example, the handwashing reduces anxiety of contamination and thereby maintains the behavior (Johnson, Schlundt, & Jarrell, 1986; Leitenberg, Gross, Peterson, & Rosen, 1984).

Given this view of bulimia nervosa, it is not surprising that it has been treated with exposure and response prevention, the methods which have been shown to be effective in the modification of anxiety disorders (see Chapters 8 and 9). Using these methods, bulimics, during planned treatment sessions, are instructed to eat their typical binge foods to the point at which they would normally vomit. They are then asked to refrain from vomiting for the remainder of the session (roughly 45 to 60 minutes) and for several hours following. Once patients have reached the point at which they would typically vomit, their attention is focused on whatever anxiety-eliciting thoughts and feelings they experience. As Leitenberg et al. (1984) put it, these thoughts and feelings usually center around "negative body image, sensations of feeling full, gross, fat, wanting to vomit, fears of weight gain and binge-eating in public, and relationship issues with spouses, parents, friends, and coworkers, including themes of anger, loss, and rejection" (p. 7). The goals of treatment are to have patients discover: (1) that the anxiety they experience does not continually increase to an intolerable level, but peaks at a manageable level and then decreases, (2) that they can eat "forbidden" foods without having to vomit afterwards, and (3) that their fear of losing control, of being overwhelmed by irresistible cravings to eat more, is groundless.

Some patients are reluctant to participate in this treatment for fear that if they do not vomit they will gain weight. This issue of resistance requires careful attention by the therapist (Wilson, 1986). These patients can be assured that most patients do not gain weight as a result of participating in the treatment. And even if they did gain a modest amount of weight, they can be helped to lose these pounds through healthier, more sensible weight control strategies than vomiting. Single-case experimental designs have shown that exposure and response prevention is a rapid and effective treatment for many bulimics, often eliminating binge-eating and vomiting completely (Leitenberg et al., 1984; Rossiter & Wilson, 1985).

Controlled Outcome Studies

Kirkley et al. (1985) compared a cognitive-behavioral treatment modeled after Fairburn's (1984) program to a nondirective control treatment. The cognitive-behavioral treatment consisted primarily of dietary management, cognitive restructuring, "interpersonal problem solving related to deficient assertive skills," and relaxation training. The nondirective control group discussed their food choices, eating patterns, vomiting rituals, and the role of stress in their bulimia, but were not instructed how to alter these behaviors. The cognitive-behavioral treatment produced significantly greater reductions in binge-eating and vomiting at post-treatment but not follow-up.

The best controlled study, by Fairburn, Kirk, O'Connor, and Cooper (in press), has yielded the most positive results. They showed that both Fairburn's (1984) cognitive-behavioral treatment (CBT) and a short-term focal psychotherapy largely eliminated binge-eating and vomiting in clients with severe cases of bulimia nervosa. Almost all of the clients had received previous psychiatric treatment. Over 33 percent had been treated for anorexia nervosa. Prior to treatment with CBT, these clients were vomiting more than once a day on average. At post-treatment, this frequency had decreased to an average of less than once a week. Most impressively, clients treated with CBT did not binge or vomit during the one-year follow-up.

Fairburn et al.'s CBT treatment was significantly more effective than focal psychotherapy in its effects on clients' general clinical status, psychopathology (e.g., depression), social adjustment, and clients' own assessment of outcome. The authors attribute the absence of a significant difference between the two therapies on binge-eating and vomiting to the inclusion in the focal psychotherapy of cognitive-behavioral strategies such as self-monitoring of eating habits and specific information about dieting and weight control.

Lacey (1983) reported that a cognitive-behavioral treatment, which included some nonbehavioral strategies, was significantly more effective than a waiting list control condition. Of thirty patients who were treated, twenty-four had stopped binge-eating and vomiting completely at the end of the ten-week program. An additional four subjects became abstinent within four weeks of the termination of treatment, and the remaining two showed significant reductions in bingeing and vomiting. No patient on the waiting list improved. A follow-up of up to two years indicated that twenty patients maintained their abstinence.

Wilson, Rossiter, Kleifield, and Lindholm (1986) compared a verbal cognitive restructuring (CR) method to CR plus exposure and vomit prevention (CR/EVP). The combined CR/EVP treatment was more effective. At one-year follow-up, CR/EVP subjects were completely abstinent. CR/EVP also resulted in significantly greater improvements on several measures of psychopathology. At one-year follow-up, CR/EVP subjects showed major changes in eating habits and cognitions and feelings about food. On these and general measures of psychopathology, CR/EVP subjects scored in the nonproblem, nonpatient range. Clients who responded to therapy showed significantly greater self-efficacy at post-treatment than those who did not. The significance of producing changes in relevant cognitive processes in addition to actual bingeing and vomiting, i.e., synchrony among measures of cognitive and behavioral functioning, is shown in Freeman, Beach, Davis, and Solyom's (1985) results. Bulimics who stopped binge-eating and vomiting at post-treatment but whose dissatisfaction with their body image did not change (a desynchronous pattern) were more likely to relapse than those whose body image also changed (a synchronous pattern).

Wilson et al.'s (1986) findings provide further support for the prediction of social learning theory that primarily verbal or symbolic methods are less effective than performance-based procedures in producing cognitive and behavioral change. Bulimic clients find that using verbal cognitive restructuring methods usually do not prevent the binge/vomiting. Some clients fail to implement cognitive strategies which, at other times, have proved effective. In the latter cases it seems as though clients have made up their minds to binge/purge before they have a chance to challenge their dysfunctional thoughts. One client described this phenomenon as "the hand being quicker than the mind" (Wilson, 1986). Cognitive methods are more likely to be effective when there is an anticipatory awareness of the binge. A lack of awareness, or "automatic" binge-eating, requires alternative treatments.

Summary. Replications with larger numbers of patients and long-term follow-up are needed. Nonetheless, the results are encouraging. Although appropriate comparative treatment studies are required, in most instances, cognitive-behavioral treatment appears to be at least equal or superior to the other major form of treatment, namely, antidepressant drugs (Agras, Dorlan, Kirkley, Arnow, & Bachman, in press; Walsh, Stewart, Roose, Gladis, et al., 1984). Moreover, drug treatment encounters the same problems as in the treatment of anxiety disorders (see Chapter 9). Some patients are reluctant to take medication, there are unpleasant side-effects, and even when drug treatment is successful, patients almost always resume binge-ing or vomiting when taken off their medication (Wilson, 1986). Except in cases in which depression, as a primary diagnosis, coexists with bulimia nervosa and antidepressant medication is indicated, cognitive-behavioral methods appear to be the treatment of choice for bulimia and bulimia nervosa (Fairburn, 1985; Wilson, 1986).

ANOREXIA NERVOSA

Diagnosis and Description

Anorexia nervosa is a relatively rare disorder marked by severe voluntary restriction of food intake. The full DSM-III criteria are listed in Table 13-2. Anorexia nervosa is a chronic, life-threatening disorder, with a mortality rate of between 15 percent and 20 percent. It is confined largely to females (95 percent). Mean age of onset is 17 to 18 years.

Clients with anorexia can be divided into those who lose weight by rigidly restricting their food intake (the restricting sub-type) and those whose severe dieting is disrupted by episodes of binge-eating (the bulimic sub-type). The latter have a poorer prognosis. Anorexia nervosa is often seen as a separate syndrome from bulimia nervosa. Yet Garner, Garfinkel, and O'Shaughnessy (1985) found that bulimic women with anorexia nervosa and bulimic normal-weight women resembled each other on many psychological characteristics, and

were more similar to each other than to women with anorexia nervosa who rigidly restricted food intake. These findings do not support the diagnostic distinction between bulimia in anorexic women and bulimia of equal severity in normal-weight women. Nevertheless clients with bulimia nervosa, as indicated in the preceding section, are much more likely to respond to treatment.

Etiology and Maintenance

In contrast to obesity, available evidence suggests that genetic factors play little role in anorexia nervosa (Crisp, 1970). Social learning and familial influences appear to be the determinants of this disorder. Perhaps the most widely accepted conceptualization of anorexia nervosa is that of a weight phobia: these individuals have an intense fear and sustained avoidance of a mature (post-pubertal) body weight and shape (Crisp, 1984). The stringent dieting, which reduces weight and stops menstruation, is seen as an attempt (not necessarily conscious) to reverse the pubertal process. Normal body weight is feared and avoided, Crisp (1984) maintains, because it represents conflict at several levels: within the individual, the family, and the broader social context. For example, at the social level, anorexia nervosa is viewed as one solution to the problems of adolescent expression within a (western) culture that has become less and less structured regarding socio-sexual roles

Table 13–2   Diagnostic Criteria for Anorexia Nervosa

A. Intense fear of becoming obese, which does not diminish as weight loss progresses.

B. Disturbance of body image, e.g., claiming to "feel fat" even when emaciated.

C. Weight loss of at least 25 percent of original body weight or, if under 18 years of age, weight loss from original body weight plus projected weight gain expected from growth charts may be combined to make the 25 percent.

D. Refusal to maintain body weight over a minimal normal weight for age and height.

E. No known physical illness that would account for the weight loss.

and customs. Crisp attributes what he and others regard as an increase in the disorder to this societal factor. Society, Crisp claims, "feeds back to teenagers views concerning female shape and with the emphasis on glorifying it as sexual on the one hand and on curbing it on the other. Perhaps this fuels the uncertain and self-doubting adolescent's fantasy that her shape is crucial to her destiny as an adult on the one hand, whilst at the same time having the potential to bring about her downfall" (1984, p. 216).

However plausible Crisp's analysis is of the etiology and maintenance of anorexia nervosa, it is not without problems. For instance, why adolescents choose this particular form of avoidance behavior for coping with the various intra- and interpersonal demands they encounter remains speculative. And while the onset of the disorder in the majority of cases is in the teen years when the conflicts Crisp emphasizes are most likely, what of the women who develop anorexia nervosa at prepuberty or as adults? Nonetheless, this weight phobia conceptualization is useful in that it leads to testable hypotheses and suggests specific treatment interventions.

Treatment

Behavioral Principles and Procedures

Treatment of anorexia nervosa may be divided into two phases: (1) immediate intervention, using reinforcement principles while the patient is hospitalized, to restore body weight and (2) more protracted therapy, mainly on an outpatient basis, to treat the many longstanding psychosocial problems that characterize anorexic patients and their families. Behavior therapy has been limited almost exclusively to the first phase of treatment.

A graphic clinical case example of behavioral treatment is provided by Bachrach, Er-win, and Mohr's (1965) report of a thirty-seven-year-old, five-feet-four-inches-tall woman who was admitted to the hospital weighing only 47 pounds. Medical and endocrinological examinations failed to reveal any disease process which could account for the patient's reduced food intake which had brought her close to death. Bachrach et al. conceptualized the patient's non-eating as operant behavior maintained by its environmental consequences, and, with the full cooperation of the patient's family, the hospital administration, and the nursing staff, devised the following treatment regime. As a first step, the patient was transferred from the "enriched environment" of an attractive hospital room which gave her access to visitors, radio, books, and T.V., which she obviously enjoyed, to the "impoverished" milieu of a barren room from which all objects which had brought her pleasure had been removed. Social interaction was reduced to the minimum level, no visitors were allowed and nurses, who only entered the room to change linen and bring her meals, ignored any attempt at conversation by the patient. Each of the three therapists ate one meal a day with the patient, during which time they tried to reinforce any approximation toward eating (e.g., lifting her fork) by talking about a topic of interest to her. If she consumed any part of the meal she was rewarded by having a radio or T.V. set brought into her room for a while, reinforcements which were made contingent on her eating increasingly larger amounts of food. The woman began to gain weight and her range of reinforcers was enhanced to include visitors, walks on the grounds, and hair care as she grew more concerned with her personal appearance. When it was discovered that her weight stabilized at 63 because she was vomiting her food (a not uncommon practice among anorexic patients) the requirement for reinforcement was made contingent on weight increase at daily weigh-ins rather than on eating.

After six weeks the patient was discharged weighing 64 pounds. Her family was coached in the use of reinforcement principles to facilitate generalization and maintenance of weight gain once she was out of the artificially controlled hospital environment. A fifteen-month follow-up found that she continued to improve; her weight was up to 88 pounds. A sixteen-year follow-up (almost unheard of in clinical psychology and psychiatry) revealed that she had lost all but 8 pounds of the weight she had gained in therapy. Her weight was 55 lbs. (instead of the normative 96 lbs.) apparently because of her failure to eat adequate amounts of food. However, she had remained socially active and independent, caring for herself and her mother (Erwin, 1977).

Brady and Rieger (1975) treated sixteen hospitalized anorexics using reinforcement principles. For nine of these patients, access to physical activity was the reinforcer made contingent on weight gain. While hospitalized for a median length of six weeks, the patients gained an average of four pounds a week. At a follow-up an average of two years later, the condition of five patients was rated as "good," five as "fair," and two as "poor." Two were dead and two could not be contacted. The absence of systematic post-hospital intervention to facilitate generalization of improvement undoubtedly contributed to these disappointing follow-up results. Agras, Barlow, Chapin, Abel, and Leitenberg (1974) treated a series of nine anorexics, attempting to experimentally isolate the effective components of behavioral treatment programs. Feedback of accurate information to the patients as to their weight and caloric intake proved to be far more effective in causing weight gains than either positive or negative reinforcement, although the latter did exert an influence. Negative reinforcement in this

instance referred to patients gaining enough weight to be discharged from the hospital.

Operant conditioning programs can be implemented in a strict or more flexible way. Touyz, Beumont, Glarin, Phillips, and Cowie (1984) compared a "strict" operant program with a "lenient" version in the treatment of hospitalized anorexics. In the former, patients were reinforced for each pound of weight they gained using a contingent, individualized schedule of reinforcement. In the latter, patients were allowed unrestricted (i.e., noncontingent) access to reinforcers provided that they gained a minimum of three pounds a week. No difference in weight gain was found, but the more lenient program was more practical and, importantly, more acceptable to patients. It can also be predicted from social learning theory that the more "lenient" the initial treatment program, the greater are the chances of fostering self-attribution of behavior change and increased self-efficacy, which, in turn, increase the likelihood that behavior change will be maintained once the patient is discharged from the hospital.

Comparative Efficacy of Behavioral Treatment

In an analysis of data from twenty-one outcome studies published between 1954 and 1982, Agras and Kraemer (1984) compared the averaged results of behavioral (reinforcement) methods with those of drug treatment and what they called "medical treatment," which included hospitalization, often combined with confinement to bed, supervised eating, psychotherapy, family therapy, and occasionally tube feeding. Given the uneven and typically flawed quality of available studies, Agras and Kraemer's analysis must be viewed with considerable caution, as the authors themselves are quick to point out. Nonetheless, the results offer useful pointers in the absence of many well-controlled studies. The behavioral and medical treatments produced better weight gain than the drug treatment but did not differ from each other. Behavioral treatment, however, was briefer and far more cost-effective than medical treatment.

The rarity of the disorder accounts in part for the relative dearth of adequately controlled outcome studies. In one of the few such studies, Eckert, Goldberg, Casper, and Davis (1981) randomly assigned eighty-one anorexic women to thirty-five days of treatment with either behavior therapy (reinforcement methods) or milieu therapy. Patients treated with behavior therapy gained weight at a rate of 4.2 kg./month, as compared with a rate of 3.6 kg./month for milieu therapy, gains which were not significantly different.

Broadening the Treatment Base

Behavior therapy for anorexia nervosa has been limited mainly to the narrow use of reinforcement procedures with hospitalized patients; yet there are persuasive reasons for extending more broadly based cognitive-behavioral strategies to both phases of treatment identified above. Procedures such as social skills and assertion training, problem-solving, self-control, and cognitive restructuring are all well-suited to helping the anorexic cope with the interpersonal demands and conflicts inherent in achieving normal weight and developing greater maturity. An early case study by Lang (1965) indicated the potential value of relaxation procedures, desensitization, and assertion training for treating anorexic problems in which the maintaining variables might be antecedant factors, such as interpersonal anxiety.

Fairburn (1984) points out that the same cognitive-behavioral techniques which have been used successfully in treating bulimia nervosa are applicable to anorexia, particularly the sub-set of anorexics who binge and vomit. He suggests that the core psychopathology of the two disorders is similar. A major difference between the two disorders is that, whereas bulimics fear gaining weight beyond what is normal for them, anorexics pursue thinness to the point of jeopardizing their lives. Also, bulimics are motivated for treatment, anorexics are not. Garner and Bemis (1982) have described a cognitive-behavioral approach, based on Beck's (1976) cognitive therapy for depression, for treating anorexics. It overlaps with Fairburn's (1984) treatment for bulimia, but incorporates several innovative features which are unique to treating anorexics, such as overcoming problems with motivation and challenging their denial about being dangerously underweight.

SUMMARY

Obesity affects one in five adult Americans and poses significant health hazards. Body-weight is biologically determined to an important degree. For many obese people, what society regards as overweight might be their "biologically normal" weight.

Behavioral treatment requires that the person make a permanent change in lifestyle—reduce caloric intake in a healthy manner; eat balanced, nutritious meals; and exercise on a regular schedule. There are no magic diets that will produce lasting weight loss. Basic treatment strategies include self-monitoring of daily caloric intake and eating patterns, the setting of realistic goals to prompt constructive self-evaluative reactions, and reinforcement of behavior change. Additional methods focus on changing dysfunctional cognitions surrounding eating and exercise, social skills training, and the use of spouse or group support to facilitate compliance with improved eating habits. Increasing physical activity is as important as reducing food intake since it might help to neutralize metabolic effects that make weight loss difficult.

Behavior therapy has been combined with drugs and a very-low-calorie-diet (VLCD) in treating more severe cases of obesity. The combination with VLCD has yielded encouraging results.

Behavioral treatment has proved more effective than alternative treatments for mild to moderate obesity. Weight loss is maintained well for at least a year, but five-year follow-ups show high rates of relapse. Other advantages of behavioral treatment are that it is safe, easily administered, and effective in reducing depression, enhances self-image, and improves cardiovascular functioning.

Bulimia nervosa afflicts mainly women and is characterized by binge-eating, purging, and excessive concern with body shape and weight.

This disorder is usefully conceptualized in terms of a cognitive-social learning model. Treatment includes restoring regular eating habits (e.g., three meals a day), challenging dysfunctional cognitions about food and weight control, developing self-control strategies, and using exposure and vomit prevention to increase clients' self-efficacy in coping with urges to binge or vomit. Behavioral treatment has produced superior results to pharmacotherapy, the other major form of treatment, including evidence of long-term improvement.

Anorexia nervosa is a life-threatening disorder, the treatment of which has been less successful than in the case of bulimia nervosa. The predominant behavioral approach has been operant conditioning. Especially in hospitalized clients, reinforcements have been made contingent on weight gain. Broader cognitive-behavioral methods are also used, but no controlled studies of their efficacy exist.

14

Alcoholism and Cigarette Smoking

ALCOHOL ABUSE AND DEPENDENCE[1]

Definition and Description

DSM-III distinguishes between alcohol dependence (usually called "alcoholism") and alcohol abuse. Both are defined by an inability to stop excessive drinking which seriously impairs social, economic, and occupational functioning. Alcohol dependence, in addition, is characterised by physical

1. In the first edition of this book we included a brief discussion of drug addiction (e.g., heroin, cocaine, etc.) in this chapter. We chose to leave out such a section from this edition for two main reasons. First, there is remarkably little research on behavior therapy for drug addiction and no empirical basis for concluding that behavioral treatment is superior to any other. Second, the behavioral conceptualization and treatment of drug addiction, in principle, follows the same logic and uses similar strategies as in the assessment and treatment of alcohol and cigarette smoking. Both alcohol and tobacco, of course, are potent drugs. For more detailed discussions of behavior therapy and drug addiction see Callahan (1980) and Callahan and Rawson (1980).

signs of addiction, such as tolerance and withdrawal symptoms. Tolerance refers to the need for significantly increased amounts of alcohol to achieve desired effects of intoxication. Withdrawal symptoms include morning shakes, nausea, and headaches after stopping or reducing alcohol consumption, symptoms relieved by resumption of drinking. The term "problem drinker," also commonly used in the literature, is roughly equivalent to the term "alcohol abuse" in DSM-III, and describes a wide range of individuals who experience life problems as a result of their alcohol consumption. Behavioral conceptualizations assume a continuum of problem drinking from mild disturbance at one end to the most serious disorder, alcoholism (alcohol dependence), at the other.

Impact and Incidence

Alcohol abuse and alcoholism are serious public health problems (U.S. Department of Health and Human Services, 1983). Beyond the countless personal human tragedies tied to alcoholism, in the United States the economic costs of alcohol-related problems as of 1977 were over $50 billion annually. Health care costs related to alcohol consumed 12 percent of this country's total adult health expenditures. Intoxication is involved in half of the fatal automobile accidents. Alcohol abuse and alcoholism are also significantly associated with suicide, homicide, wife and child abuse, and sexual violence.

Alcohol is the most widely used and abused drug in the United States. Surveys show that over two-thirds of the adult population drink at least occasionally. More men than women abuse alcohol, but the gap seems to be narrowing. By the time they are high school seniors almost all adolescents have drunk alcohol, and many have developed a drinking problem. About 12 million people are judged to be alcoholic.

A study of prevalence of psychiatric disorders in the general population in the United States has shown that alcoholism was most prevalent in men up to age 65. It was the fourth most prevalent disorder among women between the ages of 18 and 24. As the authors of this analysis state, "It would thus appear that treatments for alcoholism have a greater potential impact on society than those for any other psychiatric disorder" (Helzer, Robins, Taylor, Carey, et al., 1985, p. 1682).

Etiology and Nature

Genetic Influences

Alcoholism runs in families, a phenomenon explained by both genetic influences and social learning experiences. The evidence points to the genetic predisposition for alcoholism in many individuals. In the pioneering study, Goodwin, Schulsinger, Hermansen, Guze, and Winokur (1973) found that adopted sons of alcoholic fathers, compared to adopted sons of nonalcoholic fathers, proved three times more likely to become alcoholics. Moreover, the adopted sons of alcoholic fathers showed the same incidence of alcoholism as did their siblings who remained with the alcoholic father (Goodwin, 1985). Schuckit et al.'s (1972) study of alcoholics who had half-siblings showed that the half-siblings who were also alcoholic were three times more likely to have had an alcoholic natural parent than the nonalcoholic half-siblings. Subsequent studies have produced data consistent with genetic transmission of alcoholism in some individuals (Cloninger, Bohman, & Sigvardsson, 1981).

The foregoing studies included too few females to draw any conclusions about genetic transmission in female alcoholics. However, Bohman, Sigvardsson, & Cloninger (1981), in a study of Swedish women who were adopted by nonrelatives at an early age, found a significant increase in alcohol abuse in women whose biological mothers had been alcohol abusers. Alcoholic fathers did not have a comparable impact on their daughters as they had on their sons. Interpretation of the Bohman et al. (1981) study is complicated, since it is impossible to separate genetic influences from adverse effects the mothers' drinking may have had on their daughters during pregnancy.

The evidence on genetic determination of alcoholism has led to efforts to find behavioral or biological markers of vulnerability to alcoholism in individuals at risk for the disorder. Research has concentrated on the nonalcoholic individuals with a positive family history of alcoholism. Although the mechanisms by which an inherited tendency for alcoholism end up being expressed have not been established, individuals with a family history have been shown to differ from matched controls with no family history on some behavioral and biological dimensions (Schuckit, 1984).

The foregoing studies have also uncovered

evidence of the critical importance of socio-cultural influences. For example, in both the Bohman et al. (1981) and Cloninger et al. (1981) studies, a large percentage of identified alcohol abusers had no family history of alcohol abuse—as many as 60 percent in the Cloninger and colleagues study. Additional evidence that both heredity and social learning are determinants of alcoholism comes from rare longitudinal research, which is a powerful tool for exploring the etiology of a disorder. Vaillant (1983) has analyzed three longitudinal studies, comprising 700 men and women, 200 of whom ultimately were diagnosed as alcoholic, to examine the natural history of alcohol abuse. The individuals in these different studies were assessed at regular intervals on a wide range of measures of psychological adjustment, physical health, social and economic status, and alcohol use. Vaillant found three premorbid differences between alcoholics and nonproblem drinkers: (1) Alcoholics are "more likely to come from ethnic groups that tolerate adult drunkenness but that discourage children and adolescents from learning safe drinking habits" (p. 311), (2) Alcoholics are more likely to be related to other alcoholics, and (3) Alcoholics are "more likely to be premorbidly antisocial" (p. 311).

A Social Learning Analysis

Tension Reduction.   The initial learning theory explanation of alcohol abuse centered on the tension reduction theory (Conger, 1951). The notion that alcohol reduces tension and that people drink to obtain this effect is deeply ingrained in folklore and clinical experience. Brown (1985) found that college students' outcome expectations about the tension reducing effects of alcohol was the strongest predictor of problem drinking in this population. She also showed that alcoholics reported more

tension reduction effects of alcohol than nonproblem drinkers.

The tension reduction theory of drinking is based on two assumptions: that alcohol consumption reduces tension, and that this tension-reducing effect motivates drinking. With respect to the first assumption, any overview of the laboratory evidence must conclude that no consistent pattern of alcohol's effects on tension has been demonstrated. Alcohol has been variously shown to increase, decrease, or not affect tension (Wilson, 1982a). These apparently conflicting data are surprising only if it is assumed that there is an invariant relationship between alcohol and stress reduction. According to a social learning analysis, behavior commonly attributed to alcohol is related to it in a complex fashion. Among the many variables that determine the effect of alcohol on tension and other emotional states are the amount of alcohol that is consumed, the person's prior experience with alcohol, individual differences based on physiological responsiveness to ethanol and specific social learning histories, learned expectations about alcohol and its effects, and the social setting in which drinking occurs (Sher & Levenson, 1983; Wilson, 1982a). Alcohol consumption reliably reduces autonomic arousal (heart rate) and subjective indices of stress (anxiety) at a relatively high (.1g/kg.) dose but not at low levels (Levenson, Sher, Grossman, Newman, & Newlin, 1980; Wilson, Abrams, & Lipscomb, 1980). Alcohol consumed under stressful conditions seems to be more reinforcing for healthy, nonproblem drinking males rated at high risk for alcoholism on the MacAndrew alcoholism scale than for their counterparts at low risk (Sher & Levenson, 1983). This latter finding suggests that the stress-reducing function of alcohol may be a factor in the etiology of problem drinking.

The second assumption of the tension reduction theory is that this effect of alcohol motivates drinking. Higgins and Marlatt (1975) showed that anticipation of interpersonal evaluation produced significantly increased consumption of alcohol. Marlatt's (1985) analysis of the psychosocial determinants of relapse in alcoholics (discussed below) revealed that one of the major social stress experiences, accounting for almost a third of the relapses studied, was the experience of frustration and anger, often rising in an interpersonal context. Instead of expressing these feelings of anger or dealing with them in a constructive manner, patients began drinking again. In the laboratory Marlatt et al. (1975) demonstrated that both male and female social drinkers, when angered by a confederate in a work situation, drank significantly more alcohol than control subjects who were not angered. This study also investigated the consequences of allowing angered subjects to "retaliate" by asserting themselves with the confederate. Subjects allowed to retaliate drank significantly less than subjects without the opportunity to retaliate. These results indicate that heavy drinkers who are provided with an alternative means of coping with a social stress frequently associated with drinking will show reduced alcohol consumption.

Modeling.   Bandura (1969), in the first presentation of the social learning theory of alcohol use and abuse, noted that the tension reduction theory had been given too much explanatory weight in learning accounts and identified other powerful psychosocial influences, including modeling, differential reinforcement, and self-regulation. Modeling[2] is a powerful psychosocial influence on drinking. Both nonalcoholics (Collins & Marlatt, 1981) and alcoholics (Caudill & Lipscomb, 1980) significantly increase or decrease their

---

2. Also in 1969, MacAndrew and Edgerton published their anthropological analysis of drinking behavior in which they assigned an important role to modeling.

drinking as a function of the drinking rate of peers.

Reinforcement.   Numerous studies have shown that response-contingent positive consequences (reinforcement) reliably increase drinking, and negative consequences (punishment) decrease drinking in alcoholics (Wilson, in press a). A major contribution of the behavioral approach to the study of alcohol use and abuse was the development of behavioral measures of actual drinking by alcoholics and nonalcoholics in controlled laboratory settings (Mendelson & Mello, 1976; Nathan & O'Brien, 1971). In an example of this sort of study, Cohen, Liebson, Faillace, and Allen (1971) demonstrated that chronic alcoholics could, within a free operant situation, voluntarily restrict their drinking below five ounces per day if this moderation was positively reinforced by access to an enriched environment, as opposed to remaining in an impoverished environment. In the enriched setting a subject could earn money by working, use a private phone, eat a regular diet, obtain reading material, entertain visitors, and use the recreation room, which included television, a pool table and other games, and engage the nursing staff in conversation. Subjects drank significantly more during the periods in which the reinforcement contingencies were not in effect, even if they were allowed free (contingent) access to the enriched environment. These studies demonstrated that excessive drinking in alcoholics is, at least in part, a function of its reinforcing consequences.

These powerful social influences of modeling and differential reinforcement probably account for the differing rates of alcoholism among different ethnic groups. Chinese-, Jewish-, and Italian-Americans are much less prone to developing alcoholism than are Americans from Northern European descent.

These groups, as evidenced by Vaillant's (1983) findings, model and reward moderate drinking and disapprove of drunkeness.

Self-Regulation.   Behavior is not simply determined by external consequences, whether or not they are experienced directly or observed in connection with models. A major component of social learning theory is its emphasis on the self-regulation of behavior. Self-regulation helps explain the indisputable fact that human behavior is usually maintained and often altered in the absence of immediate external reinforcement (Bandura, 1985; Kanfer, 1977). In this motivational process, people make self-rewards or self-punishments conditional upon the attainment of specific standards of performance. The level of self-motivation generated by success or failure in matching self-prescribed standards will vary according to the specific

performance standards, the judgmental processes involved in evaluating performance, and the nature of the incentives. The performance standards themselves are a product of prior histories of differential reinforcement and modeling influences. Figure 14-1 summarizes the different component processes in the self-regulation of behavior through self-managed incentives. Dysfunctions in self-regulatory systems can explain some forms of abnormal behavior, including alcohol abuse.

Self-evaluative reactions are particularly important in the context of alcoholism because they serve as incentives that regulate socially accepted behavior. People usually strive to avoid personal actions that would elicit negative self-evaluative consequences. However, a given activity does not invariably lead to the same self-evaluative reaction in all people. Such reactions are selectively "activated" or "disengaged" depending upon the

SELF-OBSERVATION	JUDGMENTAL PROCESS	SELF-RESPONSE
Performance Dimensions	Personal Standards	Self-Evaluative Reactions
Quality	Modeling Sources	Positive
Rate	Reinforcement Sources	Negative
Quantity		
Originality	Referential Performances	Tangible Self-Applied Consequences
Authenticity		
Consequentialness	Standard Norms	Rewarding
Deviancy	Social Comparison	Punishing
Ethicalness	Personal Comparison	
	Collective Comparison	No Self-Response
	Valuation of Activity	
	Regarded Highly	
	Neutral	
	Devalued	
	Performance Attribution	
	Personal Locus	
	External Locus	

Figure 14–1 Component processes in the self-regulation of behavior. (Reprinted from Bandura, A. (1977). *Social learning theory*. Englewood Cliffs, NJ: Prentice-Hall. Reprinted with permission.)

person and the situation (Bandura & Cervone, 1985). According to this framework, negative self-evaluative reactions are most strongly activated when the causal connection between negatively sanctioned behavior and its adverse effects is clearly apparent to the person. Among the many means whereby the regulatory system of self-evaluative reactions can be disengaged is the attribution of responsibility to something or someone other than oneself. Alcohol is one such source of misattribution of personal responsibility (Wilson, 1981).

Relapse Prevention. Bandura (1969) emphasized that the evaluation of psychological treatments should distinguish among the initial induction of behavioral changes, their generalization to the natural environment, and their maintenance over time. Different variables may govern each of these processes, and generalization and maintenance can be ensured only to the degree that procedures explicitly designed to accomplish such objectives are built into the overall treatment program. Moos and Finney (1983) have shown that significant influences on treatment outcome include factors within the patient's family and work environments, both during and after treatment. For example, cohesion in the marriage and the family significantly enhances response to treatment during one- and two-year follow-ups. The work environment also affects outcome. Individuals satisfied with their jobs who perceive their work setting as involving and supportive appear to fare better. Individuals with secure families may be protected against the adverse impact of a stressful work setting. Moos, Finney, and Chan (1981) found that negative life events (e.g., deaths of friends or family) distinguish alcoholics who have relapsed compared to those who remain abstinent.

Marlatt (1985) has developed a social learning analysis of the psychological processes governing maintenance of behavior change in alcoholics and other addictive disorders. Marlatt's model is shown in Figure 14-2. Even after successful treatment, the abstinent alcoholic is faced with specific high risk situations. The model, in essence, states that the lack of a response for coping with a high-risk situation initiates a chain of events in which a decreased sense of self-efficacy leads to initial use of the alcohol. Initial consumption is even more likely to occur if the individual has positive outcome expectations for the effect of the substance.

A slip (consumption of alcohol) following a period of abstinence is likely to trigger a cognitive reaction to the transgression that Marlatt has termed the Abstinence Violation Effect (AVE). The AVE is a cognitive-affective reaction to an initial slip that influences the probability that the lapse will be followed by an increased use of the substance. There are two components to the AVE: a cognitive attribution of the perceived cause of the lapse coupled with an affective reaction to this attribution. An increased AVE is postulated when the individual attributes the cause of the lapse to internal, stable, and global factors that are perceived to be uncontrollable (e.g., lack of willpower and/or the emergence of the symptoms of an underlying addictive disease). The intensity of the AVE is decreased, however, when the individual attributes the cause of the lapse to external, unstable (changeable), and specific factors that are perceived to be controllable (e.g., a transitory deficit in coping with a specific high-risk situation). Negative (internal, stable) attributions undermine self-efficacy and increase outcome expectations of continued failure, a usually fatal combination of factors leading to resumption of substance abuse. Cognitive-behavioral treatments are designed to develop coping skills, restore self-efficacy, and

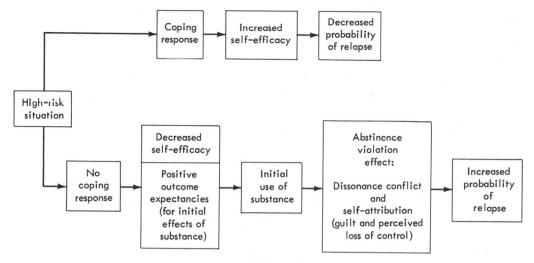

Figure 14–2 A cognitive-behavioral model of the relapse process. Reprinted from Marlatt, G. A., & Gordon, J. (eds.), (1985). *Relapse prevention.* New York: Guilford Press. Reprinted with permission.

create more constructive attributions. The latter would emphasize external (situational), unstable, and controllable causes of slips or failures. The usual strategy in cognitive behavior therapy is to encourage clients to attribute setbacks to external, unstable, and usually specific determinants, and successful coping to internal factors. Figure 14-3 summarizes some of the cognitive and behavioral methods for negating the AVE at different stages of a slip.

Social Learning Theory versus the Disease Concept

Why do alcoholics continue to drink despite serious negative consequences to their physical health, psychological well-being, and social functioning? And why, following a period of treatment-produced abstinence, do many alcoholics suddenly revert to dangerous drinking? The disease theory of alcoholism employs the concepts of craving and loss of control in trying to answer these questions.

Craving. Radical behaviorists have rejected the concept of craving as superfluous because it is inferred from the very behavior that it has been used to explain within the disease theory of alcoholism (Mello, 1975). A social learning analysis takes a broader view and redefines the concept of craving. The first drink is not an automatic, involuntary response forced upon the person by an overpowering physical demand for alcohol. Rather, the person desires and expects specific consequences, running the gamut from the reduction of aversive states (e.g., stress) to the attainment of positive states (e.g., sexual satisfaction) (Brown, 1985; Marlatt, 1984; Southwick, Steele, Marlatt, & Lindell, 1981). The abstinent alcoholic anticipates the positive or negative reinforcement that alcohol produces, or at least what he or she believes it produces. This anticipation is important, since the expectation of reinforcement may be as powerful as, if not more powerful than, actual reinforcement (Bandura, 1977b). This desire for reinforcement is assumed to be labeled by the alcoholic as craving for alcohol.

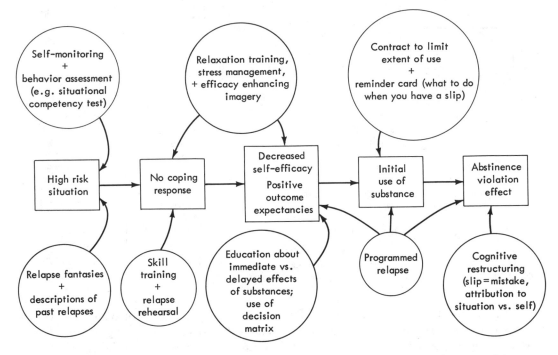

Figure 14–3 Relapse Prevention: Specific intervention strategies. (From Marlatt, G. A., & Gordon, J. (eds.), (1985). *Relapse prevention*. New York: Guilford Press. Reprinted with permission.)

In addition to expectations about alcohol's favorable effects, the alcoholic may experience conditioned reactions to environmental or emotional stimuli that have been associated with prior withdrawal states. Siegel (1982) has shown that a variety of environmental, emotional, and physiological cues can become conditioned stimuli that elicit the compensatory responses associated with the repetitive ingestion of alcohol. Classically conditioned compensatory responses are physiological reactions that are opposite in nature from the unconditioned effects of alcohol. For example, if alcohol consumption naturally decreases skin temperature, a compensatory reaction which tends to increase temperature and thus counteract the effect of alcohol, develops over time. Similarly, a drug that elicits a positive emotional state will also

later evoke a negative compensatory state. This reaction is partly responsible for what is known as acquired tolerance to drugs. These responses are classically conditioned to environmental cues that are associated with drinking. When the alcoholic who has stopped drinking is exposed to these cues, the compensatory reactions occur. Without the intoxicating effects of alcohol, these responses are experienced as aversive, and may be viewed as an important part of the psychobiological basis of craving and withdrawal symptoms.

Loss of Control According to the disease theory of alcoholism, once a drink is taken, craving is increased and the physical demand for alcohol overrides any cognitive or voluntary control (Jellinek, 1960). According to so-

---

Box 14–1

The logic of the balanced placebo design is as follows. In the past, studies of alcohol (indeed, all types of drugs) consisted essentially of comparisons between Groups I and II as shown in Figure 14-4. The actual drug was compared to a chemically inert placebo substance. Nevertheless, both groups expected that they had received the drug itself. Expectations were presumably equated but not systematically manipulated. Groups III and IV are necessary in order to study the independent effects of expectations about drug ingestion (Marlatt & Rohsenow, 1980).

	Receive Alcohol	Receive No Alcohol
Told Alcohol	I	II
Told No Alcohol	III	IV

Group I   : Receive Alcohol / Told Alcohol
Group II : Receive No Alcohol / Told Alcohol
Group III : Receive Alcohol / Told No Alcohol
Group IV : Receive No Alcohol / Told No Alcohol

Figure 14–4   The balanced placebo design.

---

cial learning theory, the consequences of one or more drinks for the abstinent alcoholic will, as in the case of any other behavior, be a function of the cognitive set of the alcoholic, the social setting in which drinking occurs, and the specific reinforcement contingencies in that environment. Nonproblem and problem drinking are viewed on the same continuum and are governed by the same cognitive processes and laws of learning (Marlatt, 1978; Wilson, in press a).

The Jellinek (1960) notion that alcohol in the blood stream automatically precipitates involuntary drinking ("one drink, one drunk") has been disconfirmed by experimental research. Marlatt, Demming, and Reid (1973) pioneered an innovative research methodology, including the balanced placebo design (see Box 14-1), to disconfirm the traditional loss-of-control concept. Nonabstinent alcoholics and matched social drinkers sampled and evaluated the taste of either alcoholic or nonalcoholic beverages during a taste-rating task. The only significant determinant of overall beverage consumption during the taste-rating test, and subjects' later estimates of the alcohol content of their respective drinks, was the expectancy factor. Regardless of the actual alcohol content of the drinks, both alcoholics and social drinkers consumed significantly more if they believed they were sampling drinks containing vodka. In a replication of this study, employing a broader range of dependent measures, Berg, Laberg, Skutle, & Ohman (1981) provided strong support for the influence of expectations on drinking by alcoholics. Berg et al. showed that alcoholics' responses to a small priming dose of alcohol was determined

> "by the expectancy of the drug effect rather than by the pharmacological properties of alcohol. The alcoholics showed reliable expectancy effects on the amount consumed, on rate of drinking, . . . on situational anxiety, . . . the experimenter's rating of craving, and on the psychiatrist's and nurses's ratings after the experiment" (p. 63).

These results demonstrate the importance of cognitive factors in regulating subsequent alcohol consumption in alcoholics following the first drink. They should not be taken to imply that the ingestion of alcohol itself is unimportant in this process. Using the balanced placebo design Stockwell, Hodgson, Rankin, and Taylor (1982) studied the responses of alcoholics to a priming dose of alcohol. Ten alcoholics were independently assessed by a psychiatrist as being severely dependent on alcohol and 10 as mildly or moderately alcohol dependent. The severely dependent alcoholics were more likely to drink after consuming a priming dose of alcohol as opposed to a nonalcoholic beverage, irrespective of what they believed the contents of the priming dose to be. The moderately dependent alcoholics, however, showed the reverse pattern, being more influenced by the instructional set they had been given than by the actual contents of the priming dose. The significance of these results is that the degree of physical dependence in alcoholics is shown to be a determinant of craving and loss of drinking control.

Treatment Effectiveness

Average Treatment Outcome

A broad spectrum of psychological and pharmacological treatment methods have been used to treat alcohol abuse and dependence. The efficacy of these diverse treatments is difficult to evaluate because the numerous controlled outcome studies vary widely in methodological quality, treatment specifications, subject populations, and outcome measures; systematic long-term follow-ups are relatively rare. Nonetheless, it is possible to reach some general conclusions regarding treatment outcome.

Effective treatments should improve upon the spontaneous remission rates or natural history of the disorder. Unfortunately, there is no agreed-upon spontaneous remission rate against which to compare behavioral treatments. Miller and Hester (1980) have estimated that an average of 19 percent of untreated problem drinkers/alcoholics are abstinent or improved after one year. Miller and Hester also estimated that on average, one third of problem drinkers/alcoholics become abstinent, and one third improve (but do not achieve abstinence) following treatment. Based on studies which included follow-up data, they concluded that only 26 percent of treated patients are successful (abstinence or marked reduction in drinking) twelve months after termination of therapy. Other assessments of treatment outcome are even less positive. Polich, Armor, and Braiker (1981), in an evaluation of 781 clients treated in public institutions in the United States, found that only 7 percent claimed to have maintained continuous abstinence over the course of a four-year follow-up.

Insight-oriented psychotherapy is contraindicated (Miller & Hester, 1980). Research has shown a high attrition rate in this form of therapy, with results that are either inferior to or no better than those achieved with more cost-effective methods (Edwards et al., 1977). Alcoholics anonymous (AA) is the largest and most popular source of alcoholism treatment in the United States, yet virtually no controlled research exists to support its efficacy. It is known that the dropout rate is very high, suggesting that the method is far from appropriate for all alcoholics.

Behavioral Treatments

Behavior therapy encompasses a variety of different methods, whose separate and interactive effects have been evaluated in numerous controlled studies.

Aversion Therapy. Electrical aversion conditioning has been shown to be ineffective in both controlled laboratory research and clinical outcome studies (Wilson, 1978a). Chemical aversion conditioning methods pair emetine, a nausea-inducing drug, with the sight, smell, and taste of alcohol, and have yielded abstinence rates of over 60 percent at one year after treatment (Lemere & Voegtlin, 1950; Wiens & Menustik, 1983). These results cannot be attributed to the specific effects of aversion conditioning, however, since they are confounded with patient selection and other nonspecific treatment influences (Bandura, 1969; Wilson, 1978).

Cannon and Baker (1981) compared the chemical aversion method with an electrical aversion conditioning and with a control condition. In addition, all subjects participated in a multifaceted alcoholism inpatient program which included individual and group therapy and assertion and relaxation training, among other components. The results showed that chemical but not electrical aversion conditioning produced an aversion to alcohol. Compared to the control group, alcoholics who received emetine conditioning exhibited greater increases in heart rate to alcohol flavors and reported more negative attitudes towards alcohol. Despite this successful conditioning of an aversion at post-treatment, six- and twelve-month follow-ups showed that

the chemical aversion conditioning group did not show greater abstinence from alcohol than the control group (Cannon, Baker, & Wehl, 1981). Chemical aversion conditioning did little to enhance the effects of the overall treatment program to which it was added, indicating that chemical aversion conditioning plays little or no role in long-term clinical outcome.

Cautela (1966) introduced the technique of covert sensitization, in which the alcoholic is instructed to imagine aversive consequences, i.e., nausea, in association with drinking. Evidence on this treatment is mixed. Wilson and Tracey (1976) failed to show a specific effect of aversive imagery on alcohol consumption in a controlled laboratory setting, but Elkins (1980) showed that clients who experienced physiological indications of nausea during covert sensitization tended to retain their sobriety. Olson, Ganley, Devine, and Dorsey (1981) found that a combination of covert sensitization and relaxation training added to the efficacy of an inpatient milieu therapy program up to eighteen months following discharge.

Exposure and Response Prevention. The concepts of craving and loss of control over drinking in alcoholics have been conceptualized as analogous to those of fear and avoidance behavior in phobic and obsessive-compulsive disorders (Hodgson, Stockwell, & Rankin, 1979). It follows that the exposure methods which have been so successful in the treatment of phobic and compulsive disorders might be applicable to alcoholics. Protracted exposure to cues that elicit craving and then alcoholic drinking might be predicted to extinguish craving and thereby remove the motivation for abusive drinking (Poulos, Hinson, & Siegel, 1981). Uncontrolled clinical studies of the effectiveness of exposure and response prevention with alcoholics are encouraging (Blakey & Baker, 1980; Cooney, Baker, &

Pomerleau, 1983). Rankin, Hodgson, and Stockwell (1983) showed that cue exposure and response prevention produced significant changes on behavioral and subjective measures of drinking in severely dependent alcoholics in a controlled laboratory setting.

Social Skills Training. Social skills training as a treatment for alcoholics was derived directly from basic clinical research and clearly illustrates the significance of the interplay between clinical work and experimental research in behavior therapy. Laboratory research had shown that heavy social drinkers consumed less alcohol when confronted with a stressful interpersonal situation if they were provided with an alternative coping strategy (Marlatt et al., 1975), as we have discussed. In a more applied study, Marlatt (1978) categorized the situations in which alcoholics relapsed. He found that relapse situations could be assigned reliably to the following types: (1) frustration and inability to express anger (29 percent), (2) inability to resist social pressure to drink (23 percent), (3) intrapersonal negative emotional state (10 percent), (4) inability to resist intrapersonal temptation to drink (21 percent), and (5) other (17 percent). Accordingly, Chaney, O'Leary, and Marlatt (1978) completed the following treatment outcome study. Hospitalized alcoholics were randomly assigned to three groups: a skill training group, a discussion group that focused on feelings such as anxiety and anger which inhibit effective assertiveness, and a control group that received the routine alcohol treatment program. The social skills program included modeling, therapist coaching, group feedback, behavioral rehearsal, and repeated practice, to teach each patient a variety of specific skills to cope effectively with high-risk situations. These were drawn from the categories of relapse situations identified by Marlatt (1978). Outcome measures included standardized tests of assertive behavior and a specially designed Situational Competency Test, administered both prior to and following the training program. In this test, subjects were instructed to respond verbally to a high-risk situation described on an audiotape. Their responses were scored for a number of components related to the quality and overall competence of the reply.

A one-year follow-up showed that the alcoholics who had received skill training showed a significant decrease in the duration and severity of relapse episodes compared to the other groups. In addition, performance on the post-treatment administration of the Situational Competency Test was found to be predictive of subjects' drinking behavior during the follow-up. Neither demographic data nor alcoholics' pre-treatment drinking history predicted outcome. Subjects who received social skills training showed progressive improvement during the follow-up. These data support a social learning analysis of treatment effects, which predicts better functioning as people increasingly cope more effectively with situations that previously had led to drinking. Presumably, subjects improved their coping skills as the year progressed. This pattern of post-treatment functioning contrasts with the traditional findings of gradual deterioration (relapse) as a function of time.

Multifaceted Treatment Programs. Contemporary treatment for alcoholics combines different procedures, such as social skills training, reinforcement, and self-control strategies in multicomponent programs. An example of such a multifaceted approach is Hunt and Azrin's (1973) community-reinforcement program, which made vocational, recreational, social, and familial reinforcers contingent upon continuing sobriety. Patients also received social skills training and behavioral marital therapy, when appropriate. Sixteen arbitrarily selected, hospitalized alcoholics were individually matched on the basis of employment history, family stability, and previous drinking history, then randomly assigned to either the community-reinforcement or the existing hospital-treatment program. A community maintenance program was instituted following a patient's discharge from the hospital, during which a counselor visited patients on a progressively less frequent basis to see that the procedures were continued and to deal with problems. These visits also served as a means of continuously monitoring the progress of the expatients in terms of number of days on which drinking occurred, days unemployed, and time spent away from home. These observations were checked against independent evaluations conducted by a reliable rater who was unaware that the patients had been treated differently.

The community-reinforcement approach was superior to the comparison treatment on measures of drinking, employment, and reinstitutionalization. These findings were replicated in a second study by Azrin (1976) that included a two-year follow-up. Although questions can be raised about the adequacy of the control groups in both studies, methodological strengths include the use of multiple measures of outcome, independent evaluation of success, and long-term follow-up.

Controlled Drinking as a Goal. The disease theory of alcoholism emphasizes above all else that the only way to recover from alcoholism is to abstain completely. Safe or controlled drinking by alcoholics is impossible. This is also the philosophy of Alcoholics Anonymous, the most influential form of treatment for alcoholism in the United States. However, in 1962, Davies, a British physician, reported that some alcoholics did maintain a long-term pattern of normal drinking following treatment. This challenge to entrenched beliefs about alcoholism initiated bitter controversy which, since the 1970s, has often been associated with the development of behavioral treatment for alcohol problems.

Research Evidence. The first major study which supported the feasibility of controlled drinking for some alcoholics was completed by Sobell and Sobell (1973). Seventy chronic male alcoholics who were inpatients at a state hospital were assigned to four different experimental conditions: a controlled drinking experimental group (CD-E), a controlled drinking control group (CD-C), a non-drinking experimental group (ND-E), and a non-drinking control group (ND-C). The two control groups received the conventional hospital treatment for alcoholics, such as large therapy groups, AA meetings, and drug therapy. The experimental groups received seventeen sessions of a multifaceted behavioral treatment program in addition to the routine hospital program. The behavior therapy sessions were devoted to making a detailed behavioral analysis and training the alcoholics to generate a series of alternative responses to problem situations.

Follow-up evaluations were obtained at each six-month interval during the first two years, then three years after the end of therapy. Estimates of daily alcohol consumption were gathered, with attempts made to corroborate subjects' reports by securing reports from significant others in the subjects' environment. For purposes of evaluating the results, abstinent and controlled drinking days (days during which six ounces or less of 86-proof liquor or its equivalent in alcohol content were consumed) were summarized as "functioning well"; drunk days (days on which ten or more ounces were consumed) or days during which subjects were incarcerated were summarized as "not functioning well." Both experimental groups were found to be significantly superior to their respective control groups in number of days functioning well at both the six-month and one-year follow-up evaluations. At the two-year mark the CD-E group was significantly different from the CD-C group. The differences between the ND-E and ND-C subjects approached but did not reach significance at either the eighteen-month or two-year follow-ups. Evaluation of adjustment to interpersonal relationships and problem situations revealed the same pattern of results as for drinking. Subjects in the CD-E group were classified as significantly more improved than CD-C group members at each follow-up over the two-year period. Subjects in the ND-E group were rated as significantly more improved than ND-C subjects during the first year, but not during the second year of follow-up. Unlike the one- and two-year follow-ups conducted by the original investigators, the three-year evaluation was an independently conducted, double-blind follow-up (Caddy et al., 1978). The results were consistent with those of the previous two years.

The limitations of this study have been noted elsewhere (Rachman & Wilson, 1980). For example, comparison between controlled drinking and abstinence as treatment goals is confounded by assignment to the controlled drinking groups of subjects who had "requested controlled drinking, had significant outside social support for such behavior, and/or had successfully practiced social drinking at some time in the past" (Sobell & Sobell, 1973, p. 54). Subjects assigned to the nondrinking conditions did not have much social support in the natural environment, which would explain the failure of ND-E subjects to continue to show superior improvement compared to control subjects over the second year of follow-up. The maintenance and generalization of treatment effects ultimately depends on the sources of reinforcement available

to support therapeutic behavior change. The strengths of the Sobells' study include the detailed, multiple measures of outcome (both alcohol consumption in particular and broader indices of personal functioning); their success in contacting well over 90 percent of their subjects for detailed follow-up evaluations; and long-term follow-up.

Different results were obtained by Foy, Nunn, and Rychtarik (1984), who treated chronic alcoholics with a multifaceted cognitive-behavioral treatment program. Half of the alcoholics received training in controlled drinking skills, half did not. During the first six months of follow-up, subjects in the controlled drinking condition experienced significantly fewer abstinent and more abusive drinking days than did their counterparts in the abstinence condition. These differences were no longer statistically significant during months seven to twelve of follow-up, although the trends persisted. Foy and colleagues attributed the less positive outcome in their study to the inclusion in their controlled drinking condition of more severely dependent alcoholics than in the Sobell and Sobell study.

Pendery, Maltzman, and West (1982) reported a ten-year follow-up of the twenty subjects in the CD-E group of Sobell and Sobell's (1978) study. This report, which disputed the possibility of controlled drinking and alleged that the Sobell and Sobell (1978) results were untrue, unleashed a major con-

---

3. On the basis of the Pendery et al. (1982) evaluation, Maltzman publicly accused the Sobells of fraud. In response, the Toronto Addiction Research Foundation, by whom the Sobells are employed, appointed a blue-ribbon panel of independent investigators to examine this allegation. The conclusion of this Committee (Dickens, Doob, Warwick, & Winegard, 1982) reads as follows: "The Committee has reviewed all of the allegations made against the Sobells by Pendery et al. in their draft manuscript, in their published papers authored by the Sobells as well as a great quantity of data which formed the basis of these pub-

troversy.[3] Pendery et al. (1982) claimed that their ten-year follow-up revealed that only one subject had maintained a pattern of controlled drinking. Eight continued to drink excessively, six abandoned their efforts to engage in controlled drinking and became abstinent, and four died from alcohol-related causes. Pendery et al. did not report follow-up data for the subjects in the CD-C group. Without this comparison standard, it is impossible to attribute these dismal long-term results either to controlled drinking or the Sobells' procedures. Even more damaging to the Pendery et al. (1982) argument is that six of the subjects in the abstinence-oriented group died (Sobell & Sobell, 1984). This is two more deaths than in the controlled drinking group, and is higher than the expected rate of mortality.

Although Pendery et al. claim that their evaluation contradicts the Sobells' two-year data, close examination of the two accounts reveals essential agreement. What is apparent is that the two groups of investigators interpreted the same findings differently. In referring to the greater number of hospitalizations and incarcerations of the CD-E than the CD-C groups during the first six months of follow-up, Sobell and Sobell speculated that this difference "might have been the result of voluntary hospitalizations among the experimental subjects, either to curb the start of a binge or to avoid starting drinking at all" (1973, pp. 65-66). Pendery et al. (1982) make

---

lished reports. After isolating each of the separate allegations, the Committee examined all of the available evidence. The Committee's conclusion is clear and unequivocal: The Committee finds there to be no reasonable cause to doubt the scientific or personal integrity of either Dr. Mark Sobell or Dr. Linda Sobell" (p. 109). A second investigation by a subcommittee of the U.S. Congress (since the research had been supported by federal funds) upheld the Dickens et al. report. Details of this controversy are summarized by Marlatt (1983).

the case that these rehospitalizations "were not isolated setbacks in persons with otherwise benign controlled drinking outcomes. Rather, they indicated the pattern of serious problems that characterized these subjects' continued attempts to practice social drinking" (p. 173).

In a major study, consisting of the results of an eighteen-month follow-up of alcoholics treated in forty-five centers in the United States, Armor, Polich, and Stambul (1978) concluded that "the majority of improved clients are either drinking moderate amounts of alcohol. . . .or engaging in alternating periods of drinking and abstention. . . .this finding suggests the possibility that for some alcoholics moderate drinking is not necessarily a prelude to relapse and that some alcoholics can return to moderate drinking with no greater chance of relapse than if they abstained" (p. 294). A four-year follow-up of this study confirmed the earlier findings and showed that approximately 18 percent of patients were drinking without problems, and that only 10 percent had remained abstinent for the entire four years. Helzer et al. (1985) have reported a far lower estimate of controlled drinking in 1289 alcoholics discharged from medical and psychiatric treatment facilities. Only 1.6 percent had been stable, moderate drinkers over a three-year period at a five- to seven-year follow-up. Only 15 percent were totally abstinent.

Miller (1983; Miller & Hester, 1980) developed a behavioral self-control treatment (BSCT) for problem drinkers, as opposed to alcoholics, in which the goal is moderate or controlled drinking. The program consists of self-monitoring of alcohol use, setting appropriate goals for drinking, self-reinforcement of safe drinking, and training in alternative coping skills to be used in situations which previously had triggered excessive drinking. This program has been extensively evaluated in a series of studies which have yielded consistent results.

Miller, Taylor, and West (1980) compared the BSCT program to a bibliotherapy condition, in which clients received self-help materials but no treatment sessions, and two treatments in which BSCT was supplemented by other behavioral methods, such as communication and assertion training. Broad assessment of outcome showed that all groups improved significantly on post-treatment drinking measures (based on subjects' self-report and self-monitoring and information from collateral sources). The only significant difference among treatments was that the bibliotherapy group was intoxicated (BAL 80 mg./percent) more hours per week than the others. The improvement rate of BSCT was roughly 70 percent (abstinent and controlled drinking). Miller and Taylor (1980) carried out a similar study to that of Miller, Taylor, and West (1980). A self-help manual was compared to the BSCT program and to the BSCT program with relaxation training. All groups showed significant improvement, but there were no differences among the groups.

Miller and Baca (1983) reported a two-year follow-up of the Miller et al. (1980) and Miller and Taylor (1980) studies. Of the eighty-two subjects, sixty-nine were interviewed and administered breathalyzer tests (all were negative). Total alcohol consumption during the three months preceding this assessment, as well as peak BALs during this period, were used as drinking measures. The major finding was that the significant improvements obtained on drinking and other measures were maintained at two years. More than 80 percent of the subjects showed improvement (abstinent or controlled drinking) at twenty-four months from any prior follow-up. Relapse rates from controlled drinking were similar to those from abstinent outcomes. Severity of problem drinking at intake remained the best single predictor of controlled drinking versus abstinent outcomes, with more severe cases tending toward abstinence. The finding that a behavioral self-control program for problem drinkers is equally effective when administered by therapists or self-administered via a detailed self-help manual has been replicated in three additional studies (Miller, 1982).

Sanchez-Craig, Annis, Bornet, and MacDonald (1984) compared the effects of a multifaceted cognitive-behavioral treatment with goals of either abstinence or controlled drinking in early-stage problem drinkers. Both treatment conditions produced significant reductions in alcohol consumption over a two-year follow-up, but did not differ from each other. Sanchez-Craig et al. concluded that, for this population, controlled drinking is the appropriate outcome goal because "it was more acceptable to the majority of the clients, and most of those assigned to abstinence developed moderate drinking on their own" (p. 390).

For Whom Is Controlled Drinking Appropriate?

Different studies carried out by different investigators have yielded a reliable pattern of results which makes it possible to answer this question. Miller (1982) has summarized the evidence as follows: "In general, clients who eventually succeed in moderating their drinking are those who are younger, have fewer alcohol-related life problems, have less family history of alcoholism, and show fewer signs of addiction and of medical deterioration. Those who become successful abstainers, on the other hand, show precisely the opposite characteristics. The picture that emerges is strikingly clear: the more advanced the drinking problem, the poorer the chances of achieving moderation and the greater the advisability of abstinence. With early stage problem drinkers, on the other hand, prognosis is generally better with moderation-oriented programs than in traditional abstinence-oriented methods" (p. 17).

Conclusion. The evidence shows that behavior therapy is an effective form of treatment for both problem drinking and alcoholism. In most cases, the outcome of behavior therapy has been clearly superior to the average nonbehavioral treatment baseline rate described. The consistent success rate of 60 percent to 80 percent achieved by behavioral self-control programs with problem drinkers suggests that it is the preferred treatment for these individuals, especially if the goal is controlled drinking. Behavior therapy has proved superior to alternative treatments, especially routine hospital treatment, in several studies (e.g., Hunt & Azrin, 1973; Pomerleau, Pertschuk, Adkins, & Brady, 1976). Nevertheless, comparative outcome studies are too few and lacking in necessary controls to permit firm conclusions about the greater efficacy of behavior therapy over other psychological methods.

Prevention

Effective efforts at preventing alcohol abuse have lagged far behind concern with treatment of alcoholism. Alcohol education programs have usually been ineffective, and even the better ones have produced changes only in attitudes towards alcohol. They have failed to change drinking behavior (Nathan, 1983). The content of public education about alcohol must be firmly based on the best available knowledge and conveyed effectively. Social learning research has yielded important findings that should be an important part of any public education effort. Even more significantly, social learning theory prescribes effective ways for disseminating knowledge and influencing people's drinking behavior. For example, take the way alcohol consumption is depicted on television: one of the most potent forms of social influence on behavior (Rubenstein, 1983).

Singer (1983) points out that "children spend more time in the U.S. watching television than they ever spend in school" (p. 815). Citing the 1982 NIMH report on "Television and Behavior," Senator Heinz (1983) draws attention to the fact that "prime-time television programs watched by children present each year about 3,000 instances of drinking alcoholic beverages. Should we be surprised that one of this nation's greatest health problems is alcohol abuse?" (p. 817). Empirical research on the specific impact of television on drinking habits is minimal, as Collins and Marlatt (1981) note. They do, however, refer to Lowery's (1980) finding that drinking is portrayed as a major positive reinforcement with no deleterious consequences.

Take beer advertising for example. Consumer Reports (1983) notes that the "money spent on beer advertising in almost all media rose from $92.7 million in 1972 to $406.5 million in 1982—an increase of 338 percent" (p. 348). The companies show a keen appreciation of social learning principles as well as the power of the dollar. The Miller Brewing Company has used former athletes as influential models drinking Miller Lite. As Consumer Reports notes, "if drinking Lite beer was the thing for Mickey Mantle, then drinking Lite must be okay for everyone else." And it works. The success of Lite beer, the magazine continues, "represents the ultimate achievement of advertising—being able to sell a lower-cost product at a high price" (p. 349).

Advertising is targeted at young drinkers, particularly the large college audience, even though many in that audience are still below the legal drinking age. Techniques include heavy advertising in college newspapers, sponsorship of campus events, and free distribution of beer ("reinforcer sampling" in the argot of operant conditioning).

The message is not confined to advertising, but pervades other heavily watched television fare. In "Dallas," the top-ranked program on commercial television in the United States in recent years, J.R. Ewing can frequently be seen reaching for a drink (without mixers) at any time and in any place (including his office). In one scene, following a stressful family conflict J.R. took a glass of champagne only to have his macho father declare, "I need something stronger than that"—to cope with the stress, one assumes. Here drinking for the most dangerous reasons is modeled and given a verbal label, thereby enhancing an already powerful modeling effect.

The same influences can be used to encourage moderate drinking under appropriate situational constraints as part of a proactive public health policy based on social learning principles. For example, Marlatt (1985) compared a skills training program based on social learning theory with an alcohol information program and a no-treatment control group in a controlled evaluation of secondary prevention methods for high-risk drinkers in a university. The skills training program was significantly more effective in modifying both the amount and pattern of alcohol consumption.

Societal efforts have been made to decrease some forms of alcohol abuse, such as drunk driving, by manipulating broad classes of response contingencies. Nathan (1983) points out that several states have raised the legal drinking age to reduce alcohol-related accidents, although the results are not clear-cut. Drunk driving laws have also been introduced, but inconsistent implementation of the law over time has attenuated their inhibitory impact. Consistency is a crucial element of an effective reinforcement program. Several countries have tried to decrease alcohol consumption by manipulating the price of alcohol. The evidence of a direct link between price change and reduction in alcohol abuse is lacking, however.

CIGARETTE SMOKING

Impact and Incidence

Cigarette smoking is the single most important cause of preventable death in the United States (U.S. Department of Health and Human Services, 1983). Smoking causes 80 percent of lung cancer in men, and lung cancer kills more people in the United States than does any other malignant disease. Even more disturbing, smoking is a greater risk factor for heart disease than is hypertension. In the United States a smoker is 70 percent more likely to die at a given age than is a comparable nonsmoker. Other hard facts are that maternal smoking during pregnancy increases the risk of stillbirth or infant death by at least 20 percent, even in light smokers (less than one pack a day). A synergistic relationship exists between smoking and alcohol use that greatly increases the risk of cancer of the larynx, oral cavity, and esophagus for those who smoke and drink heavily. A woman who smokes and uses birth control pills is twenty times more likely to suffer stroke by cerebral hemorrhage than a woman who does neither. Stopping smoking reduces or eliminates these negative health consequences.

Smoking is hazardous even for nonsmokers who breathe the same air: the evidence shows that passive smoking is hazardous, especially to children of smokers (U.S. Public Health Service, 1983). In 1980, 33 percent of the adult population smoked regularly—a decline from a figure of 43 percent in 1966. It is estimated that between 12 percent and 30 percent of teenagers smoke, even though the majority know the dangerous health consequences of smoking.

Etiology and Maintenance

There is a consensus that the onset of smoking, typically in adolescence, is a product of psychosocial influences. What maintains smoking is still a matter of controversy. One explanation is that smokers become addicted to nicotine (Schachter, 1978). In a review of the relevant research, Moss and Prue (1982) concluded that available evidence does not permit any firm conclusions. Based on the assumption that nicotine dependence maintains smoking, nicotine chewing gum has been developed to relieve smokers' physical need for nicotine as they quit inhaling it. Supplementing smoking cessation programs with this chewing gum produces superior results to a program plus a placebo (Lichtenstein, 1982). Nevertheless, although studies have shown that nicotine gum reduces withdrawal symptoms (Schneider & Jarvik, 1984), it is unclear whether it is the specific pharmacological action or psychological effect of the gum that is responsible.

A Social Learning Analysis

Behavioral assessment and treatment has been guided by the standard social learning approach to behavior change, with its emphasis on identifying and modifying the antecedants and consequences of smoking. Tracing the evolution of behavior therapy for smoking, Lichtenstein (1982) notes that "Initial naivete (a simplistic conditioning view of smoking as a simple habit) has given way to data and theory that describe a complex and tenacious phenomenon" (p. 805). In addition to behavioral self-control and reinforcement

strategies, current assessment and treatment is informed by a broader cognitive and social perspective (Bandura, 1985; Marlatt & Gordon, 1985; Shiffman, Read, Maltese, & Rapkin, 1985).

Evaluation of Treatments

Aversion Therapies

As in the treatment of alcohol dependence, different types of aversive stimuli have been used to decondition the attraction of cigarette smoking. Neither electric shock (Russell, Armstrong, & Patel, 1976), nor covert sensitization (Barbarin, 1978) has proved effective. The most effective aversive method has been rapid smoking, a procedure conducted in the clinic in which subjects are instructed to smoke continually, inhaling every six seconds until it proves too aversive to continue (Lichtenstein, Harris, Birchler, Wahl, & Schmahl, 1973).

The majority of studies on rapid smoking have yielded positive results. Danaher's (1977b) review showed that of fourteen studies in which rapid smoking was compared to a placebo condition or an alternative treatment, it was more effective in producing long-term abstinence in ten, although its superiority was not statistically significant. The best results have been reported by Lichtenstein and his group at the University of Oregon. A two- to six-year follow-up of subjects in the first four studies completed by this group showed that, compared to an abstinence rate of 54 percent at post-treatment, 34 percent of subjects were now abstinent (Lichtenstein & Rodrigues, 1977). This figure represents an improvement over the more typical 15 percent to 20 percent abstinence rate in most programs at a one-year follow-up. Yet several well-controlled studies have failed to show that rapid smoking is more effective than alternative methods (e.g., Raw & Russell, 1980). The explanation for these mixed results is not clear, although Hall, Sachs, Hall, and Benowitz (1984) have emphasized that the procedure has been implemented under different conditions. They stress the importance of individualized treatment within the context of a supportive therapeutic relationship, and proscription of smoking between clinic-based rapid smoking sessions. Following these procedures they obtained results comparable to those of Lichtenstein et al. (1973).

The side effects of rapid smoking include increases in heart rate and blood nicotine levels. However, research has shown that nicotine poisoning is highly unlikely (Russell et al., 1978), and Hall et al. (1984) proved that rapid smoking is both effective and safe even in the treatment of smokers with cardiopulmonary disease. At twelve- and twenty-four-month follow-ups, an impressive 50 percent of their patients were abstinent, compared to 0 percent in a waiting list control group. They concluded that the "frequency of arrhythmias during rapid smoking was less than during normal smoking or maximal exercise" (p. 578). In 1977, Lichtenstein and Glasgow estimated that rapid smoking had been used with approximately 35,000 individuals with no known serious consequences and relatively few reports of notable side effects" (p. 809). Nonetheless, both Lichtenstein and Glasgow (1977) and Hall and colleagues (1984) make it clear that certain smokers with heart problems should not receive this treatment, and recommend specific screening procedures to ensure its safety.

Multifaceted Programs

Most current programs consist of a number of strategies, especially behavioral self-control methods, similar to broad treatment programs for obesity and alcoholism. Among the more typical intervention strategies are self-monitoring of smoking, appropriate goal-setting, self-evaluation and reinforcement, and stimulus control. Relaxation training is often taught as a substitute behavior and a skill for coping with stress. The rationale for these programs, as in the treatment of other disorders, is that smoking is determined by complex variables which differ from person to person. No single method is likely to "fit" the needs of everyone.

Some studies have shown that multifaceted programs improve upon single methods such as rapid smoking (e.g., Lando, 1977), while others have not (e.g., Danaher, 1977a). Franks and Wilson (1978) have cautioned that "more is not always better" (p. 409) when it comes to treatment. Complex programs with too many components might confuse clients, undermine their commitment, and lead to reduced compliance (see Chapter 15). The most effective programs include rapid smoking as a component. The most systematically evaluated multifaceted program without an aversive component was that used in the multiple risk factor intervention trial (MRFIT). The methods used included both behavioral and health education tactics for middle-aged men at risk for cardiovascular disease (Hughes, Hymowitz, Ockene, Simon, & Vogt, 1981). Subjects were randomly assigned to usual care or active treatment including maintenance visits and repeat programs for relapsers. The intervention group achieved a 46 percent abstinence rate, confirmed with biochemical measures[4] after four years, compared with 27

---

4. Measures of smoking are typically based on smokers' self-report of number of cigarettes smoked. Since self-report is open to deliberate or unwitting bias, researchers have developed more objective indices of smoking. One way is to measure the amount of carbon monoxide in a person's breath. Another measure is the assessment of thiocyanate in either blood or saliva samples. Its advantage is that any smoking during the preceding 14 days will be detected.

percent for the usual care condition (Neaton et al., 1981).

Controlled Smoking and Nicotine Fading

Controlled smoking involves changing the rate, topography, even the nature of what is smoked. It was proposed as an alternative to abstinence for two reasons: (1) some people wish to smoke less but not quit, and (2) controlled reduction might benefit those who are unable to quit. Glasgow, Klesges, Godding, and Gegelman (1983) evaluated a controlled smoking procedure aimed at producing 50 percent reductions in the nicotine content of the brand of cigarette smoked, the number of cigarettes smoked per day, and the percentage of each cigarette smoked. They found significant changes in self-reported smoking and levels of carbon monoxide in subjects' breath, which were maintained at three- and six-month follow-ups. Subjects were more successful in changing brands than in reducing number and percentage of cigarettes smoked.

It appears that controlled smoking produces changes in smoking behavior that may be maintained better than smoking cessation programs. But do these changes reduce health risks? The concern is that people may change to lower tar and nicotine cigarettes, but smoke more cigarettes or draw more heavily on each puff, thereby negating any beneficial effect of treatment. Lichtenstein (1982) has concluded that "Abstinence remains the preferred goal but the extension of controlled smoking to larger and more diverse populations seems warranted" (p. 19).

Nicotine fading involves the gradual reduction of nicotine intake by switching to low nicotine cigarettes and reducing the number of cigarettes smoked on a systematic basis from week to week. Generally clients quit smoking within three to five weeks. The gradual reduction of nicotine is designed to minimize withdrawal symptoms. Foxx and Brown (1979) reported 40 percent abstinence at an eighteen month follow-up, with the remaining 60 percent smoking cigarettes lower in tar/nicotine content than their original brands. Beaver, Brown, and Lichtenstein (1981) found nicotine fading produced less long-term abstinence in a follow-up study. A more discouraging finding is reported by Brown, Lichtenstein, McIntyre, and Harrington-Kostur (1984). They compared a nicotine fading procedure to a treatment based on Marlatt's relapse prevention model. All subjects received training in standard self-control strategies. No difference was found between these groups at post-treatment or follow-up. Abstinence levels were only 15 percent and 9 percent at six- and twelve-month follow-ups.

Nicotine chewing gum has been shown to reduce the withdrawal symptoms of smokers trying to quit, as we have noted. Gottlieb, Killen, Marlatt, and Taylor (1986) used the balanced placebo design to test whether it is the gum's effect on nicotine depletion or the person's expectations about the role of the gum that causes this beneficial effect. Smokers attempting to quit received either nicotine gum or placebo gum. Half of each of these groups were told that they were receiving the gum, the other half that they were receiving the placebo. Subjects who believed that they had been given nicotine gum reported fewer withdrawal symptoms and smoked fewer cigarettes during the first week of quitting than those who thought they had the placebo gum. The real content of the gum had no affect. These results argue against the nicotine dependence view of the maintenance of cigarette smoking, and underscore the role of cognitive-social learning factors in the maintenance and modification of smoking.

Maintenance

As with obesity and alcoholism, the central problem in the treatment of cigarette smoking is maintenance of behavior change over time, i.e., preventing relapse. Success in producing long-term maintenance is greatly aided by identifying the determinants of relapse. Studies using Marlatt and Gordon's (1980) classification scheme have produced some differences, but are consistent in showing that negative affect (frustration, stress) and social pressure are overwhelmingly the most important precipitants of relapse (Cummings, Gordon, & Marlatt, 1980; Shiffman, 1982). A significant finding from Shiffman's (1982) analysis of the reports of 183 ex-smokers who called a stay-quit hotline is that withdrawal symptoms played little role in precipitating relapse and were rated as absent about 50 percent of the time. This pattern of findings suggests that the key to successful long-term smoking cessation lies not so much in the molecular study of the psychobiological processes involved in smoking (Pomerleau, 1979), but in modifying the broader psychosocial influences which largely determine relapse.

Periodic booster sessions following treatment are ineffective (Elliot & Denney, 1978), as they are in the maintenance of weight reduction. However, recent research has identified both the determinants of relapse and strategies for preventing it.

Coping Responses. Shiffman (1982) found that the extent to which ex-smokers used cognitive and behavioral coping responses was the major determinant of relapse. Ex-smokers who did not cope showed a relapse rate two-and-a-half times that of those who did try to cope. Among those who used coping responses, cognitive strategies (e.g., reminders of how hard it was to quit, images of health consequences) seemed more important (Shiff-

man, Read, Maltese, & Rapkin, 1985). Consistent with these results, Abrams, Monti, Pinto, Elder, Brown, and Jacobs (1985), in a controlled laboratory study, found that smokers who had quit showed better coping skills in high-risk smoking situations than relapsers did.

Social skills training was evaluated as a means of preventing relapse in a study by S. Hall, Rugg, Tunstall, and Jones (1984). All smokers received an aversive smoking treatment in which they smoked a maximum of three cigarettes per session with a puff rate of either every six or every thirty seconds. With the limit on three cigarettes, both of these conditions are less stressful physiologically than the usual form of rapid smoking, with the thirty-second pacing differing little from normal smoking topography. In addition, smokers in each of these aversive smoking conditions were assigned either a social skills or a discussion control treatment. The social skills treatment consisted of cue-produced relaxation training (see Chapter 15), in which smokers were taught to cope with anger and anxiety by using relaxed breathing in response to a word such as "calm," to use carbon monoxide feedback to underscore the dangers of cigarette smoking and enhance commitment to quitting, and to role-play coping responses for use in situations that typically triggered smoking.

Results showed that following treatment, smokers who received the relapse prevention training reported greater use of coping skills than their counterparts in the discussion control treatment. Also, the relapse prevention skills training produced superior abstinence rates and reductions of cigarettes smoked over a one-year follow-up. Abstinent subjects in both treatment conditions were more likely to use coping skills than nonabstinent subjects. This latter finding is consistent with Shiffman's (1982) findings as noted above. Skills training was especially effective with subjects who smoked less than twenty cigarettes a day at pre-treatment. S. Hall et al. (1984) suggest that this type of intervention, based on changes in habit patterns, is most suited to smokers who are not severely dependent on nicotine.

Programmed Relapse.   Based on his relapse prevention model, Marlatt (1978) predicted that supervising clients through a "controlled relapse" might inoculate them against the subsequent AVE or loss of control. Applied to smoking, this procedure entails a newly abstinent client deliberately smoking a single cigarette in the treatment setting, and then analyzing his or her reactions with the therapist. Cooney and Kopel (1980) compared a programmed relapse condition to an absolute abstinence condition in which the importance of avoiding even the slightest slip was stressed. Although clients in the programmed relapse condition reported greater self-efficacy and decreased craving after the "relapse," they did not show superior maintenance to the absolute abstinence condition. Shiffman et al. (1985) suggest that this procedure instills false confidence in clients, and that "confidence without competence produces failure" (p. 479). The challenge, as Bandura (1985) points out, is to foster a sense of self-efficacy based upon realistic coping ability.

Efficacy and Outcome Expectations.
Several studies have shown that efficacy expectations at post-treatment are predictors of relapse (DiClemente, 1981; Killen, Maccoby, & Taylor, 1984; McIntyre, Lichtenstein & Mermelstein, 1983). In contrast, a measure of physical dependence on nicotine did not differentiate relapsers from those who abstained. Demographics and past history of smoking also fail to predict relapse in smokers. The importance of self-efficacy is best

illustrated in a study by Condiotte and Lichtenstein (1981), who completed a three-month follow-up of seventy-eight smokers from two smoking cessation programs. Adapting the methodology used by Bandura (1977a) in his research on snake phobics, Condiotte and Lichtenstein (1981) obtained efficacy ratings on each of forty-eight situations found to be particularly problematic for cigarette smokers. Subjects were provided with this forty-eight-item list, and instructed to designate, on a 100-point probability scale ranging in ten-interval units, the probability that they would be able to resist the urge to smoke in that situation if they were to try to quit smoking at that time. These measures were made before, during, and immediately after treatment.

Predictably, efficacy ratings increased from pre- to post-treatment. Of special significance, however, was the finding that efficacy expectations at the end of treatment predicted maintenance of successful abstinence from smoking over the follow-up period. The greater the level of perceived self-efficacy at the completion of treatment, the greater was the probability that subjects would remain abstinent throughout the entire experimental period. A microanalysis of the data showed that those situations about which subjects expressed the lowest self-efficacy immediately following treatment were the situations in which they relapsed during the follow-up period. The correspondence between those smoking situations, in which subjects experienced low self-efficacy, and the situations in which they relapsed was an impressive 0.89. Subjects high in self-efficacy reinstated self-control strategies following a slip, whereas those low in efficacy showed a decrease in self-efficacy and abandoned self-control. As Condiotte and Lichtenstein conclude, "for the clinician involved in the treatment of addictive disorders, the ability to predict, through the use of a low-cost instrument, those specific situations in which clients might encounter great difficulty remaining abstinent, might be invaluable. Self-efficacy assessment during the course of treatment could be used to identify those areas toward which the greatest therapeutic effort should be addressed" (p. 657).

Resisting relapse requires not only positive but realistic efficacy expectations, but also appropriate internal standards must be set against which to evaluate performance (success or failure). Too stringent or too absolute a set of goals (e.g., "I can never make a slip") will set up clients for the AVE (Bandura, 1982; Marlatt & Gordon, 1985). The probability of a slip must be anticipated and planned for in treatment.[5] Shiffman et al. (1985) give an example of this type of anticipation and planning in smokers. Since alcohol consumption has been shown to be one of the most powerful causes of relapse in smokers, especially in social settings, Shiffman et al. point out that clients might plan to limit their alcohol intake should they attend a social function.

Social Support. According to social learning theory, the greater the degree of social support individuals have for making a change in their behavior, the more likely they are to be successful in the long run. Ockene, Benfari, Nutall, Hurwitz, and Ockene (1982) found that successful ex-smokers received more social support than those who failed to quit. Adapting a strategy used in the behavioral treatment of obesity, Mermelstein, Lichten-

stein, and McIntyre (1983) evaluated the effect of including spouses in a smoking cessation program. They found that a measure of spouse helpfulness was positively correlated with smoking status at a six-month follow-up.

In another parallel with current research on obesity, smoking cessation programs have been introduced and evaluated in worksite settings (Abrams, Elder, Lasater, Carleton, & Artz, 1985; Glasgow, Klesges, Godding, Vasey, & O'Neill, 1984). Initial results are promising, with Abrams et al. (1985) reporting abstinence rates of 54 percent at posttreatment and at a three-month follow-up.

Conclusion

The average outcome of treatment programs has been estimated at roughly 20 percent long-term abstinence (Bernstein & Glasgow, 1979). In many instances, behavioral programs have produced superior results and have made more systematic the assessment and treatment of smoking. Nevertheless, Lichtenstein (1982), in a restatement of McFall's (1978) verdict four years earlier, concluded that "we still have not achieved consistent, effective cessation programs for the motivated smoker" (p. 815). In speculating about what should be done, Lichtenstein (1982) suggests that an emphasis be placed on individual differences in nicotine dependence. But degree of nicotine dependence is a poor predictor of relapse.

A more effective strategy is to switch tactics and concentrate on broader psychosocial influences on smoking than intensive treatment programs. Leventhal and Cleary (1980) have advocated this approach.

> "It is usually assumed that intensive, individual therapy can generate the most significant impact on smoking, but the opposite may in fact be true. Intensive efforts to alter societal, community, and group values and norms might be

5. Note that this social learning analysis of maintenance or relapse is critical not only in helping smokers, but also in treating a range of other disorders, including agoraphobia (Chapter 9), bulimia (Chapter 13) and alcoholism. This commonality of core cognitive processes across so many disorders underscores the breadth and utility of a social learning approach to behavor change.

more effective in producing change in smoking behavior. Restricting smoking in public buildings, requiring nonsmoking sections in airplanes and restaurants, and changing attitudes about the rights of nonsmokers might do more to change smoking habits than intensive procedures aimed at individuals" (p. 381).

Prevention

Intervention in the Schools

Attempts to prevent teenagers and adults from starting to smoke have taken different forms. One promising approach has been to intervene in the schools. Smoking is strongly affected by social factors, the two most important sources of social influence being the family and the peer group (Evans, 1979). Family members and peers who smoke increase significantly the probability that a teenager will smoke. Teenagers themselves report that peer pressure is the major reason for starting to smoke, and junior high school seems to be the period during which smoking is usually initiated. These facts have led investigators to intervene in the junior high school years with programs based on social learning principles, designed to enable vulnerable teenagers to resist social pressure and other psychosocial determinants of smoking.

Initial efforts centered on the use of principles such as self-monitoring of smoking, role-playing in classrooms to teach students to resist invitations to smoke, and films in which peers encountered and successfully resisted social pressure (Evans, Rozelle, Mittlemark, Hansen, et al., 1978). The rationale was to inoculate teenagers against the future effects of social pressure to smoke. This basic approach was expanded by researchers at Stanford University in developing the Counseling Leadership Against Smoking Pressure (CLASP) program. The key elements of this program are as follows:

1. The program does not emphasize the negative effects of smoking on health.

2. It exposes students to the social pressures they will face in other situations and teaches them specific skills to deal with the pressures.

3. Teams of high school students teach the junior high school students the skills necessary to resist pressure. (Peers are thought to be more powerful models and reinforcers of behavior than adults.)

4. Behavioral methods of modeling, behavioral rehearsal, and role playing are the predominant teaching methods, as opposed to the lectures, movies, and worksheets used in other programs.

5. The program is administered in an entire school in the hope that a nonsmoking environment will be created.

The effects of this program were evaluated by McAlister, Perry, Killen, Slinkard, & Maccoby (1980) in a study of junior high school students. It was administered over a two-year period and included information on smoking and drug and alcohol abuse. The students receiving the CLASP program began smoking at one-half the rate of students who received no training. As shown in Figure 14-5, follow-ups at nine, twenty-one, and thirty-three months showed that the difference in favor of the program was actually increased (Telch, Killen, McAlister, Perry, & Maccoby, 1982). Other studies have corroborated the effectiveness of this type of early intervention program (Hurd, Johnson, Pehacek, Bast, et al., 1980).

The Media

We have already referred to the use of televised smoking cessation programs to reach large numbers of smokers in a cost-effective manner (Danaher, Berkanovic, & Gerber, 1983). The media can also play an important role in prevention efforts. An instructive example of this approach is the Stanford

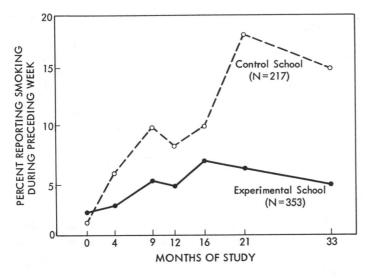

Figure 14–5 Changes in the reported prevalence of weekly smoking from a longitudinal observation of two study cohorts. The experimental school received a smoking prevention program and the control school received no program. (From "Long-Term Follow-Up of a Pilot Project on Smoking Prevention with Adolescents" by M. J. Telch, J. D. Killen, A. L. McAlister, C. L. Perry, and N. Maccoby (1982). *Journal of Behavioral Medicine, 5,* 1–8. Copyright 1982, Plenum Press. Reprinted by permission.)

Heart Disease Prevention Program's three-community study. A multimedia campaign was carried out for two years in two California communities, in one of which a supplemental face-to-face intervention program was added for high-risk subjects. A third community served as the control group. There was a 12 percent increase in smoking in the control community over the two-year period, yet there was a 5 percent decrease in smoking in the media-only community and a 17 percent decrease in the community with both the media and face-to-face interventions. There was a statistical difference between the intensive treatment and control communities, but not between the media-only and control communities. This program indicates that the media can contribute in unique fashion to the prevention and treatment of smoking.

SUMMARY

Alcohol is the most widely used and abused drug in the United States. Alcoholism is the most prevalent psychiatric disorder in the general population in the United States in men up to age 65. It is also a major problem among women. Both genetic determinants, particularly in males, and social learning influences are responsible for the development of alcoholism.

Drinking reduces anxiety, a negative reinforcing effect that motivates use and abuse of alcohol. Modeling has a strong influence on the initiation, maintenance, and modification of alcohol consumption. Similarly, contingent reinforcement and punishment has been shown reliably to alter the amount and pattern of drinking in alcoholics. Drinking is also regulated in part by the role of cognitive factors, including self-evaluative reactions, expectations, and attributions.

Although alcohol is a powerful drug, its consumption alone does not necessarily produce craving or loss of control in alcoholics. Social learning influences, such as the person's beliefs about alcohol's effects, contribute to these phenomena. Accordingly, these social learning influences have to be addressed in treatment.

A variety of behavioral methods are used in the treatment of problem drinking and alcoholism. Among the methods shown to be effective are reinforcement procedures, different self-control strategies, aversive imagery, and social skills training. Treatment programs typically combine these methods in a multifaceted approach.

Behavioral methods may be used to promote either abstinence or controlled drinking as a treatment goal. Controlled drinking is appropriate only for younger, problem drinkers who are not physically dependent on alcohol. Behavior therapy is superior to nonbehavioral treatments with this population of problem drinkers. Abstinence is the required goal for older, physically dependent alcoholics. Here the superiority of behavior therapy over other approaches has not been reliably demonstrated.

The prevention of alcohol abuse and alcoholism has lagged behind treatment efforts. A social learning analysis, especially of the influential role of television in shaping drinking practices, suggests several means of affecting alcohol consumption.

Cigarette smoking kills. The onset of smoking, in adolescence, is a product of social learning. Of the several behavioral methods that have been used to treat smokers, rapid smoking and self-control methods have been shown to be effective. Nicotine fading helps some but not all smokers, many of whom prefer to go "cold turkey." Both cognitive and behavioral coping strategies enhance the maintenance of smoking cessation. Successful treatment increases self-efficacy, and these efficacy ratings predict relapse better than estimates of nicotine dependence. Smoking prevention programs in the schools have significantly reduced smoking.

15

Behavioral Medicine

DEFINITION AND ORIGINS

One of the most important developments associated with behavior therapy in the late 1970s was the emergence of the field of behavioral medicine. Following their success in treating traditional psychiatric problems, behavioral investigators turned their attention to the assessment and treatment of medical disorders (e.g., heart disease, hypertension, and pediatric problems) that had been beyond the purview of traditional psychiatry. Significantly, many members of the medical community welcomed these contributions of behavior research and therapy. Blanchard (1982), in his analysis of the origins of behavioral medicine, stated, "It was, in my opinion, the reliability of the intervention procedures that sparked the growing interest and the acceptance of the psychological treatments by the more biologically but empirically oriented general medical community" (p. 795). This observation explains why behavioral principles and procedures have had relatively little impact on traditional psychiatry but have

been readily accepted by branches of medicine such as oncology, cardiology, and pediatrics. These medical specialties are empirically based and pragmatic, characteristics which behavior therapy shares.

Agras (1982) has also underscored the importance of behavior therapy in the development of behavioral medicine. He points out that the field of psychosomatic medicine had, since the 1940s, tried to relate research in the behavioral sciences to the practice of medicine, but with little success. The reason was that psychosomatic medicine, drawing upon largely psychodynamic views of personality, focused more on interpretations of why different people developed medical disorders than on the modification of these disorders. It was not oriented to intervention. Moreover, traditional methods of verbal psychotherapy were ineffective. Behavior therapy, by contrast, focused on intervention and brought to bear several clearly effective methods for changing behavior related to medical problems and disease.

Blanchard (1982) also credits the development of biofeedback in the 1970s with being an important precursor of behavioral medicine. Biofeedback, which developed within a broad behavioral approach to the direct modification of physiological responses (e.g., blood pressure), lent itself readily to the assessment and treatment of different physical problems.

Another indication of the intimate relationship between behavior therapy and behavioral medicine is that the Society of Behavioral Medicine was founded in 1978 and developed in close alliance with the Association for Advancement of Behavior Therapy, before it became an independent organization in 1981. So obvious is the influence of behavior therapy on the development of behavioral medicine that many authors define behavioral medicine in terms of the application of learning principles and procedures, or behavioral methods, to medical problems (e.g., Ferguson & Taylor, 1980; Melamed & Siegel, 1980; Pomerleau & Brady, 1979). Nevertheless, although behavior therapy has always had, and continues to have, a seminal influence on behavioral medicine, the field extends beyond the application of behavioral principles and procedures to encompass a much broader range of biobehavioral science research from a number of basic and applied fields (e.g., social and physiological psychology, medicine, and epidemiology, among others). A widely accepted definition of behavioral medicine, viewed within this broader context, is offered by Schwartz and Weiss (1978): "Behavioral medicine is the interdisciplinary[1] field concerned with the development and integration of behavioral and biomedical science knowledge and techniques relevant to health and illness and the

application of this knowledge and these techniques to prevention, diagnosis, treatment, and rehabilitation" (p. 250).

INTERVENTION METHODS

In this section we concentrate on two classes of the most commonly used methods for treating different problems within behavioral medicine: biofeedback and relaxation techniques. We wish to emphasize, however, that virtually all current psychological methods for preventing or treating medical disorders are based on the principles of behavior therapy. These principles define a common set of intervention strategies across widely differing problems. Basic behavioral procedures such as self-monitoring the occurrence of a particular problem or behavior, the functional analysis of the relevant antecedent and consequent variables, cognitive-behavioral analyses of compliance, and many behavior change techniques (e.g., modeling, reinforcement, self-control) are standard practice in behavioral medicine. Social learning principles are involved not only in the content of the actual intervention methods (e.g., self-control strategies and reinforcement procedures), but also in dictating how these methods can be effectively disseminated and implemented (e.g., use of the media in primary and secondary prevention efforts). Investigators who try to alter behavior that exposes people unnecessarily to health hazards invariably draw heavily upon social learning principles and procedures.

Biofeedback

Until the late 1960s, it was believed that visceral responses, e.g., heart rate or blood pressure, which were mediated by the autonomic nervous system, could be classically

---

1. A commitment to the interdisciplinary nature of the field leads us to prefer the term "behavioral medicine" to "health psychology," which is also widely used (Matarazzo, 1982), but which too narrowly emphasizes psychology only.

conditioned, but not brought under direct instrumental control, using operant conditioning procedures. Then, in a celebrated program of research, Miller (1969) showed that operant conditioning could directly modify autonomic responses.

The typical experiment to demonstrate operant control of autonomic responses in rats is one in which spontaneous fluctuations in an autonomic response, such as heart rate, are shaped or followed by reinforcing consequences, if they are in the desired direction. Under these conditions the rat can learn to increase or decrease heart rate—a physiological function previously considered "involuntary." In these experiments, the rat is curarized, which paralyzes the skeletal muscles, and maintained on artificial respiration to exclude alternative explanations of the observed changes in heart rate by the indirect effects of skeletal activity or altered respiratory patterns. The rats are rewarded either by direct electrical stimulation of rewarding areas in the brain or by termination of mild electric shocks to the tail. Rats have been trained either to increase or to decrease heart rate. Training different groups of rats to change heart rate in opposite directions controls for any classical conditioning process and for other effects of the procedure.

Following Miller's ground-breaking research, the use of operant conditioning procedures to modify physiological responses in people became known as biofeedback (Shapiro & Schwartz, 1972). An impressive range of human physiological functions has been modified by operant-feedback methods including heart rate speeding, slowing, and stabilizing; electrodermal activity; systolic and diastolic blood pressure; skin temperature; peripheral vasomotor responses; EEG rhythms; and penile tumescence (Miller, 1978; Schwartz & Beatty, 1977). The interpretation of these results was more controversial than

in animals, because it is more difficult to rule out explanation of results, such as changes in heart rate, in terms of indirect mediating influences like breathing and other skeletal responses. From a practical viewpoint, however, the specific mechanism of change was less important than the fact that different autonomic responses, which were involved in medical disorders (e.g., high blood pressure), now seemed amenable to modification.

Enthusiasm for biofeedback rapidly outdistanced empirical data on its efficacy, and it was uncritically heralded as a wonder treatment for disorders such as hypertension, headache and migraine, and other stress-related problems. The excitement and confidence shared by the early proponents of biofeedback, who believed that it represented a revolutionary advance in our ability to regulate psychobiological processes, obviously enhanced the placebo value of biofeedback methods. Unfortunately, as has all too often been the case in psychological treatments (Rachman & Wilson, 1980), subsequent controlled research has not fulfilled the ambitious claims made for biofeedback (e.g., Katkin, Fitzgerald, & Shapiro, 1979).

Here we illustrate the application and evaluation of biofeedback methods in behavioral medicine with reference to the treatment of tension headache, migraine, and hypertension.

Tension Headaches. A survey by Leviton (1978) indicated that headache was the third most frequent complaint in a prepaid medical plan, while among the general population, 31 percent of males and 44 percent of females reported severe headache. A study of college students revealed that over 50 percent suffered from headaches at least once or twice a week (Andrasik, Holroyd, & Abell, 1979).

A distinction is made between tension headache and migraine. Tension headache "is typically characterized by persistent sensations of bandlike pain or tightness located bilaterally in the occipital and/or forehead regions. It is gradual in onset and may last for hours, weeks, or even months" (Holroyd, Andrasik, & Westbrook, 1977). The exact etiology of tension headaches is not clear,[2] but in the past there has been general agreement that it might result from sustained contraction of skeletal muscles of the face, scalp, neck, and shoulders in response to psychological distress (Ad Hoc Committee on the Classification of Headache, 1962).

Biofeedback treatment of tension headache has generally been seen as one of the most successful applications of biofeedback (Birbaumer, 1977). This treatment involves auditory or visual feedback regarding muscle tension, called electromyographic (EMG) feedback. The typical procedure is to attach an electrode to the frontalis muscle area (the forehead) and provide clients with continuous visual or auditory information signalling reduction in muscle tension. This electronic feedback is then faded out as progress is made. Experimental studies have shown that EMG feedback is often effective, but no more so than alternative psychological treatments, such as progressive relaxation training or cognitive coping strategies. For example, Cox, Freundlich, and Meyer (1975) compared the effects of EMG feedback and relaxation, progressive relaxation alone, and a placebo (glucose capsule) treatment with three groups of patients. On the basis of frontalis EMG recordings, headache frequency and duration and amount of medication needed, the biofeedback and relaxation groups were superior to the pla-

cebo groups, although not different from one another.

Holroyd et al. (1977) compared the efficacy of frontalis EMG biofeedback training with "stress coping training" for tension headaches. Stress coping training emphasized that tension headaches result from stress and that stress responses are determined by cognitions about an event. Unreasonable expectations (for example, "I should be perfect and liked by everyone") were discussed and viewed as stress-producing. Clients were encouraged to view their headaches as being due to "cognitive aberrations," rather than external factors or an inner disposition to become stressed. They were taught to employ self-statements designed to minimize stress (for example, "Calm down," "Concentrate on the present," "There is no point in catastrophizing"). The biofeedback and stress coping training groups were compared with a waiting list control group; only the stress coping group showed a significant decrease in headache frequency when compared to the waiting list group. A two-year follow-up revealed good maintenance of improvement among subjects treated with the cognitive method, with an overall improvement rate of roughly 80 percent. Holroyd et al. (1977) found that only the biofeedback group showed significant reductions in frontalis EMG activity and that reduction in frontalis tension was not associated with headache improvement for either treatment group.

EMG biofeedback is effective in reducing tension headaches, but its mechanism of action is still debated. The original explanation was that this feedback reduced the muscle tension that mediated the headache. As noted above, however, muscle tension does not seem to mediate headaches, and successful treatment of tension headache is often unrelated to changes in frontalis muscle tension (Philips & Hunter, 1981). Biofeedback might work

---

2. This distinction between tension headache and migraine has been questioned (Philips, 1978), and Blanchard and Andrasik (1982) conclude that available empirical data show that psychophysiological measures do not reliably differentiate between the two groups.

not because it directly produces changes in physiological responsiveness (the original rationale of biofeedback treatment), but because it produces changes in cognitive mechanisms which then mediate reductions in headache (Meichenbaum, 1976).

Holroyd, Penzien, Hursey, Tobin, et al. (1984) tested two different explanations of biofeedback's effects on individuals who suffered from tension headache. (See Figure 15-1.) They randomly assigned forty-three subjects to one of four EMG biofeedback training conditions. Although all subjects were led to believe they were learning to decrease frontal EMG activity, actual feedback was contingent on decreased EMG activity for half of the subjects and increased EMG activity for the other half. Within each of these groups, half of the subjects were given bogus feedback indicating that they achieved high success, and the other half low success. Regardless of actual changes in EMG activity, subjects receiving high-success feedback showed substantially greater improvement in headache activity (53 percent) than subjects receiving moderate-success feedback (26 percent). The high-success feedback group showed significant increases in self-efficacy and greater internal locus of control scores, which were correlated with reductions in headache frequency following treatment. Changes in EMG levels during biofeedback training were unrelated to treatment outcome. This pattern of findings suggests that biofeedback may achieve its effects via cognitive rather than direct physiological mechanisms.

Migraine.   Migraine is described as "recurrent attacks of headache, widely varied in intensity, frequency, and duration. The attacks are commonly unilateral in onset, are usually associated with anorexia and, sometimes, with nausea and vomiting; in some are preceded by, or associated, with, conspicuous sensory, motor, and mood disturbances; and are often familial" (Blanchard & Andrasik, 1982). Migraine occurs most frequently in women and is often associated with stress and menstrual onset. It is generally felt that discomfort is caused by dilation of arteries, thus increasing blood flow to the brain.

Biofeedback treatment of migraine headaches has been designed to teach patients to warm their hands through temperature feedback. The general notion is that patients who learn to regulate skin temperature are thereby learning to moderate excessive sympathetic nervous system activity (Dalessio, Kunzel, Sternbach, & Sovak, 1979). Experimental studies have shown that, as in the case of tension headache, biofeedback is effective but no more so than relaxation training (Attfield & Peck, 1979; Blanchard, Theobald, Williamson, Silver, & Brown, 1978). There is no difference in efficacy between finger temperature biofeedback and EMG feedback. A study of the long-term (one year) maintenance of therapeutic effects of biofeedback and progressive relaxation training on both migraine and tension headache clients who had been successfully treated showed good maintenance of improvement (Andrasik, Blanchard, Neff, & Rodichok, 1984). Consistent with findings in the treatment of obesity and cigarette smoking, there was no advantage in special booster sessions over monthly contacts during the first six months of follow-up and at the end of one year.

Hypertension.   Hypertension, or high blood pressure, is a major risk factor for cardiovascular disorders (heart disease and stroke) and renal disease. It affects as many as twenty-three million people in the United States. Known as the "quiet killer" because it is asymptomatic (sufferers are unaware of it unless they have their blood pressure checked), hypertension is a chronic, life-threatening

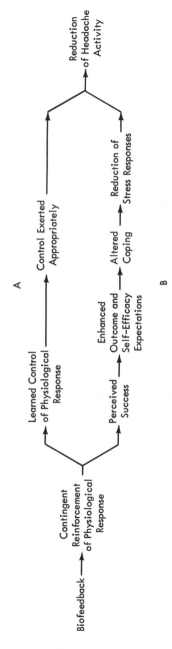

Figure 15–1 Two models of therapeutic change in EMG biofeedback training. (From Halroyd, K. et al. (1984). *Journal of Consulting and Clinical Psychology, 52,* 1039–1053, Figure 1. Copyright 1984 by the American Psychological Association. Reprinted by permission.)

disorder which can, however, be controlled through different pharmacological and non-pharmacological treatments. Any diastolic blood pressure of 90 mm Hg or above calls for treatment of some kind. Hypertension involves multiple genetic, physiological, psychosocial, and dietary factors. The result, as Shapiro and Goldstein (1982) observe, is that hypertension is a textbook example of the sort of disorder which fits the biobehavioral framework of behavioral medicine.

The treatment of hypertension involves a complex array of physiological, psychosocial, and dietary factors. Standard medical treatment is via different drugs developed to control blood pressure. These drugs are effective in lowering blood pressure, but may have negative physiological and psychological side effects (e.g., impotence). A substantial number of patients do not comply with instructions for taking antihypertensive drugs. Among the nonpharmacological approaches to treatment, weight loss reliably reduces blood pressure; hence weight reduction is a major means of controlling hypertension among the obese. A change in diet, such as reducing intake of sodium, is also a common initial treatment (Pickering, 1982). Excessive alcohol consumption is associated with hypertension, so stopping drinking may be an effective move for appropriate individuals. Increased physical exercise has also been shown to reduce high blood pressure (Martin & Dubbert, 1985).

Biofeedback aimed at direct control of high blood pressure involves providing patients with information regarding blood pressure on each heart beat. Although several studies have revealed clinically useful reductions in blood pressure using biofeedback (e.g., Blanchard & Miller, 1977), others have shown negative results (e.g., Surwit, Shapiro, & Good, 1978). Even when biofeedback has been effective, there is little evidence of long-term maintenance once treatment is discontinued. Goldstein, Shapiro, Thananopavarn and Sambhi (1982) compared biofeedback, relaxation training, standard drug treatment, and a control method consisting of self-monitoring of blood pressure, in the treatment of patients with mild hypertension. The drug treatment produced significantly greater reductions in blood pressure measured in patients' homes than the other methods did. Laboratory measures of blood pressure indicated that biofeedback was as effective as drug treatment. This finding underscores an important point about the treatment of hypertension. When and in what situation should blood pressure be assessed? Recent research has shown that blood pressure assessment at home or at work is the most sensitive in predicting health problems (Shapiro & Goldstein, 1982).

In summarizing the status of biofeedback treatment of hypertension, Agras and Jacob (1979) concluded, "biofeedback of blood pressure has no greater clinical effect than relaxation therapy, thus, the extra investment in blood pressure feedback equipment would seem unwarranted unless more sophisticated and powerful methods are developed" (p. 225).

Other Disorders. Biofeedback has been applied to a wide range of problems, including neuromuscular disorders (e.g., cerebral palsy), asthma, anxiety, and heart problems such as premature ventricular contractions. In all cases the same verdict reached by Agras and Jacob for hypertension applies: biofeedback treatments have not been shown to be more effective than simpler relaxation methods.

Raynaud's disease is a potentially serious disorder in which blood flow to the periphery of the body is restricted because of spasms in the peripheral blood vessels. Medical treatment usually necessitates major surgery or the use of powerful drugs with side effects. Both skin temperature biofeedback and simpler relaxation methods are effective treatments, although they do not differ in efficacy. Surwit (1982) concluded that "patients receiving such training report up to a 50 percent reduction in symptom frequency following training, and increases in basal digital temperature of 3°C to 4°C. These results are impressive, and they parallel the best clinical effects of many medical and surgical interventions" (p. 930).

Temporomandibular joint (TMJ) pain is a musculoskeletal disorder characterised by pain in front of the ears and around the jaw. Limitation of mouth movement, headache, and tinnitus (ringing sounds in the ear) are other common symptoms. EMG biofeedback and relaxation training have proved to be equally effective treatments. Funch and Gale (1984), in a two-year follow-up of the effects of these treatments, confirmed that they produce comparable rates of improvement; however, they also found indications that the two methods are effective with different clients. Relaxation training was more effective with younger subjects who had had prior equilibration treatment (i.e., dental grinding of the teeth for better occlusion).

Conclusion. Biofeedback is no more effective than alternative forms of relaxation training. Several critics have therefore concluded that in terms of cost-effectiveness, the simpler relaxation methods which do not require expensive electronic equipment are to be preferred to biofeedback treatment (Agras & Jacob, 1979; Silver & Blanchard, 1978; Surwit, 1982). Finally, it is important to note that whatever its immediate therapeutic benefits, and these are still being debated, biofeedback is a valuable research tool which facilitates

the detailed analysis of the functional role of psychobiological processes in behavior.

Relaxation Methods

Wolpe's (1958) technique of imaginal systematic desensitization is described in Chapter 8. The relaxation component, which Wolpe assumed would help to inhibit the client's unrealistic anxiety, was adapted from a method described by Edmund Jacobson (1938) called progressive relaxation. Jacobson's progressive relaxation training had gone virtually unnoticed before Wolpe introduced it into the behavior therapy literature. Although research subsequently showed that relaxation training was not a critical component of systematic desensitization or of successful fear reduction in general (Marks, 1981), relaxation training became an important therapeutic method in its own right for a variety of other problems.

Progressive relaxation consists of teaching an individual to alternately tense and relax different muscle groups of the body in a systematic fashion. By engaging in this tensing-relaxing procedure, the person learns to become especially attentive to feelings of tension and to substitute feelings of relaxation for the tense state. The method used in behavior therapy differs in many fundamental aspects from Jacobson's original technique (Bernstein & Given, 1984; Woolfolk & Lehrer, 1984). The typical behavior therapy version is brief (it may be taught in four to ten sessions) and emphasizes suggestion of relaxation (and therefore has a cognitive thrust). Jacobson's technique takes months, even years to master and is an exclusively somatic method based on acquiring the skill of muscle relaxation.

In its initial use in systematic desensitization (Wolpe, 1958), progressive relaxation training was administered as a series of exercises that would automatically reduce anxiety. Goldfried and Trier (1974) showed that the use of progressive relaxation as an active coping skill, in which clients were trained to implement it as a self-control strategy, produced superior results. It is as an active coping skill that progressive relaxation is now routinely used in behavior therapy. Cue-controlled relaxation involves associating a word such as "calm" or "relax" with muscle relaxation, on the assumption that the word then becomes capable of eliciting relaxation in different settings. Anxiety management training (AMT) combines relaxation training with a cognitive intervention (Suinn & Richardson, 1971). This approach combines training in live progressive relaxation with deep breathing and imagining a relaxing scene. In addition, clients are trained to imagine anxiety-provoking scenes and to use their relaxation skills to reduce the anxiety elicited. Clients also are trained to recognize "early warning" signs of stress, to use their relaxation skills when these occur, and to relax while they are imagining the anxiety scene, without avoiding it. (The Butler et al. [1984] study of social phobics described in Chapter 8 illustrates the use of AMT).

Although progressive relaxation is the most widely used method of relaxation training in behavior therapy, another approach, transcendental meditation (TM), has been studied in some of the behavior therapy literature. Benson (1975) developed a simplified form of TM in which the person gets comfortable in a quiet environment, assumes a passive attitude, and repeats a word or mantra with each exhalation. He called this simple method the "relaxation response," and it is this form of TM that has typically been used in treatment studies in behavioral medicine.

Progressive Relaxation. The section on biofeedback described how progressive relaxation has proved as effective as biofeedback methods in the treatment of problems such as headache, hypertension, Raynaud's disease, and TMJ pain. For example, in the treatment of hypertension, progressive relaxation has been shown to be superior to well-designed attention-placebo control conditions (Jacob, Kraemer, & Agras, 1977). Progressive relaxation often produces clinically significant reductions in blood pressure, depending on the pre-treatment level. Jacob et al. (1977) recommend the use of progressive relaxation only as a complement to medication, when drugs alone do not produce an optimal blood pressure or when drug side effects call for a decrease in the amount of medication taken.

Relaxation training also appears to be useful in the treatment of panic and generalized anxiety disorders (Barlow et al., 1985; Lehrer, 1978; Waddell, Barlow, & O'Brien, 1984). Positive results have also been reported for the treatment of blood phobias (Ost, Lindahl, Sterner, & Jerremalm, 1984) and social phobias (Ost et al., 1981). Progressive relaxation methods are, however, ineffective in the treatment of agoraphobia and obsessive-compulsive disorders (Marks, 1981; Rachman & Hodgson, 1980). (See Chapters 8 and 9.)

Other important therapeutic applications of relaxation training include the treatment of insomnia and the control of aversive reactions to chemotherapy in cancer patients. Progressive relaxation is more effective than stringent placebo control conditions in treating insomnia, especially when EEG rather than self-report is used as the measure of improvement (Borkovec, 1982). Knapp, Downs, and Alperson (1976), in their review of the literature, concluded that "Almost any variant of relaxation training produces statistically significant reductions in latency to sleep onset and a reduction in number of awakenings" (p. 623).

As many as 25 percent of cancer patients treated with chemotherapy acquire conditioned aversive (nausea) reactions to this treatment. They experience profound nausea and vomiting before drug administration, often in response to approaching the hospital, seeing the nurse who gives the injection, or even talking about the chemotherapy. Antiemetic drugs used to control this anticipatory or conditioned nausea are often ineffective. Accordingly, psychological procedures, including hypnosis and variations of relaxation training and guided imagery, have been used to counteract this nausea. Relaxation is the primary component of these procedures and has been shown to produce reliable reductions in distress (Redd & Andrykowski, 1982). Moreover, the effects of relaxation treatment appear to be superior to nonspecific factors, such as expectations of help and the nurse-patient relationship (Lyles, Burish, Krozely, & Oldham, 1982).

Live Versus Taped Training. It has become popular to teach relaxation by having clients listen to audiotapes of progressive relaxation instructions. Although convenient, teaching progressive relaxation via audiotapes has been shown to be inferior to relaxation taught by a live therapist. Taped relaxation instruction usually does not result in better results than control conditions (Borkovec & Sides, 1979; Lehrer, 1982).

Two explanations of the superiority of therapist-administered relaxation training have been put forward. Paul and Trimble (1970) suggested that the immediate feedback plus response-contingent pacing (going at the pace of the individual client) accounts for it. Lehrer and Woolfolk (1984) conclude that the re-

sponse-contingent element of live training alone cannot account for the difference, and suggest that nonspecific factors in the therapist-client relationship might contribute to the discrepancy.

Do Different Relaxation Methods Have Different Effects? Benson (1975) maintains that all relaxation methods have the same general effect—what he has called the "relaxation response." Schwartz, Davidson, and Goleman (1978) take another view, arguing that different methods have different and specific effects on different problems. Schwartz et al. (1978) classified alternative relaxation methods as to whether they were mainly cognitive or somatic in nature. For example, they classified TM as a cognitive method and predicted it would be most effective when applied to problems predominantly cognitive in nature. Biofeedback was classified as a somatic technique designed to alter directly the person's physiological functioning. Accordingly, biofeedback was predicted to produce greater somatic or physiological change. Progressive relaxation, too, was seen as suitable particularly for somatic problems. It should be apparent to the careful reader that this attempt by Schwartz and colleagues (1978) to match specific treatments with particular response systems represents the same type of thinking as the three response system analysis (Hugdahl, 1982) and Lazarus's (1981) multimodal therapy. As discussed in Chapter 8, both the three response systems analysis and multimodal therapy encounter problems that complicate their attempt to match a particular treatment modality with a comparable response system. Schwartz and colleagues' (1978) conceptualization fares little better.

As we have seen, biofeedback methods do not necessarily achieve their effects by directly altering physiological systems. There is evidence suggesting that they might indirectly affect these response systems via more primary cognitive changes (Holroyd et al., 1984; Meichenbaum, 1977). Another prediction from this conceptualization, which similarly is inconsistent with the data, is that a cognitive method like TM will produce the most cognitive change. Lehrer and Woolfolk (1984), in their comprehensive review of the literature on this topic, conclude that meditation does not have greater cognitive effects than progressive relaxation or biofeedback treatments. And while the same authors found that progressive relaxation and biofeedback had "slightly more powerful somatic effects" than meditation, there are a number of mixed findings. Moreover, there is little reliable evidence that progressive relaxation or biofeedback have greater somatic effects than cognitive therapy (e.g., Holroyd et al., 1984; Lehrer & Woolfolk, 1984). Finally, the Schwartz et al. specific effects view must predict that different methods would have differential effects on the treatment of different disorders, yet as we have pointed out, there is no reliable evidence that biofeedback-induced relaxation differs from progressive relaxation in the treatment of any disorder.

Despite the problematic results summarized above, Lehrer and Woolfolk (1984) conclude that "various relaxation techniques do have some distinguishing differences in their effects, but that these effects are superimposed upon a large (and often clinically much more significant) global relaxation response" (p. 463). These authors also state that a combination of different relaxation techniques, or relaxation training combined with a cognitive treatment, provides the most effective intervention.

Progressive Relaxation versus Meditation. Although there is little difference between these two methods in therapeutic efficacy, two related findings are of clinical impor-

tance. First, studies have shown that clients tend to find meditation more satisfying and continue to practice it for a longer time than progressive relaxation (Lehrer, Woolfolk, Rooney, McCann, & Carrington, 1983; Marlatt & Marques, 1977). Second, meditation may produce more negative side effects than progressive relaxation (Lehrer, Schoicket, Carrington, & Woolfolk, 1980; Lehrer et al., 1983). More people report sensations of transient anxiety during meditation than during progressive relaxation. This is consistent with the heightened physiological arousal and reactivity sometimes found in meditation. Heidi and Borkovec (1984) refer to this phenomenon as "relaxation induced anxiety" (RIA), and also report that it occurs more often during meditation. Although the explanation of RIA remains obscure, the practical solution to this unfortunate side effect is simply to switch to another form of relaxation (Heidi & Borkovec, 1983).

COMPLIANCE

It's a truism that drug therapies will not work unless patients take their medication or that other medical regimens will be unsuccessful when patients do not follow their doctor's orders. Compliance (often referred to as adherence) may be defined as "the extent to which a person's behavior (in terms of taking medications, following diets, or executing lifestyle changes) coincides with medical or health advice" (Haynes, 1979, pp. 2–3). The emergence of behavioral medicine has focused renewed attention on facilitating compliance with health-related behavior. In the process, the integration between psychosocial influences and biomedical science has been fostered.

The significance of noncompliance with medical and behavioral treatments can be gauged from the following selective examples. Hypertension can be controlled by the use of medication, yet McKenney (1981) reports that only 50 percent to 60 percent of hypertensive patients in treatment comply with their prescribed drug regimens. In a review of the literature, Ley (1977) found that only about half of all medical patients follow their doctors' advice, even when that advice has major health consequences. Diabetics often do not take their insulin as prescribed; psychiatric patients with bipolar depression frequently do not take their lithium (with adverse effects: Kocsis & Stokes, 1979); and on and on.

Facilitating Compliance

Chapter 18 provides a social learning analysis of therapeutic resistance (or noncompliance) and outlines several cognitive-behavioral strategies for facilitating better compliance with the therapist's instructions concerning behavior change. In the present chapter we confine the discussion mainly to cognitive-behavioral principles and procedures used to promote compliance with health-related behavior. These strategies, used to facilitate compliance with taking medication and other health-promoting behavior, include self-control procedures, reinforcement methods, a variety of cognitive interventions, and social support.

Keep Instructions Simple. A consistent finding in the literature on compliance with medical regimens is that as the complexity of the treatment increases, compliance decreases (Blackwell, 1976; Dunbar & Stunkard, 1979). Ley (1977) presents evidence indicating that at least part of the problem may stem from patients' failure to understand and remember what their doctor tells them. In one study, patients of general practitioners

had forgotten 50 percent of the statements made to them within five minutes of seeing their doctor. It appears that the number of statements forgotten seems to be an inverse function of the number of statements presented. Ley suggests that to increase the amount of information patients recall the medical professional should provide patients with instructions and advice at the start of the information to be presented, stress how important they are, use short words and sentences, use explicit categorization where possible, and make advice as concrete as possible. These suggestions are as relevant to the psychotherapist as to the physician.

Self-Monitoring. Self-monitoring of the symptom is widely used, often as a component of cognitive-behavioral programs for increasing compliance. For example, hypertensive patients are instructed to monitor their daily blood pressure, and patients recovering from heart attacks monitor their pulse rates as they engage in rehabilitation exercises (Baile & Engel, 1978).

Goal Setting. In social learning theory, setting realistic goals is vitally important to behavior change in general and improving compliance in particular.[3] Short-term (proximal) goals are more effective in producing behavior change than long-term (distal) goals (Bandura & Simon, 1977).

Martin, Dubbert, Katell, Thompson, et al. (1984) further evaluated the role of proximal versus distal goals in an exercise program for healthy but sedentary adults. Participants met twice weekly with instructors to receive instructions on aerobic training and proper exercise technique, followed by fifteen to forty-

---

3. See closely related discussions of goal-setting in self-regulation of behavior change in Chapter 13 on obesity and Chapter 18 on overcoming resistance to behavior change.

five minutes of brisk walking or jogging at 60 percent to 80 percent of their age-predicted maximal heart rate. They recorded their resting and exercise heart rates and graphed them to highlight their progress. Subjects randomly assigned to the proximal goal condition wrote down new mileage goals each week. They were instructed to increase their jogging so that their goal could be achieved by the following week. Subjects in the distal goal condition set distance goals at five-week intervals, or once at the beginning and again at the midpoint of the program.

At the end of the three-month program, subjects in the distal goal condition showed better adherence to exercise than their counterparts in the proximal condition, although both groups showed comparable improvements in evaluations of their aerobic conditioning. A three-month follow-up indicated better compliance in the distal goals group. In discussing the discrepancy between their findings and those of Bandura and Simon (1977), Martin and colleagues (1984) note that while the two studies are not directly comparable, with differences in type of behavior and definitions of proximal and distal goals, "the less frequent goal setting allowed greater flexibility in daily and weekly performance, prior to goal-achievement day." We can conclude from these studies that optimal goals are those which are highly specific, realistic, and short-term (exactly how proximal depending on the particular problem behavior). "Sub-goals," Bandura (1985) points out, "provide present guides and inducements for action, while sub-goal attainments produce the efficacy information and self-satisfactions that sustain one's efforts along the way" (p. 475).

Behavior change should be tailored to the needs of each individual. To take the example of exercise again, Brownell (1982) points out that programmed activities, such as jogging or aerobic dancing, are not suitable for every-one, especially obese individuals. As an alternative to programmed exercise, which is often rejected by the people most in need of exercise, Brownell and others recommend gradual changes within customary activities. These might include using stairs rather than elevators or escalators, disembarking from a bus before one's destination, and parking some distance from the entrance to shops. These activities are readily available, do not require extra time, clothing, or shoes, and can be self-paced.

Active Involvement.   Allowing patients to participate actively in establishing their own goals and treatment facilitates compliance. This strategy and the theory behind it are elaborated in Chapter 18. As an example, Haynes et al. (1976) showed hypertensive patients how to measure their blood pressure and asked them to chart their readings every day at home. This participant or self-management group showed compliance rates of 80 percent compared to 39 percent in a control group which, passively and without self-recording, had their blood pressure taken by medical staff in the customary fashion. Moreover, the self-management group achieved greater reductions in both systolic and diastolic blood pressure than the control group did.

Reinforcement Procedures.   Contingency contracting (money deposits refundable upon completion of a mutually agreed-upon task) has been used to increase compliance with taking medication or engaging in other behavior related to health. As we saw in Chapter 13, contingency contracting significantly improved obese patients' attendance at treatment sessions (Hagen et al., 1976). Similarly, Bigelow, Strickler, Liebson, and Griffiths (1976) used refundable deposits to encourage alcoholics to attend treatment sessions at which Antabuse was administered. In a related study of heroin addicts treated with methadone who also abused alcohol, Liebson, Bigelow, and Flamer (1973) administered methadone only if these cross-addicted patients also ingested Antabuse to control their alcoholism.

Contingency contracting has also been used to produce changes in the problem behavior itself. Jeffery, Wing, and Stunkard (1978) reinforced weight loss with money, while Haynes et al. (1976) reinforced hypertensive patients for having diastolic blood pressures below a cut-off point. There seems to be little doubt that reinforcement or response-cost procedures can be used to promote compliance. The inevitable question, however, is what happens when the specific reinforcement or response-cost contingency is terminated? The evidence indicates that behavior change of this sort is maintained poorly, if at all, once the contingency is withdrawn. Accordingly, procedures have to be developed that will maintain compliance over time in the person's natural environment: the omnipresent issues of generalization and maintenance of behavior change.

Cognitive Strategies. The principles of Beck's (1976) cognitive therapy have been extended to facilitating compliance. People's beliefs, expectations, and values may all influence compliance. Based on cognitive-behavioral principles, Rush (1980) offers the following advice: ". . . the practitioner would be well-advised to ask the patient to anticipate or imagine what might happen that could reduce adherence. For example, the patient should be asked to concretely imagine the steps involved in taking the medication each day. Where will it occur? Who will be around? Would a schedule change, an unexpected demand, running out of or misplacing the medication, the presence of others from whom the patient wishes to conceal medication taking derail the plan? Would any specific symptoms, side effects or intercurrent illnesses preclude adherence? Would symptomatic remission, opinions of other family members, or any other stimulus to attitude change, modify adherence? Concrete anticipation of various elements that can alter adherence allows the patient and practitioner to plan around or adapt the regimen to the individual. In addition, a detailed focus on these obstacles provides the patient with a metamessage or indirect suggestion that adhering is important enough to be planned for and discussed in detail."

Exemplifying Rush's (1980) advice, Cochran (1984) assigned patients treated with lithium for bipolar affective disorder (depression) either to a compliance intervention based on Beck's (1976) cognitive therapy principles or a control condition which only received the standard medication clinic care. Patients in the cognitive intervention received six treatment sessions devoted to altering cognitions and behavior which interfered with compliance with taking lithium. (See Chapter 10 for details of Beck's therapy.) Both at post-treatment and at a six-month follow-up, patients who received the cognitive intervention were rated as significantly more compliant than patients in the standard care condition. The cognitive intervention group also were significantly less likely to stop taking lithium against medical advice and had significantly lower rehospitalization rates than the control group. Cochran (1984) notes, "This latter finding dramatically demonstrates the cost-effectiveness, in both financial and human terms, of a preventive approach to medical noncompliance in bipolar outpatients" (p. 877).

As part of their program to increase exercise among healthy but sedentary adults, Martin et al. (1984) compared the use of what they called cognitive association to cognitive dissociation strategies. Subjects in the "association" condition were instructed to "psych" themselves up, to talk to themselves, and to be their own coach. They were to attend closely to internal sensations to ensure correct pacing and prevent injury. Subjects in the dissociation condition were also told to talk to themselves. In contrast to the other group, however, they were instructed "to attend to the environment and other pleasant distracting stimuli ('smell the flowers') rather than the ordinary discomforts of exercise. In addition, they were urged to set very realistic, short-term goals and to recognize self-defeating thoughts and replace them with more positive, externally focused, coping thoughts" (p. 805). The dissociative cognitive strategy produced significantly greater compliance than the associative strategy. Martin et al. (1984) also found evidence for the value of relapse prevention training (see Chapter 14) in facilitating compliance to physical exercise after the formal program ended.

Patients' self-efficacy is an important mediator of compliance with behavior change. For example, Kaplan, Atkins, and Reinsch (1984) showed that increased self-efficacy was significantly associated with compliance with physical exercise in patients with chronic obstructive pulmonary disease.

Social Support. Social support is a powerful maintenance strategy that can significantly improve compliance. The role that the person's family can play in facilitating maintenance and compliance in the treatment of obesity and alcohol abuse is discussed in Chapters 13 and 14. Family support increases compliance not only with treatments for these substance abuse disorders, but also with medical treatments in general (Blackwell, 1976; Brownell, 1979). Social support significantly facilitates the acquisition and maintenance of exercise habits. For example, Andrew et al. (1981) found that of their cardiac patients, those without the support of a spouse were three times more likely to drop out of rehabilitation than those with a supportive spouse.

The role of social support can be analyzed in social learning terms. In a study of men's recovery from a heart attack, Ewart, Bandura, Taylor, Debusk, and Reese (1983) examined the impact of spouses' judgments of their husbands' physical stamina during rehabilitation. One group of wives was uninvolved in their husbands' treadmill exercises; another group performed the treadmill exercises themselves. The latter group judged their husbands' physical stamina more highly than the former. Moreover, these spouse judgments predicted level of recovery of cardiac capacity six months later. These results indicate that wives who judge their husbands to have a healthy heart will encourage a more active lifestyle; wives who assume that their husband's heart is impaired will discourage physical activity.

Another source of social support we have discussed in previous chapters is the work site or industrial setting. For example, Alderman and Schoenbaum (1975) found that compliance rates in the treatment of hypertension at the work site were high, presumably because they capitalized on the naturally occurring social interactions and mutual support among employees.

Korsch and Negrete (1972) studied interactions between mothers of children with acute but usually minor medical problems and their pediatricians. They found that "Friendly treatment of the patient (e.g., the mother) generally had favorable results, harsh treatment tended to yield poor results. And there was a direct statistical relation between the amount of nonmedical (that is, sociable) conversation between doctor and patient and the patient's satisfaction with the encounter with the doctor" (p. 74). This finding underscores the relationship between mothers' satisfaction with the consultation and their compliance with pediatricians' instructions. Communication between patient and physician is often poor, and leads to lack of compliance (Ley, 1977). Dunbar (1979) summarizes evidence that nurses can provide the solution to this problem. They have direct contact with patients and their families, and are often well-placed to assess problems with compliance.

Compliance and Treatment Outcome. Treatment, whether it be taking medication or behavior therapy, depends on patient compliance. Yet Epstein and Cluss (1982) summarize numerous studies which show that while compliance and outcome of medical (drug) treatments are related, the relationship may be poor. Patients may adhere to treatment and not experience a positive outcome, and vice versa. Another assumption physicians make is that they know what an effective treatment is, and if only patients complied they would get better. Although this is often the case in medical treatment, the evidence is less clear-cut in the psychological therapies. Patients may not comply for reasons that make good sense—the treatment may be ineffective or make them worse!

Epstein and Cluss (1982) also point out that in drug treatment studies, compliance has improved treatment outcome irrespective of whether patients received the active drug or a placebo. This finding shows that there is something about the act of complying that has an effect on outcome which is independent of the medication being administered. One possible explanation is that the more compliant patient may be less sick. Another explanation suggested by Epstein and Cluss (1982) is that "the act of adhering to a treatment regimen, which allows for a person to meet a well-defined goal daily, may enhance feelings of well being [we would suggest self-efficacy] and reduce psychological side effects

of a chronic disease, which may include depression and anxiety" (p. 968).

CORONARY HEART DISEASE

Roughly 6000 Americans die of coronary heart disease (CHD) each year, and 160,000 (35 percent) of these men and women are below the age of 65—they die prematurely. CHD is the leading cause of death not only in the United States, but also in other industrialized nations, yet these premature deaths (and disability) can be prevented. Research has now firmly established that behavior—our personal lifestyle—is a significant determinant of CHD. The classic example of medical research which has revealed how lifestyle patterns influence the development of CHD is the Framingham Heart Disease Epidemiology Study (see Box 15-1).

Several of the well-known risk factors for CHD, such as cigarette smoking, hypertension, obesity, insufficient exercise, and stress, have been discussed and effective cognitive-behavioral procedures for altering these risk factors, and hence lowering the probability of CHD, have been described. Two other risk factors for CHD are a high level of serum cholesterol, discussed in Box 15-1, and a Type A behavior pattern.

Type A Behavior

This pattern of behavior was originally identified by two cardiologists, Friedman and Rosenman (1974). They defined Type A individuals as those "aggressively involved in a chronic, incessant struggle to achieve more and more in less and less time" (1974, p. 67). The pattern includes a sense of time urgency, competitive striving, and hostility. Individ-

---

Box 15–1 *Epidemiology and Behavioral Medicine: The Framingham Heart Study*

Epidemiology is a study of the prevalence, etiology, and consequences of human disease. Behavioral researchers make the assumption that specific patterns of behavior (e.g., cigarette smoking or poor nutrition) influence biological mechanisms which, in turn, are linked to disease (e.g., coronary heart disease). Much of the evidence for these assumptions comes from epidemiological research. In epidemiological research, large groups of people are examined to determine patterns of disease and factors associated with them. This can be illustrated with reference to the now-famous Framingham Heart Study.

Framingham is a town in Massachusetts in which, for the last 35 years, a substantial fraction of the adult men and women have been regularly tested for the development of heart disease. Nearly all of these people were healthy when the study began. By continuing to assess their health-related behavior and its association with CHD over the years, researchers have revealed the roles that high blood cholesterol, high blood pressure, cigarette smoking, and other risk factors play in the development of CHD.

One of the Framingham Study's most important contributions was the identification of the link between the risk of cardiovascular disease and the level and kind of cholesterol in a person's blood. In general, the higher the blood cholesterol, the greater the risk. Framingham residents with a cholesterol level of 230 milligrams (per 100 milliliters of blood serum), for example, are more than twice as likely to get heart disease as those with a level of 180. For those with a level of 300 or higher, the risk is four times greater. Epidemiological studies can never prove particular factors cause a disease; they can only show varying degrees of association and suggest which factors should be analyzed experimentally. A subsequent controlled experiment did show a cause-effect relationship between cholesterol and CHD (Lipid Research Clinics, 1984).

---

uals who did not show these characteristics were called Type B's.

Population-based studies, on balance, show that Type A behavior is a risk factor for CHD (Matthews & Haynes, 1986). In one study, data collected over an eight-and-one-half-year period showed that the annual rate of CHD was 13.2 per 1000 for Type A's versus 5.9 for Type B's (Rosenman, Brand, Jenkins, Friedman, et al., 1975). Investigators have also related Type A behavior to a specific measure of coronary artery disease using angiography.[4] Although some studies have shown a positive association between Type A behavior and degree of coronary artery disease, others have not (Matthews & Haynes, 1986).

4. Angiography involves the injection of a special dye into the coronary arteries, which are then examined under X-ray to see the extent of build-up of plaque (occlusion).

Hostility is a component of Type A behavior, and has been directly linked to CHD. Dembroski, MacDougall, Williams, Haney, and Blumenthal (1985) found that severity of CHD was a function of increasing hostility scores in Type A patients. Moreover, measures of hostility seem to predict CHD independent of Global measures of Type A behavior. The precise aspects of hostility that are related to CHD have yet to be identified, however (Matthews & Haynes, 1986).

Modification of Type A Behavior

The specific biological and psychological mechanisms that mediate the negative effect of the Type A behavior pattern remain to be identified. Nonetheless, the global Type A behavior pattern can be reliably identified using a structured interview, and treatment programs have tried to modify this behavioral pattern. If reducing Type A behavior results in lowered cardiac disease, the hypothesized role of Type A behavior as an independent risk factor is strongly supported.

The most persuasive evidence of the benefits of altering Type A behavior is a study by Friedman, Thoresen, Gill, Powell, et al. (1984). Patients who had experienced a myocardial infarction were randomly assigned either to a control condition, which received standard group cardiologic counseling, or to an experimental condition, which consisted of the same counseling plus a cognitive-behavioral intervention designed to reduce Type A behavior. The cognitive-behavioral treatment included self-control training, behavioral contracting, and cognitive as well as environmental restructuring. Decreased Type A behavior at the end of three years was observed in 43.8 percent of the 592 patients who received this intervention, a figure higher than for cardiologic counseling alone. That less than half the sample showed reductions suggests that this behavior pattern is resistant to modification. Nevertheless, the greater reduction of Type A behavior in the experimental group resulted in a three-year cumulative rate of recurrent cardiac problems (7 percent) that was significantly lower than the 13 percent in the control condition.

Multiple Risk Factor Interventions

Thus far, in our discussion of the Type A behavior pattern and a sedentary lifestyle in this chapter, and of obesity and cigarette smoking in previous chapters, we have focused on how the modification of individual risk factors may affect the probability of CHD. However, optimally effective interventions for reducing the occurrence of CHD would require programs in which multiple risk factors are simultaneously targeted for modification.

The MRFIT Study. The major example to date of such a broad-scale heart disease prevention program is the Multiple Risk Factor Intervention Trial (MRFIT) (Multiple Risk Factor Intervention Trial, 1982). This massive and very expensive study included 12,866 healthy men between the ages of 35 and 57 who were assessed to be at high risk for CHD because of their blood pressure, smoking habits, and elevated cholesterol. Their levels of these three risk factors placed them in the top 10 percent of a risk score distribution derived from data from the Framingham Heart Study. The men were randomly assigned either to a special intervention (SI) program or to a control group (UC) comprising their usual sources of health care in the community. The SI program consisted of formal attempts to lower high blood pressure through the use of antihypertensive medication, reduce cigarette smoking through behavior modification, and lower blood cholesterol levels through behavioral and dietary means.

An average follow-up evaluation of seven years showed that risk factor levels decreased in both groups, but to a greater (although statistically non-significant) degree in the SI group. Mortality from CHD was 17.9 deaths per 1000 in the SI group and 19.3 per 1000 in the UC group. That the multiple risk factor intervention program failed to produce a statistically significant improvement over usual health care came as a disappointment. One of the reasons for this lack of difference between the SI and UC groups was the unanticipated change in risk factor levels and lower-than-expected death rate in the UC group. This finding is consistent with other data indicating that CHD is on the decline in the United States. Although changes in risk factor levels, as a result of public education and awareness, might be responsible for this encouraging trend, the reasons have not been determined (Multiple Risk Factor Intervention, 1982).

The Stanford Three Community Study. In this well-known study, Meyer, Nash, McAlister, Maccoby, and Farquhar (1980) sought to evaluate the effects of a social learning-based intervention program for reducing the risk of CHD in three northern California communities. Using a quasi-experimental design,[5] one community (Gilroy) received a media-based intervention, a second (Watsonville) received the media-based intervention supplemented by an intensive program of face-to-face instruction in behavior change for participants judged to be at high risk for CHD, and the third (Tracy) served as a control community, in which no intervention, only survey assessments, were conducted. To evaluate the impact of the interventions, sample surveys were conducted to gather baseline and yearly follow-up data from a random sample of adults ages 35 to 59 in all three communities. Each survey included a behavioral interview and a medical examination of each subject. The behavioral interview assessed subjects' knowledge and self-reported change in risk factors; the medical examination included measures of plasma cholesterol and triglyceride concentrations, blood pressure, relative weight, and electrocardiograms. Both behavioral and medical data were combined into a single risk factor estimate based on one developed in the Framingham Heart Study. This statistical estimate predicts the probability of a person's developing CHD within the next twelve years.

The content of the intervention programs

5. It is a quasi-experimental design because the three groups were not randomly assigned.

was based on social learning theory and behavioral self-control principles such as self-monitoring, modeling, and reinforcement. The media campaigns were presented in both English and Spanish, using a variety of media materials. Over two years, about three hours of television programs and over fifty television spots were produced, as well as about 100 radio spots, several hours of radio programming, weekly newspaper columns, and newspaper advertisements and stories. Printed materials of many kinds were sent via direct mail to the participants and posters were used in buses, stores, and work sites.

The face-to-face intensive instruction intervention, conducted with 107 high-risk individuals and their spouses in the Watsonville community, consisted of a ten-week program of weekly, then semimonthly, sessions. The therapists who carried out this instruction were mainly college graduates who received four weeks of training in the counselling methods.

Results showed that subjects in both intervention communities showed significant gains in knowledge about risk factors for CHD. The media campaign also produced changes in self-reported consumption of cholesterol and fats. As shown in Figure 15-2, the intensive instruction plus media program achieved the best results after three years, significantly lowering risk for CHD, predominantly through reduction in number of cigarettes smoked (Meyer et al., 1980). Compared to the control community, the treated communities showed significant reductions in systolic blood pressure and dietary cholesterol. The Watsonville community showed a significant reduction in plasma cholesterol.

Three features of this innovative study require emphasis. First, Meyer et al. (1980) based their intervention on a family community rather than individual treatment model. Second, they used the local media to

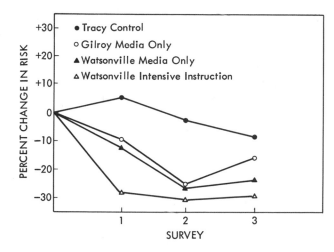

Figure 15–2 Percentage of change from baseline (0) in risk of cardiovascular disease after the three annual follow-up surveys. (Meyer, A., et al. (1980). Skills training in a cardiovascular health education campaign. *Journal of Consulting and Clinical Psychology, 48,* 129–142. Copyright 1980 by the American Psychological Association. Reprinted by permission.)

achieve maximal exposure and make the intervention cost-effective. Third, they targeted multiple risk factors (e.g., diet, cigarette smoking, blood pressure, and stress) for concurrent modification. This ground-breaking study has demonstrated the potential for producing communitywide changes in health-related behavior and has, accordingly, attracted enormous attention. Despite some criticism (Kasl, 1980; Leventhal, Safer, Cleary, & Gutmann, 1980) it has led to the implementation of several similar community studies. The available evidence strongly suggests that these preventive community efforts not only reduce behavioral risk factors, but also morbidity and mortality rates.

SUMMARY

The application of behavior therapy to medical problems helped create the field of behavioral medicine. Behavioral medicine is defined as an interdisciplinary field that applies behavioral and biomedical knowledge to the promotion of good health and the treatment and prevention of ill health.

Many of the principles and procedures of behavior therapy are used in behavioral medicine. Biofeedback has been used to modify a range of different physiological responses, including tension headache, migraine, hypertension, and neuromuscular disorders. It is an effective method, but not more so than progressive relaxation, which has been used to treat successfully an even broader range of problems (e.g., insomnia, and conditioned nausea in patients undergoing chemotherapy treatment for cancer).

Different relaxation methods (biofeedback, progressive relaxation, and transcendental meditation) achieve comparable effects, and there is little well-documented evidence of specific differences in their mode of operation or outcome.

Compliance (adherence) is a major problem in health care. Patients frequently do not take their medication or follow prescribed health-promoting behavior. Strategies for facilitating compliance include improving communication, self-monitoring and appropriate goal-setting, reinforcement, cognitive restructuring, and social support.

Coronary heart disease (CHD) is a major

cause of premature death. Different behavior patterns (e.g., cigarette smoking) have been shown to be risk factors for CHD. Another risk factor is a Type A behavior pattern, characterized by urgency, competitiveness, and hostility. Hostility may be especially related to CHD. Modification of this behavior pattern reduces CHD.

Prevention programs in the community, aimed at modifying multiple risk factors, have proved effective in promoting changes in unhealthy lifestyles and reducing mortality rates.

16

Schizophrenia

DEFINITION

Schizophrenia is a disorder which has been a puzzle to professionals for decades. It is a disorder for which there is no known cure, and it is a problem which has been the subject of billions of dollars of research by biochemists, geneticists, psychiatrists, psychologists, and sociologists. It is an especially perplexing problem to family members who thought they knew their son or daughter's personality quite well before his or her "breakdown" and who later felt they were dealing with a totally different person. Schizophrenia literally means splitting of the mind (deriving from the Greek words *schizein* [split] and *phren* [mind]). The splitting of the mind generally refers to a splitting of thought and emotion from external reality.

The single diagnostic label *schizophrenia* does not imply that there is but one unitary or common disorder. It is now held that there are several types of schizophrenia with different causes. In some of the original descriptions of the disorder now called schizophrenia

it was thought that the psychological deterioration began in one's youth, and thus the term *dementia praecox* or dementia, premature (Kraepelin, 1896). It is now known that schizophrenic disorders occur at all ages and in all cultures, though most hospital admissions for schizophrenia occur between the ages of 15 and 45.

CHARACTERISTICS

Thought Disorder. The most critically defining behavior of schizophrenia is thought disorder. The schizophrenic simply does not conform to the general rules of language; he or she will use ordinary words that may at first sound reasonable but upon close scrutiny do not make sense. The individual has what has come to be known as "cognitive slippage" and uses what is called "word salad." For example, when you ask what his name is, the schizophrenic may say, "My name is General Eisenhower. I came to this hospital ward to set things straight. I intend to use principles of war to accomplish this feat." The use of language does not conform to generally accepted facts and meanings, although the uncommon use is not a function of low intelligence or cultural deprivation.

Delusions. Some schizophrenics suffer from delusions. A delusion is the holding of a belief that is not shared by others in the culture. Such beliefs are most often held by paranoid schizophrenics. Here is an example of a delusion held by a patient in an English sanitarium.

> "There I conceived the delusion that I was about to be buried alive, not in the earth but walled in a small chamber; and I believed that "they" were coming for me. For many mornings, waking early from an artificial sleep, I heard them putting together a large box for me below, a box that, in my fantasy, had arrived in sections to be hammered together in the house with nails or pegs. . . . I was persuaded that the doctor had induced Parliament to pass a bill enabling him to bury me alive. . . ." (Kaplan, 1964, p. 86)

Motor Disturbances. Some patients simply pace like a hyperactive, troubled adult, while others who are called catatonic schizophrenics often remain motionless for hours in a stereotypic way. More typical are the stereotypic movements, ritualistic manners, grimacing, and pacing of Harding, who was an acute ward patient of Nurse Ratched, in *One Flew Over the Cuckoo's Nest.* He was described as follows:

> "Harding's face and hands are moving faster than ever now, a speeded film of gestures, grins, grimaces, sneers. The more he tries to stop it, the faster it goes. When he lets his hands and face move like they want to and doesn't try to hold them back, they flow and gesture in a way that's real pretty to watch, but when he worries about them and tries to hold back he becomes a wild, jerky puppet doing a high-strung dance.

> Everything is moving faster and faster, and his voice is speeding up to match." (Kesey, 1962, p. 58)

A motor disturbance that is often observed, called *tardive dyskinesia*, involves lip smacking, tongue protrusions, and other bizarre facial gestures. This motor disturbance is a side effect of medication taken to relieve the thought disorders associated with schizophrenia. In a review of fifty studies, Kane and Smith (1982) found this symptom occurs in about 20 percent of patients who are given the major medication used in schizophrenia, though the prevalence ranged from 0.5 percent to 56 percent. Fortunately, there are now certain predictors of tardive dyskinesia such as neurological impairment and poor performance on psychometric testing (Wegner, Catalano, Gibralter, & Kane, 1985).

Affect Disturbances. Flat affect, or absence of emotion, was found in 66 percent of schizophrenics in a World Health Organization study (Sartorius, Shapiro, & Jablonsky, 1974). Alternatively, some schizophrenics often have affect which is incongruous with the external world. They may laugh at hearing of the death of someone, or they may show no affect at an event that is extremely troubling to most persons. Flat affect is more common than incongruous affect according to Davison and Neale (1986), but incongruous affect is of special diagnostic significance when it occurs.

Perception Problems. The most common perceptual problem is an inability to selectively screen out stimuli. Thoughts and ideas race through the individual's head. As a result, the individuals complain that they cannot screen out material. Schizophrenics often report, "Everything gets through," or "My mind was filled with thoughts which seemed to race through my head."

DIAGNOSIS

The actual diagnosis of schizophrenia is based on the presence of symptoms in several of the areas already noted: thought disorders, delusions, motor disturbances, affect disturbances, and perception problems. While there are continued concerns about the utility of various diagnostic systems in predicting the course or outcome of schizophrenia, a number of diagnostic systems have considerable overlap, and different raters can arrive at similar diagnoses with the systems (Endicott, Nee, Cohen, Fleiss, & Simon, 1986). No single factor occurs in all schizophrenic patients. The onset of the problem usually is in adolescence or early adulthood, and the symptoms should exist for at least six months before a diagnosis of schizophrenia is made. Changes in personality are often noticed by friends and family. A period of social withdrawal, lack of emotional expression, and communication problems usually precede what is referred to as the active phase of psychotic symptoms, i.e., delusions and hallucinations (American Psychiatric Association, DSM-III, 1980).

During the 1980s a new system was developed for the diagnosis of schizophrenia based upon *excess symptoms* and *deficit symptoms*.[1] Excess or positive symptoms such as hallucinations and bizzare behavior have routinely been assessed in psychiatric interviews, but deficit symptoms such as lack of sociability, little interest in things and activities, asociality, flat or diminished affect, and speech blocking have not been assessed. Andreasen (1982) developed a scale which allows for reliable ratings of deficit symptoms, and this scale has shown that the major medications used to treat schizophrenics reduce excess symptoms like hallucination but leave

---

1. Often referred to as positive and negative symptoms.

the deficit symptoms such as apathy and asociality essentially unchanged. Therefore, the use of the excess and deficit symptom ratings may prove useful in tailoring treatments of a psychological and pharmacological nature for various schizophrenic patients.

Course of Schizophrenia

Blueler (1974) followed a large number of schizophrenics over their entire lives. About 35 percent of these individuals had several episodes and then recovered. About 45 percent of the schizophrenics had various episodes of severe disturbances and had residual impairment following these episodes. Finally, another 20 percent got continually worse following their initial schizophrenic disturbance. Most important, this longitudinal study leads one to conclude that while the schizophrenic problem is very debilitating, it is often episodic, and the individuals can often cope effectively with their problems.

Is There a Schizophrenic Break?

In ordinary parlance, we often hear that friends or acquaintances had a "nervous breakdown." Detailed reports by schizophrenics themselves about their past experiences indicate that the first indication of an episode is a perceptual breakdown (Chapman, 1966). Such a breakdown is reflected in a "First Person Account" of a schizophrenic by Zan Boches, a college student (Boches, 1985).

"My symptoms gradually worsened over the next 6 months. Although the depression lifted, I increasingly heard voices (which I'd always called "loud thoughts" or "impulses with words") commanding me to take destructive action. I concluded that other people were putting these "loud thoughts" in my head and controlling my behavior in an effort to ruin my life. I smelled blood and decaying matter where no blood or decaying matter could be found (for example, in the classrooms at school). I had difficulty concentrating, I fantasized excessively, and I had trouble sleeping and eating. When I began responding to the voices' commands by breaking windows in my apartment and starting fires, I was committed with a diagnosis of 'chronic hebephrenic schizophrenia.' " p. 487

Such an account typifies the experiences of individuals as they enter what is called the active phase of the psychotic symptoms, i.e., the period in which they are unable to screen out or filter sensory input.

Incidence

Approximately 1 percent of the population is diagnosed schizophrenic at some point in their lives, and about half of all psychiatric hospital patients are schizophrenics (President's Commission on Mental Health, 1978). The incidence of schizophrenics in hospitals has been decreasing during the past decade due to laws about deinstitutionalization, but many of the schizophrenics released from psychiatric hospitals require periodic readmission. Schizophrenia is a disorder observed at approximately uniform rates throughout the world. Regardless of whether the problem is observed in Africa, Denmark, India, Russia or the United States, the symptoms seem relatively uniform according to a World Health Organization report (Tsuang, 1976).

ETIOLOGY

Schizophrenia has been a puzzle to professionals for decades. There is no single factor which adequately accounts for most of the data regarding the development of this disorder. Accordingly, many psychologists and psychiatrists who were trained in a behavioral perspective view the problem as an interaction between a genetic predisposition and social stressors. This view, called the diathesis-stress model, seems most congruent with existing research on the development of schizophrenia, and we present evidence in support of this position, which links a predisposition toward disease (diathesis) and disturbing life events (stress) in the role of mental and physical disorders.

Genetic Predisposition

Twin Studies. There is considerable evidence that a predisposition for schizophrenia is genetically transmitted. Comparisons of monozygotic and dizygotic twins are the primary means of arriving at conclusions regarding the genetic transmission of schizophrenia. The concordance or agreement rates for presence of schizophrenia in monozygotic twins is almost always greater than that for dizygotic twins. While there is great variability in the concordance rates across studies, an often cited overall concordance rate in genetic texts for monozygotes is 65 percent and for dizygotes is 15 percent (Fuller & Thompson, 1978).

The actual rates of concordance will vary with the particular definition of concordance chosen as illustrated in a study of all twins treated at two London hospitals between 1948 and 1964. Gottesman and Shields (1972) used three levels of concordance as follows: The twin of the hospitalized schizophrenic was

1. Hospitalized and diagnosed schizophrenic
2. Hospitalized but not schizophrenic
3. Not hospitalized but abnormal

As seen below, regardless of the concordance definition, the rates of concordance were higher in the monozygotic twins. As one might expect, as the definition of concordance broadened from definition one to definition three, the likelihood of finding that a twin of a hospitalized schizophrenic meets a concordance definition increases.

CONCORDANCE RATES

	Monozygotic	Dizygotic
Concordance 1	42%	9%
Concordance 2	54%	18%
Concordance 3	79%	45%

As discussed in earlier chapters on the role of genetics, it is also useful to look at studies of twins reared apart, since twins reared together shared a somewhat common environment. While the number of twins reared apart at least one of whom was later diagnosed as schizophrenic is small, even when such data is used, the concordance rates are much higher than one would expect on the basis of general population data (Rosenthal, 1970).

Family Studies (Genetic).   Another method of evaluating genetic predisposition is to examine the probability of becoming schizophrenic if a nontwin relative is schizophrenic. It should be emphasized that the probability of a person in the general population being diagnosed schizophrenic is 1 percent. However, the probability of a child of a schizophrenic parent developing schizophrenia is approximately 10 percent. The risk for developing schizophrenia if your brother or sister is diagnosed schizophrenic is also roughly 10 percent. The risk for developing schizophrenia if both of your parents are schizophrenic is 35 percent (Rosenthal, 1970). In sum, family studies indicate an enhanced likelihood for developing schizophrenia if one or more blood relatives have been diagnosed for the disorder, and twin studies document an even greater likelihood for developing the

problem if you are an identical twin of an individual diagnosed as schizophrenic. Moreover, comparisons of first degree relatives of schizophrenic and surgical control patients indicate that relatives of schizophrenics are at risk not only for schizophrenia but also for paranoid disorders and schizoaffective disorders (Kendler, Gruenberg, & Tsuang, 1985).

High-Risk Studies.   A method of assessing the development of schizophrenia is to study children of schizophrenics who, as just mentioned, are at risk for developing schizophrenia. Following on the prototypic high-risk study conducted by Mednick and Schulsinger (1968), studies of children at risk have followed children of schizophrenic mothers. The children at risk are matched with children of the same sex and education and are then followed into adolescence and young adulthood, the periods in which they often begin to evidence psychological problems. It is too early to give conclusive figures on the long-term outcome of the high-risk studies, since the progeny of the schizophrenic mothers have not aged enough to be at a life stage where final figures on presence of schizophrenia can be given. However, a ten-year follow-up of Danish children who are now adults indicated that high-risk subjects were decidedly more likely to develop schizophrenia than subjects not at risk for schizophrenia (Mednick & Schulsinger, 1972; Mednick, Cudeck, Griffith, Talovic, & Schulsinger, 1984).

Biochemical Factors

Biochemical problems were thought to be causes of schizophrenia since the disorder was labeled. Kraeplin thought the problem resulted from poisons in the sex glands, and Jung felt that a toxin that he labeled "toxin X" would someday be discovered to account for schizophrenia. The current evidence that supports a genetic predisposition to develop schizophrenia also implicates biochemistry in one fashion or another. That is, if it is clear that genetics play a role in schizophrenia, biochemical factors would presumably influence the manifestation of schizophrenic symptoms. The unusual nature of the thought disorder and behavior of schizophrenics also makes the search for biochemical factors more pressing. That is, since the thought disorders are so unusual, many professionals feel some biochemical aberration must exist.

Despite the belief that schizophrenia may be due to biochemical excesses or deficiencies, there have been difficulties in finding consistent differences between schizophrenics and nonschizophrenics. When patients have been assessed for biochemical factors, the biochemical differences obtained are often confounded by long periods of hospitalization which result in different diets, exercise regimens, and social isolation. There are numerous summaries of such problems and failures to find biochemical differences between schizophrenics and community control subjects (e.g., Neale & Oltmanns, 1980).

It is now believed that dopamine, a neurotransmitter or a chemical that inhibits nerve impulses, produces bizzare symptoms in schizophrenia. When dopamine levels get too high, the thoughts apparently move through the brain in too rapid a fashion (Snyder, 1980). Animals who are given large dosages of drugs that increase dopamine activity display strange posturing and robotlike movements (McGeer & McGeer, 1980). Similarly, drugs which increase dopamine activity in humans also increase schizophreniclike symptoms.

It is important to note that the use of medication that will alter a behavior or mood does not provide direct evidence about the cause of a disorder. For example, evidence from treatment research with psychostimulant medication on hyperactive children had long been used to support the notion that hyperactive children suffer from brain abnormalities (Minimal Brain Dysfunction). However, when normal children showed similar responses to those of hyperactive children to psychostimulant medication, the etiological arguments about minimal brain dysfunction in hyperactive children were seriously questioned (Rapoport, Buchsbaum, Zahn, et al., 1978). Thus, the dopamine hypothesis in schizophrenia should be regarded as an interesting theoretical conceptualization about the possible causes of schizophrenia, but a conceptualization which awaits further and more direct support. Another reason for caution in adopting the excess dopamine hypothesis includes the fact that dopamine seems to affect only certain symptoms of schizophrenia.

Social and Family Variables

Social Class. There are a number of studies which document a relation between being schizophrenic and being from lower social classes. In the classic study of social class and mental illness by Hollingshead and Redlich (1958), schizophrenia was found to be twice as high in the lowest social class as in other social classes. This finding of an association between social class and schizophrenia has occurred in numerous areas of the United States and in Western Europe. Of special interest in this research is the finding that a great proportion of schizophrenics come from the lowest social class, and the association between social class and schizophrenia comes primarily from the prevalence of schizophrenia in the lowest social class.

Of course it is possible that individuals from lower social classes will be admitted to public hospitals and that some wealthy individuals who suffer from very serious mental problems never enter any hospital but are kept away from such facilities by having caretakers in the home. Nonetheless, even when other methods of investigation are used to examine the association between social class and mental illness, such as correlating prevalence of schizophrenia in the community and the social class of these persons, there is still an association between schizophrenia and social class.

Some believe that schizophrenics drift to lower social classes where they may find jobs and social relations with less stress. In fact, it seems reasonable that some schizophrenics feel forced to move to poverty-ridden areas as their cognitive and perceptual problems increase and they become overwhelmed with emotion. There is some, albeit inconsistent, evidence that schizophrenics are downwardly mobile socially in terms of the occupational status of their job (Turner & Wagonfeld, 1967).

The actual influence of lower social class on the etiology of schizophrenia is unclear. Most likely, variables associated with social class such as poor job opportunities, unemployment, and stress of inadequate financial resources make it more likely that members of the lower social classes will be psychologically and physically stressed and later become schizophrenic. Thus, it seems likely that variables associated with being in a lower social class will increase the likelihood of becoming schizophrenic, but it also seems that when an individual attempts to cope with the stress of the schizophrenia, he or she may drift downward in social class.

Family Variables (Behavioral)   Theories of schizophrenia in the 1950s and 1960s placed considerable emphasis on family aberration in the development of schizophrenia. Of crucial importance was the relationship of the mother to the child's development, and it was purported that mothers of schizophrenics were cold and domineering. According to psycho-dynamic theory, when children raised by a cold and domineering mother reached adolescence with its attendant stresses, they would regress and engage in the most primitive forms of thought. Such thought processes were held to be characteristic of schizophrenia. Later, in the absence of evidence for this hypothesis, emphasis switched from the mother-child relationship to the entire family. This research has indicated that schizophrenic families do not communicate as clearly as do families without a schizophrenic member (Singer & Wynne, 1965b; Hirsch & Leff, 1975), but the exact deficit or problem in communication is unclear.

More recently, work with families of schizophrenics repeatedly has revealed that readmission rates to hospitals are dependent upon the type of living or family environment to which the schizophrenic patient returned. Of greatest significance have been the analyses of interviews of the patient's parents or spouses *before* the patient returned home. Parents or spouses of schizophrenic patients who are readmitted to the hospital after going home were found to have higher rates of what is described as expressed emotion (EE), or what might best be referred to as critical and hostile comments and overinvolvement (Brown, Bone, Dalison, & Wing, 1966; Vaughn & Leff, 1976). Even when severity of symptoms is controlled for, the rates of readmission are higher for patients in homes of individuals with high EE.

High-risk studies for schizophrenia have been used to assess possible genetic and environmental factors in the etiology of schizophrenia. The essence of this research is to follow the offspring of schizophrenic mothers to determine the differences between those offspring who develop schizophrenia and those who do not. There are now fifteen major international research projects that have followed large samples of children at risk for schizophrenia. While the high-risk studies will give us some answers about the possible role of genetic factors in schizophrenia, they can also convey important information about the role of family and environmental factors in the development of schizophrenia. As summarized by Watt in the book *Children at Risk for Schizophrenia* (1984), children born to schizophrenic mothers have elevated pregnancy complications, show more aggressive/disruptive behavior in elementary school than community control subjects, and have lower performance and verbal IQs than community control subjects.

An interesting high-risk study was a comparison of the children of schizophrenic mothers who were raised in a kibbutz with a control group raised by their own parents in cities in Israel (Mirsky, Silberman, Latz, & Nagler, 1985). Twenty-six percent of the kibbutz-reared children who were at risk for schizophrenia developed schizophrenia or schizophrenic symptoms, whereas 13 percent of the at-risk children who were raised by their own parents developed schizophrenia or schizophrenic symptoms. In evaluating their results, the investigators speculated "that it may be related to the fact that the kibbutz is a relatively small, closed community, with few opportunities for individual differences that do not contribute to the common goals, and little chance for the pathological history of one's parent to be unknown or forgotten" (Mirsky et al, 1985, p. 153).

The high-risk studies have indicated several important precursors of adult schizophrenia, but more recently these studies have looked at children at risk for other adult disorders such as depression. They indicated that a number of the factors that place children at risk for schizophrenia also place children at risk for other forms of adult pathology (Rutter & Garmezy, 1983).

They also indicate, however, that certain variables such as marital discord play a critical role in the development of behavior problems of children of depressed women but not of schizophrenic women (Emery, Weintraub, & Neale, 1982). Such research does not detract from the premise that negative family variables do place children at risk for schizophrenia; instead, it raises the possibility that the development of certain disorders is dependent upon specific diathesis stress models.

TREATMENT

Psychological

There are three basic psychological approaches to the treatment of schizophrenia that are often classified under a behavioral rubric: hospital ward management, family therapy, and social skills training.

Hospital Management. The classic behavioral work on changing the behavior of schizophrenic patients was conducted by Ayllon and Azrin in the early 1960s at Anna State Hospital in Illinois (Ayllon & Azrin, 1965; 1968). A token reinforcement program was used in which patients received special privileges and activities if they engaged in certain behaviors. The token reinforcement program involved a specification of desired behaviors such as: "arriving at work on time, remaining at a job for the entire period, following instructions of supervisors, interacting with fellow employees when necessary" (p. 54). These behaviors were carefully observed. When the patients engaged in one or more of these behaviors, they were given tokens, plastic chips that were exchangeable for certain items (e.g., food or cigarettes) or privileges (hospital passes). Examples of the number of tokens necessary for various goods and privileges are described in Table 16-1.

Table 16–1   Number of Tokens Necessary to Obtain Certain Reinforcers

1. Toilet articles from commissary (e.g., Kleenex, toothpaste, comb)	1–10
2. Reading material	2- 5
3. Plants, picture holder	1–50
4. 30-minute walk on grounds	10
5. Trip to town	100

From Ayllon & Azrin, *The Token Economy*, 1968.

With the use of the reinforcement program, it was demonstrated that many behaviors could be changed. For example, improvements were evident in personal hygiene habits, social behavior, and increased work output on various hospital jobs. Like other token reinforcement programs of the 1960s, however, when the reinforcement was abruptly removed, there was a deterioration in the behavior of the patients. The value of the Ayllon and Azrin program was not in the particular behavior changes observed and the duration of these changes (or lack thereof), but rather in showing that such behaviors could be changed at all in a relatively short time.

The most comprehensive research evaluation of inpatient hospital programs for schizophrenics using behavioral methods was designed by Paul and Lentz (1977) at a regional mental health center in Illinois. There were three types of treatments being compared: (1) the standard hospital treatment, which consisted of occupational therapy, group psychotherapy, and medication; (2) a milieu program that used principles of a therapeutic community, including large group meetings in which decisions about the unit were made and resident responsibility and decision-making were maximized; and (3) a social learning approach emphasizing reinforcement of desirable behavior and prompts and instructions to shape behavior. The treatment programs lasted for four-and-a-half years.

Twenty-eight chronic schizophrenics were assigned to each of the three treatments. The patients were matched for age, sex, symptoms, and length of prior hospitalization. The staff was observed on the wards by well-trained observers who monitored the extent to which the staff adhered to the treatment regimen, and the patients were observed to assess changes in their self-care, interpersonal skills, and completion of ward assignments. When the study began, most of the patients in the three programs were receiving medication, but after periods of drug withdrawal indicated that the drugs were not having a beneficial effect for most patients, the medication was withdrawn totally for about 75 percent of the patients after eighteen months on the wards.

Two identical adjacent units were established at a mental health center to house the social learning and milieu therapy programs. Both were staffed by the same professional personnel at a level equal to that existing in a comparison state hospital where the routine hospital treatment was administered.

The remarkable degree of experimental control that Paul and Lentz built into this study can be highlighted by the following excerpt from their book:

> The milieu and social-learning programs were not only equated on all potentially relevant characteristics of the patient population, but were equally high prestige programs in identical physical settings with exact equation in the degree of operationalization, clarity, specificity, explicitness, and order provided for both staff and residents. Both programs also provided identical activity structure and focus upon specific classes of behavior, with the same staff not only conducting both programs, but equating time and focus within programs, with both running concurrently over the same time periods, subject to the same extraneous events. (p. 423)

Patients in both the psychosocial and social learning programs showed significant improvement in interpersonal skills, self-care, and ward activities (see Figure 16-1, from Paul and Lentz, 1977).

As is evident, patients in the social learning program showed greater gains than the patients in the milieu program. In addition, when overall functioning was assessed, the patients in the social learning program showed

the greatest improvement (see Figure 16-2, from Paul and Lentz, 1977).

In terms of hospital discharge, by the end of 4.5 years, 10.7 percent of the social learning group and 7.1 percent of the milieu group were discharged to *independent functioning without readmission*. None of the patients in the standard hospitalization group were re-

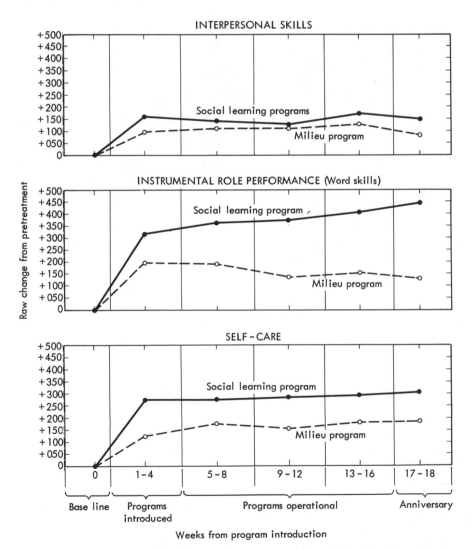

Figure 16–1 Changes in frequency of component adaptive behaviors (From Paul, G.P. & Lentz, R.J. (1978). *Psychosocial treatment of chronic mental patients: Milieu vs. social learning programs.* Cambridge, MA: Harvard University Press.)

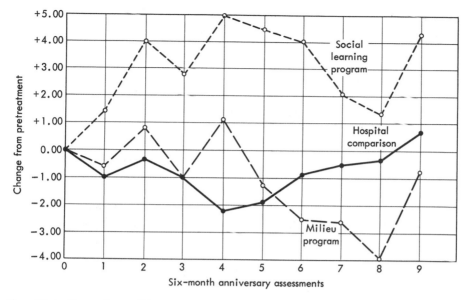

Figure 16–2 Changes in overall functioning from the Inpatient Assessment Battery during the intramural treatment period for the original equated groups—N = 28 each (From Paul, G.P. & Lentz, R.J. (1978). *Psychosocial treatment of chronic mental patients: Milieu vs. social learning programs.* Cambridge, MA: Harvard University Press.) *See note at end of chapter.

leased to independent functioning. There were many patients who were also discharged with supervision, but they were not required to hold jobs in the community. In order to be classified as having "significant release" from the hospital, patients had to remain in the community for ninety consecutive days. The release figures from the three groups were as follows:

Hospital Management Programs	Significant Release
Social Learning Program	96%
Milieu Program	68%
Standard Hospital Program	46%

Since *all* of the patients in the three programs had been rejected for community placement 4.5 years earlier, the fact that as many as 96 percent of the patients in the social learning program had a significant release was especially important. The figures are even more impressive when one considers that these patients had been so disturbed "that they were rejected for shelter care placement in the community . . . [and had] a zero probability of being released to the community" (Paul & Lentz, 1977).

Following release from the hospital, patients in all three groups showed a significant decline in functioning, most evident in the social learning and milieu program groups, which showed the greatest initial improvements. That is, patients with the greatest initial gains showed the greatest losses. However, what was learned from this research that has had lasting impact is that some schizophrenics who previously had little hope for release into the community *can* be placed in the community and function effectively with a modicum of supervised support.

While the Paul and Lentz (1977) research indicated the superiority of a social learning approach in the treatment of schizophrenics, the milieu program was also more effective than the standard hospital program. One of the successful programs with a milieu emphasis was that of Fairweather, Sanders, Maynard, and Cressler (1969). This program had an emphasis on self-management, self-evaluation, group decision-making, and a token reinforcement program in which pass privileges were made contingent upon appropriate self-directive behavior. The patients in the Fairweather et al. (1969) program learned to operate a community lodge in which formerly hospitalized patients could live together and provide peer support for each other. The lodge was organized and run by the patients themselves. They had a self-government system in which they solved daily problems by group decision. Supervision and feedback were provided by hospital and/or research staff, but only patients lived in the lodge. The patients developed their own janitorial and gardening services, which provided employment for the lodge members. Compared to standard hospital aftercare, the lodge members had less recidivism and greater employment rates (Fairweather et al., 1969). Interestingly, while the investigators described some of the lodge patients as eccentric and passive in their social interactions, Fairweather et al. note that these problems were "no deterrent . . . to their capacity to remain productively occupied in the community when an appropriately designed social situation was provided for them" (p. 209).

Other milieu programs were summarized by Magaro, Talbott, & Glick (1984), but the central themes of the successful milieu programs were high structure, shared responsibilities for group living conditions, and stress on the development of adaptive skills. It also appears that the more chronic the patient the greater the need for structure; the more acute or less disturbed patients benefit from emphasis on high decision-making and less structure. The general principle that one can draw from this research with hospitalized schizophrenics is that behavioral interventions and milieu interventions, both of which stress the development and teaching of adaptive skills, have been effective in aiding schizophrenics. In contrast, individual psychotherapy of a client-centered or psychodynamic nature has not been shown to be effective (Gomes-Schwartz, 1984). In short, teaching therapies appear to be more effective than talking therapies.

As Magaro, Talbott, and Glick noted (1984), it is now clear that chronic schizophrenics can be treated in a residential facility, but if community care with day treatment and supportive residential services exist, the community care is the treatment of choice. They further state, however, that these conditions are big "ifs" which often only exist in the minds of clinicians and planners and, as a result, the state hospital is often the treatment setting for the chronic patient. The deinstitutionalization movement of the 1950s and 1960s, involving shifts of schizophrenics from hospitals to the community residences and sometimes just to the streets, has resulted in a questioning of the utility of such a movement without very careful planning. In fact, because of the concerns in the community, many professional panels have recently recommended the hospital rather than the community as the best place for care of such patients.

Another view of care for schizophrenic patients is a two-stage process in which a brief hospital stay is followed by extended aftercare in the community (Goldstein, 1980). Since the family is often a major part of the community aftercare, consultations with families have become increasingly important. The family models used in the late 1970s and 1980s have combined an integrated approach of brief hospitalization, antipsychotic drugs, and hospital aftercare.

Family Therapy. As noted in the etiology section of this chapter, one of the early studies which illustrated the role of family functioning on relapse of schizophrenics was conducted in London by Brown and colleagues (1966). Schizophrenics who were discharged to be with their families were the targets of the study. Before they were discharged, interviews were conducted with primary family members (parents or spouses) and rated for the number of critical comments or overinvolvement by family members. The combination of these variables, called expressed emotion or *EE*, was used to separate the groups. High EE subjects had a 58 percent relapse whereas only 10 percent of low EE subjects had to return to the hospital! This research was replicated by Vaughn and Leff with schizophrenics and by Hooley, Orley and Teasdale (1985) with hospitalized depressed patients.

Based on the notion that environmental stressors may affect the outcome of schizophrenia, various family approaches have shown clear evidence of reducing regression in patients after their release into the community. For example, Falloon, Boyd, McGill, et al. (1985) developed a family-based problem-solving approach with an individualized problem-solving approach for schizophrenic patients. The goals of both the individual approach and the family approach involved the prevention of clinical morbidity and promotion of effective community functioning. The approach was based on social learning theory paradigms, and the particular strategies were tailored to the particular needs of each family. The schizophrenic patient, called the index patient, was "treated merely as one member of the family unit, usually but not always the most handicapped. His particular needs were addressed within the context of the family functioning as a whole. The major aim of the therapy was to train the family to employ a structured problem-solving method that involved sitting down together, speci-

fying a problem issue, considering a broad range of possible solutions, and agreeing on a detailed plan to implement the best solution. Where families displayed deficits in their interpersonal communication that precluded effective problem-solving discussions, training in communication skills was implemented" (pg. 868). Further, when the therapists thought it was necessary to address particular problems of family members such as parental conflict, anxiety, or depression, particular treatment strategies were devised to ameliorate these problems.

Since patients received both medication and psychosocial interventions, during the first two sessions the nature of schizophrenia and the rationale for a combined drug/psychosocial intervention were discussed. The family sessions were conducted in the home for the first nine months of treatment; all sessions were one hour long.

The individual therapy is often called supportive psychotherapy, but the emphasis was on enhancing the community functioning of the schizophrenic patient while supporting the patient's family. The approach was structured and goal oriented. Specific behavioral management strategies such as social skills training, anxiety management, and cognitive restructuring were employed as needed. Family members were frequently consulted, but not in the presence of the patient.

After stabilization on antipsychotic medication (chlorpramazine), subjects were assigned to family management (n = 18) or individual management (n = 18). In terms of changes in symptoms as recorded by therapists during the nine-month program, two-thirds of the episodes experienced by patients in individual management were considered major, whereas one-third of the episodes of the patients in the family management program had such episodes. With regard to target symptom ratings by observers unaware of the treatment condition, the family management patients also fared better (see Figure 16–3).

Finally, in terms of hospital admissions, 50 percent of the individual management patients spent some time in the hospital, whereas only 11 percent of the family management patients spent time in the hospital. This family management approach holds special promise for ameliorating the condition of schizophrenics who have been stabilized on antipsychotic medication. In addition, the approach fits well conceptually with the results seen in studies on expressed emotion and prevention of relapse discussed earlier in this chapter.

Interventions with families of schizophrenics have been used by psychologists and psychiatrists of differing theoretical orientations, but the family approaches of varying orientations have been shown to be a very effective part of aftercare programs. Certain family programs have proven effective which involved the patient little or not at all (Leff, Kuipers, Berkowitz, et al., 1982) and instead emphasized the reduction of expressed emotion (EE). Goldstein (1984) summarized the content of various family education components of programs for schizophrenic patients and their families. The programs focus on "concrete problem solving and specific helping behaviors for coping with stress." The underlying assumption of all psychoeducational programs is "giving families information about the nature of the disorder, along with specific suggestions for coping with it effectively, can decrease the intensity and conflict inherent in family life, and thus reduce the likelihood of relapse in the index patient, and the emergence of mental disorders in the previously non-affected relatives" (p. 284). Three different family programs have been shown to be effective as supplements to medication in maintaining patients in their communities. In fact, the three programs all resulted in relapse rates of approximately 10 percent or less, whereas without such programs the relapse rates were approximately 50 percent.

The common theme in the programs ranging from behavioral to structured family therapy was highly structured family sessions with a therapist who controls the level of affect in the therapy sessions. More specifically, the therapist either actively discourages or interrupts the expression of high levels of negative affect.

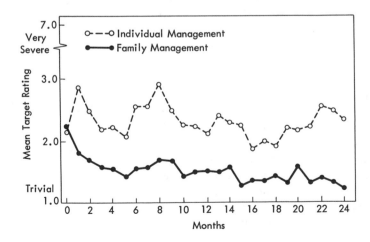

Figure 16–3 Mean blind ratings of target symptoms of schizophrenia over 24 months. (From Falloon et al. (1985). *Archives of General Psychiatry, 42*. Reprinted with permission of the American Medical Association.)

Family Intervention Programs

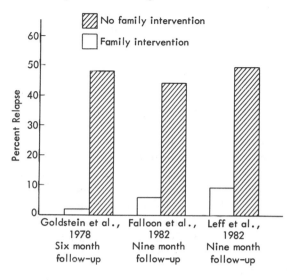

Social Skills Training. Deterioration of social functioning is one of the defining diagnostic characteristics of schizophrenia according to the 1980 *Diagnostic and Statistical Manual* of the American Psychiatric Association. Social isolation and odd or unusual behaviors are held to be prodromol or predictive signs of schizophrenia. The unusual behaviors lead to rejection, and the withdrawal places the person in question outside the usual social networks. Even when a schizophrenic is in remission or when his or her behavior is markedly improved with psychological and pharmacological treatment, there are differences in the social interactions of schizophrenic and nonschizophrenic patients (Serban, 1975; St. Lawrence, 1985).

Using the premise of social skill differences between schizophrenic and nonschizophrenic individuals, St. Lawrence (1986) built a social skills training model after a comprehensive assessment of the particular social skill deficiencies. Such an assessment is critical, but many patients do achieve satisfactory adjustments when their symptoms are in remission, i.e., when their symptoms decrease or disappear due to natural variations in the disorder or due to treatment. Social skills training is not an intervention that should be routinely prescribed for schizophrenic patients (Morrison & Bellack, 1984). Even if a social dysfunction exists, it is possible that the social problem is not a skill deficit problem but rather a dysfunction due to social anxiety, depression, or perceptual and information-processing problems. Furthermore, some psychiatric patients are able to display considerable social skill with members of the same sex rather than with the opposite sex, and with strangers rather than with family members. In brief, social skills training should be tailored to the specific needs of the patient.

There are many case studies (e.g., Edelstein & Eisler, 1976) and controlled outcome research projects (e.g., Goldsmith & McFall, 1975) which illustrate the learning of social skills by schizophrenic patients. Assessment of the social skill is generally made by role playing before and after an intervention. The typical teaching skill strategies involve instructions, modeling, role playing, feedback and positive reinforcement, and homework (Morrison & Bellack, 1984). The types of behaviors that have been taught in these programs include assertiveness, eye contact, agreement with a speaker, and problem-solving skills.

The clinical impact of social skills training has been questioned because of the frequently cited failure of patients to use the skills taught in the social skills training program in their families or their social networks. While there are reports of failure to generalize, there are also some studies which illustrate how social skills training programs can be implemented so that the patient will use his or her newly acquired skill. For example, Liberman, Lillie, Falloon, et al. (1978) showed that even with thirty hours of social skills training across a ten week period the teaching of the skills with various persons had to be taught. The training program involved hospital staff and family and community members, but it was clearly illustrated that there was not any automatic transfer of social skills learned with hospital staff to family or community members. Unlike the results with family intervention programs, there are no controlled studies which unequivocally illustrate the role of social skills training programs on relapse rates. As Morrison and Bellack (1984) note in their review of social skills training programs, the social skills deficit model and the social skills training programs as typically practiced are not sufficient to account for the complexities of the interpersonal problems of the schizophrenic person. They argue that most social skills programs have failed to address the social/perceptual problems of schizophrenics. One notable exception in this regard is the work of Wallace and colleagues (Wallace, 1978; 1982) who used videotaped social vignettes in a training program in addition to the standard social skills training discussed earlier. The patient was asked to respond to questions about what appeared on the videotape (e.g., What are the people talking about in that scene? What is the best solution to the problem?). Patients are then assisted by therapists if they cannot give reasonable answers to the questions. There is initial evidence that this program of social skills was effective in altering relapse rates, but intervention with aftercare personnel as well may have accounted for some of the relapse differences. Nonetheless, such skill programs offer promise in ameliorating the problems of the schizophrenic patient.

Pharmacological

About the time antipsychotic drugs were introduced, there was a sharp reduction in the residents of psychiatric hospitals. However, one should not conclude that the use of these medications was the cause of the deinstitutionalization. This process had begun in many places in the United States and Europe for various reasons, including the projected astronomical costs of long-term residential care, emphasis on patients' rights, and disenchantment with the mental hospitals. Nonetheless, the development of antipsychotic medication allowed many patients to have relief from their symptoms.

Phenothiazines are medications called antipsychotic drugs whose clinical efficacy is now very well documented in over 100 studies (Klein & Davis, 1969). Basically, comparisons are generally made with a placebo group and the active medication. In repeated studies, the patients were free to participate in the usual treatment regimens of the hospital such as psychotherapy and occupational therapy. Because of what are called extrapyramidal side effects such as facial rigidity and uncontrolled

---

Box 16–1 *Status of a Learning Model of Schizophrenia*

A sociopsychological formulation of schizophrenia was advanced by Ullmann & Krasner (1969; 1975), who maintained that schizophrenic behavior was learned, maintained, and modified in the same fashion as any other behavior. They hypothesized that the crucial factor in the development and maintenance of schizophrenic behavior is the absence of reinforcement for correct or appropriate behavior.

Ullmann and Krasner stressed the fact that schizophrenics withdraw and lack emotional responsiveness because they give up when other people cease being reinforcing to them. Further, when the person withdraws, his or her behavior is labeled odd or weird. In turn, to get some attention, the individual may engage in unusual behavior and thus become reinforced for a "sick role" or for "crazy behavior." Hospitals are held to foster "sick behavior" because the staff is taught to believe that a patient is sick or has some disease within himself or herself. In partial support for these positions is the evidence that certain unusual behaviors are indeed subject to the same principles of reinforcement as any "normal" behavior (Ayllon & Azrin, 1968). Second, Ullmann and Krasner (1975) presented evidence that patients learn that it is important to avoid causing trouble for the hospital aide. They argued that if you assert yourself or stand up for your rights as a patient you will be called "disturbed" and placed on a restricted, locked ward.

The sociopsychological formulation of Ullmann and Krasner (1975) has not been accepted by many behavioral psychologists because they view the position as limited and unable to account for biochemical and genetic data already discussed. Nonetheless, the sociopsychological model has been of heuristic value in hospital planning since the potential negative function of lengthy hospitalization (called an iatrogenic function) was made very clear by Ullmann and Krasner (1975). Further, highly successful hospital ward management like that of Paul and Lentz (1977) incorporated behavioral formulations of the sociopsychological model, particularly the token reinforcement program. It is our opinion that the evidence from this model for the etiology of schizophrenia is scant, but that the model does hold importance for the maintenance of apathy and withdrawal on many hospital wards.

---

tremors, physicians in these drug studies have also been free to prescribe antiparkinsonian agents to counteract such effects. Of patients treated with phenothiazines, approximately 75 percent show "much" or "very much" improvement, whereas approximately 25 percent of the patients in the placebo control groups show such improvement. Of special interest is the fact that the phenothiazines did not have a simple tranquilizing effect on the patients. Hostility and irritability were reduced, but the patients also showed increased coherent verbal behavior and greater responsivity to their social environment. Like most medications, however, the phenothiazines also have their undesired side effects, and antiparkinsonian medication had to be used in about one-third of the patients. Nonetheless,

the evidence indicated that acute schizophrenics can be aided considerably with the phenothiazines; while the mechanisms of phenothiazines are not fully understood, they clearly improve disordered thinking.

Some schizophrenic patients respond to one type of phenothiazine or antipsychotic medication but do not respond to another. However, there is no evidence that one class of such medication is more effective than another (Davis & Gierl, 1984). In most cases, the effects of the medication occur within six weeks, although additional gains are made throughout the second and third months of treatment. Following a response to medication, the issue of maintaining a patient on antipsychotic drugs must be considered. It is known from scores of studies that drug maintenance prevents relapse. Davis and Gierl (1984) indicated that relapse rates in thirty-three studies with over 3000 patients across several months of follow-up on placebo were 53 percent whereas on active medication they were 20 percent.

It is not known whether the family interventions described earlier can be used with decreasing doses of medication during aftercare. Given the often encountered problems of tardive dyskinesia and autonomic nervous system side effects such as dryness of mouth and throat and flushing of skin, the potential of decreasing antipsychotic medication with psychological and/or family therapies should certainly be explored. As Stierlin, Wynne, and Wirsching (1983) noted, "[antipsychotic medications] have serious, sometimes irreversible toxicities, . . . recovery may be impaired by them in at least some schizophrenics and . . . they have little effect on the long-term psychosocial adjustment" (p. 1). The power of the family environment to foster and to counteract the development of schizophrenic disturbances is clear, and the family environment should be explored fully to minimize the need for medications which although helpful do have serious and sometimes irreversible side effects.

SUMMARY

Schizophrenia is a serious disorder characterized by disturbances of thought, affect, motor behavior, and perception. Approximately 1 percent of the population becomes schizophrenic; the disorder is episodic in nature for many people, but nonetheless is very debilitating during the period of hallucinations and delusions. There is no single cause of schizophrenia. It is now felt that a diathesis-stress model best aids conceptualization of schizophrenia. The diathesis refers to a genetic predisposition to have the disorder;

the stress aspect of the model refers to the stressors of social and family life. Evidence from twin and family studies indicates that concordance rates for schizophrenia are much higher in monozygotic than dizgotic twins and that first degree relatives of schizophrenics also are at risk for developing schizophrenia. Research on dopamine indirectly supports a view that some symptoms of schizophrenia may be accounted for by excess levels of dopamine. Finally, being a member of a lower social class is a significant predictor of schizophrenia, and high levels of expressed emotion or negativity and overinvolvement predict relapse of schizophrenic patients.

Hospital ward management programs based upon social reinforcement systems and milieu programs have been more successful than standard hospital programs for patients who were held to have a very low probability of returning to the community. Various family therapy programs emphasizing a decrease in expressed emotion have been very successful in reducing relapse rates of schizophrenics who were also receiving antipsychotic medication. Social skills programs of a behavioral nature have been associated with learning various social skills like assertiveness, eye contact, and social problem solving. Finally, antipsychotic medication has been shown to be effective in reducing disordered thought in scores of studies, but such medication often has significant and sometimes irreversible side effects. Therefore, the power of social and family variables in altering the development and course of schizophrenia must be explored to its fullest extent.

* (See Figure 16–2, p. 351.) As Paul and Lentz (1977) noted, the greater change for the social learning group on the overall functioning measure may have been due to "lack of sensitivity to changes in objectively assessed behavior" (p. 377). Continuous objective assessment of resident behavior indicated that both the social learning and the milieu group showed improvement in overall functioning at every period through the sixth assessment.

17

Clinical Research and the Evaluation of Treatment Outcome

A defining characteristic of behavior therapy is its commitment to scientific method, measurement, and evaluation. Accordingly, a major contribution of behavior therapy has been the development of several innovative strategies for the evaluation of treatment outcome.

THE PROGRESSION OF THERAPY RESEARCH

The development of effective psychological therapies involves a number of separate but closely interrelated steps, starting with the generation of novel treatment methods, adequately testing and refining such procedures, and finally implementing them. At each stage the research question changes, and the appropriate methodological approach to that question must be taken (Agras, Kazdin, & Wilson, 1979). Figure 17-1 illustrates this multilevel process.

As illustrated in Figure 17-1, new procedures can be generated from clinical obser-

vation or from basic research and theorizing. Ideally, once new therapeutic techniques have been generated, an evaluation leads to controlled comparisons of the short-term effects of the new therapy, the identification of the effective components of therapeutic methods, and the assessment of the generality and durability of the effects produced by these methods. The next step involves comparative outcome studies with other existing treatments. Finally, the implementation of these methods in clinical practice requires evaluation. This step includes analysis of the best way to present the treatment (e.g., individual or group settings), the level of therapist training required to implement the therapy, and the cost-effectiveness of the clinical practice of the therapy.

The planned, integrated sequence of clinical research described above is only an ideal. Even behavioral treatment methods, which have been more intensively evaluated than other psychological therapies, cannot, with rare exceptions (e.g., fear reduction methods—see Chapters 8 and 9), be said to

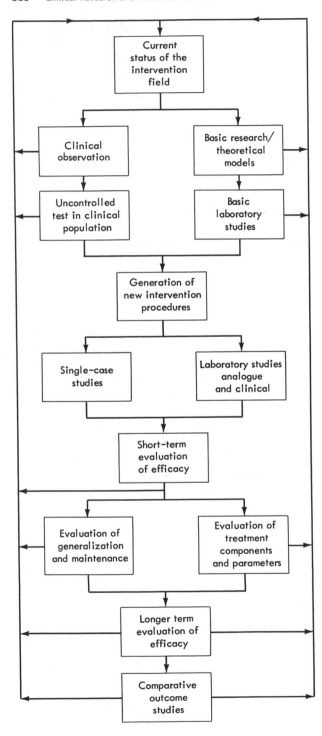

Figure 17–1   The Flow of Therapeutic Research. (From Agras, W.S., Kazdin, A.E., & Wilson, G.T. (1979). Behavior Therapy: Towards an applied clinical science. San Francisco, Freeman.)

be based upon the comprehensive research and development described in Figure 17-1. Different behavioral methods have various degrees of empirical support, ranging from techniques relying primarily on anecdotal or clinical claims to those supported by controlled outcome studies. Of the research on the techniques of behavior therapy, the major portion has been at the level of short-term laboratory or analogue investigations.

THE CLINICAL CASE STUDY

Limitations

Case studies, by their nature, are uncontrolled. Among other factors, successful outcome could be due to changes in the client's life unrelated to therapy, to the mere passage of time, or to personal characteristics of the therapist rather than the therapy. There is no way to exclude definitively (control for) these factors in a case study.

The danger of dependence on uncontrolled clinical reports is highlighted by the example of psychoanalysis. Freud's treatment of a phobic boy—the case of Little Hans—was a key element in the development of psychoanalysis. Wolpe and Rachman (1960), in a critical re-analysis of the Little Hans case, not only raised interpretive problems for psychoanalytic theory but also showed how the same events could be more parsimoniously explained in terms of conditioning theory. Another of Freud's famous cases—Anna O—was re-analyzed by Ellenberger (1972) who found that hospital records confirmed that Anna O had continued to take morphine to ease the hysterical symptoms allegedly removed by Freud's "talking cure." Ellenberger's discovery led Davison and Neale (1974) to remark that it "is fascinating and ironic to

consider that the roots of psychoanalysis may lie in an improperly reported clinical case" (p. 23).

Case studies have played an extremely influential role in the development and clinical practice of behavior therapy, too. Consider the importance once attached to the conditioning of a phobic reaction in Albert B (Watson & Rayner, 1920) and the deconditioning of Peter's phobia by Mary Cover Jones in 1924 (Chapter 3). Recall also, from Chapter 1, the historical importance of the publication in 1965 of Ullmann and Krasner's book, *Case Studies in Behavior Modification*. As the title makes clear, this was primarily an anthology of case studies.[1]

Collections or series of case studies have often had a decisive impact on the field (Barlow, 1980). The publication of the results of three consecutive series of clients (a total of 210 cases) by Wolpe (1952, 1954, 1958) and Lazarus's (1963) evaluation of his treatment of 408 clients, constituted the basis for the initial clinical practice of behavior therapy with outpatients and helped to spur subsequent experimental investigations of techniques such as systematic desensitization (Paul, 1969). Another example of the influential impact of a series of case studies was Masters and Johnson's (1970) report of 790 cases of sexual dysfunction. The influence of Masters and Johnson's findings went well beyond their data—a collection of uncontrolled case studies. Subsequent reviews have indicated important limitations and problems with the Masters and Johnson book (Chapter 11).

---

1. Follow-up reports on some of the much-quoted case studies in Ullmann and Krasner's book are available. Some of the apparent successes of behavior therapy subsequently were seen to be therapeutic failures. Yet others showed remarkably durable improvement (see Franks & Wilson, 1978, pp. 317–318).

Advantages

Clinical case studies make an invaluable contribution to clinical practice since they allow for the report of therapeutic innovations and the description of clinical methods and strategies applied to particular clients. The clinical detail and practical focus of a good case study make it especially appealing to practitioners. In serving this important clinical purpose case studies must meet some basic criteria: treatment methods must be described with sufficient detail and precision to allow replication by other therapists, the problems to which the methods are applied must be specified, and any relevant personal characteristics of the client(s) reported.

Beyond these commonly accepted functions, case studies can be reported so as to increase the likelihood that we can draw valid inferences about treatment effects (Kazdin, 1981). The dimensions said to determine the degree to which scientific inferences can be drawn from uncontrolled case studies include the type of data collected, the number of assessment occasions, past and future projections of performance, the type of effect demonstrated, and the number and heterogeneity of the patients described in case studies. Case studies should include objective measures of therapeutic change rather than anecdotal reports. Single assessments of the patient's problem(s) before or after therapy are the least secure basis for inferring treatment efficacy, since these isolated measures are most vulnerable to a host of influences aside from the particular technique in question. Repeated or continuous measurement over time before and after therapy allows one to rule out several sources of extraneous influence and increases the confidence with which we can interpret treatment-specific change.

By past projections of the patient's problem, Kazdin refers to the question of whether the history of the disorder has been stable or chronic, as opposed to acute or episodic. Consider, on the one hand, the case of an exhibitionist who has been exposing himself regularly for several years despite arrests, fines, imprisonment, and lengthy spells of expensive psychotherapy at the hands of recognized expert practitioners. Should an alternative form of therapy (e.g., behavior therapy) immediately produce a cessation of exposure incidents (presumably assessed with reliable and objective measures), it is not unreasonable to attribute the successful outcome to the behavioral methods. (Of course, even this demonstration would not be definitive, because the role of the particular therapist could not be totally discounted.) Now, on the other hand, consider a client suffering from depression of recent onset. Assume too that this client has had a history of episodic depressive spells, which have passed without the benefit of formal therapeutic intervention. Evidence that the depression lifts while the client is receiving therapy, of any variety, would not be very convincing. A plausible rival hypothesis is that history repeated itself, with therapy an unrelated concomitant of more basic change.

Projections about the natural course of clinical problems, in the absence of any treatment, similarly affect the inferences one can draw from treatment effects. Some problems show spontaneous remission over time (Rachman & Wilson, 1980).

The type of effect obtained with treatment influences our interpretation of case studies. Therapeutic change that is coincident with specific interventions makes it more likely that the effect is due to the treatment. The absence of any discernible relationship between treatment and behavioral improvement in the case of Little Hans was one of the many criticisms of Freud's highly speculative interpretation of that enormously influential case report by Wolpe and Rachman (1960). Magnitude of effect similarly lends credence to the presumed potency of therapeutic interventions.

Finally, if change is demonstrated across a diverse group of clients with heterogeneous characteristics at the time they are treated, then it becomes much more difficult to reject the inference that the treatment, and not some confounding factor, produced the change.

The influence of case studies on psychotherapeutic approaches from Freudian analysis to behavior therapy is widely accepted. A significant majority of psychotherapists would probably claim that controlled group outcome research with sophisticated statistical analyses has had relatively little impact on therapeutic practice (Barlow, 1980; Bergin & Strupp, 1970). The question is: Why is this so?

We think there are good reasons for the disproportionate influence of uncontrolled clinical case studies on thinking and practice in psychotherapy. Nisbett and Ross (1980) discuss the manner in which people, including social scientists, assign weights to different data or sources of information. Among the many valuable points they make is their conclusion that people give inferential weight to information in proportion to its vividness.

> "Research indicates that highly probative, data-summary information sometimes is ignored while less probative, case-history information has a substantial impact on inferences. Although people's responsiveness to vivid information has a certain justification and confers occasional advantages, the policy of weighting information in proportion to its vividness is risky. At best, vividness is associated imperfectly with probativeness. Consequently, highly probative but pallid information sometimes will be ignored, and conversely, evidentially weak but vivid information sometimes will have an undue impact of inferences" (p. 62).

In short, they explain the success and popularity of those charismatic therapists who rely upon the time-honored tactic of discounting "pallid" but more "probative" evidence with the response of "But I had a patient who . . ."

SINGLE-CASE EXPERIMENTAL DESIGNS

It is possible to study the individual case without sacrificing control over factors other than treatment that can affect outcome. An important contribution of the operant conditioning approach has been the development of a single-case experimental methodology with which to conduct controlled research and treatment in individual clients. The clinical adaptation of operant own-control designs demonstrates that behavior change in an individual client is the result of specific treatment interventions and not simply the passage of time, placebo reaction, or some other uncontrolled event.

The ABAB or Reversal Design

In the ABAB, or reversal design, following a period of baseline observation (A) during which no treatment of any kind is attempted, a treatment phase (B) is introduced while the behavior in question is continuously observed. Usually the behavior will show change in the desired direction, after which the treatment is withdrawn in a return to the baseline procedure (A). If the treatment per se was responsible for the observed change then the behavior should generally return almost to its former level during the original (A) period.

A pioneering study by Ayllon and Azrin (1965) provides an example of the reversal design. These investigators first increased the level of participation in rehabilitation activities in a group of hospitalized schizophrenics by making positive reinforcement contingent on participation in phase A of the study. Then, as shown in Figure 17-2, in phase B, reinforcement was administered on a noncontingent basis. In this procedure patients were given tokens at the beginning of each day regardless of their performance, which broke the contingency between reinforcer and response without eliminating the reinforcer completely. This ensured that the amount of social interaction between the attendants and ward staff, who administered the tokens, and the patients remained unchanged. Any deterioration in performance is then directly attributable to the precise functional relationship between behavior and reinforcement. Phase C marked a reversal to contingent reinforce-

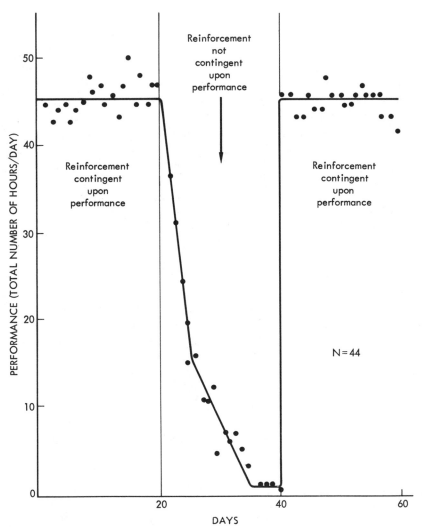

Figure 17–2 Total number of hours the group of 44 schizophrenics participated in rehabilitative activities on the ward under conditions of both contingent and noncontingent positive reinforcement. (From Ayllon and Azrin (1965). The measurement and reinforcement of behavior of psychotics. *Journal of the Experimental Analysis of Behavior, 8,* 373. Copyright 1965 by the Society for the Experimental Analysis of Behavior. Reprinted by permission.)

ment as in phase A. The results show that it was the specific reinforcing contingency that maintained these schizophrenics' behavior.

The study illustrated in Figure 17-2 demonstrates another point about single case experimental designs. Typically, the focus is on the behavior of the individual subject or client. Nevertheless, it is more the type of experimental arrangement than the number of subjects studied that defines this methodology. The number of subjects may vary widely; there were 44 in the Ayllon and Azrin study. The key point is that this group was treated as if it were a single case.

Multiple Baseline Designs

Multiple Baseline Design Across Behaviors. In this design, different responses are identified and measured over time to provide a baseline against which changes can be evaluated. Each response is then successively modified in turn; if each behavior changes maximally only when specifically treated, then a cause-effect relationship can be reliably inferred. This procedure is illustrated in Fig. 17-3. In this study of the treatment of a transvestite with sadomasochism (Brownell, Hayes, & Barlow, 1977), orgasmic reconditioning was first used to increase his heterosexual responsiveness. This left his transvestism and sadomasochism unaffected. Covert sensitization was then used to decrease transvestism, while baseline measures of sadomasochism showed no effect. Finally, sadomasochism was treated directly and successfully reduced. The different dimensions of this man's sexual disorder changed only when treated directly. (See Chapter 11.)

Multiple Baseline Design Across Individuals. In this design, baseline data are recorded for at least one behavior across several individuals in the same situation. Once the

behavior is stable for all individuals, the treatment is applied to one individual while baseline conditions are continued for the others. A cause-effect relationship between the treatment technique and behavioral change can be drawn if the behavior of each individual changes only when the technique is applied to him or her. Figure 17-4 illustrates this design. In this study by Biran, Augusto, and Wilson (1981), it was only when each of the three clients with a social phobia was treated with in vivo exposure that their behavior changed. Neither the cognitive restructuring method nor baseline assessments produced improvement.

General Characteristics of Single-Case Designs

According to Kazdin (1981), there are two central characteristics. The first is continual assessment of behavior over time. The target behavior is assessed regularly before, during, and after treatment intervention, often on a daily basis. An advantage of continual measurement is that it provides immediate information on treatment progress and makes possible data-based decisions about whether to continue or modify treatment. The second is that intervention effects are replicated within the same subject over time. Subjects act as their own controls, and comparisons of their performance are made as different interventions are implemented over time. An important exception to this latter emphasis on "own-control," however, is the widely used multiple-baseline across subjects. A third common characteristic of these designs is the emphasis on establishing both experimental and therapeutic criteria for evaluating treatment. Experimental criteria refer to demonstrating that reliable changes have been produced that are the result of the specific treatment technique. In brief, the investi-

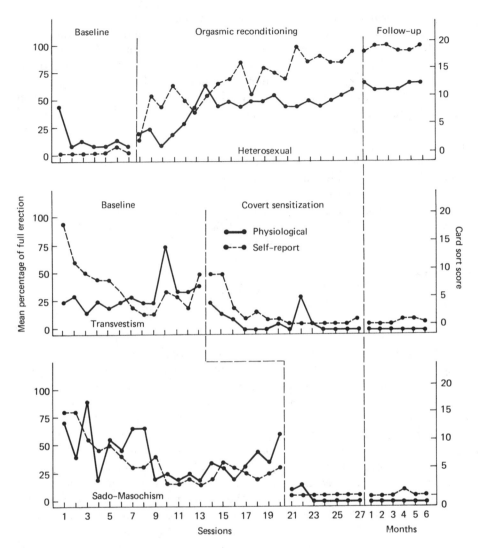

Figure 17–3 Mean penile circumference changes and card sort ratings of sexual arousal in response to deviant and heterosexual stimuli for Subject 5. (Brownell, K. D., Hayes, S. C., and Barlow, D. H. (1977). Patterns of appropriate and deviant sexual arousal: The behavioral treatment of multiple sexual deviations. Reprinted with permission from *Journal of Consulting and Clinical Psychology, 45,* 1144–1155. Copyright 1977 by the American Psychological Association.)

gator must be satisfied that the pattern of results could not plausibly be explained by variables unrelated to the specific treatment intervention.

Other features are usually identified with single-case experimental designs but, as Kaz-din (1981) points out, are not necessarily defining characteristics. One is the use of changes in overt behavior as the dependent measure. The reason for this association is straightforward. Single-case experimental methodology is the product of applied behavior analysis, a

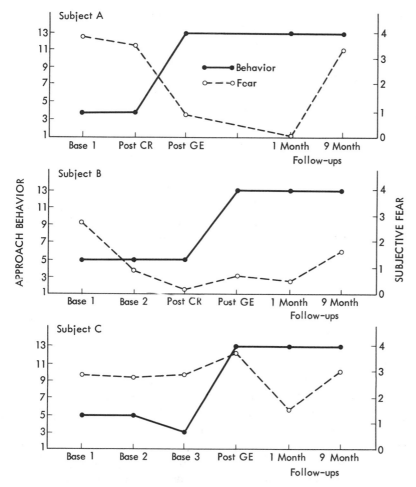

Figure 17–4   Approach behavior and subjective fear at pre-treatment assessments (BASE) after Cognitive Restructuring (CR) and Guided Exposure (GE) and at both follow-up assessments. (Biran, M., Augusto, F., and Wilson, G. T. (1981). A comparative analysis of cognitive and behavioral methods in the treatment of scriptophobia. *Behaviour Research and Therapy, 19*, 525–532. Copyright 1981 by Pergamon Journals LTD. Reprinted with permission.)

behavioristic approach defined by its emphasis on the study of overt behavior. Behavioral observations increase the objectivity of measurement. Although not totally free from bias (Kent & Foster, 1977, Chapter 2), they are less vulnerable to distortion than impressionistic or subjective evaluations typically made by therapists (Kent, O'Leary, Diament, & Dietz, 1974; Schnelle, 1974). In principle,

however, any dependent measure can be used to evaluate the effects of single-case experimental designs. Figure 17-3 illustrates the use of psychophysiological and self-report measures in this context.

Clinical Significance of Behavior Change. The therapeutic criterion referred to above reflects the emphasis in single-case experimental designs on producing change that is clinically or socially significant—change that improves the daily functioning of people and does not need to be inferred from the average performance of a group. In many instances it is self-evident when clinically significant change has been achieved, e.g., a self-injurious boy whose head-banging ceases. Clear-cut effects such as these are not always achieved, however, and the way in which clinical or social significance (the therapeutic criterion) of behavior change is evaluated has been unspecified.

Social validation has been proposed as a means of specifying the social or clinical significance of behavior change (Wolf, 1978). Social validation of treatment effects has been evaluated in two ways. In the social comparison method, the behavior of the client is compared with that of a nonproblem ("normal") peer group before and after treatment. Should treatment prove successful, the client's behavior would be indistinguishable from the nonproblem group after therapy. As an illustration of how this works, consider the treatment of children with conduct disorders. As noted in Chapter 6, these children can be reliably differentiated from their normal peers in frequency of aggressive acts, yelling, and so on. Treatment studies have shown that following treatment, these problematic behaviors are reduced to the point that they fall within normative levels (Kent & O'Leary, 1976; Patterson, 1982).

Social validation, however, is not without difficulties. In some instances the goal of making the individual indistinguishable from normal limits of functioning is unrealistic. For example, many chronic mental hospital patients will always function less effectively than normals, irrespective of the therapy. Yet this is not to say that such patients cannot be aided significantly in leading more useful and dignified lives. In other cases it is difficult to specify acceptable normative limits for different forms of behavior. What constitutes the appropriate comparison (peer) group? Whose standards or values should be used in determining what is the normative range for a particular individual or problem? Behavior therapists are concerned with the personal benefits their clients derive from treatment as well as the broader social effects of behavior change. The inescapable element of subjectivity inherent in determining treatment goals and subsequent social validation of effects must be recognized. (See Chapter 19.)

Another problem with social validation is the question of which of the client's social contacts should evaluate treatment effects. For some problems in some clients, such social contacts will be unavailable to the therapist for a variety of reasons. Another more subtle problem is that a client's social contacts, such as a spouse, might be either unable or unwilling to recognize therapeutic change. For example, it has been shown that spouses are not reliable observers of the occurrence or nonoccurrence of specific behavior in their own marriages (Jacobson & Moore, 1981). Similarly, Yeaton and Sechrest (1981), citing data showing that different sets of judges (teachers and parents of problem children) may provide different subjective evaluations of treatment effects, caution that clinicians who "use social validation techniques to argue that the goals of treatment have been reached must also be cautious in their choice of a relevant and discriminating set of judges to make the assessment" (p. 164).

Advantages

The following is a list of advantages to using single-case experimental designs in treatment evaluation.

1. The treatment of individual clients can be evaluated objectively. The personalistic quality

of the clinical case study is largely preserved without sacrificing experimental rigor.

2. Clinical problems can be studied that otherwise would be rejected as unsuitable for group methodology. Some problems are relatively rare, and insufficient numbers of subjects are available for group comparisons.

3. Effective treatment strategies can be developed by adding different therapeutic components to facilitate behavior change in a cumulative manner. This process is aided greatly by the continual, ongoing assessment of treatment outcome.

4. Different techniques can be compared in the treatment of the individual client.

5. Single-case experimental designs occupy an important place in the overall research strategy for evaluating psychological treatment methods. Innovative therapeutic techniques are often derived from basic psychological principles or uncontrolled clinical practice. Instead of making the jump from a clinical case study to an expensive, large-scale between-group study, small-scale testing with the appropriate single-case experimental design is recommended as an intermediate step. In this sense, single-case designs are useful in the development of effective behavior change methods when it is too costly or impractical to use a full-scale design. Once the efficacy of a treatment has been established, its broader value can be evaluated in a large-scale comparative outcome study.

Limitations

The limitations of these designs can be summarized as follows:

1. The possible interaction of subject variables with the specific treatment technique cannot be easily studied. Since only a single subject is studied, the effect of different subject characteristics (for example, high versus low anxiety) on the treatment procedure cannot be directly assessed. This requires group designs.

2. The generality of the findings with a single-case design is difficult to determine. One answer to this problem is the replication strategy that tests the efficacy of a single technique applied by the same therapist, under the same conditions, and to more than one client. If this technique is consistently successful with all cases, interpretation of the results is clear-cut. If the results are mixed or inconsistent, as is often the case in clinical research, problems in interpretation arise.

Even if the data from direct replications can be unambiguously interpreted, the problem of generalizing the results from the individual case to a more general population of clients remains. The solution proposed by operant conditioning is systematic replication. Systematic replication is defined as the attempt to replicate the findings from direct replication studies, varying 1) the therapists who administer the procedures, 2) the type of clients, 3) the nature of the behavior being modified, 4) the setting in which treatment occurs, or 5) any combination thereof. But there are difficulties with this strategy. The question is: When is a systematic replication series finished? Or, when can the investigator decide that the generality of a finding has been scientifically established? This question is part of the more general concern in experimental psychology with external validity (Campbell & Stanley, 1963).

3. Interpretation of the findings of single-case experimental designs is straightforward when the target behavior is stable during baseline and when treatment effects are clearly different from baseline. A problem is that these ideal conditions are not always obtained in clinical research. Marked variability in the target behavior over different phases of single-case experimental design makes it difficult to evaluate whether significant change has occurred.

4. Visual inspection is the primary basis for evaluating the data in single-case experimental designs. The reason for choosing this means of evaluation over statistical analyses is that applied behavior analysis is committed to marked and consistent changes that are of obvious social and clinical importance (Baer, 1977). The idea is not to resort to statistical analyses to uncover reliable effects that the eye can see. For this and other technical reasons related to the statistical techniques themselves, statistical analysis of single-case designs remains the exception rather than the rule (Kazdin, 1981). The problem, as Kazdin notes, is "the lack of concrete decision rules for determining whether a particular demonstration shows or fails to show a

reliable effect. The process of visual inspection would seem to permit, if not actively encourage, subjectivity and inconsistency in the evaluation of intervention effects. In fact, a few studies have examined the extent to which persons consistently judge through visual inspection whether a particular intervention demonstrated an effect. The results have shown that judges, even when experts in the field, often disagree about particular data patterns and whether the effects were reliable" (p. 239).

5. Applied behavior analysts search for large, consistent effects, and visual inspection can easily result in relatively weak, though reliable and important effects being overlooked.

6. Specific limitations attach to different designs. In the ABAB reversal design, for example, demonstrating the efficacy of the treatment requires that the treatment effect is reversible and that the target behavior returns to baseline level once the treatment is withdrawn. However, it is often ill-advised or unethical to return to a baseline condition after a treatment has been shown to be effective. For example, when a self-destructive child has responded to a particular intervention, such as praise from attendants for positive interactions with other children on the ward, it may be very detrimental to the child's physical and mental health to ask the attendants to withdraw their praise. A second problem is that the reversal design is limited to treatment conditions which can be readily reversed. There are certain treatments that lead to changes in behavior which are relatively permanent. For example, if enuretic children (bedwetters) are given certain toilet training, their bladder size increases. They no longer wet the bed, and the withdrawal of the treatment does not lead to a return to a baseline condition. This limitation applies especially to the learning of new skills. Once a child has learned to read, removal of external incentives to read will not make the child illiterate. In cases like this, the original baseline can never be reinstated. If the behavior of interest shows no reversal, little of significance can be concluded.

BETWEEN-GROUP DESIGNS

When a number of subjects is assigned to a treatment group or a control group and their outcomes then compared, the design is called a between-group design. A variety of between-group designs have been used to evaluate treatment outcome. As with other research strategies, each between-group design has its particular advantages and disadvantages.

Laboratory-Based Evaluation of Treatment Methods

At first glance it might seem that the best way to evaluate treatment outcome is to study the effects of therapy carried out by experienced practitioners with actual clients under clinical conditions. This is difficult to do for several reasons. From a methodological point of view, it is hard and often impossible to conduct highly controlled research in such service-delivery settings. From a practical point of view, it is difficult to recruit experienced therapists who have the time or desire to participate in such research. Finding sufficiently large numbers of similar clients with common problems is a formidable task. Finally, from an ethical point of view, it is difficult to assign clients to control groups which do not receive the most effective form of treatment (O'Leary & Borkovec, 1978).

An alternative research strategy to studying the clinical situation directly is to evaluate specific treatment methods applied to well-defined, circumscribed problems under controlled laboratory conditions, commonly called analogue research.

Advantages

1. The treatment method can be carefully specified and standardized. Different parameters of the technique can be systematically varied and components selectively analyzed. This makes it possible to identify the necessary and sufficient conditions of treatment success. The study of systematic desensitization, as discussed in Chapter 8, is a good example of this research strategy.

2. The selection of a homogeneous subject population with the same problem behavior permits evaluation of the particular problem for which the specific treatment is best suited.

3. Subjects can be randomly assigned to different treatment and control conditions. Unlike the actual clinical situation in which the therapist is ethically and professionally obliged to offer the client the most effective treatment in the most efficient manner possible, specific elements of therapy or even therapy itself can be selectively withheld in the laboratory setting.

Limitations

1. Concern is often expressed about whether the results from these laboratory studies can be generalized to the clinical treatment of clients. A target of such criticism has been a large number of studies on fear reduction methods using only mildly fearful college students as subjects (Bernstein & Paul, 1971). However, studies of individuals with genuine phobias that interfere with their daily lives and cause personal distress are appropriate for the evaluation of treatment outcome (Bandura, 1977a). These studies incorporate methodological rigor while still focusing on significant personal problems. Information gained in these studies has advanced our knowledge of theoretical mechanisms (e.g., self-efficacy theory) and has led to improved treatment methods (Chapter 8).

A common tactic in outcome research has been to recruit subjects by advertising the program and contacting physicians and other appropriate treatment facilities. Some critics have charged that subjects recruited in this way are intrinsically different from individuals who seek therapy of their own accord (Gurman, Knudson, & Kniskern, 1978; Marks, 1978). However, if care is taken to demonstrate that subjects recruited for clinical research are as severely distressed and motivated to change as their counterparts in the natural clinical setting are, this objection ceases to be a problem. Consistent with this view, studies with phobics, depressed patients, and obese individuals have failed to show differences in treatment effects between individuals recruited for clinical research and those who initiated treatment without such prompts (Foreyt, Goodrick, & Gotto, 1981; Grey, Sartory, & Rachman, 1979; Last, Thase, Hersen, Bellack, & Himmelhoch, 1984).

2. The question of whether the findings of a research study are generalizable to therapeutic situations applies to all clinical research, including studies conducted with clients in actual clinical settings. In evaluating therapy outcome research, the critical question is: To what degree do the conditions of the study approximate the clinical situation? The generalizability of a study has to be evaluated along several different dimensions, including the target problem, type of subject, subjects' motivation for treatment, therapist characteristics and training, nature of the treatment method and how it might vary from the way it is usually administered in clinical practice, assessment of treatment effects, and so on (Kazdin & Wilson, 1978). It is assumed that the more similar the study, the greater the generalizability of the results.

Treatment Program Research

An evaluation of the efficacy of a single treatment method applied to a circumscribed problem is an example of technique-oriented research. The relatively restricted conditions of controlled research along these lines require that all subjects be treated in the same way with the same procedure, yet clinical experience indicates that such homogeneity among a large number of clients is questionable. Usually, different variables maintain problem behavior in different individuals. Moreover, clinical disorders are typically determined by multiple factors rather than a single maintaining variable, and a multifaceted therapy program is required to change behavior. This means that clinical practice emphasizes a problem-oriented approach in which several treatment methods are tailored to the individual client's particular problem. The treatment program, or what has also been called the package research strategy, takes this into account by evaluating therapy programs that "include as many component procedures as seem necessary to obtain, ideally, a total treatment success" (Azrin, 1977). Numerous examples of effective multicomponent treatment programs have been discussed in the previous chapters. If the multicomponent treatment program proves successful, subsequent research can be directed toward identifying the effective components of the overall package.

Advantages of Multi-Component Treatment

1. It is a problem-oriented research strategy that allows for an evaluation of multiple treatment methods typically used in clinical practice. The primary emphasis is on producing clinically significant change, thus it is close to the nature and purpose of clinical practice.

2. It is logically one of the first approaches to evaluate a given treatment. If it is successful, it indicates the need for continued research; if it fails to produce therapeutic improvement, it makes little sense to try to analyze the component parts of the program. It is useful in determining whether further component analysis research is warranted.

Limitations of Multi-Component Treatment

1. From the standpoint of treatment evaluation and analysis it is important to ensure that the program is not so complex and wide-ranging that it is difficult to identify the specific techniques in complex programs. Every component of the program must be operationally defined and replicable.

2. The treatment program should not be so multifaceted that it becomes difficult to identify it as a distinctive program that is procedurally different from alternative treatments to which it might be compared.

Dismantling Research

In the dismantling strategy, specific components of the treatment package are systematically eliminated, and the associated decrement in treatment effects is measured. The relative contribution of each component to the total treatment program can then be assessed. Both the separate and combined effects of components can be analyzed (e.g., research on systematic desensitization—Chapter 8).

Comparative Research

Comparative treatment outcome studies are directed toward answering the question: Is one therapy method superior to another? Ideally, alternative treatment methods are evaluated in comparative studies after their efficacy has been established in single-case experimental designs or controlled laboratory-based research. Yet conventional comparative outcome research has been preoccupied with determining whether "psychotherapy" is more effective than "behavior therapy." This question has led to a large number of mostly uninterpretable studies that compare ill-defined treatment programs with heterogeneous clinical disorders using global and unsatisfactory outcome measures (Kazdin & Wilson, 1978).

Inadequacies of Conventional Research

The conventional comparative outcome research strategy is illustrated in a study by Sloane, Staples, Cristol, Yorkston, and Whipple (1975). Briefly, ninety-four adult clients with neurotic (anxiety) disorders were randomly assigned to one of three treatment groups, after being matched for sex and severity of disturbance. The three treatment groups consisted of (1) psychoanalytically oriented psychotherapy conducted by experienced therapists of this theoretical persuasion; (2) behavior therapy conducted by equally experienced therapists, including Wolpe and Lazarus; and (3) a waiting list control group. Therapy lasted for four months followed by a post-treatment evaluation and an eight-month follow-up. The outcome measures consisted of ratings of three primary symptoms: subjective estimates of work; social and sexual adjustment derived from a structured interview; and an overall rating of improvement. These ratings were made by therapist, client, a psychiatrist who did not know the nature of the study, and an "informant" who was a relative or close friend of the client.

On the primary symptoms, roughly 50 percent of the control group and 80 percent of the behavior therapy and psychotherapy groups were considered improved. Behavior therapy produced significant improvement in both work and social adjustment, whereas psychotherapy resulted in marginal improvement in work. Behavior therapy was significantly superior to the other groups on the overall rating of improvement. On this global measure of outcome, 93 percent of the group receiving behavior therapy were rated as significantly improved, whereas 77 percent of the psychotherapy and waiting list patients were rated as significantly improved. There were no differences among the three groups at follow-up.

In many ways the Sloane and colleagues (1975) study is the best conventional comparative outcome study yet conducted. The majority of conventional comparative outcome studies entail problems that make interpretation of the results virtually impossible (Kazdin & Wilson, 1978). However, even in the Sloane et al. (1975) study, a number of conceptual and methodological problems make it difficult to draw unambiguous conclusions.

Inadequacies of Assessment.   The failure to obtain any objective behavioral measure of treatment effects is a major shortcoming. Assessing outcome by subjective global ratings derived from a single clinical interview is unacceptable. The therapist's own ratings are obviously open to bias, as is the client's self-rating. In an improvement on these measures, which have often been the only measures used to evaluate treatment outcome, Sloane and colleagues (1975) obtained an independent assessor's ratings. The problem with these ratings is that they were based on the client's self-report during the clinical interview and not on observations of the client's behavior in real-life problem situations or on problem-specific self-monitoring by clients.

Ill-Defined Global Approaches.   Attempts to compare something called "psychotherapy" with something labeled "behavior therapy" assume that these are uniform, homogeneous approaches. However, there is no "behavior therapy" to which other approaches can be compared in any general sense. There are several different procedures that collectively can be referred to as behavior therapy. Similarly, there are different methods of psychotherapy. Sloane et al. (1975) tried to define psychotherapy and behavior therapy respectively by drawing up a list of defining characteristics of each approach. However, both approaches still encompassed a wide range of different procedures.

Some behavioral techniques are clearly more effective than others. As a result, evaluations of behavior therapy are likely to be distorted if it is assumed, as it has been (Luborsky, Singer, & Luborsky, 1975; Smith, Glass & Miller, 1980), that all behavioral methods are uniformly effective. Behavior therapy consists of numerous techniques that are constantly being developed and refined. Two of the behavioral techniques in the Sloane and colleagues study were systematic desensitization and electrical aversion conditioning. These were two of the most important methods in behavior therapy in its early stages. However, alternative methods to systematic desensitization have now been developed that appear to be even more effective. Electrical aversion conditioning, once widely used with problems like alcoholism, has been shown to be ineffective and has been abandoned.

Comparative outcome studies also require clearly defined alternative treatments. If procedural differences between contrasting techniques are blurred, it is difficult to interpret results. Replication also depends on precise specification of treatment methods. Specification is essential to determine if the treatments were implemented correctly and were procedurally distinct from each other. A well-designed study should include independent measures of whether alternative treatments were distinct from one another and of treatment integrity, i.e., the degree to which treatment was implemented as planned (Moos & Finney, 1983; Yeaton, 1982). Data can be collected either through video- or audio-tapes, transcripts, or direct observation to ensure that treatments were implemented properly (DeRubeis, Hollon, Evans, & Bemis, 1982). Sloane et al. (1975) analyzed audio-tape recordings of the fifth session of therapy to show that their psychoanalytically oriented psychotherapy was procedurally distinct from their behavior therapy condition.

In addition to monitoring the integrity of the treatment, clients' compliance with treatment must be evaluated independently of clinical outcome. Treatment effects can only be attributed to specific methods if it is shown that clients engaged in those methods. Treatment success is related to compliance with therapeutic instructions (Dubbert & Wilson, 1983).

To summarize, methodological flaws in conventional comparative outcome research have obscured differences among alternative treatment methods. As a result, these studies cannot be used to support the argument that there are no differences between behavioral methods and conventional psychotherapy in treatment outcome (Kazdin & Wilson, 1978).

What Needs To Be Done?

Instead of asking whether "behavior therapy" is more effective than "psychotherapy," the more useful question to address is *what* treatment method, applied by *whom* is most effective for *what* problem in *which* person (Paul, 1967). This formidable question cannot be answered in a single study, but it provides the framework in which outcome research can be conducted constructively. The Paul and Lentz (1977) study on the psychosocial treatment of chronic mental patients (see Chapter 16) provides an excellent example of a well-designed comparative outcome study.

Most of the clinical research in behavior therapy has addressed the question: What method is effective for what problem on what measures? Also, outcome studies of behavior therapy have increasingly included long-term follow-up evaluations of initial treatment effects—a rarity in traditional research on psychotherapy. Durability of treatment-produced improvement is an important criterion for evaluating the success of therapy (Kazdin & Wilson, 1978). If two treatments produce comparable improvement at post-treatment, but one is associated with rapid relapse whereas the other has lasting benefits, the latter is the treatment of choice. Consider the use of antidepressant drugs in the treatment of either agoraphobia or bulimia nervosa. As we saw in Chapters 9 and 13, discontinuing pharmacotherapy typically results in rapid relapse; behavioral treatment, however, shows more acceptable maintenance of treatment effects during long-term follow-ups.

Broadening Evaluation Criteria

There are, in addition to Paul's (1967) criteria for judging treatment outcome, other important considerations which have received relatively little research attention. These include the acceptability and the cost-effectiveness of treatments (Kazdin & Wilson, 1978).

Alternative treatment methods are not necessarily equally acceptable to clients. In a study by Kazdin, French, and Sherick (1981), child psychiatric inpatients, parents, and staff evaluated the acceptability of alternative treatments for children. Clinical cases of children who displayed severe behavioral problems at home and school were described together with four alternative treatments: positive reinforcement of incompatible behavior, positive practice, medication, and time out. Reinforcement of incompatible behavior was rated the most acceptable treatment (with time out the least effective) by the children, their parents, and the staff. As Kazdin et al. note, differences in degree of acceptability of alternative treatments may significantly influence compliance and hence therapeutic efficacy. Norton, Allen, and Hilton's (1982—see Chapter 9) study of the social validity of treatments of agoraphobia showed that drug treatment was significantly less acceptable to clients and nonclients alike than psychological treatment. The greater reluctance of clients to agree to drug treatment, and their higher attrition rate during pharmacotherapy, are in line with this finding.

The interaction between acceptability of treatment and compliance and efficacy is obviously complex and reciprocal. In some instances efficacy will clearly determine clients' (and society's) perception of what is "acceptable." Research on this topic is still in the early stages. In the meantime, we know that assessment of consumer satisfaction (closely related to acceptability) and assessment of treatment outcome often yield conflicting findings. Bornstein and Rychtarik (1983) observe, "A number of studies have found dif-

ferences in treatment outcome yet failed to find differences with respect to clients' satisfaction or preferences . . . Other studies have found differences in consumer satisfaction without obtaining actual outcome differences . . . while still others appear to show a correspondence between the two measures" (p. 196).

Aside from their efficacy, however this is defined, treatment methods may vary in efficiency and cost. The less costly of two equally effective treatments is to be preferred. Cost-effectiveness is a major consideration in the comparison between behavioral methods and traditional psychotherapy. There is relatively little research on cost-effectiveness in behavior therapy, although Yeaton (1982), in an analysis of the *Journal of Applied Behavior Analysis*, has shown that studies of cost-effectiveness of behavioral methods are on the increase.

The briefer the treatment the more likely it is to be cost-effective. In Chapter 13 we reported Agras and Kraemer's (1984) analysis of the treatment of anorexia nervosa. Reinforcement methods appeared to be no more effective than medical therapy, but they were briefer, and hence, the treatment Agras and Kraemer recommended. In other instances, behavior therapy has been shown to be both more effective and less costly. The Paul and Lentz (1977) study (Chapter 16) is a case in point.

Behavior therapy is usually regarded as a form of brief therapy. Butcher and Koss (1978) state, "Today, most practitioners agree that 25 sessions is the upper limit of 'brief' therapy, with as many clinicians recommending courses of treatment lasting from one to six sessions as the longer 10 to 25 session treatment" (p. 730). Given this time frame, behavior therapy unquestionably qualifies as one of the many forms of short-term therapy. As such, it tends to be relatively cost-effective versus long-term psychodynamic psychotherapy. Most of the behavioral treatment programs evaluated in controlled outcome studies in the preceding chapters were relatively brief, varying from three to six months. The clinical practice of behavior therapy, however, is not always short-term treatment. Therapy lasting from twenty-five to fifty sessions is commonplace, and still longer treatment is not unusual. Therapy in excess of 100 sessions, however, is relatively rare.

Treatment is cost-effective if it can be delivered with a minimal amount of therapist involvement. The use of self-help treatment manuals is one possible means of making treatment cost-effective. Glasgow and Rosen (1978) distinguished among self-administered programs, in which the written manual constitutes the sole basis for treatment; programs involving minimal contact, in which there is some contact with the therapist, such as phone calls or even periodic meetings; and therapist-administered programs, in which there is regular contact with the therapist, who guides the client in the use of the manual. Which of these different degrees of therapist involvement is appropriate for a particular client will depend on a number of factors, including the nature and severity of the problem and the type of self-help manual. There is, at present, no convincing evidence of the efficacy of totally self-administered programs or manuals, a disturbing finding in light of the fact that this is precisely the context in which most are likely to be used. Manuals with minimal contact, however, do have some empirical support and may offer the most prudent savings in professional time. Examples of the responsible use of treatment manuals in behavior therapy are those of Mathews, Teasdale, Munby, Johnston, and Shaw (1977) with agoraphobics (Chapter 9); Miller and Baca (1983) with problem drinkers (Chapter 14);

and Zeiss (1978) with sexual dysfunction (Chapter 11).

A major cost in evaluating therapy is the amount of professional training required of the therapist. Traditionally, becoming a therapist, whether within psychiatry or psychology, entails lengthy and expensive training. As we will discuss in the next chapter, less expensively trained individuals may in some cases achieve the same results as professionals.

Experimental Research and Clinical Practice

Thus far we have discussed the different research strategies that have characterized behavior therapy. More than any other treatment approach, behavior therapy is committed to integrating research and therapy within the context of the scientist-practitioner model of clinical training. The goal of behavior therapy was to overcome the wide gap that has always existed between experimental psychology and clinical practice in the other psychotherapies. Nevertheless, there are signs that even in behavior therapy, there is more of a gap between researchers and therapists than is desirable (Barlow, 1980).

One analysis of the apparent failure of research to influence the day-to-day functioning of clinical practitioners assumes that there has been too great a reliance on the wrong experimental methodology, one that "emphasizes factorial designs, multivariate statistics, and the 0.5 level of probability. For these will never be used in the private office or clinic" (Barlow, 1980, p. 308). The proposed solution is a greater emphasis on single-case experimental designs. Hayes (1981) goes as far as to assert that the use of single-case experimental designs will do away with the gap between researcher and therapist. Yet there are several problems with this view (Wilson, 1982b). Methodologically, completing well-controlled single-case experimental design studies that establish cause-effect relationships is usually as demanding and requires as much experimental control as more traditional group outcome research. This is not to say that on occasion the practitioner will not be able to conduct a single-case experimental study with sufficient control to make causal analyses, but these are likely to be relatively rare. Ethically, the problem is that the client be fully informed as to whether he or she is participating in a research project or receiving therapy. The therapist's activities must be identified as one or the other. If it is therapy the client is receiving, many of the critical requirements of single-case experimental designs are difficult, if not impossible, to meet. In essence, all single-case experimental designs necessitate baseline observations, holding certain conditions constant at different times, and intervening selectively in a limited manner at any one point. This conflicts with the priority in any service-delivery setting, which is to treat the client's problems in as effective and efficient a manner as possible. Clinically relevant change, produced at the least possible cost (in time, effort, money, and emotional stress), is the goal of clinical practice. Identifying the determinants of behavior change is of little relevance to the therapist

or the client in this setting. The latter is a scientific concern that need have no immediate bearing on the behavior of the practitioner.

An Integrative Framework

By virtue of its demanding nature, controlled research undertaken to identify specific cause-effect relationships, using either between-groups statistical designs or single-case experimental methodology, will be done by the clinical researcher trained in the scientist-practitioner tradition. This does not mean that the full-time practitioner does not have a vital and continuing role in the overall clinical research enterprise. He or she has an invaluable and unique role, providing the clinical researcher with novel hypotheses, unusual observations, and theoretical leads, as well as participating in field tests of experimentally tested methods (Agras et al., 1979; Barlow, 1980).

Table 17-1 describes an integrative framework for the different levels of analysis from basic scientific research to clinical practice. This framework emphasizes that each level has its unique and necessary place in the overall development of an applied clinical science.

The flow of influence along this continuum

Table 17–1 Different Levels of Scientific/Clinical Analysis along the Continuum from Basic Research to Clinical Practice

Level 1	Basic laboratory research on mechanisms of behavior change.
Level 2	Analogue treatment research to identify effective ingredients of therapeutic procedures under controlled laboratory conditions.
Level 3	Controlled clinical research with patient populations. Two sub-types can be distinguished: (1) studies of specific techniques with detailed process and outcome measures; (2) studies designed to show optimal treatment effects using multicomponent therapy packages.
Level 4	Clinical practice. Therapists may measure outcome in case studies or clinical series (an AB design), or, in rare instances, conduct single-case experimental designs.

From "Some Comments on Clinical Research" by G.T. Wilson (1981). *Behavioral Assessment, 3*, 217–226. Copyright 1981, Association for Advancement of Behavior Therapy. Reprinted by permission.

is not unidirectional. There is a reciprocal interaction between different levels. For example, novel clinical observations or uncontrolled findings by practitioners at level 4 often suggest new treatment techniques and indicate the limitations of existing methods. These observations influence the research done at levels 1 and 3. The actual flow of treatment-related research within this framework is shown in Figure 17-1. Ultimately it will prove short-sighted and self-defeating if any one level is selectively emphasized to the neglect of others.

Meta-Analysis and the Evaluation of Therapy's Effects

One of the most influential but controversial developments in the evaluation of the effects of psychological therapies has been the use of a statistical technique known as meta-analysis (Smith et al., 1980). Meta-analysis is a quantitative method for averaging and integrating the standardized results of a large number of different studies. The unit of analysis of meta-analysis is the effect size (ES), a quantitative index of the size of the effect of therapy. Most meta-analyses derive the ES by subtracting the mean of the control group from the mean of the treatment group and dividing that difference by the standard deviation of the control group. This calculation is made on the data in published studies on therapy outcome. The larger the ES, the greater the effect of therapy. An ES of 1 indicates that "a person at the mean of the control group would be expected to rise to the 84th percentile of the control group after treatment" (Smith & Glass, 1977, p. 753). For example, Smith and Glass claimed that the ES for all the psychological therapies, including behavior therapy, was 0.68., which means that the average client receiving therapy would do better than 75% of those who do not receive therapy. Once the ES's from

a large number of different studies have been calculated, statistical analyses can be carried out to answer different questions about treatment outcome, such as comparing the effects of different therapies.

The proponents of meta-analysis claim that it is inherently superior to traditional, qualitative literature reviews. A consensually validated statistical method, meta-analysis aims to eliminate or at least minimize the subjectivity and reviewer bias to which traditional "literary reviews" of the evidence are susceptible. It is argued that meta-analysis is not only fairer and more objective but also more thorough and comprehensive than other methods of reviewing diverse studies (Fiske, 1983; Shapiro & Shapiro, 1983; Smith et al., 1980). Meta-analyses have been conducted on the general literature on all psychological therapies across all problems, and on particular clinical disorders (Andrews, Moran, & Hall's [1983] meta-analysis of the treatment of agoraphobia—Chapter 9). These meta-analyses have consistently demonstrated the clear-cut superiority of behavior therapy over other psychological approaches (Wilson, 1985).[2] Several fundamental problems with the notion of meta-analysis as a means of evaluating therapy outcome and inadequacies in the way meta-analyses have been conducted, though, detract greatly from the otherwise glowing endorsement of meta-analytic findings show-

---

2. In the most flawed of the available meta-analyses, Smith et al. (1980) concluded that there are no differences among any forms of psychological therapies. Nevertheless, they contradicted themselves on this issue. Despite their insistence on the unique virtues of meta-analysis, they make the following observation, "Ex post facto statistical equating of therapies is only partly satisfactory, since many potential confounding variables remain uncontrolled. The best solution for the reduction of the influence of extraneous variables is experimental; that is, for one researcher to study the effects of two or more therapies directly, using the same kinds of client, therapy of standard duration, therapists of equivalent training, and com-

ing that behavior therapy is superior to all other forms of psychological treatment.

The many limitations and liabilities of meta-analysis in the evaluation of therapy have been the subject of several detailed critiques (Erwin, 1984; Paul, 1985; Wilson, 1983; Wilson & Rachman, 1985). We will limit the discussion that follows to three points.

1. Does Meta-Analysis Provide More Comprehensive Evaluation of Outcome? Smith et al.'s (1980) insistence on the unprecedented comprehensiveness of their review has been discredited, what with their omission of numerous well-controlled studies in the area of behavior therapy alone (Rachman & Wilson, 1980; Wilson & Rachman, 1983). Subsequent meta-analyses have wisely avoided both the exaggerated claims and rhetoric of Smith et al. about unparalleled coverage of the literature and have introduced other means of trying to develop a representative data base for statistical analysis (Shapiro & Shapiro, 1983). Unfortunately, the Shapiros, in their commendable effort to improve upon Smith et al.'s obvious inadequacies and to adopt a non-partisan set of criteria for including studies in their meta-analysis, introduced other problems that compromised the representativeness of their own data base (Wilson & Rachman, 1983). These particular problems are not inherent in meta-analysis, of course, and superior data bases could be developed

for subsequent analyses. A more fundamental limitation of meta-analysis is its apparent inability to take into account the large body of single-case experimental designs in the evaluation of treatment effects. Proponents of meta-analysis have yet to address this major problem.

2. The Question of Quality. Smith et al. included all studies in their meta-analysis, regardless of how bad or how uninterpretable their findings were. They then assigned equal weight to the good and bad studies. For example, a well-designed study such as Paul and Lentz's (1977), counted no more than literally hundreds of methodologically weak studies, many of which had no appropriate control groups. The obvious result of this policy is to swamp the relatively few good studies in the literature with the majority of bad studies.

Smith et al. defend their meta-analysis by arguing that if all studies are included in the meta-analysis, the methodological characteristics of different studies can then be empirically related to outcome (ES's). They did this, found no relation between their design criteria and ES's, and thereby concluded that high and low quality studies can be lumped together and assigned equal importance.

The overriding problem with Smith et al.'s empirical approach is that it is only as good as the subjective judgments of the quality of studies and the accuracy and representativeness of the data base, among other characteristics of the meta-analysis, on which it was based. Rachman and Wilson (1980) document the seriously deficient nature of Smith et al.'s criteria for judging the internal validity of studies. Mintz (1983) states, "It is unusual to see recommendations about inclusion or exclusion of data based on examination of the results. The recommendation appears to be that if poor-quality research agrees with good research, include it. But in that case, what information is being added? If poor research

---

mon measurements" (p. 106). When they followed this aspect on their own advice and selected "well-controlled" studies, they found that the behavioral therapies were significantly superior to both verbal (psychodynamic) and developmental therapies. In a further ad hoc analysis, they divided outcome measures into two classes: those that were "psychological" and those that were "less tractable." The superiority of the behavioral therapies was then limited to "psychological" measures. Among these measures were "fear-anxiety, self-esteem, global adjustment, personality traits, vocational-personal development" (p. 107).

disagrees, disregard it. What, then, is the benefit from including research that is obviously flawed?" (p. 74).

Landman and Dawes (1982) claimed to have addressed the quality-of-study criticism in a reanalysis of 65 randomly selected studies from Smith and Glass's (1977) data base. Among these studies, they judged 42 to be appropriately controlled. The analysis produced results similar to those of Smith et al.'s, leading Landman and Dawes to conclude, erroneously, that Smith et al.'s major conclusions were upheld in a more rigorous evaluation. Landman and Dawes's methodological criteria, the presence of a no-treatment control group and random assignment of subjects, do little to improve upon Smith et al.'s procedure. As has been widely demonstrated, an adequate attention-placebo control condition is a must if the internal validity of a treatment outcome study is to be properly assessed (Kazdin & Wilcoxon, 1976; Paul, 1969; Rachman & Wilson, 1980).

The problems with the methodological criteria used by Smith et al. (1980) and Landman and Dawes (1982) are revealed in Prioleau, Murdock, and Brody's (1983) meta-analysis of yet another sub-set of Smith et al.'s (1980) data base. Prioleau et al. limited their analysis only to psychotherapy and selected only studies that included a placebo control treatment. It is noteworthy that they still discarded fully 25 percent of the forty studies with a placebo control because they were so seriously flawed. Exactly what criteria Prioleau et al. used in making this cut are unknown, although most of the remaining studies can still be criticized on methodological grounds. In contrast to Smith et al. and Landman and Dawes (1980), Prioleau et al. found no evidence of any effects of psychotherapy greater than that of placebo.

Not all advocates of meta-analysis share Smith et al.'s particular views. Adopting yet another counter to the criticism of their quality-free approach, others have suggested that poor studies be excluded or studies weighted according to quality (Strube & Hartmann, 1983). For example, Shapiro and Shapiro (1983) observe, "each study in a meta-analysis can be weighted according to its sample size or indeed any other attribute considered important by the reviewer." They add that "care must be taken to ensure that the weightings are appropriate." But what is "appropriate"? According to whom, and using what set of ground rules? Not surprisingly, different meta-analyses, using different (and arbitrarily set) rules and standards have produced conflicting results about the value of non-behavioral therapy.

Meta-analysis may prove to be more useful than it has thus far, as subsequent analyses respond to the criticisms summarized here. An advantage of meta-analysis is that it encourages explicit statement of methodological criteria for evaluating treatment outcome. As Mintz (1983) notes, meta-analysis is a subjective method, but makes more public what has too often been the more private process of conventional reviews of the therapy outcome literature.

3. Measuring Treatment Outcome: The Dependent Variable in Meta-Analyses. Smith et al. (1980) counted every measure in each of the studies they reviewed as a separate ES. The result was that the basic unit of analysis in their meta-analysis was based on nonindependent ES estimates, so the studies were unevenly weighted according to their number of ES's. To avoid this statistical confound in the data, other meta-analyses have used a different strategy for deriving a measure of treatment effectiveness. Landman and Dawes (1980) and Prioleau et al. (1983) used as their unit of analysis the pooled ES of all measures within each study to overcome the problem of statistical nonindependence. In other words, they derived a single outcome measure for each study, regardless of how many outcome measures the original investigators had reported. This latter strategy saves the statistical purity of the meta-analysis, but only at the unacceptable cost of an analysis that has little conceptual or clinical value.

We have repeatedly stressed that treatment evaluation studies should include multiple measures of process and outcome that sample different domains of functioning. Different measures may change in response to different treatments and at different rates (Lang, 1969; Rachman, 1978). Useful theoretical and practical advances have been made by studying the nature of synchrony and desynchrony among response systems in fear and fear reduction (Lang, 1979; Rachman, 1978). And in a related vein, the analysis of response covariation promises to extend our knowledge of treatment effects (Kazdin, 1982). These lines of scientific and clinical inquiry are obliterated by pooling different measures within studies.

Some examples illustrate the problems of indiscriminately pooling different measures. Consider an evaluation of the treatment of obesity. What clinical or conceptual sense does it make to lump together measures of body-fat, body-weight, body-image, lipoproteins, systolic and diastolic blood pressure, depressed affect, and marital satisfaction into a single index (ES) of outcome? Some rapid, nonbehavioral treatments of obesity have produced weight loss but increased depression (Stunkard & Rush, 1974). Reducing these two different measures to a standard statistic (ES) not only may cancel both out, leaving a meaningless number, but it may also conceal a clinically important outcome.

As the foregoing example shows, meta-analyses have failed to consider the conceptual relevance of different measures in individual studies. Simply stated, the multiple measures included in well-designed outcome studies may have different purposes; all are not necessarily intended to reflect outcome. Paul (1985) offers an informative critique of this limitation of meta-analysis. Referring to his study of the treatment of speech anxiety (Paul, 1966, 1967), he notes that of the different scales administered at follow-up, only two were directly relevant to evaluation of outcome: focal scales of experienced and expected anxiety in the performance situation. The other measures were included "only to aid in identifying the sample of clients and to assess other changes in client behavior predicted by the competing theoretical models underlying the insight-oriented psychotherapy ('symptom-substitution' for desensitization and attention-placebo clients) and systematic desensitization treatments ('generalization' or 'no change' in nonfocal areas for all clients). Thus, to represent the conceptual integrity of the design-relevant measures, only the 'focal-experienced' scale or, at most, the two focal scales should be included in a meta-analysis of treatment outcomes" (pp. 12-13). The mistake of averaging these different measures into a single ES is obvious. Paul (1985) shows that the mean ES of the advantage of systematic desensitization over the attention-placebo control treatment at the six-week follow-up was 0.45 for the two focal scales. The mean of all scales, however, which would be the figure used by meta-analysts such as Landman and Dawes, was 0.04. Relying upon a pooled ES misrepresents the study and its results, and dramatically underestimates treatment effects.

SUMMARY

A major contribution of behavior therapy has been the development of improved strategies for analyzing and evaluating treatment outcome. No one form of methodology is appropriate for all evaluation purposes, and different strategies are required to answer different questions. Uncontrolled case studies can be reported in ways that make them more informative (e.g., using objective measures of outcome). Single-case experimental designs permit demonstration of the causal effects of specific treatments on outcome in individual clients. Behavior is continually assessed as treatments are repeated over time. Among the most commonly used are the reversal (ABAB) and multiple baselines designs. They rely upon visual inspection of graphs of treatment effects rather than statistical analyses. Variability in treatment effects makes evaluation difficult.

Laboratory-based (analogue) research allows tightly controlled studies of a specific treatment method for particular problems in restricted client populations. It is especially useful for identifying the necessary and sufficient conditions for effectiveness and the theoretical mechanisms involved.

The treatment program strategy combines a number of different methods in an attempt to show that a program is effective. Once this is done, methodologies such as the dismantling strategy can be used to test the separate components of the overall program.

Conventional comparative outcome research has pitted globally defined "psychotherapy" against "behavior therapy." Numerous conceptual and methodological inadequacies in these studies have obscured differences in effectiveness between different treatment methods. Improved comparative research must answer the question "What treatment, applied by whom is most effective for what problem in which person."

Aside from multiple measures of effectiveness, evaluation of treatment outcome must be broadened to include measures of acceptability and cost-effectiveness. Behavior therapy is often but not always a form of brief therapy. Another advantage is that its methods are more easily disseminable than those of other approaches.

There is still a gap between experimental research and clinical practice. Clinicians cannot be expected to carry out controlled research, but they can contribute to evaluation through careful case reports and field tests of methods. There are four different levels of analysis from basic scientific research to clinical practice. Each level has its place in an integrative model of an applied clinical science.

Meta-analysis is a quantitative method for averaging and integrating the standardized results of a large number of different studies. Its proponents argue that it avoids the bias inherent in traditional reviews of the literature. Critics point out that possibilities for bias still exist in meta-analysis and have uncovered other serious problems in meta-analysis (e.g., how to compare good studies with bad ones).

18

Clinical Issues and Strategies

Behavior therapy has as a defining character-istic a commitment to scientific method, measurement, and evaluation. The experi-mental evaluation of theoretical concepts and treatment outcome is fundamental. Partly as a consequence of the scientific emphasis that influences the description and application of behavioral techniques, behavior therapy has often been criticized as clinically naive or even sterile. Among the therapeutic processes which critics claimed behavior therapy ignored or could not accommodate was the importance of the therapist-patient relationship. We ad-dress this criticism in this chapter, and in our focus on major clinical issues, illustrate how both the science and art of behavior therapy blend in actual clinical practice.

In the early behavior therapy literature it was customary to refer to factors associated with the therapeutic relationship as "nonspe-cific" influences (Lazarus, 1963). Although it was recognized as significant, viewing the therapeutic relationship in this way relegated it to a position of secondary importance (Wil-son & Evans, 1977). Traditionally, the role of

placebo influences, therapeutic expectations, trust, empathy, and rapport were all sub-sumed under the label of "nonspecific influ-ences." As "nonspecifics," they were de-emphasized and held in contrast to specific behavioral techniques derived from learning theory, such as systematic desensitization or token reinforcement programs. By concep-tualizing treatment within a social learning framework, as opposed to earlier S-R condi-tioning theories, so-called nonspecific influ-ences can be viewed as an integral part of behavior therapy. Although many nonspecific influences still remain to be specified, they are neither intrinsically unspecifiable nor qualitatively very different from other inde-pendent variables involved in the treatment of clinical disorders (Wilson, 1980).

THE THERAPIST-CLIENT
RELATIONSHIP

Behavior therapists attach considerable im-portance to the therapeutic relationship, although the social learning or behavioral conceptualization of this relationship differs from the traditional psychodynamic perspective (Wilson & Evans, 1977). Brady (1980) underscores this fact:

> "There is no question that qualitative aspects of the therapist-patient relationship can greatly influence the course of therapy for good or bad. In general, if the patient's relationship to the therapist is characterized by belief in the therapist's competence (knowledge, sophistication, and training) and if the patient regards the therapist as an honest, trustworthy, and decent human being with good social and ethical values (in his own scheme of things), the patient is more apt to invest himself in the therapy. Equally important is the quality and tone of the relationship he has with the therapist. That is, if he feels trusting and warm toward the therapist, this generally will facilitate following the treatment regimen, will be associated with higher expectations of improvement, and other generally favorable factors. The feelings of the therapist toward the patient are also important. If the therapist feels that his patient is not a desirable person or a decent human being or simply does not like the patient for whatever reasons, he may not succeed in concealing these feelings and attitudes toward the patient, and in general they will have a deleterious effect. There are some exceptions to these generalizations, however. Some patients will feel frightened and vulnerable with a therapist toward whom they feel attracted, particularly if from past experience they perceive such relationships as dangerous (danger of being hurt emotionally). With such a patient, a somewhat more distant and impersonal relationship may in fact be more desirable in that it will facilitate the patient's involvement in the treatment, following the treatment regimen, etc." (p. 285).

A survey of behavior therapists by Swan and MacDonald (1978) found that the most frequently used clinical methods were reported to be relationship enhancement methods. Moreover, clients regard the relationship as important in behavior therapy (Mathews et al., 1976; Sloane, Staples, Cristol, Yorkston, & Whipple, 1975).[1]

Behavior Therapists in Practice

Therapists' actions in treatment can be judged by ratings of their performance by their clients or by independent ratings of audio- or video-tapes of therapy sessions by objective observers. In ratings by clients, O'Leary, Turkewitz, and Tafel (1973) found that virtually all parents whose children were treated at the Stony Brook Child Guidance Clinic rated their behavior therapists as understanding, warm, sincere, and interested. Several studies have evaluated therapists' actions by objective ratings of therapy tapes. In one study, behavior therapists were rated as more flex-

---

1. This latter finding is based on clients' rating of therapists at the end of treatment. Sloane et al. (1975) found that successful patients in both their behavioral and psychoanalytically oriented therapies attributed their success mainly to relationship variables such as empathy and active involvement by the therapist. Mathews et al. (1976) asked their patients to rank eight features of their treatments in the order of the perceived value. The results showed that "all patients attributed important effects to the therapists' encouragement and sympathy, and to a slightly lesser extent the practice component and learning to cope with panic" (p. 369). Lazarus (1971) and Ryan and Gizinski (1971) reported similar post hoc findings. The problem with correlational data of this sort is that clients do not necessarily know how they were helped (Wilson & Evans, 1977). Patients' attributions of success to their therapists' personalities can easily be understood by the availability heuristic. According to this concept, judgments are strongly influenced by evidence or events that are readily available, and insufficiently affected by evidence that might be important but is not easily accessible. Availability is also influenced by other less obvious factors, as Rachman (1983) points out, including biases caused by prior cognitive sets and biases introduced by imaginability and what Chapman and Chapman (1978) called "illusory correlations." It would not be far-fetched to view patients' attributions of success as reflecting prior sets that the therapist will help and to see in this an illusory correlation.

ible with and supportive of their clients than Gestalt or psychoanalytic therapists (Brunink & Schroeder, 1979). The Sloane et al. (1975) study (Chapter 17) found that behavior therapists showed higher levels of empathy, warmth, and interpersonal contact than psychoanalytically-oriented therapists.[2] DeRubeis, Hollon, Evans, and Bemis (1982) similarly showed that cognitive-behavior therapists were rated more highly on some relationship skills than a comparison group of nonbehavioral therapists.

It is often assumed that while therapists from different theoretical orientations talk very differently about treatment, they tend to act in a similar manner. This is said to be especially true in the case of experienced therapists (Goldfried, 1980b). The findings summarized above challenge this assumption and other data also contradict it. In a separate analysis of the way the therapists in the Sloane et al. (1975) study acted, the authors concluded:

> "Differences between behavior therapy and analytically oriented psychotherapy . . . involved the basic patterns of interactions between patient and therapist and the type of relationship formed. Behavior therapy is not psychotherapy with special 'scientific techniques' superimposed on the traditional therapeutic paradigm; rather, the two appear to represent quite different styles of treatment although they share common elements" (Staples et al., 1975, p. 1521).

The behavior therapists were more directive, more open, more genuine, and more

disclosing than their psychoanalytically oriented counterparts. Both sets of therapists used similar numbers of interpretations during therapy, but the quality of these interpretations differed predictably, with the psychotherapists focusing psychodynamically on feelings and the behavior therapists concentrating on behavior. Although behavior therapists are typically warm and supportive, care is exercised in suiting their style to that of a particular client's needs. Flexibility on the therapist's part is essential (Brady, 1980; Lazarus, 1971).

To summarize, the behavior therapist in clinical practice is a directive and concerned problem-solver—a coping model who tries to instigate behavioral change in the client's natural environment, and who serves as a source of emotional support.

The Therapist's Contributions

There are numerous ways in which the therapist's skill and influence directly affect treatment process and outcome.

Assessment. It is imperative that therapists develop a trusting relationship with their clients. Without trust and confidence in the therapist, clients will often be unwilling to disclose painful personal details. Clients often have to be given honest but negative feedback about aspects of their behavior and confronted on sensitive, emotionally-charged issues. Trust and confidence in the therapist makes this possible. As discussed in the next section, trust and confidence may also be crucial in encouraging the client to accept and comply with treatment.

Goal-Setting. The role of the therapist in setting treatment goals, particularly in value-laden problems (e.g., sexual preference,

---

2. Note that these ratings of warmth and empathy were not correlated with successful outcome. That therapist characteristics of warmth, empathy, and positive regard are not sufficient for effective treatment has been well-established (Lambert, de Julio, & Stein, 1978; Rachman & Wilson, 1980). This finding is particularly damaging to the Rogerian school of psychotherapy (Rogers, 1957).

abortion, or divorce) is discussed in Chapter 19. Suffice it to note here that therapists require self-understanding and social sensitivity in coping with these complex and controversial issues. Simply requiring that therapists themselves undergo therapy does not guarantee that personal requirements will be met, and behavior therapy does not require personal therapy.

Modeling. Modeling is a specific treatment technique in the modification of phobias and compulsions, teaching assertive behavior and social skills, language acquisition, and other problems (Rosenthal & Bandura, 1978). The therapist may also act as a model, implicitly and perhaps haphazardly, during therapy interactions. As Mahoney (1977) points out, modeling of behavioral, affective, and cognitive reactions—including appropriate self-disclosure by the therapist of his or her own coping strategies—may be a valuable function of the therapeutic relationship. In the cognitive realm, for example, Mahoney suggests that the therapist provide problem-solving expertise by "thinking out loud." Some empirical support for the efficacy of this strategy is provided by Meichenbaum's (1971) finding that a model who verbalized thoughts and feelings during the performance of a behavioral task exerted more influence on observers than a model who did not. Meichenbaum and Asarnouw (1979) described how models can verbalize their thoughts as they engage in problem-solving. From a social learning perspective, this modeling would be most effective to the extent that it highlights useful rules for interpreting and processing information that increases self-efficacy and promotes enhanced coping abilities and self-esteem.

Social Reinforcement. By the very nature of the therapeutic enterprise, therapists often attain a position of trust and authority. Imbued with such trust and authority, therapists are in a position to wield considerable influence on their clients' thoughts, feelings, and behavior. This is one reason they are influential models. It also means that they are powerful social reinforcers of client conduct and can use this influence to promote desired therapeutic change. Behavior therapists will often use their approval (social reinforcing value) contingently to encourage specific behavior, but it is well to point out that social reinforcement, together with other social learning principles (e.g., modeling), are an inevitable part of all psychological therapies, irrespective of whether they are described as directive or nondirective.

The classic illustration of this aspect of therapeutic interaction is Truax's (1966) analysis of one of Rogers' clinical cases. Although Rogers' theory of client-centered therapy explicitly disavows any directive intervention by the therapist or any contingent use of social influence, Truax showed that this process took place anyway. Rogers, without realizing it, responded contingently to client talk which he considered "therapeutic" with subtle forms of social reinforcement, such as smiles, nods of the head, or verbal "uh-huhs." Client material which he viewed as less "therapeutic" was followed by silence and a lack of nonverbal cues of approval.

Social learning theory emphasizes reciprocal social influence. Moos and MacIntosh (1970) demonstrated that the therapist-client relationship needs to be conceptualized as an interacting system of mutual social influence. They found that patients exercised significantly greater influence over the behavior of nonbehavioral therapists (psychiatric residents) than vice versa. Therapist behavior was not a function of any "behavioral traits" or consistently applied technique, but was situationally or client determined.

The real choice confronting the therapist is whether to use the naturally occurring social influence process in a contingent manner to produce mutually desired change or to use it haphazardly (noncontingently) in an inefficient or possibly even harmful way (Bandura, 1969).

Structuring Therapeutic Expectations. The role of clients' expectations about treatment in determining adherence to their physician's or therapist's instructions was discussed in Chapter 15. Adherence is lowered if clients' expectations are incongruent with their experience. Treatment drop-outs also increase under these conditions (Ford, 1978). Specific practical suggestions for fostering congruent expectations are offered by Goldfried and Davison (1976). Related to this point is the desirability of adequately structuring the treatment for the client (Goldstein, Heller, & Sechrest, 1966). Clients should be given an explanation of the development and treatment of their problem, a rationale for the type of therapy used, and a precise description of their own responsibilities in actively participating in treatment.

The Therapeutic Relationship as Interpersonal Learning. Both modeling and social reinforcement are important forms of learning in the therapeutic relationship. Other learning may also occur during in-session interactions between therapist and client, however.

To clarify the interpersonal learning that behavior therapists try to facilitate in appropriate cases, it is helpful to contrast this learning with the psychodynamic concept of transference. Psychodynamic therapy is largely defined by its emphasis on the transference relationship, which centers on the "reliving and modification of historically meaningful patterns (of behavior)" (Strupp, 1977, p. 17).

The therapist is assumed to elicit these patterns (e.g., relevant childhood conflicts) and the therapeutic relationship is assumed to allow the "working through" or modification of these conflicts and complexes.

Clients may benefit directly from their interactions with behavior therapists, but the content and form of this learning is different from the psychodynamic notion of transference. First, behavior therapy focuses on the present causes of problems as opposed to their putative childhood antecedents. Second, behavior therapists may well relate present functioning to relevant past learning, explaining how a client's present functioning is based on maladaptive and self-defeating perceptions and patterns acquired in previous relationships. In so doing, they focus on dysfunctional cognitions, behavioral deficits and excesses, and interpersonal patterns rather than unconscious motivation and alleged psychosexual conflicts as targets of analysis and intervention. If the client distorts his or her relationship with the therapist, these distortions and behavioral patterns are treated like any other distortions and maladaptive behavior and not accorded the special significance they receive in psychoanalysis (Arnkoff, 1983; Guidano & Liotti, 1983). Third, and most important, even if analysis and modification of the in-session relationship between therapist and client is viewed as part of cognitive-behavioral treatment, the goal is to have these changes generalize to relationships in the client's environment.

In a social learning analysis, the extent to which a focus on in-session interactions between therapist and client can directly produce behavior change will vary according to the client's specific problems and goals. In general, the more interpersonal issues are of concern, the more likely it is that a focus on in-session interactions will carry direct therapeutic potential. But this will also depend on other factors, such as the person's particular social learning history and current social relationships.

As a rule, behavior therapists see working on their interactions with the client directly as a much more limited means of change than many of their psychodynamic counterparts. Nevertheless, Arnkoff (1983) suggests three ways in which a focus on in-session therapeutic interactions may be useful. First, therapeutic interactions provide the therapist with first-hand observations about the client's current functioning. They provide a sample of actual behavior, even though the behavior therapist is keenly aware that therapy is an artificial situation with particular constraints and the behavior expressed may not necessarily be representative of the client's problem in real life. Second, "dealing with current behavior in the session rivets the attention of both therapist and client, especially because of the emotional arousal that comes from discussing the current situation. Third, a focus on in-therapy behavior allows the client to try out new behavior with the therapist. . . . To the extent that the client can make discoveries and try out new behavior that will be generalizable outside therapy" (pp. 108-109). Here again, it must be emphasized that different views of what the client's "problem" is will result in different evaluations of the value of this in-session exploration.

The Personal Factor We possess many powerful behavioral methods for treating a range of clinical disorders. In many cases, assessment of the problem and its solution is clear-cut and the appropriate method can be effectively implemented. This sort of scientific analysis and success has helped create a misleading impression of behavior therapy as simple and straightforward. There is, of course, far more to behavior therapy than the simple application of an appropriate technique.

Goldfried (1983) cautions that "Quite often, the rules for selecting the technique that is 'appropriate' are poorly spelled out. In order to make such difficult clinical decisions, one needs to depend on the sensitivity of the therapist to pick up on subtle cues within the clinical interaction, the understanding of how various behavior patterns and lifestyles interrelate, and a keen appreciation of the environmental forces and contingencies that direct people's lives. Much of this knowledge and the rules that follow from it are not readily found in the literature, but instead come from clinicians' earlier social learning experiences, their experiences as human beings, and the accumulation of actual clinical experience" (p. 45). Although some problems in some clients can be treated efficiently by minimally trained personnel, with many complex clinical cases the success of behavior therapy will hinge on the ingenuity and skill of the therapist.

RESISTANCE

Clients who seem ambivalent about therapy, fail to comply with homework assignments, withhold information, and become evasive in response to probes about sensitive material pose particular problems. These phenomena of "resistance" are an everyday clinical reality in all forms of psychological therapy. The literature on behavior therapy has had relatively little to say about resistance in any explicit fashion. The problem and strategies for addressing it have been relegated to the all-inclusive category of "nonspecific" treatment factors. Nevertheless, behavior therapists have developed clinical strategies for overcoming such obstacles, and the documented outcomes of behavioral interventions for numerous problems in children and adults attest to the success of those strategies. It is vital for both theoretical and therapeutic reasons that the phenomena of resistance be conceptualized clearly with a view to developing effective means of overcoming such difficulties. The rise of behavioral medicine as an organized field has focused serious research attention on problems of compliance or adherence with behavioral and medical interventions that are usually designed to change lifestyles, as discussed in Chapter 15. In this chapter we elaborate further on the nature of resistance or lack of compliance[3] with therapeutic prescriptions, and what to do about it.

Conceptualizing Resistance

One of the reasons the concept of resistance has usually been avoided in the behavior therapy literature has been its identification with a psychodynamic perspective that is widely rejected. The particular problems with the traditional psychoanalytic conception of resistance are neatly exposed by Lazarus and Fay (1982) as they clear the way for presenting an alternative cognitive-behavioral approach. They emphasize that it

> "is necessary to separate resistance as a postulated mechanism explaining a clinical phenomenon (negative outcomes) from resistance as a clinical phenomenon itself. Clearly, it begs the question to speak of resistance whenever positive outcomes are not achieved. Furthermore, labeling all noncompliant behavior 'resistance' obscures the essential importance of teasing out specific antecedent and maintaining factors that generate uncooperative behaviors in specific contexts." (p. 116)

The cognitive-behavioral view, as Lazarus and Fay point out, is that resistance (defined

3. The terms "resistance" and "noncompliance" are used synonymously here. Although they derive from distinctive theoretical perspectives, from a social learning viewpoint there is no real difference.

broadly as a client's failure to follow instructions or show therapeutic improvement) is usually a function of our incomplete knowledge and limited efficacy of current treatment methods. They contrast this conceptualization with the psychodynamic view, in which "resistance" is an inevitable, unconscious, internal reaction against change. The latter, they argue, has all too frequently led to rationalizations of treatment failures by therapists. Lazarus and Fay point out that different forms of resistance are a function of different variables, including the client's individual makeup or interpersonal network, the therapeutic relationship, or the absence of effective treatment methods for particular problems.

A behavior modification approach based on the model of radical behaviorism (e.g., strict operant conditioning programs) assumes unilateral therapist control over the client's behavior. The trick to overcoming resistance or noncompliance, from this point of view, is simply to rearrange the external reinforcement contingencies in a more effective manner; yet the very reality of "resistance" to attempts to change someone's behavior reflects the inadequacy of a unidirectional model of causal processes. Interpersonal behavior is, as we have emphasized throughout this book, reciprocally determined, and it follows logically that clients can resist, modify, or neutralize the therapist's attempts at influence (Bandura, 1985). As a result, successful behavior therapy depends in large part on securing the active cooperation and participation of the client in the behavior change.

Behavior therapists seek to develop open, trusting relationships with clients in which they work together in identifying problems and finding solutions. The client is an active collaborator in therapy. Feedback on the therapist's approach and behavior is encouraged; the traditional role of the (medical) patient as a relatively passive recipient of an authoritative doctor's orders is deliberately avoided. The emphasis is not on "control" but on client *choice*. This characteristic of the therapeutic relationship has a number of advantages, not the least of which is that it reduces the likelihood of resistance to the therapist's instructions. Referring to what they call "cognitive therapy," but which is also true for behavior therapy within a social learning framework, Guidano and Liotti (1983) summarize this feature of the therapeutic relationship.

"This policy (of active cooperation and collaboration) prevents many hidden competitive and resentful feelings and many artful tactics of the patient to check the therapist's 'omniscience' and 'omnipotence.' It is probably for this reason that the 'resistance' phenomenon is so remarkably uncommon in cognitive therapy (we would add also behavior therapy) as compared to psychodynamic therapies. If a cooperative relationship exists, the patient does not feel the need to 'countercontrol,' and the therapist can plainly consider any disagreement, noncompliance, or irritation on the patient's part not as a form of 'resistance,' but as a source of information on the patient's way of perceiving or construing the therapist's feelings and behavior" (p. 123).

The commitment to active collaboration between therapist and patient is also consistent with the view that therapy is analogous to scientific reasoning. Particularly in cognitive-behavioral treatment, clients are encouraged to view their cognitions as hypotheses that need to be continually tested and evaluated, in the manner that scientists presumably carry out their investigations (Meichenbaum & Gilmore, 1982). A major goal of this therapy is for clients to adopt a new conceptualization of their problems, and to this end they are prompted to be open to "anomalous data" and to reconsider key beliefs that might be responsible for their difficulties.

Mahoney (1976) and Guidano and Liotti (1983) have also put forward essentially the same "personal scientist" model of the therapeutic process. Resistance by clients to new ways of thinking is viewed, "like anomalous data for the scientist," as an additional opportunity "for examining the nature of the client's cognitions, affects, behavior, etc." The strategy for reinterpreting clients' maladaptive cognitions involves careful and planned interpretations. To quote Meichenbaum and Gilmore:

"In the same way that a lawyer carefully lays the groundwork for a brief to be presented to the jury, the therapist collects the data to present to the client. Moreover when the therapist presents the conceptualization it is not presented with certainty, but rather it is offered as reflecting the therapist's current view of what is going on. The therapist carefully checks with the client to see if indeed this view may make sense and will not seem highly unlikely to the client. The therapist may report to the client as follows: 'What I hear you saying is . . .' 'You seem to be telling me . . .' 'Am I correct in assuming that . . . ?' . . . Such queries provide the basis for involving the client in the process of collaboration and reconceptualization" (p. 136).

The "behavioral" component of treatment enters when therapists and clients mutually identify specific tasks to test their hypotheses.

This analogy of the client as a "personal scientist," which is a hallmark of cognitive-behavioral treatment, is consonant with current developments in cognitive-social psychology. In their book on human inference, Nisbett and Ross (1980) set out to explain a number of mental phenomena in simple, nonmotivational terms in contrast to less parsimonious, motivational (typically psychodynamic) constructs. One of their examples is resistance. The Freudian position assumes that patients resist (e.g., refuse to accept the therapist's interpretation) because change is threatening to the ego—patients are "well-defended" by protective psychic mechanisms. The alternative view that Nisbett and Ross present does not rely on any unconscious purposive mechanisms that can be "uncovered" (i.e., made conscious) through appropriate analysis; rather, people are simply unable to see an alternative explanation because of inherent limitations in their cognitive machinery.

Overcoming Resistance

One of the central aspects of behavior therapy, regardless of the problem being treated, is the use of homework assignments. Clients are asked to engage in new or different activities (cognitive and behavioral) between therapy sessions, and treatment success often hinges on the degree to which these assignments are carried out. Problems with clients resisting or failing to comply with treatment interventions are discussed in several preceding chapters (e.g., Chapter 11). Clients do not always comply faithfully with homework assignments, and the therapist's response to such noncompliance can serve to illustrate the general approach to resistance in the practice of behavior therapy.

Instead of assuming that this noncompliant behavior reflects purposive resistance, the behavior therapist first considers a number of other more parsimonious possibilities. Lazarus and Fay (1982, p. 119) list the following possible explanations:

1. "Was the homework assignment incorrect or irrelevant?" There are times when clients are more knowledgeable about what is good for them than their therapists. Noncompliance in these instances might even be in the clients' best interests.

2. "Was it too threatening?" Sometimes the therapist may try to move too quickly, without adequate preparation and pacing of the intervention.

3. "Was it too time-consuming in terms of its 'cost-effectiveness?' " For example, if an obese client has too much self-monitoring to complete, which interferes with her work and other essential activities, she might not comply even if it might help her with weight control.

4. "Does the patient not appreciate the value of and rationale behind homework exercises?" Clients must have the right cognitive set regarding the treatment they are to receive and their responsibilities in it.

5. "Is the therapeutic relationship at fault? (If so, the patient may display passive-aggressive behaviors toward the therapist.)" Frank discussion about how clients perceive not only the way the therapist has conceptualized the problem and the methods selected, but also the personal qualities of the therapist are called for when confronted with a therapeutic impasse.

6. "Is someone in the patient's social network undermining or sabotaging the therapy?" An example here might be the husband of an agoraphobic client who consistently fails to accompany his wife on her in vivo exposure assignments.

7. "Is the patient receiving far too many secondary gains[4] to relinquish his or her maladaptive behavior?" This problem is illustrated by an agoraphobic man who cannot travel to work, but receives disability pay and has his family doing everything for him and accompanying him when he does venture out. To overcome his agoraphobia he has to experience and conquer anxiety, then lose some of the excessive attention and support he has been receiving from his family.

An important principle reflected in Lazarus and Fay's list is the hierarchical ordering of these alternative explanations for noncompliant behavior, ranging from the relatively simple mechanics of therapy which the therapist can easily correct (e.g., the assignment was unclear) to more complex matters that may include active (and possibly unconscious)

---

4. "Secondary gain" is a term derived from psychodynamic theory which is used infrequently in the behavior therapy literature.

opposition by the client. It is only once the simpler alternatives have been ruled out that the behavior therapist is likely to tackle these latter problems.

Competing Problems. Noncompliance with some assignments may be the result of the interference of other problems that need direct treatment before compliance can be expected. Depression, for example, frequently complicates the treatment of other problems, and one of its negative effects is decreased compliance. In their study of the separate and joint effects of the behavioral and pharmacological treatment of the obsessive compulsive, Marks, Stern, Mawson, Cobb, & McDonald (1980) found that the drug clomipramine facilitated compliance with the behavioral treatment. The mechanism for this indirect therapeutic benefit of the drug treatment was improvement in the depressed mood of the clients.

Treatment Goals. The nature of treatment goals plays a significant role in influencing compliance. In social learning theory, goals serve as cognitively based sources of motivation that help initiate and sustain behavior (Bandura, 1977b). Goals should be concrete, well specified, and short-term, properties that are optimally suited to providing the incentives to carry out the required behavior. Therapeutic assignments that are vaguely described, too general, or too distal will greatly increase the chances of noncompliance.

In the treatment of an addictive disorder such as alcohol abuse, for example, clients are urged to take "one day at a time."[5] The goal is a daily one—to stay sober today and cope with tomorrow when it comes. The logic of

5. This phrase, and the philosophy it encapsulates, are at the heart of the Alcoholics Anonymous approach to rehabilitation.

this advice is that if an alcoholic (or any addict) thinks too far ahead to an entire lifetime of abstinence, the prospect may seem overwhelming. The person may then feel helpless or hopeless and revert to drinking once more.

Clients' Expectations. In social learning theory, expectations, as with goals, are a source of motivation for behavior change. Outcome expectations should be positive but realistic (Wilson, 1979). On the one hand, positive outcome expectations seem to facilitate behavior change. On the other hand, if subsequent experience is not consistent with the expectations a therapist creates, and success is not forthcoming, clients may see in this yet another confirmation of the hopelessness of their position. By developing realistic outcome expectations of ultimate success, the therapist may help to bridge the often formidable-looking gap between the short-term, demanding behavior required and eventual improvement (Mischel, 1974).

Clients' expectations affect compliance in other ways too. Efficacy expectations help determine the persistence with which coping behavior is sustained (Chapters 8, 14 and 15). Clients enter treatment with expectations not only of outcome but also of what the therapeutic process will entail. Incongruities between what clients expect and what they receive can increase drop-outs from treatment and undermine compliance (Dunbar & Stunkard, 1979; Ford, 1978).

Clients' Beliefs About their Problems. Other cognitive factors are also important in determining compliance, such as clients' beliefs about the nature of their problem, what can be done about it, and what that will mean for future adjustment (Meichenbaum & Gilmore, 1982). Chapter 15 describes cognitive-behavioral strategies for preventing noncompliance, such as the cognitive rehearsal of possible problems in completing assignments (Rush, 1980).

Doctors' Orders Or Mutual Commitments? The way in which therapeutic assignments are negotiated is probably crucial in determining compliance. Consistent with social psychological concepts such as reactance and attribution, clinical experience has shown that it is important to involve the client in making the assignment. For some oppositional clients who find fault in anything the therapist proposes, a useful strategy is to ask them to suggest a therapeutic homework assignment and to build on this. Therapists are most likely to invite noncompliance if they simply tell the client what to do. Meichenbaum and Gilmore (1982) provide a specific illustration of productive and counterproductive ways of assigning homework tasks:

> "What you are to do is . . . ," "Do the following:," "Do this . . . ,"
> versus
> "I would like you to . . . ," "I want you to . . . ," "This is what I am asking you to do . . . ,"
> versus
> "So what you have agreed to try is . . . ," "As I understand it, you will . . . ," "So you will take responsibility for . . . ." (p. 143)

As Meichenbaum and Gilmore observe, "the client's attributions concerning the change process and therapy are likely to be very different under each of these three message styles, and only the third above can facilitate looking at the resistance to homework that may be experienced while it is being attempted" (p. 143). Lazarus and Fay (1982) voice the same wisdom:

> "Telling a client to relax, imagine scenes, act more assertively, self-monitor specific behaviors, or agree on contingency management is likely to foster some degree of opposition or countercontrol . . . Asking for the same per-

formance-based responses is less likely to evoke opposition. Thus resistance or countercontrol may be a direct function of the therapist's manner and style. In our experience, at least 80 percent of patients follow our requests or suggestions without travail." (p. 122)

It is also imperative that the therapist communicate that homework assignments are an integral part of the treatment and that full compliance is expected. Most important, at the following session all homework assignments must be diligently checked first. Any difficulties the client encountered should be analyzed fully, and alternative strategies should be suggested or the nature of the assignments appropriately modified. Clients are quick to sense if a therapist is not fully committed to regular compliance with assignments, and it should come as no surprise if in such cases the therapist finds declining or inconsistent compliance.

Contingency Contracting. In this operant conditioning procedure clients agree to pay some penalty if they do not perform the mutually targeted homework assignment. In Chapter 13 we described how contingency contracting successfully decreases attrition rates in obesity treatment programs (Wilson & Brownell, 1980). The usual procedure is to make a refundable deposit contingent upon attendance at therapy sessions. However, the reliance on external regulation of behavior that this method entails is only suitable for certain clients with selected problems. To continue the obesity example, targeting actual weight loss with contingency contracting raises problems. Many clients refuse to participate in what they deride as a mechanistic or coercive process (Jeffery, Thompson, & Wing, 1978).

A Cautionary Note. The strategies summarized above usually enable the behavior therapist to overcome most forms of resistance. Nonetheless, as Lazarus and Fay (1982) state, "it is unrealistic to place the entire onus [of changing the client] on the clinician . . . There are, in short, people who do not want help, or for whom there could be too many competing factors" (p. 120). The important issues, which are still unresolved, are where and how to make this critical distinction.

Behavioral and Psychodynamic Views of Resistance. Given that noncompliance with therapeutic interventions is common in clinical practice, it might be expected that different treatment approaches overlap, at least to some degree, in the management of these problems. This overlap is probably most evident between behavior therapy and other nonbehavioral but directive approaches. Some of the similarities and differences can be seen in the following example.

Kaplan (1979) pioneered what she refers to as "psychosexual therapy" for the treatment of sexual dysfunction. Her approach draws on traditional behavioral interventions, but often integrates these methods within a psychodynamic framework. As with the general behavioral approach to treating sexual dysfunction, Kaplan's methods are directive: clients are instructed to engage in specific sexual practices with their partners. Noncompliance is a frequent obstacle to therapeutic success.

Faced with noncompliance, Kaplan follows standard behavioral practice by first simply encouraging the clients to try again. If noncompliance persists despite encouragement and after a reasonable period of time, however, Kaplan assumes that the clients may have a fear of sexual success. Insight into this sexual block is the next goal of therapy, and to this end Kaplan confronts the clients with the interpretation that noncompliance is motivated by fear of success. The following excerpt from her book illustrates how this is done:

PATIENT: We couldn't do the pleasuring this week, I had to take work home and by the time we got to bed she did not feel like it.

WIFE: Honey, it was after two o'clock each night. I was tired.

PATIENT: Well, my job is important.

THERAPIST: I am sorry you have to work so hard. Perhaps this is not a good time for treatment. Do you think we should postpone it? (At this point Kaplan noted that "Joining the resistance is often an effective confrontation method.")

PATIENT: No, this is very important. Two weeks ago I had such good erections; I was so encouraged.

THERAPIST: Yes you did, and since then you "haven't found the time" to do the exercises. Do you really think that is the true reason or do you think that your success was a little scary?

PATIENT: No, that is ridiculous. That's why I am here, to be successful.

WIFE: Honey, it always happens when we have had good sex. You always disappear afterwards for weeks.

THERAPIST: It is not unusual for a person to have some anxiety when he starts improving. Let's talk about the week it worked so well. (Giving the patient "permission" to have success anxiety may help his gaining insight.) (Kaplan, 1979, p.173)

A useful question to ask clients, before embarking on a behavior change program, is "How do you anticipate life will be when we are successful in overcoming your problem?" The purpose of this line of questioning is to elicit the client's expectations about life without the "symptoms." These expectations are frequently unrealistic and require therapeutic attention. Some clients expect improvements in their problems to change their entire lives. Others fear the changed circumstances that will result from treatment. This is the "fear of success" to which Kaplan refers.

Kaplan's intervention in the case excerpted above is consistent with what behavior therapists routinely do. "Joining the resistance" can be viewed as a mild form of paradoxical intervention, a strategy that is often employed, as Lazarus and Fay (1982) indicate. Behavior therapists part company with Kaplan when she goes on to assert that for the "more neurotic" clients, simply identifying and confronting resistance as illustrated above is insufficient. These clients, she claims, show resistance that reflects intense conflicts laid down very early (in emotional development). The answer? Long-term psychodynamic therapy that seeks to resolve these early (e.g., Oedipal) conflicts. Here is a clear case of advocacy of psychoanalytic theory of development and psychopathology that leads logically to the traditional psychoanalytic treatment of sexual problems. Neither can be shown to enjoy any acceptable scientific support in the conceptualization or treatment of sexual disorders.

BEHAVIOR THERAPY VERSUS NONBEHAVIORAL TREATMENTS

Most therapists, including behavior therapists, would agree that important therapeutic elements are common to all forms of psychological treatment. These similarities are most obvious among short-term treatments. For example, Butcher and Koss (1978) stated, "regardless of therapeutic orientation, most brief therapists are directive in their approach to patients . . . in order to make more efficient use of time and keep the session content on track" (p. 748). Aside from the directiveness of the therapist, other common characteristics of short-term therapies that Butcher and Koss list include:

- Goals are limited and are chosen, at least in part, by the patient.
- Therapy is focal in nature.
- Interviewing is "focused" with "present centeredness."
- The therapist is active and flexible in the use of diverse techniques.
- Assessment and intervention are prompt, with no lengthy psychometric evaluation.
- "Behavioral practice" is recommended.

These characteristics all apply to behavior therapy. What differences, then, are there? First, behavior therapy is committed to the principles and procedures of experimental psychology. It emphasizes scientific evaluation of concepts and methods. No other treatment method can rival this grounding in experimental psychology. Second, the clinical practice of behavior therapy is, in many key respects, different from alternative approaches. The differences between behavioral and psychodynamic approaches in the conceptualization and use of the therapeutic relationship and the nature and treatment of resistance are addressed above.

Another item in Butcher and Koss's (1978) list of commonalities among short-term therapies was "behavioral practice." Goldfried (1980b), similarly, in trying to illustrate what he views as the commonalities among all forms of psychological therapy, suggests that most approaches advocate "behavioral practice" or extratherapeutic experience. As Goldfried notes, Freud himself referred to the value of such extratherapeutic practice in the treatment of phobias. Gestalt therapy, encounter groups, and other approaches are similarly said to include an emphasis on extratherapeutic "behavioral practice," yet these comments establish only the most superficial commonality among the different psychological therapies.

Psychodynamic therapists do not recommend direct systematic exposure to anxiety-eliciting situations in treating anxiety disorders, irrespective of Freud's fleeting fancy to this effect. Some unconventional psychodynamic therapists, particularly those who practice short-term treatment, may, on occasion, recommend some form of extratherapeutic experience outside of the transference relationship, but these rare instances cannot be likened seriously to the highly structured, and systematically checked technique- and even problem-specific nature of in vivo homework assignments in behavioral assessment and therapy (Wilson, 1982d).

Clinical Inference

Consistent with the view that it would be fruitful to uncover commonalities among diverse psychological therapies, Wachtel (1977, 1982) has argued that behavior therapy and psychodynamic therapy have much to learn from each other. He asserts that behavioral techniques may increase the power of psychodynamic therapy, while psychodynamic concepts and clinical lore may enrich behavior therapy. With this in mind, he has argued that behavior therapy is based on theories that "are essentially content-free, theories concerned with basic processes, with how but not particularly with what is learned or thought or found reinforcing. Consequently, since these theories do not guide them in this respect, behavior therapists have tended to base their content assumptions on general cultural assumptions" (p. 597). Psychoanalysts, on the contrary, are very concerned with content and with inferences about people's motives, as Wachtel points out. He faults behavior therapists for naively taking too much at face value in accordance with cultural norms.

Wachtel illustrates his argument with reference to the use of praise as a reinforcer. In cultural norms, he asserts, praise is invariably viewed as positive. Since they are guided by these normative assumptions, behavior therapists are said to be "often too effusive in their praise" (p. 599). Negative therapeutic consequences may follow from this position, says Wachtel. Praise may lose its value or the therapist may be regarded as insincere. Furthermore, "if the therapist's criteria for praise are not reasonably close to the client's, praise can be noxious. To be told you have done something worthwhile when you regard it as a meager step can lead to feeling that the therapist is insulting or doesn't understand you" (p. 599). Psychoanalysts, it is said, since they are grounded in the study of non-normative, unconscious motives, would be less likely to make these errors.

Since Wachtel's analysis reflects a much broader body of clinical thinking on these issues, it warrants careful scrutiny. The first point is that Wachtel's characterization of behavior therapy is inaccurate. Consider the following statement by Beck, Rush, Shaw, and Emery (1979), who speak for behavior therapists in general:

"If the therapist is too active in demonstrating a warm, caring concern (or more importantly, if the patient thinks the warm attitude is too intense), the patient may react negatively. For example, the patient may think, 'I am undeserving of such caring,' or 'I am deceiving the therapist because he appears to like me and I know I am worthless.' Or the patient may misconstrue the therapist's motives, 'He's insincere,' or 'How can he like a worthless person like me?'. . . In essence, the therapist must strike an appropriate balance in displaying warmth. The patient may construe minimal warmth as rejection, while too hearty a display of caring may be misinterpreted in either a negative or overly positive way. Thus, the therapist must carefully attend to signs that suggest that his attitudes are counterproductive" (pp. 46–47).

Beck et al. (1979) caution the therapist about

discriminately displaying warmth toward his or her client. Although behavior therapists as a rule are warm, supportive, disclosing, and advice-giving, the need to be flexible with different clients is a given (see also Brady, 1980; Lazarus, 1971). This emphasis on flexibility would appear to distinguish behavior therapists from some other therapists who assume predetermined therapeutic postures (e.g., psychoanalysts, who are explicitly against an open, supportive, and disclosing relationship).

A second point about Wachtel's position, which is broadly representative of psychodynamic thinking, is that if he were correct, behavior therapists would be experienced as insincere, noxious, or simply naive. One would be bound to predict a greater rate of dropouts from therapy and less efficacy than that obtained by their more clinically savvy psychodynamic counterparts. Fortunately, none of these implications is true. Behavior therapists are viewed as favorably as psychodynamic practitioners by clients—if not more so. Although the data are sketchy, the case can be made that behavior therapy has decreased dropouts from treatment relative to other treatment approaches.

Third, behavior therapy has certainly not been shown to be inferior to other psychological treatments in outcome efficacy. Rather, it is demonstrably superior in the treatment of several child and adult disorders (Rachman & Wilson, 1980).

Behavior therapists do take their clients' self-reports more seriously than psychodynamic therapists do. And for good reason. Mischel (1968, 1982) has shown that self-report is often the most accurate means of personality assessment, providing more accurate information than experienced clinicians' predictions. Naturally, it is subject to limitations and distortions, but so is every method of assessment.

The tendency to de-emphasize or even dismiss self-reports of thoughts and feelings received significant support from an influential and controversial paper by Nisbett and Wilson (1977). They claimed that people do not have direct access to their own cognitive processes; they know the results of their thinking but have no consciousness of their thinking processes. Instead, when asked to give the reasons for their actions, people offer culturally normative explanations and rationalizations. Cogent criticisms of the Nisbett and Wilson position have stressed both its conceptual and methodological shortcomings. Ericsson and Simon (1980), among others, have shown that Nisbett and Wilson's procedures to probe conscious thoughts and their relationship to action were inadequate. They asked their subjects to reflect on the reasons for their behavior after they had engaged in different activities. As Bandura (1986) points out, analyses of causal thought must assess the thoughts occurring before or during the behavior people are asked to explain. In contrast to direct, specific probes of this kind, retrospective probes "requiring (people) to speculate about the causes of their past behavior, lead them to draw on all sorts of information and beliefs in formulating answers. Such conjectures may bear little resemblance to the thoughts that actually occurred during the task" (p. 124).

One of the implications of the Nisbett and Wilson position is that since people do not have access to their cognitive processes, observers who share a theory about why people engage in certain actions would predict a person's behavior as well as the person him- or herself would. The evidence, however, shows that self-reports are better predictors of subsequent behavior than are the predictions of an observer (Bandura, 1986; Mischel, 1982). "The evidence, taken as a whole, indicates that appropriate thought probes provide a rich source of data for revealing cognitive processes and their functional relation to action. While people are not fully conscious of every aspect of their thinking, neither is their thinking largely unconscious. People generally know what they are thinking. They form judgments, put them to the test, reflect on the results of their actions, and alter their judgments accordingly" (Bandura, 1986, p. 125). In a final comment on this controversial issue, we note that even if we assume that Nisbett and Wilson's (1977) thesis that people have little or no access to their cognitive processes were correct, the value of self-report of behavior is not gainsaid. Fiske and Taylor (1984) point out that people might correctly identify the determinants of their behavior, not because they have access to their cognitive processes, but because they know more than any observer about their past behavior.

Being willing to take clients' self-reports at face value does not mean that behavior therapists are not aware that these self-reports are sometimes untrue, mask hidden agendas, or provide distorted views for one or other reason. They are aware that a client's presenting problem is not always the "real problem." Behavior therapists in clinical practice have always been informed by this knowledge (Goldfried & Davison, 1976; Lazarus, 1971; Wolpe & Lazarus, 1966). They attend to the same cues as other therapists do. They are alert to patterns of functioning, to inconsistencies between verbal report and action, contradictions in accounts of events, unacknowledged emotional reactions to significant life events (desynchrony among response systems), nonverbal cues, and other signs that things don't quite fit together. Quoting Kelly (1955), Mahoney (1980) emphasizes the value of listening with the "third ear," noting the general theme as well as the specific content of what the client says. The former may be more revealing than the latter.

As in other therapeutic approaches and other walks of life, some behavior therapists will be better than others in making insightful observations and analyses, and it is likely that those therapists will achieve superior overall success. The view that training in psychodynamic theory and therapy allows therapists to make more insightful or more accurate observations or inferences about clients has little support. In one of the best known studies of clinical inference, Langer and Abelson (1974) had psychodynamic and behavior therapists watch a videotaped interview of a man who had applied for a job. Half of each group was informed that they were observing a patient, the other half a job applicant. Subsequent questionnaire-based assessment showed that the psychodynamic therapists were heavily influenced by the label assigned to the interviewee. When labeled a patient, the man was described as significantly more psychologically disturbed than when he was labeled a job applicant. In marked contrast, the behavior therapists assessed the person similarly regardless of label, suggesting that they were guided more by the person's actual behavior than pre-existing subjective set.[6]

An innovative study by Cohen and Oyster-Nelson (1981) has replicated Langer and Abelson's (1974) important finding that psychodynamically oriented therapists see more psychological disturbance in patients than behavior therapists do. Cohen and Oyster-Nelson studied the peer review process of the

---

6. The judgmental error committed by psychodynamic therapists in the Langer and Abelson (1974) study is known as confirmatory bias. Experimental research in cognitive psychology has delineated several other judgmental biases to which all therapists are vulnerable (Rachman, 1983; Turk & Salovey, 1985). Therapists and their clients would be better served if clinical training were to pay more attention to this emerging literature than to unsubstantiated psychodynamic speculation about clinical inference exemplified in Wachtel's thesis.

American Psychological Association/Civilian Health and Medical Program of the Uniformed Services (APA/CHAMPUS) program. The goal of this program is to provide high-quality, cost-effective outpatient treatment. A peer review of adult services occurs automatically after 60 sessions. Treatment reports completed after eight, twenty-four and forty sessions may also be submitted for review should questions arise. Three reviewers from the therapist's geographical region, who are authorized to review the service provided (e.g., treatment of adults), provide independent reviews, recommending, among other things, how many of the completed sessions and how many future sessions should be funded. Cohen and Oyster-Nelson suggested that this peer review process represents "a natural laboratory" in which to study clinical judgment, entailing as it does "relatively unobtrusive measurement of evaluative judgments of psychopathology and treatment necessity made by a national sample of clinicians, based on their reviews of actual clinical treatment reports" (p. 584).

Twenty-four APA/CHAMPUS reviewers from each of three theoretical orientations (behavioral, eclectic, and psychodynamic) received one of three treatment reports as part of the regular sixty-session review. The treatment reports described long-term psychodynamic therapy for depressed, middle-aged female patients. They were deliberately prepared by three experienced psychodynamic therapists from their own cases. The reviewers' evaluations showed a strikingly consistent pattern. Overall, the psychodynamic reviewers, compared with the behavioral and eclectic reviewers, rated the patients as more disturbed and in need of psychotherapy, and were consistently more positive in their ratings of treatment and more generous in their recommendations concerning the reimbursement for past and future care. Psychodynamic

reviewers recommended reimbursement of thirty-seven sessions on average, compared to only twenty-six and seventeen, respectively, by the eclectic and behavioral reviewers.

THE SCOPE OF BEHAVIOR THERAPY

The preceding chapters have documented the application of behavior therapy to a broad spectrum of child and adult disorders, including the most complex and disabling problems modern clinical psychology and psychiatry face. Nonetheless, the impression in some quarters remains that behavior therapy is most suitable for the more narrowly defined disorders (e.g., phobic disorders, substance abuse, and so on), whereas more traditional psychotherapy is the treatment of choice for less circumscribed and perhaps less easily defined problems (e.g., personality disorders). This impression is wrong.

We believe that at least part of the reason for this impression has been the tendency of the behavior therapy literature to emphasize the treatment of specific disorders. The authors, in the course of conducting clinical workshops, have often been questioned about what behavior therapy has to offer for some of the problems practicing clinicians commonly face, which, they claim, are not addressed in the published literature. In most instances, these practitioners are asking for guidance in treating what are called the personality disorders (DSM-III, 1980). Examples include antisocial, compulsive, schizoid, and borderline personality disorders. These disorders are commonly encountered in clinical practice (Turkat & Maisto, 1985). They may be diagnosed as the primary problem or seen in connection with other primary diagnoses (e.g., clients who are alcoholics or bulimics, but who could also be diagnosed as having borderline personality disorders). Personality disorders present special problems for the therapist, and in cases in which they co-exist with another primary disorder (e.g., with bulimia nervosa), they complicate treatment and probably make for a poorer prognosis (Hawkins, Fremouw, & Clement, 1984).

Compared to other major categories of clinical disorders, there is significantly less literature and research on the personality disorders in behavior therapy. Turkat and Maisto (1985) present a social learning model of these disorders, and suggest how they might be treated using many of the specific strategies described in the preceding chapters. Empirical research on treatment outcome is sparse. In their comparative outcome study of psychotherapy versus behavior therapy, Sloane et al. (1975) included twenty-five patients with a diagnosis of personality disorder. The results of this investigation showed that behavior therapy was "at least as effective, and possibly more so, than psychotherapy with the sort of . . . personality disorders that are typical of clinic populations" (Sloane et al., 1975, p. 224). Whereas psychotherapy did less well with the more disturbed patients, behavior therapy did equally well with patients with either high or low psychopathology. The impression that psychotherapy is preferred with personality disorders is further discredited by the findings of a controlled study by Strupp and Hadley (1979). Patients suffering primarily from anxieties and depression, but with personality disorders such as borderline states, were treated for the same period either by highly experienced psychoanalytically oriented psychotherapists or college professors chosen for their ability to form understanding relationships with students. There were no differences between these two groups across a variety of different outcome measures.

PROFESSIONAL ISSUES: TRAINING AND DELIVERY OF SERVICES

Training

More than any other form of psychological treatment, behavior therapy tries to blend scientific theory and research with clinical practice. Not surprisingly, within clinical psychology, training in behavior therapy has typically been offered most readily by those programs with a commitment to training clinicians with the scientist-practitioner model. Here the attempt is to train therapists both in the science and practice of therapy. These programs, and comparable ones in other disciplines such as psychiatry and social work, will continue to be the focus of training in behavior therapy. Nevertheless, alternative training models have begun to emerge.

In England, Marks (1981b) has asserted that "If we are aiming to produce scientific researchers and teachers, then a broad-based education in the behavioural sciences is essential, ranging from the biological to the psychosocial. However, for those who are mainly interested in therapy rather than in actively pursuing research, less of this detailed knowledge is necessary and much more about the clinical skills needed in therapy" (p. 286). These views are consistent with the acceptance, in the United States, of a new professional model of training in clinical psychology and the development of schools of professional psychology which offer the Doctor of Psychology (Psy.D.) degree (Peterson, Eaton, Levine, & Snepp, 1980). Different professional schools vary in their requirements for research training, but all place distinctly less importance on research activities than do more conventional Ph.D. scientist-practitioner programs.

Agras, Kazdin, and Wilson (1979) discussed the nature of training in clinical psychology from the perspective of behavior therapy as a developing clinical science. They concluded, "The developing trend in clinical psychology training toward the professional school would seem to fit nicely with developments in behavior therapy" (p. 138). Agras et al. hastened to emphasize, however, that the professional schools to which they were referring should

"... be part of a university, be located in an area large enough to afford a suitable clinical population, and reflect the relationship between the clinic and science by being closely tied to an academic department of psychology. The faculty should be capable of teaching applied psychology, and the school should offer appropriate courses in related behavioral and biological sciences that are directed to the future clinician and applied researcher. Active programs of applied research should be pursued by the faculty of such schools, as should relevant basic research, thus achieving the vigorous reciprocal interaction between the applied and basic sciences that should be a hallmark of this experimental clinical endeavor. Professional schools of psychology without this close relationship will tend to drift into the dogmatic teaching of therapeutic skills, a tendency already too frequent in the clinic. The majority of students within the professional school will become clinicians. However, a substantial minority should become clinical researchers, and the curriculum should be flexible enough to train both types of professionals" (p. 138).

Behavior therapists in clinical practice do not need to be active researchers themselves. Full-time clinical practice is essentially incompatible with completing research for several reasons. But behavior therapists do have to have a firm grounding in the behavioral sciences. They must possess an understanding of experimental research in psychology, be capable of critically evaluating research and developments in the field, and be responsive to such developments. Mere profes-

sional training in the use of techniques which happen to be in fashion at any one time is inadequate.

Delivery of Mental Health Services

Professional versus Paraprofessional Therapists. One of the advantages of behavior therapy is its precisely formulated techniques, which can be implemented by professionals and psychological assistants.[7] This has greatly aided the broad dissemination of behavioral methods in a cost-effective manner. In the United Kingdom, nurses, whose training is shorter and less costly than that of clinical psychologists and psychiatrists (the latter being by far the most expensive), have been employed as therapists. Marks, Bird, and Lindley (1978) reported that these nurse-therapists have obtained results in the treatment of phobias, obsessive-compulsive rituals, and sexual dysfunction and deviation comparable to those obtained by psychologists and psychiatrists in other studies. Gins-

---

7. In the United States, the paraprofessional's role has not been well-delineated in most mental health or educational facilities (Denner & Price, 1973). However, where that role is well-defined, the individual may execute various assessment or treatment procedures with greater professional competence than many professionals. As such, the term paraprofessional is misleading. "Para" is a prefix meaning alongside of, beside, or one side, and often carries a demeaning connotation. That is, a paraprofessional would be thought to execute rather nonessential roles, such as distributing medication, grading papers, or organizing volunteer hospital groups. In fact, as the crucial mediator of psychological, social, and educational change, a paraprofessional often executes well-defined roles (e.g., reinforcing a behavior on a specified schedule, ignoring certain behaviors, and desensitizing according to prescribed methods). As such, we prefer the term psychological assistant to paraprofessional, since the notion that the individual's function is mundane, secondary, or non-essential is inaccurate.

burg and Marks (1977) have also shown that nurse-therapists are cost-effective.

Two often competing trends seem evident in the United States. On the one hand, instead of training the psychological assistants who would provide cost-effective treatment as described by Marks, clinical psychology in the United States seems to be moving toward the alternative policy of meeting mental health needs with greatly increased numbers of expensive, highly trained professionals with doctoral degrees. On the other hand, commercial programs for the treatment of problems such as obesity (e.g., Weight Watchers, Stuart, 1980) and agoraphobia (Ross, 1982) use psychological assistants who have successfully overcome the problem. These commercial programs are flourishing, and while there are no controlled outcome studies, they are said to achieve impressive results.

SUMMARY

In addition to specific, scientifically evaluated methods, what used to be called the "non-specifics" of behavior therapy are important ingredients of clinical practice. These include factors that are said to involve the "art" that goes into therapy, such as the therapist-client relationship.

The behavior therapist is a directive and concerned problem-solver—a coping model who prompts behavioral change in the client's natural environment and provides emotional support. The basic components of a good therapeutic relationship are trust and confidence in the therapist and what is being done. A good relationship improves assessment of the client's problems, strengthens the therapist's role as a model and social reinforcer,

facilitates interpersonal learning during sessions, and improves client compliance with behavioral assignments.

Clients will often fail to comply with therapeutic assignments. In terms of social learning theory, lack of compliance or resistance is a function of our incomplete knowledge and the limited effectiveness of our treatment techniques rather than unconscious opposition by the client. Behavior therapy typically involves active and collaborative relationships with clients that reduce the liklihood of resistance to change.

Various factors cause non-compliance by clients, including the assignment of an inappropriate task, inadequate explanation and preparation for the task by the therapist, a problem with the therapist-client relationship, interference by someone in the client's social network, and other competing problems in the client's life.

Behavior therapists make inferences about their clients' motives and behavior, but they differ sharply from traditional psychodynamic therapists in the nature of these inferences. Behavior therapists tend to take client self-report at face value rather than dismissing it in a search for hidden meaning. Client self-report is often the best means of personality assessment, even though it is not always to be accepted uncritically.

Behavior therapy is applicable not only to the specific disorders described in previous chapters, but also to less clearly described personality disorders that practicing clinicians often encounter.

Behavior therapists have typically been trained in the scientist-practitioner model of clinical psychology. However, they need not be researchers, provided they have basic training in behavioral science.

19

Ethical Issues

The preceding chapters have described the application of different behavioral treatment strategies to a wide range of clinical disorders and provided an evaluation of the successes and failures of this approach. Inevitably, in discussing the practice of behavior therapy we have drawn attention to important ethical issues involved in any form of treatment. All therapists are bound by an ethical code of professional practice, and the effects of different treatment methods must be evaluated within the context of this code.

In this chapter we discuss some fundamental requirements for the ethical practice of behavior therapy. The important concerns include: (1) a definition of the problem and selection of the goals of treatment, (2) informed consent and the protection of the client's human rights, (3) accountability and quality control of treatment services, and (4) factors affecting the choice of different therapeutic strategies.

WHO DEFINES PROBLEMS AND SETS GOALS?

As an applied science, behavior therapy is simply a collection of principles and techniques about how to change behavior; it says nothing about who should modify what behavior, why, or when. It is the client, not the therapist, who ultimately should decide the goal of therapy. Selecting effective techniques with which to change behavior is an empirical judgment about which the therapist is presumably an expert; choosing therapeutic objectives is a matter of value judgement and ought to be determined primarily by the client.

While ideally the client has priority over the therapist in identifying the problem and selecting the goal of treatment, it would be naive to imagine that the therapist does not play an important role in this process. The major contribution of the therapist is in helping clients develop appropriate problem-solving strategies for establishing realistic and personally satisfying life goals for themselves. This is accomplished by helping clients to generate several alternative courses of action and attempting to analyze and predict the consequences of pursuing different objectives. The therapist performs this function particularly with those clients who enter therapy not knowing what they really want and hoping to have the therapist decide for them. In such cases, the therapist's own values will inescapably be reflected in the alternatives and consequences explored.

Take marital therapy as an example. Among the many issues that involve the therapist's judgments are extramarital sex and divorce. Stuart (1980) cites a study by Knapp (1975) showing that marriage counselors hold strong values about such client behaviors. The important finding of this study is that one of the best predictors of marriage counselors' value judgments was their personal experience. Therapists must recognize how their own experience and background may bias the process and goals of therapy. Similarly, while we know of no hard evidence on this point, it seems likely that whether therapists are married or divorced might affect the manner in which they cope with the resolution of marital conflict.

The important question, then, becomes whether the therapist is aware of this influence and the behaviors it is used to develop. The influence should be recognized, and emphasis placed on specific, client-defined objectives. The inadvertent influence of the therapist's own value system will be greater when treatment goals are not specified in clear behavioral terms. A particular problem with this form of influence in vaguely formulated and unstructured non-behavioral therapies is that it involves a subtle and often insidious manipulation of the clients' beliefs (Bandura, 1969).

It is incumbent on the behavior therapist to declare his or her own values and to state how those opinions might influence the selection of appropriate goals. Particular care should be taken in helping the client to differentiate between advice and information that has some empirical basis. The therapist might decide against furthering goals which are at odds with his or her code of ethics and refer the client elsewhere. This candor, in addition to the description of explicit treatment methods directed toward specific goals in a manner that allows continual assessment of progress (accountability), makes responsibly conducted behavior therapy consistent with the strictest ethical and professional standards. It allows the client a degree of choice in finding a suitable therapist. Performing this delicate task obviously demands self-knowledge and self-understanding on the part of the behavior therapist.

Numerous illustrations of the often controversial issues involved in deciding upon treatment goals are discussed in previous chapters. For example, Chapter 11 presents two opposing points of view about the merits of treating gender disorders in children. Specifically, should extremely effeminate little boys like Kraig be treated to make them more masculine in manner? Who should determine whether therapy is indicated and what form it should take? In this case the therapist and parents shared a common goal, one with which the little boy cooperated fully. Here the objections were registered by social scientists opposed to traditional sex-role stereotypes of "masculinity" and "femininity." But what if the therapist whom the parents consulted had not shared their values?

The controversy about whether therapists should try to help homosexuals become heterosexuals is also discussed in Chapter 11. Until recently, homosexuality was routinely viewed as a personality problem that therapists tried to "cure," i.e., make the client heterosexual. Gay activist groups and newer psychological theories of sexual development that provided an alternative to outdated Freudian notions resulted in this customary therapeutic practice being challenged. Vigorous debate broke out among professionals about whether or not to treat homosexuality. There are professionals who still insist that homosexuality is a clinical disorder (Bieber et al., 1962). At the other extreme are some gay activists and some social scientists who denounce the treatment of any homosexual as a form of social oppression (Davison, 1976). This position denies homosexuals the choice of treatment goals, which is ethically objectionable. Other mental health professionals take the view that only those homosexuals who are genuinely and sincerely committed to switching to heterosexual behavior should be offered treatment aimed at changing sexual orientation (Sturgis & Adams, 1978). Determining a client's "genuine wishes" and assessing undue pressure or social coercion on the client can be fraught with difficulties.

According to Masters and Johnson (1979), their decisions about whom to accept for conversion or reversion to heterosexuality were based not only on what clients said but also on their actions. For example, the time that elapsed between the person first deciding that a change in sexual preference was necessary or desirable and his or her subsequent action in seeking treatment was considered an important indication of motivation. A person who procrastinated about seeking treatment was seen as less motivated than a counterpart who acted promptly and decisively in entering into therapy. Clients who used therapy as camouflage, expressing a desire to change sexual preference in front of their spouse but communicating ambivalence to the therapists in private, were referred to alternative treatment sources. Yet as Barlow (1980) has pointed out, Masters and Johnson fail to specify the criteria for selecting appropriate patients in a way that would allow other investigators to replicate their research. It would be well to realize that, ultimately, the decision rests on the therapist's clinical judgment. This is one of the major reasons for sex therapists being well-versed in the specific ethical and clinical issues inherent in therapy.

INFORMED CONSENT: THE ETHICAL IMPERATIVE

Before implementing any program of behavior change, it is imperative to obtain the client's freely given informed consent, a legal term that refers to the client's right to decide whether he or she wants to participate in a proposed program, after learning what will be involved. More specifically, informed consent is considered to have three components: knowledge, volition, and competency (Friedman, 1975). Knowledge refers to the information describing the program and its goals. The client must realize that he or she may decline or withdraw from treatment at any point. Alternative treatments should be discussed and the relative merits of each fairly evaluated. For example, a therapist who proposes to treat a hyperactive child along behavioral lines should alert the parents to the benefits and risks of pharmacological treatment of hyperactivity, a widely used alternative with some empirical support. Volition refers to the absence of coercion or duress when consent is made. Competency reflects an assessment that the client can understand the information given and can make a responsible judgment about it.

Selecting therapeutic goals is considerably more difficult in institutionalized individuals (e.g., mental hospital inmates) and in clients who are too young or too disturbed (e.g., many schizophrenics) to participate meaningfully in determining behavioral objectives. In many of these instances it might be necessary to waive the requirement of obtaining the client's freely given, informed consent and seek the approval of a guardian or independent review committee that fairly represents all parties responsible for and concerned with the client's treatment.

Behavior therapy actively attempts to use influences in the client's community that affect behavior which, in turn, will influence community members. Behavior and environment interact in a reciprocal fashion. Therefore, it is important to involve relevant community groups in the planning and execution of behavior modification programs. A revealing example of how this joint decision-making procedure operates is provided by Achievement Place in Kansas, the community-based, family-style behavior modification center for predelinquent children (see Chapter 7). Relevant community interest groups cooperated with the professionals directing the project, and the delinquent boys themselves participated in establishing goals which were mutually acceptable to all parties concerned, yet beneficial in modifying behavior.

The emphasis here on the interests of the individual client, informed consent, and the right to withdraw from treatment, are the defining characteristics of therapy. As such, therapy is to be distinguished from social regulation, in which it is the social group's, rather than the individual's, interests that are recognized, and in which coercive procedures may play a prominent role.

ACCOUNTABILITY AND PEER REVIEW

The 1970s witnessed the growing demand that therapists be made accountable to their clientele and those who share the cost of these increasingly expensive services. Closely related to this demand was the growing concern with the protection of the rights of patients, particularly those in institutions. Behavior therapists have been in the forefront of attempts to bring the application of psychological procedures for clinical and educational problems under critical scrutiny and to develop guidelines for the humane and effective practice of psychological therapies. Specific efforts towards this end included the publication of a report, *Ethical Issues in Behavior Modification*, by an American Psychological Association commission composed largely of behaviorally-oriented professionals (Stolz et al., 1978) and the release, by the Association for Advancement of Behavior Therapy (AABT), of a statement on ethical practice (Azrin, Stuart, Risley, & Stoltz, 1977). Like the APA Commission, and for similar reasons, AABT decided that there was no need to establish guidelines peculiar to behavior therapy, and that a set of questions of importance to the provision of human services in general (independent of the conceptual basis of treatment, the types of clients, and the nature of the treatment setting) would be appropriate.

In view of its fundamental commitment to accountability and evaluation of treatment programs, AABT, in 1978, formed the Professional Consultation and Peer Review Committee to provide authoritative interpretation of behavior therapy practice and research. The results of this innovative peer review process, which has been provided free of charge as a professional service, have been described by Risley and Sheldon-Wildgen (1982). Among the types of consultation offered are on-site reviews of both noncontroversial and controversial treatment programs. So-called controversial programs typically involve aversive or deprivation procedures in institutional settings. The programs often receive financial support from the state or federal government, and the officials charged with regulatory control have to rely on qualified professionals to evaluate the adequacy of the procedures used. The AABT Committee requires that four principles be agreed to by all parties involved in the controversy before they send a specially selected task force to conduct the on-site review. First, the parties of interest (e.g., the administrators of the program as well as the state licensing personnel) must agree with the request for review. Second, the members of the reviewing task force must be selected by the Professional Consultation and Peer Review Committee to represent a range of expertise appropriate to review the treatment procedures. Third, the task force will review the program and make pertinent professional interpretations and recommendations. Finally, the reviewing task force's report will be issued only to the relevant parties.

The task force has three missions: (1) to provide expert information on behavior therapy practice and research, (2) to interpret both general and specific ethical and legal issues as they relate to the issues raised in the controversy, and (3) to make recommendations that will facilitate the optimal care and treatment of clients. AABT does not assume responsibility for monitoring the program to ensure that its recommendations, assuming that they are accepted, have been followed; this is the responsibility of the regulatory agency, be it a state or federal agency.

Based on experience gained in conducting these on-site reviews, the Committee concluded that treatment programs that use controversial techniques should establish two committees. The first would be a peer review committee consisting of external, independent professionals who would periodically review program procedures. The second would be a human rights committee consisting of laypersons who would be aware of the relevant ethical and legal issues. Such a committee would monitor clients' rights, ensure due process in difficult decisions, and review all aversive or deprivation techniques. These recommendations are in line with previously proposed policies. Risley and Sheldon-Wildgen go further, however, in urging that this committee also review the treatment progress of individual clients on a regular basis. The following statement deserves emphasis. "It should be incumbent on the treatment staff to demonstrate not only that the type of treatment is appropriate but also that it is the best possible treatment for each particular client" (p. 130). Parenthetically, it seems most appropriate that Risley and Sheldon-Wildgen link this function of ensuring the selection of appropriate and preferred treatment methods with "human rights." It is insufficiently recognized that one of the most important ethical guidelines in the delivery of mental health services is the use of the most effective (and safest) treatments possible.

However desirable or well-intentioned the establishment of Human Rights Committees is, the reality is that they are saddled with extremely difficult tasks. As Reese (1982) commented, "Clients or guardians and Human Rights Committees are asked to make these decisions without fully realizing what considerations are relevant in making the decisions. They might be told to weigh the effectiveness of a treatment option against its intrusiveness, but what is effectiveness and intrusiveness?" (p. 98). Criteria of effectiveness are not all that easily agreed upon, as the many often lively discussions of this topic in the professional literature indicate, but neither are criteria of intrusiveness always straightforward. Towards this end, Reese proposes that the intrusiveness of a procedure be evaluated along three major dimensions: public acceptability, amount of restriction of liberty, and degree of discomfort or stress inherent in its application.

SELECTION OF INTERVENTION METHODS

Once the problem is defined and the goals of treatment set, the appropriate therapeutic techniques have to be selected by the therapist. The efficacy, efficiency, and safety of a treatment method are the most important factors to be taken into account. There are, however, additional factors that need to be considered.

Relative Intrusiveness of Alternative Methods

An important legal and ethical consideration is the relative intrusiveness of alternative methods. Intrusiveness refers to methods that involve a high degree of obvious external control, especially those based on aversive control. Self-administered relaxation therapy, for example, would be a benign, minimally intrusive technique, whereas therapist-administered punishment using aversive electric shock would be highly intrusive and restrictive. Similarly, praise or social reinforcement is less intrusive than is a token economy program based on tangible rewards. Recent legal rulings have emphasized the importance of using the least intrusive of available treatment methods (Wexler, 1973).

This principle of the "least intrusive alternative treatment" dictates that more intrusive methods be applied only after less intrusive methods have been shown to be ineffective.

There are occasions, however, when more intrusive, or even aversive, procedures are appropriate. An example of this is provided by the case study of Peter, a self-injurious six-year-old boy described in Box 19-1.

In this case the more benign procedure, differential positive reinforcement, proved ineffective. In the absence of alternative methods and given the life-threatening nature of the problem, a more restrictive and aversive technique was adopted. Note that in making this decision, the therapist obtained informed consent from the parents, tried an alternative method first, and documented the fact that previous experimental and clinical research showed that response-contingent electric shock was an effective form of treatment (Bachman, 1972). Although a treatment might be effective in changing a target behavior, it is important to assess whether any adverse side effects are associated with its use. In other words, likely benefits must be weighed against possible risks. This risk-benefit analysis will vary according to the nature of the target behavior, the particular treatment technique, and the therapeutic setting. In Peter's case, the research literature indicated that negative side effects of the punishment procedure were unlikely (Risley, 1968). In view of the severity of the problem, the lack of an alternative, and the availability of an effective method with little probability of negative side effects, the use of the momentarily painful punishment procedure was professionally responsible and humane (Friedman, 1975).

Intrusiveness is usually understood in terms of obvious external control, especially that involving the use of aversive methods. Nevertheless, some critics have used the notion of intrusiveness in a much broader and less exact sense. For example, behavioral sex therapy has been critized as highly intrusive com-

Box 19–1. *The Case of Peter the Self-Injurious Six-Year-Old*

Six-and-a-half years old, Peter was referred to the Psychological Clinic at Rutgers University because of his self-injurious behavior. Peter's language was nonfunctional; he had no self-help skills and had to be force-fed since he would spit out all food he was offered. More disturbing, however, was the fact that he would hit and scratch himself unless physically restrained. He hit his head so hard with his hand or knee, or against any solid object, that it posed a threat to his life. His condition had been diagnosed by a previous treatment agency as "infantile autism with functional retardation."

Initial treatment focused on counseling the parents and attempting to reinforce behavior incompatible with hitting and scratching, using food as a reward (differential reinforcement of other behavior). At the end of one treatment session, while Peter was in the care of both his mother and the therapist, he hit his head with sufficient force to require immediate hospitalization. Since even constant adult supervision could not ensure Peter's safety, it was decided that differential reinforcement was an inappropriate method. Elimination or suppression of life-threatening, self-injurious behavior was urgently required. After consulting with Peter's parents and gaining their fully informed consent and following the advice of other professional behavior therapists and the child's pediatrician, the therapist decided to use reponse-contingent electric shock as a treatment method. Experimental evidence showed that this was an effective means of reducing severe self-injurious behavior.

The details of this complex and time-consuming treatment program are beyond the scope of this book. To summarize, shock electrodes were strapped to the hand Peter used to hit himself. Each self-injurious response was punished by a brief, nonharmful shock. As the self-injurious behavior decreased, Peter's mother was taught to administer the treatment at home. Both parents observed all details of the treatment procedure. Following approximately three months of this treatment, Peter had improved enough to be admitted to the Child Behavior Research and Learning Center at Rutgers University, a special school for severely disturbed children. Two months later, Peter almost completely ceased self-injurious behavior, scratching, spitting, screaming, and throwing things. He was eating solid foods and had made considerable progress in speech, self-help, and simple academic and social skills. Detailed records were kept of Peter's behavior during all treatment phases, both at home and in the clinic, to evaluate the effects of treatment.

For reasons that remain unclear, Peter's behavior began to deteriorate at this point. The reintroduction of electric shock helped somewhat but failed to suppress self-injurious behavior as effectively as before. Because of the constant supervision now involved and the limited effectiveness of the punishment procedure, Peter's parents had him admitted to an institution on the advice of the therapist. With partial restraint, Peter was able to attend the school at the institution and engage in simple tasks. A careful follow-up revealed that during home visits, the intensity and frequency of Peter's self-injurious behavior remained considerably improved, compared to pre-treatment level. Details of the treatment and results of this case are described by Romanczyk and Goren (1975).

pared to traditional psychotherapy, which is allegedly far less intrusive (Bailey, 1978). A closer analysis reveals that the intrusiveness here refers to the directive nature of behavior therapy, namely the targeting of a specific response for direct modification. This objection falls away when it is realized that behavioral treatment methods for sexual problems are well-specified techniques that are jointly agreed to by the couple and then ultimately self-administered. Far from being "intrusive" in any negative sense, these methods are clearly stated, understandable, and most important, safe and effective. This desirable state of affairs can be contrasted with some traditional approaches, the goals of which are more ambigious and rarely explicitly agreed upon by the client.

Strategies Based On Social Versus Tangible Rewards

In general, methods directed towards developing positive, alternative behavior are favored over aversive techniques aimed at reducing or suppressing unwanted or undesirable behavior. In turn, there is a hierarchy of preferred methods within each of these general categories of treatment procedures. Consider the use of reinforcement programs in the classroom as an illustration of positive methods for increasing appropriate behavior. The sequencing of intervention strategies from the least to the most intrusive requires that a token reinforcement program using tangible rewards be instituted only if systematic attempts to praise good behavior and ignore bad behavior have failed. This advice is given for several reasons: (1) token reinforcement programs require considerable teacher effort and the fading of external rewards, (2) the use of external rewards may reduce the likelihood that behavioral improvements will generalize to other situations in which there are no token reinforcement programs (O'Leary, Poulous, & Devine, 1972), and (3) laboratory studies have shown that external (tangible) rewards can undermine intrinsic interest in the rewarded activity (Lepper, Green, & Nisbett, 1973); however, when made contingent on behavior in which students have little initial intrinsic interest, external rewards reliably increase interest in and performance of that behavior (Bandura & Schunk, 1981; Fisher, 1979).

This principle of sequencing of interventions is best viewed as a general guide for treatment, not an iron-clad rule. The possibility exists that this sequencing strategy may,

under some circumstances, undermine the efficacy of a program. For example, O'Leary, Becker, Evans, and Saudargas (1969) introduced rules, structure, and a combination of praising and ignoring as treatment components prior to instituting a token economy. The question remained whether an earlier introduction of the token program might not have produced more efficient and effective behavior change than a sequence of less powerful procedures did. Although controlled comparisons were not made, the token economy eventually introduced in the O'Leary et. al. (1969) study may have resulted in less behavior change than had occurred in previous studies with similar populations in which token programs were introduced earlier in the treatment. Thus, inflexibly sequencing intervention strategies from the least to the most intrusive might well have adverse effects, in the sense that a program so sequenced might be less effective than one begun with a stronger intervention.

Conventional Versus Unconventional Methods

We have stressed that the most important criteria for selecting treatment methods are their efficacy and safety. Unfortunately, however, not all currently available techniques enjoy the unequivocal empirical support that would allow the therapist to make clear-cut choices. Often the evidence is more ambiguous. When this applies to unconventional techniques, problems may arise. Consider the use of the method of "aversive behavior rehearsal" or "controlled exposure" in the treatment of exhibitionists described in Chapter 11. One of the reasons for the lack of acceptance of this technique is its unconventional nature. Many people, including professionals, find it distasteful to put a patient through such a procedure. A dispassionate look at the available evidence reveals that in the treatment of exhibitionists and other paraphilias, there is no compelling evidence that traditional psychotherapy is effective. Nevertheless, psychotherapy continues to be the treatment of choice in most therapeutic settings. In the case of aversive behavioral rehearsal there has been no controlled evaluation of its efficacy. Nevertheless, the favorable clinical findings in the literature and the theoretical basis of aversive counterconditioning would suggest that aversive behavior rehearsal be used under the appropriate circumstances.

Consider the case of a persistent exhibitionist described by Wilson and O'Leary (1980). This man faced life imprisonment because of his deviant behavior. He had been arrested repeatedly for exposing himself, received over ten years of psychoanalytically oriented psychotherapy without any success, and had been diagnosed as "incorrigible" by a psychiatrist. He had served six years in prison for his repeated sexual offenses. The final straw was when he exposed himself to a group of children. Given his previous legal record and his failure to respond to treatment, the prosecution requested life imprisonment. He was, however, allowed an additional course of behavior therapy prior to being sentenced. Under these circumstances, the therapists were obliged to use whatever techniques they considered potentially effective, making sure, of course, to obtain the patient's informed consent. In addition to the routine use of self-control methods, aversive imagery, and other behavioral procedures, aversive behavior rehearsal was recommended in view of clinical reports of its efficacy. Since it was an unconventional technique, the therapists obtained the patient's informed consent specifically for this method. He was told that were he to

refuse to participate in the procedure, he would be treated with all the other methods, but the therapists made clear their view that he should try the technique.

In presenting this case to a group of fellow professionals, the therapists were criticized by some colleagues for subjecting the patient to a "degrading" experience. Yet consider the alternative. Had the treatment failed—fortunately it proved successful and the patient had his prison sentence dropped—he would have been sent to a prison for sexual offenders. Anyone familiar with these institutions in the United States can testify to the "humiliating" and "degrading" experiences individuals like this exhibitionist would receive. In his previous term of imprisonment he had been threatened repeatedly with rape by other inmates and had been constantly harrassed. The point, and it applies to the evaluation of any form of psychological treatment, is that in some special instances we must bear in mind what the consequences are of *not* using a particular technique for a given problem. Many therapists arbitrarily reject direct, intrusive methods because they are not to their personal liking. We believe that it is unprofessional and unethical not to use an effective technique when one exists.

ACCOUNTABILITY AND QUALITY CONTROL IN TREATMENT

There are two important issues here: appropriate assessment of the effects of treatment intervention and implementation of treatment methods by competent and qualified therapists or other behavior-change agents. To resolve these issues and ensure quality control, it is necessary to collect data on the effects of treatment on both the target behavior and other behaviors.

Assessment of Treatment Effects

One of the defining characteristics of behavior therapy is a commitment to the continual measurement and evaluation of the specific effects of treatment. This concern with assessment is illustrated in the treatment of Peter, the self-injurious boy (Box 19-1). Detailed records were kept showing the frequencies of operationally defined self-injurious behavior and the number of punishments administered in both the home and the clinic. These data showed that, compared to Peter's behavior prior to treatment (baseline), the introduction of the punishment procedure greatly reduced self-injurious behavior. On the basis of these detailed behavioral observations, changes were made in the treatment program; these observations also provided an early warning of Peter's deterioration following his earlier progress.

Side Effects

Treatments aimed at changing particular problems may have effects on other behaviors not targeted for change. In Chapter 1, these correlated changes in untreated behavior were analyzed as response covariation (Kazdin, 1982). They are also known more commonly as side effects. Side effects are a more general phenomenon associated with medical and pharmacological treatments, as well as with psychological interventions; they may be either positive or negative. Numerous examples of positive or beneficial response covariation are discussed in the preceding chapters. For example, Dubbert and Wilson (1983) showed that a behavioral weight loss program not only produced reductions in body weight, but also significantly decreased depression and improved cardiovascular functioning. It is important for the therapist to know of these correlated forms of improvement associated with treatment, yet the more essential reason for monitoring possible side effects is that they may be detrimental to the client's well-being. Nonbehavioral treatments for obesity, particularly those emphasizing sudden and rapid weight loss, have been reported to cause increases in depression (Stunkard & Rush, 1974). This possibility made it vital for behavior therapists to assess the relationship between weight loss and negative psychological effects in their treatment programs. These assessments have demonstrated that behavior therapy appears to be a safe and benign form of treatment (Wilson & Brownell, 1980).

The available evidence suggests that negative side effects of behavioral treatments are relatively rare, yet they do occur, and therapists must be on the lookout for their appearance. Occasionally, treatment might produce both positive and negative side effects. Wahler (1975), for example, reported a case in which a behavioral program that succeeded in improving a child's behavior at school was associated with increases in peer interactions at home (a positive effect) and in oppositional behavior at school (a negative effect). In addition, a change in clients' behavior may precipitate negative reactions in spouses or other family members. These must be carefully evaluated in treatment planning. An example of this form of covariation was discussed in Chapter 11. Husbands became impotent after their wives' sexual responsiveness was increased (Brady, 1971). Behavior change does not occur in a vacuum but within the context of a network of complicated social relationships. More often than not, the development of behavioral competence engenders positive, reinforcing social feedback; it may also, however, draw attention to behavioral deficits in a marital partner for whom the original problem was of functional value. This partner, then, will often require treatment in his or her own right. This requires careful assessment of the effects of therapy on both the client's functioning and the spouse's behavior.

It is easy to emphasize how important it is for therapists to be alert to possible side effects of treatment. The practical problem, however, is how broad this assessment of possible changes in concomitant behavior should be. Where do you draw the line? No simple or uniform answer can be given: It will depend on the particular problem in a specific individual. As in so many instances of clinical practice, there can be no substitute for an informed therapist's wisdom and judgment in making such decisions. In addition, familiarity with the clinical literature on the treatment of different disorders can provide useful, albeit rough, guides of what to monitor.

Information on the targeted and correlated effects of treatment makes the therapist or treatment agency accountable to the consumer. This consumer may be the person receiving treatment, parents, or representatives of institutions who are employing the therapist to change someone else's behavior. Another advantage of collecting data on treatment effects is that it may allow the therapist to make more informed decisions about treatment. Data provide feedback about client progress and can be used to indicate whether therapy should be continued, intensified, or completely altered. In most traditional approaches, which are less empirically oriented, a switch in therapeutic tactics, if this occurs at all, is usually made according to more arbitrary and subjective criteria.

Of course, clinical practitioners are not always able to collect objective data on a continuous basis as they were in the case of Peter, who was treated in university facilities where the therapists had the necessary time and backup resources (a psychophysiological laboratory and trained behavioral observers). Asking the client to keep daily records of problem behaviors (self-monitoring) or obtaining reports from a spouse or family member (with the client's permission) are acceptable alternatives that yield valuable information.

CRITICAL CONSIDERATIONS FOR ETHICAL TREATMENT

The ethical issues raised here on the therapist's specific contribution to treatment are summarized in the AABT publication reproduced in Box 19–2. These issues should be borne in mind in the practice of all forms of psychological treatment, not just behavior therapy.

CAUSAL MODELS OF HUMAN BEHAVIOR

In part, behavior therapy was a reaction against the psychoanalytic model of human behavior. According to this causal model, behavior is determined by largely autonomous and unconscious intrapsychic forces. Logically, therapy focuses on these internal processes to the relative neglect of environmental factors. In rejecting this model, many behavior therapists adopted the causal model of radical behaviorism. However, like the psychoanalytic model, radical behaviorism, or the strict operant conditioning approach, is basically a unidirectional causal model of human behavior. Whereas the psychoanalytic view emphasizes internal, psychic determinants of behavior, the behavioristic approach holds that the environment is the ultimate determinant of behavior. As Skinner (1971) bluntly put it, "A person does not act upon the world, the world acts upon him" (p. 211). Not surprisingly, often exaggerated descriptions of this model evoked unflattering images of people as passive automatons, responding reflexively to external

---

Box 19–2   *Ethical Issues for Human Services*

A. Have the goals of treatment been adequately considered?
  1. To insure that the goals are explicit, are they written?
  2. Has the client's understanding of the goals been assured by having the client restate them orally or in writing?
  3. Have the therapist and client agreed on the goals of therapy?
  4. Will serving the client's interests be contrary to the interests of other persons?
  5. Will serving the client's immediate interests be contrary to the client's long-term interest?
B. Has the choice of treatment methods been adequately considered?
  1. Does the published literature show the procedure to be the best one available for that problem?
  2. If no literature exists regarding the treatment method, is the method consistent with generally accepted practice?
  3. Has the client been told of alternative procedures that might be preferred on the basis of significant differences in discomfort, treatment time, cost, or demonstrated effectiveness?
  4. If a treatment procedure is publicly, legally, or professionally controversial, has formal professional consultation been obtained, the reaction of the affected segment of the public adequately considered, and the alternative treatment methods more closely reexamined and reconsidered?
C. Is the client's participation voluntary?
  1. Have possible sources of coercion on the client's participation been considered?
  2. If treatment is legally mandated, has the available range of treatments and therapists been offered?
  3. Can the client withdraw from treatment without a penalty or financial loss that exceeds actual clinical costs?
D. When another person or agency is empowered to arrange for therapy, have the interests of the subordinated client been sufficiently considered?
  1. Has the subordinated client been informed of the treatment objectives and participated in the choice of treatment procedures?
  2. When the subordinated client's competence is limited, have the client as well as the guardian participated in the treatment discussions to the extent that the client's abilities permit?
  3. If the interests of the subordinated person and the superordinate persons or agency conflict, have attempts been made to reduce the conflict by dealing with both interests?
E. Has the adequacy of treatment been evaluated?
  1. Have quantitative measures of the problem and its progress been obtained?
  2. Have the measures of the problem and its progress been made available to the client during treatment?
F. Has the confidentiality of the treatment relationship been protected?
  1. Has the client been told who has access to the records?
  2. Are records available only to authorized persons?
G. Does the therapist refer the clients to other therapists when necessary?
  1. If treatment is unsuccessful, is the client referred to other therapists?
  2. Has the client been told that if dissatisfied with the treatment, referral will be made?
H. Is the therapist qualified to provide treatment?
  1. Has the therapist had training or experience in treating problems like those of the client?
  2. If deficits exist in the therapist's qualifications, has the client been informed?
  3. If the therapist is not adequately qualified, is the client referred to other therapists or has supervision by a qualified therapist been provided? Is the client informed of the supervisory relation?
  4. If the treatment is administered by mediators, have the mediators been adequately supervised by a qualified therapist?

Reprinted by permission from Ethical issues for human services, *Behavior Therapy*, (1977) *8*, v–vi.

influences beyond their control. Such a position seems to deny our experience that we at least partly determine our own actions.

As discussed in Chapter 1, the social learning approach to behavior therapy is based on the model of reciprocal determinism. According to this model, psychological functioning involves a continuous reciprocal interaction among behavioral, cognitive, and environmental influences. There is not an inevitable prime determinant of behavior, although the relative influence of cognitive, behavioral, and environmental factors will vary across individuals, activities, and situations. The importance of this social learning model is that people are viewed as having the capability of self-direction—of being able to shape their own destinies by affecting the external environment. Behavior therapy is devoted to the development of self-regulatory skills for more personally satisfying emotional and behavioral adjustment—what Mahoney and Thoresen (1974) aptly called "power to the person."

The reciprocal determinism model of causal processes in human behavior must be borne in mind in evaluating ethical issues in behavior therapy. One of the major objections critics had of behavior therapy was that a scientific technology of behavior modification would give treatment agencies unilateral power to change the behavior of clients. Happily, this fear is greatly exaggerated and based upon grossly distorted interpretations of the field. The fundamental flaw in charges of this nature is that they assume a unidirectional causal model of behavior and exaggerate the reality of automatic conditioning processes. The automatic nature of both classical and operant conditioning has been shown to be largely false. The alleged power of behavior modification methods to control human behavior has been exaggerated by both extreme proponents as well as the opponents of behavior therapy.

Even an extreme behaviorist such as Skinner (1971) has acknowledged what he calls the capacity for countercontrol. To countercontrol means to react against environmental influence. However, this concept does not go far enough in accommodating the well-documented ability of people to resist unwanted external control over their lives (Bandura, 1977b). In therapy, for example, it is vital that the behavior therapist have the cooperation and active participation of the client. This is one of the reasons the therapist-client relationship is important in behavior therapy. One of its hallmarks is that the client is asked to do something, such as imagine aversive scenes in desensitization, refuse to accede to an unreasonable request in assertion training, self-monitor caloric intake in self-control programs for the treatment of obesity, and so on. If the client does not follow these specific treatment suggestions, little if any change can be expected. This is especially true with adult outpatients. Whenever possible, the behavior therapist is also well-advised to seek out the active cooperation of children and even institutionalized clients whose own behavior is to be altered, despite the fact that someone else (parents or institutional authorities) has initiated the therapy (Stolz et al., 1978). It is clear, then, that for behavior therapy to be successful, the client's freely given, informed consent and continued cooperation with a trusted therapist are minimal necessities.

In an attempt to emphasize the links between laboratory research and applied behavior analysis, some investigators have described the behavior therapist as a "social reinforcement machine," a "behavioral engineer," or a behavioral "programmer." The use of this operant jargon has been doubly unfortunate. First, these figurative terms are misleading, since they emphasize the therapist's unilateral control over a relatively passive and powerless client. As we have indicated, this model of human behavior is one-sided; it does not reflect the interdependence among behavior, cognitive processes, and the environment. Second, this language of "control" helps perpetuate an unfavorable (and inaccurate) image of behavior therapy. People are so put off that they might reject behavioral methods that can contribute significantly to a happier and more rewarding life.

There is no need to resort to mechanistic metaphors and technocratic jargon to describe behavior in precise and accurate terms. In contemporary behavior therapy, with its explicit recognition of cognitive mediation and its emphasis on self-control processes, therapists are no longer seen as simple "shapers" of attitudes and behavior, although their influence on the client may be profound. Instead, the therapist is seen as a consultant, not as a controller.

BEHAVIOR THERAPY AS A HUMANISTIC SCIENCE

Bandura (1969) has pointed out that, far from being inconsistent with a humanistic philosophy, behavior therapy is a very effective means of promoting personal freedom and emotional growth because of its efficacy in enhancing freedom of choice. Consider, for example, the agoraphobic client who is at the mercy of her unpredictable terrors and confined to her home, or the unassertive person who cannot express his genuine feelings and is often treated like a doormat. To remove the agoraphobic's crippling fears, or to teach the dependent person to be appropriately assertive and hence experience a sense of human dignity rather than personal humiliation, is to increase dramatically the range of activities in which those individuals can engage.

They can now choose to stay at home or travel; they can now elect to refuse an unreasonable request or freely express approval or disapproval, joy or sorrow, without experiencing guilt or embarrassment.

Or, think of the psychotic or retarded child, who, as a result of not knowing basic self-care skills, having learning deficiencies, and being unable to talk or communicate properly, is destined to a life of squalid emptiness in some understaffed, impersonal state institution. A behavior therapy program which can successfully teach self-care, social skills, and communicative competencies can give that child a chance to avoid institutionalization and find a rewarding role in society (Lovaas, Koegel, Simmons, & Long, 1973). Behavior therapy, when successfully applied, does not oppressively mold clients according to some rigid, impersonal formula. Rather, it seeks to free clients from the restrictions placed upon them by their problems by helping them to overcome obstacles to self-fulfillment.

As with any body of knowledge, the principles and procedures of behavior therapy can be abused. Specific instances of the unethical and illegal use of behavior modification methods have been reported in institutions. In response to these abuses, behavior therapists have been active in attempts to formulate procedures that guarantee the human rights and personal dignity of all clients, especially those retarded and mental hospital populations often subjected to relative neglect (Azrin, Stuart, Risley, & Stolz, 1977; Davison and Stuart, 1975; May et al., 1975; Stolz et al., 1978). Finally, it must be remembered that these ethical imperatives of informed consent, accountability, and quality control of treatment should be common to all forms of psychological and psychiatric treatment. There is little unique about behavior therapy when it comes to concern about these matters.

SUMMARY

There is more to the practice of clinical behavior therapy than the simple application of the principles and procedures of experimentally based psychology. Ethical and legal considerations require that the therapist be concerned about how these procedures are applied, toward what ends, and for which purposes. Four areas in particular demand attention: who determines the goals of treatment, was informed consent given, which therapeutic techniques were selected, and what are the guidelines for the quality control of treatment.

In behavior therapy, the goal of treatment is determined primarily by the client. The role of the therapist is to help the client generate alternative courses of action and to attempt to analyze their probable consequences. The therapist does influence the client in setting goals, however, the therapist attempts to indicate what his or her personal biases are and how they might influence goal selection.

Informed consent is defined legally as consent given by a competent and knowledgeable person on a strictly voluntary basis. With young children or individuals who are too disturbed (e.g., some schizophrenics) or too retarded to participate meaningfully in the selection of treatment goals, the right to informed consent has to be modified or waived. In the case of young children, the parents must give their informed consent for treatment. With institutionalized clients, a review committee representing those people responsible for and concerned about the client's treatment should approve treatment goals and procedures.

The guiding ethical and legal principle in the selection of treatment methods is that the least intrusive method should be used to accomplish therapeutic objectives. In those instances in which more restrictive or intrusive procedures are warranted (e.g., punishment procedures with a self-injurious child), the anticipated benefits must be weighed carefully against potential risks or adverse side effects.

Accountability requires that the effects of treatment on the target behavior and other related activities be systematically monitored and assessed. Quality control necessitates that the therapist be competent and well-trained in scientific psychology and general clinical skills. In behavioral programs in which the procedures are implemented by psychological assistants (e.g., parents and teachers), the behavior therapist is responsible for ensuring that the assistants are well-trained and closely supervised.

Behavior therapists often arouse concern because they avowedly change behavior. However, all forms of psychological treatment involve therapist influence on the client. In explicitly acknowledging this influence and in emphasizing specific, client-defined goals, behavior therapy is an open and "up-front" approach in which the client is an active and cooperative participant.

Rather than imposing arbitrary therapeutic goals or molding clients according to some impersonal formula, behavior therapy expands clients' life choices by reducing debilitating inhibitions and fears and broadening behavioral repertoires.

References

A

Abrams, D. B., Elder, J. P., Lasater, E., Carleton, R., & Artz, R. (1985). A comprehensive framework for conceptualizing and planning organizational health promotion programs. In M. Cataldo & T. Coates (Eds.). *Behavioral medicine in industry*. New York: John Wiley & Sons.

Abrams, D. B., Follick, M., & Thompson, C. (1983). Work site weight loss intervention. *Journal of Consulting and Clinical Psychology, 51*, 226–233.

Abrams, D. B., Monti, P. M., Pinto, R. P., Elder, J. P., Brown, R. A., & Jacobs, S. (1985) *Psychosocial stress and coping in smokers who relapse or quit.* Unpublished manuscript, Miriam Hospital, Providence, RI.

Abrams, R., Taylor, M. A., Faber, R., Tso, T. O. T., Williams, R. A., & Almy, G. (1983). Unilateral versus bilateral ECT: The controversy continues. In P. J. Clayton and J. E. Barrett (Eds.), *Treatment of depression: Old controversies and new approaches*. New York: Raven Press.

Abramson, L. Y., Seligman, M. E. P., & Teasdale, J. D. (1978). Learned helplessness in humans: Critique and reformulation. *Journal of Abnormal Psychology, 87*, 49–74.

Adams, P. L. (1973). *Obsessive children: A sociopathic study*. New York: Brunner/Mazel.

Ad Hoc Committee on Classification of Headache. (1962). Classification of headache. *Journal of American Medical Association, 179*, 127–128.

Agras, W. S. (1979). President's message. *Behavioral Medicine Update, 1*, p. 3.

Agras, W. S. (1982). Behavioral medicine in the 1980s: Nonrandom connections. *Journal of Consulting and Clinical Psychology, 50*, 797–803.

Agras, W. S., Barlow, D. H., Chapin, H. N., Abel, G. G., & Leitenberg, H. (1974). Behavior modification of anorexia nervosa. *Archives of General Psychiatry, 30*, 279–286.

Agras, W. S., Dorlan, B., Kirkley, B., Arnow, B., & Bachman, J. (in press). Imipramine in the treatment of bulimia: A double-blind controlled study. *International Journal of Eating Disorders*.

Agras, W. S., & Jacob, R. G. (1979). Hypertension. In O. F. Pomerleau & J. P. Brady (Eds.), *Behavioral medicine: Theory and practice*. Baltimore: Williams and Wilkins.

Agras, W. S., Kazdin, A. E., & Wilson, G. T. (1979). *Behavior therapy: Towards an applied clinical science*. San Francisco: Freeman.

Agras, W. S., & Kraemer, H. (1984). The treatment of anorexia nervosa: Do different treatments have different outcomes. In A. J. Stunkard & E. Stellar (Eds.), *Eating and its disorders*. New York: Raven Press.

Alderman, N. H., & Schoenbaum, E. E. (1975). Detection and the treatment of hypertension at the work site. *New England Journal of Medicine, 293*, 65–68.

Alexander, J. F. (1970, May). *A systems approach to family interaction*. Paper presented at the meeting of the Rocky Mountain Psychological Association, Salt Lake City.

Alexander, J. F., & Parsons, B. V. (1973). Short term behavioral intervention with delinquent families: Impact on family process and recidivism. *Journal of Abnormal Psychology, 81*, 219–226.

Allen, K. E., Hart, B. M., Buell, J. S., Harris, F. R., & Wolf, M. M. (1964). Effects of social reinforcement on isolate behavior of a nursery school child. *Child Development, 35*, 511–518.

Allen, R. R., & Hasazi, J. (1978). *Bladder capacity and awakening behavior as outcome variables in the conditioning treatment of enuresis*. Unpublished manuscript, University of Vermont.

American Psychiatric Association. (1980). *Diagnostic and statistical manual of mental disorders* (3rd ed.). Washington, DC: American Psychiatric Association.

Amies, P. L., Gelder, M. G., & Shaw, P. M. (1983). Social phobia: A comparative clinical study. *British Journal of Psychiatry, 142*, 174–179.

Andrasik, F., Blanchard, E. B., Neff, D. F., & Rodichok, L. D. (1984). Biofeedback and relaxation training for chronic headache: A controlled comparison of booster treatments and regular contacts for long-term maintenance. *Journal of Consulting and Clinical Psychology, 52*, 609–615.

Andrasik, F., Holroyd, K. A., & Abell, T. (1979). Prevalence of headache within a college student population: A preliminary analysis. *Headache, 20*, 384–387.

Andreasen, N. C. (1982). Negative symptoms in schizophrenia: Definition and reliability. *Archives of General Psychiatry, 39*, 784–788.

Andreasen, N. C. (1984). Concepts, diagnosis and classification. In E. S. Paykel (Ed.), *Handbook of affective disorders*. New York: Guilford Press.

Andrew, G. M., Oldridge, N. B., Parker, J. O., Cunningham, D. A., Rechnitzer, P. A., Jones, N. L., Buck, C., Kavanagh, T., Shepard, R. J., & Sutton, J. R. (1981). Reasons for dropout from exercise programs in post-coronary patients. *Medicine and Science in Sports and Exercise, 13*, 164–168.

Andrews, G., Moran, C., & Hall, W. (1983). Agoraphobia: *A meta-analysis of treatment outcome studies*. Unpublished manuscript, University of New South Wales Medical School, Australia.

Andry, R. G. (1960). *Delinquency and parental pathology*. London: Methuen.

Anthony, E. J. (1978). From birth to breakdown: A perspective study of vulnerability. In E. J. Anthony & T. Benedick (Eds.), *Parenthood*. Boston: Little, Brown & Co.

Arias, I., & O'Leary, K. D. (1983). *Prevalence rates of hyperactivity across cultures*. Unpublished manuscript, State University of New York at Stony Brook.

Armor, D. J., Polich, J. M., & Stambul, H. B. (1978). *Alcoholism and treatment*. New York: John Wiley & Sons.

Arnkoff, D. (1983). Common and specific factors in cognitive therapy. In M. J. Lambert (Ed.), *Psychotherapy and patient relationships*. Homewood, IL: Dorsey.

Arnow, B., Taylor, C. B., Agras, W. S., & Telch, M. (1985). Enhancing agoraphobia treatment outcome by changing couple communication patterns. *Behavior Therapy, 16*, 452–467.

Arrindell, W. A., & Emmelkamp, P. M. G. (1985). *Marital adjustment, intimacy and needs in female agoraphobics and their partners: A controlled study*. Unpublished manuscript, State University of Groningen, The Netherlands.

Ashby, W. A., & Wilson, G. T. (1977). Behavior therapy for obesity: Booster sessions and long-term maintenance of weight loss. *Behaviour Research and Therapy, 15*, 451–466.

Ashkenazi, Z. (1975). The treatment of encopresis using a discrimination stimulus and positive reinforcement. *Journal of Behavior Therapy and Experimental Psychiatry, 6*, 155–157.

Attfield, M., & Peck, D. F. (1979). Temperature self-regulation and relaxation with migraine patients and normals. *Behaviour Research and Therapy, 17*, 591–595.

Auerbach, R., & Kilmann, P. R. (1977). The effects of group systematic desensitization on secondary erectile failure. *Behavior Therapy, 8*, 330–339.

Ayllon, T., & Azrin, N. H. (1965). The measurements and reinforcement of behavior of psychotics. *Journal of the Experimental Analysis of Behavior, 8,* 357–383.

Ayllon, T., & Azrin, N. H. (1968). *The token economy: A motivational system for therapy and rehabilitation.* New York: Appleton-Century-Crofts.

Ayllon, T., Smith, D., & Rogers, M. (1970). Behavioral management of school phobia. *Journal of Behavior Therapy and Experimental Psychiatry, 1,* 125–128.

Azrin, N. H. (1976). Improvements in the community-reinforcement approach to alcoholism. *Behaviour Research and Therapy, 14,* 339–348.

Azrin, N. H. (1977). A strategy for applied research: Learning based but outcome oriented. *American Psychologist, 32,* 140–149.

Azrin, N. H., & Foxx, R. M. (1971). A rapid method of toilet training the institutionalized retarded. *Journal of Applied Behavior Analysis, 4,* 89–99.

Azrin, N. H., & Foxx, R. M. (1974). *Toilet training in less than a day.* New York: Simon & Schuster.

Azrin, N. H., Holz, W., Ulrich, R., & Goldiamond, I. (1961). The control of the content of conversation through reinforcement. *Journal of Experimental Analysis of Behavior, 4,* 25–30.

Azrin, N. H., Naster, B., & Jones, R. (1973). Reciprocity counseling: A rapid learning-based procedure for marital counseling. *Behaviour Research and Therapy, 11,* 365–382.

Azrin, N. H., & Powell, J. (1968). Behavioral engineering: The reduction of smoking behavior by a conditioning apparatus and procedure. *Journal of Applied Behavior Analysis, 1,* 193–200.

Azrin, N. H., & Powell, J. (1969). Behavioral engineering: The use of response priming to improve prescribed self-medication. *Journal of Applied Behavior Analysis, 2,* 39–42.

Azrin, N. H., Sneed, T. J., & Foxx, R. M. (1973). Dry Bed: A rapid method of eliminating bedwetting (enuresis) of the retarded. *Behaviour Research and Therapy, 11,* 427–434.

Azrin, N. H., Sneed, T. J., & Foxx, R. M. (1974). Dry bed training: Rapid elimination of childhood enuresis. *Behaviour Research and Therapy, 12,* 147–156.

Azrin, N. H., Stuart, R. B., Risley, T. R., & Stolz, S. B. (1977). Ethical issues for human services. *Behavior Therapy, 8,* v–vi.

B

Bachman, J. A. (1972). Self-injurious behavior: A behavioral analysis. *Journal of Abnormal Psychology, 80,* 211–224.

Bachrach, A. J., Erwin, W. J., & Mohr, J. P. (1965). The control of eating behavior in an anorexic by operant conditioning techniques. In L. P. Ullmann & L. Krasner (Eds.), *Case Studies in behavior modification.* New York: Holt, Rinehart & Winston.

Baer, D. (1977). Perhaps it would be better not to know everything. *Journal of Applied Behavior Analysis, 10,* 167–172.

Baile, W. F., & Engel, B. T. (1978). A behavioral strategy for promoting treatment compliance following myocardial infarction. *Psychosomatic Medicine, 40,* 413–419.

Bailey, J. S., Wolf, M. M., & Phillips, E. L. (1970). Home-based reinforcement and the modification of predelinquents' classroom behavior. *Journal of Applied Behavior Analysis, 3,* 223–233.

Bailey, K. G. (1978). Psychotherapy or massage palor technology: Comments on the Zeiss, Rosen, and Zeiss treatment procedure. *Journal of Consulting and Clinical Psychology, 46,* 1502–1506

Baker, B. L. (1969). Symptom treatment and symptom substitution in enuresis. *Journal of Abnormal Psychology, 74,* 42–49.

Baker, H., & Wills, U. (1978). School phobia: Classification and treatment. *British Journal of Psychiatry, 132,* 492–499.

Bakwin, H., & Bakwin, R. M. (1967). *Clinical management of behavior disorders in children.* (3rd ed.). Philadelphia: W. B. Saunders Co.

Baldwin, A. (1955). *Behavior and development in childhood.* New York: Dryden Press.

Ball, J. R. B., & Kiloh, L. G. (1959). A controlled trial of imipramine in the treatment of depressed state. *British Medical Journal, 2,* 1052–1055.

Baller, W. R., & Giangreco, J. C. (1970). Correction of nocturnal enuresis in deaf children. *The Volta Review, 72,* 9:545–547.

Bancroft, J. H. (1974). *Deviant sexual behaviour.* Oxford: Oxford University Press.

Bandura, A. (1969). *Principles of behavior modification.* New York: Holt, Rinehart & Winston.

Bandura, A. (1973). *Aggression: A social learning approach.* Englewood Cliffs, NJ: Prentice-Hall.

Bandura, A. (1977a). Self-efficacy: Toward a

unifying theory of behavioral change. *Psychological Review, 84*, 191–215.

Bandura, A.   (1977b). *Social learning theory.* Englewood Cliffs, NJ: Prentice-Hall.

Bandura, A.   (1978). The self system in reciprocal determinism. *American Psychologist, 33*, 344–358.

Bandura, A.   (1982). Self-efficacy mechanisms in human agency. *American Psychologist, 37*, 122–147.

Bandura, A.   (1986). *Social foundations of thought and action: A social cognitive theory.* Englewood Cliffs, NJ: Prentice-Hall.

Bandura, A., & Adams, N. E.   (1977). Analysis of self-efficacy theory of behavioral change. *Cognitive Therapy and Research, 1*, 287–310.

Bandura, A., Adams, N. E., & Beyer, J.   (1977). Cognitive processes mediating behavioral change. *Journal of Personality and Social Psychology, 35*, 125–139.

Bandura, A., Adams, N. E., Hardy, A., & Howells, G.   (1980). Tests of the generality of self-efficacy theory. *Cognitive Therapy and Research, 4*, 39–66.

Bandura, A., Blanchard, E. B., & Ritter, B.   (1969). The relative efficacy of desensitization and modeling approaches for inducing behavioral, affective, and cognitive changes. *Journal of Personality and Social Psychology, 13*, 173–199.

Bandura, A., & Cervone, D.   (1985). *Differential engagement of self-reactive influences in cognitive motivation.* Unpublished manuscript, Stanford University.

Bandura, A., Grusec, J. E., & Menlove, F. L.   (1967). Vicarious extinction of avoidance behavior. *Journal of Personality and Social Psychology, 5*, 16–23.

Bandura, A., & Menlove, F. L.   (1968). Factors determining vicarious extinction of avoidance behavior through symbolic modeling. *Journal of Personality and Social Psychology, 8*, 99–108.

Bandura, A., Reese, L., & Adams, N. E.   (1982). Microanalysis of action and fear arousal as a function of differential levels of perceived self-efficacy. *Journal of Personality and Social Psychology, 43*, 5–21.

Bandura, A., Ross, D., & Ross, S. A.   (1963). Imitation of film-mediated aggressive models. *Journal of Abnormal and Social Psychology, 66*, 3–11.

Bandura, A., & Schunk, D.   (1981). Cultivating competence, self-efficacy, and intrinsic interest through proximal self-motivation. *Journal of Personality and Social Psychology, 41*, 586–598.

Bandura, A., & Simon, K. M.   (1977). The role of proximal intentions in self-regulation of refractory behavior. *Cognitive Therapy and Research, 1*, 177–193.

Bandura, A., Taylor, C. B., Williams, L., Mefford, I., & Barchas, J.   (1985). Catecholamine secretion as a function of perceived coping self-efficacy. *Journal of Consulting and Clinical Psychology, 53*, 406–414.

Bandura, A., & Walters, R. H.   (1959). *Adolescent aggression.* New York: Ronald Press.

Bandura, A., & Walters, R. H.   (1963). *Social learning and personality development.* New York: Holt, Rinehart & Winston.

Barabasz, A. F.   (1973). Group desensitization of text anxiety in elementary school. *Journal of Psychology, 83*, 295–301.

Barabasz, A. F.   (1974). Quantifying hierarchy stimuli in systematic desensitization via GSR: A preliminary investigation. *Child Study Journal, 4*, 207–211.

Barbarin, O. A.   (1978). Comparison of symbolic and overt aversion in the self-control of smoking. *Journal of Consulting and Clinical Psychology, 46*, 1569–1571.

Barkley, R. A., & Cunningham, C. E.   (1978). Do stimulant drugs improve the academic performance of hyperkinetic children? *Clinical Pediatrics, 17*, 85–92.

Barling, J., & Abel, M.   (1983). Self-efficacy beliefs and performance. *Cognitive Therapy and Research, 7*, 265–272.

Barling, J., O'Leary, S. G., & Cowen, R. A.   (1985). *Factor structure of the Stony Brook Scale: Replication and extension.* Unpublished manuscript, State University of New York at Stony Brook.

Barlow, D. H.   (1977). Behavioral assessment in clinical settings: Developing issues. In J. D. Cone & R. P. Hawkins (Eds.), *Behavioral assessment: New directions in clinical psychology.* New York: Brunner/Mazel.

Barlow, D. H.   (1980a). Behavior therapy: The next decade. *Behavior Therapy, 11*, 315–328.

Barlow, D. H.   (1980b). Review of Masters and Johnson's "Homosexuality in perspective." *Contemporary Psychology, 25*, 355–357.

Barlow, D. H.   (1986). Causes of sexual dysfunction: The role of anxiety and cognitive interference. *Journal of Consulting and Clinical Psychology, 54*, 140–148.

Barlow, D. H. (Ed.).   (1985). *Clinical handbook*

of psychological disorders. New York: Guilford Press.

Barlow, D. H., Abel, G. G., & Blanchard, E. B. (1979). Gender identity change in transsexuals. *Archives of General Psychiatry, 36,* 1001–1007.

Barlow, D. H., & Beck, J. G. (1984). The psychosocial treatment of anxiety disorders: Current status, future directions. In J. Williams and R. Spitzer (Eds.), *Psychotherapy Research* New York: Guilford Press.

Barlow, D. H., Cohen, A. J., Waddell, M. T., Vermilyea, B. B., Klosko, J., Blanchard, E. B., & DiNardo, P. A. (1984). Panic and generalized anxiety disorders: Nature and treatment. *Behavior Therapy, 15,* 431–449.

Barlow, D. H., O'Brien, G. T., Last, C. G., & Holden, A. E. (1983). Couples treatment of agoraphobia: Initial outcome. In K. D. Craig and R. J. McMahon (Eds.), *Advances in clinical behavior therapy.* New York: Brunner/Mazel.

Barlow, D. H., Reynolds, E. J., & Agras, W. S. (1973). Gender identity change in a transsexual. *Archives of General Psychiatry, 28,* 569–576.

Barlow, D. H., Vermilyea, J., Blanchard, E. B., Vermilyea, B., Dinardo, P. A., & Cerney, J. A. (1985). The phenomenon of panic. *Journal of Abnormal Psychology, 94,* 320–328.

Barnard, J. D., Gant, B. L., Kuehn, F. E., Jones, H. H., Ford, D., & Christopherson, E. R. (1986). Homebased treatment of the juvenile probationer. Unpublished manuscript, University of Kansas, Laurence, Kansas.

Barton, E. S., Guess, D., Garcia, E., & Baer, D. M. (1970). Improvement of retardates mealtime behaviors by time-out procedures using multiple baseline techniques. *Journal of Applied Behavior Analysis, 3,* 77–84.

Baucom, D. H. (1982). A comparison of behavioral contracting and problem-solving/communications training in behavioral marital therapy. *Behavior Therapy, 13,* 162–174.

Baum, C. G., & Forehand, R. (1981). Long term follow-up assessment of parent training by use of multiple outcome measures. *Behavior Therapy, 12,* 643–652.

Baumeister, A., & Klosowski, R. (1965). An attempt to group toilet train severely retarded patients. *Mental Retardation, 3,* 24–26.

Beach, S. R. H., Arias, I., & O'Leary, K. D. (in press). The role of marital satisfaction and social support in depressive symptomatology, *Journal of Psychopathology and Behavior Assessment.*

Beach, S. R. H., Arias, I., & O'Leary, K. D. (1983). *Risk for depression as a function of social support.* Paper presented at the Eastern Psychological Association, Philadelphia, PA.

Beach, S. R. H., Jouriles, E. N., & O'Leary, K. D. (1985). Extra-marital sex: Impact on depression and commitment in couples seeking marital therapy. *Journal of Sex and Marital Therapy, 11,* 99–108.

Beach, S. R. H., & O'Leary, K. D. (1986). The treatment of depression occurring in the context of marital discord. *Behavior Therapy, 17,* 43–49.

Beaver, C., Brown, R. A., & Lichtenstein, E. (1981). Effects of monitored nicotine fading and anxiety management training on smoking reduction. *Addictive Behaviors, 6,* 301–305.

Beck, A. T. (1967). *Depression: Clinical, experimental, and theoretical aspects.* New York: Harper & Row.

Beck, A. T. (1976). *Cognitive therapy and the emotional disorders.* New York: International Universities Press.

Beck, A. T., & Emery, G. (1985). *Anxiety disorders and phobias.* New York: Basic Books.

Beck, A. T., Hollon, S. D., Young, J. E., Bedrosian, R. C., & Budenz, D. (1985). Treatment of depression with cognitive therapy and amitriptyline. *Archives of General Psychiatry, 42,* 142–152.

Beck, A. T., Rush, A. J., Shaw, B. F., & Emery, G. (1979). *Cognitive therapy of depression.* New York: Guilford Press.

Beck, G., Barlow, D. H., & Sakheim, D. K. (1983). The effects of attentional focus and partner arousal on sexual responding in functional and dysfunctional men. *Behaviour Research and Therapy, 21,* 1–8.

Beck, G., & Barlow, D. H. (1984). Current conceptualizations of sexual dysfunction: A review and an alternative perspective. *Clinical Psychology Review, 4,* 363–378.

Bekhterev, V. M. (1970). Cited in A. J. Yates, *Behavior therapy.* New York: John Wiley & Sons.

Bem, D. J., & Funder, D. C. (1978). Predicting more of the people more of the time: Assessing the personality of situations. *Psychological Review, 85,* 485–510.

Bennett, F. C., & Sherman, R. (1983). Management of childhood "hyperactivity" by primary care physicians. *Developmental and Behavioral Pediatrics, 4,* 88–93.

Benson, H. (1975). *The relaxation response.* New York: William Morrow.

Berg, G., Laberg, J. C., Skutle, A., & Ohman, A. (1981). Instructed versus pharmacological effects of alcohol in alcoholics and social drinkers. *Behaviour Research and Therapy, 19*, 55–66.

Bergin, A. E., & Strupp, H. H. (1970). New directions in psychotherapy research. *Journal of Abnormal Psychology, 76*, 13–26.

Bernstein, D., & Given, B. A. (1984). Progressive relaxation: Abbreviated methods. In R. L. Woolfolk & P. M. Lehrer (Eds.), *Principles and Practice of Stress Management.* New York: Guilford Press.

Bernstein, D., & Glasgow, R. (1979). Smoking. In O. Pomerleau & J. P. Brady (Eds.), *Behavioral medicine: Theory and practice.* Baltimore: Williams and Wilkins.

Bernstein, D. A., & Paul, G. L. (1971). Some comments on therapy analogue research with small animal "phobias." *Journal of Behavior Therapy and Experimental Psychiatry, 2*, 225–237.

Bernstein, L., Bernstein, R. S., & Dana, R. H. (1974). *Interviewing: A guide for health professionals.* (2nd ed.). New York: Appleton-Century-Crofts.

Berryman, E. (1959). School phobia: Management problems in private practice. *Psychological Reports, 5*, 19–25.

Bieber, I., Dain, H. J., Dince, P. R., Drellich, M. G., Grand, H. G., Gundlach, R. H., Kremer, M. W., Rifkin, A. H., Wilbur, C. G., & Bieber, T. B. (1962). *Homosexuality: A psychoanalytic study.* New York: Basic Books.

Bigelow, G., Strickler, D., Liebson, I., & Griffiths, R. (1976). Maintaining disulphiram ingestion among outpatient alcoholics: A security-deposit contingency contracting procedure. *Behaviour Research and Therapy, 14*, 378–381.

Biglan, A., Hops, H., & Sherman, L. (1985). *Coercive family processes and maternal depression.* Unpublished manuscript, Oregon Research Institute.

Biglan, A., Hops, H., Sherman, L., Friedman, L. S., Arthur, J., & Osteen, V. (1985). Problem-solving interactions of depressed women and their husbands. *Behavior Therapy, 16*, 431–451.

Bijou, S. W. (1965). Experimental studies of child behavior, normal and deviant. In L. Krasner & L. P. Ullmann (Eds.), *Research in behavior modification.* New York: Holt, Rinehart & Winston.

Bijou, S. W. (1965, March). *Social variables and the beginnings of self-control.* Paper presented to Society for Research in Child Development, Bowling Green, OH.

Bijou, S. W., & Baer, D. M. (1961). *Child development: A systematic and empirical theory.* New York: Appleton-Century-Crofts.

Biran, M., Augusto, F., & Wilson, G. T. (1981). A comparative analysis of cognitive and behavioral methods in the treatment of scriptophobia. *Behaviour Research and Therapy, 19*, 525–532.

Biran, M., & Wilson, G. T. (1981). Cognitive versus behavioral methods in the treatment of phobic disorders: A self-efficacy analysis. *Journal of Consulting and Clinical Psychology, 49*, 886–899.

Birbaumer, H. (1977). Biofeedback training: A critical review of its clinical applications and some possible future directions. *European Journal of Behavioural Analysis and Modification, 4*, 235–251.

Birchler, G. R., Weiss, R. L., & Vincent, J. P. (1975). A multimethod analysis of social reinforcement exchange between maritally distressed and nondistressed spouse and stranger dyads. *Journal of Personality and Social Psychology, 31*, 349–360.

Birk, L., Stolz, S. B., Brady, J. P., Brady, J. V., Lazarus, A. A., Lynch, J. J., Rosenthal, A. J., Skelton, W. D., Stevens, J. B., & Thomas, E. J. (1973). *Behavior therapy in psychiatry.* Washington, DC: American Psychiatric Association.

Bistrian, B. (1978). Clinical use of a protein sparing modified fast. *Journal of the American Medical Association, 21*, 2299–2302.

Blackburn, I. M., Bishop, S., Glen, A. I. M., Whally, L. J., & Christie, J. E. (1981). The efficacy of cognitive therapy in depression: A treatment trial using cognitive therapy and pharmacotherapy, each alone and in combination. *British Journal of Psychiatry, 139*, 181–189.

Blackwell, B. (1976). Treatment adherence. *British Journal of Psychiatry, 129*, 513–531.

Blakey, R., & Baker, R. (1980). An exposure approach to alcohol abuse. *Behaviour Research and Therapy, 18*, 319–326.

Blanchard, E. B. (1982). Behavioral medicine: Past, present, and future. *Journal of Consulting and Clinical Psychology, 50*, 795–796.

Blanchard, E. B., & Andrasik, F. (1982). Psychological assessment and treatment of headache: Recent developments and emerging issues. *Journal of Consulting and Clinical Psychology, 50*, 859–879.

Blanchard, E. B., Andrasik, F., Ahles, T. A.,

Teders, S. J., & O'Keefe, D. (1980). Migraine and tension headache: A meta-analytic review. *Behavior Therapy, 11,* 613–631.

Blanchard, E. B., & Miller, S. T. (1977). Psychological treatment of cardiovascular disease. *Archives of General Psychiatry, 34,* 1402–1413.

Blanchard, E. B., Theobald, D. E., Williamson, D. A., Silver, B. V., & Brown, D. A. (1978). Temperature biofeedback in the treatment of migraine headaches. *Archives of General Psychiatry, 35,* 581–588.

Blanchard, R., Steiner, B., & Clemmensen, L. (1985). Gender dysphoria, gender reorientation, and the clinical management of transsexualism. *Journal of Consulting and Clinical Psychology, 53,* 295–304.

Bland, K., & Hallam, R. (1981). Relationship between response to graded exposure and marital satisfaction in agoraphobics. *Behaviour Research and Therapy, 19,* 335–338.

Bloom, B. L., Asher, S. J., & White, S. W. (1978). Marital disruption as a stressor: A review and analysis. *Psychological Bulletin, 85,* 867–894.

Blueler, M. (1974). The long term course of the schizophrenic psychoses. *Psychological Medicine, 4,* 244–254.

Boches, Z. (1985). First person account: "Freedom" means knowing you have a choice. *Schizophrenia Bulletin, 11,* 487–488.

Bohman, M., Sigvardsson, S., & Cloninger, C. R. (1981). Maternal inheritance of alcohol abuse: Cross-fostering analysis of adopted women. *Archives of General Psychiatry, 38,* 965–969.

Bollard, R. J., & Nettelbeck, T. (1981). A comparison of dry-bed training and standard urine-alarm conditioning treatment of childhood bed-wetting. *Behaviour Research and Therapy, 19,* 215–226.

Bonham, G. S., & Wilson, R. W. (1981). Children's health in families with cigarette smokers. *American Journal of Public Health, 71,* 290–293.

Borkovec, T. D. (1978). Self-efficacy: Cause or reflection of behavioral change? *Advances in Behaviour Research and Therapy, 1,* 163–170.

Borkovec, T. D. (1982). Insomnia. *Journal of Consulting and Clinical Psychology, 50,* 880–895.

Borkovec, T. D., & O'Brien, G. T. (1977). Relation of autonomic perception and its manipulation to the maintenance and reduction of fear. *Journal of Abnormal Psychology, 86,* 163–171.

Borkovec, T. D., & Sides, J. K. (1979). Critical procedural variables related to the physiological effects of progressive relaxation: A review. *Behaviour Research and Therapy, 17,* 119–126.

Bornstein, P. H., & Rychtarik, R. G. (1983). Consumer satisfaction in adult behavior therapy: Procedures, problems, and future perspectives. *Behavior Therapy, 14,* 191–208.

Bower, G. H. (1981). Mood and memory. *American Psychologist, 36,* 129–148.

Bowlby, J. (1969). *Attachment.* New York: Basic Books.

Bowlby, J. (1977). The making and breaking of affectional bonds: II. Some principles of psychotherapy. *British Journal of Psychiatry, 130,* 421–431.

Bradbury, T. N., & Fincham, F. D. (1986). *Assessing the effects of behavioral marital therapy: Assumptions and measurement strategies.* Unpublished manuscript, University of Illinois at Urbana-Champaign.

Brady, J. P. (1971). Brevital-aided systematic desensitization. In R. D. Rubin, H. Fensterheim, A. A. Lazarus, & C. M. Franks (Eds.), *Advances in Behavior Therapy.* New York: Academic Press.

Brady, J. P. (1976). Behavior therapy and sex therapy. *American Journal of Psychiatry, 133,* 896–899.

Brady, J. P. (1980). Some views on effective principles of psychotherapy. In M. R. Golfried (Ed.). *Cognitive Therapy and Research, 4,* 271–306.

Brady, J. P., & Rieger, W. (1975). Behavioral treatment of anorexia nervosa. In T. Thompson & W. Dockens (Eds.), *Application of behavior modification.* New York: Academic Press.

Brady, J. P., & Wienckowski, L. A. (1978). Update on the teaching of behavior therapy in medical student and psychiatric resident training. *Journal of Behavior Therapy and Experimental Psychiatry, 9,* 125–127.

Braginsky, D. D., & Braginsky, B. M. (1971). *Hansels and Gretels: Studies of children in institutions for the mentally retarded.* New York: Holt, Rinehart & Winston.

Bray, G. A. (1976). *The obese patient.* Philadelphia: Saunders.

Bregman, E. O. (1934). An attempt to modify the emotional attitudes of infants by the conditioned response technique. *Journal of Genetic Psychology, 45,* 169–198.

Bridger, W. H., & Mandel, I. J. (1964). A comparison of GSR fear responses produced by threat and electric shock. *Journal of Psychiatric Research, 2,* 31–40.

Broderick, J. E. (1981). A method for derivation of areas for assessment in marital relationships. *American Journal of Family Therapy, 14,* 191–208.

Broderick, J. E., & O'Leary, K. D. (1986). Contributions of affect, attitude, and behavior to marital satisfaction. *Journal of Consulting and Clinical Psychology, 54,* 514–517.

Brody, J. E. (1985). Heart disease: Big study produces new data. *The New York Times,* January 8, C1.

Brown, G. W., Bone, M., Dalison, B., & Wing, J. K. (1966). *Schizophrenia and social care.* Maudsley Monograph No. 17. London: Oxford University Press.

Brown, G. W., Harris, T. O., & Copeland, J. R. (1977). Depression and loss. *British Journal of Psychiatry, 130,* 1–18.

Brown, G. W., Harris, T. O., & Peto, J. (1973). Life events and psychiatric disorders. Part II: Nature of causal link. *Psychological Medicine, 3,* 159–176.

Brown, R. A., Lichtenstein, E., McIntyre, K. O., & Harrington-Kostur, J. (1984). Effects of nicotine fading and relapse prevention on smoking cessation. *Journal of Consulting and Clinical Psychology, 52,* 307–308.

Brown, S. A. (1985). Expectancies versus background in prediction of college drinking patterns. *Journal of Consulting and Clinical Psychology, 53,* 123–130.

Brownell, K. D. (1979). Compliance: Measurement and intervention. *Behavioral Medicine Update, 2,* 16–18.

Brownell, K. D. (1981). Assessment of eating disorders. In D. H. Barlow (Ed.), *Behavioral assessment.* New York: Guilford Press.

Brownell, K. D. (1982). The addictive disorders. In C. M. Franks, G. T. Wilson, P. Kendall, & K. D. Brownell (Eds.), *Annual review of behavior therapy: Theory and practice,* Vol. 8. New York: Guilford Press.

Brownell, K. D. (1982). Behavioral medicine. In C. M. Franks, G. T. Wilson, P. Kendall, & K. D. Brownell (Eds.), *Annual review of behavior therapy: Theory and practice,* Vol. 8. New York: Guilford Press.

Brownell, K. D., & Foreyt, J. (Eds.) (1986).

Physiology, psychology, and treatment of the eating disorders. New York: Basic Books.

Brownell, K. D., Greenwood, M., Stellar, E., & Shrager, E. (1986). *Diet-induced obesity: The effects of repeated cycles of weight loss and regain.* Unpublished manuscript, University of Pennsylvania.

Brownell, K. D., Hayes, S. C., & Barlow, D. H. (1977). Patterns of appropriate and deviant sexual arousal: The behavioral treatment of multiple sexual deviations. *Journal of Consulting and Clinical Psychology, 45,* 1144–1155.

Brownell, K. D., Heckerman, C., Westlake, R. J., Hayes, S. C., & Monti, P. (1978). The effect of couples training and partner cooperativeness in the behavioral treatment of obesity. *Behaviour Research and Therapy, 16,* 323–333.

Brownell, K. D., & Stunkard, A. J. (1980). Exercise in the development and control of obesity. In A. J. Stunkard (Ed.), *Obesity for clinicians.* Philadelphia: Saunders.

Brownell, K. D., & Stunkard, A. J. (1981a). Couples training, pharmacotherapy, and behavior therapy in the treatment of obesity. *Archives of General Psychiatry, 38,* 1224–1229.

Brownell, K. D., & Stunkard, A. J. (1981b). Differential changes in plasma high-density lipoprotein-cholesterol levels in obese men and women during weight reduction. *Archives of Internal Medicine, 141,* 1142–1146.

Brunink, S., & Schroeder, H. (1979). Verbal therapeutic behavior of expert psychoanalytically oriented, gestalt, and behavior therapists. *Journal of Clinical and Consulting Psychology, 47,* 567–574.

Bucher, B., & Lovaas, O. I. (1968). Use of aversive stimulation in behavior modification. In M. R. Jones (Ed.), *Miami symposium on the prediction of behavior, 1967: Aversive stimulation.* Coral Gables, Florida: University of Miami Press.

Buglass, D., Clarke, J., Henderson, A., Kreitman, N., & Presley, A. (1977). A study of agoraphobic housewives. *Psychological Medicine, 7,* 73–86.

Burgess, R. L., & Ackers, R. L. (1966). A differential association-reinforcement theory of criminal behavior. In R. L. Burgess & D. Bushell (Eds.), *Behavioral Sociology: The experimental analysis of social process.* New York: Columbia University Press.

Burns, D. D. (1980). *Feeling good.* New York: William Morris.

Burt, C. G., Gordon, W. F., Holt, N. F., & Horden, A. (1962). Amitriptyline in depressive stages: A controlled trial. *Journal of Mental Science, 108,* 711–730.

Butcher, J. N., & Koss, M. P. (1978). Research on brief and crisis-oriented psychotherapies. In S. L. Garfield & A. E. Bergin (Eds.), *Handbook of psychotherapy and behavior change.* New York: John Wiley & Sons.

Butler, G., Cullington, A., Munby, M., Amies, P., & Gelder, M. (1984). Exposure and anxiety management in the treatment of social phobia. *Journal of Consulting and Clinical Psychology, 52,* 642–649.

C

Caddy, G., Addington, H., & Perkins, D. (1978). Individualized behavior therapy for alcoholics: A third-year independent double-blind follow-up. *Behaviour Research and Therapy, 16,* 345–363.

Callahan, E. (1980). Alternative strategies in the treatment of narcotic addiction: A review. In W. R. Miller (Ed.), *The Addictive Behaviors.* New York: Pergamon Press.

Callahan, E., & Rawson, R. (1980). Behavioral assessment of narcotic addiction and treatment outcome. In L. C. Sobell & M. B. Sobell (Eds.). *Treatment outcome evaluation in alcohol and drug abuse.* New York: Plenum Press.

Cameron, N. (1963). *Personality development and psychopathology.* Boston: Houghton Mifflin.

Camp, B. W. (1977). Verbal mediation in young aggressive boys. *Journal of Abnormal Psychology, 86,* 145–153.

Campbell, D. T., & Stanley, J. C. (1963). *Experimental and quasi-experimental designs for research.* Chicago: Rand McNally.

Cannon, D., & Baker, T. (1981). Emetic and electric shock alcohol aversion therapy: Assessment of conditioning. *Journal of Consulting and Clinical Psychology, 49,* 20–33.

Cannon, D., Baker, T., & Wehl, C. K. (1981). Emetic and electric shock alcohol aversion therapy: Six- and twelve-month follow-up. *Journal of Consulting and Clinical Psychology, 49,* 360–368.

Cantwell, D. P., Baker, L., & Rutter, M. (1978). Family Factors. In M. Rutter & E. Schopler (Eds.), *Autism: A reappraisal of concepts and treatment.* New York: Plenum Publishing.

Cantwell, D. P., & Carlson, G. A. (1978). Stimulants. In J. S. Werry (Ed.), *Pediatric psychopharmacology: The use of behavior modification drugs on children.* New York: Brunner/Mazel.

Caplan, G. (1974). *Support systems and community mental health.* New York: Behavioral Publications.

Cappell, H. (1975). An evaluation of tension models of alcohol consumption. In R. J. Gibbins, Y. Israel, H. Kalant, R. E. Popham, W. Schmidt, & R. G. Smart (Eds.), *Research Advances in alcohol and drug problems,* Vol. II. New York: John Wiley & Sons.

Carr, A. C., & Ghosh, A. (1983). Accuracy of behavioral assessment by computer. *British Journal of Psychiatry, 142,* 66–70.

Carr, E. G. (1985). Behavioral approaches to language and communication. In E. Schopler and G. B. Mesibov (Eds.), *Communication problems in autism.* New York: Plenum Publishing.

Carr, E. G., & Durand, V. M. (1983, August). *The application of pragmatics to conceptualization and treatment of severe behavior problems in children.* Invited address presented at the meeting of the American Psychiatric Association, Anaheim, CA.

Carter, C., & McCarthy, D. (1951). Incidence of mongolism and its diagnosis in the newborn. *British Journal of Preventative Social Medicine, 5,* 83–90.

Carver, C. S., & Scheier, M. F. (1981). *Attention and self-regulation: A control theory approach to human behavior.* New York: Springer.

Caudill, B., & Lipscomb, T. L. (1980). Modeling influences on alcoholics' rates of consumption. *Journal of Applied Behavior Analysis, 13,* 355–365.

Cautela, J. (1966). Treatment of compulsive behavior by covert sensitization. *Psychological Record, 16,* 33–41.

Chambless, D. L., & Goldstein, A. (Eds.). (1982). *Agoraphobia.* New York: John Wiley & Sons.

Chambless, D. L. (1985). The relationship of severity of agoraphobia to associated psychopathology. *Behaviour Research and Therapy, 23,* 305–310.

Chambless, D. L., Foa, E. B., Groves, G. A., & Goldstein, A. J. (1982). Exposure communications training in the treatment of agoraphobia. *Behaviour Research and Therapy, 20,* 219–231.

Chaney, E., O'Leary, M., & Marlatt, G. A. (1978). Skill training with alcoholics. *Journal of Consulting and Clinical Psychology, 46,* 1092–1104.

Chapman, L. J. (1966). Schizomimetic conditions in schizophrenia. *Journal of Consulting and Clinical Psychology, 33,* 646–650.

Chapman, L. J., & Chapman, J. P. (1969). Illusory correlation as an obstacle to the use of valid psychodiagnostic signs. Journal of Abnormal Psychology, *74,* 271–287.

Chazan, M. (1962). School phobia. *British Journal of Educational Psychology, 32,* 209–217.

Christensen, A., & Nies, D. C. (1980). The spouse observation checklist: Empirical analysis and critique. *American Journal of Family Therapy, 8,* 69–79.

Christensen, A., Sullaway, M., & King, C. E. (1982, November). *Dysfunctional interaction patterns and marital happiness.* Paper presented at the annual convention of the Association for the Advancement of Behavior Therapy, Los Angeles.

Christensen, K. O. (1968). In N. Walker, *Crime and punishment in britain.* (rev. ed.). Edinburgh: University Press.

Ciminero, A. R., Nelson, R. O., & Lipinski, D. P. (1977). Self-monitoring procedures. In A. R. Ciminero, K. S. Calhoun, & H. E. Adams, (Eds.), *Handbook of behavioral assessment.* New York: John Wiley & Sons.

Clark, D. M., Salkovskis, P. M., & Chalkley, A. J. (1985). Respiratory control as a treatment for panic attacks. *Journal of Behavior Therapy and Experimental Psychiatry, 16,* 23–30.

Clark, L. P. (1933). *Lincoln: A Psycho-biography,* New York: Charles Scribner's Sons.

Clarke, R. V. G., & Cornish, D. B. (1978). The effectiveness of residential treatment for delinquents. In L. A. Hersov & M. Berger (Eds.), *Aggression and anti-social behavior in childhood and adolescence.* New York: Pergamon Press.

Cloninger, C. R., Bohman, M., & Sigvardsson, S. (1981). Inheritance of alcohol abuse: Cross-fostering analysis of adopted men. *Archives of General Psychiatry, 38,* 861–868.

Coates, T. J., & Thoresen, C. E. (1984). Assessing daytime thoughts and behavior associated with good and poor sleep: Two exploratory case studies. *Behavioral Assessment, 6,* 153–167.

Cobb, J., Mathews, A. M., Childs-Clarke, A., & Blowers, C. M. (1984). The spouse as co-therapist in the treatment of agoraphobia. *British Journal of Psychiatry, 144,* 282–287.

Cobb, J., McDonald, R., Marks, I., & Stern, R.

(1980). Marital versus exposure therapy: Psychological treatments of co-existing marital and phobic obsessive problems. *European Journal of Behavioural Analysis and Modification, 4,* 3–17.

Cochran, S. E. (1984). Preventing medical noncompliance in the outpatient treatment of bipolar affective disorders. *Journal of Consulting and Clinical Psychology, 52,* 873–878.

Cohen, A. (1955). *Delinquent boys.* New York: Free Press.

Cohen, D. J., Caparulo, B., Shaywitz, B. A., & Bowers, M. B. (1977). Dopamine and serotonin metabolism in neuropsychiatrically disturbed children. *Archives of General Psychiatry, 34 (5),* 545–550.

Cohen, D. J., & Shaywitz, B. A. (1982). Preface to special issue on neurobiological research in autism. *Journal of Autism and Developmental Disorders, 12,* 103–107.

Cohen, D. J., Young, G., & Roth, J. A. (1977). Platelet monoamine oxidase in early childhood autism. *Archives of General Psychiatry, 34 (5),* 534–537.

Cohen, H. L., & Filipczak, J. (1971). *A new learning environment.* San Francisco: Jossey-Bass.

Cohen, H. L. (1972). Programming consequences to punishment: The design of competence through consequences. In S. W. Bijou & E. Ribes-Inesta (Eds.). *Behavior Modification: Issues and Extensions.* New York: Academic Press.

Cohen, H. L., Filipczak, J., & Bis, J. S. (1967). *CASE I: An initial study of contingencies applicable to special education.* Silver Spring, MD: Educational Facility Press, IBR.

Cohen, L., & Oyster-Nelson, C. (1981). Clinicians' evaluations of psychodynamic psychotherapy: Experimental data on psychological peer review. *Journal of Consulting and Clinical Psychology, 49,* 583–589.

Cohen, M., Liebson, I. A., Faillace, L. A., & Allen, R. P. (1971). Moderate drinking by chronic alcoholics. *Journal of Nervous and Mental Disease,* 53, 434–444.

Coleman, R. E., & Beck, A. T. (1981). Cognitive therapy for depression. In J. F. Clarkin & H. I. Glazer (Eds.), *Depression: behavioral and directive intervention strategies.* New York: Garland Press.

Collins, R. L., & Marlatt, G. A. (1981). Social modeling as a determinant of drinking behavior:

Implications for prevention and treatment. *Addictive Behaviors, 6,* 233–240.

Condiotte, M. M., & Lichtenstein, E. (1981). Self-efficacy and relapse in smoking cessation programs. *Journal of Consulting and Clinical Psychology, 49,* 648–658.

Cone, J. D., Anderson, J. A., Harris, F. C., Goff, D. K., & Fox, S. R. (1978). Developing and maintaining social interaction in profoundly retarded young males. *Journal of Abnormal Child Psychology, 6,* 351–360.

Conger, J. C. (1970). The treatment of encopresis by the management of social consequences. *Behavior Therapy, 1,* 386–390.

Conger, J. (1951). The effects of alcohol on conflict behavior in the albino rat. *Quarterly Journal of Studies on Alcohol, 12,* 1–29.

Conger, J., & Keane, S. (1981). Social skills intervention in the treatment of isolated or withdrawn children. *Psychological Bulletin, 90,* 478–495.

Conley, R. W. (1973). *The economics of mental retardation.* Baltimore: Johns Hopkins University Press.

Conners, C. K. (1969). A teacher rating scale for use in drug studies with children. *American Journal of Psychiatry, 6,* 884–888.

Conners, C. K. (1980). Artificial colors in the diet and disruptive behavior. In R. M. Knights & D. J. Bakker (Eds.), *Treatment of Hyperactive and Learning Disabled Children.* Baltimore: University Park Press.

Conners, C. K., & Blouin, A. G. (1983). Nutritional effects on behavior of children. *Journal of Psychiatric Research, 17,* 193–201.

Consumer Reports. (1983). Beer advertising: Coming through for you? *Consumer Reports,* July, 348–351.

Cooney, N., Baker, L., & Pomerleau, O. (1983). Cue exposure for relapse prevention in alcohol treatment. In K. Craig & R. McMahon (Eds.), *Advances in Clinical Behavior Therapy.* New York: Brunner/Mazel.

Cooney, N., & Kopel, S. (1980, September). *Controlled relapse: A social learning approach to preventing smoking recidivism.* Paper presented at the annual meeting of the American Psychological Association, Montreal, Canada.

Coppen, A., Metcalfe, M., & Wood, K. (1980). Lithium. In E. S. Paykel (Ed.), *Handbook of Affective Disorders.* New York: Guilford Press.

Cortes, J. B., & Gatti, F. M. (1972). *Delinquency and crime: A biosocial approach.* New York: Seminar Press.

Couchells, S. M., Johnson, S. B., Carter, R., & Walker, D. (1981). Behavioral and environmental characteristics of treated and untreated enuretic children and matched nonenuretic controls. *Journal of Pediatrics, 99,* 812–816.

Cox, D. J., Freundlich, A., & Meyer, R. G. (1975). Differential effectiveness of electromyographic feedback, verbal relaxation instructions, and medication placebo with tension headaches. *Journal of Consulting and Clinical Psychology, 43,* 892–898.

Coyne, J. C. (1976). Depression and the response of others. *Journal of Abnormal Psychology, 85,* 186–193.

Coyne, J. C. (1985). Strategic marital therapy for depression. In N. S. Jacobsen & A. S. Gurman (Eds.), *Clinical Handbook of Marital Therapy.* New York: Guilford Press.

Craighead, L. W. (1984). Sequencing of behavior therapy and pharmacotherapy for obesity. *Journal of Consulting and Clinical Psychology, 52,* 190–199.

Craighead, L. W., Stunkard, A. J., & O'Brien, R. (1981). Behavior therapy and pharmacotherapy of obesity. *Archives of General Psychiatry, 38,* 763–768.

Craighead, W. E. (1984). Affective disorders—unipolar. In S. M. Turner & M. Hersen (Eds.), *Adult psychopathology: A Behavioral Perspective.* New York: John Wiley & Sons.

Craighead, W. E. (1985, November). *Unipolar Depression: Why is it so complicated?* Paper presented at the meetings of the Association for Advancement of Behavior Therapy, Houston, TX.

Craske, M. G., & Craig, K. D. (1984). Musical performance anxiety: The three-systems model and self-efficacy theory. *Behaviour Research and Therapy, 22,* 267–280.

Crisp, A. H. (1970). Anorexia nervosa: Feeding disorder, nervous malnutrition, or weight phobia? *World Review of Nutrition and Dietetics, 12,* 452–504.

Crisp, A. H. (1984). The psychopathology of anorexia nervosa: Getting the 'heat' out of the system. In A. J. Stunkard & E. Stellar (Eds.), *Eating and eating disorders.* New York: Raven Press.

Crowe, M. J. (1978). Conjoint marital therapy: A controlled outcome study. *Psychological Medicine, 8,* 623–636.

Crowe, M. J., Gillan, P., & Golombok, S. (1981).

Form and content in the conjoint treatment of sexual dysfunction: A controlled study. *Behaviour Research and Therapy, 19,* 47–54.

Cummings, C., Gordon, J., & Marlatt, G. A. (1980). Relapse: Prevention and prediction. In W. Miller (Ed.), *The addictive behaviors.* Oxford: Pergamon Press.

D

Dahlkoeter, J., Callahan, E., & Linton, J. (1979). Obesity and and the unbalanced energy equation: Exercise vs. eating habit change. *Journal of Consulting and Clinical Psychology, 47,* 898–905.

Dalessio, D. J., Kunzel, M., Sternbach, R., & Sovak, M. (1979). Conditioned adaptation-relaxation in migraine therapy. *Journal of American Medical Association, 242,* 2102–2104.

Danaher, B. G. (1977a). Rapid smoking and self-control in the modification of smoking behavior. *Journal of Consulting and Clinical Psychology, 45,* 1068–1075.

Danaher, B. G. (1977b). Research on rapid smoking: An interim summary and recommendations. *Addictive Behaviors, 2,* 151–166.

Danaher, B. G., Berkanovic, E., & Gerber, B. (1983). Smoking and television: Review of extant literature. *Addictive Disorders, 8,* 173–182.

Davies, D. L. (1962). Normal drinking in recovered alcohol addicts. *Quarterly Journal of Studies in Alcohol, 23,* 94–104.

Davis, J. M., & Gierl, B. (1984). Pharmacological treatment in the care of schizophrenic patients. In A. S. Bellack (Ed.), *Schizophrenia: Treatment, Management and Rehabilitation.* New York: Grune & Stratton.

Davison, G. C. (1986). Systematic desensitization as a counterconditioning process. *Journal of Abnormal Psychology, 73,* 91–99.

Davison, G. C. (1976). Homosexuality: The ethical challenge. *Journal of Consulting and Clinical Psychology, 44,* 157–162.

Davison, G. C., & Neale, J. M. (1974). *Abnormal psychology: An experimental approach,* (2nd ed.). New York: John Wiley & Sons.

Davison, G. C., & Neale, J. M. (1986). *Abnormal psychology.* (4th ed.). New York: John Wiley & Sons.

Davison, G. C., & Stuart, R. B. (1975). Behavior therapy and civil liberties. *American Psychologist, 30,* 755–763.

Davison, G. C., & Wilson, G. T. (1973). Attitudes of behavior therapists towards homosexuality. *Behavior Therapy, 4,* 686–696.

Dawson, M. E., & Biferno, M. A. (1973). Concurrent measurement of awareness and electrodermal classical conditioning. *Journal of Experimental Psychology, 101,* 55–62.

Dayan, M. (1964). Toilet training retarded children in a state residential institution. *Mental Retardation, 2,* 116–117.

DeKaban, A., O'Rourke, J., & Cornman, T. (1958). Abnormalities of offspring related to maternal rubella during pregnancy. *Neurology, 8,* 837.

Deleon, G., & Mandell, W. (1966). A comparison of conditioning and psychotherapy in the treatment of functional enuresis. *Journal of Clinical Psychology, 22,* 326–330.

Deleon, G., & Sacks, S. (1972). Conditioning functional enuresis: A four year follow-up. *Journal of Clinical Psychology, 39,* 299–300.

Dember, W. N. (1974). Motivation and the cognitive revolution. *American Psychologist, 29,* 161–168.

Dembroski, T. M., MacDougall, J. M., Williams, R. B., Haney, T. L., Blumenthal, J. A. (1985). Components of Type A, hostility, and anger in relationship to angiographic findings. *Psychosomatic Medicine, 47,* 219–233.

DeMonbreun, B. G., & Craighead, W. E. (1977). Selective recall of positive and negative feedback, self-control behaviors, and depression. *Cognitive Therapy & Research, 1,* 311–329.

DeMyer, M. K., Barton, S., DeMyer, W. E., Norton, J. A., Allen, J., & Steele, R. (1973). Prognosis in autism: A follow-up study. *Journal of Autism and Childhood Schizophrenia, 3,* 199–246.

Denner, B., & Price, R. (1973). *Community mental health: Social action and reaction.* New York: Holt, Rinehart & Winston.

Derry, P. A., & Kuiper, N. A. (1981). Schematic processing and self-reference in clinical depression. *Journal of Abnormal Psychology, 90,* 286–297.

DeRubeis, R., Hollon, S., Evans, M., & Bemis, K. (1982). Can psychotherapies for depression be discriminated? A systematic investigation of cognitive therapy and interpersonal therapy. *Journal of Consulting and Clinical Psychology, 50,* 744–752.

de Silva, P., & Rachman, S. (1981). Is exposure a necessary condition for fear-reduction? *Behaviour Research and Therapy, 19,* 227–232.

de Silva, P., & Rachman, S. (1984). Does escape behaviour strengthen agoraphobic avoidance? A preliminary study. *Behaviour Research and Therapy, 22,* 87–92.

de Silva, P., Rachman, S., & Seligman, M. E. P. (1977). Prepared phobias and obsessions: Therapeutic outcome. *Behaviour Research and Therapy, 15,* 65–77.

Dickens, B. M., Doob, A. N., Warwick, O. H., & Winegard, O. H. (1982). *Report of the Committee of Inquiry into allegations concerning Drs. Linda and Mark Sobell.* Toronto: Addiction Research Center.

DiClemente, C. C. (1981). Self-efficacy and smoking cessation maintenance. *Cognitive Therapy and Research, 5,* 175–187.

DiLoreto, A. (1971). *Comparative psychotherapy.* New York: Aldine-Atherton.

Doleys, D. M. (1977). Behavioral treatments for nocturnal enuresis in children: A review of the recent literature. *Psychological Bulletin, 84,* 30–54.

Doleys, D. M., Ciminero, A. R., Tollison, C. L., & Wells, K. C. (1977). Dry bed training & retention control training: A comparison. *Behavior Therapy, 8,* 541–548.

Dollard, J., & Miller, N. E. (1950). *Personality and psychotherapy.* New York: McGraw Hill.

Donahoe, C. P., Lin, D. H., Kirschenbaum, D. S., & Keesey, R. E. (1984). Metabolic consequences of dieting and exercise in the treatment of obesity. *Journal of Consulting and Clinical Psychology, 52,* 827–836.

Douglas, J. W. B., & Bloomfield, J. M. (1958). *Children under five.* London: George Allen and Unwin.

Douglas, V. I. (1979). Treatment and training approaches to hyperactivity: Establishing internal or external control. In C. K. Whalen & B. Henker (Eds.), *Hyperactive children.* New York: Academic Press.

Drabman, R., Spitalnik, R., Hageman, M. B., & Van Witsen, B. (1973). The five-two program: An integrated approach to treating severely disturbed children. *Hospital & Community Psychiatry, 24,* 33–36.

Dubbert, P., & Wilson, G. T. (1983). Treatment failures in behavior therapy for obesity: Causes, correlates, and consequences. In E. Foa & P. M. G. Emmelkamp (Eds.), *Treatment Failures in Behavior Therapy.* New York: John Wiley & Sons.

Dubey, D. R., Kent, R. D., O'Leary, S. G., Brod-erick, J., & O'Leary, K. D. (1977). Reactions of children observers: A series of controlled investigations. *Behavior Therapy, 8,* 887–897.

Dubey, D. R., O'Leary, S. G., & Kaufman, K. F. (1983). Training parents of hyperactive children in child management: A comparative outcome study. *Journal of Abnormal Child Psychology, 11,* 229–246.

Dumas, J. E., & Wahler, R. G. (1985). Indiscriminate mothering as a conceptual factor in aggressive-oppositional child behavior: "Damned if you do and damned if you don't." *Journal of Abnormal Child Psychology, 13,* 1–18.

Dunbar, J. (1979). Compliance: Nursing intervention and research. *Behavioral Medicine Update, 2,* 18–20.

Dunbar, J. M., & Stunkard, A. J. (1979). Adherence to medical regimen. In R. Levy, B. Rifkind, B. Dennis, & N. Ernst (Eds.), *Nutrition, Lipids, and Coronary Heart Disease.* New York: Raven Press.

Dunlap, K. (1932). *Habits: Their making and unmaking.* New York: Liveright.

Durand, V. M., & Carr, E. G. (1982). Differential reinforcement of communicative behavior. In R. L. Koegel, (Chair), *Research on clinical intervention with autistic and psychotic children.* Symposium presented at the meeting of the American Psychiatric Association, Washington, DC.

E

Eckert, E. D., Goldberg, S. C., Casper, R. C., & Davis, J. M. (1979). Behavior therapy in anorexia nervosa. *British Journal of Psychiatry, 134,* 55–59.

Edelman, R. I. (1971). Operant conditioning treatment of encopresis. *Behavior Therapy and Experimental Psychiatry, 1,* 71–73.

Edelstein, B. A., & Eisler, R. M. (1976). Effects of modeling and modeling with instructions and feedback on the behavioral components of social skills. *Behavior Therapy, 7,* 382–389.

Edwards, G., Orford, J., Egert, S., Guthrie, S., Hawker, A., Hensman, C., Mitcheson, M., Oppenheimer, E., & Taylor, C. (1977). Alcoholism: A controlled trial of "treatment" versus "advice." *Journal of Studies on Alcohol, 38,* 1004–1031.

Eisenberg, J. M., & Zingle, H. W. (1975). Marital adjustment and irrational ideas. *Journal of Marriage and Family Counseling, 1,* 81–91.

Eisenberg, L. (1958). School phobia: A study in

the communication of anxieties. *American Journal of Psychiatry, 114,* 712–718.

Elkin, I., Parloff, M. B., Hadley, S. W., & Autry, J. H. (1985). NIMH treatment of depression collaborative research program. *Archives of General Psychiatry, 42,* 305–316.

Ellis, A. (1962). *Reason and emotion in psychotherapy.* New York: Lyle Stuart.

Ellis, A., & Harper, R. A. (1962). *Creative marriage.* New York: Lyle Stuart.

Elkins, R. (1980). Covert sensitization and alcoholism: Contributions of successful conditioning to subsequent abstinence maintenance. *Addictive Behaviors, 5,* 67–89.

Ellenberger, H. F. (1972). The story of "Anna O": A critical review with new data. *Journal of the History of the Behavior Sciences, 8,* 267–279.

Elliot, C. H., & Denney, D. R. (1978). A multiple-component treatment approach to smoking reduction. *Journal of Consulting and Clinical Psychology, 46,* 1330–1339.

Elliot, D. S. (1966). Delinquency, school attendance, and dropout. *Social Problems, 13,* 307–314.

Ellis, A. (1962) *Reason and emotion in psychotherapy.* New York: Lyle Stuart.

Ellis, A. (1970). *The essence of rational psychotherapy: A comprehensive approach to treatment.* New York: Institute for Rational Living.

Ellis, A. (1977). Rational-emotive therapy research data that supports the clinical and personality hypothesis of RET and other modes of cognitive-behavior therapy. *The Counseling Psychologist, 7,* 2–42.

Emery, R. E., & O'Leary, K. D. (1982). Children's perception of marital discord and behavior problems of boys and girls. *Journal of Abnormal Child Psychology, 10,* 11–24.

Emery, R. E., & O'Leary, K. D. (1984). Marital discord and child behavior problems in a nonclinic sample. *Journal of Abnormal Child Psychology, 12,* 411–420.

Emery, R. E., Weintraub, S., & Neale, J. M. (1982). Effects of marital discord on the school behavior of children of schizophrenic, affectively disordered, and normal parents. *Journal of Abnormal Child Psychology, 10,* 215–228.

Emmelkamp, P. M. G. (1982). *Phobic and obsessive-compulsive disorders.* New York: Plenum Press.

Emmelkamp, P. M. G., & Kuipers, A. C. M. (1979). Agoraphobia: A follow-up study four years after treatment. *British Journal of Psychiatry, 134,* 325–355.

Emmelkamp, P. M. G., & Kraanen, J. (1977). Therapist-controlled exposure in vivo versus self-controlled exposure in vivo: A comparison with obsessive-compulsive patients. *Behaviour Research and Therapy, 15,* 491–495.

Emmelkamp, P. M. G., & Mersch, P. P. (1982). Cognition and exposure in vivo in the treatment of agoraphobia: Short term and delayed effects. *Cognitive Therapy and Research, 6,* 77–90.

Emmelkamp, P. M. G., van der Helm, M., van Zanten, B. L., & Plochg, I. (1980). Treatment of obsessive-compulsive patients: The contribution of self-instructional training to the effectiveness of exposure. *Behaviour Research and Therapy, 18,* 61–66.

Endicott, J., Nee, J., Cohen, J., Fleiss, J. L., & Simon, R. (1986). Diagnosis of schizophrenia. *Archives of General Psychiatry, 43,* 13–19.

English, H. B. (1929). Three cases of the conditioned fear response. *Journal of Abnormal Social Psychology, 24,* 221–225.

Epstein, L., & Cluss, P. (1982). A behavioral medicine perspective on adherence to long-term medical regimens. *Journal of Consulting and Clinical Psychology, 50,* 950–971.

Epstein, N., & Eidelson, R. J. (1981). Unrealistic beliefs of clinical couples: Their relationship to expectations, goals, and satisfaction. *American Journal of Family Therapy, 9,* 13–22.

Ericsson, K. A., & Simon, H. A. (1980). Verbal reports as data. *Psychological Review, 87,* 215–251.

Eron, L. D., Walder, L. O., Huesmann, L. R., & Lefkowitz, M. M. (1974). The convergence of laboratory and field studies of the development of aggression. In J. DeWitt & W. W. Hartup (Eds.), *Determinants and Origins of Aggression.* The Hague, Paris: Mouton.

Ersner-Hershfield, R., & Kopel, S. (1979). Group treatment of preorgasmic women: Evaluation of partner involvement and spacing of sessions. *Journal of Consulting and Clinical Psychology, 47,* 750–759.

Erwin, E. (1978). *Behavior therapy: Scientific, philosophical and moral foundations.* New York: Cambridge University Press.

Erwin, E. (1986). Establishing causal connections: Meta-analysis and psychotherapy. *Midwest Studies in Philosophy, 9,* 421–436.

Erwin, W. J. (1977). A 16-year follow-up of a case of severe anorexia nervosa. *Journal of Behavior Therapy and Experimental Psychiatry, 8,* 157–160.

Evans, I. M. (1985). Building systems models as a strategy for target behavior selection in clinical assessment. *Behavioral Assessment, 7,* 21–32.

Evans, R. I. (1979). Smoking in children and adolescents. Psychological determinants and prevention strategies. In *Smoking and Health: Report of the Surgeon General.* Washington, DC: U.S. Government Printing Office.

Evans, R. I., Rozelle, R. M., Mittelmark, M. B., Hansen, W. B., Bane, A. L., & Navis, J. (1978). Deterring the onset of smoking in children: Coping with peer pressure, media pressure, and parent modeling. *Journal of Applied Social Psychology, 8,* 126–135.

Ewart, C., Taylor, C. B., Reese, L., & DeBusk, R. (1983). Effects of early post-myocardial infarction exercise testing on self-perception and subsequent physical activity. *American Journal of Cardiology, 51,* 1076–1080.

Eysenck, H. J. (1952). The effects of psychotherapy: An evaluation. *Journal of Consulting Psychology, 16,* 319–324.

Eysenck, H. J. (1959). Learning theory and behaviour therapy. *British Journal of Marital Science, 105,* 61–75.

Eysenck, H. J. (1960). *Behaviour therapy and the neuroses.* London: Pergamon Press.

Eysenck, H. J. (1964). *Crime and personality.* London: Routledge & Kegan Paul.

Eysenck, H. J. (1982). The neo-behaviouristic (S-R) theory of behaviour therapy. In G. T. Wilson & C. M. Franks (Eds.), *Contemporary Behavior Therapy: Theoretical Foundations of Clinical Practice.* New York: Guilford Press.

Eysenck, H. J., & Rachman, S. (1965). *The causes and cures of the neuroses.* London: Routledge & Kegan Paul.

Eysenck, H. J., & Eysenck, S. B. G. (1976). *Psychoticism as a dimension of personality.* London: Hodder and Stoughton.

F

Fairburn, C. G. (1981). A cognitive behavioral approach to the treatment of bulimia. *Psychological Medicine, 11,* 707–711.

Fairburn, C. G. (1984). Bulimia: Its epidemiology and management. In A. J. Stunkard & E. Stellar (Eds.). *Eating and its Disorders.* New York: Raven Press.

Fairburn, C. G. (1985). A cognitive-behavioural treatment for bulimia. In D. M. Garner & P. E. Garfinkel (Eds). *Handbook on Psychotherapy for Anorexia Nervosa and Bulimia.* New York: Guilford Press.

Fairburn, C. G., & Cooper, P. J. (1984). The clinical features of bulimia nervosa. *The British Journal of Psychiatry, 144,* 238–246.

Fairburn, C. G., Kirk, J., O'Connor, M., Cooper, P. (in press). A comparison of two psychological treatments for bulimia nervosa. *Behaviour Research and Therapy.*

Fairweather, G. W., Sanders, D. H., Maynard, H., & Cressler, D. L. (1969). *Community life for the mentally ill.* Chicago: Aldine.

Falloon, I. R. H., Boyd, J. L., McGill, C. W., Williamson, M., Razani, J., Moss, H. B., Gilderman, A. M., & Simpson, G. M. (1985). Family management in the prevention of morbidity of schizophrenia. *Archives of General Psychiatry, 42,* 887–896.

Feighner, J. P., Robins, E., Guze, S. B., Woodruff, R. A., Jr., Winokur, G., & Munoz, R. (1972). Diagnostic criteria for use in psychiatric research. *Archives of General Psychiatry, 26,* 57–63.

Feingold, B. (1975). *Why your child is hyperactive.* New York: Random House.

Feldman, M. P., & MacCulloch, M. J. (1971). *Homosexual behaviour: Therapy and assessment.* New York: Pergamon Press.

Feldman-Summers, S., Gordon, P. E., & Meagher, J. R. (1979). The impact of rape on sexual satisfaction. *Journal of Abnormal Psychology, 88,* 101–105.

Ferguson, J. M., & Taylor, C. B.(Eds.).—(1980). *The comprehensive handbook of behavioral medicine.* New York: Spectrum.

Ferster, C. B. (1965). Classification of behavior pathology. In L. Krasner & L. P. Ullmann (Eds.), *Research in Behavior Modification.* New York: Holt, Rinehart & Winston.

Ferster, C. B., Nurnberger, J., & Levitt, E. (1962). The control of eating. *Journal of Mathetics, 1,* 87–109.

Fincham, F. D., Beach, S. R. H., Nelson, G. (in press). Attributional processes in distressed and nondistressed couples: Three causal and evaluative inferences for spouse behavior. *Cognitive Therapy and Research.*

Fincham, F. D. (1985). Attribution processes in distressed and nondistressed couples: 2. Responsibility for marital problems. *Journal of Abnormal Psychology, 94,* 183–190.

Fincham, F. D., & O'Leary, K. D. (1983). Causal inferences for spouse behavior in maritally distressed and nondistressed couples. *Journal of Social and Clinical Psychology, 1,* 42–57.

Fink, M. (1977). Myths of shock therapy. *American Journal of Psychiatry, 134,* 991–996.

Finley, W. W., Besserman, R. L., Bennett, L. F., Clap, R. K., & Finley, P. M. (1973). The effects of continuous, intermittent, and "placebo" reinforcement on the effectiveness of the conditioning treatment for enuresis nocturna. *Behavior Research and Therapy, 11,* 289–297.

Fisher, E. B. (1979). Overjustification effects in token economics. *Journal of Applied Behavior Analysis, 12,* 407–415.

Fisher, L., & Wilson, G. T. (1985). A study of the psychology of agoraphobia. *Behaviour Research and Therapy, 23,* 97–108.

Fiske, D. W. (1983). The meta-analytic revolution in outcome research. *Journal of Consulting and Clinical Psychology, 51,* 65–70.

Fiske, S. T., & Taylor, S. E. (1984). *Social cognition.* Menlo Park, CA: Addison-Wesley.

Flood, R., & Saeger, C. (1968). A retrospective examination of psychiatric case records of patients who subsequently commit suicide. *British Journal of Psychiatry, 114,* 443–450.

Foa, E. B., & Goldstein, A. (1978). Continuous exposure and complete response prevention in the treatment of obsessive-compulsive neurosis. *Behavior Therapy, 9,* 821–829.

Foa, E. B., Grayson, J. B., Steketee, G. S., Doppelt, H. G., Turner, R. M., & Latimer, P. R. (1983). Success and failure in the behavioral treatment of obsessive-compulsives. *Journal of Consulting and Clinical Psychology, 51,* 287–297.

Foa, E. B., & Tilmanns, A. (1980). The treatment of obsessive-compulsive neurosis. In A. Goldstein & E. Foa (Eds.), *Handbook of Behavioral Interventions: A Clinical Guide.* New York: John Wiley & Sons.

Follich, M. J., Abrams, D. B., Smith, T. W., Henderson, L. O., & Herbert, P. N. (1984). Contrasting short- and long-term effects of weight loss on lipoprotein levels. *Archives of Internal Medicine, 144,* 1571–1574.

Folstein, S., & Rutter, M. (1977). Infantile autism: A genetic study of 21 twin pairs. *Journal of Child Psychology & Psychiatry & Allied Disciplines, 18,* 297–321.

Ford, J. (1978). Therapeutic relationship in behavior therapy: An empirical analysis. *Journal of Consulting and Clinical Psychology, 46,* 1302–1314.

Foreyt, J. P., Goodrick, K., & Gotto, A. M. (1981). Limitations of behavioral treatment of obesity: Review and analysis. *Journal of Behavioral Medicine, 4,* 159–174.

Foreyt, J. P., Mitchell, R. E., Garner, D., Gee, M., Scott, L., & Gotto, A. M. (1982). Behavioral treatment of obesity: Results and limitations. *Behavior Therapy, 13,* 153–163.

Forrester, R. M., Stein, Z., & Susser, M. W. (1964). A trial of conditioning therapy in nocturnal enuresis. *Developmental Medicine and Child Neurology, 6,* 158–166.

Foster, S. L., Prinz, R. J., & O'Leary, K. D. (1983). Impact of problem-solving communication training and generalization procedures on family conflict. *Child & Family Behavior Therapy, 5,* 1–23.

Fowler, R. D. (1985). Landmarks in computer-assisted psychological assessment. *Journal of Consulting and Clinical Psychology, 61,* 948–959.

Foxx, R. M., & Azrin, N. H. (1973a). *Toilet training the retarded.* Champaign, Il: Research Press.

Foxx, R. M., & Azrin, N. H. (1973b). Dry pants: A rapid method of toilet training children. *Behaviour Research and Therapy, 11,* 435–442.

Foxx, R. M., & Brown, R. A. (1979). Nicotine fading and self-monitoring for cigarette abstinence or controlled smoking. *Journal of Applied Behavior Analysis, 12,* 111–125.

Foy, D. W., Nunn, L. B., & Rychtarik, R. G. (1984). Broad-spectrum behavioral treatment for chronic alcoholics: Effects of training controlled drinking skills. *Journal of Consulting and Clinical Psychology, 52,* 218–230.

Framo, J. L. (1975). Personal reflections of a family therapist. *Journal of Marriage and Family Counseling, 1,* 15–28.

Frank, J. (1979). The present status of outcome studies. *Journal of Consulting and Clinical Psychology, 47,* 310–316.

Franks, C. M., & Wilson, G. T. (1973). *Annual review of behavior therapy: Theory and practice,* Vol. 1. New York: Brunner/Mazel.

Franks, C. M., & Wilson, G. T. (1974). Annual review of behavior therapy: Theory and practice, Vol. 2. New York: Brunner/Mazel.

Franks, C. M., & Wilson, G. T. (1975). *Annual review of behavior therapy: Theory and practice,* Vol. 3. New York: Brunner/Mazel.

Franks, C. M., & Wilson, G. T. (1976). *Annual review of behavior therapy: Theory and practice,* Vol. 4. New York: Brunner/Mazel.

Franks, C. M., & Wilson, G. T. (1978). *Annual review of behavior therapy: Theory and practice.* Vol. 6. New York: Brunner/Mazel.

Freeman, R. J., Beach, B., Davis, R., & Solyom, L. (1985). The prediction of relapse in bulimia nervosa. *Journal of Psychiatric Research, 19,* 349–353.

Freud, S. (1916). *Three contributions to the theory of sex.* New York: Nervous and Mental Disease Publishing Co.

Friedman, B. J. (1974). *An analysis of social-behavioral skill deficits in delinquent and non-delinquent adolescent boys.* Unpublished doctoral dissertation, University of Wisconsin, Madison.

Friedman, J., & Hogan, D. (1985). Sexual dysfunction: Low sexual desire. In D. H. Barlow (Ed.), *Adult Clinical Disorders.* New York: Guilford Press.

Friedman, M., & Rosenman, R. (1974). *Type A behavior and your heart.* New York: Knopf.

Friedman, M., Thoresen, C. E., Gill, J., Powell, L. H., Ulmer, D., Thompson, L., Price, V. A., Rabin, D. D., Breall, W. J., Dixon, T., Levy, R., & Bourg, E. (1984). Alteration of type A behavior and reduction in cardiac recurrences in post-myocardial infarction patients. *American Heart Journal, 108,* 237–248.

Friedman, P. R. (1975). Legal regulation of applied behavior analysis. *Arizona Law Review, 17,* 39–204.

Fuller, J. L., & Thompson, W. R. (1978). *Foundations of behavior genetics.* St. Louis, MO: C. V. Mosby.

Funabiki, D., & Calhoun, J. (1979). Use of behavior-analytic procedure in evaluating two models of depression. *Journal of Consulting and Clinical Psychology, 47,* 183–185.

Funch, D., & Gale, E. (1984). Biofeedback and relaxation therapy for chronic temporomandibular joint pain: Predicting successful outcomes. *Journal of Consulting and Clinical Psychology, 52,* 928–935.

Furman, W., Rahe, D., & Hartup, W. (1979). Rehabilitation of socially withdrawn preschool children through mixed-age and same-age socialization. *Child Development, 50,* 915–922.

G

Gadow, K. D., & Loney, J. (1981). *Psychosocial aspects of drug treatment for hyperactivity.* Boulder, CO: Westview Press.

Gagnon, J. (1977). *Human sexualities.* Chicago: Scott, Foresman.

Garcia, J. (1981). Tilting at the paper mills of academe. *American Psychologist, 36,* 149–159.

Garner, D. M., & Bemis, K. M. (1982). A cognitive-behavioral approach to anorexia nervosa. *Cognitive Therapy and Research, 6,* 123–150.

Garner, D. M., Garfinkel, P., & O'Shaughnessy, M. (1985). The validity of the distinction between bulimia with and without anorexia nervosa. *American Journal of Psychiatry, 142,* 581–587.

Garner, D. M., Rockert, W., Olmsted, M., Johnson, C., & Coscina, D. (1985). Psychoeducational principles in the treatment of bulimia and anorexia nervosa. In D. M. Garner & P. Garfinkel (Eds.), *Handbook of Psychotherapy for Anorexia and Bulimia.* New York: Guilford Press.

Garry, J. W., & Leonard, T. J. (1963). Trial of amitriptyline in chronic depression. *British Journal of Psychiatry, 109,* 55–55.

Geer, J. H. (1965). The development of a scale to measure fear. *Behaviour Research and Therapy, 3,* 45–53.

Geer, J. H. (1977). Sexual functioning: Some data and speculations on psychophysiological assessment. In J. D. Cone & R. P. Hawkins, (Eds.), *Behavioral Assessment: New Directions in Clinical Psychology.* New York: Brunner/Mazel.

Geer, J. H., Morokoff, D., & Greenwood, P. (1974). Sexual arousal in women. The development of a measurement device for vaginal blood-volume. *Archives of Sexual Behavior, 3,* 559–564.

Gelder, M. G., Bancroft, J. H. L., Gath, D., Johnston, D. W., Mathews, A. M., & Shaw, P. M. (1973). Specific and non-specific factors in behaviour therapy. *British Journal of Psychiatry, 123,* 445–462.

Gelder, M. G., Marks, I. M., & Wolff, H. H. (1967). Desensitization and psychotherapy in the treatment of phobic states: A controlled inquiry. *British Journal of Psychiatry, 113,* 53–73.

Gibbons, D. C. (1976). *Delinquent behavior* (2nd ed.). Englewood Cliffs, NJ: Prentice-Hall.

Gillan, P., & Rachman, S. (1974). An experimental investigation of desensitization in phobic patients. *British Journal of Psychiatry, 124,* 392–401.

Ginsberg, G., & Marks, I. (1977). Costs and benefits of behavioral psychotherapy. *Psychological Medicine, 7,* 685–700.

Girardeau, F. L., & Spradlin, J. E. (1964). Token rewards on a cottage program. *Mental Retardation, 2,* 345–351.

Gittleman-Klein, R., & Klein, D. (1973). School phobia: Diagnostic considerations in the light of imipramine effects. *Journal of Nervous and Mental Diseases, 156,* 199–215.

Gittelman-Klein, R., Klein, D. F., Abikoff, H., Katz, S., Gloisten, A. C., & Kates, W. (1976). Relative efficacy of methylphenidate and behavior modification in hyperactive children: An interim report. *Journal of Abnormal Child Psychology, 4,* 361–79.

Gittelman, R., Mannuzza, S., Shenker, R., & Bonagura, N. (1985). Hyperactive boys almost grow up. *Archives of General Psychiatry, 42,* 937–947.

Glasgow, R. E., Klesges, R., Godding, P., & Gegelman, R. (1983). Controlled smoking, with or without carbon monoxide feedback, as an alternative for chronic smokers. *Behavior Therapy, 14,* 386–397.

Glasgow, R. E., Klesges, R., Godding, P., Vasey, M., & O'Neill, K. (1984). Evaluation of a work-site-controlled smoking program. *Journal of Consulting and Clinical Psychology, 52,* 137–138.

Glasgow, R. E., & Rosen, G. M. (1978). Behavioral bibliotherapy: A review of self-help behavior therapy manuals. *Psychological Bulletin, 85,* 1–24.

Glick, P. G., & Norton, A. J. (1978). Marrying, divorcing, and living together in the United States today. *Population Bulletin, 32,* 3–38.

Godding, P. R., & Glasgow, R. E. (1985). Self-efficacy and outcome expectancy as predictors of controlled smoking status. *Cognitive Therapy and Research, 9,* 583–590.

Goldfried, M. R. (1979). Anxiety reduction through cognitive-behavioral intervention. In P. C. Kendall & S. D. Hollon (Eds.), *Cognitive-behavioral Interventions: Theory, Research, and Procedures.* New York: Academic Press.

Goldfried, M. R. (Ed.) (1980a). Some views on effective principles of psychotherapy. *Cognitive Therapy and Research, 4,* 271–306.

Goldfried, M. R. (1980b). Toward the delineation of therapeutic change principles. *American Psychologist, 35,* 991–999.

Goldfried, M. R. (1983). The behavior therapist in clinical practice. *The Behavior Therapist, 6,* 45–46.

Goldfried, M. R., & Davison, G. C. (1976). *Clinical behavior therapy.* New York: Holt, Rinehart & Winston.

Goldfried, M. R., & Linehan, M. M. (1977). Basic issues in behavioral assessment. In A. R. Ciminero, K. S. Calhoun, & H. E. Adams, (Eds.), *Handbook of Behavioral Assessment.* New York: Wiley-Interscience.

Goldfried, M. R., & Robins, C. (1983). Self-schemas, cognitive bias, and the processing of therapeutic experiences. In P. C. Kendall (Ed.), *Advances in Cognitive-behavioral Research and Therapy,* Vol. 2. New York: Academic Press.

Goldfried, M. R., & Sobocinski, D. (1975). Effect of irrational beliefs on emotional arousal. *Journal of Consulting and Clinical Psychology, 53,* 504–510.

Goldfried, M. R., & Trier, C. S. (1974). Effectiveness of relaxation as an active coping skill. *Journal of Abnormal Psychology, 83,* 348–355.

Goldsmith, J. B., & McFall, R. M. (1975). Development & evaluation of an interpersonal skill-training program for psychiatric inpatients. *Journal of Applied Psychology, 84,* 51–58.

Goldstein, A. (1982). Agoraphobia: Treatment success, treatment failures, and theoretical implications. In D. Chambless & A. Goldstein (Eds.), *Agoraphobia.* New York: John Wiley & Sons.

Goldstein, A. P., Heller, K., & Sechrest, L. (1966). *Psychotherapy and the psychology of behavior change.* New York: John Wiley & Sons.

Goldstein, I. B., Shapiro, D., Thananopavarn, C., & Sambhi, M. P. (1982). Comparison of drug and behavioral treatments of essential hypertension. *Health Psychology, 1,* 7–26.

Goldstein, M. J. (1980). Family therapy during the aftercare treatment of acute schizophrenia. In J. S. Strauss, M. Bowers, T. W. Downey, S. Fleck, S. Jackson, and I. Levine (Eds.). *Psychotherapy of Schizophrenia: Current Status and New Directions.* New York: Plenum Medical.

Goldstein, M. J. (1984). Family intervention programs. In A. S. Bellack (Ed.), *Schizophrenia: Treatment, Management and Rehabilitation.* New York: Grune & Stratton.

Goldstein, M. J., & Kopeikin, H. S. (1981). Short- and long-term effects of combining drug and family therapy. In M. J. Goldstein (Ed.). *New Developments in Interventions with Families of Schizophrenics.* San Francisco: Jossey-Bass.

Golin, S., Hartmann, S. A., Klatt, E. N., Munz, K., & Wolfgang, G. L. (1977). Effects of self-esteem manipulation on arousal and reactions to sad models in depressed and nondepressed college students. *Journal of Abnormal Psychology, 86*, 435–439.

Gomes-Schwartz, B. (1984). Individual psychotherapy of schizophrenia. In A. S. Bellack (Ed.). *Schizophrenia: Treatment, Management, and Rehabilitation*. New York: Grune and Stratton.

Goodwin, D. W. (1985). Alcoholism and genetics. *Archives of General Psychiatry, 42*, 171–174.

Goodwin, D. W., Schulsinger, F., Hermansen, L., Guze, S., & Winokur, G. (1973). Alcohol problems in adoptees raised apart from alcoholic biological parents. *Archives of General Psychiatry, 28*, 238–243.

Gottesman, I. I., & Shields, J. (1972). *Schizophrenia and genetics: A twin study vantage point*. New York: Academic Press.

Gottlieb, A., Killen, J., Marlatt, G. A., & Taylor, C. B. (1986). *Psychological and pharmacological influences in smoking: The effects of nicotine gum and expectancy on smoking withdrawal symptoms and relapse*. Unpublished manuscript, Stanford University School of Medicine.

Gottman, J. M., Gonso, J., & Rasmussen, B. (1975). Social interaction, social competence and friendship in children. *Child Development, 46*, 709–718.

Gottman, J. M., & Levenson, R. W. (1985). A valid procedure for obtaining self-report of affect in marital interaction. *Journal of Consulting and Clinical Psychology, 53*, 151–160.

Gottman, J. M., Notarius, C., Markman, H., Bank, S., Yoppi, B., & Rubin, M. E. (1976). Behavior exchange theory and marital decision making. *Journal of Personality and Social Psychology, 34*, 14–23.

Grayson, J. , Foa, E. B., & Steketee, G. (1982). Habituation during exposure treatment: Distraction vs. attention-focusing. *Behaviour Research and Therapy, 20*, 323–328.

Graziano, A. M., DeGiovanni, I. S., & Garcia, K. A. (1979). Behavioral treatment of children's fear: A review. *Psychological Bulletin, 86*, 804–830.

Graziano, A. M., & Mooney, K. C. (1980). Family self-control instruction for children's nighttime fear reduction. *Journal of Consulting and Clinical Psychology, 48*, 206–213.

Green, L. (1978). Temporal and stimulus factors in self-monitoring by obese persons. *Behavior Therapy, 9*, 328–341.

Green, R., & Money, J. (1969). *Transsexualism and sex reassignment*. Baltimore, MD: Johns Hopkins Press.

Green, R., Newman, L., & Stoller, R. (1972). Treatment of boyhood "transsexualism." *Archives of General Psychiatry, 26*, 213–217.

Greenfeld, J. (1972). *A child called Noah*. New York: Holt, Rinehart & Winston.

Grey, S., Sartory, G., & Rachman, S. (1979). Synchronous and desynchronous changes during fear reduction. *Behaviour Research and Therapy, 78*, 137–148.

Guidano, V. F., & Liotti, G. (1983). *Cognitive processes and emotional disorders*. New York: Guilford Press.

Gurin, G., Veroff, J., & Feld, S. (1960). *Americans view their health: A nationwide interview survey*. New York: Basic Books.

Gurman, A. S., Knudson, R. M., & Kniskern, D. P. (1978). Behavioral marriage therapy. IV. Take two aspirin and call us in the morning. *Family Process, 17*, 165–180.

H

Hafner, R. J. (1976). Fresh symptom emergence after intensive behaviour therapy. *British Journal of Psychiatry, 129*, 378–383.

Hagen, R. L. (1974). Group therapy versus bibliotherapy in weight reduction. *Behavior Therapy, 5*, 222–234.

Hagen, R. L., Foreyt, J. P., & Durham, T. W. (1976). The dropout problem: Reducing attrition in obesity research. *Behavior Therapy, 7*, 463–471.

Hagglund, T. B., & Parkkulainen, K. (1965). Enuretic children treated with imipramine. *Annales Paediatia Fennica, 2*, 53.

Hagman, C. (1932). A study of fears of children in preschool age. *Journal of Experimental Psychology, 1*, 110–130.

Hahlweg, K., Schindler, L., & Revenstorf, D. (1980). *Comparison of reciprocity training and communication skills training in the treatment of marital discord*. Unpublished manuscript, Max Planck Institut fur Psychiatrie, Psychologische Abteilung. Kraepilinstrasse 10, D-8000 München 40.

Hall, R. G., Sachs, D., Hall, S. M., & Benowitz, N. L. (1984). Two-year efficacy and safety of rapid smoking therapy in patients with cardiac and pulmonary disease. *Journal of Consulting and Clinical Psychology, 52*, 574–581.

Hall, S., Hall, R., Hanson, R., & Borden, B. (1974). Permanence of two self-managed treatments of overweight in university and community populations. *Journal of Consulting and Clinical Psychology, 42*, 781–786.

Hall, S., Rugg, D., Turnstall, C., & Jones, R. (1984). Prevention of relapse to cigarette smoking by behavioral skill training. *Journal of Consulting and Clinical Psychology, 52*, 372–382.

Hallam, R., & Rachman, S. (1976). Current status of aversion therapy. In M. Hersen, R. M. Eisler, & P. M. Miller (Eds.), *Progress in Behavior Modification*, Vol. 2. New York: Academic Press.

Halmi, K. A., Falk, J. R., & Schwartz, E. (1981). Binge-eating and vomiting: A survey of a college population. *Psychological Medicine, 11*, 697–706.

Hammen, C. L., & Cochran, S. D. (1981). Cognitive correlates of life stress and depression in college students. *Journal of Abnormal Psychology, 90*, 286–297.

Hand, I., Lamontagne, Y., & Marks, I. M. (1974). Group exposure (flooding) in vivo for agoraphobics. *British Journal of Psychiatry, 124*, 588–602.

Hare, R. D. (1965). Psychopathy, fear arousal, and anticipated pain. *Psychological Reports, 16*, 499–502.

Hare, R. D. (1968a). Psychopathy, autonomic functioning, and the orienting response. *Journal of Abnormal Psychology Monograph Supplement, 73*, Part 2: 1–24.

Hare, R. D. (1968b). Detection threshold for electric shock in psychopaths. *Journal of Abnormal Psychology, 73*, 268–272.

Hare, R. D., & Quinn, M. J. (1971). Psychopathy and autonomic conditioning. *Journal of Abnormal Psychology, 71*, 223–235.

Harlow, H. F., & Harlow, M. K. (1965). The affectional systems. In A. M. Schrier, H. F. Harlow, & F. Stolnitz (Eds.), *Behavior of Nonhuman Primates*, Vol. 2. New York: Academic Press.

Harris, E. L., Noyes, R., Crowe, R. R., & Chaundry, D. R. (1983). Family study of agoraphobia. *Archives of General Psychiatry, 40*, 1061–1064.

Harris, L. S., & Purohit, A. P. (1977). Bladder training and enuresis: A controlled trial. *Behaviour Research and Therapy, 15*, 485–490.

Harris, M. B., & Hallbauber, E. S. (1973). Self-directed weight control through eating and exercise. *Behaviour Research and Therapy, 11*, 523–529.

Hart, B., & Risley, T. (1982). *How to use incidental teaching for elaborating language.* Lawrence, KS: H & H Enterprises.

Haynes, S. N., Chavez, R. E., & Samuel, V. (1984). Assessment of marital communication and distress. *Behavioral Assessment, 6*, 315–322.

Hauri, P. (1976). Dreams of patients remitted from reactive depression. *Journal of Abnormal Psychology, 85*, 1–10.

Hawkins, R. C., Fremouw, W. J., & Clement, P. F. (1984). *The binge-purge syndrome: Treatment, research, and theory.* New York: Springer.

Haynes, R. B. (1979). Strategies to improve compliance with referrals, appointments, and prescribed medical regimens. In R. B. Haynes, D. W. Taylor, & D. L. Sackett (Eds.), *Compliance in Health Care.* Baltimore: Johns Hopkins Press.

Hedbring, C., & Newsom, C. (1985). Visual overselectivity: A comparison of two instructional remediation procedures with autistic children. *Journal of Autism and Developmental Disorders, 15*, 9–22.

Heidi, F. J., & Borkovec, T. D. (1983). Relaxation-induced anxiety: Paradoxical anxiety enhancement due to relaxation training. *Journal of Consulting and Clinical Psychology, 51*, 171–182.

Heidi, F. J., & Borkovec, T. D. (1984). Relaxation-induced anxiety: Mechanisms and theoretical implications. *Behaviour Research and Therapy, 22*, 1–12.

Heiman, J., LoPiccolo, L., & LoPiccolo, J. (1976). *Becoming orgasmic: A sexual growth program for women.* Englewood Cliffs, NJ: Prentice-Hall.

Heiman, J., & Rowland, D. (In press). Affective and physiological sexual response patterns: The effects of instructions on sexually functional and dysfunctional men. *Journal of Psychosomatic Research.*

Heinz, J. (1983). National leadership for children's television. *American Psychologist, 38*, 817–819.

Helzer, J. E., Robins, L. N., Taylor, J. R., Carey, K., Miller, R., Combs-Orne, T., & Farmer, A. (1985). The extent of long-term moderate drinking among alcoholics discharged from medical and psychiatric facilities. *The New England Journal of Medicine, 312*, 1678–1682.

Henderson, S., Duncan-Jones, P., McAuley, H., & Richie, K. (1978). The patient's primary group. *British Journal of Psychiatry, 132*, 74–86.

Henn, F. A., Bardwell, R., & Jenkins, R. L.

(1980). Juvenile delinquents revisited: Adult criminal activity. *Archives of General Psychiatry, 37,* 1160–1163.

Henricksen, K., & Doughty, R. (1967). Decelerating undesirable mealtime behavior in a group of profoundly retarded boys. *American Journal of Mental Deficiency, 72,* 40–44.

Herbert, M. (1978). *Conduct disorders of childhood and adolescence.* New York: John Wiley & Sons.

Herjanic, B., Herjanic, M., Brown, F., & Wheatt, T. (1975). Are children reliable reporters? *Journal of Abnormal Child Psychology, 3,* 41–48.

Herrnstein, R. J. (1969). Method and theory in the study of avoidance. *Psychological Review, 76,* 46–69.

Hersov, L. A. (1960). Persistant non-attendance at school. *Journal of Child Psychology and Psychiatry, 1,* 130–136.

Heshe, J., & Roeder, E. (1976). Electroconvulsive therapy in Denmark. *British Journal of Psychiatry, 128,* 241–245.

Hetherington, E. M., & Parke, R. D. (1979). *Child psychology: A contemporary viewpoint* (2nd ed.). New York: McGraw-Hill.

Higgins, R., & Marlatt, G. A. (1975). Fear of interpersonal evaluation as a determinant of alcohol consumption in male social drinkers. *Journal of Abnormal Psychology, 84,* 664–651.

Himaldi, W. G., Boice, R., & Barlow, D. H. (1985). Assessment of agoraphobia: Triple response measurement. *Behaviour Research and Therapy, 23,* 311–324.

Hindley, C. B., Fillozat, A., Klackenberg, G., Nicolet-Meister, D., & Sand, E. A. (1965). Some differences in infant feeding and elimination training in five European longitudinal samples. *Journal of Child Psychiatry and Psychology, 6,* 179–201.

Hingtgen, J. N., Saunders, B. J., & DeMyer, M. K. (1965). Shaping cooperative responses in early childhood schizophrenics. In L.P. Ullmann & L. Krasner, (Eds.), *Case Studies in Behavior Modification.* New York: Holt, Rinehart & Winston.

Hinshaw, S. P., Henker, B., & Whalen, C. K. (1984). Self-control in hyperactive boys in anger-inducing situations: Affects of cognitive-behavioral training and of methylphenidate. *Journal of Abnormal Child Psychology, 12,* 55–78.

Hirsch, J. (1985). *Time Magazine.* February 25.

Hirschi, T. (1969). *Causes of delinquency.* Berkeley: University of California Press.

Hobbs, S. A., Moguin, L. E., Tyroler, M., & Lahey, B. B. (1980). Cognitive Therapy with Children. *Psychological Bulletin, 87,* 147–165.

Hodgson, R. J., Stockwell, T. R., & Rankin, H. J. (1979). Can alcohol reduce tension? *Behaviour Research and Therapy, 17,* 459–466.

Hogan, R., DeSoto, C., & Solanto, C. (1977). Traits, tests, and personality research. *American Psychologist, 32,* 255–264.

Holden, A. E., O'Brien, G. T., Barlow, D. H., Stetson, D., & Infantino, A. (1983). Self-help manual for agoraphobia: A preliminary report of effectiveness. *Behavior Therapy, 14,* 545–556.

Hollingshead, A. B., & Redlich, S. C. (1958). *Social class and mental illness: A community study.* New York: John Wiley & Sons.

Holmes, T. H., & Rahe, R. H. (1967). The social readjustment rating scale. *Journal of Psychosomatic Research, 11,* 213–218.

Holroyd, K., Andrasik, R., & Westbrook, T. (1977). Cognitive control of tension headache. *Cognitive Therapy and Research, 1,* 121–133.

Holroyd, K., Penzien, D., Hursey, K., Tobin, D., Rogers, L., Holm, J., Marcille, P., Hall, J., & Chila, A. (1984). Change mechanisms in EMG biofeedback training: Cognitive changes underlying improvements in tension headache. *Journal of Consulting and Clinical Psychology, 52,* 1039–1053.

Homan, W. E. (1969). *Child sense.* New York: Bantam Books.

Hooley, J. M., Orley, J., & Teasdale, J. D. (1986). Levels of expressed emotion and relapse in depressed patients. *British Journal of Psychiatry, 148,* 642–647.

Hops, S., & Greenwood, C. R. (1981). Social skills deficits. In E. J. Mash & L. G. Terdal (Eds.), *Behavioral assessment of childhood disorders.* New York: Guilford Press.

Houts, A. C., Liebert, R. M., & Padawer, W. (1983). A delivery system for the treatment of primary enuresis. *Journal of Abnormal Child Psychology, 11,* 513–519.

Houts, A. C., Peterson, J. K., & Liebert, R. M. (1984). The effect of prior imipramine treatment on the results of conditioning therapy in children with enuresis. *Journal of Pediatric Psychology, 9,* 505–509.

Howard, A. N., & Bray, G. (Eds.) (1981). Proceedings of a symposium on evaluation of very-low-calorie diets. *International Journal of Obesity, 5,* 193–352.

Howard, J. R., Jones, R. R., & Weinrott,

M. R. (1982). Cost-effectiveness of teaching family programs for delinquents: Results of a national evaluation. *Evaluation Review, 6*, 173–201.

Hubert, H. B., Feinlieb, M., McNamara, P., & Castelli, W. (1983). Obesity as an independent risk factor for cardiovascular disease: A 26 year follow-up of participants in the Framingham Heart Study. *Circulation, 67*, 968–977.

Hudson, J. I., Pope, H. G., & Jonas, J. M. (1984). Treatment of bulimia with antidepressants: Theoretical considerations and clinical findings. In A. J. Stunkard and E. Stellar (Eds.), *Eating and Its Disorders.* New York: Raven Press.

Hugdahl, K. (1978). Electrodermal conditioning to potentially phobic stimuli: Effects of instructed extinction. *Behaviour Research and Therapy, 16*, 315–321.

Hugdahl, K. (1981). The three-systems model of fear and emotion—a critical examination. *Behaviour Research and Therapy, 19*, 75–86.

Hughes, G. H., Hymowitz, N., Ockene, J., Simon, N., & Vogt, T. (1981). The multiple risk factor intervention trial (MRFIT): V. Intervention on smoking. *Preventive Medicine, 10*, 476–500.

Hunt, G. H. & Azrin, N. H. (1973). The community-reinforcement approach to alcoholism. *Behaviour Research and Therapy, 11*, 91–104.

Hurd, R. D., Johnson, C., Pehacek, T., Bast, L., Jacobs, D., & Luetker, R. (1980). Prevention of cigarette smoking in seventh grade students. *Journal of Behavioral Medicine, 3*, 14–28.

Hutchings, B., & Mednick, S. A. (1974). Registered criminality in the adoptive and biological parents of registered male adoptees. In S. A. Mednick, F. Schulsinger, J. Higgins, & B. Bell (Eds.), *Genetics. Environment and Psychopathology.* Amsterdam: North Holland

I

Inhof, B. (1957). Enuretics in child guidance. *Heilpadag Werkbl, 1956, 2*, 122–127. (Psychological Abstracts, *31*, no. 8322.)

J

Jacobs, R., Kraemer, H., & Agras, W. S. (1977). Relaxation therapy in the treatment of hypertension. *Archives of General Psychiatry, 34*, 1417–1427.

Jacobs, M., & Schneider, J. (1985). Medical complications of bulimia: A prospective evalua-

tion. *Quarterly Journal of Medicine, 54*, 177–182.

Jacobs, P.A., Brunton, M., Melville, M.M., Brittain, R.P., & McClemont, W.F. (1965). Aggressive behavior, mental subnormality, and the XYY male. *Nature, 208*, 1351–1352

Jacobson, E. (1938). *Progressive relaxation.* Chicago: University of Chicago Press.

Jacobson, J. W. (1982). Problem behavior and psychiatric impairment within a developmentally disabled population: I. Behavior frequency. *Applied Research in Mental Retardation, 3*, 121–139.

Jacobson, N. S. (1977, December). *The role of problem solving in behavior marital therapy.* Paper presented at the Annual Meeting of the Association for Advancement of Behavior Therapy, Atlanta, GA.

Jacobson, N. S. (1978). Specific and nonspecific factors in the effectiveness of a behavioral approach to the treatment of marital discord. *Journal of Consulting and Clinical Psychology 46*, 442–452.

Jacobson, N. S., Follette, W. C., & Elwood, R. W. (1984). Outcome research in behavioral marital therapy: Methodological and conceptual reappraisal. In K. Halweg & N. S. Jacobson (Eds.). *Marital interaction: Analysis and modification.* New York: Guilford Press.

Jacobson, N. S., & Margolin, G. (1979). *Marital therapy: Strategies based on social learning and behavior exchange principles.* New York: Brunner/Mazel.

Jacobson, N. S., McDonald, D. W., Follette, W. C., & Berley, R. A. (1985). Attribution processes in distressed and nondistressed married couples. *Cognitive Therapy and Research, 9*, 35–50.

Jacobson, N., & Moore, D. (1981). Spouses as observers of the events in their relationship. *Journal of Consulting and Clinical Psychology, 49*, 269–277.

Jannoun, L., Munby, M., Catalan, J., & Gelder, M. (1980). A home-based treatment program for agoraphobia: Replication and controlled evaluation. *Behavior Therapy, 11*, 294–305.

Jannoun, L., Oppenheimer, C., & Gelder, M. (1982). A self-help treatment program for anxiety state patients. *Behavior Therapy, 13*, 103–111.

Jarvik, L. F., Klodin, V., & Matsuyama, S. S. (1973). Human aggression and the extra Y chromosome: Fact or fantasy? *American Psychologist, 28*, 674–682.

Jeffery, R. W., Bjornson-Benson, W., Rosenthal, B., Lindquist, R., et al. (1984). Correlates of weight loss and its maintenance over two years of follow-up among middle-aged men. *Preventive Medicine, 13,* 155–168.

Jeffery, R. W., Folsom, A., Luepker, R., Jacobs, D., et al. (1984). Prevalence of overweight and weight loss behavior in a metropolitan adult population: The Minnesota heart survey experience. *American Journal of Public Health, 74,* 349–352.

Jeffery, R. W., Thompson, P. D., & Wing, R. R. (1978). Effects on weight reduction of strong monetary contracts for calorie restriction or weight loss. *Behaviour Research and Therapy, 16,* 363–370.

Jeffery, R., Wing, R., & Stunkard, A. J. (1978). Behavioral treatment of obesity. *Behavior Therapy, 6,* 189–199.

Jellinek, E. M. (1960). *The disease concept of alcoholism.* New Brunswick, NJ: Hillhouse Press.

Jersild, A. J., & Holmes, F. B. (1935). Children's fears. Child Development Monographs.

Johns, J. H., & Quay, H. C. (1962). The effect of social reward on verbal conditioning in psychopathic and neurotic military offenders. *Journal of Consulting Psychology, 26,* 217–220.

Johnson, C., Lewis, C., & Hagman, J. (1984). The syndrome of bulimia: Review and synthesis. *Psychiatric Clinics of North America, 7,* 247–273.

Johnson, J. H., & Williams, T. A. (1980). Using on-line computer technology in a mental health admitting system. In J. B. Sidowski, J. H. Johnson, & T. A. Williams (Eds.), *Technology in Mental Health Care Delivery Systems.* Norwood, NJ: Ablex.

Johnson, P., & O'Leary, K. D. (1986). *An individualized approach to assessing behavioral components of marital satisfaction.* Unpublished manuscript. State University of New York, Stony Brook, NY.

Johnson, S. B. (1981). Enuresis. In Daitzman Reid (Ed.). *Clinical Behavior Therapy and Behavior Modification,* Vol I. New York: Garland Publications.

Johnson, S. B. & Melamed, D. G. (1979). The assessment and treatment of children's fears. In B. Lahey & A. E. Kazdin (Eds.), *Advances in clinical psychology,* Vol 2. New York: Plenum Press.

Johnson, W., Schlundt, D., & Jarrell, M. (1986). Exposure and response prevention, training in energy balance, and problem solving therapy for bulimia nervosa. *International Journal of Eating Disorders, 5,* 35–46.

Jones, H. E. (1931). The conditioning of overt emotional responses. *Journal of Educational Psychology, 22,* 127–130.

Jones, H. G. (1960). The behavioral treatment of enuresis nocturna. In H. J. Eysenck (Ed.), *Behavior therapy and the neuroses.* Oxford: Pergamon Press.

Jones, M. C. (1924a). The elimination of children's fears. *Journal of Experimental Psychology, 7,* 383–390.

Jones, M. C. (1924b). A laboratory study of fear: The case of Peter. *Journal of Genetic Psychology, 31,* 308–315.

Jones, M. C. (1978). Invited address: John B. Watson. American Psychological Association, Division 26, Toronto, Canada.

Jones, R. G. (1968). *A factored measure of Ellis' irrational belief system, with personality and maladjustment correlates.* Unpublished doctoral dissertation, Texas Technological College.

K

Kagan, J., & Moss, H. (1962). *Birth to maturity.* New York: John Wiley & Sons.

Kahn, J., Coyne, J. C., & Margolin, G. (1983). *Depression and marital conflict.* Unpublished manuscript, Mental Research Institute, Palo Alto, CA.

Kahn, J. H., & Narsten, J. P. (1962). School refusal: A comprehensive view of school phobia and other failures of school attendance. *American Journal of Orthopsychiatry, 32,* 707–718.

Kalish, H. I. (1981). *From behavioral science to behavior modification.* New York: McGraw-Hill.

Kane, J. M., & Smith, J. M. (1982). Tardive dyskinesia: Prevalence and risk factors. *Archives of General Psychiatry, 20,* 39–40.

Kanfer, F. (1977). The many faces of self-control. In R.B. Stuart (Ed.), *Behavioral self-management.* New York: Brunner/Mazel.

Kanfer, F. H. (1979). A few comments on the current status of behavioral assessment. *Behavioral Assessment, 1,* 37–40.

Kanter, N. J., & Goldfried, M. R. (1979). Relative effectiveness of rational restructuring and self-control desensitization in the reduction of interpersonal anxiety. *Behavior Therapy, 14,* 84–91.

Kantorovich, N. V. (1930). An attempt at associative–reflex therapy in alcoholism. *Psychological Abstracts, 4,* 493.

Kaplan, B. (Ed.) (1964). *The inner world of mental illness.* New York: Harper & Row.

Kaplan, H. (1974). *The new sex therapy.* New York: Brunner/Mazel.

Kaplan, H. (1979). *Disorders of sexual desire.* New York: Brunner/Mazel.

Kaplan, R. M., Atkins, C. J., & Reinsch, S. (1984). Specific efficacy expectations mediate exercise compliance in patients with COPD. *Health Psychology, 3,* 223–242.

Kardish, S., Hillman, E., & Werry, J. (1968). Efficacy of imipramine in childhood enuresis. *Canadian Medical Association Journal, 99,* 263–266.

Kasl, S. V. (1980). Cardiovascular risk reduction in a community setting: Some comments. *Journal of Consulting and Clinical Psychology, 48,* 143–149.

Katell, A., Callahan, E., Fremouw, W., & Zitter, R. (1979). The effects of behavioral treatment and fasting on eating behaviors and weight loss: A case study. *Behavior Therapy, 10,* 579–587.

Katkin, E. S., Fitzgerald, C. R., & Shapiro, D. (1979). Clinical applications of biofeedback: Current status and future prospects. In H. Pick, H. Leibowitz, J. Singer, A. Stein-Schneider, & H. Stevenson (Eds.), *Psychology: From research to practice.* New York: Plenum Publishing.

Kavanagh, D. J., & Bower, G. (1985). Mood and self-efficacy. *Cognitive Therapy and Research, 9,* 507–526.

Kazdin, A. E. (1978a). *History of behavior modification.* Baltimore, MD: University Park Press.

Kazdin, A. E. (1978b). The application of operant techniques in treatment, rehabilitation, and education. In S. L. Garfield & A. E. Bergin (Eds.), *Handbook of Psychotherapy and Behavior Change,* (2nd. ed.). New York: John Wiley & Sons.

Kazdin, A. E. (1978c). Conceptual and assessment issues raised by self-efficacy theory. *Advances in behaviour research and therapy, 1,* 177–186.

Kazdin, A. E. (1981). Drawing valid inferences from case studies. *Journal of Consulting and Clinical Psychology, 49,* 183.

Kazdin, A. E. (1982). Symptom substitution, generalization, and response co-variation: Implications for psychotherapy outcome. *Psychological Bulletin, 91,* 349–365.

Kazdin, A. E., French, N., & Sherick, R. (1981). Acceptability of alternative treatments for children: Evaluations by inpatient children, parents and staff. *Journal of Consulting and Clinical Psychology, 49,* 900–906.

Kazdin, A. E., & Wilcoxon, L. A. (1976). Systematic desensitization and nonspecific treatment effects: A methodological evaluation. *Psychological Bulletin, 83,* 729–758.

Kazdin, A. E., & Wilson, G. T. (1978). *Evaluation of behavior therapy: Issues, evidence, and research strategies.* Cambridge, MA: Ballinger.

Keefe, P., Wyshogrod, D., Weinberger, E., & Agras, W. S. (1984). Binge eating and outcome of behavioral treatment of obesity: A preliminary report. *Behaviour Research and Therapy, 22,* 319–322.

Kelly, G. A. (1955). *The psychology of personal constructs.* New York: Norton.

Kelly, R. (1982). Behavioral reorientation of pedophiliacs: Can it be done? *Clinical Psychology Review, 2,* 387–408.

Kendall, P. C., & Norton-Ford, J. D. (1982). *Clinical psychology: Scientific and professional dimensions.* New York: John Wiley & Sons.

Kendler, K. S., Gruenberg, A. M., & Tsuang, M. T. (1985). Psychiatric illness in first-degree relatives of schizophrenic and surgical control patients. *Archives of General Psychiatry, 42,* 770–779.

Kennedy, W. A. (1965). School phobia: Rapid treatment of fifty cases. *Journal of Abnormal Psychology, 70,* 285–289.

Kennedy, W. A. (1971). *Child psychology.* Englewood Cliffs, NJ: Prentice-Hall.

Kent, R. N. (1976). A methodological critique of "Interventions for boys with conduct problems." *Journal of Consulting and Clinical Psychology, 44,* 297–299.

Kent, R. N., & Foster, S. L. (1977). Direct observational procedures: Methodological issues in naturalistic settings. In A. R. Ciminero, K. S. Calhoun, & H. E. Adams (Eds.), *Handbook of behavioral assessment.* New York: John Wiley & Sons.

Kent, R. N., & O'Leary, K. D. (1976). A controlled evaluation of behavior modification with conduct problem children. *Journal of Consulting and Clinical Psychology, 44,* 586–596.

Kent, R. N., O'Leary, K. D., Diament, C., & Dietz, A. (1974). Expectation biases in observational evaluation of therapeutic change. *Journal of Consulting and Clinical Psychology, 42,* 774–780.

Kesey, K. (1962). *One flew over the cuckoo's nest.* New York: Viking Press.

Keys, A. (1979). Is overweight a risk factor for coronary heart disease? *Cardiovascular Medicine, 4,* 1233–1242.

Keys, A., Brozek, J., Henschel, A., Mickelsen, O., & Taylor, H. (1950). *The biology of human starvation*. Minneapolis: University of Minnesota Press.

Kihlstrom, J., & Nasby, W. (1981). Cognitive tasks in clinical assessment: An exercise in applied psychology. In P. Kendall & S. D. Hollon (Eds.), *Assessment strategies for cognitive-behavioral interventions*. New York: Academic Press.

Killen, J., Maccoby, N., & Taylor, C. (1984). Nicotine gum and self-regulation training in smoking relapse prevention. *Behavior Therapy, 15*, 234–248.

Kiloh, L. G. (1980). Electroconvulsive therapy. In E.S. Paykel (Ed.), *Handbook of affective disorders*. New York: Guilford Press.

Kimmel, H. D., & Kimmel, E. (1970). An instrumental conditioning method for the treatment of enuresis. *Journal of Behavior Therapy and Experimental Psychiatry, 6*, 121–123.

Kingsley, R. G., & Wilson, G. T. (1977). Behavior therapy for obesity: A comparative investigation of long-term efficacy. *Journal of Consulting and Clinical Psychology, 45*, 288–298.

Kinsey, A. C., Pomeroy, W. B., Martin, C. E., & Gebhard, P. H. (1953). *Sexual behavior in the human female*. Philadelphia: Saunders.

Kirigin, K. A., Braukman, C. J., Atwater, J. D., & Wolf, M. M. (1982). An evaluation of teaching-family (Achievement Place) group homes for juvenile offenders. *Journal of Applied Behavior Analysis, 15*, 1–16.

Kirk, J. W. (1983). Behavioural treatment of obsessional-compulsive patients in routine clinical practice. *Behaviour Research and Therapy, 21*, 57–62.

Kirk, S. A. (1972). *Educating exceptional children*. Boston: Houghton-Mifflin.

Kirkley, B. G., Schneider, J. A., Agras, W. S., & Bachman, J. A. (1985). A comparison of two group treatments for bulimia. *Journal of Consulting and Clinical Psychology, 53*, 43–48.

Klaber, M. M. (1969). The retarded and institutions for the retarded: A preliminary research report. In S. B. Sarason & J. Doris (Eds.), *Psychological problems in mental deficiency*. New York: Harper & Row.

Klein, D. F., & Davis, J. M. (1969). *Diagnosis and drug treatment of psychiatric disorders*. Baltimore, MD: Williams and Wilkins.

Klein, D. F., Zitrin, C. M., Woerner, M. G., &

Ross, D. C. (1983). Treatment of phobias. *Archives of General Psychiatry, 40*, 139–145.

Klein, N. C., Alexander, J. F., & Parsons, B. V. (1977). Impact of family systems intervention on recidivism and sibling delinquency: A model of primary prevention and program evaluation. *Journal of Consulting and Clinical Psychology, 45*, 469–474.

Klerman, G. L. (1980). Practical issues in the treatment of depression and mania. In E. S. Paykel (Ed.), *Handbook of affective disorders*. New York: Guilford Press.

Klerman, G. L., & Weissman, M. W. (1982). Interpersonal psychotherapy: Theory and Research. In A. J. Rush (Ed.), *Short-term psychotherapies for depression*. New York: Guilford Press.

Knapp, J. (1975). Some non-monogamous marriage styles and related attitudes and practices of marriage counselors. *The Family Coordinator, 24*, 505–514.

Knapp, T. J., Downs, D. L., & Alperson, J. R. (1976). Behavior therapy for insomnia: A review. *Behavior Therapy, 7*, 614–625.

Knopf, I. J. (1979). *Childhood psychopathology: A developmental approach*. Englewood Cliffs, NJ: Prentice-Hall.

Knutson, J. F., & Hyman, M. (1973). Predatory aggression and irritable aggression: Shock-induced fighting in mouse-killing rats. *Physiology and Behavior, 11*, 113–115.

Kocsis, J. H., & Stokes, P. E. (1979). Lithium maintenance: Factors affecting outcome. *American Journal of Psychiatry, 136*, 563–566.

Korsch, B., & Negrete, V. (1972). Doctor-patient communication. *Scientific American, 227*, 66.

Kraepelin, E. (1896). *Dementia praecox*. Translated by R. M. Barclay. Edinburgh: E.S. Livingston, Ltd.

Krager, J. M., Safer, D., & Earhardt, J. (1979, Spring). *Medication used to treat hyperactive children: Follow up survey results*. Paper presented at School Health Association Annual Meeting, Detroit, MI.

Krantz, S., & Hammen, C. (1979). The assessment of cognitive bias in depression. *Journal of Abnormal Psychology, 88*, 611–619.

Krasner, L. (1971). Behavior therapy. In P. H. Mussen, & M. R. Rosenzweig. (Eds.). *Annual review of psychology*, (pp. 498–491). California: Annual Reviews, Inc.

Kuhn, T. S. (1962). *The structure of scientific revolutions.* Chicago: Chicago University Press.

L

Lacey, J. H. (1983). Bulimia nervosa, binge eating, and psychogenic vomiting: A controlled treatment study and long-term outcome. *British Medical Journal, 286,* 1609–1613.

LaGreca, A. M., & Santogrossi, D. A. (1981). Social skills training with elementary school students: A behavioral group approach. *Journal of Consulting and Clinical Psychology, 48,* 220–227.

Lambert, M., de Julio, S., & Stein, D. (1978). Therapist interpersonal skills. *Psychological Bulletin, 85,* 467–489.

Landman, J. T., & Dawes, R. (1982). Psychotherapy outcome: Smith and Glass's conclusions stand up under scrutiny. *American Psychologist, 37,* 504–516.

Lando, H. A. (1977). Successful treatment of smokers with a broad-spectrum behavioral approach. *Journal of Consulting and Clinical Psychology, 45,* 361–366.

Lang, P. J. (1965). Behavior therapy with a case of anorexia nervosa. In L. P. Ullmann & L. Krasner (Eds.), *Case studies in behavior modification.* New York: Holt, Rinehart & Winston.

Lang, P. J. (1969). The mechanics of desensitization and the laboratory study of fear. In C. M. Franks (Ed.). *Behavior therapy: Appraisal and status.* New York: McGraw-Hill.

Lang, P. J. (1971). The application of psychophysiological methods to the study of psychotherapy and behavior modification. In A. E. Bergin & S. L. Garfield (Eds.), *Handbook of psychotherapy and behavior change.* New York: John Wiley & Sons.

Lang, P. J. (1977). Physiological measurement of anxiety and fear. In J. P. Cone & R. P. Hawkins, (Eds.), *Behavioral assessment.* New York: Brunner/Mazel.

Lang, P. J. (1978). Self-efficacy theory: Thoughts on cognition and unification. *Advances in Behaviour Research and Therapy, 1,* 187–192.

Lang, P. J. (1979). A bio-informational theory of emotional imagery. *Psychophysiology, 16,* 495–512.

Lang, P. J., Lazovick, A. D., & Reynolds, D. J. (1965). Desensitization, suggestibility and pseudotherapy. *Journal of Abnormal Psychology, 70,* 395–402.

Lang, P. J., Melamed, B. G., & Hart, J. A. (1970). A psychophysiological analysis of fear modification using an automated desensitization procedure. *Journal of Abnormal Psychology, 76,* 220–234.

Lange, J. (1931). *Crime as destiny.* London: Allen and Unwin.

Langer, E., & Abelson, W. (1974). A patient by any other name: Clinician group differences in labeling bias. *Journal of Consulting and Clinical Psychology, 42,* 4–9.

Langhorne, J. E., & Loney, J. (1979). A fourfold model for subgrouping the hyperkinetic MBD syndrome. *Child Psychiatry and Human Development, 9,* 153–159.

Largo, R. H., & Stutzle, W. (1977). Longitudinal study of bowel and bladder control by day and night in first six years of life. *Developmental Medicine and Child Neurology, 19,* 607–613.

Lasagna, L. (1980). Drugs in the treatment of obesity. In A. J. Stunkard (Ed.), *Obesity.* Philadelphia: Saunders.

Last, C. G., Thase, M. E., Hersen, M., Bellack, A. S., & Himmelhoch, J. M. (1984). Treatment outcome for solicited versus nonsolicited unipolar depressed female outpatients. *Journal of Consulting and Clinical Psychology, 52,* 134.

Lazarus, A. A. (1958). New methods in psychotherapy: A case study. *South African Medical Journal, 32,* 660–664.

Lazarus, A. A. (1963). The results of behaviour therapy in 126 cases of severe neurosis. *Behaviour Research and Therapy, 1,* 65–78.

Lazarus, A. A. (1968). Scientism and psychotherapy. *Psychological Reports, 22,* 1015–1016.

Lazarus, A. A. (1971). *Behavior therapy and beyond.* New York: McGraw-Hill.

Lazarus, A. A. (1976). *Multimodal behavior therapy.* New York: Springer.

Lazarus, A. A. (1981). *The practice of multimodal therapy.* New York: McGraw-Hill.

Lazarus, A. A., & Abramovitz, A. (1962). The use of "emotive imagery" in the treatment of children's phobias. *Journal of Mental Science, 108,* 191–195.

Lazarus, A. A., Davison, G. C., & Polefka, D. (1965). Classical and operant factors in the treatment of a school phobia. *Journal of Abnormal and Social Psychology, 70,* 225–229.

Lazarus, A. A., & Fay, A. (1982). Resistance or rationalization? A cognitive-behavioral perspective. In P. I. Wachtel (Ed.), *Resistance: Psycho-*

dynamic and behavioral approaches. New York: Plenum Publishing.

Lazarus, A. A., & Fay, A. (1984). Behavior therapy. In T. B. Karasu (Ed.). *The psychiatric therapies.* Washington, DC: American Psychiatric Press.

Lee, C. (1984a). Accuracy of efficacy and outcome expectations in predicting performance in a simulated assertiveness task. *Cognitive Therapy and Research, 8,* 37–48.

Lee, C. (1984b). Efficacy expectations and outcome expectations as predictors of performance in a snake-handling task. *Cognitive Therapy and Research, 8,* 509–516.

Leff, J., Kuipers, L., Berkowitz, R., Eberlein-Fries, R., & Sturgeon, D. (1982). A controlled trial of social intervention in the families of schizophrenic patients. *British Journal of Psychiatry, 141,* 121–134.

Lefkowitz, M. M., Eron, L. D., Walden, L.O., & Heusmann, L.R. (1977). *Growing up to be violent.* New York: Pergamon Press.

Lehrer, P. M. (1978). Psychophysiological effects of progressive relaxation in anxiety neurotic patients and of progressive relaxation and alpha feedback in nonpatients. *Journal of Clinical and Consulting Psychology, 46,* 389–404.

Lehrer, P. M. (1982). How to relax and how not to relax: A re-evaluation of the work of Edmund Jacobson. *Behaviour Research and Therapy, 20,* 417–428.

Lehrer, P. M., Schoicket, S., Carrington, P., & Woolfolk, R. L. (1980). Psychophysiological and cognitive responses to stressful stimuli in subjects practicing progressive and relaxation and clinically standardized meditation. *Behaviour Research and Therapy, 18,* 293–303.

Lehrer, P. M., Woolfolk, R. L., Rooney, A., McCann, B., & Carrington, P. (1983). Progressive relaxation and meditation. A study of psychophysiological and therapeutic differences between two techniques. *Behaviour Research and Therapy, 21,* 651–662.

Lehrer, P. M., & Woolfolk, R. L. (1984). Are stress reduction techniques interchangeable, or do they have specific effects? A review of the comparative empirical literature. In R. L. Woolfolk & P. M. Lehrer (Eds.), *Principles and practices of stress management.* New York: Guilford Press.

Leiblum, S. R., Rosen, R. C., & Pierce, D. (1976). Group treatment format: Mixed sexual dysfunctions. *Archives of Sexual Behavior, 5,* 313–322.

Leiblum, S. R., & Pervin, L. A. (Eds.). (1980). *Principles and practice of sex therapy.* New York: Guilford Press.

Leitenberg, H. (1976). Behavioral approaches to treatment of neuroses. In H. Leitenberg (Ed.). *Handbook of behavior modification and behavior therapy.* Englewood Cliffs, NJ: Prentice-Hall.

Leitenberg, H., Agras, S., Butz, R., & Wincze, J. (1971). Relationship between heart rate and behavioral change during the treatment of phobias. *Journal of Abnormal Psychology, 78,* 59–68.

Leitenberg, H., Gross, J., Peterson, J., & Rosen, J. C. (1984). Analysis of an anxiety model and the process of change during exposure plus response prevention treatment of bulimia nervosa. *Behavior Therapy, 15,* 3–20.

Lemere, F., & Voegtlin, W. (1950). An evaluation of the aversion treatment of alcoholism. *Quarterly Journal of Studies on Alcohol, 11,* 199–204.

Lemert, E. M. (1981). Diversion in juvenile justice: What hath been wrought. *Journal of Research in Crime and Delinquency, 18,* 34–46.

Lepper, M., Green, D., & Nisbett, R. (1973). Undermining children's intrinsic interest with external rewards: A test of the "overjustification hypothesis." *Journal of Personality and Social Psychology, 28,* 129–137.

Levantal, T., & Sills, M. (1964). Self-image in school phobia. *American Journal of Orthopsychiatry, 34,* 685–695.

Levenson, R. W., & Gottman, J. M. (1983). Marital interaction: Physiological linkage and affective exchange. *Journal of Personality and Social Psychology, 45,* 587–597.

Levenson, R. W., Sher, K. J., Grossman, L., Newman, J., & Newlin, D. (1980). Alcohol and stress response dampening: Pharmacological effects, expectancy, and tension reduction. *Journal of Abnormal Psychology, 89,* 528–538.

Leventhal, H., & Cleary, P. (1980). The smoking problem: A review of the research and theory in behavioral risk modification. *Psychological Bulletin, 88,* 370–405.

Leventhal, H., Safer, M., Cleary, P., & Gutmann, M. (1980). Cardiovascular risk modification by community-based programs for life-style change: Comments on the Stanford Study. *Journal of Consulting and Clinical Psychology, 48,* 150–158.

Levis, D. J., & Malloy, P. F. (1982). Experimental foundations of behavior therapy: Infrahuman and human conditioning research. In G. T. Wilson & C. M. Franks (Eds.), *Contemporary behavior therapy: Conceptual and empirical foundations.* New York: Guilford Press.

Leviton, A. (1978). Epidemiology of headache. In *Advances in Neurology*, Vol. 19. New York: Raven Press.

Levitsky, A. S., & Perls, F. S. (1970). The rules and games of Gestalt therapy. In J. Fagan & I. L. Shepard (Eds.). *Gestalt therapy now.* Palo Alto, CA: Science and Behavior Books.

Levitt, E. E. (1957). The results of psychotherapy with children: An evaluation. *Journal of Consulting Psychology, 21,* 189–196.

Levitt, E. E. (1963). Psychotherapy with children: A further evaluation. *Behaviour Research and Therapy, 1,* 45–51.

Levitz, L. S., & Stunkard, A. J. (1974). A therapeutic coalition for obesity: Behavior modification and patient self-help. *American Journal of Psychiatry, 131,* 423–427.

Lew, E. A., & Garfinkel, L. (1979). Variations in mortality by weight among 750,000 men and women. *Journal of Chronic Diseases, 32,* 563–576.

Lewin, K. (1935). *Principles of topological psychology.* New York: McGraw-Hill.

Lewinsohn, P. M. (1974). A behavioral approach to depression. In R. J. Friedman & M. M. Katz (Eds.), *The psychology of depression: Contemporary theory and research.* New York: John Wiley & Sons.

Lewinsohn, P. M. (1975). Engagement in pleasant activities and depression level. *Journal of Abnormal Psychology, 84,* 729–731.

Lewinsohn, P. M., & Amenson, C. S. (1978). Some relations between pleasant and unpleasant mood–related events and depression. *Journal of Abnormal Psychology, 87,* 644–654.

Lewinsohn, P. M., Antonuccio, D. O., Steinmetz, J. L., & Teri, L. (1984). *The coping with depression course.* Eugene, OR: Castalia Publishing Co.

Lewinsohn, P. M., & Arconad, M. (1981). Behavioral treatment of depression: A social learning approach. In J. F. Clarkin and H.I. Glazer (Eds.), *Depression: Behavioral and directive intervention strategies,* New York: Garland Press.

Lewinsohn, P. M., Sullivan, J. M., & Grosscup, S. J. (1982). Behavioral therapy: Clinical applications. In A.J. Rush (Ed.), *Short term psychotherapies for the depressed patient.* New York: Guilford Press.

Ley, P. (1977). Psychological studies of doctor patient communication. In S. Rachman (Ed.), *Contributions to medical psychology.* London: Pergamon Press.

Liberman, R. P., Lillie, F., Falloon, I., Vaughn, C., Harpin, E., Leff, J., Hutchinson, W., Ryan, P., & Stoute, M. (1978). *Social skills training for schizophrenic patients and their families.* Unpublished manuscript. Camarillo, California.

Lichtenstein, E. (1982). The smoking problem: A behavioral perspective. *Journal of Consulting and Clinical Psychology, 50,* 804–819.

Lichtenstein, E., & Glasgow, R. E. (1977). Rapid smoking: Side effects and safeguards. *Journal of Consulting and Clinical Psychology, 45,* 815–821.

Lichtenstein, E., Harris, D. E., Birchler, G. R., Wahl, J. H., & Schmahl, D. P. (1973). Comparison of rapid smoking, warm smoky air, and attention placebo in the modification of smoking behavior. *Journal of Consulting and Clinical Psychology, 40,* 92–98.

Lichtenstein, E., & Rodrigues, M. P. (1977). Long-term effects of rapid smoking treatment for dependent cigarette smokers. *Addictive Behaviors, 2,* 109–112.

Liebowitz, M. R., Fyer, A. J., Gorman, J. M., Dillon, D., Davies, S., Stein, J. M., Cohen, B. S., & Klein, D. F. (1985). Social phobia. *American Journal of Psychiatry, 142,* 947–950.

Liebowitz, M. R., Gorman, J. M., Fyer, A. J., & Klein, D. (1985). Social phobia. *Archives of General Psychiatry, 42,* 729–736.

Liebson, I., Bigelow, G., & Flamer, G. (1973). Alcoholism among methadone patients: A specific treatment method. *American Journal of Psychiatry, 130,* 483–485.

Linden, W. (1973). Practicing of meditation by school children and their levels of field dependence-independence, test anxiety, and reading achievement. *Journal of Consulting and Clinical Psychology, 41,* 139–143.

Lindner, P. G., & Blackburn, G. L. (1976). An interdisciplinary approach to obesity utilizing fasting modified by protein-sparing therapy. *Obesity and Bariatric Medicine, 5,* 198–216.

Lindsley, O. R., Skinner, B. F., & Solomon, H. C. (1953). Studies in behavior therapy. Status Report 1. Waltham, MA: Metropolitan State Hospital.

Linehan, M. M. (1977). Issues in behavioral interviewing. In J. D. Cone & R. P. Hawkins, (Eds.),

Behavioral assessment: New directions in clinical psychology. New York: Brunner/Mazel.

Lipid Research Clinics Program. (1984). The Lipid Research Clinics coronary primary prevention trial results. I. Reduction in incidence of coronary heart disease. *Journal of the American Medical Association, 251,* 351–364.

Lipinski, D., & Nelson, R. (1974). The reactivity and unreliability of self-recording. *Journal of Consulting and Clinical Psychology, 42,* 110–123.

Lobitz, G. K., & Johnson, S. M. (1975). Normal versus deviant children: A multimethod comparison. *Journal of Abnormal Child Psychology, 3,* 353–373.

Loeb, A., Beck, A. T., Diggory, J. C., & Tuthill, R. (1967). Expectancy, level of aspiration, performance, and self-evaluation in depression. In *Proceedings. 75 Annual Convention, APA.*

Loney, J., Langhorne, J. E., & Paternite, C. S. (1978). An empirical basis for subgrouping the hyperkinetic minimal brain disfunction syndrome. *Journal of Abnormal Psychology, 87,* 431–441.

LoPiccolo, J., & Daiss, S. (in press). The assessment of sexual dysfunction. In K. D. O'Leary (Ed.), *Assessment of marital discord.* Hillsdale, NJ: Erlbaum.

LoPiccolo, J., Heiman, J., Hogan, D., & Roberts, C. (1985). Effectiveness of single therapists versus co-therapy teams in sex therapy. *Journal of Consulting and Clinical Psychology, 53,* 287–294.

Lopiccolo, J., & LoPiccolo, L. (Eds.) (1978). *Handbook of sex therapy.* New York: Plenum Publishing.

Loro, A. D., Fisher, E. B., & Levenkron, J. C. (1979). Comparison of established and innovative weight-reduction treatment procedures. *Journal of Applied Behavior Analysis, 12,* 141–155.

Lovaas, O. I. (1982). Comments on self-destructive behaviors. *Analysis and Intervention in Developmental Disabilities, 2*(1), 115–124.

Lovaas, O. I. (In press). Behavioral treatment and apparent recovery in young autistic children. *Journal of Consulting and Clinical Psychology.*

Lovaas, O. I., Freitag, G., Gold, V. J., & Kassorla, I. C. (1965). Experimental studies in childhood schizophrenia: Analysis of self-destructive behavior. *Journal of Experimental Child Psychology, 2,* 67–84.

Lovaas, O. I., Koegel, R., Simmons, J. Q., & Long, J. S. (1973). Some generalization and follow-up measures on autistic children in behavior therapy. *Journal of Applied Behavior Analysis, 6,* 131–166.

Lovaas, O. I., Schreibman, L., Koegel, R. L., & Rehm, R. (1971). Selective responding by autistic children to multiple sensory input. *Journal of Abnormal Psychology, 77,* 211–222.

Lovibond, S. H. (1963). The mechanism of conditioning treatment of enuresis. *Behaviour Research and Therapy, 1,* 17–21.

Lovibond, S. H. (1964). *Conditioning and enuresis.* Oxford: Pergamon Press.

Lovibond, S. H. (1972). Critique of Turner, Young, & Rachman's conditioning treatment of enuresis. *Behaviour Research and Therapy, 10,* 287–291.

Lowery, S. (1980). Soap and booze in the afternoon. *Journal of Studies on Alcohol, 41,* 829–838.

Luborsky, L., Singer, B., & Luborsky, L. (1975). Comparative studies of psychotherapies: Is it true that everyone has won and all must have prizes? *Archives of General Psychiatry, 32,* 995–1008.

Lyerly, R., & Skipper, J. K., Jr. (1982). Differential rates of rural-urban delinquency: A social-control approach. *Criminology, 19,* 385–394.

Lyles, J. N., Burish, T. G., Krozely, M. G., & Oldham, R. K. (1982). Efficacy of relaxation training and guided imagery in reducing the aversiveness of cancer chemotherapy. *Journal of Consulting and Clinical Psychology, 50,* 509–524.

M

MacAndrew, C., & Edgerton, R. B. (1969). *Drunken comportment.* Chicago: Aldine-Atherton.

MacDonald, M. (1978). Measuring assertion: A model and method. *Behavior Therapy, 9,* 889–899.

MacFarlane, J. W., Allen, L., & Honzik, M. P. (1954). A developmental study of the behavior problems of normal children between twenty-two months and fourteen years. *University of California Publications in Child Development, Vol. II.* Berkeley: University of California Press.

MacLean, R. E. G. (1960) Imipramine hydrochloride (Tofranil) and enuresis. *American Journal of Psychiatry, 117,* 551.

Madsen, C. H. (1965). Positive reinforcement in the toilet training of a normal child: A case report. In L. P. Ullmann & L. Krasner (Eds.). *Case studies in behavior modification.* New York: Holt, Rinehart & Winston.

Madsen, C. H., Becker, W. C., Thomas, D. R., Koser, L., & Plager, E. (1968). An analysis of the reinforcing function of "sitdown" commands. In R. K. Parker (Ed.). *Readings in educational psychology.* Boston: Allyn and Bacon.

Madsen, C. H., Hoffman, M., Thomas, D. R., Koropsak, E., & Madsen, C. K. (1969). Comparisons of toilet training techniques. In D. M. Gelfand (Ed.), *Social learning in childhood.* Belmont, CA: Brooks and Cole.

Magaro, P. A., Talbott, T. A., & Glick, I. (1984). The inpatient care of chronic schizophrenia. In A. S. Bellack (Ed.). *Schizophrenia: Treatment management and rehabilitation.* Orlando, FL: Grune & Stratton.

Mahoney, K., Van Wagenen, R. K., & Meyerson, L. (1971). Toilet training of normal and retarded children. *Journal of Applied Behavior Analysis, 4,* 173–181.

Mahoney, M. J. (1974). *Cognition and behavior modification.* Cambridge, MA: Ballinger.

Mahoney, M. J. (1976). *The scientists as subject: The psychological imperative.* Cambridge, MA: Ballinger.

Mahoney, M. J. (1977). Reflections on the cognitive-learning trend in psychotherapy. *American Psychologist, 32,* 5–13.

Mahoney, M. J. (1980). Psychotherapy and the structure of personal revolutions. In M. J. Mahoney (Ed.), *Cognition and clinical science.* New York: Plenum Publishing.

Mahoney, M. J., & Arnkoff, D. (1978). Cognitive and self-control therapies. In S. L. Garfield & A. E. Bergin (Eds.), *Handbook of psychotherapy and behavior change,* (2nd ed.). New York: John Wiley & Sons.

Mahoney, M. J., & Thoresen, C. E. (1974). *Self-control: Power to the person.* Monterrey, CA: Brooks/Cole.

Maier, S. F., & Seligman, M. E. P. (1976). Learned helplessness: Theory and evidence. *Journal of Experimental Psychiatry: General, 105,* 3–46.

Maletzky, B. (1980). Self-referred versus court-referred sexually deviant patients: Success with assisted covert sensitization. *Behavior Therapy, 11,* 302–314.

Mann, J., & Rosenthal, T. (1969). Vicarious and direct counter-conditioning of test anxiety through individual and group desensitization. *Behaviour Research and Therapy, 7,* 359–367.

Mann, R. A. (1972). The behavior-therapeutic use of contingency contracting to control an adult behavior problem: Weight control. *Journal of Applied Behavior Analysis, 5,* 99–109.

Margolin, G. (1983). The reciprocal relationship between marital and child problems. In J. P. Vincent (Ed.), *Advances in family intervention, Assessment and theory,* Vol. 3. London: J. A. I. Press.

Markman, H. (1977). *A behavioral exchange model applied to the longitudinal study of couples planning to marry.* Unpublished doctoral dissertation, University of Indiana, Bloomington, IN.

Marks, I. (1971). Phobic disorders four years after treatment: A prospective follow-up. *British Journal of Psychiatry, 18,* 683–688.

Marks, I. (1981a). Behavioural concepts and treatments of neuroses. *Behavioural Psychotherapy, 9,* 137–154.

Marks, I. (1981b). Behavioural psychotherapy and the behavioural sciences. *Behavioural Psychotherapy, 9,* 285–286.

Marks, I., Bird, J., & Lindley, P. (1978). Psychiatric nurse therapy: Developments and implications. *Behavioral Psychotherapy, 6,* 25–36.

Marks, I., Hodgson, R., & Rachman, S. (1975). Treatment of chronic obsessive-compulsive neurosis by in vivo exposure. *British Journal of Psychiatry. 127,* 349–364.

Marks, I. M. (1969). *Fears and phobias.* New York: Academic Press.

Marks, I. M. (1971). Phobic disorders four years after treatment. *British Journal of Psychiatry, 118,* 683–688.

Marks, I. M. (1978). Behavioral psychotherapy of adult neurosis. In S. L. Garfield & A. E. Bergin (Eds.), *Handbook of psychotherapy and behavior change* (2nd. ed.). New York: John Wiley & Sons.

Marks, I. M. (1981). *Cure and care of the neuroses.* New York: John Wiley & Sons.

Marks, I. M., Gelder, M. G., & Bancroft, J. (1970). Sexual deviants two years after aversion. *British Journal of Psychiatry, 117,* 173–185.

Marks, I. M., Hallam, R. S., Connolly, J., & Philpott, R. (1977). *Nursing in behavioural therapy.* London: The Royal College of Nursing of the United Kingdom.

Marks, M., Gray, S., Cohen, D., Hill, R., Mawson, D., Ramm, E., & Stern, R. S. (1983). Imipramine and brief therapist-aided exposure in agoraphobics having self-exposure homework. *Archives of General Psychiatry, 40,* 153–162.

Marlatt, G. A. (1978). Craving for alcohol, loss of control, and relapse: A cognitive-behavioral analysis. In P. E. Nathan, G. A. Marlatt, & T. Loberg (Eds.), *Alcoholism: New directions in behavioral research and treatment.* New York: Plenum Publishing.

Marlatt, G. A. (1983). The controlled-drinking controversy: A commentary. *American Psychologist, 38,* 1097–1110.

Marlatt, G. A. (1984). *Alcohol, the magic elixir: Stress, expectancy, and the transformation of emotional states.* Unpublished manuscript, University of Washington.

Marlatt, G. A. (1985). Personal communication.

Marlatt, G. A., Demming, B., & Reid, J. (1973). Loss of control drinking in alcoholics. *Journal of Abnormal Psychology, 81,* 233–241.

Marlatt, G. A., & Gordon, J. (Eds.) (1980). Determinants of relapse: Implications for the maintenance of behavior change. In P. Davidson & S. Davidson (Eds.), *Behavioral medicine.* New York: Brunner/Mazel.

Marlatt, G. A., & Gordon, J. (1985). *Relapse prevention: Maintenance strategies in addictive behavior change.* New York: Guilford Press.

Marlatt, G. A., Kosturn, C. F., & Lang, A. R. (1975). Provocation to anger and opportunity for retaliation as determinants of alcohol consumption in social drinkers. *Journal of Abnormal Psychology, 84,* 652–659.

Marlatt, G. A. and Marques, J. K. (1977). Meditation, self-control, and alcohol use. In R. B. Stuart (Ed.), *Self-management: Strategies, Techniques, and Results.* New York: Brunner/Mazel.

Marlatt, G. A., & Rohsenow, D. (1980). Cognitive processes in alcohol use: Expectancy and the balanced placebo design. In N. K. Mello (Ed.), *Advances in substance abuse* (Vol. 1). Greenwich, Conn: JAI Press.

Marmor, J. (1973). *Psychiatry in transition.* New York: Brunner/Mazel.

Marshall, W. L., Gauthier, J., Christie, M., Currie, D., & Gordon, P. (1977). Flooding therapy: effectiveness, stimulus characteristics, and the value of brief in vivo exposure. *Behaviour Research and Therapy, 15,* 79–87.

Marshall, W. L., Presse, L., & Andrews, W. R. (1976). A self-administered program for public speaking anxiety. *Behaviour Research and Therapy, 14,* 33–39.

Martin, J. E., & Dubbert, P. M. (1985). Exercise in hypertension. *Annals of Behavioral Medicine, 7,* 13–18.

Martin, J. E., Dubbert, P. M., Katell, A. D.,

Thompson, J. K., Racqynski, J. R., Lake, M., Smith, P. O., & Webster, J. S. (1984). Behavioral control of exercise in sedentary adults: Studies 1–6. *Journal of Consulting and Clinical Psychology, 52,* 795–811.

Martin, S. E. (1981). Restitution and community service sentences: Promising sentencing alternative or passing fad. In S. E. Martin, L. B. Sechrest, & R. Redner (Eds.), *New directions in the rehabilitation of criminal offenders.* Washington, DC: National Academy Press.

Masserman, J. H. (1943). *Behavior and neurosis.* Chicago: University of Chicago Press.

Masters, W. H., & Johnson, V. E. (1970). *Human sexual inadequacy.* Boston: Little, Brown & Company.

Masters, W. H., & Johnson, V. E. (1979). *Homosexuality in perspective.* Boston: Little, Brown & Company.

Matarazzo, J. D. (1982). Behavioral health's challenge to academic, scientific, and professional psychology. *American Psychologist, 37,* 1–14.

Matarazzo, J. (1986). Computerized clinical psychology tests interpretations. *American Psychologist, 41,* 14–24.

Mathews, A. M., Bancroft, J., Whitehead, A., Hackmann, A., Julier, D., Bancroft, J., Gath, D., & Shaw, P. (1976). The behavioural treatment of sexual inadequacy: A comparative study. *Behaviour Research and Therapy, 14,* 427–436.

Mathews, A. M., Gelder, M. G., & Johnston, D. W. (1981). *Agoraphobia: Nature and treatment.* New York: Guilford Press.

Mathews, A. M., Johnston, D. W., Lancashire, M., Munby, M., Shaw, P. M., & Gelder, M. G. (1976). Imaginal flooding and exposure to real phobic situations: Treatment outcome with agoraphobic patients. *British Journal of Psychiatry, 129,* 362–371.

Mathews, A. M., Teasdale, J., Munby, M., Johnston, D., & Shaw, P. (1977). A home based treatment program for agoraphobia. *Behavior Therapy, 8,* 915–924.

Matson, J. L., & Ollendick, T. H. (1977). Issues in toilet training normal children. *Behavior Therapy, 8,* 549–553.

Matthews, K. A., & Haynes, S. G. (1986). Type A behavior pattern and coronary risk: Update and critical evaluation. *American Journal of Epidemiology, 123,* 923–960.

Matison, R., Cantwell, D. P., Russell, A. T., & Will, L. (1979). A comparison of DSM-II and

DSM-III in the diagnosis of childhood psychiatric disorders. II. Interrater agreement. *Archives of General Psychiatry, 36,* 1217–1222.

Mavissakalian, M., & Michelson, L. (1983). Self-directed in vivo exposure practice in behavioral and pharmacological treatments of agoraphobia. *Behavior Therapy, 14,* 506–519.

Mavissakalian, M., Michelson, L., & Dealy, R. S. (1983). Pharmacological treatment of agoraphobia: Imipramine versus imipramine with programmed practice. *British Journal of Psychiatry, 143,* 348–355.

Mavissakalian, M., & Perel, J. (1985). Imipramine in the treatment of agoraphobia: Dose-response relationships. *American Journal of Psychiatry, 142,* 1032–1036.

May, J. G., Risley, T. R., Twardosz, S., Friedman, P., Bijou, S. W., Wexler, D., et al. (1975). Guidelines for the use of behavioral procedures in state programs for retarded persons. *M.R. Research, 1.*

McAlister, A., Perry, C., Killen, J., Slinkard, L., & Maccoby, N. (1980). Pilot study of smoking, alcohol, and drug abuse prevention. *American Journal of Public Health, 70,* 719–721.

McCord, J., & McCord, W. (1958). The effects of parental role models on criminality. *Journal of Social Issues, 14,* 66–74.

McCrae, R. R., & Costa, P. T., Jr. (1983). Social desirability scales: More substance than style. *Journal of Consulting and Clinical Psychology, 51,* 882–888.

McFall, R. M. (1970). Effects of self-monitoring on normal smoking behavior. *Journal of Consulting and Clinical Psychology, 35,* 135–142.

McFall, R. M. (1978). Smoking-cessation research. *Journal of Consulting and Clinical Psychology, 46,* 703–712.

McFall, R. M., & Lillesand, D. B. (1971). Behavior rehearsal with modeling and coaching in assertive training. *Journal of Abnormal Psychology, 77,* 313–323.

McGeer, E., & McGeer, P. L. (1980). Neurotransmitter metabolism in the aging brain. In R. D. Terry & S. Gershion (Eds.). *Aging* (Vol. 3). New York: Raven Press.

McIntyre, K., Lichtenstein, E., & Mermelstein, R. (1983). Self-efficacy and relapse in smoking cessation: A replication and extension. *Journal of Consulting and Clinical Psychology, 51,* 632–633.

McKenney, J. M. (1981). Methods of modifying compliance behavior in hypertensive patients. *Drug Intelligence and Clinical Pharmacy, 15,* 8–16.

McLean, P. D., & Hastigan, A. R. (1979). Clinical depression: Comparative efficacy of outpatient treatments. *Journal of Consulting and Clinical Psychology, 47,* 818–836.

McMullen, S., & Rosen, R. C. (1979). Self-administered masturbation training in the treatment of primary orgasmic dysfunction. *Journal of Consulting and Clinical Psychology, 47,* 912–918.

McPherson, F. M., Brougham, L., & McLaren, L. (1980). Maintenance of improvements in agoraphobic patients treated by behavioural methods in a four year follow-up. *Behaviour Research and Therapy, 18,* 150–152.

Medical Research Council of England (1965). Clinical trial of the treatment of depressive illness. *British Medical Journal, 1,* 881–886.

Mednick, S. A., Cudeck, J. J., Griffith, J., Talovic, S. A., & Schulsinger, F. (1984). The Danish high-risk project: Recent methods and findings. In N. F. Watt, E. J. Anthony, L. C. Wynne, & J. E. Rolf (Eds.), *Children at risk for schizophrenia: A longitudinal perspective.* Cambridge, MA: Cambridge University Press.

Mednick, S. A., & Schulsinger, F. (1968). Some premorbid characteristics related to breakdown in children with schizophrenic mothers. *Journal of Psychiatric Research* (Supplement 1), *6,* 354–362.

Mednick, S. A., & Schulsinger, F. (1972). Studies of children at high risk for schizophrenia. In S. R. Dean (Ed.), *Schizophrenia: The first ten dean award lectures.* New York: M.S.S. Information Corporation.

Meichenbaum, D. (1971). Examination of model characteristics in reducing avoidance behavior. *Journal of Personality and Social Psychology, 17,* 298–307.

Meichenbaum, D. (1976). Cognitive factors in biofeedback therapy. *Biofeedback and self-regulation. 1,* 201–215.

Meichenbaum, D. (1977). *Cognitive-behavior modification.* New York: Plenum Publishing.

Meichenbaum, D., & Asarnouw, J. (1979). Cognitive-behavioral modification and metacognitive development: Implications for the classroom. In P. C. Kendall & S. D. Hollon (Eds.), *Cognitive-behavioral interventions: Theory, research, and procedures.* New York: Academic Press.

Meichenbaum, D., & Cameron, R. (1982). Cognitive behavior modification: Current issues. In G. T. Wilson & C. M. Franks (Eds.), *Contem-*

porary behavior therapy: Conceptual and empirical foundations. New York: Guilford Press.

Meichenbaum, D., & Gilmore, J. (1982). Resistance: From a cognitive-behavioral perspective. In Wachtel (Ed.), *Resistance: Psychodynamic and behavioral approaches.* New York: Plenum Publishing.

Melamed, B. G. (1979). Behavioral approaches to fear in dental settings. In M. Hersen, R. M. Eisler, & P. M. Miller (Eds.), *Progress in behavior modification* (Vol. 7). New York: Academic Press.

Melamed, B. G., & Siegel, L. J. (1975). Reduction of anxiety in children facing hospitalization and surgery by use of filmed modeling. *Journal of Consulting and Clinical Psychology, 43,* 511–521.

Melamed, B. G., & Siegel, L. J. (1980). *Behavioral medicine.* New York: Springer.

Mello, N. (1975). A semantic aspect of alcoholism. In H. D. Cappell & A. E. LeBlanc (Eds.), *Biological and behavioral approaches to drug dependence.* Toronto: Addiction Research Foundation.

Mendelson, J. H., & Mello, N. K. (1976). Behavioral and biochemical interrelations in alcoholism. In W. P. Creger, C. H. Coggins, & E. W. Hancock (Eds.), *Annual review of medicine.* Palo Alto, CA: Annual Reviews Inc.

Mercatoris, M., & Craighead, W. E. (1974). The effects of nonparticipant observation on teacher and pupil classroom behavior. *Journal of Educational Psychology, 66,* 512–519.

Mermelstein, R., Lichtenstein, E., & McIntyre, K. (1983). Partner support and relapse in smoking-cessation programs. *Journal of Consulting and Clinical Psychology, 51,* 465–466.

Metropolitan Life Insurance. (1960). Frequency of overweight and underweight. *Statistical Bulletin, 41,* 4–7.

Meyer, A. (1957). *Psychobiology: A science of man.* E. E. Winters & A. M. Bowers (Eds.). Springfield, IL: Thomas.

Meyer, A., Nash, J., McAlister, A., Maccoby, N., & Farquhar, J. (1980). Skills training in a cardiovascular health education campaign. *Journal of Consulting and Clinical Psychology, 48,* 129–142.

Meyer, J. K., & Reter, D. J. (1979). Sex reassignment. *Archives of General Psychiatry, 36,* 1010–1015.

Meyer, V., Levy, R., & Schnurer, A. (1974). The behavioural treatment of obsessive-compulsive disorder. In H. R. Beech (Ed.), *Obsessional states.* London: Methuen.

Milich, R. E., & Pelham, W. E. (1985). Effects of sugar ingestion on the classroom and playgroup behavior of attention deficit disorder boys. *Journal of Consulting and Clinical Psychology, 54.*

Miller, L. C., Barrett, C. L., Hampe, E., & Noble, H. (1972). Comparison of reciprocal inhibition, psychotherapy, and waiting list control for phobic children. *Journal of Abnormal Psychology, 79,* 269–279.

Miller, N. E. (1951). Learnable drives and rewards. In S. S. Stevens (Ed.), *Handbook of experimental psychology.* New York: John Wiley & Sons.

Miller, N. E. (1969). Learning of visceral and glandular responses. *Sciences, 163,* 434–445.

Miller, P., & Ingham, J. G. (1976). Friends, confidants, and symptoms. *Social Psychiatry, 11,* 51–58.

Miller, P., & Sims, K. (1981). Evaluation and component analysis of a comprehensive weight control program. *International Journal of Obesity, 5,* 57–66.

Miller, W. R. (1982). Treating problem drinkers: What works? *The Behavior Therapist, 5,* 15–18.

Miller, W. R. (1983). Controlled drinking. *Journal of Studies on Alcohol, 44,* 68–83.

Miller, W. R., & Baca, L. M. (1983). Two-year follow-up of bibliotherapy and therapist-directed controlled drinking training for problem drinkers. *Behavior Therapy, 14,* 441–448.

Miller, W. R., & Hester, R. K. (1980). Treating the problem drinkers: Modern approaches. In W. R. Miller (Ed.), *The Addictive Behaviors.* Oxford: Pergamon.

Miller, W. R., Taylor, C. A., & West, J. C. (1980). Focused versus broad-spectrum behavior therapy for problem drinkers. *Journal of Consulting and Clinical Psychology, 48,* 590–601.

Miller, W. R., & Taylor, C. A. (1980). Relative effectiveness of bibliotherapy, individual and group self-control training in the treatment of problem drinkers. *Addictive Behaviors, 5,* 13–24.

Mills, H. L., Agras, W. S., Barlow, D. H., & Mills, J. R. (1973). Compulsive rituals treated by response prevention. *Archives of General Psychiatry, 28,* 524–529.

Mindham, R. H. S. (1979). Tricyclic antidepressants and amine precursors. In E. S. Paykel (Ed.), *Handbook of Affective Disorders.* New York: Guilford Press.

Mineka, S., Davidson, M., Cook, M., & Keir,

R.   (1984). Observational conditioning of snake fear in rhesus monkeys. *Journal of Abnormal Psychology, 93,* 355–372.

Mintz, J.   (1983). Integrating research evidence. *Journal of Consulting and Clinical Psychology, 51,* 71–75.

Mirsky, A. F., Silberman, E. K., Latz, A., & Nagler, S.   (1985). Adult outcomes of high-risk children: Differential effects of town or kibbutz rearing. *Schizophrenia Bulletin, 11,* 150–154.

Mischel, W.   (1968). *Personality and assessment.* New York: John Wiley & Sons.

Mischel, W.   (1973). Toward a cognitive social learning reconceptualization of personality. *Psychological Review, 80,* 252–283.

Mischel, W.   (1974). Processes in the delay of gratification. In L. Berkowitz (Ed.), *Advances in experimental social psychology* (Vol. 7). New York: Academic Press.

Mischel, W.   (1981). A cognitive social learning approach to assessment. In T. V. Merluzzi, C. R. Glass, & M. Genest (Eds.). *Cognitive assessment.* New York: Guilford Press.

Mischel, W., & Bentler, P.   (1960). *The ability of persons to predict their own behavior.* Unpublished manuscript. Stanford University, Stanford, CA.

Mischel, W., Ebbesen, E. B., & Zeiss, A.   (1972). Comparative effects of the reward stimulus and its cognitive presentation in voluntary delay. *Journal of Personality and Social Psychology, 21,* 204–218.

Mischel, W., & Peake, P. K.   (1982). Beyond *deja vu* in the search for cross situational consistency. *Psychological Review, 89,* 730–755.

Mitchell, C., & Stuart, R.   (1984). Effect of self-efficacy on dropout from obesity treatment. *Journal of Consulting and Clinical Psychology, 52,* 1100–1101.

Moos, R. H., & Finney, J. W.   (1983). The expanding scope of alcoholism treatment evaluation. *American Psychologist, 38,* 1036-1044.

Moos, R. H., Finney, J. W., & Chan, D. A.   (1981). The process of recovery from alcoholism. *Journal of Studies on Alcohol, 42,* 383–402.

Moos, R., & MacIntosh, S.   (1970). Multivariate study of the patient-therapist system. *Journal of Consulting and Clinical Psychology, 35,* 298–307.

Moreno, J. L.   (1946). *Psychodrama.* Beacon, NY: Beacon House.

Morrison, R. L., & Bellack, A. S.   (1984). Social skills training. In A. S. Bellack (Ed.), *Schizophrenia: treatment, Management and rehabilitation.* New York: Grune & Stratton.

Morrison, J. R., & Stewart, M. A.   (1973). The psychiatric status of the legal families of adopted hyperactive children. *Archives of General Psychiatry, 28,* 888–891.

Moss, R., & Prue, D.   (1982). Research on nicotine regulation. *Behavior Therapy, 13,* 31–46.

Mowrer, O. H.   (1939). A stimulus-response analysis of anxiety and its role as a reinforcing agent. *Psychological Review, 46,* 553–565.

Mowrer, O. H.   (1947). On the dual nature of learning—a reinterpretation of "conditioning" and "problem-solving." *Harvard Educational Review, 17,* 102–148.

Mowrer, O. H.   (1980). Enuresis: The beginning work: What really happened. *Journal of the History of the Behavioral Sciences, 16,* 25–30.

Mowrer, O. H., & Mowrer, W. M.   (1938). Enuresis: A method for its study and treatment. *American Journal of Orthopsychiatry, 8,* 436–459.

Moyer, K. E.   (1976). *The psychobiology of aggression.* New York: Harper & Row.

Muellner, S. R.   (1960). Development of urinary control in children: A new concept in cause, prevention and treatment of primary enuresis. *Journal of Urology, 84,* 714–716.

Multiple Risk Factor Intervention Trial Research Group.   (1982). Multiple risk factor intervention trial: Risk factor changes and mortality results. *Journal of the American Medical Association, 248,* 1465–1477.

Munby, M., & Johnston, D. W.   (1980). Agoraphobia: The long-term follow-up of behavioural treatment. *British Journal of Psychiatry, 137,* 418–427.

Munjack, D., Cristol, A., Goldstein, A., Phillips, D., Goldberg, A., Whipple, K., Staples, F., & Kanno, P.   (1976). Behavioural treatment of orgasmic dysfunction: A controlled study. *British Journal of Psychiatry, 129,* 497–502.

N

Nathan, P. E.   (1983). Failures in prevention. *American Psychologist, 38,* 459–467.

Nathan, P. E., & O'Brien, J. S.   (1971). An experimental analysis of the behavior of alcoholics and nonalcoholics during prolonged experimental drinking. *Behavior Therapy, 2,* 455–476.

National Institute of Health Consensus Conference on Obesity (1985). Consensus conference statement. *Annals of Internal Medicine, 103,* 1073–1077.

Neale, D. H. (1963). Behavior therapy and encopresis in children. *Behavior Research and Therapy, 1,* 139–149.

Neale, J. M. & Oltmanns, T. F. (1980). *Schizophrenia.* New York: John Wiley & Sons.

Neaton, J. D., Broste, S., Cohen, L., Fishman, E., Kjelsberg, M. D., & Schoenberger, J. (1981). The multiple risk factor intervention trial. VII. A comparison of changes between two study groups. *Preventive Medicine, 11,* 13–28.

Nedelman, D., & Sulzbacher, S. I. (1972). Dicky at thirteen years of age: A long term success following early application of operant conditioning procedures. In G. Semb (Ed.), *Behavior analysis and education.* Lawrence, KS: Follow-through Project.

Neidig, P. H. (1985). Domestic violence in the military. Part II: The impact of high levels of work-related stress on family functioning. *Military Family, 5,* 3–5.

Nelson, R. E., & Craighead, W. E. (1977). Selective recall of positive and negative feedback, self-control behaviors, and depression. *Journal of Abnormal Psychology, 86,* 379–388.

Nelson, R. O., Kapust, J. A., & Dorsey, B. L. (1978). Minimal reactivity of overt classroom observations on student and teacher behavior. *Behavior Therapy, 9,* 695–702.

Nemetz, G. H., Craig, K. D., & Reith, G. (1978). Treatment of female sexual dysfunction through symbolic modeling. *Journal of Consulting and Clinical Psychology, 46,* 62–73.

Nettelbeck, T., & Langeluddecke, P. (1979). Dry-bed training without an enuresis machine. *Behaviour Research and Therapy, 17,* 403–404.

Newsday, "Happily Unmarried", March 15, 1976, p. 7.

Nies, A., & Robinson, D. L. (1980). Monamine oxidase inhibitors. In E. S. Paykel (Ed.), *Handbook of affective disorders.* New York: Guilford Press.

Nietzel, M. T. (1979). *Crime and its modification: A social learning perspective.* New York: Pergamon.

Nisbett, R., & Ross, L. (1980). *Human inference: Strategies and shortcomings of social judgement.* Englewood Cliffs, NJ: Prentice-Hall.

Nisbett, R., & Wilson, T. (1977). Telling more than we can know: Verbal reports on mental processes. *Psychological Review, 84,* 231–259.

Norman, D. K., & Herzog, D. B. (1983). Bulimia, anorexia nervosa, and anorexia nervosa with bulimia: A comparative analysis of MMPI profiles. *International Journal of Eating Disorders, 2,* 43–52.

Norton, A. J. (1976, January 15). United States Census Bureau, personal communication.

Norton, G. R., Allen, G. E., & Hilton, J. (1983). The social validity of treatments for agoraphobia. *Behaviour Research and Therapy, 21,* 393–399.

Nunn, J. D., Stevenson, R. J., & Whalan, G. (1984). Selective memory effects in agoraphobic patients. *British Journal of Clinical Psychology, 23,* 195–201.

O

Obler, M. (1973). Systematic desensitization in sexual disorders. *Journal of Behavior Therapy and Experimental Psychiatry, 4,* 93–101.

Ockene, J. K., Benfari, R. C., Nutall, R. L., Hurwitz, I., & Ockene, I. S. (1982). Relationship of psychosocial factors to smoking behavior change in an intervention program. *Preventive Medicine, 11,* 13–28.

O'Connor, R. D. (1969). Modification of social withdrawal through symbolic modeling. *Journal of Applied Behavior Analysis, 2,* 15–22.

O'Connor, R. D. (1972). The relative efficacy of modeling, shaping, and combined procedures. *Journal of Abnormal Psychology, 79,* 327–334.

Offer, D., Sabshin, M., & Marcus, D. (1965). Clinical evaluation of normal adolescents. *American Journal of Psychiatry, 121,* 864–872.

O'Hara, M. W., & Rehm, L. P. (1979). Self-monitoring, activity levels, and mood in the development and maintenance of depression. *Journal of Abnormal Psychology, 88,* 450–453.

O'Leary, K. D. (1978). Token reinforcement programs in the classroom. In A. C. Catania & T. A. Brigham (Eds.), *Handbook of applied behavior analysis: Social and instructional processes.* New York: Irvington Publishers.

O'Leary, K. D. (1980). Pills or skills for hyperactive children. *Journal of Applied Behavior Analysis, 13,* 191–204.

O'Leary, K. D. (1984a). The image of behavior therapy: It is time to take a stand. *Behavior Therapy, 15,* 219–233.

O'Leary, K. D. (1984b). Marital discord and children: Problems, strategies, methodologies, and results. In A. Doyle, D. Gold, & D. S. Moscowitz (Eds.), *Children in families under stress. New directions for child development*, no. 24. San Francisco: Jossey–Bass.

O'Leary, K. D., (in press). Physical aggression between spouses: A social learning theory perspective. In V. B. Van Hasselt, R. L. Morrison, A. S. Bellack, & M. Hersen (Eds.), *Handbook of Family Violence*. New York: Plenum Publishing.

O'Leary, K. D., & Arias, I. (1983). The influence of marital therapy on sexual satisfaction. *Journal of Sex and Marital Therapy, 9,* 171–181.

O'Leary, K. D., Arias, I., Rosenbaum, A., & Barling, J. (1986). *Premarital physical aggression.* Unpublished manuscript.

O'Leary, K. D., Becker, W. C., Evans, M. B., & Saudargas, R. A. (1969). A token reinforcement program in a public school: A replication and systematic analysis. *Journal of Applied Behavior Analysis, 2,* 3–13.

O'Leary, K. D., & Borkovec, T. (1978). Conceptual, methodological, and ethical problems of placebo groups in psychotherapeutic research. *American Psychologist, 33,* 821–830.

O'Leary, K. D., & Curley, A. (in press). Assertion and family violence: Correlates of spouse abuse. *Journal of Marital and Family Therapy. 12,* 281–290.

O'Leary, K. D., & Emery, R. (1982). Children's perceptions of marital discord and behavior problems of boys and girls. *Journal of Abnormal Child Psychology, 10,* 11–24.

O'Leary, K. D., & Johnson, S. B. (1979). Psychological assessment. In H. C. Quay & J. S. Werry (Eds.), *Psychopathological disorders of children.* (2nd ed.). New York: John Wiley & Sons.

O'Leary, K. D., & Johnson, S. B. (1986). Assessment and assessment of change. In H. C. Quay & J. S. Werry (Eds.), *Psychopathological disorders of children,* (3rd ed.). New York: John Wiley & Sons.

O'Leary, K. D., Kent, R. N., & Kanowitz, J. (1975). Shaping data collection congruent with experimental hypotheses. *Journal of Applied Behavior Analysis, 1,* 92–100.

O'Leary, K. D., Pelham, W. E., Rosenbaum, A., & Price, G. H. (1976). Behavioral treatment of hyperkinetic children. *Clinical Pediatrics, 15,* 510–515.

O'Leary, K. D., Poulos, R., & Devine, V. T. (1972). Tangible reinforcers: Bonuses or bribes? *Journal of Consulting and Clinical Psychology, 38,* 1–8.

O'Leary, K. D., & Turkewitz, H. (1978). Methodological errors in marital and child treatment research. *Journal of Consulting and Clinical Psychology, 46,* 747–758.

O'Leary, K. D., Turkewitz, H., & Tafel, S. (1973). Parent and therapist evaluation of behavior therapy in a child psychological clinic. *Journal of Consulting and Clinical Psychology, 41,* 289–293.

O'Leary, K. D., & Wilson, G. T. (1975). *Behavior therapy: Application and outcome* (1st ed.). Englewood Cliffs, NJ: Prentice-Hall.

O'Leary, S. G. (1985, November). *It is time to stop avoiding punishment.* Invited address: Association for Advancement of Behavior Therapy, Houston, TX.

O'Leary, S. G., & Dubey, D. R. (1979). Applications of self-control procedures by children: A review. *Journal of Applied Behavior Analysis, 12,* 449–465.

O'Leary, S. G., & Pelham, W. E. (1978). Behavioral therapy and withdrawal of stimulant medication with hyperactive children. *Pediatrics, 61,* 211–217.

O'Leary, S. G., & Steen, P. L. (1982). Subcategorizing hyperactivity: The Stony Brook scale. *Journal of Consulting and Clinical Psychology, 50,* 426–432.

Olson, R. P., Ganley, R., Devine, V., & Dorsey, G. (1981). Long-term effects of behavioral versus insight-oriented therapy with inpatient alcoholics. *Journal of Consulting and Clinical Psychology, 49,* 866–877.

Oltmanns, T. F., Broderick, J. E., & O'Leary, K.D. (1977). Marital adjustment and the efficacy of behavior therapy with children. *Journal of Consulting and Clinical Psychology, 45*(5), 724–729.

Ost, L. G., & Gotestam, K. (1976). Behavioral and pharmacological treatments for obesity: An experimental comparison. *Addictive Behaviors, 1,* 331–338.

Ost, L. G., & Hugdahl, K. (1981).Acquisition of phobias and anxiety response patterns in clinical patients. *Behaviour Research and Therapy, 19,* 439–447.

Ost, L. G., & Hugdahl, K. (1983). Acquisition of agoraphobia, mode of onset and anxiety response patterns. *Behaviour Research and Therapy, 21,* 623–631.

Ost, L. G., Jerremalm, A., & Johansson, J. (1981). Individual response patterns and the effects of different behavioral methods in the treatment of social phobia. *Behaviour Research and Therapy, 19,* 1–16.

Ost, L. G., Jerremalm, A., & Jansson, L. (1984). Individual response patterns and the effects of different behavioral methods in the treatment of agoraphobia. *Behaviour Research and Therapy, 22,* 697–708.

Ost, L. G., Lindahl, I. L., Sterner, U., & Jerremalm, A. (1984). Exposure in vivo vs. applied relaxation in the treatment of blood phobia. *Behaviour Research and Therapy, 22,* 205–216.

P

Paschalis, A. Ph., Kimmel, H. D., & Kimmel, E. (1972). Further study of diurnal instrumental conditioning in the treatment of enuresis nocturna. *Journal of Behavior Therapy and Experimental Psychiatry, 3,* 253–256.

Patterson, G. R. (1963). *State institutions as teaching machines for delinquent behavior.* Unpublished manuscript, University of Oregon.

Patterson, G. R. (1974). Interventions for boys with conduct problems: Multiple settings, treatments, and criteria. *Journal of Consulting and Clinical Psychology, 42,* 471–481.

Patterson, G. R. (1982). *Coercive family processes.* Eugene, OR: Castaba Publishing Co.

Patterson, G. R., & Bank, L. (1986). Bootstrapping your way in the nomalogical thicket. *Behavioral Assessment, 8,* 49–73.

Patterson, G. R., Cobb, J. A. & Ray, R. S. (1972). Direct intervention in the classroom: A set of procedures for the aggressive child. In E. N. Clark, D. R. Evans, & L. A. Hamerlynck (Eds.). *Implementing Behavioral Programs in Educational and Clinical Settings.* Champaign, IL: Research Press.

Patterson, G. R., & Fleischman, M. J. (1979). Maintenance of treatment effects: Some considerations concerning family systems and follow-up data. *Behavior Therapy, 10,* 168–85.

Patterson, G. R., & Gullion, M. E. (1968). *Living with children.* Champaign, IL: Research Press.

Patterson, G. R., Littman, R. A., & Bricker, W. (1967). Assertive behavior in children: A step toward a theory of aggression. *Monographs for the Society for Research in Child Development, 32,* 1–43.

Patterson, G. R., Ludwig, M., & Sonoda, B. (1961). *Reinforcement of aggression in children.* Unpublished manuscript, University of Oregon.

Patterson, G. R., & Reid, J. B. (1970). Reciprocity and coercion: Two facets of social systems. In C. Neuringer & J. Michael (Eds.), *Behavior Modification in Clinical Psychology.* New York: Appleton-Century-Crofts.

Patterson, G. R., & Reid, J. B. (1973). Intervention for families of aggressive boys: A replication study. *Behaviour Research and Therapy, 11,* 383–394.

Paul, G. L. (1966). *Insight versus desensitization in psychotherapy.* Stanford: Stanford University Press.

Paul, G. L. (1967). Insight vs. desensitization in psychotherapy two years after termination. *Journal of Consulting Psychology, 31,* 333–348.

Paul, G. L. (1969). Behavior modification research: Design and tactics. In C. M. Franks (Ed.), *Behavior therapy: Appraisal and status.* New York: McGraw-Hill.

Paul, G. L. (1985). Can pregnancy be a placebo effect? Terminology, designs, and conclusions in the study of psychosocial and pharmacological treatments of behavioral disorders. In L. White, B. Tursky, & G. F. Schwartz (Eds.), *Placebo: Clinical Phenomena and New Insights.* New York: Guilford Press.

Paul, G. L., & Lentz, R. J. (1978). *Psychosocial treatment of chronic mental patients: (Milieu vs. social learning programs).* Cambridge, MA: Harvard University Press.

Paul, G. L., & Trimble, R. W. (1970). Recorded versus "live" relaxation training and hypnotic suggestion: Comparative effectiveness for reducing physiological arousal and inhibiting stress response. *Behavior Therapy, 1,* 285–302.

Paykel, E. S., Emms, E. M., Fletcher, J., & Rassaby, E. S. (1980). Life events and social support in puerperal depression. *British Journal of Psychiatry, 136,* 339–346.

Paykel, E. S., Myers, J. K., Dienelt, M. N., Klerman, G. L., Lindenthal, J. J., & Pepper, M. P. (1969). Life events and depression. *Archives of General Psychiatry, 21,* 753–760.

Pearce, J. W., LeBow, M., & Orchard, J. (1981). Role of spouse involvement in the behavioral treatment of overweight women. *Journal of Consulting and Clinical Psychology, 49,* 236–244.

Pendery, M., Maltzman, I., & West, L. J. (1982). Controlled drinking by alcoholics? New findings and a reevaluation of a major affirmative study. *Science, 217,* 169–174.

Penick, S., Fillon, R., Fox, S., & Stunkard, A. J. (1971). Behavior modification in the treatment of obesity. *Psychosomatic Medicine, 33,* 49–55.

Peplau, L. A., Rubin, Z., & Hill, C. T. (1977). Sexual intimacy in dating relationships. *The Journal of Social Issues, 33,* 86–109.

Perri, M. G., Shapiro, R. M., Ludwig, W. W., Twentyman, C. T., & McAdoo, W. G. (1984). Maintenance strategies for the treatment of obesity: An evaluation of relapse prevention training and posttreatment contact by mail and telephone. *Journal of Consulting and Clinical Psychology, 52,* 404–413.

Peterson, C., & Seligman, M. E. P. (1984). Causal explanations as a risk factor for depression: Theory and evidence. *Psychological Review, 91,* 347–374.

Peterson, D. R., Eaton, M. M., Levine, A. R., & Snepp, F. P. (1980). Development of doctor of psychology programs and experiences of graduates through 1980. *The Placebo: Clinical phenomena and new insights.* New York: Guilford Press.

Peterson, D. R., & London, P. (1964). Neobehaviorist psychotherapy: quasi hypnotic suggestion and multiple reinforcement in the treatment of a case of post infantile dyscopresis. *Psychological Record, 14,* 469–474.

Peterson, D. R., Quay, H. C., & Cameron, G. R. (1959). Personality and background factors in juvenile delinquency as inferred from questionnaire reports. *Journal of Consulting and Clinical Psychology, 23,* 395–399.

Philips, C. (1977). The modification of tension headache pain using EMG biofeedback. *Behaviour Research and Therapy, 15,* 119–129.

Philips, C. (1978). Tension headache: Theoretical problems. *Behaviour Research and Therapy, 16,* 249–262.

Philips, C., & Hunter, M. (1981). The treatment of tension headache—I. Muscular abnormality in biofeedback. *Behaviour Research and Therapy, 19,* 485–498.

Phillips, D., & Wolpe, S. (1981). Multiple behavioral techniques in severe separation anxiety of a twelve-year-old. *Journal of Behavior Therapy and Experimental Psychiatry, 12,* 329–332.

Phillips, E. L. (1968). Achievement Place: Token reinforcement procedures in a home-style rehabilitation setting for "predelinquent" boys. *Journal of Applied Behavior Analysis, 1,* 213–223.

Phillips, E. L., Phillips, E. A., Fixsen, D. L., &

Wolf, M. M. (1971). Achievement Place: Modification of the behaviors of predelinquent boys within a token economy. *Journal of Applied Behavior Analysis, 4,* 45–59.

Phillips, E. L., Wolf, M. M., & Fixsen, D. L. (1973). Achievement Place: Development of the elected manager system. *Journal of Applied Behavior Analysis, 6,* 541–561.

Physicians Desk Reference. (1984). Oradell, NJ: Medical Economics Company.

Pickering, T. G. (1982). Nonpharmacologic methods of treatment of hypertension: Promising but unproved. *Cardiovascular Reviews and Reports, 3,* 82–88.

Piggott, L. R. (1979). Overview of selected basic research in autism. *Journal of Autism and Developmental Disorders, 9,* 199–218.

Piotrowski, C., & Keller, J. W. (1984). Attitudes toward clinical assessment by members of the AABT. *Psychological Reports, 55,* 831–838.

Pokalow, R., & Doctor, R. (1974). A behavioral modification program for adult drug offenders. *Journal of Research in Crime and Delinquency, 11,* 63–69.

Polich, J. M., Armor, D. J., & Braiker, H. B. (1981). *The course of alcoholism: Four years after treatment.* New York: John Wiley & Sons.

Polivy, J., & Herman, C. P. (1985). Dieting and bingeing: A causal analysis. *American Psychologist, 40,* 193–201.

Polivy, J., Herman, C. P., Olmsted, M., & Jazwinski, C. (1984). Restraint and binge eating. In R. C. Hawkins, W. J. Fremouw, & P. Clement (Eds.). *The Binge-purge Syndrome.* New York: Springer.

Pomerleau, O. F. (1979). Why people smoke: Current psychosocial models. In P. Davidson (Ed.), *Behavioral Medicine: Changing Health Lifestyles.* New York: Brunner/Mazel.

Pomerleau, O. F., & Brady, S. P. (Eds.). (1979). *Behavioral medicine: Theory and practice.* Baltimore: Williams & Wilkins.

Pomerleau, O. F., Pertschuk, M., Adkins, D., & Brady, J. P. (1976 December). *Comparison of behavioral and traditional treatment for problem drinking.* Paper presented at the Annual Meeting of the Association for the Advancement of Behavior Therapy, New York.

Pomerleau, O. F., Pertschuk, M., Adkins, D., & D'Aquili, E. (1978). Treatment for middle income problem drinkers. In P. E. Nathan, G. A. Marlatt, & T. Loberg (Eds.), *Alcoholism: New Di-*

rections in *Behavioral Research and Treatment*. New York: Plenum Press.

Poussaint, A., & Dittman, K. (1965). A controlled study of imipramine (tofranil) in the treatment of childhood enuresis. *Journal of Pediatrics*, 67, 283–290.

Poulos, C. X., Hinson, R. E., & Siegel, S. (1981). The role of Pavlovian processes in drug tolerance and dependence: Implications for treatment. *Addictive Behaviors*, 6, 205–212.

President's Commission on Mental Health (1978). *Report to the President* (Vol. 1). Washington, DC: U.S. Government Printing Office.

Price, W. H., & Whatmore, P. B. (1967). Behavior Disorders and patterns of crime among XYY males identified at a maximum security hospital. *British Medical Journal*, 1, 533–536.

Prinz, R. J., Myers, D., Holden, E. W., Tarnowski, K. J., & Roberts, W. A. (1983). Marital disturbance and child problems. A cautionary note regarding hyperactive children. *Journal of Abnormal Child Psychology*, 11, 393–399.

Prinz, R. J., Roberts, W. A., & Hantman, E. (1980). Dietary correlates of hyperactivity behavior in children. *Journal of Consulting and Clinical Psychology*, 48, 760–769.

Prioleau, L., Murdock, M., & Brody, N. (1983). An analysis of psychotherapy versus placebo studies. *The Behavioral and Brain Sciences*, 6, 275–310.

Pueschel, S. M., Herman, R., & Groden, G. (1985). Brief Report: Screening children with autism for fragile-X syndrome and phenylketonuria. *Journal of Autism and Developmental Disorders*, 15, 335–338.

Pyle, R. L., Halvorson, P., Neuman, P., & Mitchell, J. (1986). The increasing prevalence of bulimia in freshman college students. *International Journal of Eating Disorders*, 5, 631–648.

Pyle, R. L., Mitchell, J. E., & Eckert, E. D. (1981). Bulimia: A report of 34 cases. *Journal of Clinical Psychiatry*, 42, 60–64.

Pyle, R. L., Mitchell, J. E., Eckert, E. D., Halvorson, L., et al. (1983). The incidence of bulimia in freshman college students. *International Journal of Eating Disorders*, 2, 75–85.

Q

Quay, H. C. (1964). Personality dimensions in delinquent males as inferred from the factor analysis of behavior ratings. *Journal of Research on Crime and Delinquency*, 1, 33–37.

Quay, H. C. (1972). Patterns of aggression, withdrawal, and immaturity. In H. C. Quay & J. S. Werry (Eds.), *Psychopathological disorders of childhood*. New York: John Wiley & Sons.

Quay, H. C. (1979). Classification. In H. C. Quay & J. S. Werry (Eds.), *Psychopathological disorders of children*. (2nd ed.). New York: John Wiley & Sons.

Quay, H. C., & Quay, L. C. (1965). Behavior problems in early adolescence. *Child Development*, 36, 215–220.

Quay, H. C., & Werry, J. S. (1986). *Psychopathological disorders of children*, (3rd ed.) New York: John Wiley & Sons.

Quilitch, H. R., & Risley, T. R. (1973). The effects of play material on social play. *Journal of Applied Behavior Analysis*, 6, 573–578.

Quinsey, V. L., & Marshall, W. (1983). Procedures for reducing inappropriate sexual arousal: An evaluative review. In J. Greer & I. Stuart (Eds.), *The sexual aggressor*. New York: Van Nostrand.

R

Rachman, S. (1977). The conditioning theory of fear-acquisition: A critical examination. *Behaviour Research and Therapy*, 15, 375–388.

Rachman, S. (1978). *Fear and courage*. San Francisco: Freeman.

Rachman, S. (1983). Behavioural medicine, clinical reasoning and technical advances. *Canadian Journal of Behavioural Science*, 15, 318–333.

Rachman, S., Cobb, J., Grey, S., McDonald, D., Mawson, D., Sartory, G., & Stern, R. (1979). The behavioural treatment of obsessional-compulsive disorders, with and without clomipramine. *Behaviour Research and Therapy*, 17, 467–478.

Rachman, S., & Hodgson, R. (1974). Synchrony and desynchrony in fear and avoidance: I. *Behaviour Research and Therapy*, 12, 311–318.

Rachman, S., & Hodgson, R. (1980). *Obsessions and compulsions*. Englewood Cliffs, NJ: Prentice-Hall.

Rachman, S., & Levitt, K. (1985). Panics and their consequences. *Behaviour Research and Therapy*, 23, 585–600.

Rachman, S., & Wilson, G. T. (1980). *The effects of psychological therapy*. Oxford: Pergamon Press.

Rankin, H., Hodgson, R., & Stockwell, T. (1983). Cue exposure and response prevention with alcoholics: A controlled trial. *Behaviour Research and Therapy, 21*, 435–466.

Rapee, R. (1986). Differential response to hyperventilation in panic disorder and generalized anxiety disorder. *Journal of Abnormal Psychology, 95*, 24–28.

Rapoport, J. L., Buchsbaum, M. S., Zahn, T. P., Weingartner, H., Ludlow, D., & Mikkelson, E. J. (1978). Dextroamphetamine: Cognitive and behavioral effects in normal prepubertal boys. *Science, 199*, 560–563.

Raskin, M., Bali, L. R., & Peeke, H. V. (1980). Muscle biofeedback and transcendental meditation. *Archives of General Psychiatry, 37*, 93–97.

Rathus, S. A. (1973). A thirty-item schedule for assessing assertive behavior. *Behavior Therapy, 4*, 398–406.

Raw, M., & Russell, M. A. H. (1980). Rapid smoking, cue exposure, and support in the modification of smoking. *Behaviour Research and Therapy, 18*, 363–372.

Raymer, R., & Poppen, R. (1985). Behavioral relaxation training with hyperactive children. *Journal of Behavior Therapy and Experimental Psychiatry, 16*, 309–316.

Redd, W., & Andrykowski, M. A. (1982). Behavioral intervention in cancer treatment: Controlling aversion reactions to chemotherapy. *Journal of Consulting and Clinical Psychology, 50*, 1018–1029.

Reese, M. (1982). Helping human rights committees and clients balance intrusiveness and effectiveness: A challenge for research and therapy. *The Behavior Therapist, 5*, 95–99.

Rehm, L. P. (1977). A self control model of depression. *Behavior Therapy, 8*, 787–804.

Rehm, L. P. (1981). A self-control therapy program for treatment of depression. In J. F. Clarkin & H. I. Glazer (Eds.), *Depression: Behavioral and directive intervention strategies*. New York: Garland Press.

Reid, J. B., & Hendricks, A. F. (1973). Preliminary analysis of the effectiveness of direct home intervention for the treatment of predelinquent boys who steal. In L. A. Hamerlynck, L. C. Handy, & E. J. Mash (Eds.), *Behavior change: Methodology, concepts and practice*. Champaign, IL: Research Press.

Reid, J. B., Hinojosa-Rivero, G., & Lorber, R. A. (1980). *A social learning approach to the outpatient treatment of children who steal*. Unpublished manuscript. (Available from Oregon Social Learning Center, 207 East 5th, Eugene, OR.)

Rekers, G. A. (1975). Stimulus control over sex-typed play in cross-gender identified boys. *Journal of Experimental Child Psychology, 20*, 136–148.

Rekers, G. A., & Lovaas, O. I. (1974). Behavioral treatment of deviant sex-role behaviors in a male child. *Journal of Applied Behavior Analysis, 7*, 173–190.

Rescorla, R., & Solomon, R. (1967). Two-process learning theory: Relationships between Pavlovian conditioning and instrumental learning. *Psychological Review, 74*, 151–182.

Rescorla, R., & Wagner, A. (1972). A theory of Pavlovian conditioning. In A. Black & W. Prokasy (Eds.), *Classical conditioning*, Vol. II. New York: Appleton-Century-Crofts.

Rice, K. M., & Blanchard, E. B. (1982). Biofeedback in the treatment of anxiety disorders. *Clinical Psychology Review, 2*, 557–577.

Riley, A., & Riley, E. (1978). A controlled study to evaluate directed masturbation in the management of primary orgasmic failure in women. *British Journal of Psychiatry, 133*, 404–409.

Rimland, B. (1964). *Infantile autism*. New York: Appleton-Century-Crofts.

Risley, T. R. (1968). The effects and side effects of punishing the autistic behaviors of a deviant child. *Journal of Applied Behavior Analysis, 1*, 21–34.

Risley, T. R., & Sheldon-Wildgen, J. (1982). Invited peer review: The AABT experience. *Professional Psychology, 13*, 125–131.

Ritvo, L. R., Yuwiler, A., Geller, E., Ornitz, E. M., Saeger, K., & Plotkin, S. (1970). Increased blood serotonin and platelets in early infantile autism. *Archives of General Psychiatry, 23*, 566–572.

Rivera, G. (1972). *Willowbrook*. New York: Random House.

Robbins, L. (1979). Follow-up studies. In H. C. Quay & J. S. Werry, (Eds.), *Psychopathological Disorders of Children*, (2nd ed.), New York: John Wiley & Sons.

Robertiello, R. C. (1956). Some psychic interrelations between the urinary and sexual systems with special reference to enuresis. *Psychiatric Quarterly, 30*, 61–62.

Roberts, R. R., Jr., & Renzaglia, G. A. (1965). The influence of tape-recording on counseling. *Journal of Counseling Psychology, 12*, 10–16.

Robin, A. L., O'Leary, K. D., Kent, R. N., Foster, S. L., & Prinz, R. J. (1977). Communication training: An approach to problem solving for parents and adolescents. *Behavior Therapy, 8,* 639–643.

Robin, A. L., Schneider, M., & Dolnick, M. (1976). The turtle technique: An extended case study of self-control in the classroom. *Psychology in the Schools, 13,* 444–453.

Robins, E., & Guze, S. G. (1972). Classification of affective disorders: The primary-secondary, the endogenous-reactive, and the neurotic-psychotic concepts. In T. A. Williams, M. M. Katz, & J. A. Shield (Eds.), *Recent advances in the psychobiology of the depressive illnesses,* (DHEW publication No. HSM 70–9053). Washington, DC: U.S. Government Printing Office.

Robinson, H. B., & Robinson, N. M. (1965). *The mentally retarded child.* New York: McGraw-Hill.

Rodin, J. (1980). *The Yale weight control program.* Unpublished manuscript, Yale University.

Rogers, C. (1957). The necessary and sufficient conditions of therapeutic personality change. *Journal of Consulting Psychology, 21,* 95–103.

Rogers, S. C., & Clay, P. M. (1975). A statistical review of controlled trials of imipramine and placebo in the treatment of depressive illness. *British Journal of Psychiatry, 127,* 599–603.

Rogers, T., & Craighead, W. E. (1977). Physiological responses to self-statements: The effects of statement valence and discrepancy. *Cognitive Therapy and Research, 1,* 99–120.

Romanczyk, R. G., & Goren, E. R. (1975). Severe self-injurious behavior: The problem of clinical control. *Journal of Consulting and Clinical Psychology, 43,* 730–739.

Roos, P., & Oliver, M. (1965). *Evaluation of operant conditioning with institutionalized retarded children.* Unpublished manuscript, Austin, Texas: Austin State School.

Rooth, F. G., & Marks, I. M. (1974). Persistent exhibitionism: Short-term response to self-regulation and relaxation treatment. *Archives of Sexual Behavior, 3,* 227–248.

Rosen, G. M., Glasgow, R. E., & Barrera, M. (1976). A controlled study to assess the clinical efficacy of totally self-administered systematic desensitization. *Journal of Consulting and Clinical Psychology, 44,* 208–217.

Rosen, J. C., & Leitenberg, H. (1982). Bulimia nervosa: Treatment with exposure and response prevention. *Behavior Therapy, 13,* 117–124.

Rosen, L. A., Booth, S. R., Bender, M. E., McGrath, M. L., Sorrell, S., & Drabman, R. S. (1985). *The effects of sugar (sucrose) on children's behavior.* Unpublished manuscript, Colorado State University, Fort Collins, CO.

Rosen, L. A., O'Leary, S. G., Joyce, S. A., Conway, G., & Pfiffner. The importance of prudent negative consequences for maintaining the appropriate behavior of hyperactive students. *Journal of Abnormal Child Psychology, 12,* 581–604.

Rosen, R. C. (1983). Clinical issues in the assessment and treatment of impotence: A new look at an old problem. *The Behavior Therapist, 6,* 81–85.

Rosen, R. C. (1986). Personal communication.

Rosenbaum, A., O'Leary, K. D., & Jacob, R. C. (1975). Behavioral intervention with hyperactive children: Group consequences as a supplement to individual contingencies. *Behavior Therapy, 6,* 315–323.

Rosenbaum, M. S., & Drabman, R. S. (1979). Self-control in the classroom. *Journal of Applied Behavior Analysis, 12,* 467–485.

Rosenman, R. H., Brand, R. J., Jenkins, C. D., Friedman, M., Strauss, K., Wurm, M. (1975). Coronary heart disease in the Western Collaborative Group Study: Final follow-up experience of 8½ years. *Journal of the American Medical Association, 233,* 872–877.

Rosenthal, B. S., & Marx, R. D. (1978). Differences in eating patterns of successful and unsuccessful dieters, untreated overweight, and normal weight individuals. *Addictive Behaviors, 3,* 129–134.

Rosenthal, D. (1970). *Genetic theory and abnormal behavior.* New York: McGraw-Hill.

Rosenthal, R. (1969). Interpersonal expectations: Effects of the experimenter's hypothesis. In R. Rosenthal & R. L. Rosnow (Eds.), *Artifact in Behavioral Research.* New York: Academic Press.

Rosenthal, T. L. (1982). Social learning theory and behavior therapy. In G. T. Wilson & C. M. Franks (Eds.), *Contemporary Behavior Therapy: Conceptual and Empirical Foundations.* New York: Guilford Press.

Rosenthal, T., & Bandura, A. (1978). Psychological modeling: Theory and practice. In S. L. Garfield & A. E. Bergin (Eds.), *Handbook of psychotherapy and behavior change.* New York: John Wiley & Sons.

Ross, J. (1982). The role of the family member in the supported approach to the treatment of phobias. In J. Boulougouris (Ed.), *Learning theory approaches to psychiatry*. London: John Wiley & Sons.

Rossiter, E., & Wilson, G. T. (1985). Cognitive restructuring and exposure in the treatment of bulimia nervosa. *Behaviour Research and Therapy, 23*, 349–360.

Roth, D., & Rehm, L. P. (1980). Relationships between self-monitoring processes, memory and depression. *Cognitive Therapy & Research, 4*, 149–158.

Rowe, D. C. (1983). Biometrical genetic models of self-reported delinquent behavior: A twin study. *Behavior Genetics, 13*, 473–489.

Rowe, D. C., & Osgood, D. W. (1984). Heredity and sociological theories of delinquency: A reconsideration. *American Sociological Review, 49*, 526–540.

Rubenstein, E. A. (1983). Television and behavior. *American Psychologist, 38*, 820–825.

Ruderman, A. (1985). Dysphoric mood and overeating: A test of restraint theory's disinhibition hypothesis. *Journal of Abnormal Psychology, 94*, 78–85.

Rush, A. J. (1980). Identifying obstacles to health behavior. New York: BMA Audio Cassettes.

Rush, A. J. (1982). *Short-term psychotherapies for depression*. Chichester, U.K.: John Wiley & Sons.

Rush, A. J., Beck, A. T., Kovacs, M., & Hollon, S. (1977). Comparative efficacy of cognitive therapy and imipramine in the treatment of depressed outpatients. *Cognitive Therapy and Research, 1*, 17–37.

Rush, A. J., & Giles, D. E. (1982). Cognitive therapy: Theory and research. In A. J. Rush (Ed.), *Short-term psychotherapies for depression*. New York: Guilford Press.

Russell, M. A. H., Armstrong, E., & Patel, U. A. (1976). The role of temporal contiguity in electrical aversion therapy for cigarette smoking: Analysis of behavior changes. *Behaviour Research and Therapy, 14*, 103–123.

Russell, M., Raw, M., Taylor, C., Feyerabend, C., & Saloojee, Y. (1978). Blood nicotine and carboxyhemoglobin levels after rapid-smoking aversion therapy. *Journal of Consulting and Clinical Psychology, 46*, 1423–1431.

Russell, A., & Winkler, R. (1977). Effectiveness of assertive training and homosexual guidance service groups designed to improve homosexual functioning. *Journal of Consulting and Clinical Psychology, 45*, 1–13.

Russo, D. C., & Koegel, R. L. (1977). A method for integrating an autistic child into a normal public school classroom. *Journal of Applied Behavior Analysis, 10*, 569–590.

Rutter, M. (1975). Epidemiology. In H. C. Quay & J. S. Werry (Eds.), *Psychopathological Disorders of Children*, New York: John Wiley & Sons.

Rutter, M. (1984). The family, the child, and the school. In M. D. Levine & P. Satz (Eds.), *Middle Childhood: Development and Dysfunction*. Baltimore, MD: University Park Press.

Rutter, M. R., & Garmezy, N. (1983). Childhood psychopathology. In M. Hetherinton & P. H. Mussen (Eds.), *Carmichael's Manual of Child Psychology, 4*. New York: John Wiley & Sons.

Rutter, M., & Garmezy, N. (1983). Developmental psychopathology. Paul Mussen (Ed.), *Handbook of Child Psychology* (Vol. 4). Socialization, personality, and social development. (E. M. Hetherington, Vol. ed.).

Ryan, V., & Gizynski, M. (1971). Behavior therapy in retrospect: Patients' feelings about their behavior therapies. *Journal of Consulting and Clinical Psychology, 37*, 1–9.

S

Sackett, D. L., & Snow, J. C. (1979). The magnitude of compliance and noncompliance. In R. B. Haynes, D. W. Taylor, & D. L. Sackett (Eds.), *Compliance in health care*. Baltimore: Johns Hopkins Press.

Sager, C. (1976). *Marriage contracts and couple therapy*. New York: Brunner/Mazel.

St. Lawrence, J. S. (1986). Assessment and treatment of social dysfunctions in chronic schizophrenics. *The Behavior Therapist, 9*, 85–86.

Salk, L. (1972). *What every child would like his parents to know*. New York: David McKay.

Salmon, M. A. (1975). An historical account of nocturnal enuresis and its treatments. *Proceedings of the Royal Society of Medicine, 68*, 443–445.

Salter, A. (1949). *Conditioned reflex therapy*. New York: Farrar, Straus.

Sanchez-Craig, M., Annis, H., Bornet, A., & MacDonald, K. (1984). Random assignment to abstinence and controlled drinking: Evaluation of a cognitive-behavioral program for problem drinkers. *Journal of Consulting and Clinical Psychology, 52,* 390–403.

Santulli, T. V. (1972). Anorectal malformations. In H. L. Barnett & A. H. Einhorn (Eds.), *Pediatrics.* (15th ed.). New York: Appleton-Century-Crofts.

Sartorius, N., Shapiro, R., & Jablonsky, A. (1974). The international pilot study of schizophrenia. *Schizophrenia Bulletin, 1,* 21–35.

Satterfield, J. H., Cantwell, D. P., & Satterfield, B. Y. (1979). Multimodality treatment. *Archives of General Psychiatry, 36,* 965–974.

Saunders, M. R., & Dadds, M.R. (1982). The effects of planned activities and child management procedures in parent training: An analysis of setting generality. *Behavior Therapy, 13,* 452–461.

Schacter, J., & O'Leary, K. D. (1985). Affective intent and impact in marital communication. *The American Journal of Family Therapy, 13,* 17–23.

Schachter, S. (1978). Pharmacological and psychological determinants of smoking. *Annals of Internal Medicine, 88,* 104–114.

Schachter, S. (1982). Recidivism and self-cure of smoking and obesity. *American Psychologist, 37,* 436–444.

Schacter, S., & Latane, B. (1964). Crime, cognition, and the autonomic nervous system. In D. Levine (Ed.), *Nebraska symposium on motivation,* Lincoln: University of Nebraska Press.

Schilling, D., & Poppen, R. (1983). Behavioral relaxation training and assessment. *Journal of Behavior Therapy and Experimental Psychiatry, 14,* 99–107.

Schneider, N., & Jarvik, M. (1984). Nicotine versus placebo gum in the alleviation of withdrawal during smoking cessation. *Addictive Behaviors, 9,* 149–156.

Schnelle, J. (1974). A brief report on invalidity of parent evaluations of behavior change. *Journal of Applied Behavior Analysis, 7,* 341–343.

Schover, L. R., & LoPiccolo, J. (1982). Treatment effectiveness for dysfunctions of low sex drive. *Journal of Sex and Marital Therapy, 8,* 179–187.

Schuckit, M. (1984). Genetic and biochemical factors in the etiology of alcoholism. In L. Grinspoon (Ed.), *Psychiatry update* (Vol. III). Washington, DC: American Psychiatric Press.

Schuckit, M., Goodwin, D., & Winokur, G. (1972). A study of alcoholism in half-siblings. *American Journal of Psychiatry, 128,* 1132–1136.

Schulmann, J. L., & Reisman, J. M. (1959). An objective measurement of hyperactivity. *American Journal of Mental Deficiency, 64,* 455–456.

Schwartz, G. E., & Beatty, J. (1977). *Biofeedback: Theory and research.* New York: Academic Press.

Schwartz, G. E., Davidson, R. J., & Coleman, D. T. (1978). Patterning of cognitive and somatic processes in the self-regulation of anxiety: Effects of meditation versus exercise. *Psychosomatic Medicine, 40,* 321–328.

Schwartz, G. E., & Weiss, S. M. (1978). Behavioral medicine revisited: An amended definition. *Journal of Behavioral Medicine, 1,* 249–252.

Schwitzgebel, R., & Kolb, D. A. (1964). Inducing behavior change in adolescent delinquents. *Behaviour Research and Therapy, 1,* 297–304.

Science Times, The New York Times, September 17, 1985.

Scott, P. M., Burton, R. V., & Yarrow, M. R. (1967). Social reinforcement under natural conditions. *Child Development, 38,* 53–63.

Sears, R. R., Maccoby, E., & Levin, H. (1957). *Patterns of child rearing.* New York: Harper & Row.

Seligman, M. E. P. (1971). Phobias and preparedness. *Behavior Therapy, 2,* 307–320.

Seligman, M. E. P. (1981). A learned helplessness point of view. In L. P. Rehm (Ed.), *Behavior therapy for depression.* New York: Academic Press.

Serban, G. (1975). Stress in schizophrenics and normals. *British Journal of Psychiatry, 126.* 397–407.

Shapiro, D., & Goldstein, I. B. (1982). Biobehavioral perspectives on hypertension. *Journal of Consulting and Clinical Psychology, 50,* 841–858.

Shapiro, D., & Schwartz, G. E. (1972). Biofeedback and visceral learning: Clinical applications. *Seminars in Psychiatry, 4,* 171–184.

Shapiro, D. A., & Shapiro, D. (1983). Comparative therapy outcome research: Methodological implications of meta-analysis. *Journal of Consulting and Clinical Psychology, 51,* 42–53.

Shaw, P. (1979). A comparison of three behaviour therapies in the treatment of social phobia. *British Journal of Psychiatry, 134,* 620–623.

Sheldon, W. H. (with the collaboration of E. M. Hartl & E. McDermott) (1949). *Varieties of delinquent youth.* New York: Harper.

Shepard, M., Oppenheim, A. N., & Mitchell,

S. (1966). Childhood behavior disorders and the child guidance clinic: An epidemiological study. *Journal of Child Psychology and Psychiatry, 7,* 39–52.

Sher, K., & Levenson, R. (1983). Alcohol and tension reduction: The importance of individual differences. In L. Pohorecky & J. Brick (Eds.), *Stress and alcohol use.* New York: Elsevier.

Shiffman, S. M. (1979). The tobacco withdrawal syndrome. In N. A. Krasnegor (Ed.), *Cigarette smoking as a dependence process* (NIDA Research Monograph 23, DHEW Publication No. ADM 79–800). Washington, DC: U.S. Government Printing Office.

Shiffman, S. M. (1982). Relapse following smoking cessation: A situational analysis. *Journal of Consulting and Clinical Psychology, 50,* 71–86.

Shiffman, S. M., Read, L., Maltese, J., & Rapkin, D. (1985). Preventing relapse in ex-smokers: A self-management approach. In G. A. Marlatt & J. Gordon (Eds.), *Relapse prevention.* New York: Guilford Press.

Shrauger, J. S., & Osberg, T. M. (1982). Self-awareness: The ability to predict one's future behaviour. In G. Underwood (Ed.), *Aspects of consciousness (Vol. 3), Awareness and self-awareness.* New York: Academic Press.

Siegel, S. (1982). Classical conditioning, drug tolerance, and drug dependence. In R. Smart, F. Glaser, Y. Israel, H. Kalant, R. Popham, & W. Schmidt (Eds.), *Research advances in alcohol and drug problems* (Vol. 7). New York: Plenum Publishing.

Sims, E., Goldman, R., Gluck, C., Horton, E., Kelleher, P. & Rowe, D. (1968). Experimental obesity in man. *Transcript of American Physicians, 81,* 153.

Singer, D. G. (1983). A time to re-examine the role of television in our lives. *American Psychologist, 38,* 815–816.

Singer, M. T., & Wynne, L. C. (1965a). Thought disorder and family relations of schizophrenics: III. Methodology using projective techniques. *Archives of General Psychiatry, 12,* 187–200.

Singer, M. T., & Wynne, L. C. (1965b). Thought disorder and family relations of schizophrenics: IV. Results and implications. *Archives of General Psychiatry, 12,* 201–212.

Singer, M. T., & Wynne, L. C. (1966). Principles for scoring communication defects and devi-ances in parents of schizophrenics: Rorschach and TAT scoring manuals. *Psychiatry, 29,* 260–288.

Skinner, B. F. (1948). *Walden Two.* New York: Macmillan Co.

Skinner, B. F. (1953). *Science and human behavior.* New York: Macmillan.

Skinner, B. F. (1963). Behaviorism at fifty. *Science, 140,* 951–958.

Skinner, B. F. (1967). *Cumulative record: A selection of papers.* New York: Appleton-Century-Crofts.

Skinner, B. F. (1971). *Beyond freedom and dignity.* New York: Alfred A. Knopf.

Slack, C. W. (1960). Experimenter-subject psychotherapy: A new method of introducing intensive office treatment for unreachable cases. *Mental Hygiene, 44,* 238–256.

Sloane, R. B., Staples, F. R., Cristol, A. H., Yorkston, N. J., & Whipple, K. (1975). *Psychotherapy versus behavior therapy.* Cambridge, MA: Harvard University Press.

Smith, D. (1982). Trends in counseling and psychotherapy. *American Psychologist, 37,* 802–810.

Smith, M. L., & Glass, G. V. (1977). Meta-analysis of psychotherapy outcome studies. *American Psychologist, 32,* 752–760.

Smith, M. L., Glass, G., & Miller, T. (1980). *The benefits of psychotherapy.* Baltimore: Johns Hopkins University Press.

Snyder, S. H. (1980). *Biological aspects of mental disorder.* New York: Oxford University Press.

Sobell, L. C., & Sobell, M. B. (1983). Behavioral research and therapy: Its impact on the alcohol field. In K. D. Craig & R. J. McMahon (Eds.), *Advances in clinical behavior therapy.* New York: Brunner/Mazel.

Sobell, M. B., & Sobell, L. C. (1973). Individualized behavior therapy for alcoholics. *Behavior Therapy, 4,* 49–72.

Sobell, M. B., & Sobell, L. C. (1978). *Behavioral treatment of alcohol problems.* New York: Plenum Press.

Sobell, M. B., & Sobell, L. C. (1984). The aftermath of heresy: A response to Pendery et al.'s (1982) critique of "Individualized Behavior Therapy for Alcoholics." *Behaviour Research and Therapy, 22,* 413–440.

Society of Actuaries. (1983). *Build and blood pressure study.* Chicago: Society of Actuaries.

Solyom, I., Beck, P., Solyom, C., & Hugel, R. (1974). Some etiological factors in phobic neurosis. *Canadian Psychiatry Association Journal, 19,* 69–78.

Southwick, L., Steele, C., Marlatt, A., & Lindell, M. (1981). Alcohol-related expectancies: Defined by phase of intoxication and drinking experience. *Journal of Consulting and Clinical Psychology, 49,* 713–721.

Spark, R., White, R., & Connolly, P. (1980). Impotence is not always psychogenic: Newer insights in hypothalamic-pituitary gonadal dysfunction. *Journal of the American Medical Association, 243,* 750–755.

Sperling, M. (1971). Sleep disturbances in children. In J. G. Howells (Ed.), *Modern perspectives in international child psychiatry.* New York: Brunner/Mazel.

Spradlin, J. E., & Girardeau, F. L. (1966). The behavior of moderately and severely retarded persons. In N. R. Ellis (Ed.), *International review of research in mental retardation, 1.* New York: Academic Press.

Stalonas, P. M., Johnson, W. G., & Christ, M. (1978). Behavior modification for obesity: The evaluation of exercise, contingency management, and program adherence. *Journal of Consulting and Clinical Psychology, 46,* 463–469.

Stalonas, P. M., Perri, M., & Kerzner, A. (1984). Do behavioral treatments of obesity last? A five-year follow-up investigation. *Addictive Behaviors, 9,* 175–183.

Stampfl, T., & Levis, D. (1967). Essentials of implosive therapy: A learning-theory-based psychodynamic behavioral therapy. *Journal of Abnormal Psychology, 72,* 496–503.

Staples, F. R., Sloane, R. B., Whipple, K., Cristol, A. H., & Yorkston, N. (1975). Differences between behavior therapists and psychotherapists. *Archives of General Psychiatry, 32,* 1517–1522.

Starfield, B. (1972). Enuresis: Its pathogenesis and management. *Clinical Pediatrics, 11,* 343–349.

Steen, P. L. (1982). *Validation of the Stony Brook Hyperactivity Scale.* Unpublished doctoral dissertation, State University of New York, Stony Brook, NY.

Stein, A. (1885). Enuresis or incontinence of urine. *The Medical Record, 27,* 701.

Stene, J., Stene, E., Stengel-Rutkowsky, S., & Muiken, J. D. (1981). Paternal age and Down's syndrome: Data from prenatal diagnoses (DFG). *Human Genetics, 59,* 119–124.

Stern, R., Lipsedge, M., & Marks, I. (1973). Thought stopping of neutral and obsessive thoughts: A controlled trial. *Behaviour Research and Therapy, 11,* 659–661.

Stern, R., & Marks, I. (1973). Brief and prolonged flooding. *Archives of General Psychiatry, 28,* 270–276.

Sternberg, B. S. (1985). Relapse in weight control: Definitions, processes, and prevention strategies. In G. A. Marlatt, & J. Gordon (Eds.), *Relapse prevention.* New York: Guilford Press.

Stierlin, H., Wynne, L. C., & Wirsching, M. (Eds.) (1983). *Psychosocial intervention in schizophrenia: An international overview.* Berlin, Heidelberg: Springer-Verlag.

Still, G. F. (1902). The Goulstonian lectures on some abnormal physical conditions in children. *Lancet, 1,* 1008–1012.

Stockwell, T. R., Hodgson, R., Rankin, H., & Taylor, S. (1982). Alcohol dependence, beliefs, and the priming effect. *Behaviour Research and Therapy, 20,* 513–522.

Stolz, S. B. & Associates. (1978). *Ethical issues in behavior modification.* San Francisco: Jossey-Bass.

Stone, L. J., & Church, J. (1973). *Childhood and adolescence.* New York: Random House.

Stone, N., & Borkovec, T. D. (1975). The paradoxical effect of brief CS exposure on analogue phobic subjects. *Behaviour Research and Therapy, 13,* 51–54.

Striegel-Moore, R., Silberstein, L., & Rodin, J. (1986). Toward an understanding of risk factors for bulimia. *American Psychologist, 41,* 246–263.

Strube, M. J., & Hartmann, D. (1983). Meta-analysis: Techniques, applications, and functions. *Journal of Consulting and Clinical Psychology, 51,* 14–27.

Strupp, H. H. (1977). A reformulation of the dynamics of the therapist's contribution. In A. Guman & A. Razin (Eds.), *Effective psychotherapy,* New York: Pergamon Press.

Strupp, H. H., & Hadley, S. (1979). Specific versus non-specific factors in psychotherapy. *Archives of General Psychiatry, 36,* 1125–1136.

Stuart, R. B. (1968). Token reinforcement in marital treatment. In R. Rubin & C. Franks (Eds.),

Advances in behavior therapy. New York: Academic Press.

Stuart, R. B. (1969). Operant-interpersonal treatment of marital discord. *Journal of Consulting and Clinical Psychology, 33,* 675–682.

Stuart, R. B. (1971). Behavioral contracting within families of delinquents. *Journal of Behavior Therapy and Experimental Psychiatry, 2,* 1–11.

Stuart, R. B. (1977). (Ed.) *Behavioral self-management.* New York: Brunner/Mazel.

Stuart, R. B. (1980). *Act thin, stay thin.* New York: Norton.

Stuart, R. B. (1980). *Helping couples change: A social learning approach.* New York: Guilford Press.

Stuart, R. B., & Davis, B. (1972). *Slim chance in a fat world.* Champaign, IL: Research Press.

Stuart, R. B., & Guire, K. (1978). Some correlates of the maintenance of weight loss through behavior modification. *International Journal of Obesity, 2,* 225–235.

Stuart, R. B., & Jacobson, B. (1979). Sex differences in obesity. In E. Gomberg, & V. Franks (Eds.), *Gender and disordered behavior: Sex differences in psychopathology.* New York: Brunner/Mazel.

Stuart, R. B., & Mitchell, C. (1978). A professional and a consumer perspective on self-help weight control programs. In A. J. Stunkard (Ed.), *The psychiatric clinics of North America symposium on obesity.* Philadelphia: Saunders.

Stuart, R. B., & Tripodi, T. T. (1973). Experimental evaluation of three time-constrained behavioral treatments for predelinquents and delinquents. In R. D. Rubin, J. P. Brady, & J. D. Henderson (Eds.), *Advances in behavior therapy,* (Vol 4). New York: Academic Press.

Stumphauzer, J. S. (1979). *Behavior therapy with delinquents.* Springfield, IL: Thomas.

Stunkard, A. J. (1975). From explanation to action in psychosomatic medicine: The case of obesity. *Psychosomatic Medicine, 37,* 195–236.

Stunkard, A. J. (1980). (Ed.) *Obesity.* Philadelphia: Saunders.

Stunkard, A. J., & Brownell, K. D. (1979). Behaviour therapy and self-help programmes for obesity. In J. F. Munno (Ed.), *Treatment of obesity.* Lancaster, England: MTP Press.

Stunkard, A. J., & Brownell, K. D. (1980). Work site treatment for obesity. *American Journal of Psychiatry, 137,* 252–253.

Stunkard, A. J., Foch, T. T., & Hrubec, Z. (1986).

A twin study of human obesity. *Journal of the American Medical Association, 256,* 51–54.

Stunkard, A. J., & Penick, S. (1979). Behavior modification in the treatment of obesity: The problem of maintaining weight loss. *Archives of General Psychiatry, 36,* 801–806.

Stunkard, A. J., & Rush, J. (1974). Dieting and depression re-examined: A critical review of reports of untoward responses during weight reduction for obesity. *Annals of Internal Medicine, 81,* 526–533.

Stunkard, A. J., Sorensen, T., Hanis, C., Teasdale, T. W., Chakraborty, R., Schull, W. J., & Schulsinger, F. (1986). An adoption study of human obesity. *New England Journal of Medicine, 314,* 193–198.

Sturgis, E., & Adams, H. (1978). The right to treatment: Issues in the treatment of homosexuality. *Journal of Consulting and Clinical Psychology, 46,* 165–169.

Suinn, R. M., & Richardson, F. (1971). Anxiety management training: A nonspecific behavior therapy program for anxiety control. *Behavior Therapy, 2,* 498–510.

Surwit, R. S. (1982). Behavioral treatment of Raynaud's syndrome in peripheral vascular disease. *Journal of Consulting and Clinical Psychology, 50,* 922–932.

Surwit, R. S., Shapiro, D., & Good, M. I. (1978). A comparison of cardiovascular biofeedback, neuromuscular biofeedback, and meditation in the treatment of borderline essential hypertension. *Journal of Consulting and Clinical Psychology, 46,* 252–263.

Sutherland, E. H. (1939). *Principles of criminology.* Philadelphia: Lippincott.

Swan, G. E., & MacDonald, M. L. (1978). Behavior therapy in practice: A national survey of behavior therapists. *Behavior Therapy, 9,* 799–807.

Swanson, J. M., & Kinsbourne, M. (1980). Food dyes impair performance of hyperactive children on a laboratory learning test. *Science, 207,* 1485–1487.

T

Tasto, D. L., Hickson, R., & Rubin, S. E. (1971). Scaled profile analysis of fear survey schedule factors. *Behavior Therapy, 2,* 543–549.

Tate, B. G., & Baroff, G. S. (1966). Aversive

control of self-injurious behavior in a psychotic boy. *Behaviour Research and Therapy, 4,* 281–287.

Taylor, C. B., Bandura, A., Ewart, C., Miller, M. H., & Debusk, R. (1985). Raising spouse's and patient's perception of his cardiac capabilities following a myocardial infarction. *American Journal of Cardiology, 55,* 635–638.

Taylor, C. B., Ferguson, J. M., & Reading, J. C. (1978). Gradual weight loss and depression. *Behavior Therapy, 9,* 622–625.

Taylor, F. G., & Marshall, W. L. (1977). Experimental analysis of a cognitive-behavioral therapy for depression. *Cognitive Therapy and Research, 1,* 59–72.

Teasdale, J. D. (1985). Psychological treatments for depression: How do they work? *Behaviour Research and Therapy, 23,* 157–165.

Telch, M. J., Agras, W. S., Taylor, C. B., Roth, W. T., & Gallen, C. C. (1985). Combined pharmacological and behavioral treatment for agoraphobia. *Behaviour Research and Therapy, 23,* 325–336.

Telch, M. J., Killen, J., McAlister, A., Perry, C., & Maccoby, N. (1982). Long-term follow-up of a pilot project on smoking prevention with adolescents. *Journal of Behavioral Medicine, 5,* 1–8.

Telch, M. J., Tearnan, B. H., & Taylor, C. B. (1983). Antidepressant medication in the treatment of agoraphobia: A critical review. *Behaviour Research and Therapy, 21,* 505–518.

Thomas, A., Chess, S., Birch, H. G., Hertzig, M. E., & Korn, S. (1963). *Behavior individuality in early childhood.* New York: New York University Press.

Thompson, J. K., & Blanton, P. D. (1984). The effect of dieting and exercise on metabolic rate. *Behavioral Medicine Abstracts, 5,* v-viii.

Thompson, J. K., Jarvie, G. J., Lahey, B. B., & Cureton, K. J. (1982). Exercise and obesity: Etiology, physiology, and intervention. *Psychological Bulletin, 91,* 55–79.

Thompson, P. D., Jeffery, R. W., Wing, R., & Wood, P. D. (1979). Unexpected decrease in plasma high-density lipoprotein cholesterol with weight loss. *American Journal of Clinical Nutrition, 32,* 2016.

Thorpe, G., & Burns, L. (1983). *The nature and treatment of agoraphobia.* London: Wiley.

Tomlinson, J. R. (1970). Bowel retention. *Behavior Therapy and Experimental Psychiatry, 1,* 83–85.

Touyz, S. W., Beumont, F. J. V., Glarin, D., Phillips, T., & Cowie, I. (1984). A comparison of lenient and strict operant conditioning programmes in refeeding patients with anorexia nervosa. *British Journal of Psychiatry, 144,* 517–520.

Truax, C. B. (1966). Reinforcement and non-reinforcement in Rogerian psychotherapy. *Journal of Abnormal and Social Psychology, 71,* 1–9.

Tsuang, M. (1976). Schizophrenia around the world. *Comparative Psychiatry, 17,* 477–481.

Tuma, J., & Cohen, R. (1981). Pediatric psychology. Cited in O'Leary, K. D. (1984), The image of behavior therapy: It is time to take a stand. *Behavior Therapy, 15,* 219–233. Louisiana State University, Baton Rouge.

Tuma, J., & Pratt, J. (1982). Clinical child psychology practice and training: A survey. *Journal of Clinical Child Psychology, 11,* 27–34.

Turk, D. C., & Salovey, P. (1985). Cognitive structures, cognitive processes, and cognitive-behavior modification. *Cognitive Therapy and Research, 9,* 19–34.

Turkat, I. D., & Maisto, S. A. (1985). Personality disorders: Application of the experimental method to the formulation and modification of personality disorders. In D. H. Barlow (Ed.), *Clinical disorders.* New York: Guilford Press.

Turkewitz, H. (1982). Family systems: Conceptualizing child problems within the family context. In A. Meyers & W. E. Craighead, (Eds.), *Cognitive behavior therapy for children.* New York: Plenum Publishing.

Turkewitz, H., & O'Leary, K. D. (1981). A comparative outcome study of behavioral marital therapy and community therapy. *Journal of Marital and Family Therapy, 7,* 159–169.

Turner, R. J., & Wagonfeld, M. O. (1967). Occupational mobility and schizophrenia: An assessment of the social causation and social selection hypotheses. *American Sociological Review, 32,* 104–113.

Turner, R. K., Young, G. C., & Rachman, S. (1970). Treatment of nocturnal enuresis by conditioning techniques. *Behaviour Research and Therapy, 8,* 367–381.

U

Ullmann, L. P., & Krasner, L. (1965). (Eds.), *Case studies in behavior modification.* New York: Holt, Rinehart & Winston.

Ullmann, L. P., & Krasner, L. (1969). *A psy-*

chological approach to abnormal behavior. Englewood Cliffs, NJ: Prentice-Hall.

Ullmann, L. P., & Krasner, L.   (1975). *A psychological approach to abnormal behavior.* (2nd ed.) Englewood Cliffs, NJ: Prentice-Hall.

Uniform Crime Reports.   (1979). Washington, DC: U.S. Government Printing Office, annual editions, 1957–1979.

U.S. Department of Health, Education, & Welfare.   (1971). *Report on the conference on the use of stimulant drugs in the treatment of behaviorally disturbed young school children.* Washington, DC: U.S. Government Printing Office.

U.S. Department of Health and Human Services.   (1983). *Alcohol and health.* Washington, DC.

U.S. Public Health Service.   (1983). The health consequences of smoking: A report of the Surgeon General. *Washington, DC.*

V

Vaillant, G. E.   (1983). *The natural history of alcoholism: Causes, patterns, and paths to recovery.* Cambridge, MA: Harvard University Press.

Valentine, C. W.   (1930). The innate bases of fear. *Journal of Genetic Psychology, 37,* 394–419.

Van Itallie, T. B.   (1979). Obesity: Adverse effects on health and longevity. *American Journal of Clinical Nutrition, 32,* 2723–2733.

Van Itallie, T. B., & Kral, J. G.   (1981). The dilemma of morbid obesity. *Journal of the American Medical Association, 246,* 999–1003.

Vaughn, C. E., & Leff, J. P.   (1976a). The influence of family and social factors on the course of psychiatric illness: A comparison of schizophrenic and depressed neurotic patients. *British Journal of Psychiatry, 129,* 125–137.

Vaughn, C. E., & Leff, J. P.   (1976b). The measurement of expressed emotion in the families of psychiatric patients. *British Journal of Social and Clinical Psychology, 15,* 157–65.

Venn, J. R., & Short, J. G.   (1973). Vicarious classical conditioning of emotional responses in nursery school children. *Journal of Personality and Social Psychology, 28,* 249–255.

Vernon, D. J.   (1973). Use of modeling to modify children's responses to a natural, potentially stressful situation. *Journal of Applied Psychology, 58,* 351–356.

Vernon, D. J., & Bailey, W. C.   (1974). The use of motion pictures in the psychological preparation of children for induction of anesthesia. *Anesthesiology, 40,* 68–72.

Vital Statistics, Volume III. (1978). Washington, DC: U.S. Government Printing Office.

Vivian, D., Fischel, J. E., & Liebert, R. M.   (in press). Effect of "wet nights" on daytime behavior during concurrent treatment of enuresis and conduct problems. *Journal of Behavior Therapy and Experimental Psychiatry.*

W

Wachtel, P. L.   (1977). *Psychoanalysis and behavior therapy: Toward an integration.* New York: Basic Books.

Wachtel, P. L.   (1982). What can dynamic therapies contribute to behavior therapy? *Behavior Therapy, 13,* 594–609.

Waddell, M. T., Barlow, D. H., & O'Brien, G. T.   (1984). A preliminary investigation of cognitive and relaxation treatment of panic disorder: Effects on intense anxiety vs. 'background' anxiety. *Behaviour Research and Therapy, 22,* 393–402.

Wadden, T. A., Stunkard, A. T., & Brownell, K. D.   (1983). Very low calorie diets: Their efficacy, safety, and future. *Annals of Internal Medicine, 99,* 675–684.

Wadden, T. A., Stunkard, A. J., Brownell, K. D., & Day, S. C.   (1984). Treatment of obesity by behavior therapy and very low calorie diet: A pilot investigation. *Journal of Consulting and Clinical Psychology, 52,* 692–694.

Wahler, R. G.   (1975). Some structural aspects of deviant child behavior. *Journal of Applied Behavior Analysis, 8,* 27–42.

Wahler, R. G.   (1980). The insular mother: Her problems in child management. *Journal of Applied Behavior Analysis, 13,* 207–220.

Wallace, C. J.   (1982). The social skills training project of the Mental Health Clinical Research Center for the study of schizophrenia. In J. P. Curran & P. M. Monti (Eds.), *Social skills training: A practical handbook for assessment and treatment.* New York: Guilford Press.

Wallace, C. J., Nelson, C. J., Lukoff, D., Webster, C., Rappe, S., & Ferris, C.   (1978) *Cognitive skills training. Paper presented at the Annual Meeting of the Association for Advancement of Behavior Therapy, Chicago, Ill.*

Wallace, I. (1977). Self-control techniques of famous novelists. *Journal of Applied Behavior Analysis, 10,* 515–525.

Walsh, B. T., Stewart, J. W., Roose, S. P., Gladis, M., & Glassman, A. H. (1984). Treatment of bulimia with phenelzine: A double-blind, placebo-controlled study. *Archives of General Psychiatry, 41,* 1105–1109.

Walster, E., & Walster, G. W. (1978). *A new look at love.* Reading, MA: Addison-Wesley.

Walters, R. H., & Demkov, L. F. (1963). Timing of punishment as a determinant of response inhibition. *Child Development, 34,* 207–214.

Walters, R. H., Parke, R. D., & Cane, V. A. (1965). Timing of punishment and the observation of consequences to others as determinants of response inhibition. *Journal of Experimental Child Psychology, 2,* 10–30.

Walzer, S., Wolff, P. H., Bowen, D., Silbert, A. R., Bashir, A. S., Gerald, P. S., & Richmond, J. B. (1978). A method for the longitudinal study of behavioral development in infants and children: The early development of XYY children. *Journal of Child Psychology & Psychiatry & Allied Disciplines, 19*(3), 213–229.

Wardlaw, G. R., & Miller, P. J. (1978). A controlled exposure technique in the elimination of exhibitionism. *Journal of Behavior Therapy and Experimental Psychiatry, 9,* 27–32.

Warren, N. T. (1976). Self-esteem and sources of cognitive bias in the evaluation of past performance. *Journal of Consulting and Clinical Psychology, 44,* 966–975.

Watson, J. B. (1930). *Behaviorism.* Chicago: University of Chicago Press.

Watson, J. B., & Rayner, R. (1920). Conditioned emotional reactions. *Journal of Experimental Psychology, 3,* 1–14.

Watson, L. S. (1973). *Child behavior modification: A manual for teachers, nurses and parents.* New York: Pergamon Press.

Watt, N. F., Anthony, E. J., Wynne, L. C., & Rolf, J. E. (Eds.), (1984). *Children at risk for schizophrenia: A longitudinal perspective.* Cambridge, MA: Cambridge University Press.

Wegner, J. T., Catalano, F., Gibralter, J., & Kane, J. M. (1985). Schizophrenics with tardive dyskinesia. *Archives of General Psychiatry, 42*(3), 860–865.

Weiss, G., Hechtman, L., Perlman, T., Hopkins, J., & Wener, A. (1979). Hyperactives as young adults. *Archives of General Psychiatry, 36,* 675–681.

Weiss, R. L., Hops, H., & Patterson, G. R. (1973). A framework for conceptualizing marital conflict, a technology for altering it, some data for evaluating it. In L. A. Hamerlynch, L. C. Handy & E. J. Mash (Eds.), *Behavior change: Methodology, concepts, and practice.* Champaign, IL: Research Press.

Weissman, M. M., Klerman, G. L., Paykel, E. S., et al. (1974). Treatment effects on the social adjustment of depressed patients. *Archives of General Psychiatry, 30,* 771–778.

Weissman, M. M., & Paykel, E. S. (1974). *The depressed woman.* Chicago: University of Chicago Press.

Weissman, M. M., Prusoff, B. A., DiMascio, A., Neu, C., Goklaney, M., & Klerman, G. L. (1979). The efficacy of drugs and psychotherapy in the treatment of acute depressive episodes. *American Journal of Psychiatry, 136,* 555–558.

Weltman, A., Matter, S., & Stamford, B. A. (1980). Caloric restriction and/or mild exercise: Effects on serum lipids and body composition. *American Journal of Clinical Nutrition, 33,* 1002–1009.

Werry, J. S. (1972). Psychosomatic disorders (with a note on anesthesia, surgery, and hospitalization). In H. C. Quay & J. S. Werry (Eds.), *Psychopathological disorders of childhood,* New York: John Wiley & Sons.

Werry, J. S., & Cohrssen, J. (1965). Enuresis —an etiologic and therapeutic study. *Journal of Pediatrics, 67,* 423–431.

West, D. J., & Farrington, D. P. (1973). *Who becomes delinquent?* London: Heinemann.

Wexler, D. B. (1973). Token and taboo: Behavior modification, token economies, and the law. *California Law Review, 61,* 81–109.

Whalen, C. K., & Henker, B. (1980). *Hyperactive children.* New York: Academic Press.

Whalen, C. K., Henker, B., & Hinshaw, S. P. (1985). Cognitive therapy for hyperactive children: Premises, problems and prospects. *Journal of Abnormal Child Psychology, 13,* 391–410.

White, G. D. (1977). The effects of observer presence on the activity level of families. *Journal of Applied Behavior Analysis, 10,* 734.

Wickramasekera, I. (1976). Aversive behavior rehearsal for sexual exhibitionism. *Behavior Therapy, 7,* 167–176.

Wiens, A., & Menustik, C. (1983). Treatment outcome and patient characteristics in an aversion therapy program for alcoholism. *American Psychologist, 38,* 1089–1096.

Wiggins, J. S. (1973). *Personality and prediction: Principles of personality assessment.* Reading, MA: Addison-Wesley.

Willerman, L. (1973). Activity level and hyperactivity in twins. *Child Development, 44,* 288–293.

Williams, C. D. (1959). The elimination of tantrum behavior by extinction procedures. *Journal of Abnormal and Social Psychology, 59,* 269.

Williams, L., Dooseman, G., & Kleifield, E. (1984). Comparative effectiveness of mastery and exposure treatments for intractable phobias. *Journal of Consulting and Clinical Psychology, 52,* 505–518.

Williams, S. L., & Rappaport, J. A. (1983). Behavioral practice with and without thought modification for agoraphobics. *Behavior Therapy, 15,* 299–313.

Williams, S. L., & Watson, M. (1985). Perceived danger and perceived self-efficacy as cognitive determinants of acrophobic behavior. *Behavior Therapy, 16,* 136–146.

Wilson, G. T. (1978a). Aversion therapy for alcoholism: Issues, ethics, and evidence. In G. A. Marlatt & P. E. Nathan (Eds.), *Behavioral assessment and treatment of alcoholism.* New Brunswick, NJ: Center for Alcohol Studies.

Wilson, G. T. (1978b). Ethical and professional issues in sex therapy: Comments on Bailey's "Psychotherapy or massage parlor technology?" *Journal of Consulting and Clinical Psychology, 46,* 1510–1514.

Wilson, G. T. (1979). Perceived control and the theory and practice of behavior therapy. In L. C. Perlmuter & R. A. Monty (Eds.), *Choice and perceived control.* Hillsdale, NJ: Lawrence Erlbaum.

Wilson, G. T. (1980). Toward specifying the "nonspecifics" in behavior therapy: A social learning analysis. In M. J. Mahoney (Ed.), *Psychotherapy process.* New York: Plenum Publishing.

Wilson, G. T. (1981a). Behavior therapy as a short-term therapeutic approach. In S. Budman (Ed.), *Forms of brief therapy.* New York: Guilford Press.

Wilson, G. T. (1981b). The effects of alcohol on human sexual behavior. In N. K. Mello (Ed.), *Advances in Substance Abuse: Behavioral and biological research.* Greenwich, CT: JAI Press.

Wilson, G. T. (1982a). Alcohol and anxiety: Recent evidence on the tension reduction theory of alcohol use and abuse. In J. Polivy & K. Blankstein (Eds.), *Self control of emotional behavior.* New York: Plenum Press.

Wilson, G. T. (1982b). Clinical issues and strategies in the practice of behavior therapy. In C. M. Franks, G. T. Wilson, P. C. Kendall, & K. D. Brownell (Eds.), *Annual review of behavior therapy: Theory and practice* (Vol. 8). New York: Guilford Press.

Wilson, G. T. (1982c). Fear reduction methods and the treatment of anxiety disorders. In C. M. Franks, G. T. Wilson, P. Kendall, & K. Brownell (Eds.), *Annual review of behavior therapy* (Vol. 8). New York: Guilford Press.

Wilson, G. T. (1982d). Psychotherapy process and procedure: The behavioral mandate. *Behavior Therapy, 13,* 291–312.

Wilson, G. T. (1984). Clinical issues and strategies in the practice of behavior therapy. In G. T. Wilson, C. M. Franks, K. D. Brownell, & P. Kendall (Eds.), *Annual review of behavior therapy,* (Vol. 9). New York: Guilford Press.

Wilson, G. T. (1985a). Limitations of meta-analysis in clinical psychology. *Clinical Psychology Review, 5,* 35–47.

Wilson, G. T. (1985b). Psychological prognostic factors in the treatment of obesity. In J. Hirsch & T. Van Itallie (Eds.), *Recent advances in obesity research, IV.* London: John Libbey & Co.

Wilson, G. T. (1986). Cognitive-behavioral and pharmacological therapies for bulimia. In K. D. Brownell, & J. P. Foreyt (Eds.), *Physiology, Psychology, and Treatment of the Eating Disorders.* New York: Basic Books.

Wilson, G. T. (in press a). Alcohol use and abuse: A social learning analysis. In A. Wilkinson & D. Chaudron (Eds.), *Theories of alcoholism.* Toronto: Addiction Research Foundation.

Wilson, G. T. (in press b). Psychosocial treatment of anxiety disorders. In B. Shaw, F. Cashman, Z. Segal, & M. Vallis (Eds.), *Anxiety disorders: Theory, diagnosis, and treatment.* New York: Plenum Publishing.

Wilson, G. T. (in press c). Social psychological concepts in the theory and practice of behavior therapy. In P. Eelen (Ed.), *Behavior therapy and social cognition*. New York: Erlbaum.

Wilson, G. T. (in press d). The treatment of bulimia nervosa: A cognitive-social learning analysis. In A. J. Stunkard & A. Baum (Eds.), *Eating, sleep, and sexual disorders*. New York: Erlbaum.

Wilson, G. T., Abrams, D. B., & Lipscomb, T. (1980). Effects of intoxication levels and drinking pattern on social anxiety in men. *Journal of Studies on Alcohol, 41*, 250–264.

Wilson, G. T., & Brownell, K. (1980). Behavior therapy for obesity: An evaluation of treatment outcome. *Advances in Behaviour Research and Therapy, 3*, 49–86.

Wilson, G. T., & Evans, I. M. (1976). Adult behavior therapy and the therapist-client relationship. In C. M. Franks & G. T. Wilson (Eds.), *Annual review of behavior therapy: Theory and practice* (Vol. 4). New York: Brunner/Mazel.

Wilson, G. T., & Evans, I. M. (1977). The therapist-client relationship in behavior therapy. In R. S. Gurman & A. M. Razin (Eds.), *The therapist's contribution to effective psychotherapy: An empirical approach*. New York: Pergamon Press.

Wilson, G. T., & Franks, C. M. (Eds.). (1982). *Contemporary behavior therapy: Conceptual and empirical foundations*. New York: Guilford Press.

Wilson, G. T., & Lawson, D. M. (1976). The effects of alcohol on sexual arousal in women. *Journal of Abnormal Psychology, 85*, 489–497.

Wilson, G. T., & O'Leary, K. D. (1980). *Principles of Behavior Therapy*. Englewood Cliffs, NJ: Prentice-Hall.

Wilson, G. T., & Rachman, S. (1983). Meta-analysis and the evaluations of psychotherapy outcome: Limitations and liabilities. *Journal of Consulting and Clinical Psychology, 51*, 54–64.

Wilson, G. T., Rossiter, E., Kleifield, E., & Lindholm, L. (1986). Cognitive-behavioral treatment of bulimia: A controlled evaluation. *Behaviour Research and Therapy, 24*, 277–288.

Wilson, G. T., & Tracey, D. A. (1976). An experimental analysis of aversive imagery versus electrical aversive conditioning in the treatment of chronic alcoholics. *Behaviour Research and Therapy, 14*, 41–51.

Wilson, J. Q., & Herrnstein, R. J. (1985). *Crime and human nature*. New York: Simon & Schuster.

Wing, R., Epstein, L., Marcus, M., & Shapira, B. (1981). Strong monetary contingencies for weight loss during treatment and maintenance. *Behavior Therapy, 12*, 702–710

Wolberg, L. R. (1967). *Short-term psychotherapy*. New York: Grune & Stratton.

Wolchick, S. A., & Harris, S. L. (1982). Language environments of autistic and normal children matched for language age: A preliminary investigation. *Journal of Autism and Developmental Disorders, 12*, 43–55.

Wolf, M. M. (1978). Social validity: The case for subjective measurement. Or how applied behavior analysis is finding its heart. *Journal of Applied Behavior Analysis, 11*, 203–214.

Wolf, M. M., Risley, T. R., & Mees, H. L. (1964). Application of operant conditioning procedures to the behavior problems of an autistic child. *Behaviour Research and Therapy, 1*, 305–312.

Wolpe, J. (1952). Objective psychotherapy of the neuroses. *South African Medical Journal, 26*, 825–829.

Wolpe, J. (1954). Reciprocal inhibition as the main basis of psychotherapeutic effects. *Archives of Neurology and Psychiatry, 72*, 205–226.

Wolpe, J. (1958). *Psychotherapy by reciprocal inhibition*. Stanford: Stanford University Press.

Wolpe, J. (1978). Cognition and causation in human behavior and its therapy. *American Psychologist, 33*, 437–446.

Wolpe, J., & Lang, P. J. (1964). A fear survey schedule for use in behavior therapy. *Behaviour Research and Therapy, 2*, 27–30.

Wolpe, J., & Lazarus, A. A. (1966). *Behavior therapy techniques*. New York: Pergamon Press.

Wolpe, J., & Rachman, S. (1960). Psychoanalytic "evidence": A critique based on Freud's case of Little Hans. *Journal of Nervous and Mental Disease, 131*, 135–148.

Wolraich, M., Milich, R., Stumbo, P., & Schultz, F. (1985). The effects of sucrose ingestion on the behavior of hyperactive boys. *The Journal of Pediatrics, 106*, 675–682.

Woodward, R., & Jones, R. B. (1980). Cognitive restructuring treatment: A controlled trial with anxious patients. *Behaviour Research and Therapy, 18*, 401–407.

Wooley, S. C., & Wooley, O. W. (1986). Understanding and treatment of bulimia. In K. D. Brownell & J. P. Foreyt (Eds.), *Physiology, psychology, and treatment of the eating disorders*. New York: Basic Books.

Wooley, S. C., Wooley, O. W., & Dyrenforth, S. R. (1979). Theoretical, practical, and social issues in behavioral treatments of obesity. *Journal of Applied Behavior Analysis, 12,* 3–25.

Woolfolk, R. L., & Lehrer, P. M. (Eds.). (1984). *Principles and practice of stress management.* New York: Guilford Press.

Wright, L., & Walker, C. E. (1976). Behavioral treatment of encopresis. *Journal of Pediatric Psychology, 4*(1), 35–37.

Y

Yates, A. J. (1970). *Behavior therapy,* New York: John Wiley & Sons.

Yates, G. (1978). Improving the cost-effectiveness of obesity programs: Three basic strategies for reducing the cost per pound. *International Journal of Obesity, 2,* 249–266.

Yeaton, W. H. (1982). A critique of the effectiveness of applied behavior analysis research. *Advances in Behaviour Research and Therapy, 4,* 75–96.

Yeaton, W. H., & Sechrest, L. (1981). Critical dimensions in the choice and maintenance of successful treatments: Strength, integrity, and effectiveness. *Journal of Consulting and Clinical Psychology, 49,* 156–167.

Young, G. C. (1965). Conditioning treatment of enuresis. *Developmental Medicine and Child Neurology, 7,* 557–562.

Young, C. G., & Morgan, R. T. (1972a). Overlearning in the conditioning treatment of enuresis. *Behavior Research and Therapy, 10,* 147–151.

Young, G. C., & Morgan, R. T. (1972b). Overlearning in the conditioning treatment of enuresis: A long term follow-up study. *Behaviour Research and Therapy, 10,* 419–420.

Young, G. C., & Turner, R. K. (1965). CNS stimulant drugs and the conditioning treatment of nocturnal enuresis. *Behaviour Research and Therapy, 3,* 93–101.

Young, G. C., & Turner, R. K. (1973). Nocturnal enuresis in childhood. *Health and Social Service Journal,* April 7, 1973.

Young, I. L., & Goldsmith, A. D. (1972). Treatment of encopresis in a day treatment program. *Psychotherapy: Theory, Research and Practice, 9,* 231–235.

Young, J. E., & Beck, A. T. (1982). Cognitive therapy: Clinical Applications. In A. J. Rush (Ed.), *Short-term psychotherapies for depression.* New York: Guilford Press.

Young, J. G., Kavanagh, M. E., Anderson, G. M., Shaywitz, B. A., & Cohen, D. J. (1982). Clinical neurochemistry of autism and associated disorders. *Journal of Autism and Developmental Disorders, 12* 147–165.

Z

Zeiss, R. A. (1978). Self-directed treatment for premature ejaculation. *Journal of Consulting and Clinical Psychology, 46,* 1234–1241.

Zeiss, R. A., & Zeiss, A. M. (1978). *Prolong Your Pleasure.* New York: Pocket Books.

Zilbergeld, B., & Evans, M. (1980). The inadequacy of Masters and Johnson. *Psychology Today, 14,* 28–43.

Zis, A. P., & Goodwin, F. K. (1980). The amine hypothesis. In E. S. Paykel (Ed.), *Handbook of Affective Disorders.* New York: Guilford Press.

Zitrin, C. M. (1981). Combined pharmacological and psychotherapeutic treatment of phobias. In M. Mavissakalian & D. Barlow (Eds.), *Phobia: Psychological and pharmacological treatment.* New York: Guilford Press.

Zitrin, C. M., Klein, D. E., Woerner, M. G., & Ross, D. C. (1983). Treatment of phobias. *Archives of General Psychiatry, 40,* 125–138.

Zubin, J., Eron, L. D., & Schumer, F. (1965). *An experimental approach to projective techniques.* New York: John Wiley & Sons.

Name Index

Subject Index